T0296897

Advances in Computer Vision and Pattern Recognition

For further volumes:
www.springer.com/series/4205

An illustration of the power of perceptual grouping. Individually, the black, amorphous blobs carry very little information. However, when grouped into parts, the emergent part structure allows each figure to be quickly interpreted without any a priori knowledge of scene content. The figures are reproduced with kind permission from Teachers College Press, Columbia University, New York: A gestalt completion test: a study of a cross section of intellect, 1931, Roy F. Street, p. 41, Fig. 1, p. 61, Fig. 11, p. 47, Fig. 4, p. 55, Fig. 8).

Sven J. Dickinson • Zygmunt Pizlo
Editors

Shape Perception in Human and Computer Vision

An Interdisciplinary Perspective

 Springer

Editors
Sven J. Dickinson
Department of Computer Science
University of Toronto
Toronto, Ontario
Canada

Zygmunt Pizlo
Department of Psychological Sciences
Purdue University
West Lafayette, IN
USA

Series Editors
Prof. Sameer Singh
Research School of Informatics
Loughborough University
Loughborough
UK

Dr. Sing Bing Kang
Microsoft Research
Microsoft Corporation
Redmond, WA
USA

ISSN 2191-6586   ISSN 2191-6594 (electronic)
Advances in Computer Vision and Pattern Recognition
ISBN 978-1-4471-6168-4   ISBN 978-1-4471-5195-1 (eBook)
DOI 10.1007/978-1-4471-5195-1
Springer London Heidelberg New York Dordrecht

Printed on acid-free paper

Springer is part of Springer Science+Business Media (www.springer.com)

In memory of my mother, Ursula Dickinson (1936–2012), who always wanted to know about the vision problems I worked on.

From Sven

To my wife, Irmina Agnieszka, who has always shared my passion for natural sciences.

From Zygmunt

Preface

Shape has a long and rich history in vision research. On the computer vision side, shape was the backbone of classical object recognition systems in the 1960s, 1970s, and 1980s. However, the advent of appearance-based recognition in the 1990s drew the spotlight away from shape. While an active shape community continued in the periphery, only recently has shape re-entered the mainstream with a return to contours, shape hierarchies, shape grammars, shape priors, and even 3-D shape inference. On the human vision side, shape research was also affected by paradigm changes. Unlike the computer vision community, psychologists have usually agreed that shape is important, but it has been less clear to them what it is about shape that should be studied: surfaces, invariants, parts, multiple views, learning, simplicity, shape constancy or shape illusions? The growing interest in mathematical formalisms and computational models has begun to provide the long overdue common denominator for these various paradigms.

In an effort to foster greater dialog between these two communities of shape researchers, we co-organized a very successful series of four International Workshops on Shape Perception in Human and Computer Vision, in conjunction with ECCV 2008 (http://viper.psych.purdue.edu/workshops/iwsphcv08/), ECVP 2009 (http://viper.psych.purdue.edu/workshops/iwsphcv09/), ECCV 2010 (http://viper.psych.purdue.edu/workshops/iwsphcv2010/), and VSS 2011 (http://www.visionsciences.org/satellite_shape_perception.htm), two computer vision venues and two human vision venues. The format of each workshop was identical: 12 distinguished invited speakers, 6 from human vision and 6 from computer vision. Each speaker was invited not to present their latest and greatest research, but to reflect more broadly on the issues and challenges they've faced over their careers and the major challenges ahead. Moreover, the speakers were chosen to cover the topic from all sides rather than promote a particular paradigm. The workshops were a great success and received funding from a number of sources.

The goal had always been to have the union of the four workshops' authors each submit a chapter to an interdisciplinary collection modeled after the workshops. What follows is a collection that is the realization of that goal, offering 33 chapters by a set of world-class shape researchers from both sides of the aisle. Most of the authors have worked on the problem of shape perception for many years (decades), and have a unique perspective to offer researchers and students alike on what issues have shaped the field, the trends we've followed, the progress we've made, and the challenges we face. Just like the four workshops, this collection offers a unique, interdisciplinary perspective that is essential for young researchers to understand the broader landscape of the problem so that they can build on a firm foundation. We hope you find the collection as exciting and as useful as we do.

There are a number of people and organizations who we'd like to thank for helping to make this volume possible. Wayne Wheeler and Simon Rees from Springer have been incredibly supportive of this initiative, providing valuable guidance and support throughout the process of assembling this collection. We'd like to sincerely thank the Air Force Office of Scientific Research (AFOSR), the Purdue University Department of Psychological Sciences, and the German Association for Pattern Recognition (*DAGM*) for their generous financial support of the workshops. Finally, we'd like to thank the Organizers of the ECCV, ECVP and VSS conferences for accommodating our workshops. Our sincere thanks to you all.

University of Toronto, Canada   Sven J. Dickinson
Purdue University, USA   Zygmunt Pizlo

Contents

Contributors

Ronen Basri Department of Computer Science and Applied Mathematics, Weizmann Institute of Science, Rehovot, Israel

Irving Biederman Department of Psychology and Neuroscience Program, University of Southern California, Los Angeles, CA, USA

Erica Briscoe Aerospace, Transportation and Advanced Systems Laboratory, Georgia Tech Research Institute, Atlanta, GA, USA

Laura Cacciamani Department of Psychology, University of Arizona, Tucson, USA

Corrado Caudek Department of Psychology, Università degli Studi di Firenze, Firenze, Italy

Elias H. Cohen SUNY College of Optometry, Graduate Center for Vision Research, State University of New York, New York, NY, USA

Daniel Cremers Departments of Computer Science & Mathematics, TU Munich, Garching, Germany

Doug DeCarlo Department of Computer Science and Center for Cognitive Science, Rutgers University, Piscataway, NJ, USA

Sven J. Dickinson Department of Computer Science, University of Toronto, Toronto, Canada

Fulvio Domini Center for Neuroscience and Cognitive Systems@UniTn, Istituto Italiano di Tecnologia, Rovereto, Italy; Department of Cognitive, Linguistic and Psychological Sciences, Brown University, Providence, RI, USA

Gregory L. Dudek Centre for Intelligent Machines, McGill University, Montreal, Canada

James H. Elder Centre for Vision Research, York University, Toronto, Canada

Gennady Erlikhman Department of Psychology, University of California, Los Angeles, USA

Jacob Feldman Department of Psychology, Center for Cognitive Science, Rutgers University, New Brunswick, USA

Pedro F. Felzenszwalb Department of Engineering, Brown University, Providence, RI, USA

Vicky Froyen Department of Psychology, Rutgers University, New Brunswick, USA

Patrick Garrigan Department of Psychology, St. Joseph's University, Philadelphia, PA, USA

Andrew Glennerster School of Psychology and Clinical Language Sciences, University of Reading, Reading, UK

Martial Hebert Robotics Institute, Carnegie Mellon University, Pittsburgh, USA

Donald D. Hoffman Department of Cognitive Science, University of California, Irvine, CA, USA

Edward Hsiao Robotics Institute, Carnegie Mellon University, Pittsburgh, USA

Wenze Hu University of California, Los Angeles, CA, USA

David Jacobs Department of Computer Science, University of Maryland, College Park, MD, USA

Ian H. Jermyn Department of Mathematical Sciences, Durham University, Durham, UK

Anne Jorstad Department of Computer Science, University of Maryland, College Park, MD, USA

Philip J. Kellman Department of Psychology, University of California, Los Angeles, USA

Ira Kemelmacher-Shlizerman Department of Computer Science and Engineering, University of Washington, Seattle, WA, USA

Seha Kim Department of Psychology, Rutgers University, New Brunswick, USA

Jan Koenderink Laboratory of Experimental Psychology, University of Leuven (K.U. Leuven), Leuven, Belgium; Faculteit Sociale Wetenschappen, Afdeling Psychologische Functieleer, Utrecht University, Utrecht, The Netherlands

Sebastian Kurtek Department of Statistics, Florida State University, Tallahassee, FL, USA

Alex Levinshtein Department of Computer Science, University of Toronto, Toronto, Canada

Andrea Li SUNY College of Optometry, Graduate Center for Vision Research, State University of New York, New York, NY, USA

Yunfeng Li Department of Psychological Sciences, Purdue University, West Lafayette, IN, USA

Giacomo Mazzilli School of Psychology, University of Birmingham, Birmingham, UK

Xin Meng SUNY College of Optometry, Graduate Center for Vision Research, State University of New York, New York, NY, USA

Richard F. Murray Centre for Vision Research, York University, Toronto, Canada

Boaz Nadler Department of Computer Science and Applied Mathematics, Weizmann Institute of Science, Rehovot, Israel

Björn Ommer Heidelberg Collaboratory for Image Processing (HCI) & Interdisciplinary Center for Scientific Computing (IWR), University of Heidelberg, Heidelberg, Germany

Thomas V. Papathomas Department of Biomedical Engineering and Center for Cognitive Science, Rutgers University, Piscataway, NJ, USA

Nikos Paragios Center for Visual Computing, Ecole Centrale Paris, Châtenay-Malabry Cedex, France; LIGM Laboratory, University Paris-East & Ecole des Ponts Paris-Tech, Marne-la-Vallée, France; GALEN Group, INRIA Saclay - Île-de-France, Rocquencourt, France

Nadia Payet School of Electrical Engineering and Computer Science, Oregon State University, Corvallis, OR, USA

Mary A. Peterson Department of Psychology, University of Arizona, Tucson, USA

Zygmunt Pizlo Department of Psychological Sciences, Purdue University, West Lafayette, IN, USA

Morteza Rezanejad McGill University, Montreal, QC, Canada

Antonio J. Rodríguez-Sánchez Intelligent and Interactive Systems, University of Innsbruck, Innsbruck, Austria

Pablo Sala Department of Computer Science, University of Toronto, Toronto, Canada

Dimitris Samaras Dept. of Computer Science, Stony Brook University, Stony Brook, USA

Tadamasa Sawada Department of Psychological Sciences, Purdue University, West Lafayette, IN, USA

Andrew J. Schofield School of Psychology, University of Birmingham, Birmingham, UK

Jianbo Shi Department of Computer and Information Science, University of Pennsylvania, Philadelphia, USA

Yun Shi Department of Psychological Sciences, Purdue University, West Lafayette, IN, USA

Zhangzhang Si University of California, Los Angeles, CA, USA

Kaleem Siddiqi McGill University, Montreal, QC, Canada

Manish Singh Department of Psychology and Center for Cognitive Science, Rutgers University, New Brunswick, NJ, USA

Cristian Sminchisescu Institute of Numerical Simulation, University of Bonn, Bonn, Germany

Anuj Srivastava Department of Statistics, Florida State University, Tallahassee, FL, USA

Robert M. Steinman Department of Psychological Sciences, Purdue University, West Lafayette, IN, USA

Jingyong Su Department of Statistics, Florida State University, Tallahassee, FL, USA

Peng Sun Department of Cognitive Science, University of California Irvine, Irvine, CA, USA

Sinisa Todorovic School of Electrical Engineering and Computer Science, Oregon State University, Corvallis, OR, USA

Alain Trouvé CMLA, École normale supérieure de Cachan, Cachan, France

John K. Tsotsos Dept. of Electrical Engineering and Computer Science, and Center for Vision Research, York University, Toronto, Canada

Christopher W. Tyler Brain Imaging Center, Smith-Kettlewell Institute, San Francisco, CA, USA

Andrea van Doorn Industrial Design, Delft University of Technology, Delft, The Netherlands

Johan Wagemans Laboratory of Experimental Psychology, University of Leuven, Leuven, Belgium

Christian Wallraven Cognitive Systems Lab, Dept. of Brain and Cognitive Engineering, Korea University, Seol, Republic of Korea

Chaohui Wang Vision Lab, University of California, Los Angeles, USA

John Wilder Department of Psychology, Rutgers University, New Brunswick, USA

Carson Wong SUNY College of Optometry, Graduate Center for Vision Research, State University of New York, New York, NY, USA

Qasim Zaidi SUNY College of Optometry, Graduate Center for Vision Research, State University of New York, New York, NY, USA

Yun Zeng Dept. of Computer Science, Stony Brook University, Stony Brook, USA

Song-Chun Zhu University of California, Los Angeles, CA, USA

Steven W. Zucker Yale University, New Haven, CT, USA

Sven J. Dickinson is Professor and Chair of the Department of Computer Science, University of Toronto. His research program in computer vision includes shape-based object recognition, and the related problems of perceptual grouping, shape segmentation, shape modeling, shape abstraction, and shape indexing. He has published over 150 papers on these and other topics in computer vision.

Zygmunt Pizlo is a Professor in the Department of Psychological Sciences and in the School of Electrical and Computer Engineering at Purdue University. His primary research interest is in human vision, with a special emphasis on 3D shape perception. His secondary interests are in human problem solving, motor control, as well as image and video quality. He has published over 100 papers as well as a monograph on human shape perception.

Chapter 1
The Role of Mid-Level Shape Priors
in Perceptual Grouping and Image Abstraction

Sven J. Dickinson, Alex Levinshtein, Pablo Sala, and Cristian Sminchisescu

1.1 Introduction

Have a look at the image in Fig. 1.1(a) (taken from [29]) and don't read any further until you recognize the object(s) in the scene. For most people, the image of a horse and rider quickly emerges. This is remarkable considering that each individual black fragment is practically meaningless in terms of its indexing power to suggest a horse or rider (or *any* object, for that matter). Only when the fragments are *grouped* together and *abstracted* to yield meaningful parts and relations do the objects begin to emerge. Moreover, these grouping and abstraction processes are primarily bottom-up, and do not require a priori knowledge of scene content. Nobody told you what object to look for, and you certainly didn't run through tens of thousands of category detectors to decide that it was a horse and rider and not a table and chair. Somehow, your visual system grouped the fragments to form a set of abstract parts, then grouped those parts into larger configurations, then "queried" your visual memory for similar configurations, and only then used a priori knowledge of a promising candidate to "detect", i.e., verify, the object.

Perceptual grouping is a critical function in the human visual system, offering a powerful heuristic for grouping together causally related image features in support of both figure-ground segmentation and 3-D inference. In the mid-to-late 1990s, perceptual grouping was a thriving subcommunity in computer vision, as illustrated in Fig. 1.1(b). However, over the past 10 years, there's been a steady decline in the number of perceptual grouping papers appearing in the computer vision community's main conferences. The reason for this is the reformulation of object recogni-

S.J. Dickinson (✉) · A. Levinshtein · P. Sala
Department of Computer Science, University of Toronto, Toronto, Canada
e-mail: sven@cs.toronto.edu

C. Sminchisescu
Institute of Numerical Simulation, University of Bonn, Bonn, Germany

S.J. Dickinson, Z. Pizlo (eds.), *Shape Perception in Human and Computer Vision*,
Advances in Computer Vision and Pattern Recognition,
DOI 10.1007/978-1-4471-5195-1_1, © Springer-Verlag London 2013

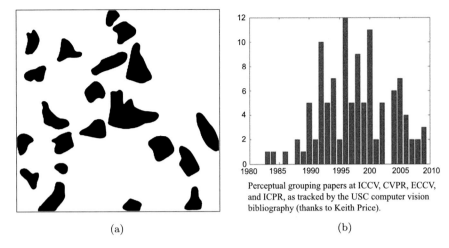

(a)   (b)

Fig. 1.1 (**a**) An illustration of the power of perceptual grouping. Individually, the black, amorphous blobs carry very little information. However, when grouped into parts, the emergent part structure allows the scene (horse and rider) to be quickly interpreted *without* any a priori knowledge of scene content (figure reproduced with kind permission from Teachers College Press, Columbia University, New York: *A gestalt completion test: a study of a cross section of intellect*, 1931, Roy F. Street, p. 55, Fig. 8); (**b**) The rise and fall of perceptual grouping. Tracking perceptual grouping papers in the computer vision community's four main conferences indicates a growing interest in perceptual grouping, peaking in the late 1990s. However, since then, interest in this critically important problem has waned

tion, historically cast as the problem of recognizing an object from a large database, as a detection problem, cast as the search for a particular target object.

The classical formulation of the object recognition problem, which defined the mainstream from the mid-1960s through to the late-1990s, was the recognition of an unexpected object from a database of objects. As illustrated in Fig. 1.2, the feature extraction process began by extracting categorical or generic features, as the recognition community aspired to recognize categories, not exemplars. As far back as the seminal work of Roberts [23] in the mid-1960s, the recognition community understood that across the exemplars that belong to a category, shape is a more invariant property than appearance. As a result, the majority of recognition systems from the mid-1960s to the late 1990s attempted to extract shape features, typically beginning with the extraction of edges, for at occluding boundaries and surface discontinuities, edges capture shape information. However, unlike today's distinctive local image features, e.g., SIFT [20], a local edgel carries very little information with which to index into a database of objects in an attempt to select a small number of promising object models that might account for the edgels.

The need for perceptual grouping in these early systems was critical, for only when the edgels were grouped into longer contours, perhaps parsed at high-curvature points, and grouped with other causally related contours, did distinctive indexing features emerge. Lowe's thesis [21] was the first to introduce computational models of perceptual grouping processes, e.g., proximity, collinearity, and

Classical Categorization Model

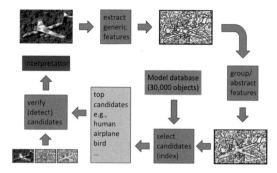

Fig. 1.2 In the classical recognition model, the desire to extract shape features, considered more generic than appearance, began with edge detection. Because edgels were not discriminative, they were perceptually grouped and abstracted to form distinctive indexing structures that could prune a large database of objects down to a small number of promising candidates. (figure reproduced with kind permission from Springer Science+Business Media: *Proceedings, 4th Mexican Conference on Pattern Recognition (MCPR)*, Perceptual Grouping using Superpixels, 2012, S. Dickinson, A. Levinshtein, and C. Sminchisescu, p. 14, Fig. 1)

parallelism, derived from image statistics. By grouping contour features into more distinctive groups (in Lowe's case, proximity followed by collinearity followed by parallelism), more discriminating indexing (using parallel lines instead of, say, triples of corners [11]) was possible. The more that features were grouped, perhaps first into parts and then into multipart groups [8, 9], the more powerful the resulting indexing structure and the fewer candidates that ultimately needed to be verified. Each candidate was verified, yielding a score (typically reflecting the degree to which a model could be aligned with image features), and the top-scoring candidate, if sufficiently strong, gave the final interpretation.

The formulation of object recognition as the detection of a specific target object has dominated the recognition community over the past 10 years. As illustrated in Fig. 1.3(top) and working backwards from the verification module, instead of having to verify a number of candidate object hypotheses, the detection problem identifies only a single hypothesis that needs to be verified (or detected). This, in turn, means that the indexing step, in which a large database of candidate objects is pruned down to a small set of candidates for verification, is superfluous, as the database effectively has a single object (target). Continuing to work our way backwards, as illustrated in Fig. 1.3(middle), if discriminative indexing features are not required to select promising candidates, the perceptual grouping stage is also superfluous. Instead, as illustrated in Fig. 1.3(bottom), the detector, i.e., verification, can be applied directly to the edgels, e.g., [6], to give the final score, thereby short-circuiting the entire perceptual grouping process.

The existence of an object detector, representing a strong shape prior, eliminates the need for perceptual grouping, representing a much weaker, domain-independent shape prior. However, as the categorization community moves from single object

4 S.J. Dickinson et al.

Fig. 1.3 The classical formulation of object recognition from a large database has given way to a more recent formulation of object recognition as target detection: (*top*) rather than verifying a number of candidates, the target candidate is known, rendering the process of indexing (or model selection) obsolete. (*Middle*) Without the need for domain-independent recovery, grouping, and abstraction of structure in order to prune a large database down to a small number of promising candidates, perceptual grouping is unnecessary. (*Bottom*) As a result, verification (detection) can be applied directly to the ungrouped, low-level edge features. (Figure reproduced with kind permission from Springer Science+Business Media: *Proceedings, 4th Mexican Conference on Pattern Recognition (MCPR)*, Perceptual Grouping using Superpixels, 2012, S. Dickinson, A. Levinshtein, and C. Sminchisescu, p. 14, Fig. 1)

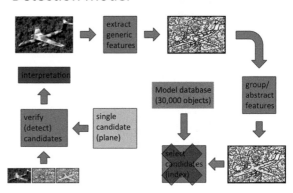

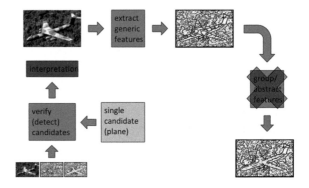

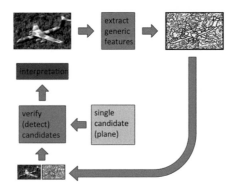

spatial proximity (Fig. 1.4(e)). Each edge is assigned an affinity, this time reflecting the degree to which two nearby parts are believed to be physically attached. Like in the first phase, the associated, higher granularity affinities are learned from the regularities of attached symmetric parts identified in training data. A graph segmentation yields a set of part clusters, each representing a set of regularized symmetric elements and their hypothesized attachments (Fig. 1.4(f)).

Our approach offers clear advantages over competing approaches. For example, classical multiscale blob and ridge detectors, such as [19] (Fig. 1.4(g)), yield many spurious parts, a challenging form of noise for any graph-based indexing or matching strategy. And even if an opportunistic setting of a region segmenter's parameters yields a decent object silhouette (Fig. 1.4(h)), the resulting skeleton may exhibit spurious branches and may fail to clearly delineate the part structure. From a cluttered image, our two-phase approach recovers, abstracts, and groups a set of medial branches into an approximation to an object's skeletal part structure, enabling the application of skeleton-based categorization systems to more realistic imagery. Details of the approach can be found in [13].

Some qualitative results are shown in Fig. 1.5. Proceeding left to right, top to bottom, we see excellent part recovery and grouping for the starfish, the plane, the windmill, and the runner, respectively. In the case of the windmill, a second, singleton cluster, representing the entire body of the human, is recovered; however, the distant windmills are not recovered, for their scale is smaller than the smallest superpixel scale. The final two figures represent failure modes. In the case of the lizard, the curved symmetric tail is oversegmented into piecewise linear symmetric parts. In the case of the lake scene, the symmetric parts making up the horizon tree line are incorrectly grouped with the dock structure due to a lack of apparent occlusion boundary between the dock structure and the tree line parts.

1.3 Contour Closure

In this section, we review our framework for efficiently searching for optimal contour closure; details can be found in [14, 15]. Figure 1.6 illustrates an overview of our approach to computing contour closure. Given an image of extracted contours (Fig. 1.6(a)), we begin by restricting contour closures to pass along boundaries of superpixels computed over the contour image (Fig. 1.6(b)). In this way, our first contribution is to reformulate the problem of searching for cycles of contours as the problem of searching for a subset of superpixels whose collective boundary has strong contour support in the contour image; the assumption we make is that those salient contours that define the boundary of the object (our target closure) will align well with superpixel boundaries. However, while a cycle of contours represents a single contour closure, our reformulation requires a mechanism to encourage superpixel subsets that are spatially coherent.

Spatial coherence is an inherent property of a cost function that computes the ratio of perimeter to area. We modify the ratio cost function of Stahl and Wang [28]

Fig. 1.5 Detected medial parts and their clusters. Parts with the same color axis have been grouped together (through high attachment affinities) and are hypothesized to belong to the same object. (Figure reproduced with kind permission from Springer Science+Business Media: *Proceedings, 4th Mexican Conference on Pattern Recognition (MCPR)*, Perceptual Grouping using Superpixels, 2012, S. Dickinson, A. Levinshtein, and C. Sminchisescu, p. 18, Fig. 3)

to operate on superpixels rather than contours, and extend it to yield a cost function that: (1) promotes spatially coherent selections of superpixels; (2) favors larger closures over smaller closures; and (3) introduces a novel, learned gap function that accounts for how much agreement there is between the boundary of the selection and the contours in the image. The third property adds cost as the number and sizes of gaps between contours increase. Given a superpixel boundary fragment (e.g., a side of a superpixel) representing a hypothesized closure component, we assign a gap cost that's a function of the proximity of nearby image contours, their strength,

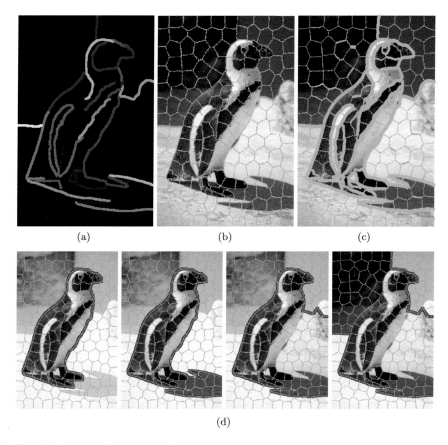

(a)   (b)   (c)

(d)

Fig. 1.6 Overview of our approach for image closure: (**a**) contour image: while we take as input only this contour image, we will overlay the original image in the subsequent figures to ease visualization; (**b**) superpixel segmentation of contour image, in which superpixel resolution is chosen to ensure that target boundaries are reasonably well approximated by superpixel boundaries; (**c**) a novel, learned measure of gap reflects the extent to which the superpixel boundary is supported by evidence of a real image contour (line thickness corresponds to the amount of agreement between superpixel boundaries and image contours); (**d**) our cost function can be globally optimized to yield the largest set of superpixels bounded by contours that have the least gaps. In this case the solutions, in increasing cost (decreasing quality), are organized left to right. (Figure reproduced with kind permission from Springer Science+Business Media: *Proceedings, 4th Mexican Conference on Pattern Recognition (MCPR)*, Perceptual Grouping using Superpixels, 2012, S. Dickinson, A. Levinshtein, and C. Sminchisescu, p. 19, Fig. 4)

and their orientation (Fig. 1.6(c)). It is in this third property that our superpixel reformulation plays a second important role—by providing an appropriate scope of contour over which our gap analysis can be conducted.

In our third contribution, the two components of our cost function, i.e., area and gap, are combined in a simple ratio that can be efficiently optimized using parametric maxflow [12] to yield the global optimum. The optimal solution yields the

Fig. 1.7 Example results of superpixel closure. (Figure reproduced with kind permission from Springer Science+Business Media: *Proceedings, 4th Mexican Conference on Pattern Recognition (MCPR)*, Perceptual Grouping using Superpixels, 2012, S. Dickinson, A. Levinshtein, and C. Sminchisescu, p. 20, Fig. 5)

largest set of superpixels bounded by contours that have the least gaps (Fig. 1.6(d)). Moreover, parametric maxflow can be used to yield the top k solutions (see [4], for example). In an object recognition setting, generating a small set of such solutions can be thought of as generating a small set of promising shape hypotheses which, through an indexing process, could invoke candidate models that could be verified (detected). The use of such multiscale hypotheses was shown to facilitate state-of-the-art object recognition in images [18].

In Fig. 1.7, we illustrate results of our superpixel closure (SC) method. In the case of the carriage, swimmer, plane, golfer, baseball player, plane, and spider, we see that the algorithm nearly correctly segments figure from background, and is able to capture the deep concavities of the object, which is particularly visible with the spider. In the case of the horse, elephant, and giraffe, we see evidence of undersegmentation due to the properties of the objective function that we're optimizing. In each case, there are false boundaries (e.g., horizon) that can increase the area of the figure without introducing additional gap. In other words, if the algorithm can follow a gap-free contour that yields a larger area, e.g., following the contour between ground and sky in the giraffe image, it will do so, yielding a bias towards compact objects.

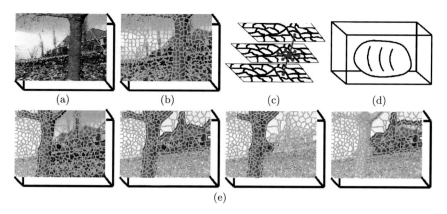

Fig. 1.8 Overview of our approach for spatiotemporal closure. (**a**) Spatiotemporal volume; (**b**) spatiotemporal superpixels; (**c**) superpixel graph with edges encoding appearance and motion affinity; (**d**) optimizing our spatiotemporal closure corresponds to finding a closed surface cutting low affinity graph edges; (**e**) our optimization framework results in multiple multiscale hypotheses, corresponding to objects, objects with their context, and object parts. (Figure reproduced with kind permission from Springer Science+Business Media: *Proceedings, 10th Asian Conference on Computer Vision (ACCV)*, 4th Mexican Conference on Pattern Recognition (MCPR), Spatiotemporal Closure, 2010, A. Levinshtein, C. Sminchisescu, and S. Dickinson, p. 370, Fig. 1)

We have extended this framework to detect spatiotemporal closure [15, 16]. Similar to detecting contour closure in images, we formulate spatiotemporal closure detection inside a spatiotemporal volume (Fig. 1.8(a)) as selecting a subset of spatiotemporal superpixels whose collective boundary falls on such discontinuities (Fig. 1.8(b)). Our spatiotemporal superpixels, extending our superpixel framework in [17], provide good spatiotemporal support regions for the extraction of appearance and motion features, while limiting the undersegmentation effects exhibited by other superpixel extraction techniques due to their lack of compactness and temporal stability.

We proceed by forming a superpixel graph whose edges encode appearance and motion similarity of adjacent superpixels (Fig. 1.8(c)). Next, we formulate spatiotemporal closure. The notion of contour gap from image closure detection is generalized to the cost of a cut of a set of spatiotemporal superpixels from the rest of the spatiotemporal volume, where the cut cost is low for superpixel boundaries that cross appearance and motion boundaries. Similarly, instead of normalization by area, we choose to normalize by a measure of internal motion and appearance homogeneity of the selection, which is more appropriate for video segmentation. The cost is again minimized using parametric maxflow [12] which is not only able to efficiently find a globally optimal closure solution, but returns multiple closure hypotheses (Fig. 1.8(e)). This not only eliminates the need for estimating the number of objects in a video sequence, as all objects with the best closure are extracted, but can result in hypotheses that oversegment objects into parts or merge adjacent objects. Multiple spatiotemporal segmentation hypotheses can serve tasks such as action recognition, video synopsis, and indexing [22].

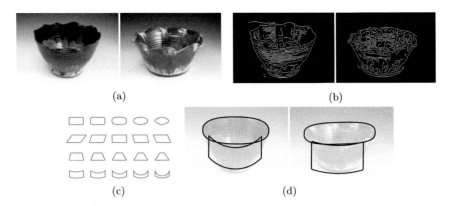

(a)   (b)

(c)   (d)

Fig. 1.9 Recovering abstract shape parts from an image: (**a**) input image of two exemplars that show considerable within-class variation; (**b**) extracted contours: note that corresponding contour-based features are seldom in one-to-one correspondence; (**c**) a simple example vocabulary of 2-D part models that will drive the perceptual grouping and shape abstraction processes; (**d**) the resulting abstract surfaces recovered by our framework; contour correspondence exists not at the level of individual contours, but at a much higher level of abstraction. (Figure reproduced with kind permission from Springer Science+Business Media: *Proceedings, 11th European Conference on Computer Vision (ECCVC)*, Contour Grouping and Abstraction using Simple Part Models, 2010, P. Sala and S. Dickinson, p. 604, Fig. 1)

1.4 Abstract Part Recovery

In the previous two sections, we reviewed approaches based on traditional Gestalt grouping principles such as symmetry and closure. But consider Fig. 1.9(a), which shows images of two object exemplars belonging to the same class (bowl). If we examine their extracted contours, shown in Fig. 1.9(b), we notice that corresponding contour-based features are seldom in one-to-one correspondence. Despite this lack of contour correspondence, the two objects are perceived as having similar shape *without any a priori knowledge of object class*, i.e., you did not run a successful bowl detector on both images. Somehow, you not only grouped this plethora of contours into surfaces, but *abstracted* the groups to yield emergent shapes that were common to both images. While cues such as symmetry and closure are indeed powerful mid-level regularities that could drive perceptual grouping of these contours, the complexity of the contours begs the question: Is there some sort of higher-level regularity, lying somewhere between low-level perceptual grouping and knowledge of the target object, that can be used to not only group the contours but recover their abstract shape?

In this third and final section of this chapter, we review our approach to the perceptual grouping and abstraction of image contours using a set of 2-D part models; details can be found in [24]. We assume no object-level prior knowledge and, like the perceptual grouping community, assume only a mid-level shape prior. However, our shape prior is slightly stronger than such classical Gestalt features as symmetry, parallelism, proximity, collinearity, etc. Specifically, our mid-level shape prior takes the form of a user-defined vocabulary of simple 2-D shape models, representing a

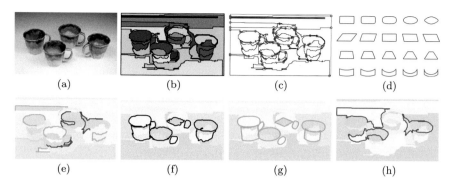

Fig. 1.10 Problem formulation: (**a**) input image; (**b**) region oversegmentation; (**c**) region boundary graph; (**d**) example vocabulary of shape models (used in our experiments); (**e**) example paths through the region boundary graph that are consistent (*green*) and inconsistent (*red*); (**f**) example detected cycles that are consistent with some model in the vocabulary; (**g**) abstractions of cycles consistent with some model; (**h**) example cycles inconsistent with all models. (Figure reproduced with kind permission from Springer Science+Business Media: *Proceedings, 11th European Conference on Computer Vision (ECCVC)*, Contour Grouping and Abstraction using Simple Part Models, 2010, P. Sala and S. Dickinson, p. 606, Fig. 2)

fixed set of parts from which a large database of object models can be constructed. In that sense, our vocabulary can be seen as a high-level nonaccidental regularity—a common denominator set of part shapes that can be used to model a large collection of objects in the world [7–9]. But since different domains may demand different vocabularies of parts, it's essential that our framework be *independent* of the part vocabulary; therefore, the vocabulary is an input to our framework.

Returning to our illustrative example, in Fig. 1.9(c), we show sample instances from a simple, example vocabulary of 2-D shapes that will be used to group and abstract the contours in Fig. 1.9(b). In Fig. 1.9(d), we overlay the abstract shapes recovered by our algorithm. It is at this level, i.e., the abstracted parts and their relations, that commonality exists between the two images. Moreover, the boundaries of these abstract parts may not correspond to explicit image boundaries in the image. Rather, they can be viewed as *hallucinations* of the actual image boundaries, after they're appropriately selected and grouped.

Our approach begins by computing a region oversegmentation (Fig. 1.10(b)) of the input image (Fig. 1.10(a)). The resulting region boundaries yield a *region boundary graph* (Fig. 1.10(c)), in which nodes represent region boundary junctions where three or more regions meet, and edges represent the region boundaries between nodes; the region boundary graph is a multigraph, since there may be multiple edges between two nodes. Our approach can be formulated as finding simple cycles in the region boundary graph whose shape is consistent with one of the model shapes in the input vocabulary (Fig. 1.10(d)); these are called *consistent cycles*. There is an exponential number of simple cycles in a planar graph [3], and simply enumerating all cycles (e.g., [30]) and comparing their shapes to the model shapes is intractable. Instead, we start from an initial set of starting edges and extend these paths, called *consistent paths* (or CPs), as long as their shapes are consistent with a part of *some* model. To determine whether a given path is consistent (and therefore extendable), we approximate the path at multiple scales with a set of polylines (piecewise linear approximations), and classify each polyline using a one-class classifier trained on the set of training shapes (Fig. 1.10(e)). When a consistent path is also a simple cycle, it is added to the set of output consistent cycles (Fig. 1.10(f)).

Figure 1.10(d) shows the input vocabulary used in our experiments: four part classes (superellipses plus sheared, tapered, and bent rectangles, representing the rows) along with a few examples of their many within-class deformations (representing the columns). Each shape model is allowed to anisotropically scale in the horizontal and vertical directions as well as rotate in the image plane. Since we employ scale-, rotation-, and translation-invariant features to train the classifiers, we need to generate only (approximately) 1,500 instances (by varying the aspect ratio and deformation parameters) belonging to these four shape classes. A *single* classifier is trained on all the component polylines (computed at multiple scales) of length (i.e., number of piecewise linear segments) k spanning the *complete* set of shape models and their deformations. Therefore, if K is the upper bound on the length of a polyline approximating a shape in the vocabulary, then K classifiers are trained. An ideal vocabulary defines a small set of "building blocks" common to a large database of objects. As such, the complexity of the vocabulary shapes is low, and even at the finest scale of polyline partitioning of a vocabulary shape's contour, K remains low; for our vocabulary, K is 13.

The algorithm outputs cycles of contours that are consistent with one of the model (training) shapes. A cycle consists of actual contours (edges in the region boundary graph) in the image, and therefore does not explicitly capture the abstract shape of the contours. Moreover, the cycle has not yet been categorized according to the shapes in the vocabulary. To abstract (or regularize) the shape of a cycle and to categorize it, we employ an active shape model (ASM) [5] trained on about 600,000 model instances (generated by varying their aspect ratio, orientation, and a finer sweeping of the deformation parameters than the one used to train the polyline classifiers). We iterate over the classical two-step ASM procedure, consecutively aligning and deforming the mean training shape with the cycle until convergence. However, we depart from a standard ASM framework in two key ways.

In a standard ASM framework, the training shapes belong to a single shape class, and the allowable, often limited, deformations are typically captured (using PCA) in a low-dimensional shape space that can be approximated by a multidimensional Gaussian distribution. Moreover, at run time, the model must be properly initialized, for if the model is grossly misaligned, the deformations required to warp the model into the image may fall outside the space of allowable deformations. In our case, given a consistent cycle, we don't know which category of vocabulary shape it belongs to, and hence which ASM model to apply (if we assumed one model per category in the vocabulary). Moreover, even if we knew its category, we assume no correct or near-correct initial landmark correspondence. We overcome the first problem by having a single ASM that's trained on all instances of all the shapes in the vocabulary, and overcome the second problem by training on all possible landmark correspondences (alignments) across these shapes.

After ASM convergence, the training shape closest to the deformed model identifies the category of the cycle. In the previous step, the consistent cycle classifier's precision rate is never 100 % at reasonable recall rates, and some of the recovered consistent cycles (of contours) may yield shapes that are qualitatively different from those in the vocabulary. Therefore, following ASM convergence, shapes that are still significantly different from the training shapes are discarded. Figure 1.10(g) illustrates the vocabulary shapes abstracted from the consistent cycles in Fig. 1.10(f); for each detected shape, the algorithm also yields its shape category. Finally, Fig. 1.10(h) illustrates some of the false positives discarded by the shape abstraction process.

In order to evaluate our framework, we created an annotated dataset with 67 images containing object exemplars whose 3-D shape can be qualitatively described by cylinders and bent or tapered cubic prisms. The abstract visible surfaces of each 3-D shape were hand-labeled using 2-D models drawn from our vocabulary. Figure 1.11 illustrates the output of our system on a number of examples in the dataset: column (a) shows the input image; column (b) shows the region oversegmentation used as input to our algorithm, computed using the local variation approach by Felzenszwalb and Huttenlocher [10] with a fixed parameterization on all images; column (c) shows the consistent cycles from which the shapes in column (d) were abstracted, representing the recovered parts closest to the ground truth in column (e). The numbers inside recovered abstract parts in column (d) indicate the rank of the part among all recovered parts in that image, computed as a function of the distance to the contours of the cycles that they are abstracting. The target regions can sometimes rank low if their degree of abstraction is high compared to non-target regions in the image (whether real or segmentation artifacts) that require less abstraction. Note that in some cases, e.g., the blender body in row 8, the ideal ground truth part (e.g., corresponding to the projection of the body of a tapered cylinder) did not exist in the vocabulary.

Exploring the results in more detail, we see that Fig. 1.11(d) shows the ability of our approach to abstract object surfaces that are locally highly irregular due to noise or within-class variation, but capture a model shape at a higher level of abstraction. In some cases (e.g., rows 5, 6, and 8), we see misalignment with a neighboring shape. This can be due to two reasons: (1) the vocabulary may not contain the appropriate shape to model the surface; and (2) the shapes are recovered independently, with no alignment constraints exploited; such constraints, as well as other constraints, will play an aggressive role in pruning/aligning hypotheses in our future work. In all the examples, we can see that the model abstraction process is able to cope with region undersegmentation when it is restricted to a relatively small section of the contour.

Our ability to abstract the shape of a cycle of contours with high local irregularity (shape "noise") means that many false positive parts will be recovered. In [25], we addressed this precision problem by moving the camera and exploiting spatiotemporal constraints in the grouping process. We introduced a novel probabilistic, graph-theoretic formulation of the problem of spatiotemporal contour grouping, in which the spatiotemporal consistency of a perceptual group under camera motion is

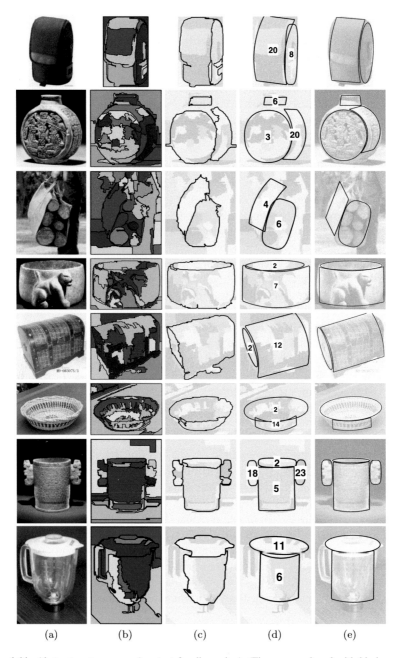

Fig. 1.11 Abstract part recovery (see text for discussion). (Figure reproduced with kind permission from Springer Science+Business Media: *Proceedings, 11th European Conference on Computer Vision (ECCVC)*, Contour Grouping and Abstraction using Simple Part Models, 2010, P. Sala and S. Dickinson, p. 613, Fig. 4)

(a) (b) (c) (d) (e)

learned from a set of training sequences. In future work, we plan to explore powerful contextual relations, including proximity, alignment, and 3-D shape information to prune many of these false positives. For example, if the surfaces in our images can indeed be the projections of volumetric parts, such as cylinders or prisms, then there are strong constraints on the shapes and relations of the component faces (parts) of their aspects. Other constraints are also possible, such as pruning smaller surfaces that are subsumed by larger surfaces.

1.5 Conclusions

The perceptual grouping of contours has long been a problem of interest to human and computer vision researchers alike. In computer vision, classical approaches have addressed the problem by first extracting contours and then grouping the contours, leading to prohibitive combinatorial complexity. We have explored this problem from the dual standpoint of region-based grouping, where regions are superpixels that minimize undersegmentation. In the case of symmetry-based grouping, the superpixels represent deformable, maximally inscribed disks (medial points), and we learn to group them when they belong to the same symmetric part. In the case of closure-based grouping, the superpixels represent "chunks" of boundary, and when the right subset of superpixels is found, those chunks of boundary will form a closure with minimal gap. Finally, in the case of part-based grouping and abstraction, the superpixels define an intractable space of contour cycles from which those whose coarse shape matches a model part are efficiently found. In each case, oversegmented regions, or superpixels, not only help manage the combinatorial complexity of traditional contour grouping, but support the inclusion of appearance information.

As the community moves from single category detection to recognition from very large databases, the strong priors provided by object detectors will have to give way to domain-independent intermediate shape priors that can yield discriminative shape structures that, in turn, are required for efficient indexing. These mid-level shape priors represent a return to perceptual grouping, and we expect research activity in this area of critical importance to rise again. Shape is clearly the most powerful and the most invariant feature of most categories, but a single shape part, unlike a SIFT feature, carries very little distinctiveness. Only when shape primitives are nonaccidentally grouped together do the resulting higher-order structures possess the indexing power required to prune a large database down to a few promising candidates. In each of the frameworks reviewed in this chapter, the perceptual grouping of superpixels yields a rich shape structure (in the case of a closed contour, a set of parts and relations can be easily extracted [27]) that will support powerful shape indexing and categorization.

Acknowledgements   The authors gratefully acknowledge the support of NSERC, Mitacs, and DARPA. Sven Dickinson would like to thank Keith Price for providing the data in Fig. 1.1(b).

References

1. Binford TO (1971) Visual perception by computer. In: Proceedings, IEEE conference on systems and control, Miami, FL
2. Blum H (1967) A transformation for extracting new descriptors of shape. In: Wathen-Dunn W (ed) Models for the perception of speech and visual form. MIT Press, Cambridge, pp 362–380
3. Buchin K, Knauer C, Kriegel K, Schulz A, Seidel R (2007) On the number of cycles in planar graphs. In: In proceedings, COCOON, LNCS, vol 4598. Springer, Berlin, pp 97–107
4. Carreira J, Sminchisescu C (2012) Cpmc: automatic object segmentation using constrained parametric min-cuts. IEEE Trans Pattern Anal Mach Intell 34(7):1312–1328
5. Cootes TF, Taylor CJ, Cooper DH, Graham J (1995) Active shape models–their training and application. Comput Vis Image Underst 61(1):38–59
6. Dalal N, Triggs B (2005) Histograms of oriented gradients for human detection. In: CVPR, pp 886–893
7. Dickinson S, Pentland A, Rosenfeld A (1990) A representation for qualitative 3-d object recognition integrating object-centered and viewer-centered models. In: Leibovic K (ed) Vision: a convergence of disciplines. Springer, New York
8. Dickinson S, Pentland A, Rosenfeld A (1992) From volumes to views: an approach to 3-d object recognition. CVGIP, Image Underst 55(2):130–154
9. Dickinson S, Pentland A, Rosenfeld A (1992) 3-d shape recovery using distributed aspect matching. IEEE Trans Pattern Anal Mach Intell 14(2):174–198
10. Felzenszwalb P, Huttenlocher D (2004) Efficient graph-based image segmentation. Int J Comput Vis 59(2):167–181
11. Huttenlocher D, Ullman S (1990) Recognizing solid objects by alignment with an image. Int J Comput Vis 5(2):195–212
12. Kolmogorov V, Boykov YY, Rother C (2007) Applications of parametric maxflow in computer vision. In: IEEE international conference on computer vision, pp 1–8
13. Levinshtein A, Dickinson S, Sminchisescu C (2009) Multiscale symmetric part detection and grouping. In: IEEE international conference on computer vision, September 2009
14. Levinshtein A, Sminchisescu C, Dickinson S (2010) Optimal contour closure by superpixel grouping. In: ECCV, pp 480–493
15. Levinshtein A, Sminchisescu C, Dickinson S (2012) Optimal image and video closure by superpixel grouping. Int J Comput Vis 100(1):99–119
16. Levinshtein A, Sminchisescu C, Dickinson SJ (2010) Spatiotemporal closure. In: ACCV, pp 369–382
17. Levinshtein A, Stere A, Kutulakos KN, Fleet DJ, Dickinson SJ, Siddiqi K (2009) Turbopixels: fast superpixels using geometric flows. IEEE Trans Pattern Anal Mach Intell 31(12):2290–2297
18. Li F, Carreira J, Sminchisescu C (2010) Object recognition as ranking holistic figure-ground hypotheses. In: CVPR, June 2010
19. Lindeberg T, Bretzner L (2003) Real-time scale selection in hybrid multi-scale representations. In: Scale-space. LNCS, vol 2695. Springer, Berlin, pp 148–163
20. Lowe D (2004) Distinctive image features from scale-invariant keypoints. Int J Comput Vis 60(2):91–110
21. Lowe DG (1985) Perceptual organization and visual recognition. Kluwer Academic, Norwell
22. Pritch Y, Rav-Acha A, Peleg S (2008) Nonchronological video synopsis and indexing. IEEE Trans Pattern Anal Mach Intell 30:1971–1984
23. Roberts L (1965) Machine perception of three-dimensional solids. In: Tippett J et al (eds) Optical and electro-optical information processing. MIT Press, Cambridge, pp 159–197
24. Sala P, Dickinson S (2010) Contour grouping and abstraction using simple part models. In: Proceedings, European conference on computer vision (ECCV), Crete, Greece, September 2010

25. Sala P, Macrini D, Dickinson S (2010) Spatiotemporal contour grouping using abstract part models. In: Proceedings, Asian conference on computer vision (ACCV), Queenstown, New Zealand, November 2010
26. Shi J, Malik J (2000) Normalized cuts and image segmentation. IEEE Trans Pattern Anal Mach Intell 22(8):888–905
27. Siddiqi K, Shokoufandeh A, Dickinson S, Zucker S (1999) Shock graphs and shape matching. Int J Comput Vis 35:13–32
28. Stahl JS, Wang S (2007) Edge grouping combining boundary and region information. IEEE Trans Image Process 16(10):2590–2606
29. Street R (1931) A gestalt completion test: a study of a cross section of intellect. Teachers College Press, Columbia University, New York
30. Tiernan J (1970) An efficient search algorithm to find the elementary circuits of a graph. Commun ACM 13(12):722–726

Chapter 2
Symmetry Is the *sine qua non* of Shape

Yunfeng Li, Tadamasa Sawada, Yun Shi, Robert M. Steinman, and Zygmunt Pizlo

2.1 Introduction

"Shape" is one of those concepts that seem intuitively obvious, but prove to be surprisingly difficult to define. In this paper, we propose a solution of this seemingly insoluble definitional problem. Our definition of shape is based on a fundamentally new first principle. By starting from scratch, we avoided what had been an insurmountable problem inherent in the traditional way of thinking about shape. In our definition, shape is characterized by a *similarity of the object to itself not to other objects* as had always been done previously. This new characterization is done by specifying how spatial features of the object are transformed, spatially or temporally, to its other spatial features. Such transformations, which are called *symmetries*, are the object's *self-similarities*. In order to anticipate objections of some readers that our definition is too narrow because it excludes objects that are completely asymmetrical from the class of objects having shape, we can point out that our definition explains what is surely the most fundamental perceptual phenomenon of shape called, "shape constancy".

By the way of reminder, *shape constancy refers to the fact that the perceived shape of a given 3D object is constant despite changes in the shape of the object's 2D retinal image. The retinal image changes when the 3D viewing orientation changes.* Conventional wisdom holds that our perceptual systems always strive for perceptual constancy and it also accepts empirical results showing that perceptual constancy in general, and shape constancy in particular, is never fully achieved. Constancy always falls far short of perfection. But note that if shape is not defined properly, a putative study of "shape constancy" is likely to produce failures of constancy simply because shape was not actually being studied. It would be completely unreasonable to expect that the observer's visual system is able to achieve shape constancy when what is meant by "shape" changes from study to study often in ad

Y. Li · T. Sawada · Y. Shi · R.M. Steinman · Z. Pizlo (✉)
Department of Psychological Sciences, Purdue University, West Lafayette, IN 47907, USA
e-mail: pizlo@psych.purdue.edu

S.J. Dickinson, Z. Pizlo (eds.), *Shape Perception in Human and Computer Vision*,
Advances in Computer Vision and Pattern Recognition,
DOI 10.1007/978-1-4471-5195-1_2, © Springer-Verlag London 2013

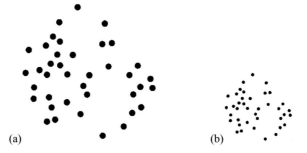

(a)   (b)

Fig. 2.1 (a) An irregular set of scattered points. (b) Is a scaled down version of (a). According to most conventional definitions, (b) has the same shape as (a). It is not clear, however, what this shape actually is, or whether either of these two dot patterns actually possesses the property we mean when we say a visual stimulus has "shape"

hoc, arbitrary ways. A better way of dealing with this confusion is to determine how shape *should* be defined so as to make it possible to show in the laboratory, what commonsense tells us happens in everyday life where shape constancy is perfect. This is what *we* did. We started by accepting that shape constancy is the *sine qua non* of shape, without shape constancy there is no shape. By starting this way, we were able to define shape *operationally* [16]. This worked well for planning shape experiments and evaluating their results but it was less than ideal because one cannot know whether an object has shape until shape constancy with the stimulus used was verified by viewing it from more than one direction.

Using an operational, rather than analytical, definition presented us with two problems, namely: (i) it can be argued that our definition was circular, and (ii) this, like all, operational definitions did not provide any *analytical* tools that could be used to formulate a mathematical or computational model of shape constancy. The first problem can be partially circumvented by pointing out that our operational definition, at the very least, allows identification of the class of objects that satisfy the shape constancy criterion. Recall, that for centuries common wisdom believed that shape constancy could *never* be achieved with *any* object. Our operational definition made it possible for us to show convincingly that shape constancy could be achieved with many objects. The second problem made it clear that an analytical definition of shape was needed. This chapter explains how this was done by proposing that *there is as much shape in an object as there is symmetry* (*regularity*) *in it*. Note that the complete *failure* of shape constancy will *never* be observed once you accept our new definition of shape. In fact, when our new definition is used, shape constancy is *almost always perfect*, and when shape constancy does fall short of perfection, we know why it does and we can explain the extent of the failure in every case. Should you worry about excluding objects that have no regularities in them from a definition of shape? The answer is "no" because our definition of shape applies to *all* natural objects important to human beings, including, animal bodies and plants, as well as to the tools we use.

Our new definition questions whether *all* objects and *all* patterns exhibit the property called "shape". Does the spatial arrangement of the points in Fig. 2.1a

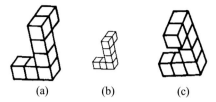

Fig. 2.2 The object in (**b**) is identical to the object in (**a**) except for its overall size. The object in (**c**) was produced by computing a 3D reflection of (**a**). According to the conventional definition of shape, all three objects have the same "shape" (after [22])

have shape? According to conventional definitions it does. If the pattern of points in Fig. 2.1a has shape, is it the same visual quality as the shape of, say, a butterfly or of an airplane? No matter which conventional definition of shape you prefer, your *commonsense* will tell you that the answer to this question is a resounding "No". The quality of shape inherent in a butterfly or in an airplane is nothing like any shape you can make out in the dotted pattern shown in Fig. 2.1. So, if we want to include *all* patterns and *all* objects in a comprehensive discussion of shape, some objects will surely have more shape than others, and there will even be *amorphous* objects without any shape, whatsoever. Bent wires and crumpled papers will fall on, or near, the amorphous end of this continuum. Prior definitions of shape will be reviewed before our new definition of shape is explained.

2.2 Prior Definitions of Shape

Most contemporary shape theorists agree that the property we have in mind when we refer to some visual arrangement as having shape refers to some aspect of this arrangement that is "invariant under transformations". Consider first, an example of what is probably the most appropriate transformation that can be used when we try to define shape. This transformation is produced by the rigid motion of an object within a 3D space. Pulling a chair away from a table is a good example. The position of the chair within the room has changed (this is what we mean by the "transformation"), but the chair, itself, did not. We call this kind of transformation a "rigid motion" because all of the geometrical properties of the chair (what the conventional definition calls the chair's "shape") stay the same. These properties are "invariant." The size of the chair stays the same, as well as all the distances and angles between the individual parts that made it up. The legs are not broken or bent, and the individual parts are not stretched by this kind of transformation. It follows that if there are two identical chairs in the room, we would say that they have the same shape.

Note that this conventional definition of shape is often generalized, slightly, by including a 3D reflection of the object and the change of its overall size. This results in a "similarity transformation." Look at Fig. 2.2. According to the conventional definition of shape, all three objects seen in Fig. 2.2 have the same shape. All angles remain the same in a similarity transformation, so an angle formed by two line segments is an invariant of this transformation. If all corresponding angles in two objects are equal, one object can be produced by transforming the other by using a similarity transformation. These two objects are said to have the same "shape" because such a transformation is possible.

This is by far the most commonly used definition of shape. There are several variants of this definition that use more general groups of transformations, leading some shape experts to suggest that shape refers to invariants of an affine transformation:

$$x' = ax + by + cz + d$$
$$y' = ex + fy + gz + h \qquad\qquad (2.1)$$
$$z' = kx + ly + mz + n$$

Affine transformation allows for uniform stretching of an object along an arbitrary direction. As a result, angles, surface areas and volumes are no longer invariant. What is invariant is the ratio of areas of two figures residing on parallel planes or the ratio of the volumes of two objects. According to this definition, any two rectangular boxes, say a shoebox and a pizza box have the same shape. This definition obviously violates our commonsense. Most people would say that a pizza box and a shoebox have very different shapes. Few, if any, people would look for their pie in the shoebox, or try to put their foot in the pizza box. Despite the obvious fact that the affine definition of shape is counterintuitive, this definition has been used in shape perception research and applications for two reasons. The first reason is geometrical. A camera image of a planar figure can be approximated by a 2D affine transformation of the figure [16]. It follows that affine invariants of planar figures will be preserved (approximately) in any camera image. This could serve as a tool for recognizing planar figures in camera (or retinal) images. The second reason was suggested by the results of psychophysical experiments. When an observer is asked to judge depth relations of points on 3D surfaces, the judgments are *always* quite *unreliable*. This poor performance was taken to indicate that metric aspects of depth are not reconstructed by the observer, which has led many, probably most, researchers to conclude that metric aspects of depth are not represented in the visual system. The smallest non-metric group is the affine group, so the observer's failure to judge metric properties led many shape experts to claim that shape is represented by affine invariants in the human visual system. The first reason just described is acceptable to us, but the second is not. We believe that *the definition of shape, including perceived shape, should be based on what the human visual system can do very well, not on what the visual system cannot do*. Very many, quite different, reasons are probably responsible for failures in visual perception, and using the failure of shape perception does not seem to be a good way to derive a useful definition. Affine invariants obviously cannot form the basis of a useful definition of shape, at least not shape as we humans perceive it. A transformation that shows that shoe and pizza boxes have the same shape cannot apply to human shape perception.

The affine group is not the end of the line when it comes to trying to use more and more abstract properties to define shape. Another definition of shape uses a

Fig. 2.3 An image of a 3D projective transformation of a cube (from Pizlo [16])

projective group of transformations:

$$x' = \frac{ax + by + cz + d}{px + qy + rz + s}$$

$$y' = \frac{ex + fy + gz + h}{px + qy + rz + s} \qquad (2.2)$$

$$z' = \frac{kx + ly + mz + n}{px + qy + rz + s}$$

The motivations for using this group are essentially the same as those used with the affine group. The advantage of using a projective group is that, unlike an affine transformation, a projective transformation provides an accurate description of image formation in a camera or in the human eye (but see [17, 18] for a detailed discussion of the limitations of the projective group as the model of retinal image formation). The disadvantage is that the projective group is larger than the affine group. Comparing them, a 3D *affine group* is characterized by 12 parameters, 5 of which affect the 3D shape as defined by a 3D rigid motion plus size scaling while a 3D *projective group* is characterized by 15 independent parameters, 8 of which affect the 3D shape as defined by a 3D rigid motion plus size scaling. Note that all hexahedra with 8 vertices and 6 quadrilateral faces are valid 3D projective transformations of a cube as long as the planarity of quadruples of points in the cube is preserved. According to the projective definition of shape, the object in Fig. 2.3 should look like a cube. This, obviously, is not the case. The fact that a 3D projective transformation of a cube does not look like a cube is precisely the reason why the Ames's room demo is so striking. According to a projective definition of shape, there is nothing special in Ames's distorted room. Ames's trapezoidal room has, according to this definition, the same shape as a normal rectangular room. So, despite the fact that the projective transformation is an essential tool for describing the relation between the 3D space and the 2D retinal image, the projective group, like the affine group, cannot provide the foundation needed for the study of human shape perception.

Shape is sometimes defined by an even more general group of transformations, namely, the topological group. The topological transformation is a continuous transformation. When used in a 2D space, this transformation is often called "rubber sheet geometry", because the rubber can be stretched arbitrarily without tearing or cutting. The main reason for using a topological group to define shape is that it allows one to identify two different postures of an animal body as the same shape. But the "price" paid for being able to handle non-rigid objects is very high: for example, when a topological definition is used, a needle and a coffee cup have identical shapes! Both are 3D surfaces with one hole. It is obviously the *metric* properties which allow one to use a cup to drink and a needle to sew. Obviously, the topological transformation, like the affine and the projective transformations, is not without its problems when human shape perception is under study.

There is a way to avoid the excessive generality inherent in the topological transformation (just described) while preserving the ability to handle non-rigid and piecewise rigid objects, namely, the shape under consideration can be characterized by geodesics along a surface. Recall that the shortest path between two points on a surface is a geodesic curve of the surface. When an animal changes its posture, all geodesic lines stay the same, or nearly the same. Similarly, when the stem of a flower bends, the geodesics along its surface stay approximately the same. So, geodesic lines are much more attractive than topological properties for describing shapes. There are, however at least two serious shortcomings in using geodesic lines. First, finding geodesic lines is computationally difficult, so using them beyond toy examples is impractical. Second, defining a 3D shape by using lines, which are 1D properties, will not work because geodesic lines do not convey any information about the volumetric aspects of the object. For example, all *origami* shapes (3D shapes produced by folding paper) are identical in a "geodesic" definition of their shape, and they *all* have the same shape as an unfolded, flat piece of paper.

Clearly, there are multiple problems with all of the conventional definitions in use for describing shape: some are too restrictive and others too general. Recall what we really want our definition to do. We want it to exclude random dot patterns like the pattern shown in Fig. 2.1, but we want it to include non-rigid objects such as walking animals and human beings. Furthermore, if we do not want to exclude *any* objects, whatsoever, can we find a way to assign some degree of shape to all objects, even to objects with very little or even no shape? It can be done but this requires us to adopt an entirely new way of thinking about shape. The way we adopted goes as follows: *If shape is to capture permanent (invariant) properties of an object's geometry, properties that will allow us to recover the object, recognize it, remember it and identify its function, shape must refer to the object's intrinsic characteristics in a way that does not require comparing one object with other objects. The way to do this, perhaps the only way, is to define shape by object's self-similarities.*

2.3 Explanation of the New Definition and How We Worked It out

Recall that all conventional definitions of shape have assumed that *all* objects have shape. Intuitively, even commonsensically, something seems to be missing from this very strong claim. Namely, there are patterns and objects that actually have no shape at all, or at most, they have very little of this property. Asking someone about the shape of the pattern of randomly generated points like the pattern shown in Fig. 2.1, makes little sense. Commonsense tells us that there is little, if any, shape in Fig. 2.1. We also "know" that shapeless common objects exist in everyday life. A crumpled piece of paper, a bent paperclip, or a rock before it is shaped by a human hand do not

Fig. 2.4 Eight
differently-shaped
meaningless objects
characterized by translational
symmetry. The shape of the
cross section is constant for
each cone, but the size is not
necessarily constant. The axis
is orthogonal to the cross
sections and it is a planar
curve or a straight line (from
Pizlo [16])

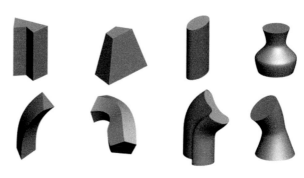

have what we really mean when we refer to an object's shape. All of these objects, as well as random patterns like the pattern in Fig. 2.1, are, and should be, called "amorphous" or "shapeless." Why? They are amorphous simply because they are *completely "irregular."*

This observation makes it very clear that the term *"shape" refers to the spatial regularity (self-similarity) possessed by an object.* We have all had lots of experience dealing with such regularities in our everyday life. The bodies of *all* animals are mirror-symmetrical. By "mirror-symmetrical" we simply mean that one symmetrical half is the mirror image (the reflection) of the other with respect to the animal's plane of symmetry. But there is more to symmetry than mirror symmetry and reflection. Limbs of animals, trunks of trees, and stems of flowers are characterized by what we call "translational symmetry". An object with translational symmetry is produced by taking a planar shape and sweeping it through a 3D space using rigid motion along an axis. During the sweeping process, the size of the cross section may change. Figure 2.4 shows several examples of objects with translational symmetry. They are called "Generalized Cones" (GC) [2, 4].

Take one of the 8 objects in Fig. 2.4, say the second from the left in the top row. All cross sections of this object are *similar* to each other. The technical meaning of *similar* here is that the members of any pair of cross sections in this object are related to each other by a similarity transformation (rigid motion and size scaling). So, *we can use rigid motion, reflection and size-scaling of the "parts" within the object, itself, to define the shape of the object as its "spatial self-similarity"(regularity)* instead of using rigid motion, reflection and size-scaling of the entire object in 3D space to define the shape of this object by comparing it to another object. *Put simply, shape is an intrinsic characteristic of an object because it refers to its self-similarity, rather than to the similarity of one object to another.* A small-scale model of an airplane has the same shape as a real airplane not merely because the model is a scaled version of the plane, but because both the model and a real airplane are characterized by the same symmetries.

Self-similarity of biological forms seems to be their inherent characteristic. It is the result of the natural process called "growth" (D'Arcy Thompson [24]). Growth explains why all flowers and plants are characterized by one or more types of symmetry. They have the shape they have because of *how they grow.* All animal bodies are mirror symmetrical because of the *way they move.* A dog without a mirror symmetrical body could not run straight along a straight path. *All biological forms have shape because all of them are symmetrical.* Inanimate objects such as rocks and crumpled papers, which have no trace of symmetry, are obviously shapeless. It is also important to note that many inanimate objects actually do have shape. All objects that serve some useful function, such objects as furniture and tools, have one or more types of symmetry, without which they would probably be dysfunctional.

Symmetry relations among parts of objects imply the presence of invariants of 3D symmetry transformations. These invariants can be represented as the eigenvectors of the 3D transformation matrix. We will analyze their 2D perspective images to derive the perspective invariants of their symmetries after we derive the formulas for the eigenvectors characterizing their 3D symmetries. These invariants are needed for the veridical recovery of 3D shapes. This approach leads naturally to the two essential aspects that are required to characterize shape perception, namely, (i) properties of the retinal image that provide *visual data* about the *invariants* of symmetries, and (ii) the kind of *a priori knowledge* that is needed to produce the 3D shape percept which provides information about the symmetry transformations characterizing the self-similarities of the particular object. The reader should appreciate the fact that our new definition of shape is *richer* than any of the previous definitions because our definition uses *both* invariants and the transformations, whereas all previous definitions only used invariants.

2.4 Symmetry Groups for 3D Shapes, Their Invariants and Invariants of the Perspective Projection

Our analytical definition of shape states that the shape of an object refers to all of its spatially-global symmetries (its self-similarities) as measured by the group of rigid motions, reflections and size-scaling of the "parts" within the object itself.

Groups of transformations are known to have invariants. Unlike all conventional approaches to shape, we begin *not* with invariants of transformations from one object to another, but with invariants of transformations of one part of an object to another part of the same object. This makes sense because we defined 3D shape as the presence of self-similarity. It is known that a similarity transformation is a linear transformation and that it can be represented by a matrix. Furthermore, it is known that eigenvectors are the only invariant vectors of a linear transformation. It follows that it is natural to look for invariants by analyzing the properties of the eigenvectors characterizing the transformation matrices. Consider the three basic symmetries: mirror, translational and rotational. We begin with a symmetrical shape, whose repeated part is planar, and then extend the results to general symmetrical shapes. Some invariants are limited and exist only for the symmetries with a planar configuration, and the others are general.

Assume that c is a point on a plane π, n_X and n_Y are two perpendicular axes in π. The normal of π is n_Z (see Fig. 2.5). c, n_X and n_Y define a 2D Cartesian coordinate system, in which c is the origin and n_X and n_Y are the two axes. Let a

Fig. 2.5 Illustration of a 3D translation of a point from one plane to the other

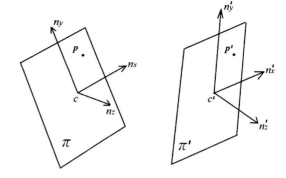

3×3 matrix A represent this coordinate system

$$A = (n_X \quad n_Y \quad c) \tag{2.3}$$

Then any point in π can be expressed as

$$P = Ap \tag{2.4}$$

where $p = (p_X, p_Y, 1)^{\mathrm{T}}$ in which p_X and p_Y are the Cartesian coordinates of P in π. Assume that π' is the resulting plane after some rigid transformation of π. The normal of π' is n'_Z and the Cartesian coordinate system is expressed as

$$A' = \left(n'_X \quad n'_Y \quad c'\right) \tag{2.5}$$

The resulting point P after the rigid transformation is obtained as:

$$P' = A'p \tag{2.6}$$

Combining Eqs. (2.4) and (2.6), we obtain the transformation from the point P to P'

$$P' = A'A^{-1}P \tag{2.7}$$

which means that the transformation from P to P' is a 3D affine transformation.

Next, we use A and A' to define the three types of symmetries, translational, mirror and rotational, and identify the invariants for those symmetry transformations.

(a) If $n_X = n'_X$, the transformation from π to π' is a translational symmetry (see Fig. 2.6a). The translation axis (the red curve in Fig. 2.6a) is a planar curve and n_X coincides with the normal of the plane containing the axis. If the translation axis is not a planar curve, the transformation is a mixture of a translational symmetry and a rotational symmetry. It is easy to prove that n_X is one of the eigenvectors of the transformation matrix $A'A^{-1}$. Since n_X is constant and is only determined by the plane in which the translation axis resides (see Fig. 2.6a), n_X is an invariant of the projective transformation from one cross section to another.

(b) If $n_X = n'_X$ and cc' bisects the angle formed by n_Z and n'_Z, the transformation from π to π' is a mirror symmetry (see Fig. 2.6b). Compared with the translational symmetry, an additional constraint is added in the mirror symmetry. It follows that a mirror symmetry with a planar configuration is a special case of the translational symmetry. The fact that cc' bisects the angle formed by n_Z and n'_Z is equivalent to the fact that a symmetry plane (the plane in red in Fig. 2.6b) bisects the planes π to π'. The normal of the symmetry plane is $n_Y - n'_Y$. Both n_X and $n_Y - n'_Y$ are the eigenvectors of $A'A^{-1}$.

(c) If $c = c'$, $n_Z = n'_Z$ and $n_X \neq n'_X$, the transformation from π to π' is a rotational symmetry (see Fig. 2.6c). It is easy to prove that c is an eigenvector of $A'A^{-1}$. Since c is the rotation center of a planar rotationally symmetrical object and it is a fixed point, c is an invariant of a rotationally symmetric transformation. The other two eigenvectors of $A'A^{-1}$ are $n_X + in_Y$ and $n_X - in_Y$. They are not invariant because n_X or n_Y could be an arbitrary direction (or vector) on the plane π. However, their cross product n_Z is. The geometrical application of the cross product (n_Z) will be discussed in the next part.

Up to this point, we characterized the invariants of the three types of symmetries in 3D space. This is a transformation from one part of an object to another. We are also interested in the invariants of 2D perspective images of 3D symmetry relations—the invariants of the transformation from the image of one part of an object to an image of another part of the same object. This will be essential for detecting 3D symmetries in perspective images and for recovering 3D symmetrical shapes from perspective images.

Assume that a pair of symmetric corresponding points P and P' in π and π' are projected to an image through a camera and that the camera matrix is K. A camera matrix is an upper triangular 3×3 matrix, consisting of a camera's intrinsic parameters, such as its focal length and principal point. Then, the images of P and P' are

$$v = KAp \tag{2.8}$$

$$v' = KA'p \tag{2.9}$$

Note that the image points v and v' are expressed in homogeneous coordinates and they are 3-element vectors (refer to [9], for the details of differences between Euclidean coordinates and homogeneous coordinates). Combining Eqs. (2.8) and (2.9), we obtain

$$v' = KA'A^{-1}K^{-1}v \tag{2.10}$$

Equation (2.10) implies that the relation between images of the planes π to π' is a 2D projective transformation. By analyzing the eigenvectors of $KA'A^{-1}K^{-1}$, we look for the invariants for the above three types of symmetries in their 2D perspective images. It is known that an eigenvector has the following property: if m is an eigenvector of $A'A^{-1}$, then Km is an eigenvector of $KA'A^{-1}K^{-1}$. Therefore, it is easy to identify the invariants in the 2D image from the invariants of 3D symmetry transformations. Next, we list the invariants in the 2D image and explain their geometrical meaning.

(a) In the case of translational symmetry, since n_X is an invariant vector of the symmetry transformation in 3D, Kn_X is an invariant of the projective transformation from one perspective image of a cross section to a perspective image of another cross section. Geometrically, Kn_X represents the vanishing point of the lines that are parallel to n_X. This means that for a 2D projective transformation between the images of any two cross sections, the vanishing point is projected to itself (the invariant point under projective transformation). Identifying the vanishing point Kn_X should help recover translationally symmetrical 3D shapes from their images [23].

(b) In the case of mirror symmetry, n_X and $n_Y - n'_Y$ are the invariant eigenvectors of $A'A^{-1}$. So are Kn_X and $K(n_Y - n'_Y)$ for $KA'A^{-1}K^{-1}$. Kn_X and $K(n_Y - n'_Y)$ are the vanishing points for those lines that are parallel to n_X and $n_Y - n'_Y$, respectively. In particular, $K(n_Y - n'_Y)$ is the vanishing point for those lines that are perpendicular to the symmetry plane. Because $K(n_Y - n'_Y)$ is determined by the normal of the symmetry plane, it is independent of the orientation of π or π'. This means that $K(n_Y - n'_Y)$ can be used with mirror-symmetrical objects whose symmetrical halves are not planar. For example, for the polyhedron in Fig. 2.6e, its lateral side is non-planar and it consists of three planar faces. From the image of each face and its symmetrical counterpart, we compute a 2D projective transformation matrix. For the three matrices representing the relations between images of the three pairs of symmetrical faces, $K(n_Y - n'_Y)$ is their common eigenvector. In a perspective image, once the vanishing point $K(n_Y - n'_Y)$ is identified and the symmetry correspondences in the image are established, the shape of a 3D mirror symmetrical object can be uniquely determined [14]. Because Kn_X and $K(n_Y - n'_Y)$ are invariant, their cross product $K^{-T}((n_Y - n'_Y) \times n_X)$, representing a line passing through Kn_X and $K(n_Y - n'_Y)$, is also invariant under the projective transformation $KA'A^{-1}K^{-1}$.[1] This means that any point on this line projects onto this line again. The points Kn_X and $K(n_Y - n'_Y)$ are two special points on this line because they project onto themselves.

(c) In the case of rotational symmetry, Kc is the invariant eigenvector of $KA'A^{-1}K^{-1}$. It is the image of c (the image of the rotation center) and it is an invariant point under the projective transformation between the images of a repeated part of a rotationally symmetrical shape. The other two eigenvectors of $KA'A^{-1}K^{-1}$, $K(n_X + in_Y)$ and $K(n_X - in_Y)$ are not invariant. But, their cross product $K^{-T}n_Z$ is and it represents an invariant line. n_Z is the direction of the rotation axis and it is fixed for a rotationally symmetrical shape. $K^{-T}n_Z$ is

---

[1] The magnitude of a vector is unimportant in a homogeneous coordinate system. So, we can ignore $\det(K)$, which is a constant, from the cross product $\det(K)K^{-T}((n_Y - n'_Y) \times n_X)$ of Kn_X and $K(n_Y - n'_Y)$.

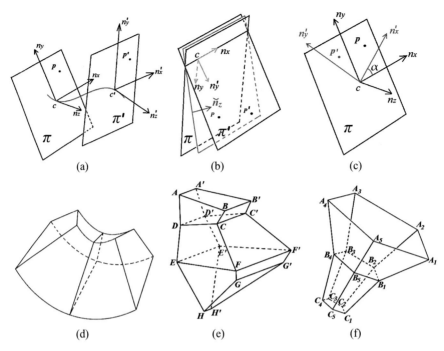

Fig. 2.6 Three types of symmetries and their symmetry transformations. (**a**) Translational symmetry. The *red planar curve* represents the translation axis. (**b**) Mirror symmetry. The *red plane* represents the symmetry plane. (**c**) Rotational symmetry. c is the rotation center. (**d**) A translational symmetrical 3D shape with a quadrilateral cross sections. (**e**) A mirror-symmetrical 3D shape that consists of three pairs of mirror-symmetrical planes. (**f**) A rotationally symmetrical 3D shape that consists of three planes

more general than the invariant Kc and it can be applied to the non-planar rotational shape like the one in Fig. 2.6f. $K^{-T}n_Z$ is an invariant line for the plane $A_1A_2A_3A_4A_5$ and it is also the invariant line for the planes $B_1B_2B_3B_4B_5$ and $C_1C_2C_3C_4C_5$.

It is known that at least four points and their correspondences are needed to compute the 2D projective transformation matrix. Therefore, four planar points "out there" and their symmetrical counterparts are needed to identify the invariance in a perspective image. The invariants for the three types of symmetries are listed in Table 2.1. Those invariants representing lines are marked by *.

Table 2.1 shows the invariants of symmetry transformations under a perspective projection. Because an orthographic projection is a special case of a perspective projection, these equations can also be applied to the orthographic projection after making two changes in the camera matrix K, and the matrices A and A'. First, in the case of an orthographic projection, the principal point is undefined. So, we set the elements in the camera matrix K that represent the principal points to zero. Second, the last row in vectors A and A' is replaced by $(0, 0, 1)$, which means that the change of Z values of vertices doesn't change their image. As a result, $KA'A^{-1}K^{-1}$ has

Table 2.1 The invariants for the three types of symmetries

Type	Planar configuration	Non-planar configuration
Translation	$K n_X$	$K n_X$
Mirror	$K n_X, K(n_Y - n'_Y), K^{-T}((n_Y - n'_Y) \times n_X)^*$	$K(n_Y - n'_Y)$
Rotation	$K c, K^{-T} n_Z^*$	$K^{-T} n_Z^*$

the same format as A and A', in which the last row vector is $(0, 0, 1)$. It follows that the symmetry transformation under an orthographic projection is a 2D affine transformation, instead of a 2D projective transformation. For an affine transformation, three points and their correspondences are enough to determine the transformation matrix and then identify the invariants. It follows that in the case of an orthographic projection, co-planarity of points or curves is not required.

2.5   Inferring 3D Shape from a 3D Object

With a real object, its shape (its symmetries) must be inferred (abstracted). The symmetries are not given. The best (perhaps the only) way to do this is by using a Bayesian formalism and a closely-related concept called "Minimum Description Length" [11]. This method will be analogous to the "generative" model formulated by Feldman & Singh [8] and used for their 2D medial axis transform (identification of a "shape skeleton"). The main differences are that our model applies to 3D shapes and it handles several 3D symmetries. We start by formulating the problem as a Bayesian inference [10]. Our task is to estimate the 3D symmetries (we call this the "shape" of the object) that best describe a given 3D "object". This means that we try to maximize the posterior probability, $p(\text{shape}|\text{object})$. Take a generalized cone like the one on the top-left of Fig. 2.4. This 3D object has two possible descriptions, one based on translational symmetry and the other based on mirror symmetry (this object has both symmetries). Translational symmetry seems to capture its 3D structure better, so the maximum of the posterior will probably be higher when translational symmetry serves as the shape description than when the description is based on its mirror symmetry. The planar cross section (pentagon) of this Generalized Cone (GC) is a simple 2D figure whose contour information is fairly low [7]. The same is true with the axis of this GC, which is a straight-line segment. It follows that the prior, $p(\text{shape})$, for translational symmetry will be high in this case. This object does not have any random perturbations, which means that the likelihood, $p(\text{object}|\text{shape})$, will be equal to 1.0. As a result, the maximum of the posterior will also be high:

$$p(\text{shape}|\text{object}) = c \cdot p(\text{object}|\text{shape}) \cdot p(\text{shape}) \qquad (2.11)$$

Note that what we call "an object", Feldman & Singh [8] call a "shape", but this difference is only terminological. By taking the negative logarithm of both sides of (2.11), we can express our problem in terms of the description length, DL:

$$DL(\text{shape}|\text{object}) = DL(\text{object}|\text{shape}) + DL(\text{shape}) + c' \qquad (2.12)$$

Now we can look for the shortest description length, $DL(\text{shape}|\text{object})$, instead of looking for a maximum of the posterior probability. The "shape" solution is the same.

If we consider the maximum of the posterior, $p(\text{shape}|\text{object})$, for mirror symmetry, we will get a smaller value (a more complex description) because mirror symmetry will lead to lower "compression" of the shape of this object. Mirror symmetry will not "know" about the simplicity of its cross section. The only redundancy represented by mirror symmetry is the fact that one half is the same as the other half. Note that this is less obvious than it sounds because the actual prior, $p(\text{shape})$, in this case, depends on how we describe one half of this mirror-symmetrical object. One could do this by using a large number of points on the surface, or by using straight lines, the object's contours, interpolated by planar surface patches. Mirror symmetry might become a better description of an object like the one on the top-left in Fig. 2.4, when the mirror-symmetrical cross-section becomes less regular. This can be done by introducing random perturbation of the object's contours, while keeping these perturbations mirror-symmetrical. Such perturbations will be counted as random noise in the likelihood, $p(\text{object}|\text{shape})$, when translational symmetry, but not when mirror symmetry is used. This will lower the value of the posterior. It should be obvious that the formalisms (2.11) and (2.12) allow both the object's regularities (symmetries) and random perturbations to be handled naturally. In other words, all objects, no matter how irregular, can be described in this way. Less regular objects will have more complex descriptions and the maximum of the posterior, $p(\text{shape}|\text{object})$, ranging between 0 and 1, can be used as a measure of the object's "shapeness".

In this approach, similarities among different shapes can be evaluated by simply comparing the objects' symmetries. In Sect. 2.2, we discussed how metric symmetries can be generalized to affine and projective groups. Recall that all symmetries are defined by the underlying groups of transformations, where "group" has a specific meaning. Group refers to a set of transformations that satisfies the group's axioms, like closure and associativity. It follows that the change from one "shape" to another (where "shape" means a description of an object's symmetries, using a particular symmetry group) will be represented by a transformation of its characteristics (cross section, axis) by using one of the groups, namely, Euclidean, similarity, affine, projective or topological. At this point it is not clear whether this approach will naturally lead to a one-dimensional dissimilarity metric representing the currently conventional way of thinking about similarity in cognitive psychology (e.g., [1]), or whether it will turn out to be a parameterized (geometrical) measure making explicit use of the concepts of transformation groups. After all, when we compare a pizza box to a shoebox, we may be more comfortable saying that "they have different aspect ratios" than that their "dissimilarity is about 7.4".

2.6 Computational and Psychophysical Implications of the New Definition

Now that we have explained both geometrical and algebraic characteristics of shape based on symmetry, we will discuss several interesting implications of our new definition. Two of these implications were anticipated in our recent papers (Sects. 2.6.1 and 2.6.4), and two are new (Sects. 2.6.2 and 2.6.3).

2.6.1 Veridical Perception of 3D Shapes

Recovering a 3D shape from one or more 2D retinal images is an ill-posed inverse problem [15, 20]. This is the case with all difficult inverse problems, so producing a unique and correct interpretation requires the application of constraints to the family of possible solutions. When a 3D symmetry constraint is applied to a single 2D perspective image of a 3D shape, the 3D interpretation is unique and always very close to veridical! The shape recovered is said to be "veridical" because it is the same as the object's shape "out there". During the last 6 years we provided empirical, both simulation and psychophysical evidence, showing how symmetry leads to veridical 3D shape recovery. This includes the recovery of 3D mirror-symmetrical shapes from: (i) a single image [12], and (ii) a pair of images [13], as well as (iii) the recovery of nearly symmetrical shapes [21] and (iv) 3D shapes characterized by translational symmetry [23]. The claim that 3D shapes can be, and actually are, perceived veridically is completely new [19] and until very recently, the "veridical perception of shape" was considered by most shape researchers to be "science fiction", something that does not exist, never has existed, and never will exist. This conventional "wisdom" was based on hundreds of years of reporting failures to achieve shape constancy in the laboratory. Everyone believed that human shape perception could never be perfect or even nearly so. We now know that all of these reported failures came about because everybody was studying the perception of depth, not the perception of shape [16]. Once shape is defined properly, by it symmetries, this confusion is removed and a "miracle" ensues. Shape perception *is* perfect when the viewing conditions and psychophysical measurements are done correctly. How this can be done was explained in our papers (referenced just above) in which we described computational models that use the mathematical properties of symmetry to recover 3D shape and presented extensive psychophysical data on 3D shape recovery and on shape constancy.

2.6.2 Shapes of Non-rigid Objects

When shape is defined by self-similarity, rather than by the similarity of one object to another, it becomes much easier to talk about the shapes of "non-rigid" and

Fig. 2.7 Three snapshots from a range of articulations of non-rigid objects: *Top*—the axis of a GC is changing, but the shape of the cross-section is the same (this looks like a gymnast on uneven bars at the Olympic Games). *Middle*—the shape of the cross-section is changing, but the axis is not (this looks like a flying bird). *Bottom*—the local size of the cross-section is changing, but the shape of the cross-section and the axis of the GC is constant (this looks like a snake that swallowed a large belly-bulging prey)

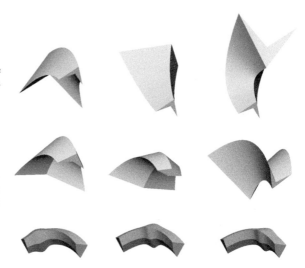

"piece-wise rigid" objects. If an object is non-rigid, like the stem of a flower, bending the stem does not remove its translational symmetry. All of the flower's cross-sections are still circular. Bending only changes the curvature of the axis of the flower's stem. If an object is piece-wise rigid, like the body of a dog, changes in the articulations of its legs distorts the mirror symmetry of the dog's body, but it does *not* eliminate the symmetry altogether. After all, the dog still has two legs on the right side of his body and two legs on the left side. This obviously applies as well to your body as to your dog's. Our new analytical definition of shape removes the fundamental difficulty inherent in all other conventional definitions of shape. None of them can deal with the non-rigidity of objects, objects that are both common and often very important throughout our natural environment.

Consider some examples (Fig. 2.7). Three snapshots of non-rigid, unfamiliar objects are shown. It is easy to see that the three objects in a given row have something in common. They share symmetries. The objects on top have the same shape of their cross-sections, the objects in the middle have the same axis, and the objects at the bottom have the same axis as well as the same shape of their cross-sections. If an observer is able to see the similarities of the symmetries of an object despite the non-rigidity of this object, he may be able to conclude that the shape of the object being viewed is constant despite its non-rigidity. This is what we mean by perceiving the shape of a non-rigid object.

2.6.3 Symmetry as an Objective, but Informative, Prior

"Objective priors" have a special status in Bayesian methods used to solve inverse problems, probably simply because "objective" sounds more reliable and more scientific than "subjective". But there is another pair of terms for these two types of priors, namely, "uninformative" and "informative". Uninformative priors are objective in the sense that these priors are derived from some basic statistical and mathematical principles, rather than from some special domain such as knowledge about lung cancer or about earthquakes. Such domain specific knowledge is less interesting because it results in a Bayesian inference method that is specific to a particular domain. Also, it is often difficult to quantify this kind of subjective prior. If the prior is unreliable, the posterior will also be unreliable. The good news in the conventional approach, is that there is an objective way to learn the subjective prior. One begins with an objective, uninformative prior and starts collecting evidence. The posterior computed after the first piece of evidence is acquired is used as a prior for the second piece of evidence. Bayesian inference, including updating priors is optimal in the sense that it extracts all relevant information contained in the data. By the time that the learning has been completed, we have a very good, informative prior that is based on hard data without any "subjective" guessing.

With shape recovery, however, we are presented with a unique situation in which an *objective prior is actually informative*. It seems likely that this unique situation only applies to a symmetry prior. No other prior has this unique characteristic. All other priors in all other inverse problems, can be *either* objective *or* informative. This fact, alone, is responsible both for the special and unique status of shape in visual perception and for the fact that shapes are perceived veridically (see [16], for the uniqueness of shape in visual perception). Once we realize that *all* important objects are symmetrical, the *informative* prior of 3D symmetry becomes an *objective* prior because it refers to mathematical invariants, specifically to invariants of transformation groups. There is no need, whatsoever, to learn group invariants from examples. We can derive them analytically, and once the invariants are derived, we can prove their invariance and examine the necessary and sufficient conditions for them to operate. Symmetries are also informative because they represent the fundamental (permanent, invariant, and intrinsic) characteristics of the 3D objects "out there". So, once we know that all objects are symmetrical, it makes no sense, whatsoever, to start with any uninformative priors because symmetry, alone, is sufficiently informative, and once symmetry is used as a prior, it also makes no sense, whatsoever, to update it. How could you improve (update) a definition of a mirror symmetry? It simply cannot be done. Note that the symmetry prior can be applied to infinitely many shapes in a finite amount of time, and this includes unfamiliar shapes and even the shapes of non-existent objects.

2.6.4 Shape Constancy: View-Invariant vs. View-Dependent Shape Perception

Note that shape constancy is typically tested with novel (unfamiliar) objects in order to avoid allowing familiarity to influence the shape perceived. All studies of shape constancy prior to ours focused efforts on determining the availability of invariant properties in the 2D image (see [16], for a review). If invariants cannot be extracted reliably from the 2D retinal image, shape constancy fails or, at least, degrades when the size of the change of the viewing direction increases. This result encouraged investigators to accept what is known as the "view-point dependence of shape perception". Before we explain what is missing in this view-point dependent view of shape perception, we will remind the reader about a basic aspect of conventional shape constancy methodology. In a typical experiment of this kind, the subject is shown the same object twice, with the second viewing direction different from the first by an "angle α". The angle α refers to the rotation of the object in depth, that is, a rotation around an axis that is orthogonal to the line of sight. Only then will the shape of the 2D retinal image change, and a change in the shape of the retinal image is the necessary condition for studying shape constancy. When the object is rotated around the line of sight, not orthogonal to it, the 2D retinal shape does not change; only its 2D orientation changes, so such an experiment cannot have any bearing on the shape constancy phenomenon.

Appropriate methodology for performing experiments to test shape constancy introduces a complication that has never been discussed explicitly in the past. For large values of α, shape constancy may be difficult to achieve because some parts of an opaque object that were visible in the first presentation, are not visible after the object is rotated, and new parts may become visible in the second presentation. So, shape constancy, in such cases, may not be perfect for a trivial reason: the relevant information was simply not available to the observer. But if the object is symmetrical, or if it is composed of symmetrical parts, as it was in Biederman & Gerhardstein's [3] experiment, it may be possible to recover the entire 3D shape, including the back, invisible parts. In such cases, shape constancy might be perfect because the entire 3D shape could be recovered correctly in both presentations. This problem has not been studied in the past because there was no computational theory that could predict when an entire shape, back as well as front, can be recovered. We now know that the symmetry of an object is the key concept involved in recovering the invisible backs of 3D objects. These objects must have a sufficient degree of redundancy (regularity and self-similarity) to permit an observer to correctly "guess" (recover) the shape of the hidden part. We already have a computational model that can *usually* recover the entire 3D shape of a mirror-symmetrical object [12]. It can also recover a translationally symmetrical object [23]. However, the entire shape may not be recovered, even if the object is symmetrical, if the object does not have a sufficient degree of regularity. This is precisely what happens with irregular objects like symmetrical polyhedra, whose faces are not planar [5] or with symmetrical irregular "potatoes" and "bell peppers" [6]. It follows that shape constancy is actually much more concerned with invariants in the 3D representation, after the 3D shape is recovered, than with the presence of invariants in the 2D retinal image. For those symmetrical objects, whose entire shape can be recovered, shape constancy will not be affected by the degree of rotation in depth. Put simply, performance will be view-invariant. For objects, like irregular polyhedra, or potatoes and bell peppers, whose back parts cannot be recovered, performance will be view-dependent. This analysis should clarify, once and for all, the apparent controversy between the proponents of both theories. The key to understanding what is going on resides in the recovery of 3D shapes rather than in the presence of cues or invariants in the 2D retinal image.

2.7 Conclusion

In the past, the only thing that everyone agreed about when trying to define shape was that shape refers to the spatially-global geometrical characteristics of an object or a figure. Once one appreciates that all important objects in our natural environment are symmetrical, it follows that any meaningful definition of shape must be based on the concept of symmetry. Imagine how difficult it would be to describe spatially-global geometrical characteristics of a symmetrical object adequately without mentioning its symmetry? It is probably impossible to do this! But using symmetry to describe an object cannot be the whole story because a definition of shape should go beyond a mere description of the object's geometry. The concept called "shape" is used in many ways. We use it to identify objects, we use it to compare similar objects, we use it to remember and to recognize objects, we use it to infer an object's functions, and we use it to identify the permanence of objects in the presence of non-rigidities. We conclude by claiming that *all* of these things can be done *only* when shape is defined by the object's symmetries, as we explained in detail above. Furthermore, all of these things can be done very well, and they can be done in a very principled way because "symmetry groups", with their concepts of transformations and invariants, provide the foundation of large parts of mathematics. By excluding only the very few objects in our natural environment that are completely devoid of symmetries, you can use our new definition of shape to accomplish a great deal more than had been possible before we explained the significance and utility of symmetry in the visual perception of shape. You will have to use experience and learning with irregular rocks and crumpled papers to discriminate their shapes, but with *all* other shapes, you can depend entirely on symmetry.

References

1. Ashby FG, Perrin NA (1988) Toward a unified theory of similarity and recognition. Psychol Rev 95(1):124–150
2. Biederman I (1987) Recognition-by-components: a theory of human image understanding. Psychol Rev 94(2):115–147
3. Biederman I, Gerhardstein PC (1993) Recognizing depth-rotated objects: evidence and conditions from three-dimensional viewpoint invariance. J Exp Psychol Hum Percept Perform 19(6):1162–1182
4. Binford TO (1971) Visual perception by computer. In: IEEE conference on systems and control, Miami
5. Chan MW, Stevenson AK, Li Y, Pizlo Z (2006) Binocular shape constancy from novel views: the role of a priori constraints. Percept Psychophys 68(7):1124–1139
6. Egan E, Todd J, Phillips F (2012) The role of symmetry in 3D shape discrimination across changes in viewpoint. J Vis 12(9):1048

7. Feldman J, Singh M (2005) Information along curves and closed contours. Psychol Rev 112(1):243–252
8. Feldman J, Singh M (2006) Bayesian estimation of the shape skeleton. Proc Natl Acad Sci 103(47):18014–18019
9. Hartley R, Zisserman A (2003) Multiple view geometry in computer vision. Cambridge University Press, Cambridge
10. Knill DC, Richards W (1996) Perception as Bayesian inference. Cambridge University Press, New York
11. Li M, Vitanyi P (1997) An introduction to Kolmogorov complexity and its applications. Springer, New York
12. Li Y, Pizlo Z, Steinman RM (2009) A computational model that recovers the 3D shape of an object from a single 2D retinal representation. Vis Res 49(9):979–991
13. Li Y, Sawada T, Shi Y, Kwon T, Pizlo Z (2011) A Bayesian model of binocular perception of 3D mirror symmetrical polyhedra. J Vis 11(4):1–20
14. Li Y, Sawada T, Latecki LM, Steinman RM, Pizlo Z (2012) Visual recovery of the shapes and sizes of objects, as well as distances among them, in a natural 3D scene. J Math Psychol 56(4):217–231
15. Pizlo Z (2001) Perception viewed as an inverse problem. Vis Res 41(24):3145–3161
16. Pizlo Z (2008) 3D shape: its unique place in visual perception. MIT Press, Cambridge
17. Pizlo Z, Rosenfeld A, Weiss I (1997) The geometry of visual space: about the incompatibility between science and mathematics. Comput Vis Image Underst 65:425–433
18. Pizlo Z, Rosenfeld A, Weiss I (1997) Visual space: mathematics, engineering, and science. Comput Vis Image Underst 65:450–454
19. Pizlo Z, Sawada T, Li Y, Kropatsch W, Steinman RM (2010) New approach to the perception of 3D shape based on veridicality, complexity, symmetry and volume. Vis Res 50(1):1–11
20. Poggio T, Torre V, Koch C (1985) Computational vision and regularization theory. Nature 317(6035):314–319
21. Sawada T (2010) Visual detection of symmetry of 3D shapes. J Vis 10(6):4 (22pp)
22. Shepard RN, Cooper LA (1982) Mental images and their transformations. MIT Press, Cambridge
23. Shi Y (2012) Recovering a 3D shape of a generalized cone from a single 2D image. Master's thesis, Department of Psychological Sciences, Purdue University, Indiana
24. Thompson DW (1942) On growth and form. Cambridge University Press, Cambridge

Chapter 3
Flux Graphs for 2D Shape Analysis

Morteza Rezanejad and Kaleem Siddiqi

3.1 Introduction

Medial representations, introduced by Blum [2], simultaneously capture properties of an object's outline and its interior. Abstractions of medial representations into graphs have become popular in the computer vision literature and have successfully been applied to view-based object recognition [12, 14]. Recent extensions and applications include alterations of medial graphs to capture salient object parts [8] and the use of medial fragments for perceptual grouping to form object part hypotheses directly from images [11].

Motivated by the success of medial representations, this chapter revisits a quantity related to medial axis computations—the limiting behavior of the average outward flux (AOF) of the gradient of the Euclidean distance function to the object's boundary as the region through which it is computed is shrunk [4]. We exploit the property that at skeletal points the AOF reveals the object angle and thus can be viewed as a scalar descriptor from which the complete boundary can be reconstructed. We then introduce a novel measure of salience for a skeletal point by combining the AOF with a check on uniqueness of the inscribed medial disk to the host skeletal branch. The simplified skeletons are used to derive a directed graph-based representation of the object which we term the flux graph. Our experiments show that flux graphs are a good deal simpler than competing skeletal graphs such as shock graphs, by a number of standard complexity measures, with little loss in representational power. Furthermore, they yield competitive performance in object recognition experiments.

We begin by discussing mathematical properties of the geometry of the medial axis of an object and by introducing the appropriate notation.

M. Rezanejad (✉) · K. Siddiqi
McGill University, Montreal, QC, Canada, H3A 2A7
e-mail: morteza@cim.mcgill.ca

K. Siddiqi
e-mail: siddiqi@cim.mcgill.ca

S.J. Dickinson, Z. Pizlo (eds.), *Shape Perception in Human and Computer Vision*,
Advances in Computer Vision and Pattern Recognition,
DOI 10.1007/978-1-4471-5195-1_3, © Springer-Verlag London 2013

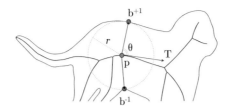

Fig. 3.1 Local geometry of a maximal inscribed disk centered at the skeletal point **p** with radius r and with object angle θ. The maximal inscribed disk touches the boundary at two points $\mathbf{b}^{\pm 1}$ ($\Pi(\mathbf{p}) = \{\mathbf{b}^{+1}, \mathbf{b}^{-1}\}$) (adapted from [13])

Definition 3.1 Assume an n-dimensional object denoted by Ω with its boundary given by $\partial\Omega \in \mathbb{R}^n$. A closed disk $D \in \mathbb{R}^n$ is a *maximal inscribed disk* in Ω if $D \subseteq \Omega$ but for any disk D' such that $D \subset D'$, the relationship $D' \subseteq \Omega$ does not hold.

Definition 3.2 The *Blum medial locus* or *skeleton*, denoted by $Sk(\Omega)$, is the locus of centers of all maximal inscribed disks in $\partial\Omega$.

As illustrated in Fig. 3.1, a skeletal point is characterized by its location **p**, the maximal inscribed disk radius r, the object angle θ, the direction of the unit tangent vector **T**, and the object angle θ given by $\arccos(-\frac{dr}{ds})$, where s is the arc length along a branch of the medial axis. The projection $\Pi(\mathbf{p})$ is the set of closest points on the boundary $\partial\Omega$ to **p**, i.e., $\Pi(\mathbf{p}) \overset{\triangle}{=} \{\mathbf{q} \in \partial\Omega : \|\mathbf{p} - \mathbf{q}\| = \min\{\|\mathbf{p} - \mathbf{q}\| \forall \mathbf{q} \in \partial\Omega\}\}$. For a skeletal point **p** the projection set $\Pi(\mathbf{p})$ is the set of points on the boundary touched by the maximal inscribed disk centered at **p** (the points $\mathbf{b}^{\pm 1}$ in Fig. 3.1). According to the "Maxwell set" definition of the medial locus [10], each skeletal point $\mathbf{p} \in Sk(\Omega)$ must have at least two closest boundary points ($|\Pi_\Omega(\mathbf{p})| \geq 2$).

Topologically $Sk(\Omega)$ consists a set of branches that join to each other at branch points to form the complete skeleton. A *skeletal branch* denoted by χ is a set of contiguous regular points from the skeleton that lie between a pair of junction points, a pair of end points or an end point and a junction point. As shown by Dimitrov et al. in [4] these three classes of points can be analyzed by considering the behavior of the average outward flux of the gradient of the Euclidean distance function to the boundary of a 2D object, given by $\frac{\int_{\partial R} \langle \dot{\mathbf{q}}, \mathbf{N} \rangle ds}{\int_{\partial R} ds}$, when shrunk to a circular neighborhood, where $\dot{\mathbf{q}} = \nabla D$ [4], with **D** the Euclidean distance function to the object's boundary. In particular:

1. **p** is a *regular point* if the maximal inscribed disk at **p** touches the boundary at two corresponding boundary points such that $|\Pi_\Omega(\mathbf{p})| = 2$. The computed AOF at a regular point **p** is given by $\lim_{\varepsilon \to 0} \frac{\mathbf{F}_\varepsilon(\mathbf{p})}{2\pi\varepsilon} = -\frac{2}{\pi}\sin\theta$.
2. **p** is an *end point* if there exists δ ($0 < \delta < r$) such that for any ε ($0 < \varepsilon < \delta$) the circle centered at **p** with radius ε intersects $Sk(\Omega)$ just at a single point (r is the radius of the maximal inscribed disk at **p**). The computed AOF at an end point **p** is given by $\lim_{\varepsilon \to 0} \frac{\mathbf{F}_\varepsilon(P)}{2\pi\varepsilon} = -\frac{1}{\pi}(\sin\theta_P - \theta_P)$.

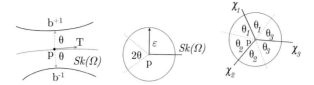

Fig. 3.2 Different types of skeletal points are illustrated using segments of the skeleton $Sk(\Omega)$ of a given shape Ω. *Left*: A regular skeletal point. *Middle*: An end point. *Right*: A junction point. (Adapted from [4])

3. $\mathbf{p}$ is a *junction point* if $\Pi_\Omega(\mathbf{p})$ has three or more corresponding closest boundary points. Generically a junction point has degree 3. All other branch points are unstable. The computed AOF at a junction point $\mathbf{p}$ is given by $\lim_{\varepsilon \to 0} \frac{F_\varepsilon(P)}{2\pi\varepsilon} = -\frac{1}{\pi} \sum_{i=1}^{n} \sin\theta_i$.

These different classes of skeletal points are shown in Fig. 3.2.

We now enumerate the main contributions of this chapter. First, previous approaches to compute flux-based skeletons and use them for boundary representation are not entirely complete. Section 3.2 addresses these limitations and presents a method that gives more complete boundary reconstruction results. Second, a new method for skeletal simplification which in turn leads to a simplified graph representation is presented in Sect. 3.3. Underlying this simplification is a measure of saliency that combines a notion of uniqueness of the inscribed medial disk to the host branch with the limiting AOF value.

3.2 Full Boundary Reconstruction

According to the Maxwell set definition of the medial axis, each point on the skeleton has two or more corresponding boundary points. Therefore, given a mapping between boundary points to skeletal points, it is possible to invert that mapping to reconstruct the boundary purely from skeletal points and their properties. Dimitrov et al. [4] attempted to do this by exploiting the relationship between regular points of the medial axis and the object angle. In this section, we will review the basic algorithm for doing this and then extend it to obtain a more complete boundary reconstruction by adding the cases of end points and junction points.

3.2.1 Boundary Representation Through Regular Points with First-Order Approximation of the Tangent Vector

Taking a regular point $\mathbf{p}$ on the skeleton, Dimitrov et al. outlined the reverse transform to obtain corresponding boundary points by $\mathbf{b}^{\pm 1} = \mathbf{p} + r\mathrm{Rot}(\pm\theta)\mathbf{T_p}$. To reconstruct $\mathbf{b}^{\pm 1}$ from a regular point on a parametrized skeleton, the following parameters

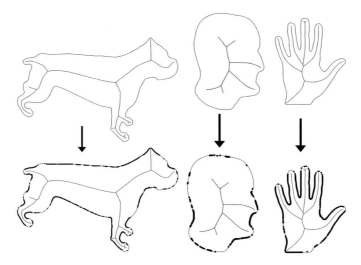

Fig. 3.3 *Top row*: Outlines of binary images of a dog, a profile and a hand object, along with their derived skeletons using flux based skeletonization. *Bottom row*: Reconstructed boundary points (filled black disks) overlayed on the original outlines, using the method of Dimitrov et al. [4]

of a skeletal point ought to be numerically computed: the coordinates of the point **p**, the radius value r, the object angle θ, and the unit tangent vector $\mathbf{T_p}$. During the skeletonization process, a parametrized discrete skeleton is computed where each skeletal point includes its position **p**, the radius at that point r, and the limiting AOF value. For the object angle θ, a numerical estimate is obtained based on the relationship for regular skeletal points: $\theta = \arcsin\left(-\frac{\mathbf{F}_\varepsilon(P)}{4\varepsilon}\right)$. Finally, the tangent vector is estimated as the slope of the line that connects the prior (discrete) skeletal point $\mathbf{p}_{-1}$ to the subsequent (discrete) skeletal point $\mathbf{p}_{+1}$, i.e., $\mathbf{T_p} = \frac{\mathbf{p}_{+1} - \mathbf{p}_{-1}}{\|\mathbf{p}_{+1} - \mathbf{p}_{-1}\|}$. Figure 3.3 shows results from these skeletonization and boundary reconstruction algorithms, using the original implementations.

3.2.2 Full Boundary Reconstruction

As is evident from the results in Fig. 3.3, the reconstruction of regular points, though promising, does not provide a complete representation of the boundary. In this subsection, we extend this approach by considering all types of skeletal points and providing a better numerical approximation of the parameters required for reconstruction. To achieve this aim, three limitations of the boundary reconstruction method are considered and addressed:

1. *Sensitivity of first-order approximation of tangent estimation*: The two point stencil computation of the tangent vector is very sensitive to discretization effects along the skeleton, and can often fail at regular points. To mitigate these

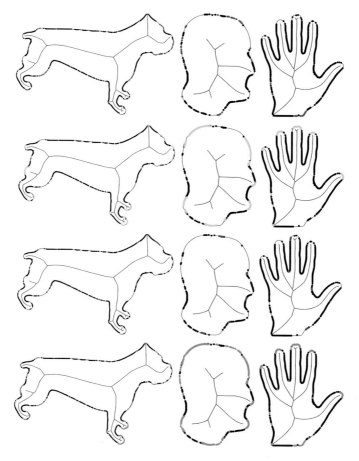

Fig. 3.4 *Top row*: Along with the reconstructed points in Fig. 3.3 shown with black disks, newly reconstructed points resulting from the improved tangent estimation are shown with *blue disks*. *Second row*: Along with the reconstructed points in Fig. 3.3 shown with black disks, newly reconstructed boundary circular segments corresponding to end points are shown with *green disks*. *Third row*: Along with the reconstructed points in Fig. 3.3 shown with black disks, newly reconstructed boundary points corresponding to junction points are shown with *violet disks*. *Bottom row*: Along with reconstructed points in Fig. 3.3 shown with black disks, all the additional reconstructed boundary points are shown in *orange*

numerical errors, we deploy higher order methods for approximating the unit tangent. For those medial loci for which the two point method fails, we use a four point (discrete) stencil approximation [1] given by $\mathbf{T_p} = \frac{2}{3}\left(\frac{\mathbf{p}_{+1}-\mathbf{p}_{-1}}{\|\mathbf{p}_{+1}-\mathbf{p}_{-1}\|}\right) + \frac{1}{3}\left(\frac{P_{+2}-P_{-2}}{\|P_{+2}-P_{-2}\|}\right)$ where $\mathbf{p}_{+2}$ and $\mathbf{p}_{-2}$ represent the subsequent and the previous skeletal points to $\mathbf{p}_{+1}$ and $\mathbf{p}_{-1}$, respectively. Using the second-order of approximation of tangent estimation results in a number of newly reconstructed boundary points (see Fig. 3.4, top row).

2. *Boundary points that map to an end point*: The boundary reconstruction method
   by Dimitrov et al. [3] does not explicitly consider the other two types of skeletal
   points (end points and junction points). This decision results in a number of
   circular segments missing from the boundary, which map to the end points. We
   present a numerical approach to recover such missing boundary points. Assume
   p is an end point such as the one shown in Fig. 3.2. Then, there would be a
   circular arc segment from the boundary corresponding to this skeletal point. The
   osculating disk at **p** touches the boundary along that circular segment, and the
   limiting tangent vector to the skeleton at that point bisects the angle that subtends
   the circular arc. Let γ represent the curve of that circular arc segment, then

$$\gamma : I \to \Omega \tag{3.1}$$

$$\gamma(\theta) = \mathbf{p} + r \operatorname{Rot}(\theta)\mathbf{T_p} \tag{3.2}$$

where I is an interval $I = [-\theta_\mathbf{p}, \theta_\mathbf{p}]$. The coordinates of the point **p**, and the radius value r are parameters that are computed during the skeletonization process.
To compute γ, the following parameters need to be computed numerically other
than **p**, and r: the object angle $\theta_\mathbf{p}$, and the unit tangent vector $\mathbf{T_p}$. To compute
the object angle, we use the end point equation $\frac{F_\varepsilon(P)}{2\pi\varepsilon} = -\frac{1}{\pi}(\sin\theta_p - \theta_p)$. For
the tangent vector $\mathbf{T}_P$, we simply use the tangent estimation of the (discrete)
skeletal point prior to the end point, i.e., $\mathbf{T_p} = \mathbf{T_{p_{-1}}}$. Figure 3.4 (second row)
shows boundary reconstruction results with the newly found circular boundary
segments corresponding to end points shown in green.

3. *Boundary points that map to a junction point*: Junction points are also not included in the initial boundary reconstruction method by Dimitrov et al. [3]. We
   compute the corresponding boundary points of a junction point the same way that
   we compute the corresponding boundary points of a regular point, with the difference that the tangent vectors near junction points are approximated by those at
   the prior points on the skeleton. The rest of the procedure is the same as that for
   computing boundary points for a regular point. Figure 3.4 (third row) shows the
   improvement with the newly found boundary points corresponding to junction
   points shown in violet.

The contribution of this approach to reconstructing boundary points is threefold:
improved approximation of tangents for many regular points of the skeleton, the
computing of circular segments that correspond to end points of the skeleton, and
the computing of extra boundary points from junction points. In Fig. 3.4 (bottom
row), the additional skeletal points added by these steps are shown in orange, which
together with the original reconstructed points demonstrate a far more complete representation of the boundary (compare with Fig. 3.3). The remaining gaps between
the reconstructed boundary points can be attributed to the fact that they are mappings of discretely sampled skeletal points.

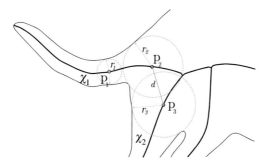

Fig. 3.5 A part of the dog shape is shown with maximal inscribed disks corresponding to unique and non-unique skeletal points. The maximal inscribed disk centered at $\mathbf{p}_1 (\in \chi_1)$ does not intersect with any maximal inscribed disk from branches other than χ_1 so $\mathbf{p}_1$ is a unique skeletal point. In contrast, $\mathbf{p}_2 (\in \chi_1)$ is not a unique skeletal point because the maximal inscribed disk centered at $\mathbf{p}_2 (\in \chi_1)$ intersects with the maximal inscribed disk centered at $\mathbf{p}_3 (\in \chi_2)$

3.3 Salient Parts of the Medial Axis

We now build on the previous results to obtain a novel measure of saliency for medial axis points that combines two criteria: (1) The object angle, which by the characterization of [4] is obtained directly from the computation of the AOF and (2) A notion of uniqueness of the maximal inscribed disk at a skeletal point to the host branch.

Definition 3.3 A *unique skeletal point* has the property that the maximal inscribed disk centered at it does not intersect the maximal inscribed disk associated with any skeletal point on any other branch.

Whereas the object angle has often been used as a criterion for saliency [13], the second notion is novel. The intuition here is that unique skeletal points are salient because without them a significant portion of the object's area would not be represented. Examples of unique and non-unique skeletal points are shown in Fig. 3.5.

As explained in Sect. 3.1, the limiting average outward flux at a regular skeletal point $\mathbf{p}$ is computed by: $\lim_{\varepsilon \to 0} \frac{\mathbf{F}_\varepsilon(\mathbf{p})}{2\pi\varepsilon} = -\frac{2}{\pi}\sin\alpha$. This equation determines a relationship between the AOF and the object angle. The bigger the AOF, the higher the object angle and the more likely the shape silhouette is to be elongated locally. Since elongated parts admit a simple and stable medial axis structure, skeletal points with high AOF are salient.

3.3.1 Simplifying the Skeleton

We combine these two measures of saliency to simplify flux based skeletons using the following procedure: when the considered skeletal point is unique or its normalized AOF is greater than a certain threshold, the skeletal point is retained. In

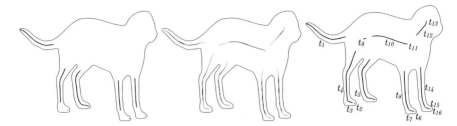

Fig. 3.6 *Left*: The skeletal points found to be unique are shown in *black* on the medial axis of a dog example. *Middle*: Normalized flux values of a skeleton are shown in a range starting from *white* (minimum AOF) and ending in *black* (maximum AOF). *Right*: Several salient segments labeled as t_i are shown as the result of simplifying the medial axis by retaining only those skeletal points that are unique or have AOF above a threshold

our experiments, we use the threshold $\tau = 0.9045$ for the AOF, which means that all non-unique skeletal points with object angle α greater than about $60°$ will be retained in the simplified skeleton. Figure 3.6 illustrates the result of applying this simplification procedure on the dog shape.

3.4 Flux Graphs

Our main motivation for simplifying the flux-based skeleton is to extract a graph representation which is simpler than but otherwise as complete and effective as popular existing approaches such as the shock graph [14] and the bone graph [8]. We propose a "Flux Graph" that uses the simplification process to describe a shape as a set of connected parts while preserving the topology of the original skeleton.

3.4.1 Nodes and Edges

The simplification process can result in a number of skeletal fragments, as illustrated by the example in Fig. 3.6. Not all these fragments described distinct parts, rather, those that share a significant portion of their volumes (obtained as the union of the associated medial disks) and are in close proximity of one another can be combined via a merging process. The segments which remain at the end of the merging process are treated as the nodes of a flux graph. The results of merging fragmented parts associated with the simplified skeleton of the dog shape are shown in Fig. 3.7 (left). The set of edges between nodes are then determined based on their connectivities on the original medial axis. To direct edges, we consider the average radii of inscribed disks associated with two adjacent nodes and compare them. The one with larger magnitude is chosen as the parent and the other as the child. The resulting directed flux graph for the dog shape is shown in Fig. 3.7 (right).

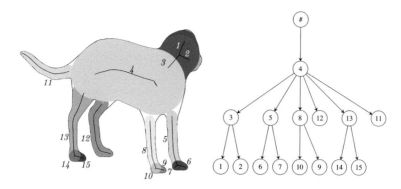

Fig. 3.7 The flux graph of the dog shape. *Left*: The set of nodes is shown with the distinct parts depicted in different colors, each representing a union of medial disks. *Right*: The directed flux graph. The dummy node ♯ carries no geometrical information but serves as a parent to all the top level nodes

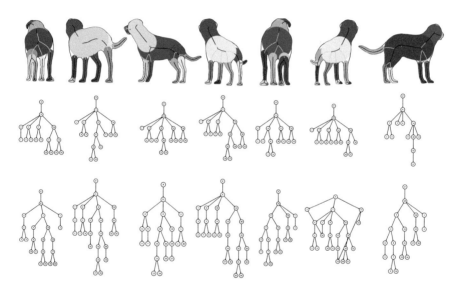

Fig. 3.8 *Top row*: A view of a dog (*middle*) with adjacent views obtained by rotating around it in the clockwise and anti-clockwise directions. For each view, the parts reconstructed by each node of the flux graph are shown as a colored union of disks. *Middle row*: The flux graph corresponding to the view in the *top row*. *Bottom row*: The shock graph corresponding to the view in the *top row*

3.4.2 Qualitative Stability with Viewpoint Changes

We provide a qualitative demonstration that flux graphs remain stable under small changes in viewpoint, while providing an intuitive part structure. We consider a view of the dog (Fig. 3.8 (top row, middle)) and adjacent views obtained by rotating around it in clockwise and anti-clockwise directions. For each view the top row

Table 3.1 Efficiency of flux graphs over shock graphs. The measures in the first six columns are obtained by taking the ratios of the average values of these complexity measures for flux graphs and shock graphs, subtracting these ratios from 1, and then averaging over all the 1664 silhouettes in the database. The last column indicates the percentage of area of the original object reconstructed by flux graphs

	Nodes	Edges	$\Sigma \deg(v)d$	Depth	Skeletal point	TSV	Coverage
Efficiency	% 49.87	% 56.08	% 59.99	% 26.38	% 24.08	% 48.52	% 99

depicts the parts represented by each node of the flux graph, the second row the flux graph and the bottom row the shock graph. Changes to the flux graph typically occur when new parts, such as the tail, come into view (or disappear) but the overall graph structure is much simpler than that of the shock graph. This is essentially because the shock graph utilizes and hence represents the entire skeleton, without any simplification. The experimental results in Table 3.1 which shows averages over 1664 view-based silhouettes of objects used in [8] demonstrate that the flux graph representation is essentially complete, reconstructing 99 % of an object's area. This will be discussed in further detail in Sect. 3.5.3.

3.5 Flux Graphs for Matching

A skeletal graph abstraction can be used as a tool in many visual shape problems including view-based object recognition. We now examine the potential of using flux graphs for matching, in comparison against the well established shock graphs. To carry out a comparative experiment against shock graphs, we used the same graph matching setup and database used for shock graphs in [5, 14].

3.5.1 Topological and Geometrical Similarity

Given two flux graphs, which are directed acyclic graphs (DAGs) a bipartite graph is constructed between their nodes in a hierarchical manner. Each edge is weighted based on the structural similarity between nodes; the weight is the normalized length of difference of the topological signature vectors (TSVs) introduced in [14]. The best matching of a maximum weighted bipartite matching is when the sum of the values of the edges is maximized. In a DAG representation, the TSV is defined as the vector of eigenvalue-sums derived from the corresponding adjacency matrix for the sub-DAG of the considered node. The matching algorithm used is a greedy algorithm [5] which has the benefit of finding a largest maximal matching in polynomial time. The similarity is computed by matching a query with a model node and then normalizing by the number of matched nodes according to the order of the model graph.

3.5.2 The DAG Matcher

To match a query shape with other shapes, we must develop a DAG matcher. The DAG matcher receives two DAGs as input and computes a value representing their similarity, as well as a list of corresponding nodes in the two DAGs. This analysis considers both topological structure (Γ) and geometric information (Δ) associated with a flux graph's vertices. Each of these two measures returns a value normalized in the interval [0 1]. The final similarity score is a weighted combination of these two $S(G_1, G2) = \omega \Gamma(G_1, G_2) + (1 - \omega)\Delta(G_1, G_2)$, where $S(G_1, G2)$ represents the similarity between DAGs derived from two given shapes, and ω is a tuning weight in the interval [0 1]. At the end of the process, a list of corresponding nodes and a similarity measure are obtained.

3.5.3 The Dataset and Experimental Results

The matching problem we consider is to recognize unseen 2-D query views of 3-D objects by matching a query view against all the available silhouettes (reviewed in Sect. 3.5). We compare results of these experiments with those obtained using shock graphs in [6, 8].

The dataset used for our experiments is the same dataset used for experiments carried out for Bone Graphs in [7, 9] and Shock Graphs [5] and has 13 3-D models. Perspective projection of each 3-D object is computed onto the image plane where each model is centered in a uniformly tessellated view sphere. With 128 uniformly sampled views per object, the data set contains a total of 1664 2-D projected views.

3.5.4 Flux Graphs versus Shock Graphs

We begin by demonstrating that by a number of complexity measures the flux graph is simpler and hence more efficient than the shock graph, while essentially providing a complete reconstruction of the original object. To do this, in Table 3.1, for each of the 1664 views we compare: the count of graph vertices, the count of graph edges, the cumulative sum of number of nodes at each depth multiplied by the depth, the depth, total number of skeletal points on the graph, and the average of the TSV (topological signature vectors) values. The numbers reported in the table reflect the efficiency gained by using flux graphs over shock graphs, e.g., flux graphs have 50 % fewer nodes, 56 % fewer edges and 24 % fewer skeletal points. The last column shows the fraction of the area of the original object reconstructed by flux graphs (99 %), indicating that there is essentially no less in representational power.

Fig. 3.9 Using the experimental set up of [6, 8], we compare the use of flux graphs versus shock graphs in a view-based object recognition experiment involving a total of 128 views of each of 13 3-D graphical objects (1664 silhouettes in total). The flux graphs, which are considerably simpler, provide recognition results that are a few percentage points below those of shock graphs

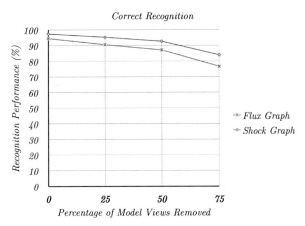

3.5.5 Matching 2-D Views of 3-D Models

We now evaluate the flux graph against the shock graph in a set of view-based object recognition experiments. This comparison follow the matching framework of [7]. The recognition task is performed by: (a) Each view removed sequentially from the database (1664 2-D view-based shapes), and compared to all other remaining views (b) if the class of the closest matching view is the same as that of the query, then the recognition is interpreted as being correct. In the next set of trials, in each step 25 % of the total views are removed randomly from the database. The same experiment is then carried out with further subsampled databases. Figure 3.9 plots the recognition estimation success rates for both shock graphs and flux graphs, averaged over all views of all objects in the database. See [6] for a more detailed explanation of the experimental set up. We also note that the results reported in [6, 8] show that the use of bone graphs, which require a more elaborate construction process, outperforms shock graphs in this experiment.

Flux graphs offer the advantage of efficiency in terms of fewer nodes, edges, depth levels and skeletal points than shock graphs, while still allowing for intuitive hierarchical part-to-part correspondences. However, in terms of the quantitative results, shock graphs outperform flux graphs slightly in this experiment. This could be in part because the matcher used has been tuned to shock graphs and their detailed features and has not been changed in any way to exploit the simplicity of flux graphs. A particular issue is that the geometric node similarity measure used in the matcher [6] implicitly assumes that a node contains a continuous locus of skeletal points. This assumption fails for flux graph nodes that arise from the simplification process we have outlined because the underlying skeletal segments maybe fragmented. The greedy matching approach may also suffer from some limitations and alternate hierarchical matching algorithms could be explored.

3.6 Conclusion

We have presented a novel skeletal shape representation that can be used to faithfully reconstruct the original object's boundary from medial entities. The comprehensive recovery of the object's boundary supports the integrity of using the average outward flux at skeletal points for shape analysis. In addition, a complete representation suggests a way of directly relating medial quantities to boundary features, because the medial features are easier to handle, to store and to compare with other represented objects than the shape boundaries directly.

We have suggested the use of the uniqueness of an inscribed disk to the host skeletal branch as a novel measure of saliency. Combining this measure with the limiting AOF leads to simplified skeletons which can be abstracted as graphs that are simpler than popular skeletal graphs in the literature such as shock graphs. In contrast with methods that carry out ligature analysis for simplification based on the limited number of configurations of the placement of ligature and non-ligature parts, such as the bone graph in [8], our investigation has the advantage that the notion of saliency is defined for each skeletal point separately. The flux graph representation has been evaluated using a matching framework designed for shock graphs ([8, 9]) to recognize 2D views of 3D objects and the results show that flux graphs are almost as good as shock graphs for matching. However, more work could be done to improve the robustness of the merging process of fragments left by our simplification method, which is presently based on a heuristic.

To advance the use of flux graphs for matching, a number of directions could be explored including the use of appropriate node similarity measures, the incorporation of a notion of types for nodes (those resulting from simplification, and those not) and the use of alternate hierarchical matching algorithms. The qualitative simplicity and stability of flux graphs with changes in viewpoint suggests their potential for view-based partitioning of the view sphere and view abstraction.

Acknowledgements We are grateful to Diego Macrini for many stimulating discussions, and for sharing his shock graph matching code and his database of 3-D model silhouettes to allow the comparisons in this paper to be carried out. This work was supported by NSERC, the Natural Sciences and Engineering Research Council of Canada.

References

1. Abramowitz M, Stegun IA (1970) Handbook of mathematical functions—with formulas, graphs, and mathematical tables. Dover, New York. 0-486-61272-4
2. Blum H (1967) A transformation for extracting new descriptors of shape. In: Wathen-Dunn W (ed) Models for the perception of speech and visual form. MIT Press, Cambridge, pp 362–380
3. Dimitrov P (2003) Flux invariants for shape. Master's thesis, McGill University, Montreal, July 2003
4. Dimitrov P, Damon JN, Siddiqi K (2003) Flux invariants for shape. In: Proceedings of the IEEE conference on computer vision and pattern recognition, vol 1, pp 835–841
5. Macrini DA (2003) Indexing and matching for view-based 3-d object recognition using shock graphs. Master's thesis, University of Toronto

6. Macrini D (2010) Bone graphs: Medial abstraction for shape parsing and object recognition. PhD thesis, University of Toronto
7. Macrini D, Dickinson S, Fleet D, Siddiqi K (2011) Bone graphs: medial shape parsing and abstraction. Comput Vis Image Underst 115(7):1044–1061
8. Macrini D, Dickinson S, Fleet D, Siddiqi K (2011) Object categorization using bone graphs. Comput Vis Image Underst 115(8):1187–1206
9. Macrini D, Siddiqi K, Dickinson S (2008) From skeletons to bone graphs: medial abstraction for object recognition. In: Proceedings of the IEEE conference on computer vision and pattern recognition, June 2008, pp 1–8
10. Mather JN (1983) Distance from a submanifold in Euclidean space. In: Proceedings of symposia in pure mathematics, vol 40, pp 199–216
11. Narayanan M, Kimia B (2012) Bottom-up perceptual organization of images into object part hypotheses. In: European conference on computer vision, pp 257–271
12. Sebastian T, Klein P, Kimia B (2004) Recognition of shapes by editing their shock graphs. IEEE Trans Pattern Anal Mach Intell 26:551–571
13. Siddiqi K, Pizer SM (2008) Medial representations: mathematics, algorithms and applications. Springer, Berlin
14. Siddiqi K, Shokoufandeh A, Dickinson SJ, Zucker SW (1999) Shock graphs and shape matching. Int J Comput Vis 35:13–32

Chapter 4
An Integrated Bayesian Approach to Shape Representation and Perceptual Organization

Jacob Feldman, Manish Singh, Erica Briscoe, Vicky Froyen, Seha Kim, and John Wilder

4.1 Shape and Perceptual Organization

The visual representation of shape is a complex problem, requiring the reduction of an essentially infinite-dimensional object (the geometry of the shape) to a few perceptually meaningful dimensions. Human infants can recognize shape from line drawings without any prior experience [17], suggesting that the ability to abstract form from the bounding contour is innate. Much research in the study of shape has involved a quest for a set of shape descriptors that will allow just the right aspects of shape to be extracted—a representation that retains enough information to support recognition, shape similarity, and other key functions. Each of these techniques— geons [3], codons [37], medial axes [4], curvature extrema [18], Fourier descriptors

J. Feldman (✉)
Department of Psychology, Center for Cognitive Science, Rutgers University, New Brunswick, USA
e-mail: jacob.feldman@rutgers.edu

M. Singh
Department of Psychology, Rutgers University, New Brunswick, USA
e-mail: manish.singh@rutgers.edu

E. Briscoe · V. Froyen · S. Kim · J. Wilder
Aerospace, Transportation and Advanced Systems Laboratory, Georgia Tech Research Institute, Atlanta, GA, USA

E. Briscoe
e-mail: erica.briscoe@gtri.gatech.edu

V. Froyen
e-mail: vickyf@rutgers.edu

S. Kim
e-mail: sehakim@rutgers.edu

J. Wilder
e-mail: jdwilder@rutgers.edu

S.J. Dickinson, Z. Pizlo (eds.), *Shape Perception in Human and Computer Vision*, Advances in Computer Vision and Pattern Recognition, DOI 10.1007/978-1-4471-5195-1_4, © Springer-Verlag London 2013

[8], and so forth—has merits. Some have compelling mathematical motivations, while others (unfortunately not usually the same ones) have demonstrable agreement with human data. Still, broadly speaking, a complete computational characterization of human shape representation remains elusive.

The approach we lay out below aims to address two inadequacies in the existing literature. First, many existing theories of shape lack a persuasive "theory of the computation," in Marr's influential phrase [34]—that is, an explanation of why, in principle, the proposed shape descriptors solve the shape problem better than alternatives. To provide such an account, one must adopt a particular definition of "the shape problem"—i.e., a model of what it is that we are actually trying to estimate when we describe a shape. Second, many shape theories have suffered from a lack of connection to other closely related problems in perceptual organization, including perceptual grouping and figure/ground. The shape literature in both psychology and computer science has generally focused on isolated shapes segregated from their backgrounds. But a great deal of evidence suggests that the problem of shape is, at least in the human visual system, intimately connected with the problems of figure/ground and perceptual organization more generally. The representation of a shape is in part determined by the factors that make it perceived as an integral, figural object in the first place, suggesting that shape and perceptual organization are intertwined.

In what follows we describe a framework that is both (a) principled, meaning that it stems from basic considerations of the nature of the shape inference, and (b) unified, in that it aims to approach a broad class of interrelated problems in a coherent way. We first briefly explain the principles of the Bayesian approach to shape representation, and then illustrate how it naturally gives rise to solutions to several related problems, including (i) shape similarity (ii) figure/ground, and (iii) 3D shape from line drawings.

4.2 Bayesian Estimation of the Shape Skeleton

Skeletal or medial-axis representations were first introduced by Blum [4, 5]. Blum's basic insight was that many aspects of contour shape are intuitively captured by a representation that extracts the *local symmetries* of the bounding contour. The medial axis transform (MAT), originally defined as the union of centers of inscribed circles, is highly suggestive of global shape structure, in that its branches often seem to correspond intuitively distinct shape parts such as limbs (and indeed Blum initially conceived it as a compact representation of animal morphology). Medial representations relate to many other problems in perceptual organization [23], and have both psychophysical correlates [25, 50] as well as known neural representations in brain areas V4 and IT [19, 26]. But as has long been recognized [5], the conventional MAT reflects global part structure very imperfectly; in particular, its branches do not reliably correspond to perceptually distinct shape parts. Many improvements on Blum's original MAT have been developed (e.g., [21]), including some that represent mathematically deep generalizations of the "grassfire" procedure that underlies it [40].

But most contemporary medial axis models inherit the basic limitations of Blum's approach, because (with some exceptions [53]) they share its essentially *deterministic* conception, which aims to define an information-preserving transformation of the shape, rather than an abstraction of the shape's underlying structure.

In contrast, we view skeleton computation as a *probabilistic estimation* problem, the goal of which is to estimate the shape skeleton from which the shape is most likely to have been generated—that is, the skeleton that *best explains* the shape. Many natural shapes, especially biological ones, are effectively described as combinations of elongated parts [35]. We view the skeletal structure underlying such shapes as the "signal" which is combined with noisy local contour perturbations to yield the eventual shape. Specifically, we conceive of the shape skeleton as the *generating source* of the contour, which then "extrudes" the shape via a partly stochastic process akin to growth (cf. [28]). We then adopt an inverse-probability framework, taking as our goal the recovery of the skeleton that gave rise to the observed shape. The problem then becomes a standard Bayesian inverse probability problem, with the goal being to estimate the skeleton with maximum posterior probability (called the MAP skeleton) as the best interpretation of the shape. The rest of the approach flows from this central conception: we define a model of the shape-generating process, and estimate the model.

4.2.1 Sketch of the Theory

In our formalism, a shape $\text{SHAPE} = \{(x_1, t_1), (x_2, t_2), \ldots, (x_n, t_n)\}$ is a set of edges each of which is defined by a location x_i and a tangent vector t_i. A *skeleton* $\text{SKEL} = \{A_1, A_2, \ldots\}$ is a set of hierarchically connected axial curves, with a root axis, child axes, grandchildren, etc., branching off from it. Skeletons have a prior probability $p(\text{SKEL})$ and generate shapes stochastically via the likelihood model $p(\text{SHAPE}|\text{SKEL})$ explained below. Our computational goal is to find the best "explanation" of SHAPE by estimating the skeleton SKEL that is *most likely* to have generated it, i.e., that maximizes the product $p(\text{SKEL})p(\text{SHAPE}|\text{SKEL})$ of prior and likelihood.

We begin by adopting a prior $p(\text{SKEL})$. As in all Bayesian approaches, the prior encodes our assumptions about which models (here, skeletons) are more and less likely to be encountered in the environment—assumptions that can then be easily modified to reflect different contexts or knowledge. In [15], we adopted a simple "vanilla" prior that assigns higher probability to simpler skeletons and lower probability to more complex ones, meaning ones with *more* axes or *more curved* axes (Fig. 4.1). This prior is a simple hierarchical extension of our prior for smooth contours, which has been validated in a number of empirical settings (see [12–14, 43, 44]). Specifically, we assume that each of the N component axes A_i contains a series of points $A_i = \{a_{i,1}, a_{i,2}, \ldots\}$, which defines a sequence of turning angles $\alpha_{i,j}$ (e.g., $\alpha_{1,2}$ is the angle between the vector $a_{i,3} - a_{i,2}$ and the vector $a_{i,2} - a_{i,1}$) with the turning angles following a von Mises distribution $p(\alpha_{i,j}) \propto \exp \beta \cos \alpha$ (the analog of the normal for circular variables, see [33]) and assumed independent.

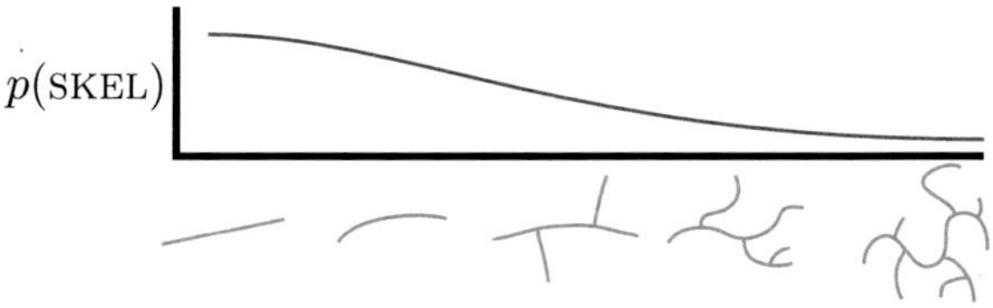

Fig. 4.1 "Vanilla" prior
$p(\text{SKEL})$ for skeletons,
favoring skeletons with fewer,
straighter axes (*left*) and
penalizing those with more
numerous and curvier
branches (*right*)

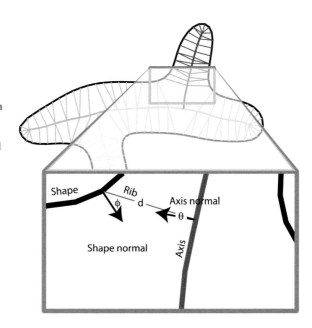

Fig. 4.2 Generative
(likelihood) model
$p(\text{SHAPE}|\text{SKEL})$, modeling a
process of stochastic lateral
growth. Random deviates
("ribs") sprout bilaterally
from each axis, terminating in
edges that taken together
constitute the shape contour.
The sprouting direction θ and
edge orientation ϕ are each
von Mises distributed
(respectively
$\theta \sim \exp[\beta_\theta \cos\theta]$ and
$\phi \sim \exp[\beta_\phi \cos\phi]$), and the
rib length d is assumed
Gaussian with a mean and
variance estimated from the
data ($d \sim N(\hat{d}, \sigma_d^2)$)

So the prior for axis A_i is the product of the probabilities of its component turning angles, $p(A_i) = \prod_j p(\alpha_{i,j})$. Each axis is "born" with fixed probability p_A, leading to an overall prior $p(\text{SKEL}) = p_A^N \prod_{i=1}^{N} \prod_j p(\alpha_{i,j})$. This prior favors skeletons with fewer axes (low N) and relatively straight axes (small αs, see Fig. 4.1).

The next component is the likelihood model $p(\text{SHAPE}|\text{SKEL})$, which quantifies how likely each shape is given a hypothesized skeleton. Our likelihood model expresses the idea of shape "growth" contour points sprout laterally from each axial segment. The growth process is formalized via a set of random lateral vectors that sprout from both sides of a skeletal axis, referred to as "ribs" (Fig. 4.2). The ribs point in a stochastically chosen direction (we use a von Mises distribution, centered on perpendicular to the axis) and have a stochastically chosen length (we use a normal distribution, centered on an expected shape-part half-width whose value varies continuously over the length of the axis). The ribs thus represent *correspondences* between contour points and axial points that explain them—i.e., are interpreted as having generated them. This notion of "explanation" is central to the framework: the skeleton is understood as a hypothesis that explains the data, i.e. the observed contour points. We assume conditional independence of contour points given the

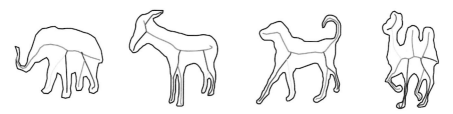

Fig. 4.3 Examples of the MAP skeleton for simple animal shapes (ribs not shown)

skeleton, so the likelihood of the shape is simply the product of the likelihoods of all its component points,

$$p(\text{SHAPE}|\text{SKEL}) = \prod_{i=1}^{n} p\big((x_i, t_i)|\text{SKEL}\big). \tag{4.1}$$

The likelihood quantifies the degree of fit between a shape and a hypothetical skeleton that might explain it.

Finally the degree of belief in a given skeleton—that is, the degree to which the system ought to adopt that skeleton as an explanation for the given shape—is given by the posterior $p(\text{SKEL}|\text{SHAPE})$, which is proportional to the product of the prior and the likelihood,

$$p(\text{SKEL}|\text{SHAPE}) \propto p(\text{SKEL})p(\text{SHAPE}|\text{SKEL}). \tag{4.2}$$

To select a single best explanation of the shape, we estimate the skeleton with maximum posterior probability, referred to as the MAP skeleton (Fig. 4.3). The MAP skeleton represents the optimal skeletal interpretation of the shape, meaning that—given the assumptions captured by the prior and likelihood model—it identifies the single skeleton most likely to have generated the shape. Critically, the choice of the MAP involves a tradeoff between the prior, which favors simple skeletons, and the likelihood, which favors more complex skeletons that can fit the shape better. The axes that are included in the MAP skeleton, i.e., those whose contribution to the likelihood outweighs their penalization in the prior, represent statistically meaningful parts of the shape. That is, each distinct axis in the MAP skeleton represents what the procedure interprets as a distinct part of the shape (depicted with different colors in the figures).

4.3 Applications and Extensions

We next describe preliminary work extending the basic shape theory to key shape problems. Each of these applications grows directly out of the basic theory, illustrating the fecundity of the approach.

Fig. 4.4 The estimated
skeleton divides the shape
into sections "owned" by
distinct axes (*color coding*).
The entailed part boundaries
tend to correspond to negative
curvature minima and
correspond to short part cuts,
suggesting that skeleton
estimation can subsume these
principles

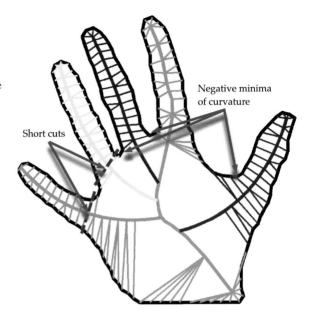

Negative minima
of curvature

Short cuts

4.3.1 Decomposing Shapes into Parts

Notwithstanding the success of appearance-based recognition models (e.g. [30]), there is substantial evidence that human object recognition uses structural representations based on combinations of shape parts [1, 3]. But though many factors are known to influence the decomposition of shapes into parts [9, 41, 45, 46], we still lack a comprehensive account of part decomposition. A simple and principled account of part decomposition is directly entailed by the Bayesian approach to shape representation, encompassing several well-known part-decomposition rules as side-effects. The MAP skeleton implies a part decomposition, because the shape contour naturally decomposes into regions that are "owned" by distinct component axes. For example, in Fig. 4.4 contour sections indicated with different-colored ribs are owned (explained) by distinct axes. As explained above, the axial makeup of the winning skeleton reflects a Bayesian decision about which branches benefit the posterior; the MAP includes only those axes whose contribution to the likelihood outweighs their penalization by the prior.

The skeleton-based decomposition of shapes into component parts concurs with, and arguably subsumes, certain rules of part decomposition obeyed by the human visual system [42]. For example, transitions between axial ownership (e.g., the boundary between red and green ribs in the hand in Fig. 4.4) tend to occur at within deeply concave sections of the contour, near negative curvature extrema, in accordance with the well-known minima rule [18] (even though curvature plays no overt role in skeleton estimation). In this sense skeleton-based shape decomposition explains both the successes of the minima rule, i.e., the fact that part boundaries tend to occur near minima, and also its failures, for example, part boundaries that occur where there are no curvature minima and curvature minima that are not perceived as part boundaries (see [45]). Similarly, regions of common axial ownership tend to be relatively convex, subsuming the part convexity principle [38], and part cuts tend to be relatively short, subsuming the short-cut rule [46]. All of these known characteristics of intuitive part decomposition arise naturally from skeletal estimation, rather requiring additional assumptions, leading to a more principled and unified account than was previously possible.

4.3.2 Tuning the Shape Model to the Environment

The results given above are based on a very simple "vanilla" skeleton prior and likelihood, but both the prior and likelihood model can be modified to accommodate more realistic models of natural shape classes. Some shape classes tend systematically to have more axial branches, or fewer; or more curved branches, or straighter; or smoother contours (smaller variance in rib lengths), or rougher; and so forth, all suggesting modifications to the generative model. To illustrate the approach, we estimated the skeletal parameters of the shapes in several large databases of natural shapes [52], including one of animals and one of leaves (Fig. 4.5a). Tabulations of skeletal parameters show substantial differences between the two shape classes. For example the distribution of number of branches show not only different means but also qualitatively different distributional forms (Fig. 4.5b): Gaussian for animals (with a mean near 5, about the number of intuitively distinct parts in the typical animal body plan) but exponential for leaves (suggesting a recursively branching process). Such differences show how the skeletal generative model can be "tuned" to natural shape classes.

We have also found that human subjects' classification of novel shapes can be predicted from their skeletal representations. We showed subjects composite shapes created by morphing animals and leaves in controlled proportions, and asked them to classify them into animal or leaf categories. (There is no correct answer since the shapes are actually novel composites.) Their responses closely match Bayesian classifications based on skeletal parameters, but disregard or even contradict predictions based on more conventional shape parameters such as aspect ratio or compactness. This suggests that human observers do indeed extract skeletal parameters and use category-specific probabilistic knowledge to classify novel shapes.

4.3.3 Shape Similarity

An essential application of shape representation is the evaluation of shape similarity. Measures of shape matching abound in the computational literature, where they form the basis of shape recognition [10], including some with properties suggestive of human intuitions, like robustness to part articulation [29]. But though similarity

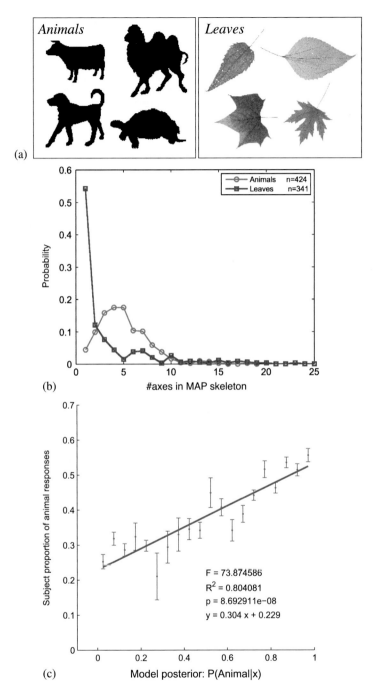

Fig. 4.5 (**a**) Samples of the shapes from which skeletal statistics were drawn. (**b**) Animals and leaves show systematic statistical differences, such as in the distribution of the number of axial branches. (**c**) A classifier based on these differences predicts human subjects' classifications of morphed (composite) shapes

based on skeletal representations has been found effective [39], few if any algorithmic similarity measures have been validated against human similarity judgments.

Our skeletal representation provides a natural measure of shape similarity [6]. Because each skeletal estimate represents a "model" of the observed shape, it is natural to ask how well this model explains *another* shape. Specifically, given two shapes SHAPE$_1$ and SHAPE$_2$, with associated skeletal estimates SKEL$_1$ and SKEL$_2$, we define the similarity of SHAPE$_1$ to SHAPE$_2$ as the likelihood

$$\text{sim}(\text{SHAPE}_1, \text{SHAPE}_2) = p(\text{SHAPE}_1|\text{SKEL}_2), \tag{4.3}$$

that is, the probability that shape SHAPE$_1$ would "grow" from skeleton SKEL$_2$. This gives an asymmetric assessment of the first shape's fit to the second shape's representation (potentially accommodating the asymmetric similarity judgments that are well-known in the psychological literature). A symmetric similarity measure can be defined by taking the average

$$d(\text{SHAPE}_1, \text{SHAPE}_2) = \frac{1}{2}\big[\text{sim}(\text{SHAPE}_1, \text{SHAPE}_2) + \text{sim}(\text{SHAPE}_2, \text{SHAPE}_1)\big].$$
$$\tag{4.4}$$

In [6], we tested the psychological validity of this shape similarity measure by asking subjects to rate similarity of all pairs drawn from several collections of shapes. For example, Fig. 4.6a shows a set of shapes generated from a 2-axis skeleton, in which the length of the secondary axis was modulated from very small to large. The red border shows the boundary between shapes whose MAP skeletons contain one axis (that is, in which the second part was too small to be included in the estimated skeleton) and those that contain two distinct axes. Figure 4.6b shows the similarity space of the same shapes, computed via multidimensional scaling from subjects' similarity judgments. The exaggerated division (marked in red) between shapes perceived to have one part and those perceived to have two parts is plainly visible, and as can be seen in the figure corresponds exactly to the division between 1-axis and 2-axis MAP skeletons. Finally, Fig. 4.6c shows the very close linear relationship between judged similarity and similarity computed via Eq. (4.4). Experiments with several other classes of shapes also show close matches between computed and perceived shape similarity [6].

4.3.4 Figure and Ground

Figure/ground (f/g) assignment is intrinsically intertwined with the representation of shape, in part because figural polarity (border ownership) determines the sign of curvature, which plays a central role in shape representation [18]. Indeed because figural regions "own" the border [2, 11], only figural regions' shapes are overtly represented [36], with ground regions perceived as extending indefinitely behind. F/g assignment is known to be influenced by a number of shape factors, including region size [24] convexity [20] and symmetry [20]. But nonetheless theoretical connections between shape and f/g remain largely unexplored.

Fig. 4.6 Shape similarity
model. (**a**) Shapes tested,
showing MAP skeletons
including ribs and entailed
part decomposition. The *red
border* divides the shapes
estimated to have 1 part from
those estimated to have 2
parts. (**b**) Results of
multidimensional scaling
based on human similarity
ratings; the *red border* here
corresponds to the border in
(**a**), showing the exaggerated
psychological distance
between 1- and 2-part shapes.
(**c**) Plot showing
approximately linear
relationship between human
and computed similarity
ratings

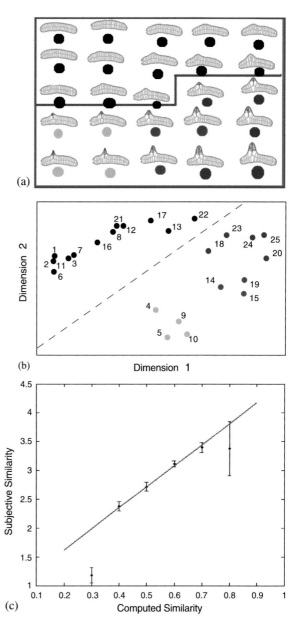

Our approach to contour interpretation can easily be extended to encompass geometric factors on f/g assignment in a simple but principled way. Above, we have
assumed that f/g assignment along the contour is known, and that shapes have to be
explained from their interiors—that is, by skeletons in their interiors. Instead, we
now (a) relax the assumption that border ownership is known, and instead treat it
as a parameter to be estimated; and (b) relax the assumption that there is a single

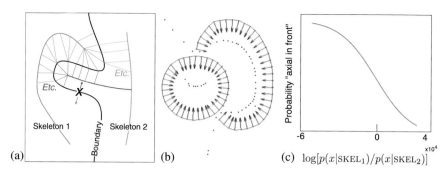

Fig. 4.7 (**a**) A contour point x can be "explained" by the skeleton on one side or the other, determining its border ownership. (**b**) Belief estimation of border ownership from skeletons, showing the medial structure present (on both sides of all contours) and estimated border ownership (*arrows* point towards figure). (**c**) Human judgments of figural status depend on the log posterior ratio (relative axiality) of the skeletons on either side of a boundary, favoring the side with the stronger posterior

shape to be explained by a single skeleton, and instead attempt to explain the entire set of image contours by an ensemble of skeletons. More specifically, we no longer assume that the sign of each tangent vector t_i (which defines which side of each contour is figural) is given as part of the data, and instead treat it as an unknown parameter to be estimated. The formal problem of image explanation now reduces to the estimation of the ensemble of skeletons that, collectively, best explain the observed image structure. That is, we seek the set of skeletons that best explains all the observed edges, with each edge being explained from *whichever side* provides the best overall posterior, which determines its perceived border ownership.

In this expanded view of the problem, the MAP interpretation assigns (skeletal models) conjointly with f/g assignments over the entire ensemble of edges. The winning interpretation explains as much the contour as possible "from within"— that is, with each contour owned by a skeleton in what is perceived as its interior— while also maximizing everything else that the Bayesian model maximizes, such as the simplicity of the skeletons and the fit between the skeletons and the contours.

Because figural surfaces are perceived as closer, the induced figural assignment induces depth differences among skeletal axes: the axis that "wins" a given edge is interpreted as closer. This in turn allows the 3D relations among objects in the scene to be estimated. More specifically, each contour point (x, t) can be explained by skeletons on either side of it, and whichever skeleton assigns it a higher posterior will be interpreted as "owning" the point, thus determining the direction of t, the polarity of local f/g, and the relative (qualitative) depth (Fig. 4.7a). Recall that the direction of the normal at the contour point influences the posterior in part because the likelihood function penalizes contour normals that point "away" from the generating skeleton (see Fig. 4.2). Figure 4.7b shows results of a Bayesian belief network that implements a version of this computation [16]. The belief network estimates border ownership at each contour point, propagating the f/g estimate along each contour in a manner similar to previous f/g belief networks [51], but here including the skeleton-based likelihood function as a determinant of f/g status. As can be seen in the illustration, the procedure assigns border ownership to the perceived interiors of both overlapping shapes, critically including assigning the common boundary to the region human observers judge to be in front.

An empirical prediction derived directly from this framework is that more "axial" regions, that is, regions with stronger skeletal posteriors, are more likely to be perceived as figural. We tested this by constructing displays in which a symmetric region abutted a more "axial" one, and asked subjects which side appeared to own their common boundary [22], while manipulating the shape of the axial side so as to modulate the skeletal posterior. In the Bayesian model, ownership of a point (x, t) along the common boundary should follow the posterior ratio $p((x, t)|\text{SKEL}_1)/p((x, t)|\text{SKEL}_2)$, where SKEL_1 and SKEL_2 are MAP skeletons on respectively the axial and symmetric sides. Figure 4.7c gives a representative plot showing the observed decrease in f/g responses as a function of (log) posterior ratio, confirming the basic claim that axiality under the Bayesian model tends to "draw" figural status.

4.3.5 3D Shape

Our approach to skeleton estimation, like virtually all medial approaches, is based on two-dimensional silhouettes, which do not generally give rise to strong 3D interpretations. But much richer 3D interpretations arise from images that include interior contours, including T-junctions stemming from self-occlusions. Even without texture, shading, or other surface cues, human subjects can interpret 3D shape from such line drawings about as well as from natural images [7]. Yet interpretation of such figures remains a virtually unsolved problem. The extensive early literature on line and junction labeling [31, 32, 49] largely failed to solve it due to reliance on hard-and-fast junction classification rules. Our framework replaces these deterministic rules with a probabilistic inference in which the goal is to estimate the 3D skeleton that best explains the ensemble of contours and junctions in the image.

The first step is to extend the generative (likelihood) model to 3D. A direct 3D generalization of the conventional MAT [27] results in a complex and psychologically implausible combination of space curves and 2D medial "scaffolds." In contrast, the skeletal generative model generalizes to 3D in an intuitive way. The key idea is simply to assume that the ribs (random deviates), rather than being generated laterally on both sides of the skeleton as in the 2D model, are instead generated in all directions in the plane orthogonal to the skeleton, thus "inflating" the skeleton into a 3D shape (Fig. 4.8a, b) (cf. [48]). The inverse problem is to estimate the 3D skeleton that is most likely, when inflated, to yield the observed contour when projected, including both outer silhouette, internal contours, and other contour features such as T-junctions. The resulting estimate can be substantially non-planar (Fig. 4.8c). A suitable estimation procedure for this model is of course a difficult problem, but in principle one that can be solved by conventional Bayesian techniques.

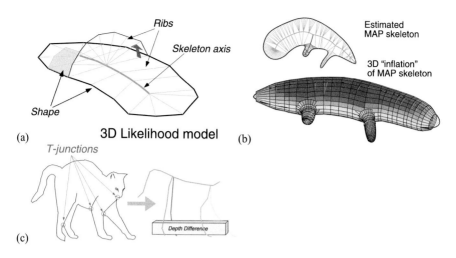

Fig. 4.8 (**a**) 3D likelihood model, yielding (**b**) inflation of the skeleton into a 3D shape. (**c**) When T-junctions and internal contours are included, the estimated skeleton can be non-planar

4.4 Discussion and Conclusion

We have described a principled probabilistic conception of shape representation, which provides natural approaches to part decomposition, shape similarity, and figure/ground, and can be extended in a conceptually simple way to 3D. The main idea is to view contour elements as data generated by a skeletal growth process, and then estimate the structure of the skeleton. The best representation of a shape is the skeleton that best explains it; the similarity of two shapes is the degree to which one shape's skeletal interpretation explains the other shape; and the best interpretation of multiple shapes is the collection of skeletons that best explains the ensemble of contours, thus inducing estimates of f/g and depth relations.

Many aspects of our framework are present in other approaches, including stochastic estimation of skeletal structure [47, 53], belief propagation for f/g [51], and inflation of 2D skeletal representations into 3D shape [48]. But the main attraction of our approach is its simplicity, comprehensiveness, and coherence: all the applications derive from the central conception of shape as a rational inference problem. Broadly speaking, the aim is to make some assumptions about shape-generating processes in the environment; express these assumptions as a probability model; and estimate the model. As mentioned, the probability model can then be tuned to natural shape statistics, used to model shape similarity, extended to multiple shapes in a way that yields f/g estimates and depth relations, and easily extended to 3D. None of these extensions require elaborate new hacks, nor indeed any change to the basic principles. The psychological literature attests a wealth of connections among these different aspects of perceptual organization, and we would argue that our approach integrates them in a way that properly respects their interconnections.

It is important to understand that our approach does not intrinsically require mediality; axial forms are simply a reasonable model for many natural shapes. For others, alternative (non-medial) generative models might be adopted without changing the essentials of the approach. All the extensions we have presented derive from the central probabilistic estimation problem, not from specific aspects of medial geometry or local symmetry. The ultimate goal of this work is thus not to deepen our understanding of medial representations specifically, but rather to "probabilize" shape and related problems of perceptual organization, thus unifying them with the growing literature on probabilistic and Bayesian approaches to visual perception.

References

1. Barenholtz E, Tarr MJ (2008) Visual judgment of similarity across shape transformations: evidence for a compositional model of articulated objects. Acta Psychol 128(2):331–338
2. Baylis G, Driver J (1995) Obligatory edge assignment in vision: the role of figure and part segmentation in symmetry detection. J Exp Psychol Hum Percept Perform 21(6):1323–1342
3. Biederman I (1987) Recognition by components: a theory of human image understanding. Psychol Rev 94:115–147
4. Blum H (1973) Biological shape and visual science (part I). J Theor Biol 38:205–287
5. Blum H, Nagel RN (1978) Shape description using weighted symmetric axis features. Pattern Recognit 10:167–180
6. Briscoe E (2008) Shape skeletons and shape similarity. PhD thesis, Rutgers University
7. Cole F, Sanik K, DeCarlo AFD, Funkhouser T, Rusinkiewicz S, Singh M (2009) How well do line drawings depict shape? In: ACM transactions on graphics (Proc. SIGGRAPH), vol 28
8. Cortese JM, Dyre BP (1996) Perceptual similarity of shapes generated from Fourier descriptors. J Exp Psychol Hum Percept Perform 22(1):133–143
9. de Winter J, Wagemans J (2006) Segmentation of object outlines into parts: a large-scale integrative study. Cognition 99(3):275–325
10. Demirci F, Shokoufandeh A, Keselman Y, Bretzner L, Dickinson S (2006) Object recognition as many-to-many feature matching. Int J Comput Vis 69(2):203–222
11. Driver J, Baylis GC (1996) Edge-assignment and figure-ground segmentation in short-term visual matching. Cogn Psychol 31:248–306
12. Feldman J (1997) Curvilinearity, covariance, and regularity in perceptual groups. Vis Res 37(20):2835–2848
13. Feldman J (2001) Bayesian contour integration. Percept Psychophys 63(7):1171–1182
14. Feldman J, Singh M (2005) Information along contours and object boundaries. Psychol Rev 112(1):243–252
15. Feldman J, Singh M (2006) Bayesian estimation of the shape skeleton. Proc Natl Acad Sci 103(47):18014–18019
16. Froyen V, Feldman J, Singh M (2010) A Bayesian framework for figure-ground interpretation. In: Lafferty J, Williams CKI, Shawe-Taylor J, Zemel R, Culotta A (eds) Advances in neural information processing systems, vol 23, pp 631–639
17. Hochberg J, Brooks V (1962) Pictorial recognition as an unlearned ability: a study of one child's performance. Am J Psychol 75(4):624–628
18. Hoffman DD, Richards WA (1984) Parts of recognition. Cognition 18:65–96
19. Hung CC, Carlson ET, Connor CE (2012) Medial axis shape coding in macaque inferotemporal cortex. Neuron 74(6):1099–1113
20. Kanizsa G, Gerbino W (1976) Convexity and symmetry in figure-ground organization. In: Henle M (ed) Vision and artifact. Springer, New York
21. Katz RA, Pizer SM (2003) Untangling the Blum medial axis transform. Int J Comput Vis 55(2/3):139–153
22. Kim S (2011) The influence of axiality on figure/ground assignment. Master's thesis, Rutgers University

23. Kimia BB (2003) One the role of medial geometry in human vision. J Physiol (Paris) 97:155–190

24. Koffka K (1935) Principles of gestalt psychology. Harcourt, New York

25. Kovács I, Fehér A, Julesz B (1970) Medial-point description of shape: a representation for action coding and its psychophysical correlates. Vis Res 38:2323–2333

26. Lescroart MD, Biederman I (2012) Cortical representation of medial axis structure. In: Cerebral cortex

27. Leymarie FF, Kimia BB (2007) The medial scaffold of 3d unorganised point clouds. IEEE Trans Pattern Anal Mach Intell 29(2):313–330

28. Leyton M (1989) Inferring causal history from shape. Cogn Sci 13:357–387

29. Ling H, Jacobs DW (2007) Shape classification using the inner-distance. IEEE Trans Pattern Anal Mach Intell 29(2):286–299

30. Lowe DG (2004) Distinctive image features from scale-invariant keypoints. Int J Comput Vis 60(2):91–110

31. Mackworth A (1973) Interpreting pictures of polyhedral scenes. Artif Intell 4:121–137

32. Malik J (1987) Interpreting line drawings of curved objects. Int J Comput Vis 1:73–103

33. Mardia KV (1972) Statistics of directional data. Academic Press, London

34. Marr D (1982) Vision: a computational investigation into the human representation and processing of visual information. Freeman, San Francisco

35. Marr D, Nishihara HK (1978) Representation and recognition of the spatial organization of three-dimensional shapes. Proc R Soc Lond B 200:269–294

36. Palmer S, Davis J, Nelson R, Rock I (2008) Figure-ground effects on shape memory for objects versus holes. Perception 37(10):1569–1586

37. Richards W, Dawson B, Whittington D (1988) Encoding contour shape by curvature extrema. In: Natural computation. MIT Press, Cambridge

38. Rosin PL (2000) Shape partitioning by convexity. IEEE Trans Syst Man Cybern, Part A, Syst Hum 30:202–210

39. Sebastian TB, Kimia BB (2005) Curves vs. skeletons in object recognition. Signal Process 85:247–263

40. Siddiqi K, Shokoufandeh A, Dickinson S, Zucker S (1999) Shock graphs and shape matching. Int J Comput Vis 30:1–24

41. Siddiqi K, Tresness KJ, Kimia BB (1996) Parts of visual form: psychophysical aspects. Perception 25:399–424

42. Singh M, Froyen V, Feldman J (2013, forthcoming) Unifying parts and skeletons: a Bayesian approach to part decomposition

43. Singh M, Fulvio JM (2005) Visual extrapolation of contour geometry. Proc Natl Acad Sci USA 102(3):939–944

44. Singh M, Fulvio JM (2007) Bayesian contour extrapolation: geometric determinates of good continuation. Vis Res 47:783–798

45. Singh M, Hoffman DD (2001) Part-based representations of visual shape and implications for visual cognition. In: Shipley T, Kellman P (eds) From fragments to objects: segmentation and grouping in vision, advances in psychology, vol 130. Elsevier, New York, pp 401–459

46. Singh M, Seyranian GD, Hoffman DD (1999) Parsing silhouettes: the short-cut rule. Percept Psychophys 61(4):636–660

47. Telea A, Sminchisescu C, Dickinson S (2004) Optimal inference for hierarchical skeleton abstraction. In: Proceedings IEEE international conference on pattern recognition, Cambridge

48. Twarog NR, Tappen MF, Adelson EH (2012) Playing with puffball: simple scale-invariant inflation for use in vision and graphics. In: Proceedings of the ACM symposium on applied perception, pp 47–54

49. Waltz D (1975) Understanding line drawings of scenes with shadows. In: Winston PH (ed) The psychology of computer vision, pp 19–91

50. Wang X, Burbeck CA (1998) Scaled medial axis representation: evidence from position discrimination task. Vis Res 38(13):1947–1959

51. Weiss Y (1997) Interpreting images by propagating Bayesian beliefs. In: Adv. in neural information processing systems, pp 908–915
52. Wilder J, Feldman J, Singh M (2011) Superordinate shape classification using natural shape statistics. Cognition 119:325–340
53. Zhu S-C (1999) Stochastic jump-diffusion process for computing medial axes. IEEE Trans Pattern Anal Mach Intell 21(11):1158–1169

Chapter 5
Perceptual Organization of Shape

James H. Elder

5.1 Introduction

Computing the correct bounding contours of objects in complex natural scenes is generally thought to be one of the harder computer vision problems, and the state of the art is still quite far from human performance, when human subjects are given an arbitrary amount of time to delineate the shape of these contours [1]. How do we explain this gap? One possibility is that, when given enough time, humans fall back on high-level, deliberative reasoning processes. If this is true, then it is possible that when faced with detecting and recognizing objects in an active vision timeframe (hundreds of milliseconds), we may rely upon a simpler "bag of tricks", using appearance cues such as texture and color to discriminate objects.

To address this possibility, let us consider the specific task of rapidly detecting animals in natural scenes. Humans perform this task remarkably well: evoked potential studies indicate that the corresponding neural signals can emerge in the brain within 150 msec of stimulus onset [32], and eye movements toward animal targets can be initiated in roughly the same timeframe [20].

Until recently, little was known about the cues that humans use to achieve this impressive level of performance. However, a recent study by Elder & Velisavljević [10] sheds some light on this question. This study made use of a standard computer vision image dataset called the Berkeley Segmentation Dataset (BSD) [26]. For each image in the dataset, the BSD provides hand segmentations created by human subjects, each of which carves up the image into meaningful regions. Elder & Velisavljević used this dataset to create new images in which luminance, color, texture and shape cues were selectively turned on or off (Fig. 5.1—top). They then measured performance for animal detection using these various modified images over a range of stimulus durations (Fig. 5.1—bottom left), and estimated the weight of each cue using a multiple regression technique (Fig. 5.1—bottom right).

J.H. Elder (✉)
Centre for Vision Research, York University, Toronto, Canada
e-mail: jelder@yorku.ca

S.J. Dickinson, Z. Pizlo (eds.), *Shape Perception in Human and Computer Vision*,
Advances in Computer Vision and Pattern Recognition,
DOI 10.1007/978-1-4471-5195-1_5, © Springer-Verlag London 2013

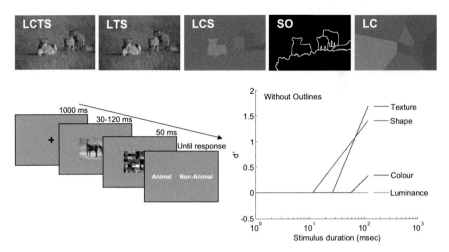

Fig. 5.1 Psychophysical animal detection experiment. *Top*: Example stimuli. The *letters* indicate the cues available: Luminance, Color, Texture, Shape. 'SO' stands for 'Shape Outline'. *Bottom left*: Stimulus sequence. *Bottom right*: Estimated loadings for four cues to animal detection. From [10]

The results show that humans do not use simple luminance or color cues for animal detection, but instead rely on shape and texture cues. Interestingly, shape cues appear to be the first available, influencing performance for stimulus durations as short as 10 msec, within a backward masking paradigm. These results suggest that contour shape cues are not "luxury items" used only when time is not a factor, but rather underlie our fastest judgements about the objects around us. So the question remains: how does the brain rapidly and reliably extract contour shape information from complex natural scenes?

5.2 Computational Models

Computer vision algorithms for contour grouping typically assume as input a map of the local oriented elements to be grouped into chains corresponding to the boundaries of objects in the scene. This is a combinatorial problem—exhaustive methods have exponential complexity and are thus infeasible as algorithms or models for information processing in the brain.

To tame this complexity, most research has focused on modelling and exploiting only the first-order probabilistic relations between successive elements on bounding contours, in other words, modelling contours, either explicitly or implicitly, as first-order Markov chains. In the psychophysics community, this has led to the notion of an "association field" encoding these local relations [13, 28], identified with long-range lateral connections known to link compatible orientation hypercolumns in primate striate cortex [16]. The probabilistic expression of this model has been supported by studies of the ecological statistics of contour grouping, which have also focused principally upon first-order cues [7, 15, 21, 35].

Input Image   **Spatial Prior**   **Multi–scale**   **Single–scale**

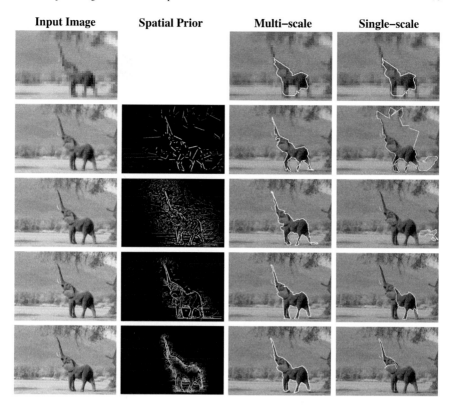

Fig. 5.2 Contour grouping algorithms. *Right column*: Single scale. *Left three columns*: multi-scale, with coarse-to-fine feedback. From [12]

Similarly, many computer vision algorithms for contour grouping have employed a Markov assumption and have focused on first-order cues [3, 4, 8, 11, 18, 24, 28, 33, 41, 43]. However, these first-order Markov algorithms have generally not performed well unless augmented by additional problem-domain knowledge [8] or user interaction [5]. An example from [8] is shown in Fig. 5.2 (right column). The algorithm proceeds by greedy search over the exponential space of possible contours, monotonically increasing the length of the contour hypotheses, and pruning those of lower probability. As can be seen in this example, closed contours corresponding to *parts* of objects can sometimes be computed in this way, but for complex scenes it is rare that the entire object boundary is recovered exactly, unless additional domain-specific constraints are brought to bear.

Recently, however, Estrada & Elder [12] demonstrated that the same algorithm performs much more effectively when placed within a coarse-to-fine scale-space framework (Fig. 5.2—left three columns). In this framework, a Gaussian scale-space over the image is formed, and greedy search is first initiated at the coarsest scale. Since the number of features at this scale is greatly reduced, the search space is much smaller and the algorithm generally finds good, coarse blob hypotheses that code the

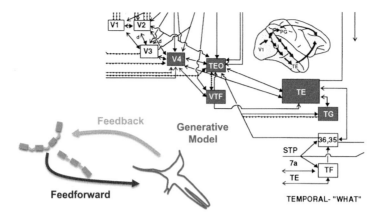

Fig. 5.3 Feedback in the human object pathway. The *diagram on the upper right* is modified from [39]. *Solid arrowheads* indicate feedforward connections, *open arrowheads* indicate feedback connections

rough location and shape of the salient objects in the scene. These hypotheses are then fed back to the next finer level of resolution, where they serve as probabilistic priors, conditioning the likelihoods and effectively shrinking the search space to promising regions of the image.

The success of this simple framework raises the possibility that the brain may also use a feedback mechanism to transmit global shape constraints to the early visual mechanisms involved in contour grouping.

5.3 Feedback in the Primate Object Pathway

Physiologically, it is certainly plausible that feedback might be involved in the perceptual organization of contours in the human brain. Figure 5.3 (right) shows the known connectivity of visual areas in the object pathway of primate brain. While processing is often described by default as a feedforward sequence V1 → V2 → V4 → TE/TEO [37], in fact there are feedback connections from each of the later areas to each of the earlier areas, as well as additional feedforward connections.

While some have argued that animal detection by humans and other primates is too fast to allow time for feedback [20, 32, 37], behavioral and physiological reaction times are always broadly dispersed, with a long positive tail. Thus even if the very fastest reactions (perhaps on the easy conditions) are strictly feedforward, there is time for feedback on the rest. Furthermore, recent evidence suggests that visual signals arrive in higher areas much faster than previously thought [14], allowing sufficient time for feedback even on the fastest trials.

What exactly are the grouping computations effected by the recurrent circuits in primate object pathway? We are far from being able to answer this question, but Fig. 5.3 (left) illustrates one specific conceptual model (see also [2, 22, 38, 42]). For concreteness, let us suppose that earlier areas (e.g., V1, V2) in the visual pathway compute and encode specific partial grouping hypotheses corresponding to fragments of contours. These fragment hypotheses are communicated to higher-order areas (e.g., V4 or TEO), which use them to generate more complete hypotheses of the global shape. These global hypotheses are then fed back to earlier visual areas to sharpen selectivity for other fragments that might support these global hypotheses.

A central component of this architecture is a generative model of shape that is capable of producing probable global shape hypotheses given partial shape information. This generative shape module will be our focus for the remainder of the chapter.

5.4 Generative Models of Shape

While there are many computational theories and algorithms for shape representation, few are truly generative, and those that are or could be have not been fully developed and tested (e.g., [23]). An important exception is the shapelet theory proposed by Dubinskiy & Zhu [6]. The theory is based upon the representation of a shape by a summation of component *shapelets*. A shapelet is a primitive curve defined by Gabor-like coordinate functions that map arclength to the plane. Shifting and scaling shapelets over the arclength parameter produces a basis set that, when combined additively, can model arbitrarily complex shapes.

The shapelet approach has many advantages. For example, components are localized, albeit only in arclength, and scale is made explicit in a natural way. However, like other contour-based methods, the shapelet theory does not explicitly capture regional properties of shape. Perhaps most crucially, the model does not respect the topology of object boundaries: sampling from the model will in general yield non-simple, i.e., self-intersecting, curves.

5.4.1 Localized Diffeomorphisms: Formlets

A different class of model that could be called region-based involves the application of coordinate transformations of the planar space in which a shape is embedded. This idea can be traced back at least to D'Arcy Thompson, who considered specific classes of global coordinate transformations to model the relationship between the shapes of different animal species [36]. Coordinate transformation methods for representing shape have been explored more recently in the field of computer vision (e.g., [19, 34]), but these methods do not in general preserve the topology of embedded contours.

While general smooth coordinate transformations of the plane will not preserve the topology of an embedded curve, it is possible to design a specific family of diffeomorphic transformations that will [9, 17, 27]. It then follows immediately by induction that a generative model based upon arbitrary sequences of diffeomorphisms will preserve topology.

Specifically, let us consider a family of diffeomorphisms we will call *formlets* [9, 27], in tribute to D'Arcy Thompson's seminal book *On Growth and Form* [36]. A formlet is a simple, isotropic, radial deformation of planar space that is localized within a specified circular region of a selected point in the plane. The family comprises formlets over all locations and spatial scales. While the gain of the deformation is also a free parameter, it is constrained to satisfy a simple criterion that guarantees that the formlet is a diffeomorphism. Since topological changes in an embedded figure can only occur if the deformation mapping is either discontinuous or non-injective, these diffeomorphic deformations are guaranteed to preserve the topology of embedded figures.

This formlet model is closely related to recent work by Grenander and colleagues [17], modeling changes to anatomical parts over time. There the problem is: given two MRI images I_t and I_{t+1} of an anatomical structure taken at two successive times t and $t + 1$, first (a) compute the deformation vector field that associates each pixel of I_t with a pixel of I_{t+1}, and then (b) represent this deformation field by a sequence of local and radial diffeomorphisms. They demonstrated their method, which they called Growth by Random Iterated Diffeomorphisms (GRID), on the problem of tracking growth in the rat brain, as revealed in sequential planar sections of MRI data. Subsequent work has focused on the generalization of this method to other coordinate systems [29], on establishing the existence and uniqueness of a continuous 'growth flow' given a specified forcing function [31] and on investigating regularized versions of the GRID formulation [30].

The underlying mathematics here are very similar, although there are some important differences in the exact nature of the localized diffeomorphisms and the manner in which parameters are estimated. But the crucial question of interest here is whether these ideas can be extended to model not just differential deformations between two successive images, but to serve as the framework for a generative model over the entire space of smooth shapes, based upon a universal embryonic shape in the plane such as an ellipse.

5.5 Formlet Coding

5.5.1 Formlet Bases

We represent the image by the complex plane $\mathbb{C}$, and define a formlet $f : \mathbb{C} \to \mathbb{C}$ to be a diffeomorphism localized in scale and space. Such a deformation can be realized by centering f about the point $\zeta \in \mathbb{C}$ and allowing f to deform the plane within a ($\sigma \in \mathbb{R}^+$)-region of ζ. A Gabor-inspired formlet deformation can be defined as

$$f(z; \zeta, \sigma, \alpha) = \zeta + \frac{z - \zeta}{|z - \zeta|} \rho(|z - \zeta|; \sigma, \alpha), \quad \text{where}$$

$$\rho(r; \sigma, \alpha) = r + \alpha \sin\left(\frac{2\pi r}{\sigma}\right) \exp\left(\frac{-r^2}{\sigma^2}\right).$$

(5.1)

Fig. 5.4 Example formlet deformations. The location ζ of the formlet is indicated by the *red marker*. From [27]

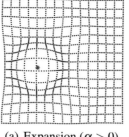
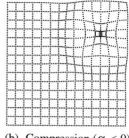

(a) Expansion ($\alpha > 0$)   (b) Compression ($\alpha < 0$)

Thus, each formlet $f : \mathbb{C} \to \mathbb{C}$ is a localized isotropic and radial deformation of the plane at location ζ and scale σ. The magnitude of the deformation is controlled by the gain parameter $\alpha \in \mathbb{R}$. Figure 5.4 demonstrates formlet deformations of the plane with positive and negative gain.

5.5.2 Diffeomorphism Constraint

Without any constraints on the parameters, these deformations, though continuous, can fold the plane on itself, changing the topology of an embedded contour. In order to preserve topology, we must constrain the gain parameter to guarantee that each deformation is a diffeomorphism. As the formlets defined in Eq. (5.1) are both isotropic and angle preserving, it is sufficient to require that the radial deformation ρ be a diffeomorphism of $\mathbb{R}^+$, i.e., that $\rho(r; \sigma, \alpha)$ be strictly increasing in r. It can be shown [9, 17, 27] that this requirement leads to a very simple *diffeomorphism constraint*:

$$\alpha \in \sigma\left(-\frac{1}{2\pi}, 0.1956\right). \tag{5.2}$$

By enforcing this constraint, we guarantee that the formlet $f(z, \zeta, \sigma, \alpha)$ is a diffeomorphism of the plane.

Figures 5.5(a) and (b) show the radial deformation function $\rho(r; \sigma, \alpha)$ as a function of r for a range of gain α and scale σ values respectively. Figures 5.5(c) and (d) show the corresponding trace of the formlet deformation of an ellipse in the plane.

5.5.3 Formlet Composition

The power of formlets is that they can be composed to produce complex shapes while preserving topology. Given an embryonic shape $\Gamma^0(t)$ and a sequence of K formlets $\{f_1, \ldots, f_K\}$, the new shape $\Gamma^K(t)$, defined as

$$\Gamma^K(t) = (f_K \circ f_{K-1} \circ \cdots \circ f_1)\left(\Gamma^0(t)\right), \tag{5.3}$$

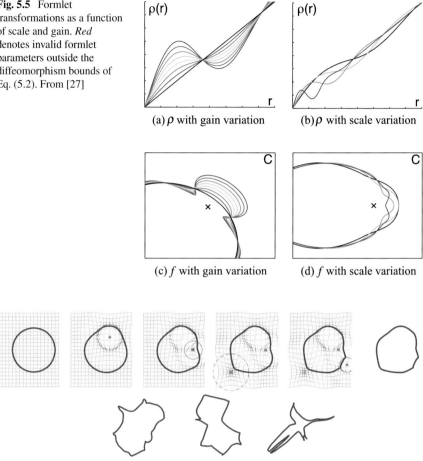

Fig. 5.5 Formlet transformations as a function of scale and gain. *Red* denotes invalid formlet parameters outside the diffeomorphism bounds of Eq. (5.2). From [27]

(a) ρ with gain variation (b) ρ with scale variation

(c) f with gain variation (d) f with scale variation

Fig. 5.6 Shapes generated by random formlet composition over the unit circle. *Top row*: shapes resulting from a sequence of five random formlets. The *red dot* and *circle* indicate formlet location ζ and scale σ, respectively. *Bottom row*: example shapes produced from the composition of many random formlets. From [27]

is guaranteed to have the same topology as the original embryonic shape $\Gamma^0(t)$.

Figure 5.6 shows an example of forward composition from a circular embryonic shape, where the formlet parameters ζ, σ, and α have been randomly selected. Note that a rich set of complex shapes is generated without leaving the space of valid shapes (simple, closed contours).

A more difficult but interesting problem is inverse formlet composition: given an *observed* shape $\Gamma^{\mathrm{obs}}(t)$, determine the sequence of K formlets $\{f_1, \ldots, f_K\}$, drawn from a formlet dictionary $\mathcal{D}$ producing the new shape $\Gamma^K(t)$ that best approximates $\Gamma^{\mathrm{obs}}(t)$, according to a specified error measure ξ. Here, we measure error as the L^2 norm of the residual.

5.6 Formlet Pursuit

To explore the inverse problem of constructing formlet representations of planar shapes, Oleskiw et al. [9, 27] employed a set of 391 blue-screened images of animal models from the Hemera Photo-Object database. The boundary of each object was sampled at 128 points at regular arc-length intervals. The full dataset of object shapes used is available at www.elderlab.yorku.ca/formlets.

To estimate the optimal formlet sequence $\{f_1, \ldots, f_K\}$, a version of matching pursuit for sparse approximation was employed [25]. Specifically, given an observed target shape Γ^{obs}, the model was initialized as a an embryonic elliptical shape Γ^0 minimizing the L^2 error $\xi(\Gamma^{\text{obs}}, \Gamma^0)$. At iteration k of the formlet pursuit algorithm, the formlet $f_k(z; \zeta_k, \sigma_k, \alpha_k)$ is selected that, when applied to the current model Γ^{k-1}, maximally reduces the approximation error.

This is a difficult non-convex optimization problem with many local minima. Fortunately, the error function is quadratic in the formlet gain α, so that, given a specified location ζ and scale σ, the optimal gain α^* can be computed analytically [9, 27]. Thus, the problem comes down to a search over location and scale parameters. In practice, this problem can be solved effectively by a *dictionary descent* method, which combines a coarse grid search with local gradient descent at promising locations in the parameter space [9].

5.7 Evaluation

This shape model can be evaluated by addressing the problem of *contour completion*, using the animal shape dataset. In natural scenes, object boundaries are often fragmented by occlusion and loss of contrast: contour completion is the process of filling in the missing parts. Note that this is precisely the task of the generative model in the feedback process illustrated in Fig. 5.3.

Oleskiw and colleagues [9, 27] compared the formlet model with the shapelet model described in Sect. 5.4 [6]. For each shape in the dataset, they simulated the occlusion of a section of the contour, and allowed the two methods to pursue only the remaining visible portion. They then measured the residual error between the model and target for both the visible and occluded portions of the shapes. Performance on the occluded portions, where the model is under-constrained by the data, reveals how well the structure of the model captures properties of natural shapes. Implementations for both the formlet and shapelet models are available at www.elderlab.yorku.ca/formlets.

Figure 5.7 shows example qualitative results for this experiment. While shapelet pursuit introduces topological errors in both visible and occluded regions, formlet pursuit remains topologically valid, as predicted. Figure 5.8 shows quantitative results. While the shapelet and formlet models achieve comparable error on the visible portions of the boundaries, on the occluded portions the error is substantially lower for the formlet representation. This suggests that the structure of the formlet model

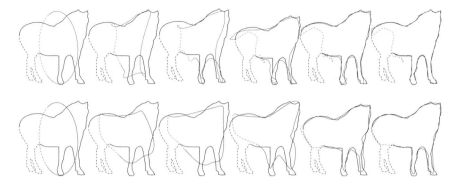

Fig. 5.7 Example of 30 % occlusion pursuit with shapelets (*red*) and formlets (*blue*) for $k = 0, 2, 4, 8, 16, 32$. *Solid lines* indicate visible contour, *dashed lines* indicate occluded contour. From [9]

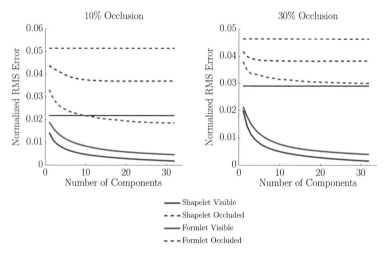

Fig. 5.8 Results of occlusion pursuit evaluation. *Black* denotes error for $\Gamma^0(t)$, the affine-fit ellipse. From [9]

better captures regularities in the shapes of natural objects. The two principal reasons for this are thought to be [9] (a) respecting the topology of the shape prunes off many inferior completion solutions and (b) by working in the image space, rather than arc length, the formlet model is better able to capture important regional properties of shape.

5.8 Discussion

Strictly feedforward algorithms for contour grouping based upon first-order Markov models of contours tend to work poorly on complex natural scenes, yet humans are able to make effective use of contour shape information for object detection [10]. Proven performance advantages of coarse-to-fine methods for contour grouping [12], together with the massive feedback connections that are known to pervade primate object pathway [39, 40] suggest that the human brain may employ a recurrent computation to group contours and efficiently extract shape information from natural scenes.

A key requirement for this recurrent network is a generative model of shape capable of producing global shape "hallucinations" based on contour fragments computed in early visual cortex. These global shape hypotheses can then be fed back to early visual areas to condition search for additional fragments that might support the hypotheses.

The main problem in establishing such a generative model has been topology: prior models do not guarantee that sampled shapes are simple closed contours (e.g., [6]). Recently, however, a novel framework for shape representation has been introduced that guarantees that sampled shapes will have the correct topology. The theory [9, 27], based upon localized diffeomorphic deformations of the image called *formlets*, has its roots in early investigations of biological shape transformation [36], and is closely related to recent work modelling growth in biomedical imaging data [17]. The formlet representation is seen to yield more accurate shape completion than an alternative contour-based generative model of shape, which should make it more effective at generating global shape hypotheses to guide feedforward contour grouping processes.

These findings suggest a number of future experiments and computational investigations: (1) Is there any psychophysical evidence that humans exploit higher-order shape features to segment contours in complex, cluttered scenes? If we do, is there any evidence that this involves a feedback circuit? (2) Many shapes have highly elongated parts that are not efficiently modelled by isotropic formlets. Is there a way to generalize the theory to incorporate oriented formlets? (3) Applying the theory effectively for problems of grouping, detection and recognition will require a probabilistic model over formlet sequences. What is an appropriate structure for this model, and how can its parameters be learned?

Answers to these questions will bring us considerably closer to an understanding of the perceptual organization of shape.

Acknowledgements   The author would like to thank Francisco Estrada, Tim Oleskiw, Gabriel Peyré, Ljiljana Velisavljević and Alexander Yakubovich for their contributions to the work reviewed in this chapter. This work was supported by NSERC, OCE and GEOIDE.

References

1. Arbelaez P, Maire M, Fowlkes C, Malik J (2011) Contour detection and hierarchical image segmentation. IEEE Trans Pattern Anal Mach Intell 33(5):898–916. doi:10.1109/TPAMI. 2010.161
2. Cavanagh P (1991) What's up in top-down processing. In: Gorea A (ed) Representations of vision. Cambridge University Press, Cambridge, pp 295–304

3. Cohen LD, Deschamps T (2001) Multiple contour finding and perceptual grouping as a set of energy minimizing paths. In: Energy minimization methods workshop, CVPR
4. Crevier D (1999) A probabilistic method for extracting chains of collinear segments. Comput Vis Image Underst 76(1):36–53
5. Deschamps T, Cohen LD (2000) Minimal paths in 3d images and application to virtual endoscopy. In: Proceedings of the 6th European conference on computer vision
6. Dubinskiy A, Zhu SC (2003) A multiscale generative model for animate shapes and parts. In: Proc. 9th IEEE ICCV, vol 1, pp 249–256
7. Elder JH, Goldberg RM (2002) Ecological statistics of Gestalt laws for the perceptual organization of contours. J Vis 2(4):324–353
8. Elder JH, Krupnik A, Johnston LA (2003) Contour grouping with prior models. IEEE Trans Pattern Anal Mach Intell 25(25):661–674
9. Elder JH, Oleskiw TD, Yakubovich A, Peyré G (2013) On growth and formlets: sparse multiscale coding of planar shape. Image Vis Comput 31:1–13
10. Elder JH, Velisavljević L (2009) Cue dynamics underlying rapid detection of animals in natural scenes. J Vis 9(7):1–20
11. Elder JH, Zucker SW (1996) Computing contour closure. In: Proceedings of the 4th European conference on computer vision. Springer, New York, pp 399–412
12. Estrada FJ, Elder JH (2006) Multi-scale contour extraction based on natural image statistics. In: IEEE conference on computer vision and pattern recognition workshop
13. Field DJ, Hayes A, Hess RF (1993) Contour integration by the human visual system: evidence for a local "association field". Vis Res 33(2):173–193
14. Foxe JJ, Simpson GV (2002) Flow of activation from V1 to frontal cortex in humans. Exp Brain Res 142:139–150
15. Geisler WS, Perry JS, Super BJ, Gallogly DP (2001) Edge co-occurence in natural images predicts contour grouping performance. Vis Res 41(6):711–724
16. Gilbert CD, Wiesel TN (1989) Columnar specificity of intrinsic horizontal and corticocortical connections in cat visual cortex. J Neurosci 9(7):2432–2443
17. Grenander U, Srivastava A, Saini S (2007) A pattern-theoretic characterization of biological growth. IEEE Trans Med Imaging 26(5):648–659
18. Cox IJ, Rehg JM, Hingorani S (1993) A Bayesian multiple hypothesis approach to contour segmentation. Int J Comput Vis 11(1):5–24
19. Jain AK, Zhong Y, Lakshmanan S (1996) Object matching using deformable templates. IEEE Trans Pattern Anal Mach Intell 18(3):267–278
20. Kirchner H, Thorpe SJ (2006) Ultra-rapid object detection with saccadic eye movements: visual processing speed revisited. Vis Res 46:1762–1766
21. Kruger N (1998) Collinearity and parallelism are statistically significant second order relations of complex cell responses. Neural Process Lett 8:117–129
22. Lee TS, Mumford D (2003) Hierarchical Bayesian inference in the visual cortex. J Opt Soc Am A 20(7):1434–1448
23. Leyton M (1988) A process-grammar for shape. Artif Intell 34(2):213–247
24. Mahamud S, Thornber KK, Williams LR (1999) Segmentation of salient closed contours from real images. In: IEEE international conference on computer vision. IEEE Computer Society, Los Alamitos, pp 891–897
25. Mallat SG, Zhang Z (1993) Matching pursuits with time frequency dictionaries. IEEE Trans Signal Process 41(12):3397–3415
26. Martin D, Fowlkes C, Malik J (2004) Learning to detect natural image boundaries using local brightness, color and texture cues. IEEE Trans Pattern Anal Mach Intell 26(5):530–549
27. Oleskiw TD, Elder JH, Peyré G (2010) On growth and formlets. In: Proceedings of the IEEE conference on computer vision and pattern recognition (CVPR)
28. Parent P, Zucker SW (1989) Trace inference, curvature consistency, and curve detection. IEEE Trans Pattern Anal Mach Intell 11:823–839
29. Portman N, Grenander U, Vrscay ER (2009) Direct estimation of biological growth properties from image data using the "GRID" model. In: Kamel M, Campilho A (eds) Image analysis

and recognition, proceedings. Lecture notes in computer science, vol 5627, pp 832–843. 6th international conference on image analysis and recognition, Halifax, Canada, Jul 06–08, 2009

30. Portman N, Grenander U, Vrscay ER (2011) GRID macroscopic growth law and it application to image inference. Q Appl Math 69(2):227–260

31. Portman N, Vrscay ER (2011) Existence and uniqueness of solutions to the grid macroscopic growth equation. Appl Math Comput 217(21):8318–8327. doi:10.1016/j.amc.2011.03.021. http://www.sciencedirect.com/science/article/pii/S0096300311003754

32. Thorpe S, Fize D, Marlot C (1996) Speed of processing in the human visual system. Nature 381:520–522

33. Sha'ashua A, Ullman S (1988) Structural saliency: the detection of globally salient structures using a locally connected network. In: Proceedings of the 2nd international conference on computer vision, pp 321–327

34. Sharon E, Mumford D (2004) 2d-shape analysis using conformal mapping. In: Computer vision and pattern recognition, IEEE Comp. Soc. Conf., vol 2, pp 350–357

35. Sigman M, Cecchi GA, Gilbert CD, Magnasco MO (2001) On a common circle: natural scenes and Gestalt rules. Proc Natl Acad Sci 98(4):1935–1940

36. Thompson DW (1961) On growth and form. Cambridge University Press, Cambridge

37. Thorpe S (2002) Ultra-rapid scene categorization with a wave of spikes. In: Bülthoff HH et al (eds) Proceedings of the biologicaly-motivated computer vision conference. LNCS, vol 2525, pp 1–15

38. Tu Z, Chen X, Yuille AL, Zhu SC (2005) Image parsing: unifying segmentation, detection, and recognition. Int J Comput Vis 63(2):113–140

39. Ungerleider L (1995) Functional brain imaging studies of cortical mechanisms for memory. Science 270(5237):769–775

40. Van Essen DC, Olshausen B, Anderson CH, Gallant JL (1991) Pattern recognition, attention, and information processing bottlenecks in the primate visual search. SPIE 1473:17–28

41. Williams LR, Jacobs DW (1997) Stochastic completion fields: a neural model of illusory contour shape and salience. Neural Comput 9(4):837–858

42. Yuille A, Kersten D (2006) Vision as Bayesian inference: analysis by synthesis? Trends Cogn Sci 10(7):301–308

43. Zucker SW, Hummel R, Rosenfeld A (1977) An application of relaxation labeling to line and curve enhancement. IEEE Trans Comput 26:394–403

Chapter 6
Two-Dimensional Shape as a Mid-Level Vision Gestalt

Johan Wagemans

6.1 General Introduction

In this chapter, I consider two-dimensional (2-D) shape as a mid-level vision Gestalt. There is an extensive literature on the projection of three-dimensional (3-D) objects on 2-D images and how human and computer vision can recover 3-D objects and shapes from 2-D images (e.g., [34]). However, 2-D shape in itself is also a very rich phenomenon. Here, I will argue that 2-D shape constitutes an interesting case of visual Gestalts, in the sense of structured percepts where global properties dominate, where local features or parts interact with one another or are coded relative to a reference frame. I will also argue that 2-D shape is a prototypical case of a mid-level vision phenomenon, meaning that its essential properties are processed somewhere mid-way along the cortical hierarchy, receiving inputs from low-level visual areas where simple stimulus attributes (or "features" such as orientation and curvature) are processed, and sending outputs to high-level visual areas for recognition and further interpretation. This formulation suggests a rather static system of relatively well-delineated and isolated processing modules, with a series of sequential input-output processors, but what I will show here instead is that the way in which 2-D shapes are processed in human vision is really much more flexible and dynamical, in the sense that most processes at this level show an intricate interplay between low- and high-level aspects of processing. Studying these processes in isolation, which has been the dominant approach in much research so far, has been masking much of the richness of 2-D shape processing as a mid-level Gestalt. I will argue for a more integrated approach by showing some examples of our research program on this theme.

The chapter consists of a brief overview of three lines of research under this umbrella. First, I will discuss our work on the perception of contours of outline

J. Wagemans (✉)
Laboratory of Experimental Psychology, University of Leuven, Leuven, Belgium
e-mail: johan.wagemans@psy.kuleuven.be

S.J. Dickinson, Z. Pizlo (eds.), *Shape Perception in Human and Computer Vision*,
Advances in Computer Vision and Pattern Recognition,
DOI 10.1007/978-1-4471-5195-1_6, © Springer-Verlag London 2013

shapes derived from everyday objects, showing strong interactions between local and global aspects of processing. Second, I will illustrate some of our projects on 2-D shape as a mid-level vision phenomenon, using Gabor arrays, which allow to link shape with perceptual grouping, texture processing, and figure-ground organization. Third, I will briefly review some studies that relate 2-D shape processing to more high-level processes such as categorization.

6.2 Part I. Contours of Outline Shapes Derived from Everyday Objects

6.2.1 Introduction

A few well-placed line segments on a flat canvas are often sufficient to identify objects but not all points along an object's boundary contour are equally informative about shape. Attneave [1] was probably the first to explicitly formulate the hypothesis that curvature extrema (i.e., points along the contour where curvature reaches a local maximum) are most informative about shape. He used two demonstrations to support this hypothesis. In one demonstration, he asked participants to mark salient points along the contour of a random shape and showed that frequencies of participants' responses were highest on the curvature extrema. In a second demonstration, which has become known as Attneave's sleeping cat, he created a version of a line drawing of his sleeping cat by connecting the curvature extrema by straight lines and showed that this straight-line version was still easy to recognize.

To test the role curvature singularities, special values of curvature such as extrema (maxima and minima) but also inflections (i.e., points where curvature changes sign and goes through zero locally) for shape perception, we studied an extensive stimulus set on many observers in a variety of tasks (reviewed in [3]). This way we overcame limitations of previous studies that often tested a small set of shapes and observers with a single task.

6.2.2 The Role of Curvature Singularities in Shape Perception

We derived various stimulus sets from line drawings of everyday objects and asked large groups of observers to identify and segment them. We manipulated information about shape in different ways and tested hypotheses about the role of curvature singularities for object identification and segmentation.

Silhouette and Outline Versions   As a point of departure, we have taken a well-known set of line drawings from Snodgrass and Vanderwart [39], turned these into black silhouettes, extracted their contours and spline-fitted them to obtain smoothly curved, closed contours, with known curvature values at all points along the contour

Fig. 6.1 For all line-drawings of everyday objects in the set by Snodgrass and Vanderwart [39] Rossion and Pourtois [36] created version with additional surface qualities (gray-level or color). In this example, different versions of a frog are shown. We reduced the amount of information about 3-D and 2-D shape in several ways in subsequent studies. On the *top row at the right* are silhouette and outline versions [42]. On the *bottom row at the left* are straight-line versions (analogous to Attneave's sleeping cat) with *straight-line segments* connecting the curvature extrema or the inflections that are, respectively, easy or hard to identify [6]. On the *bottom row at the right* are fragmented versions with fragments centered on extrema or inflections that are, respectively, hard or easy to identify [30]. This pattern of result was typically but not always found for other items in the set

(see Fig. 6.1, top row). Not all of these boundary shapes can still be identified. Identifiability ranged from 0 % to 100 %. We have established norms for identification of these silhouette and outline versions and explored why identifiability of different stimuli was highly variable [42]. These benchmark data are useful for testing computational theories of 3-D object recognition, because they illustrate a wide range of difficulties having to do with diagnostic versus degenerate 2-D views, surface structure, texture, diagnostic features, different types of line segments, junctions, etc.

Salient Points   We then asked subjects to mark salient points along the contours of these shapes and noted that they often picked points in the neighborhood of curvature extrema, confirming Attneave's original observation. But we also found that more global shape factors also played a significant role [5]. The saliency of a point along the contour did not only depend on how high the maximum or how low the minimum was but it also depended on the local neighborhood (e.g., the contour segment within which it was embedded) and the part structure (e.g., how much a part is seen to be protruding or how deep the perceived indentation between two parts is). Such data evidently constrain computational theories of shape representation. Additionally, these benchmark data reveal the spatial scale at which object outlines are perceived (e.g., level of smoothness).

Straight-Line Versions   We then created figures consisting of straight-line segments connecting different points along the contour, such as curvature extrema versus inflection points, or salient points versus points midway between them (Fig. 6.1, bottom row, two left images). Again, we have established norms for identification of these straight-line figures and discussed some reasons for the large differences in identifiability between different stimuli that we found [6]. The straight-line figures based on extrema or salient points were generally easier to identify, again confirming Attneave's intuitions as illustrated in his famous drawing of a sleeping cat. However, we also noted that the degree in which the straight-line version represented the overall part-structure of the outline shape strongly affects the degree of identifiability. In some cases, the straight lines connecting the selected points still preserved the overall structural description of the shape (i.e., same parts in more or less the same relative spatial positions and orientations), while in others they created a different structural description. Hence, adding line-segments between two consecutive points along the contour does much more to the resulting shape than just marking these points, which may be a trivial point but one that is often forgotten in discussions regarding Attneave's cat.

Fragmented Versions   Next, we created versions of these stimuli consisting of small fragments, centered either on curvature extrema or salient points on the one hand or on inflection points or midpoints on the other hand. Once again, we have established norms for identification of these fragmented figures and explored the reasons for the large variability of identifiability between different stimuli [30]. This time, however, we found that the fragmented figures with contour elements centered on extrema or salient points were generally more difficult to identify than those where contour elements were centered on inflections or midpoints (Fig. 6.1, bottom row, two right images), contradicting the idea that most information is carried by the curvature extrema. Apparently, the fact that the fragments require some perceptual grouping to occur yields effects opposite to those obtained in figures with closed contours. This observation illustrates the general point that a computational theory about the importance of geometric sources of information also requires a consideration of task demands. In the context of visual perception, information is not a general, abstract notion but one that requires a computational analysis of the constraints provided to the visual system carrying out a particular function.

Microgenesis of Fragmented Picture Identification   The role of perceptual grouping and the effects of different types of fragments in different types of shape (simple versus complex, natural versus artificial) were later studied in much more detail. Here we used a discrete identification paradigm, which means that we presented a series of fragmented pictures with increasing exposure duration (first for 80 ms, when the answer was incorrect, for 93 ms, then for 106 ms, etc.), until correct identification occurred [33]. In combination with a discrete-time survival analysis, this method allowed us to get a handle on the gradual emergence or microgenesis of fragmented picture identification, including interesting time-course contingencies between component processes (such as perceptual grouping of image fragments) to build a shape description on the one hand and the matching of the resulting shape description to existing object representations in visual memory on the other hand. In addition, different geometric measures of the stimuli were incorporated in the statistical models to analyze the data, which allowed us to investigate their role at different points in time. For instance, configural properties such as symmetry dominated early grouping processes, compared to local fragment properties such as fragment curvature or local relational properties such as proximity. The complexity of shape also played a role that changed over time. For instance, low-complexity objects showed a decreasing disadvantage compared to medium-complexity objects (because there are more possible matches for simpler objects), while high-complex objects showed an increasing advantage (due to a low number of activated candidates). Similar results were subsequently obtained in a version of the discrete identification paradigm in which the fragmented pictures were gradually build up from very sparse, short fragments to longer fragments and almost complete contours [40].

6.2.3 Conclusion

Contours provide considerable information about outline shapes, especially at the points where contour curvature has singular values (inflections and extrema). However, no matter how much one reduces the available information (e.g., by presenting only contour fragments), human perception always extracts and encodes relational properties such as relative distance, parallelism, and so forth. Curvature singularities play a role which is significantly modulated by the local neighborhood and global configuration in which they are embedded. This was also very obvious in an extensive study on the segmentation of objects into parts which we performed with these stimuli [4]. Hence, shape perception, shape-based object identification and segmentation are all tasks that require perceptual organization.

6.3 Part II. From Mid- to Lower-Level Vision: Linking Shape Perception to Perceptual Organization

6.3.1 Introduction

In an extensive research program, we are explicitly connecting our earlier work on perceptual grouping (e.g., [2]) and figure-ground organization (e.g., [16]) to issues in shape perception. It is obvious that in real-life, both of these mid-level processes play a significant role in detecting, localizing and identifying objects. Usually, objects are not presented to us as delineated outlines without a background, which implies that the visual system has to do significant preprocessing to deliver a shape percept which can then be interpreted. As is well known to the computer vision community, this can be a very difficult task. In the photograph in Fig. 6.2, for instance, the segregation and grouping cues would give rise to the perception of a stick in the foreground and some segments of twigs may be grouped in elliptic or circular configurations, but the grouping of elements belonging to the frog (in the center of

Fig. 6.2 Find the frog

the image) with elements from the background prevents to segregate the frog from the background.

To mimic this interplay between perceptual grouping, figure-ground organization, and object detection and identification, we have created so-called Gaborized object outlines. Starting from the same contours derived from line-drawings of everyday objects as in Part I, we can place Gabor patches on the contour and in the interior surface of the object. When we embed these target patches in an array of randomly oriented Gabor patches in the background, the task can become shape detection or identification but it would also require grouping and segregation (as in the frog example). We can then manipulate the orientation of the Gabor elements on the contour separately from the orientation of the Gabor elements forming the interior surface of the figure, and examine the interplay between curvilinearity-based contour grouping and isolinearity-based texture segregation or surface grouping (Fig. 6.3, top panel). Software tools have been made to create such displays, with easy control over low-level parameters like contrast, frequency, phase and orientation of the Gabor elements and mid-level parameters like density and distribution of their placement [7]. The power of this approach is the combination of the following characteristics:

(1) By using Gabor displays, we can mimic the processes that are necessary to group elements that belong together and segregate them from the background. We can slow down the processes that are usually occurring too quickly for measurements in the lab.

(2) By using Gabor patches as the primitive element, we can relate our work to the huge psychophysical and neurophysiological literature on how these stimuli are processed at early levels in the visual system.

(3) By placing Gabor patches on the contour or in the interior surface of object outlines, we can also study the contribution of perceptual organization processes to object identification, and vice versa. We can study the interplay between mid-level and high-level processes in more or less controlled circumstances.

(4) The natural variation of object outlines, which implies a reduced level of parametric control, can still be studied more or less systematically by incorporating all kinds of geometric measures of the shapes (e.g., contour length, surface area, degree of curvature variation along the contour, degree of symmetry, complexity, etc.) in the statistical models to analyze the data.

(5) In principle, the same stimuli can be used to tap into different levels of processing: from detecting a regularity or structure in noise, to grouping and figure-ground organization, to shape discrimination and object identification.

Here, I summarize only some headlines of some of the studies we have done so far within this on-going research program. In extensive benchmark studies we have provided norms for the detectability and identifiability for these stimuli [37, 38], in which the structure were made more or less obvious by manipulating the degree of grouping of the elements along the contour as well as inside (surface) and outside (background). In more psychophysical experiments, we have studied the effect of different levels of misalignment of the elements along the contour for both static and dynamic stimuli, and for both detection and identification [21]. In a subsequent study, we have also tested the effect of local flicker rates on the strength of grouping and how that affects both detection and identification (see [20]). In another line of work, we have examined the role of contour and surface grouping as cues to figure-ground organization with random shapes [18]. As illustrated in Fig. 6.3 (bottom panel), grouping of surface elements is sufficient to see "something" against a background, but a closed contour seems important to really see a clear "shape" or "figure". Psychophysical results indicated that both cues were combined optimally.

6.3.2 Conclusion

In the context of this chapter, I could not do justice to this line of research but I do hope to have shown that the development of such stimuli and tasks can help to bridge the gaps between the traditionally separated domains of perceptual organization (perceptual grouping, texture segregation, figure-ground organization) and shape detection. Gaborized object arrays like these are particularly suited to study mid-level vision as a relay station between low-level vision and high-level vision.

6.4 Part III. From Mid- to Higher-Level Vision: Linking Shape Perception to Categorization

6.4.1 Introduction

Human shape perception is intrinsically relational (e.g., [15]). Not only is the perception of an individual shape often determined by how the different features and

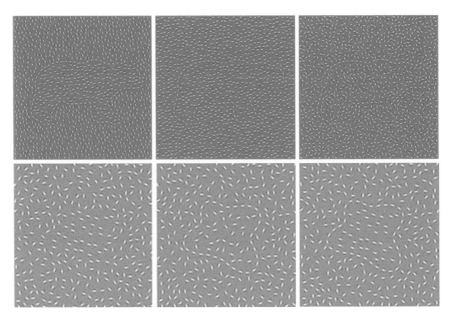

Fig. 6.3 Figure-ground organization in Gabor arrays. On *top* are three examples of Gaborized outlines [37, 38], with the contour and surface clearly segregated from the background (*left*), and only the contour segregated from a regular (*middle*) or noisy (*right*) background. *Below* are three examples of surface only, contour only, and combined surface-contour displays, used in target detection [18]

parts are coded relative to one another within a spatial reference frame or structural description. Human perceivers also spontaneously encode similarities and differences between shapes (e.g., [19]). Indeed, shape similarity is at the heart of a remarkable cognitive capacity, namely to categorize shapes into groups that are sufficiently similar to be treated as exemplars of the same fundamental kind (e.g., apples, bottles) and to distinguish these as a group from other shapes that are similar in some respects and different in others (e.g., pears, cups). Categorization facilitates perceptual and cognitive processing by supporting inferences about behaviorally relevant features of objects one has never encountered. For instance, if it looks like a duck and quacks like a duck, it is (probably) a duck, and then it will fly away when approached by a human, it will swim rather than sink when thrown in the water, etc.

In this section, I will briefly review studies pertaining to the relationship between shape similarity and categorization. This relationship is far from trivial: shape similarity at least partially determines categorization but categorization also affects perceived shape similarity. For example, when shapes are grouped together in a single category, they are perceived to be more similar. Before getting into this relationship, I will first address the question what aspects of visual shape form the basis of perceived shape similarity (e.g., features, dimensions, or yet other aspects).

6.4.2 Shape Features, Dimensions, and Generative Transformations

There is considerable controversy in the perceptual literature about whether differences between shapes are perceived holistically or analytically. In an analytic processing mode, a shape is analyzed into its constituent features or dimensions, and shape similarity is assessed feature-by-feature or dimension-by-dimension. In a holistic processing mode, the processing depends on the nature of the dimensions [9]. So-called integral dimensions cannot be perceived independently. Well-known examples are color brightness and saturation, or for the shape domain, a rectangle's width and height. So-called separable dimensions, on the other hand, allow for separate or independent judgments (e.g., shape and color). In a holistic processing mode, integral dimensions are processed holistically, whereas separable dimensions can be processed analytically [9].

In one study, we created a shape space of novel 2-D shapes varying in aspect ratio and medial axis curvature, and asked whether the two dimensions could be processed independent of one another in various tasks [22]. In general, the two dimensions behaved as separable and they could be extracted consistently from a large set of different contour shapes. The latter finding indicated that shape dimensions could be thought of as generic shape transformations or generative operations that can be applied to a variety of visual objects. We tested this hypothesis in subsequent studies.

In one series of experiments, we introduced two kinds of transformations: one used linear transformations of the image plane (i.e., affine transformations), generally limiting shape variations within the boundaries of basic-level categories; the other used curvilinear continuous transformations of the image plane that preserved local affine structure (i.e., diffeomorphisms), allowing shape variations that crossed and did not cross the boundaries of basic-level categories (for more details, see Appendix in [23]). We created shape quartets, in which two contours of object outlines (e.g., lamp and wineglass) were paired and two other outlines were derived from them by applying corresponding linear and curvilinear transformations (Fig. 6.4). Similar quartets, with corresponding transformation parameters, were created for non-existing shapes. We administered stimulus pairs from within these shape quartets to children of 3 to 7 years old in a delayed match-to-sample task [23]. With increasing age, especially between 5 and 6 years, children became more sensitive to the curvilinear shape deformations that are relevant for between-category distinctions, indicating that acquired categorical knowledge in early years induces perceptual learning of the relevant generic shape differences between categories. Such a distinction was also found in a word-stimulus association learning task in a subsequent study, where errors in a naming task reflected the visual structure of categories [24]. In an earlier study [14], we had applied a similar logic to simpler shapes (e.g., triangles, trapezoids) and simpler shape transformations (e.g., stretching, tapering), and found that infants and toddlers (between 2.5 months and 2.5 years) were more sensitive to categorical than metric shape changes.

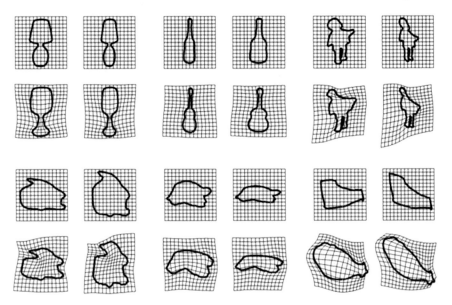

Fig. 6.4 Some of the stimuli that are used in the experiments on shape transformations. The *horizontal pairs* reflect planar linear shape differences (affine transformations) and the *vertical pairs* reflect planar curvilinear shape differences (diffeomorphisms). The *upper three panels* are derived from existing objects (lamp-wineglass, bottle-guitar, doll-ostrich); the *lower three panels* use non-existing shapes assembled from contour fragments of object outlines

6.4.3 Shape Similarity and Categorization Learning

We have investigated the relationship between shape similarity and categorization in two lines of work, one using artificial shapes (which observers have never encountered) and one using outlines of everyday objects (see "Within-category shape discrimination").

Shape Similarity of Fourier Boundary Descriptors   In many of the studies we have performed on this topic, we have created random shapes using the so-called Fourier Boundary Descriptors (or FBDs). These shapes are defined by radial frequency components, describing the shape's contour as a sum of sinusoidal modulations, which are turned into a closed shape by connecting the end point to the starting point [43]. This method allows one to parametrically vary the stimulus shape (by the number, amplitude, and phase of the frequency components), although it is very unlikely that human shape perception makes use of these parameters (Fig. 6.5).

Instead, the family resemblance seems to be based on the overall structure or configuration of the shapes, i.e., the number of parts and their relative positions within some structural description of the shape, whereas the within-family exemplars are all variations of the same global structure in terms of the relative size, degree of curvature and protrusion of the parts, etc. Surprisingly, the similarity structure of such shape spaces showed a clear correspondence between similarity ratings by

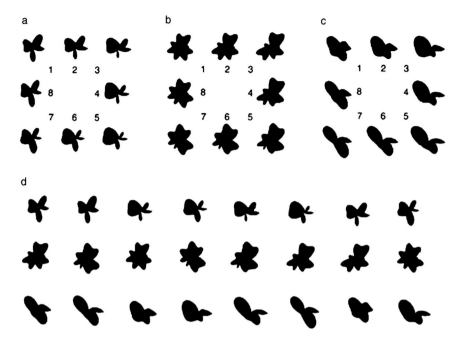

Fig. 6.5 Novel 2-D shapes created by Fourier Boundary Descriptors (FBDs). Although one can easily see in (**d**) that shapes within a row are more similar to one another than between rows, the specific relations between the shapes belonging to a family of similar shapes become clear only when they are presented in an ordered way as in (**a-b-c**), where the shape variations are captured by two dimensions and all pairwise differences between two shapes are more or less the same

human observers, shape confusions revealed in shape discrimination by macaque monkeys, and responses of single neurons in the infero-temporal (IT) cortex in the same macaque monkeys [27]. All of these (behavioral and neural) similarity spaces corresponded (at least at an ordinal level) with the 2-D structure of the shape space defined by the sum of the local, pixel-by-pixel dissimilarities (as reflected by the arrangements in panels a, b, and c of Fig. 6.5, with equal pairwise differences between all consecutive shapes within the space).

Shape Similarity and Categorization Learning   In subsequent studies, we have investigated relations between shape encoding and category learning in such shape spaces. For example, we examined how the difficulty of a categorization task depended on the way a categorization rule divided the shape space. When a linear separation rule was used, separating half of the shapes from the other half by a linear boundary in the shape space (e.g., shapes 1–4 versus 5–8 in Fig. 6.5a–c), categorization learning proceeded quickly. In the absence of such a linear separation rule, categorization learning was much slower and did not reach perfect performance, although performance was still better when the rule divided the space into quadrants (e.g., shapes 1, 2, 5, and 6 versus 3, 4, 7, and 8 in Fig. 6.5a–c), as compared to an arbitrary rule in which every nearest neighbor of a shape belonged to the opposite category (e.g., shapes 1, 3,5, and 7 versus 2, 4, 6, and 8 in Fig. 6.5a–c). This pattern of results clearly supports the relevance of perceptual similarity for categorization: It is much easier to group shapes into categories depending on their perceived similarity. The categorization learning rate in monkeys could be modeled on the basis of the similarity of neural responses in the cortical area IT, in a version of a neural network model derived from ALCOVE [17], but only when the variability of their firing rate and tuning selectivity was taken into account (for more details, see [29]).

In another line of work, the reverse influence was studied, i.e., how categorization affected perceived shape similarity. After learning to categorize some shapes as members of category A and others as members of category B, two shapes from different categories were perceived as more different from one another. However, the nature of the perceived shape dimensions was important: With so-called integral shape dimensions of shapes made from FBDs, both the relevant and the irrelevant shape differences became more distinguishable, whereas in so-called separable shape dimensions (such as aspect ratio and curvature) only the relative differences were enhanced (for more details, see [28]). This provides evidence for another link between shape perception and categorization.

6.4.4 Within-Category Shape Discrimination

In a second set of studies, we investigated shape similarity effects within existing categories of objects. Previous research of object identification has been primarily concerned with basic-level identification: identification of objects as members of a larger class, usually made of different exemplars with similar overall shapes and usually named by simple nouns, learned in the young age (e.g., dog, chair). Of course, many natural categories consist of different exemplars, which can also be distinguished (e.g., German shepherd, Labrador, Golden retriever, etc.; kitchen chair, arm chair, office chair, etc.). Moreover, these basic-level categories themselves can also be grouped into larger categories, usually containing much more shape variation (e.g., mammals, furniture). The former is called subordinate-level categorization; the latter is called superordinate-level categorization [35]. We have conducted several studies on subordinate-level categorization and shape similarity.

First, we developed a stimulus set that allows one to study identification at the subordinate-category level [26]. This set consists of 269 line-drawings of 25 different basic-level categories, both natural objects and artifacts. In an fMRI study, we investigated the additional perceptual processes and representations that are recruited when exemplars have to be discriminated at the subordinate-category level [25].

In subsequent studies, we derived silhouette and outline versions of these subordinate-level exemplars and had a large sample of subjects perform similarity ratings on them. Using Multi-Dimensional Scaling or MDS [8], we derived two-dimensional representations of those families of shapes such as cars (Fig. 6.6A). Then we extracted four extreme exemplars and created intermediated shapes by morphing the extreme exemplars (Fig. 6.6B). In a set of 6 × 4 morph sequences

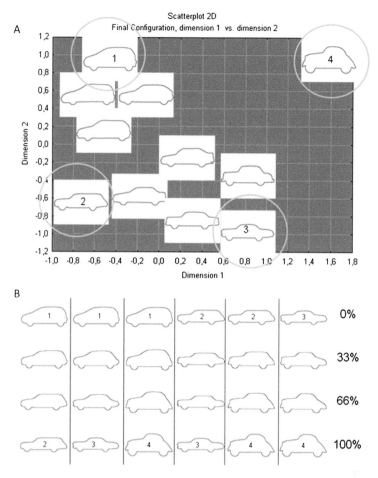

Fig. 6.6 (**A**) The similarity ratings between all the exemplars of one basic-level object (e.g., car) can be analyzed by MDS to create a shape space (with distance representing dissimilarity). (**B**) Taking the four most extreme shapes in such a shape space, one can then create 6 morph sequences between each pair

with equal parametric changes from one exemplar to another for each basic-level category, we collected similarity ratings, typicality ratings and basic-level matching responses [32].

In an fMRI study using an event-related adaptation design, we confirmed that within-category shape similarity is represented in the cortical area LOC, previously identified as the locus for shape-based object identification [31]. When pairs of these object outlines were presented consecutively, the BOLD activations in this area decreased monotonically as a function of the distance between objects on the morph line (small decrease for large distance, larger decrease for smaller distance). This finding of shape-similarity encoding in human LOC corresponds to a similar correlation that was established in the study mentioned earlier [27], between 2-D shape similarity at the behavioral level for both humans and macaque monkeys and single-cell responses in cortical area IT in the macaque monkey.

In an additional study in this series, we trained subjects to partition each basic-level category into two subsets, using a horizontal or vertical boundary in the 2-D shape space. Compared to a control condition in which the different exemplars were presented equally often, the categorized shapes were discriminated better and, more importantly, between-category pairs were discriminated better than within-category pairs. Moreover, LOC was more selective for differences among the categorized objects than among control objects [10]. These results indicate that the task context modulates the extent to which shape similarity is altered as a result of training, both at the behavioral and neural levels.

6.4.5 Shape Interpretation and Perceptual Switching

In all of the above studies where we created morphed between identifiable stimuli (e.g., two cars), we implicitly assumed that the intermediate shapes formed a smooth stimulus continuum. In another line of work, we explicitly studied the possibility of a categorical shift from one interpretation to another, and the role of ambiguity in the transition stage. The source of inspiration for this work came from traditional ambiguous figures like Boring's old-young woman, Jastrow's duck-rabbit, and so forth (see Fig. 6.7, top). An interesting aspect of these ambiguous figures is that one can manipulate the degree of ambiguity. This can be done in two opposite ways. First, starting from a classic ambiguous figure and its two unambiguous interpretations, one can construct gradually less ambiguous versions in both directions (e.g., from classic duck-rabbit in the middle to clear duck at one side and clear rabbit at the other side; see Fig. 6.7, middle). Eleven such series were made [13], normative data on the level of perceptual ambiguity of each exemplar in a series were collected, and interesting biases were obtained [41].

Second, starting from pairs of outlines of everyday objects (e.g., airplane–crocodile; [42]), fifteen series of morphed objects were made with ambiguous figures arising in-between the extremes [11], also at several levels of ambiguity (see Fig. 6.7, below). The degree of categorical perception differed between the different series: For some series, the transition between the two alternative interpretations changed abruptly, somewhere in the middle, with very few other responses than the two dominant ones, while for other series, the transition occurred much more gradually, and the morphs in the middle region of the continuum gave rise to quite a few additional response alternatives). In subsequent studies, we have used a double-naming task to reveal whether the non-dominant alternative enters response competition (becomes suppressed) and a Bayesian selection model to distinguish continuous versus discrete processing of alternatives and accounts of switching [12].

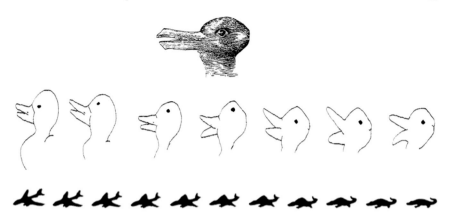

Fig. 6.7 On *top* is the classic duck-rabbit ambiguous figure. In the *middle*, a morph sequence created in-between the ambiguous middle figure and one extreme (clear duck) in one direction and another extreme (clear rabbit) in the other direction. *Below* is another kind of morph sequence, starting from one clear picture (e.g., airplane) to another clear picture (e.g., crocodile) with gradual transitions in-between

6.4.6 Conclusion

Several conclusions can be drawn from this review on our work on the link between shape perception and categorization. First, shape encoding is essentially relational. Few changes can be made to a local feature of a shape without influencing the overall shape percept, so features and parts of shapes are encoded configurally. Moreover, shapes are usually encoded relative to other similar shapes, and properties of sets of shapes (the average, the overall degree of variation, the strength of different sources of variation) are extracted from the input images without much effort. Second, how shapes are encoded affects several cognitive tasks. The mental representation of a family of shapes (i.e., mental shape space) and how the categorization rule divides it influence the difficulty of category learning by way of the nature of the separation of the space. Third, similar shapes are often categorized together and category learning increases perceived similarity of shapes within a category. In sum, there is a mutual influence between shape similarity and categorization.

6.5 General Conclusion

Shape is a beautiful thing. Even simple outline drawings induce a wealth of processes and representations within the human visual system. When fragments of shapes and objects must be extracted from a noisy and cluttered input images, the interplay between low-level image processing, mid-level perceptual organization, and high-level interpretations is truly stunning. Much of this is still way too complex for computer vision systems but they can resort to simpler brute-force methods to solve more delineated problems. Human vision, in contrast, is probably less good at isolated tasks but by combining subprocesses in generic and flexible ways, it can handle the much more complex tasks of visual processing encountered in everyday life. Laboratory experiments usually scratch only the surface of what human perceivers can do and there is still a great deal to learn about why things look the way they do [15].

Acknowledgements I am supported by long-term structural funding from the Flemish Government (METH/08/02). This chapter was written during my sabbatical, with support from the Research Foundation–Flanders (K8.009.12N). I would also like to acknowledge the hospitality of the Department of Psychology at the University of California, Berkeley, the "Institut d'études avancées" (IEA), Paris, and the Department of Experimental Psychology at the University of Oxford.

References

1. Attneave F (1954) Some informational aspects of visual perception. Psychol Rev 61:183–193
2. Claessens PM, Wagemans J (2005) Perceptual grouping in Gabor lattices: proximity and alignment. Percept Psychophys 67:1446–1459
3. De Winter J, Wagemans J (2004) Contour-based object identification and segmentation: stimuli, norms and data, and software tools. Behav Res Methods Instrum Comput 36:604–624
4. De Winter J, Wagemans J (2006) Segmentation of object outlines into parts: a large-scale, integrative study. Cognition 99:275–325
5. De Winter J, Wagemans J (2008) Perceptual saliency of points along the contour of everyday objects: a large-scale study. Percept Psychophys 70:50–64
6. De Winter J, Wagemans J (2008) The awakening of Attneave's sleeping cat: identification of everyday objects on the basis of straight-line versions of outlines. Perception 37:245–270
7. Demeyer M, Machilsen B (2012) The construction of perceptual grouping displays using GERT. Behav Res Methods 44:439–446. doi:10.3758/s13428-011-0167-8
8. Everitt BS, Dunn G (2001) Multidimensional scaling. In: Everitt BS, Dunn G (eds) Applied multivariate data analysis. Arnold, London, pp 93–124
9. Garner WR (1974) The processing of information and structure. Wiley, New York
10. Gillebert CR, Op de Beeck HP, Panis S, Wagemans J (2009) Subordinate categorization enhances the neural selectivity in human object-selective cortex for fine shape differences. J Cogn Neurosci 21:1054–1064
11. Hartendorp MO, Van der Stigchel S, Burnett HG, Jellema T, Eilers PHC, Postma A (2010) Categorical perception of morphed objects using a free-naming experiment. Vis Cogn 18:1320–1347
12. Hartendorp MO, Van der Stigchel S, Wagemans J, Klugkist I, Postma A (2012) The activation of alternative response candidates: when do doubts kick in? Acta Psychol 139:38–45
13. Hogeboom MM (1995) On the dynamics of static pattern perception. PhD Thesis, University of Amsterdam, Amsterdam, The Netherlands
14. Kayaert G, Wagemans J (2010) Infants and toddlers show enlarged visual sensitivity to categorical compared to metric shape changes. i-Perception 1:149–158. doi:10.1068/i0397
15. Koffka K (1935) Principles of Gestalt psychology. Lund Humphries, London
16. Kogo N, Strecha C, Van Gool L, Wagemans J (2010) Surface construction by a 2-d differentiation-integration process: a neurocomputational model for perceived border ownership, depth, and lightness in Kanizsa figures. Psychol Rev 117:406–439
17. Kruschke JK (1992) ALCOVE: an exemplar-based connectionist model of category learning. Psychol Rev 99:22–44
18. Machilsen B, Wagemans J (2011) Integration of contour and surface information in shape detection. Vis Res 51:179–186

19. Medin DL, Goldstone RL, Gentner D (1993) Respects for similarity. Psychol Rev 100:254–278

20. Nygård GE, Sassi M, Wagemans J (2011) The influence of orientation and contrast flicker on contour saliency of outlines of everyday objects. Vis Res 51:65–73

21. Nygård GE, Van Looy T, Wagemans J (2009) The influence of orientation jitter and motion on contour saliency and object identification. Vis Res 49(20):2475–2484

22. Ons B, De Baene W, Wagemans J (2011) Subjectively interpreted shape dimensions as privileged and orthogonal axes in mental shape space. J Exp Psychol Hum Percept Perform 37:422–441

23. Ons B, Wagemans J (2011) Development of differential sensitivity for shape changes resulting from linear and nonlinear planar transformations. i-Perception 2:121–136. doi:10.1068/i0407

24. Ons B, Wagemans J (2012) A developmental difference in shape processing and word-shape associations between 4 and 6.5 year olds. i-Perception 3:481–494. doi:10.1068/i0481

25. Op de Beeck H, Béatse E, Wagemans J, Sunaert S, Van Hecke P (2000) The representation of shape in the context of visual object categorisation tasks. NeuroImage 12:28–40

26. Op de Beeck H, Wagemans J (2001) Visual object categorization at distinct levels of abstraction: a new stimulus set. Perception 30:1337–1361

27. Op de Beeck H, Wagemans J, Vogels R (2001) Macaque inferotemporal neurons represent low-dimensional configurations of parameterized shapes. Nat Neurosci 4:1244–1252

28. Op de Beeck H, Wagemans J, Vogels R (2003) The effect of category learning on the representation of shape: dimensions can be biased but not differentiated. J Exp Psychol Gen 4:491–511

29. Op de Beeck HP, Wagemans J, Vogels R (2008) The representation of perceived shape similarity and its role for category learning in monkeys: a modelling study. Vis Res 48:598–610

30. Panis S, De Winter J, Vandekerckhove J, Wagemans J (2008) Identification of everyday objects on the basis of fragmented versions of outlines. Perception 37:271–289

31. Panis S, Vangeneugden J, Op de Beeck H, Wagemans J (2008) The representation of subordinate shape similarity in human occipitotemporal cortex. J Vis 8(10):9. doi:10.1167/8.10.9

32. Panis S, Vangeneugden J, Wagemans J (2008) Similarity, typicality, and category-level matching of outlines of everyday objects. Perception 37:1822–1849

33. Panis S, Wagemans J (2009) Time-course contingencies in perceptual organization and identification of fragmented object outlines. J Exp Psychol Hum Percept Perform 35:661–687

34. Pizlo Z (2008) 3-d shape: its unique place in visual perception. MIT Press, Cambridge

35. Rosch E, Mervis CB, Gray WD, Johnson DM, Boyes-Braem P (1976) Basic objects in natural categories. Cogn Psychol 8:382–439

36. Rossion B, Pourtois G (2004) Revisiting Snodgrass and Vanderwart's object pictorial set: the role of surface detail in basic-level object recognition. Perception 33:217–236

37. Sassi M, Machilsen B, Wagemans J (2012) Shape detection of Gaborized outline versions of everyday objects. i-Perception 3:745–764. doi:10.1068/i0499

38. Sassi M, Vancleef K, Machilsen B, Panis S, Wagemans J (2010) Identification of everyday objects on the basis of Gaborized outline versions. i-Perception 1:121–142. doi:10.1068/i0384

39. Snodgrass JG, Vanderwart M (1980) A standardized set of 260 pictures: norms for name agreement, image agreement, familiarity, and visual complexity. J Exp Psychol Hum Learn Mem 6:174–215

40. Torfs K, Panis S, Wagemans J (2010) Identification of fragmented object outlines: a dynamic interplay between different component processes. Vis Cogn 18:1133–1164

41. Verstijnen I, Wagemans J (2004) Ambiguous figures: living versus nonliving objects. Perception 33:531–546

42. Wagemans J, De Winter J, Op de Beeck HP, Ploeger A, Beckers T, Vanroose P (2008) Identification of everyday objects on the basis of silhouette and outline versions. Perception 37:207–244

43. Zahn CT, Roskies RZ (1972) Fourier descriptors for plane closed curves. IEEE Trans Comput 21:269–281

Chapter 7
Shape Priors for Image Segmentation

Daniel Cremers

7.1 Image Analysis and Prior Knowledge

The segmentation of images into meaningful regions is among the most studied problems in image analysis. The term *meaningful* typically refers to a semantic partitioning where the computed regions correspond to individual objects in the observed scene. Unfortunately, generic purely low-level segmentation algorithms often do not provide the desired segmentation results, because the traditional low level assumptions like intensity or texture homogeneity and strong edge contrast are not sufficient to separate objects in a scene.

To stabilize the segmentation process with respect to missing and misleading low-level information, researchers have proposed to impose prior knowledge into low-level segmentation methods. In the following, we will review methods which allow to impose knowledge about the *shape* of objects of interest into segmentation processes.

In the literature there exist various definitions of the term *shape*, from the very broad notion of shape of Kendall [37] and Bookstein [5] where shape is whatever remains of an object when similarity transformations are factored out (i.e., a geometrically normalized version of a gray value image) to more specific notions of shape referring to the geometric outline of an object in 2D or 3D. In this work, we will adopt the latter view and refer to an object's silhouette or boundary as its shape. Intentionally we will leave the exact mathematical definition until later, as different representations of geometry actually imply different definitions of the term *shape* and will require different algorithms. In fact, we will see that the question of how to *represent* shapes is closely coupled to the question of finding efficient algorithms for shape optimization.

One can distinguish three kinds of shape knowledge:

D. Cremers (✉)
Departments of Computer Science & Mathematics, TU Munich, Garching, Germany
e-mail: cremers@tum.de

S.J. Dickinson, Z. Pizlo (eds.), *Shape Perception in Human and Computer Vision*,
Advances in Computer Vision and Pattern Recognition,
DOI 10.1007/978-1-4471-5195-1_7, © Springer-Verlag London 2013

Table 7.1 Shapes can be represented explicitly or implicitly, in a spatially continuous or a spatially discrete setting. More recently, researchers have adopted hybrid representations [67], where objects are represented both in terms of their interior (implicitly) and in terms of their boundary (explicitly)

	Spatially continuous	Spatially discrete	
Explicit	polygons [15, 74], splines [3, 26, 36]	edgel labeling & dyn. progr. [1, 53, 60, 64, 66]	hybrid repres. LP relaxation [67]
Implicit	level-set methods [27, 51], convex relaxation [12, 23]	graph cut methods [6, 33]	

- *Low-level shape priors* typically favor shorter boundary length, that is, curves with shorter boundary have lower shape energy [4, 6, 33, 36, 48].
- *Mid-level shape priors* characterize a certain class of shapes without specifying their exact shape. For example, thin and elongated structures can be preferred to facilitate the segmentation of roads in satellite imagery or of blood vessels in medical imagery [30, 49, 55]. Similarly one can impose a prior on the low-order shape moments without otherwise constraining the shape [41].
- *High-level shape priors* favor similarity to previously observed shapes, such as hand shapes [15, 26, 34], silhouettes of humans [18, 21] or medical organs like the heart, the prostate, the lungs or the cerebellum [42, 58, 59, 71].

Among a wealth of works on shape priors for image segmentation we will focus in this chapter on high-level shape priors. Specifically, we will present a range of representative works—with many of the examples taken from the author's own work—and discuss their advantages and shortcomings.

7.2 Explicit versus Implicit Shape Representation

Among mathematical representations of shape, one can distinguish between *explicit* and *implicit* representations. In the former case, the boundary of the shape is represented explicitly as a mapping from a chart into the embedding space. Alternatively, shapes can be represented implicitly in the sense that points in the ambient space are labeled as part of the interior or the exterior of the object. In the spatially continuous setting, the optimization of such implicit shape representations is solved by means of partial differential equations. Among the most popular representatives are the level-set method [27, 51] or alternative convex relaxation techniques [11, 12]. In the spatially discrete setting, implicit representations have become popular through the graph cut methods [7, 33]. More recently, researchers have also advocated hybrid representations where objects are represented both explicitly and implicitly [67]. Table 7.1 provides an overview of a few representative works on image segmentation using explicit and implicit representations of shape.

Figure 7.1 shows examples of shape representations using an explicit parametric representation by spline curves (spline control points are marked as black boxes),

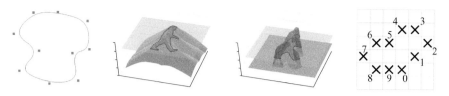

Fig. 7.1 Examples of shape representations by means of a parametric spline curve (*1st image*), a signed distance function (*2nd image*), a binary indicator function (*3rd image*), and an explicit discrete representation (*4th image*)

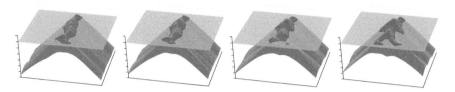

Fig. 7.2 The linear interpolation of the signed distance functions associated with two human silhouettes also gives rise to intermediate shapes, yet it does not constrain the shape's topology. The interpolation of signed distance functions is generally no longer a signed distance function

implicit representations by a signed distance function or a binary indicator function and an explicit discrete representation (4th image).

Both explicit and implicit shape representations can be used for *statistical shape learning* where one can generalize a family of plausible shapes from a few sample shapes—see Fig. 7.2.

In the following, we will give an overview of some of the developments in the domain of shape priors for image segmentation. In Sect. 7.3, we will discuss methods to impose statistical shape priors based on explicit shape representations. In Sect. 7.4, we discuss methods to impose statistical shape priors in level-set based image segmentation including the concept of *dynamical shape priors* to learn temporal models of shape evolution as priors for image sequence segmentation. And lastly, in Sect. 7.5, we will present a method to compute polynomial-time optimal segmentations with elastic shape priors.

7.3 Statistical Shape Priors for Explicit Shape Representations

Over the last decades Bayesian inference has become an established paradigm to tackle the problem of image segmentation—see [22, 76], for example. Given an input image $I : \Omega \to \mathbb{R}$ on a domain $\Omega \subset \mathbb{R}^2$, a segmentation C of the image plane Ω can be computed by maximizing the posterior probability $\mathscr{P}(C \mid I) \propto \mathscr{P}(I \mid C) \, \mathscr{P}(C)$, where $\mathscr{P}(I \mid C)$ denotes the data likelihood for a given segmentation C and $\mathscr{P}(C)$ denotes the prior probability which allows to impose knowledge about which segmentations are a priori more or less likely.

Maximizing the posterior distribution can be performed equivalently by minimizing its negative logarithm given by a cost function of the form

$$E(C) = E_{\text{data}}(C) + E_{\text{shape}}(C), \tag{7.1}$$

where $E_{\text{data}}(C) = -\log \mathscr{P}(I \mid C)$ and $E_{\text{shape}}(C) = -\log \mathscr{P}(C)$ are typically referred to as *data fidelity term* and *regularizer* or *shape prior*. By maximizing the posterior, one aims at computing the most likely solution given data and prior.

Over the years various data terms have been proposed. In the following, we will simply use a piecewise-constant approximation of the input intensity I [48]. More sophisticated data terms based on color likelihoods [8, 40, 50, 75] or texture likelihoods [2, 22] are conceivable.

7.3.1 Linear Shape Priors

Among the most straightforward ways to represent a shape is to model its outline as a parametric curve, for example a spline curve of degree k [14, 26, 29, 46]. For $k = 1$, we simply have a polygonal shape [74]. Such parametric representations are quite *compact* in the sense that very detailed silhouettes can be represented by a few control points. This representation can be made invariant to translation, rotation and scale by appropriate normalizations often called *procrustes analysis* [28].

With this contour representation, the image segmentation problem boils down to computing an optimal spline control point vector for a given image. The segmentation process can be constrained to familiar shapes by imposing a statistical shape prior computed from the set of training shapes. The most popular shape prior is based on the assumption that the training shapes are Gaussian distributed—see for example [15, 26, 38]. One can define a shape prior that is invariant to similarity transformations (translation, rotation and scaling) by applying the Gaussian assumption to the similarity-normalized control point vector [26]. Since the space of similarity-normalized shapes is no longer a vector-space, however, the resulting distribution will not be exactly Gaussian.

Figure 7.3 shows several intermediate steps in a gradient descent evolution on the energy (7.1) combining the piecewise constant intensity model with a Gaussian shape prior constructed from a set of sample hand shapes. Note how the similarity-invariant shape prior constrains the evolving contour to hand-like shapes without constraining its translation, rotation or scaling. We refer to this as a *linear* shape prior since admissible shapes are linear combinations of respective eigen-shapes.

Figure 7.4 shows the gradient descent evolution with the same shape prior for an input image of a partially occluded hand. Here the missing part of the silhouette is recovered through the statistical shape prior. The curve converges to the desired segmentation over rather large spatial distance.

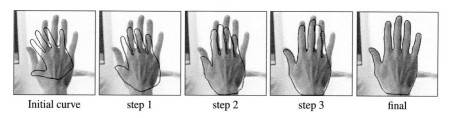

| Initial curve | step 1 | step 2 | step 3 | final |

Fig. 7.3 Evolution of a parametric spline curve during gradient descent on the energy (7.1) combining a piecewise constant intensity data term model with a Gaussian shape prior constructed from a set of sample hand shapes [26]. Since the shape prior is by construction invariant to similarity transformations, the contour easily undergoes translation, rotation and scaling during energy minimization

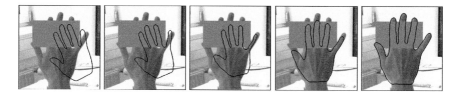

Fig. 7.4 Gradient descent evolution of a parametric curve with similarity invariant shape prior. The statistical shape prior permits a reconstruction of the hand silhouette in places where it is occluded

7.3.2 Nonlinear Shape Priors

In general, a given set of shapes—say the various projections of a 3D object observed from different view points or the various silhouettes of a walking person—will not be Gaussian-distributed. There are many ways to go beyond the Gaussian distribution—using mixtures of Gaussians, kernel density estimators or manifold learning techniques. Alternatively one can introduce nonlinearity by means of Mercer kernel methods. In [20], it was proposed to model the shape prior not by a Mahalanobis distance in the input space (arising from the Gaussian model), but by a corresponding distance upon a transformation $\psi : \mathbb{R}^n \to Y$ of the control point vector $z \in \mathbb{R}^n$ to some generally higher-dimensional *feature space* Y. This gives rise to a Mahalanobis distance of the form:

$$E(z) = \big(\psi(z) - \psi_0\big)^t \, \Sigma_\psi^{-1} \, \big(\psi(z) - \psi_0\big) \tag{7.2}$$

with $\hat{z}$ being the similarity-normalized control point vector. Here ψ_0 and Σ_ψ denote the mean and covariance matrix computed for the transformed shapes:

$$\psi_0 = \frac{1}{m} \sum_{i=1}^{m} \psi(z_i), \qquad \Sigma_\psi = \frac{1}{m} \sum_{i=1}^{m} \big(\psi(z_i) - \psi_0\big)\big(\psi(z_i) - \psi_0\big)^\top. \tag{7.3}$$

As shown in [20], the energy $E(z)$ above can be evaluated without explicitly specifying the nonlinear transformation ψ. It suffices to define the corresponding

Fig. 7.5 Tracking a familiar object over a long image sequence with a nonlinear statistical shape prior constructed from a set of sample silhouettes. In contrast to commonly used Gaussian shape priors, the nonlinear prior allows the emergence of a multitude of familiar shapes which are not merely a linear combination of familiar shapes

Mercer kernel [17, 47]:

$$k(x, y) := \langle \psi(x), \psi(y) \rangle, \quad \forall x, y \in \mathbb{R}^n, \tag{7.4}$$

representing the scalar product of pairs of transformed points $\psi(x)$ and $\psi(y)$. A popular choice of k is a Gaussian kernel function: $k(x, y) \propto \exp(-\frac{1}{2\sigma^2} \|x - y\|^2)$. It was shown in [20], that the resulting energy is related to the classical Parzen-Rosenblatt density estimators. As shown in Fig. 7.5, this nonlinear shape prior allows the emergence of multiple very different shapes and therefore better preserves small-scale shape details.

7.4 Statistical Priors for Level-Set Representations

Parametric representations of shape such as those presented above have numerous favorable properties. In particular, they allow the representation of rather complex shapes with few parameters, resulting in low memory requirements and low computation time. Nevertheless, the explicit representation of shape has several drawbacks: Firstly, explicit shapes require a specific choice of curve (or surface) parameterization. To factor out this dependency in the representation and in respective algorithms gives rise to computationally challenging problems of regridding or reparameterization. This becomes particularly difficult for higher-dimensional shapes. Secondly, parametric representations are difficult to adapt to varying topology of the represented shape. Numerically topology changes require sophisticated splitting and remerging procedures. Thirdly, the commonly used energies are not convex with respect to a parametric boundary representation. Gradient descent algorithms will therefore only determine locally optimal solutions.

A mathematical representation of shape which is independent of parameterization was pioneered in the analysis of random shapes by Fréchet [31] and in the school of mathematical morphology founded by Matheron and Serra [45, 70]. The level-set method [27, 51] provides a means of propagating contours C (independent of parameterization) by evolving associated embedding functions ϕ via partial differential equations—see Fig. 7.2 for a visualization of the level-set function associated with a human silhouette. It has been adapted to segment images based on numerous low-level criteria such as edge consistency [10, 39, 44], intensity homogeneity [13, 73], texture information [9, 35, 52, 57] and motion information [24].

7.4.1 Nonparametric Shape Priors

For level-set based shape representations, researchers have fit a linear sub-space to the sampled signed distance functions [43, 59, 72]. These approaches were shown to capture some shape variability. Yet, they exhibit two limitations: Firstly, they rely on the assumption of a Gaussian distribution which is not well suited to approximate shape distributions encoding more complex shape variation—see above. Secondly, they work under the assumption that shapes are represented by signed distance functions. Yet, the space of signed distance functions is not a linear space. Therefore, in general, neither the mean nor the linear combination of a set of signed distance functions will correspond to a signed distance function.

In the following, we will propose an alternative approach for generating a statistical shape dissimilarity measure for level-set based shape representations. It is based on classical methods of (so-called non-parametric) kernel density estimation and overcomes the above limitations.

Given a set of training shapes $\{\phi_i\}_{i=1,\dots,N}$, one can introduce a nonparametric shape prior on the space of signed distance functions [25] by means of a Parzen-Rosenblatt kernel density estimator [54, 56]:

$$\mathscr{P}(\phi) \propto \frac{1}{N} \sum_{i=1}^{N} \exp\left(-\frac{1}{2\sigma^2} d^2(\phi, \phi_i)\right), \qquad (7.5)$$

with an appropriate distance d to measure the dissimilarity of two given level-set functions. The kernel density estimator is among the theoretically most studied density estimation methods. In the finite-dimensional case, it was shown to converge to the true distribution in the limit of infinite samples (and $\sigma \to 0$).

As in the case of parametric curves, segmentation can be cast as a problem of maximum aposteriori inference which boils down to an energy minimization problem of the form

$$E(\phi) = E_{\text{data}}(\phi) + E_{\text{shape}}(\phi), \qquad (7.6)$$

with $E_{\text{shape}}(\phi) = -\log \mathscr{P}(\phi)$ and an appropriate data term E_{data}.

Figure 7.6 shows a direct comparison of a level-set segmentation process without and with the non-parametric shape prior in (7.5). The shape prior permits the accurate reconstruction of an entire set of fairly different shapes. Since the shape prior is defined on the level-set function ϕ, it can easily handle topological changes of the represented curve.

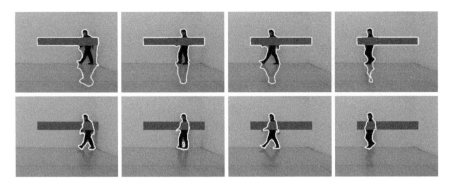

Fig. 7.6 By extending a purely data driven level set segmentation (*top row*) with a nonparametric shape prior (*bottom row*) the resulting segmentation method is robust to misleading low-level information such as shadows or partial occlusion

7.4.2 Dynamical Shape Priors for Implicit Shapes

Although the above shape priors can be applied to tracking objects in image sequences, they are not suited for this task, because they neglect the *temporal coherence of silhouettes* which characterizes many deforming shapes. In the following, we will present temporal statistical shape models for implicitly represented shapes that were first introduced in [18]. At any given time, the shape probability depends on the shapes observed at previous time steps. The integration of such dynamical shape models into the segmentation process can be formulated within a Bayesian framework for image sequence segmentation: Let $I_t : \Omega \to \mathbb{R}$ denote the input image at time t and let $\hat{\phi}_{1:t-1} := (\hat{\phi}_1, \ldots, \hat{\phi}_{t-1})$ denote the segmentations obtained for the previous frames. Under the assumption that these segmentations are correct and that no knowledge about future data is available, the most likely segmentation at time t can be computed as follows:

$$\hat{\phi}_t = \arg\max_{\phi_t} \mathscr{P}(\phi_t \mid I_t, \hat{\phi}_{1:t-1}) = \arg\max_{\phi_t} \mathscr{P}(I_t \mid \phi_t) \mathscr{P}(\phi_t \mid \hat{\phi}_{1:t-1}). \qquad (7.7)$$

Under certain assumptions, it is even possible to reinterpret the past observations in closed form [61]. The intuition is then to find the segmentation which best partitions the current image and all past images (when propagated backward in time with the dynamical model). Similarly one could take into account future observations (if available) by propagating the model forward in time.

Again, one can equivalently minimize the negative logarithm of the above expression. Gradient descent induces an evolution of the level set function which is driven both by the intensity information of the current image as well as by a dynamical shape prior which relies on the segmentations obtained for the preceding frames. Experimental evaluation demonstrates that the resulting segmentations are not only similar to previously learned shapes, but they are also consistent with the temporal correlations estimated from sample sequences. The resulting segmentation

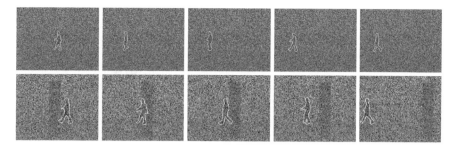

Fig. 7.7 Variational image sequence segmentation with a dynamical shape prior on noisy and partially occluded data. 90 % noise means that nine out of ten intensity values were replaced by a random intensity. The statistically learned dynamical model allows for reliable segmentation results despite large amounts of noise (*above*) and prominent occlusion (*below*)

process can cope with large amounts of noise and occlusion because it exploits prior knowledge about *temporal* shape consistency and because it aggregates information from the input images over time (rather than treating each image independently).

As in the case of static shape priors, one can consider linear [18] or nonlinear [19] dynamical shape priors. As shown in Fig. 7.7, a linear dynamical shape prior allows reliable tracking of a walking person in an image sequence degraded by large amounts of noise and prominent occlusion.

7.5 Parametric Representations Revisited: Combinatorial Solutions for Segmentation with Shape Priors

In previous sections, we saw that shape priors improve the segmentation and tracking of familiar deformable objects, biasing the segmentation process to favor familiar shapes or even familiar shape evolutions. Unfortunately these approaches are based on locally minimizing the respective energies via gradient descent. Since these energies are generally non-convex, the computed locally optimal solutions typically depend on an initialization and may be suboptimal in practice. One exception based on implicit shape representations as binary indicator functions and convex relaxation techniques was proposed in [23]. Yet, the linear interpolation of shapes represented by binary indicator functions will generally not give rise to plausible intermediate shapes: For example, linearly interpolating two human silhouettes with one arm in different locations will fade out the arm in one location and make it emerge again in the other location. It will not translate the arm from one location to the other which would be desirable. In this sense, there is no generalization to plausible intermediate shapes.

Moreover, while implicit representations like the level-set method circumvent the problem of computing correspondences between points on either of two shapes, it is well-known that the aspect of point correspondences plays a vital role in human notions of shape similarity. For matching planar shapes, there is abundant literature

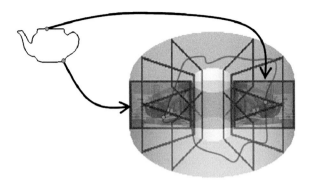

Fig. 7.8 A polynomial-time solution for matching shapes to images: matching a template curve $C : \mathbb{S}^1 \to \mathbb{R}^2$ (*left*) to the image plane $\Omega \subset \mathbb{R}^2$ is equivalent to computing an orientation-preserving cyclic path $\Gamma : \mathbb{S}^1 \to \Omega \times \mathbb{S}^1$ in the product space spanned by the image domain and the template domain. The latter problem can be solved in polynomial time—see [66] for details

on how to solve this correspondence problem in polynomial time using dynamic programming techniques [32, 62, 69].

Similar concepts of dynamic programming can be employed to localize deformed template curves in images. Coughlan et al. [16] detected open boundaries by shortest path algorithms in higher-dimensional graphs. Felzenszwalb et al. used dynamic programming in chordal graphs to localize shapes, albeit not on a pixel level.

Polynomial-time solutions for localizing deformable closed template curves in images using minimum ratio cycles or shortest circular paths were proposed in [66], with a further generalization presented in [65]. There the problem of determining a segmentation of an image $I : \Omega \to \mathbb{R}$ that is elastically similar to an observed template $cc : \mathbb{S}^1 \to \mathbb{R}^2$ is computed as a cycle

$$\Gamma : \mathbb{S}^1 \to \Omega \times \mathbb{S}^1 \tag{7.8}$$

of minimum ratio in the product space spanned by the image domain Ω and template domain $\mathbb{S}^1$. See Fig. 7.8 for a schematic visualization. All points along this circular path provide a pair of corresponding template point and image pixel. In this manner, the matching of template points to image pixels is equivalent to the estimation of orientation-preserving cyclic paths, which can be solved in polynomial time using dynamic programming techniques such as ratio cycles [63] or shortest circular paths [68].

Figure 7.9 shows an example result obtained with this approach: The algorithm determines a deformed version (right) of a template curve (left) in an image (center) in globally optimal manner. An initialization is no longer required and the best conceivable solution is determined in polynomial time.

Figure 7.10 shows further examples of tracking objects: Over long sequences of hundreds of frames the objects of interest are tracked reliably—despite low contrast, camera shake, bad visibility and illumination changes. For further details, we refer to [66].

Template curve   Close-up of input image   Optimal segmentation

Fig. 7.9 Segmentation with a single template: despite significant deformation and translation, the initial template curve is accurately matched to the low-contrast input image. The globally optimal correspondence between template points and image pixels is computed in polynomial time by dynamic programming techniques [66]

frame 1   frame 10   frame 80   frame 110

frame 1   frame 100   frame 125   frame 200

Fig. 7.10 Tracking of various objects in challenging real-world sequences [66]. Despite bad visibility, camera shake and substantial lighting changes, the polynomial-time algorithm allows to reliably track objects over hundreds of frames. Image data taken from [66]

7.6 Conclusion

In the previous sections, we have discussed various ways to include statistical shape priors in image segmentation methods. We have made several observations:

- By imposing statistically learned shape information one can generate segmentation processes which favor the emergence of familiar shapes—where familiarity is based on one or several training shapes.
- Statistical shape information can be elegantly combined with the input image data in the framework of Bayesian maximum aposteriori estimation. Maximizing the posterior distribution is equivalent to minimizing a sum of two energies representing the data term and the shape prior. A further generalization allows to impose

dynamical shape priors so as to favor familiar deformations of shape in image sequence segmentation.

- While linear Gaussian shape priors are quite popular, the silhouettes of typical objects in our environment are generally not Gaussian distributed. In contrast to linear Gaussian priors, nonlinear statistical shape priors based on Parzen-Rosenblatt kernel density estimators or based on Gaussian distributions in appropriate feature spaces [20] allow to encode a large variety of rather distinct shapes in a single shape energy.

- Shapes can be represented explicitly (as points on the object's boundary or surface) or implicitly (as the indicator function of the interior of the object). They can be represented in a spatially discrete or a spatially continuous setting.

- The choice of shape representation has important consequences regarding the tractability of the resulting optimization problem. Moreover, different notions of shape similarity and shape interpolation are more easily expressed with respect to one or the other shape representation. As a result, there is no single ideal representation of shape. In fact, a good compromise between *desirable* and *tractable* cost functions may be obtained using hybrid representations such as the one proposed in [67]. It is an overcomplete shape representation which combines an explicit (albeit not parametric) and an implicit representation coupled via linear constraints. As a consequence, properties of both the object's interior and its boundary can be directly accessed in the respective cost function. If this cost function is linear then LP relaxation can provide minimizers of bounded optimality.

Acknowledgements   The work described here was done in collaboration with numerous researchers. The author would like to thank T. Schoenemann, F.R. Schmidt, C. Schnoerr, S. Soatto, N. Sochen, T. Kohlberger, M. Rousson and S.J. Osher for their support.

References

1. Amini AA, Weymouth TE, Jain RC (1990) Using dynamic programming for solving variational problems in vision. IEEE Trans Pattern Anal Mach Intell 12(9):855–867
2. Awate SP, Tasdizen T, Whitaker RT (2006) Unsupervised texture segmentation with nonparametric neighborhood statistics. In: European conference on computer vision (ECCV), Graz, Austria, May 2006. Springer, Berlin, pp 494–507
3. Blake A, Isard M (1998) Active contours. Springer, London
4. Blake A, Zisserman A (1987) Visual reconstruction. MIT Press, Cambridge
5. Bookstein FL (1978) The measurement of biological shape and shape change. Lect notes in biomath, vol 24. Springer, New York
6. Boykov Y, Kolmogorov V (2003) Computing geodesics and minimal surfaces via graph cuts. In: IEEE int conf on computer vision, Nice, pp 26–33
7. Boykov Y, Kolmogorov V (2004) An experimental comparison of min-cut/max-flow algorithms for energy minimization in vision. IEEE Trans Pattern Anal Mach Intell 26(9):1124–1137
8. Brox T, Rousson M, Deriche R, Weickert J (2003) Unsupervised segmentation incorporating colour, texture, and motion. In: Petkov N, Westenberg MA (eds) Computer analysis of images and patterns, Groningen, The Netherlands, August 2003. LNCS, vol 2756. Springer, Berlin, pp 353–360

9. Brox T, Weickert J (2004) A TV flow based local scale measure for texture discrimination. In: Pajdla T, Hlavac V (eds) European conf. on computer vision, Prague. LNCS, vol 3022. Springer, Berlin, pp 578–590
10. Caselles V, Kimmel R, Sapiro G (1995) Geodesic active contours. In: Proc IEEE intl conf on comp vis, Boston, USA, pp 694–699
11. Chambolle A, Cremers D, Pock T (2012) A convex approach to minimal partitions. SIAM J Imaging Sci 5(4):1113–1158
12. Chan T, Esedoğlu S, Nikolova M (2006) Algorithms for finding global minimizers of image segmentation and denoising models. SIAM J Appl Math 66(5):1632–1648
13. Chan TF, Vese LA (2001) Active contours without edges. IEEE Trans Image Process 10(2):266–277
14. Cipolla R, Blake A (1990) The dynamic analysis of apparent contours. In: IEEE int. conf on computer vision. Springer, Berlin, pp 616–625
15. Cootes TF, Taylor CJ, Cooper DM, Graham J (1995) Active shape models—their training and application. Comput Vis Image Underst 61(1):38–59
16. Coughlan J, Yuille A, English C, Snow D (2000) Efficient deformable template detection and localization without user initialization. Comput Vis Image Underst 78(3):303–319
17. Courant R, Hilbert D (1953) Methods of mathematical physics, vol 1. Interscience, New York
18. Cremers D (2006) Dynamical statistical shape priors for level set based tracking. IEEE Trans Pattern Anal Mach Intell 28(8):1262–1273
19. Cremers D (2008) Nonlinear dynamical shape priors for level set segmentation. J Sci Comput 35(2–3):132–143
20. Cremers D, Kohlberger T, Schnörr C (2003) Shape statistics in kernel space for variational image segmentation. Pattern Recognit 36(9):1929–1943
21. Cremers D, Osher SJ, Soatto S (2006) Kernel density estimation and intrinsic alignment for shape priors in level set segmentation. Int J Comput Vis 69(3):335–351
22. Cremers D, Rousson M, Deriche R (2007) A review of statistical approaches to level set segmentation: integrating color, texture, motion and shape. Int J Comput Vis 72(2):195–215
23. Cremers D, Schmidt FR, Barthel F (2008) Shape priors in variational image segmentation: convexity, Lipschitz continuity and globally optimal solutions. In: IEEE conference on computer vision and pattern recognition (CVPR), Anchorage, Alaska, June 2008
24. Cremers D, Soatto S (2005) Motion Competition: a variational framework for piecewise parametric motion segmentation. Int J Comput Vis 62(3):249–265
25. Cremers D, Sochen N, Schnörr C (2006) A multiphase dynamic labeling model for variational recognition-driven image segmentation. Int J Comput Vis 66(1):67–81
26. Cremers D, Tischhäuser F, Weickert J, Schnörr C (2002) Diffusion Snakes: introducing statistical shape knowledge into the Mumford–Shah functional. Int J Comput Vis 50(3):295–313
27. Dervieux A, Thomasset F (1979) A finite element method for the simulation of Raleigh-Taylor instability. Springer Lect Notes in Math, vol 771. pp 145–158
28. Dryden IL, Mardia KV (1998) Statistical shape analysis. Wiley, Chichester
29. Farin G (1997) Curves and surfaces for computer–aided geometric design. Academic Press, San Diego
30. Franchini E, Morigi S, Sgallari F (2009) Segmentation of 3d tubular structures by a pde-based anisotropic diffusion model. In: Intl. conf. on scale space and variational methods. LNCS, vol 5567. Springer, Berlin, pp 75–86
31. Fréchet M (1961) Les courbes aléatoires. Bull Inst Int Stat 38:499–504
32. Geiger D, Gupta A, Costa LA, Vlontzos J (1995) Dynamic programming for detecting, tracking and matching deformable contours. IEEE Trans Pattern Anal Mach Intell 17(3):294–302
33. Greig DM, Porteous BT, Seheult AH (1989) Exact maximum a posteriori estimation for binary images. J R Stat Soc B 51(2):271–279
34. Grenander U, Chow Y, Keenan DM (1991) Hands: a pattern theoretic study of biological shapes. Springer, New York
35. Heiler M, Schnörr C (2003) Natural image statistics for natural image segmentation. In: IEEE int. conf. on computer vision, pp 1259–1266

36. Kass M, Witkin A, Terzopoulos D (1988) Snakes: active contour models. Int J Comput Vis 1(4):321–331
37. Kendall DG (1977) The diffusion of shape. Adv Appl Probab 9:428–430
38. Kervrann C, Heitz F (1999) Statistical deformable model-based segmentation of image motion. IEEE Trans Image Process 8:583–588
39. Kichenassamy S, Kumar A, Olver PJ, Tannenbaum A, Yezzi AJ (1995) Gradient flows and geometric active contour models. In: IEEE int. conf. on computer vision, pp 810–815
40. Kim J, Fisher JW, Yezzi A, Cetin M, Willsky A (2002) Nonparametric methods for image segmentation using information theory and curve evolution. In: Int. conf. on image processing, vol 3, pp 797–800
41. Klodt M, Cremers D (2011) A convex framework for image segmentation with moment constraints. In: IEEE int. conf. on computer vision
42. Kohlberger T, Cremers D, Rousson M, Ramaraj R (2006) 4d shape priors for level set segmentation of the left myocardium in SPECT sequences. In: Medical image computing and computer assisted intervention, October 2006. LNCS, vol 4190, pp 92–100
43. Leventon M, Grimson W, Faugeras O (2000) Statistical shape influence in geodesic active contours. In: Int. conf. on computer vision and pattern recognition, Hilton Head Island, SC, vol 1. pp 316–323
44. Malladi R, Sethian JA, Vemuri BC (1995) Shape modeling with front propagation: a level set approach. IEEE Trans Pattern Anal Mach Intell 17(2):158–175
45. Matheron G (1975) Random sets and integral geometry. Wiley, New York
46. Menet S, Saint-Marc P, Medioni G (1990) B–snakes: implementation and application to stereo. In: Proc. DARPA image underst workshop, April 6–8, pp 720–726
47. Mercer J (1909) Functions of positive and negative type and their connection with the theory of integral equations. Philos Trans R Soc Lond A 209:415–446
48. Mumford D, Shah J (1989) Optimal approximations by piecewise smooth functions and associated variational problems. Commun Pure Appl Math 42:577–685
49. Nain D, Yezzi A, Turk G (2003) Vessel segmentation using a shape driven flow. In: MICCAI, pp 51–59
50. Nieuwenhuis C, Cremers D (2013) Spatially varying color distributions for interactive multilabel segmentation. IEEE Trans Pattern Anal Mach Intell 35(5):1234–1247
51. Osher SJ, Sethian JA (1988) Fronts propagation with curvature dependent speed: algorithms based on Hamilton–Jacobi formulations. J Comp Physiol 79:12–49
52. Paragios N, Deriche R (2002) Geodesic active regions and level set methods for supervised texture segmentation. Int J Comput Vis 46(3):223–247
53. Parent P, Zucker SW (1989) Trace inference, curvature consistency, and curve detection. IEEE Trans Pattern Anal Mach Intell 11(8):823–839
54. Parzen E (1962) On the estimation of a probability density function and the mode. Ann Math Stat 33:1065–1076
55. Rochery M, Jermyn I, Zerubia J (2006) Higher order active contours. Int J Comput Vis 69(1):27–42
56. Rosenblatt F (1956) Remarks on some nonparametric estimates of a density function. Ann Math Stat 27:832–837
57. Rousson M, Brox T, Deriche R (2003) Active unsupervised texture segmentation on a diffusion based feature space. In: Proc. IEEE conf. on comp. vision patt. recog, Madison, WI, pp 699–704
58. Rousson M, Cremers D (2005) Efficient kernel density estimation of shape and intensity priors for level set segmentation. In: MICCAI, vol 1, pp 757–764
59. Rousson M, Paragios N, Deriche R (2004) Implicit active shape models for 3d segmentation in MRI imaging. In: MICCAI. LNCS, vol 2217. Springer, Berlin, pp 209–216
60. Rosenfeld A, Zucker SW, Hummel RA (1977) An application of relaxation labeling to line and curve enhancement. IEEE Trans Comput 26(4):394–403
61. Schmidt FR, Cremers D (2009) A closed-form solution for image sequence segmentation with dynamical shape priors. In: Pattern recognition (Proc. DAGM), September 2009

62. Schmidt FR, Farin D, Cremers D (2007) Fast matching of planar shapes in sub-cubic runtime. In: IEEE int. conf. on computer vision, Rio de Janeiro, October 2007
63. Schoenemann T, Cremers D (2007) Globally optimal image segmentation with an elastic shape prior. In: IEEE int. conf. on computer vision, Rio de Janeiro, Brasil, October 2007
64. Schoenemann T, Cremers D (2007) Introducing curvature into globally optimal image segmentation: minimum ratio cycles on product graphs. In: IEEE int conf on computer vision, Rio de Janeiro, October 2007
65. Schoenemann T, Cremers D (2008) Matching non-rigidly deformable shapes across images: a globally optimal solution. In: IEEE conference on computer vision and pattern recognition (CVPR), Anchorage, Alaska, June 2008
66. Schoenemann T, Cremers D (2009) A combinatorial solution for model-based image segmentation and real-time tracking. IEEE Trans Pattern Anal Mach Intell
67. Schoenemann T, Kahl F, Masnou S, Cremers D (2012) A linear framework for region-based image segmentation and inpainting involving curvature penalization. Int J Comput Vis 99:53–68
68. Schoenemann T, Schmidt FR, Cremers D (2008) Image segmentation with elastic shape priors via global geodesics in product spaces. In: British machine vision conference, Leeds, UK, September 2008
69. Sebastian T, Klein P, Kimia B (2003) On aligning curves. IEEE Trans Pattern Anal Mach Intell 25(1):116–125
70. Serra J (1982) Image analysis and mathematical morphology. Academic Press, London
71. Tsai A, Wells W, Warfield SK, Willsky A (2004) Level set methods in an EM framework for shape classification and estimation. In: MICCAI
72. Tsai A, Yezzi A, Wells W, Tempany C, Tucker D, Fan A, Grimson E, Willsky A (2001) Model–based curve evolution technique for image segmentation. In: Comp vision patt recog, Kauai, Hawaii, pp 463–468
73. Tsai A, Yezzi AJ, Willsky AS (2001) Curve evolution implementation of the Mumford-Shah functional for image segmentation, denoising, interpolation, and magnification. IEEE Trans Image Process 10(8):1169–1186
74. Unal G, Krim H, Yezzi AY (2005) Information-theoretic active polygons for unsupervised texture segmentation. Int J Comput Vis, May
75. Unger M, Pock T, Cremers D, Bischof H (2008) TVSeg—interactive total variation based image segmentation. In: British machine vision conference (BMVC), Leeds, UK, September 2008
76. Zhu SC, Yuille A (1996) Region competition: unifying snakes, region growing, and Bayes/MDL for multiband image segmentation. IEEE Trans Pattern Anal Mach Intell 18(9):884–900

Chapter 8
Observations on Shape-from-Shading in Humans

Andrew J. Schofield, Peng Sun, and Giacomo Mazzilli

Humans are able to judge the shape of an undulating surface from variations in the amount of light reflected from it due to changes in its orientation/position relative to the light source. Here, we are concerned more with the shape of undulations on a surface than the solid shapes of objects as a whole. The latter may support object recognition and coarse grasping actions whereas the former may relate more to fine grasping and finger placement.

The study of shape-from-shading in humans has a long history but remains an open problem. It is clear that humans can estimate surface undulations from patterns of shading but less clear what mechanisms support this process. This knowledge gap is also found in the computer vision literature where despite many years' of effort and the existence of many good algorithms to deal with special cases, a robust, generic solution to shape-from-shading remains somewhat elusive.

The central problem of shape-from-shading is that shape must be estimated from luminance variations in the image but the origin of such variations is highly ambiguous. Even in the most restricted cases (e.g., Lambertian surfaces with uniform albedo illuminated by a single collimated light source) the amount of light reflected to the eye depends on the angle between the surface normal and the lighting direction. Potentially, vision faces the task of simultaneously estimating two unknowns (the direction of the light source and the orientation of the surface) from a single luminance value. This problem is mathematically ill posed and can only be solved with additional information or constraints. Vision of course has access to more than

A.J. Schofield (✉) · G. Mazzilli
School of Psychology, University of Birmingham, Birmingham, UK, B15 2TT
e-mail: a.j.schofield@bham.ac.uk

G. Mazzilli
e-mail: GXM947@bham.ac.uk

P. Sun
Department of Cognitive Science, University of California Irvine, Irvine, CA 92697-5100, USA
e-mail: sunp2@uci.edu

S.J. Dickinson, Z. Pizlo (eds.), *Shape Perception in Human and Computer Vision*,
Advances in Computer Vision and Pattern Recognition,
DOI 10.1007/978-1-4471-5195-1_8, © Springer-Verlag London 2013

Fig. 8.1 A photograph of a convexity and a concavity both lit from above-left. People tend to see both as convexities with the one on the left lit from below-right even though this requires two light sources

one luminance value at a time, but no surface is truly Lambertian, surface albedo varies, and scenes are lit by a multitude of spatially localized light sources. All of these factors complicate the estimation of shape-from-shading. Thus, a given pattern of luminance variations, can arise from changes in surface properties, illumination intensity and direction, and surface orientation. The task of extracting surface orientation with no knowledge of the light field or surface reflectance properties is mathematically intractable.

That humans can apparently perform shape-from-shading implies that we can also perform a number of other related tasks such as (1) decompose the luminance image into reflectance changes and illumination changes; (2) discriminate shading from shadows; (3) estimate the light field; and (4) locate boundary points in the image to both separate surfaces one from another and to provide vital constraints to solve the shape-from-shading problem. Each of these tasks is difficult in its own right and it is by no means certain that the human visual system solves them all independently or veridically. What is clear is that the visual system can solve this constellation of problems well enough to produce useful solutions most of the time.

The human visual system also seems to employ prior knowledge to fill in gaps in the sensory input thus allowing shape-from-shading to proceed even in highly impoverished scenes. Human vision degrades gracefully. For example, the simple case of a sinusoidal luminance grating of moderate contrast is seen as an undulating surface even when there is no physical surface or light source generating the 'shading', and when boundary information is at best incomplete [25, 29, 32]. In such reduced cases, the visual system must assume a light source and estimate surface shape despite the lack of boundary constraints. However, these surface estimates may not be veridical to the physical surface, where one exists. The ambiguities and inaccuracies of shape-from-shading are well illustrated by Fig. 8.1 which shows a photograph of a bump and a dip lit by a single light source but which often appears as two bumps lit from different directions.

In this review, we will first consider which shape properties are estimated by human shape-from-shading. We will then review the human visual system's ability to extract shape-from-shading and estimate light source direction; the importance of boundary conditions; the nature and role of default assumptions; and the estimation of shape in sub-optimal circumstances.

8.1 Shape Properties

Marr's [20] hierarchal approach to vision suggests that low-order scene properties, such as the orientation of surfaces are extracted from the image and that these estimates are then used to compute higher properties such a surface curvature and overall object shape. More recent theories of shape perception such as Pizlo's [26] account of the extraction of object shape from 2D outlines suggest that no such hierarchy exists. Human vision need not, and does not, compute higher order shape properties from surface orientations. Johnston and Passmore [9, 10] had observers measure both surface orientation and curvature and found that the two appeared to be estimated separately. This dissociation persisted even when stereoscopic and texture cues were added to the displays. They concluded that curvature judgments do not rely on estimates of surface orientation. People can derive both surface orientation and curvature from shading, but the two processes are separate. Perhaps unfortunately, most studies of shape-from-shading (including our own) have measured the perceived orientation of surfaces. Other studies have used relative depth judgments between probe points to estimate surface shape and a few have asked participants to estimate curvature directly. Johnston & Passmore's result suggest that findings based on one type of shape estimate cannot be assumed to translate to other measurement methods.

Summary   Human vision estimates surface orientation and curvature directly and separately from shading, it does not derive curvature estimates from changes in orientation.

8.2 Veridicality and Stability

While the visual system seems to reconstruct surface shape from shading if at all possible, it does not necessarily do so veridically. Orientation settings for a given image do not necessarily match the orientations of the original surface that generated the image. However, given that any shading image can be generated from an infinite number of shape and lighting combinations (see, for example, [2]) this lack of veridical perception is not surprising. As Koenderink, van Doorn, and Kappers [14] put it, the information in an image can only deliver shape estimates up to a certain level of ambiguity, after that the observer must apply their 'beholders share' (some internal estimate of the missing information) to interpret the shape before them.

Koenderink, van Doorn and Kappers [13] side stepped the question of veridical perception and asked only if observers' shape judgments were consistent over repeated observations and across observers. They found that observers were internally consistent for a given task and that tilt settings were reasonably consistent between observers. In contrast, the inter-observer variability in slant settings was quite high. Tilt measures the direction or axis along which the surface is oriented whereas slant measures the degree to which the surface is oriented away from the observer. Thus, Koenderink et al.'s [13] result shows that observers tend to perceive the same basic shape but apply a different depth scaling to it. Koenderink et al. [14] extended this work to consider variations across different tasks for the same shape. As well as the expected inter-observer variations, Koenderink et al. found considerable within observer variations for the same shape estimated using different measurement methods. This result would seem to suggest that shape-from-shading is unreliable, however, the estimated shapes were almost always affine transformations of one another (both across tasks and observers). That is, all the estimates represented the same basic shape with a scale factor in depth (z) and a shear in x, y. Koenderink et al. [14] associated this affine transformation with the 'beholders share' and the application of prior assumptions.

It is interesting that the particular affine transformation adopted by an observer varied between measurement methods and stimuli. This finding suggests that the set of prior assumptions adopted by human vision is to some large extent determined by both the stimulus and the measurement task. There were, however, marked similarities among the transformations adopted by each observer: for example, shears tended to be in the same direction. Koenderick et al. [14] concluded that, affine transformations notwithstanding, estimates of surface shape are very reliable.

Summary Human shape-from-shading does not always yield veridical solutions but it does yield reliable ones up to an affine transformation. Because of the ill-posed nature of shape-from-shading, and the consequent need to employ prior assumptions about the scene and lighting conditions which may be idiosyncratic, we must expect variations in perceived shape across participants and between tasks within participants. Thus, we must be careful about the choice of task and should probably test more people than is typical in psychophysics. However, for reasonably well-articulated stimuli, we should expect a high degree of stability once affine transformations of perceived surfaces are allowed. We should not be too concerned by inter- and intra-subject variability that can be explained by such transformations.

8.3 Boundary Conditions and Contours

Although it is possible to make some estimate of shape directly from shading alone, the presence of contours in an image can have a profound effect on the percept formed. Erens, Kappers and Koenderick [5] asked people to make shape judgments about isolated patches of surface free from boundary and lighting information and found that they were unable to distinguish between convex, concave, quadric and hyperbolic structures. Adding lighting information in the form of cast shadows improved performance but participants were still unable to distinguish the quadric and hyperbolic cases. Knill [11] provides an interesting example case: a sinusoidal shading pattern provides an ambiguous shape percept; it might either represent two bumps under frontal lighting or four bumps lit from above. Curved stripes added to the image disambiguate the percept such that the curvature frequency of the contours determines the number of bumps perceived.

Occluding contours and edge contours also disambiguate shape-from-shading. Occluding contours, such as those found at the perimeters of objects, are especially important for helping to define shape. At such points, surface slant is a maximal 90 degrees and tilt is perpendicular to the contour. Thus, occluding contours provide useful seed points where both slant and tilt are known independently of shading. Slant and tilt values can then be propagated from such points and, modified appropriately by the intervening shading values, producing more veridical solutions than might be obtained using shading alone [8].

In our own work on boundary constraints [32], we presented observers with simple periodic stimuli—not rendered images—and found that shape estimates often conformed to the linear shading or 'slant proportional to luminance' rule. However, shape estimates were also affected by luminance edges in the image. For example, truncating the image so that only one cycle of luminance variation was visible changed the perceived shape. We conclude that even when edge features do not define occluding boundaries and are not interpreted as surface marking they can still affect shape perception.

Summary   Contours due to both occluding boundaries and surface markings strongly determine perceived surface shape and serve to disambiguate, perhaps even override, shape-from-shading. Luminance edges, even when they are part of the shading pattern and do not define contours, may also be critical in determining the computations used to extract shape-from-shading.

8.4 The Role of Lighting

Gerardin, Kourtzi and Mamassian [6] have shown that lighting direction and shape judgments are processed in separate brain areas with the former being processed in early retinotopic areas while the latter is processed in higher areas. This might support a degree of independence between the estimation of lighting direction and shape-from-shading but also suggest that shape-from-shading may depend on an estimate of the light source. In this section, we discuss the relationship between shape-from-shading and the nature of the light source.

The pattern of shading produced by a surface clearly depends on the direction and nature of the illuminant that shines upon it. A robust shape-from-shading algorithm should produce stable shape estimates despite variations in the composition of the light field. Such robustness might be achieved by estimating the light field and then using this information when extracting shape-from-shading. If this process were perfect, shape estimates would be independent of lighting. However, it is by no means certain that humans use lighting information so directly. For example, Todd and Mingolla [33] asked observers to judge curvature and lighting direction for shiny and dull surfaces and found that whereas curvature estimates varied between the two surface treatments judgments of lighting direction did not; suggesting that the two estimates are decoupled. Further Mingolla and Todd [21] found that the accuracy on shape judgment tasks correlated only weakly with that for judgments of lighting direction. This correlation fell to zero when the stimuli represented elongated ellipsoids suggesting a disassociation between lighting judgments and shape judgments. We note, however, that accuracy was relatively low for both tasks when the ellipsoids were elongated and that judgments of lighting direction have since been shown to be poor for elongated stimuli.

Curran and Johnston [3] assessed the lighting dependence of shape judgments using a curvature estimation task. Curvature estimates reduced when the tilt of the illuminant was increased (away from vertical) but increased with increasing illuminant slant (zero slant representing lighting along the line of sight). This variation in perceived depth with lighting slant could indicate a relationship between perceived curvature and contrast. Low lighting slant corresponds to more frontal lighting which tends to produce low contrast shading signals. Similarly, for a given lighting slant, reducing the overall depth of the surface will reduce contrast. It is possible then that changes in lighting slant are mistaken for changes in surface depth with overall depth being set proportional to image contrast. It is less clear why increased tilt should reduce perceived curvature.

Christou and Koenderink [4] showed that shape estimates for elliptical solids were biased by the illuminant direction such that regions of high luminance were seen as closer to the observer and darker regions as further away (a dark-is-deep interpretation). For directional lighting, highlights occur on surfaces pointing towards the light source and so move with changes in lighting direction. Knowledge of the lighting direction should stabilize the perceived surface shape. The finding that perceived shape varied with lighting direction suggests that no such stabilization occurred. However, the observers produced a dark-is-deep interpretation which is something of a special case as it is associated with diffuse illumination rather than directional illumination (Langer and Bülthoff [16]). Diffuse illumination is, by definition, non-directional and therefore under diffuse lighting any variation in shading must be due to the surface shape rather than changes in lighting direction. Therefore, the lack of shape constancy found by Christou and Koenderink may have been caused by observers falsely perceiving the illuminant as diffuse and therefore, at least partially, attributing shading variations between images of the same object to changes in surface shape.

Summary   Perceived shape is not always independent of lighting direction. It may be that such variations are most prevalent when changes in the lighting direction are misattributed to changes in the surface profile. This might occur when changes in lighting slant result in reduced image contrast which is falsely associated with low surface relief and where a directional light source is mistaken for a diffuse one.

8.5 Estimating Lighting Direction and Diffuseness

We now consider the human ability to estimate lighting diffuseness and direction. Langer and Bülthoff [16] used well-articulated isotropic surfaces and had people make relative depth judgments for pairs of probe points. When the surface was lit by a directional source, observers responded accordingly indicating that light parts of the surface were slanted towards the light source (slant proportional to luminance). However, when a diffuse source was used, observers adopted an approximation to the dark-is-deep rule whereby light regions are seen as closest to the observer and thus often oriented towards them. The contrast between these two cases suggests that observers can both tell the difference between directional and diffuse lighting and that they process shape-from-shading accordingly. Few if any models of shape-from-shading accommodate such a switch.

Koenderink, Pont, van Doorn, Kappers and Todd [12] have shown that humans are sensitive to many parameters of the physical light field in terms of their ability to correctly set the pattern of shading on a probe sphere introduced into a well-articulated scene; people can estimate both lighting direction and diffuseness. Lighting direction can also be estimated accurately for images of isotropic rough surfaces Koenderink, van Doorn, and Pont [15]. Directional lighting produces anisotropies in the shading pattern even for isotropic textures and these can be used to infer the direction of the light source as coming from one of two orientations 180 degrees apart. However, if the texture is anisotropic the resulting shading pattern will be dominated by anisotropies in the texture itself and people will estimate the light source orientation incorrectly, but systematically, to be orthogonal to the dominant orientation of the surface/shading pattern. We conclude, after Pentland [23] and Koenderink, van Doorn, and Pont [15], that humans assume that surfaces are isotropic and therefore use anisotropies in the shading image to estimate the location of the light source. This logic might extend to ellipsoid surfaces where we would expect elongated ellipsoids to support judgments of lighting direction less well than more isotropic examples, as is indeed the case [21].

Summary   Humans are quite good at estimating the direction and diffuseness of lighting in well-articulated and globally isotropic scenes. When the surfaces themselves are highly anisotropic the dominant orientation of the surface undulations largely determines the perceived direction of the light source.

8.6 Prior Assumptions

As an alternative to estimating the position of the light source the human visual system sometimes assumes the lighting parameters and is thus able to process shape-from-shading without estimating the light source at all, but with the consequence that all images will be interpreted as if lit from the same default location. While this is unlikely to be the case in well-articulated scenes it seems likely that some sort of default illumination is assumed when there are insufficient cues in the image to specify the light source. There are, however, other potential prior assumptions, such as the assumption that objects will tend to be convex, which might also influence shape-from-shading.

The crater illusion, first reported by Gemlin at the Royal Society in 1744 and in print by Rittenhouse [28], describes a compelling effect whereby surface relief as perceived from shading is inverted (that is, convexities become concavities) when the image is rotated through 180 degrees. This much studied illusion is taken as evidence that humans have a bias for seeing lighting from above. Experimental versions of the crater illusion have been used to determine the precise direction of the assumed light source. Early studies put it above the observers head [27, 31] suggesting that it corresponds to the average location of the sun. More recent studies have suggested a consistent leftward bias [19] although the ecological reason for this left-bias is unknown. Adams, Graf and Ernst [1] have shown that the lighting bias can be somewhat modified by experience in humans.

Studies related to the crater illusion often assume, at least implicitly, that the default lighting assumption is quite strongly directional. Tyler [34] by contrast suggests that the most basic lighting assumption is for a diffuse source although this was argued on the basis of a stimulus (a radial sine wave or rosette) which strongly promoted such an interpretation. Schofield, Rock and Georgeson [29] observed the perceived shape obtained from images of linear sine waves (that is sinusoidal luminance variations not rendered sinusoidal surfaces) and concluded that changes in the perceived locations of surface peaks relative to luminance peaks could not be explained by the assumption of any highly directional point source alone, nor by a fully diffuse source alone, but could be explained by a combination of diffuse and directional sources with the precise location of each person's preferred directional element responsible for idiosyncratic variations in the data.

Although the dominance of the lighting from above assumption is often presented as the cause of the crater illusion, Liu and Todd [18] note that there are other prior assumptions with equally strong ecological validity that could explain many examples of the effect. For example, due to gravity and the tendency to view surfaces from above, observers have a tendency to interpret ambiguous surfaces such that overall depth increases with height in the image. Further, because objects tend to be globally convex there is a bias towards seeing ambiguous stimuli as convexities rather than concavities [7, 17]. Lui and Todd tested naturalistic renderings of simple concave and convex surfaces which produced ambiguous shading profiles. They found a strong perceptual bias for convexity and a much weaker perceptual bias for lighting from above. The convexity bias is seen in Fig. 8.1 where many people see two convexities lit from different directions even though this greatly complicates the perceived light field. If lighting from above dominated, the left disk would be seen as concave—which is in fact the ground truth for this image. Lui and Todd's most striking finding was that perceived shape was strongly influenced by perceptual biases even when specular highlights and cast shadows were present suggesting, somewhat counter intuitively, that stimulus properties are rather unimportant for shape-from-shading. However, it should be noted that, while realistically rendered, these scenes were highly reduced in content, containing one shape only. In this sense, they were not well articulated and this may be why prior assumptions seemed to dominate in Lui and Todd's study.

In contrast, Morgenstern, Murray and Harris [22] examined the combination of default illumination assumptions with estimates of the actual illuminant in well- articulated scenes. They found evidence for a maximum likelihood combination of assumed and actual illumination but noted that the weight given to the prior assumption is low such that it can be overridden by relatively weak lighting cues. This suggests that in most everyday cases, shape estimates will be dominated by the observer's estimate of the actual lighting direction not by their any prior assumption.

Summary   For poorly articulated scenes, shape-from-shading most likely employs prior assumptions in some way. The assumptions that surface depth increases with height in the image, that objects are convex and that lighting is from above all seem to assist shape-from-shading in certain circumstances. The idea that we a have a strong preference for seeing shaded objects as if lit from above has strong currency but may be a relatively weak assumption, easily overridden by image information relating to lighting and less strong that the convexity assumption. Even when the default lighting assumption is applied it most likely represents a mixed diffuse and directional source rather than a strongly directional one.

8.7 Computation of Shape-from-Shading

We now consider the mechanisms that might underlie shape-from-shading at the most basic level. Although many have attempted to derive computer vision algorithms for shape-from-shading relatively few studies have directly considered the algorithm employed by human vision. Pentland [24] noted that the visual field is tiled with local small scale sensors that compute centre surround Laplacian of Gaussian (retina) and oriented 2nd derivatives (early cortex) of image intensity and that, assuming Lambertian surfaces, such local operators are sufficient to compute slant and tilt provided the illumination direction can also be estimated. The method produces plausible relief maps from natural scenes and is quite robust to deviations from its operating assumptions. Remarkably, this result is achieved working directly from the image itself with no recourse to top-down information or requirement for boundary conditions to constrain the solution. However, to our knowledge the validity of this algorithm as a model for human shape-from-shading has not been fully tested.

Pentland [25] proposed an alternative model for shape-from-shading based on a Fourier decomposition of the image. In this model, the Fourier spectrum of the surface height function is linearly related to the Fourier spectrum of the image plus some constant (Pentland set the constant to zero). Pentland also provided a biologically plausible mechanism by which this relationship might be calculated which comprised the type of filters found in early vision. This method rests on the assumption that there is a linear relationship between luminance and surface orientation and both Pentland and Seyama and Sato [30] present data to suggest that human vision may make such an assumption. Pentland's method also introduces a 90 degree phase shift between the luminance and height spectra such that, when linearity is also assumed, points of maximum luminance will typically correspond to points of maximum perceived slant. This phase shift implies that estimated surface gradient should be proportional to luminance. This relationship between surface gradient and luminance is now often implicitly assumed in the literature although there are important cases where it does not hold.

As with his 1984 method, Pentland's Fourier model presents a powerful shape-from-shading tool which does not rely on top-down processing or strong in-built assumptions and yet can produce plausible relief maps from input images. Both models are robust to violations of their own assumptions about the surface composition. However, like the human visual system, model solutions may not always be veridical.

Langer and Bülthoff [16] showed that shape-from-shading can switch between operating under a point source lighting assumption and a diffuse lighting assumption. They offered an alternative model for the diffuse case in which surface height (not slant) is proportional to luminance. In this model, the image was blurred to remove high frequency information from the luminance signal, thus better modeling visual systems tendency to ignore the slight increases in luminance found at the very bottom of valleys under diffuse lighting.

Summary   Relatively simple linear mechanisms which set either surface slant or surface height proportional to image luminance have been proposed as models for human shape-from-shading although few studies have directly tested such models against human performance. Pentland has presented methods based on both local luminance differentials and Fourier decomposition that relate slant to luminance via a linear transformation. The modified dark-is-deep transformation proposed by Langer and Bülthoff might account for cases were surface height is proportional to luminance.

8.8 Operation in Sub-optimal Conditions

Shape-from-shading gives better (more veridical) solutions that are less dependent on prior assumptions and more stimulus driven when the stimulus is well articulated. Well-articulated stimuli should contain lots of shapes and, globally, be sufficiently isotropic to allow the identification of the principle illuminants. It can be argued that testing shape-from-shading in less well articulated circumstances is, in effect, testing a broken system. However, it is clear that people perceive shape even in the most reduced images: shape-from-shading degrades gracefully. Anything that looks at all like a shaded pattern will drive shape-from-shading mechanisms which, with the aid of prior assumptions, do their best to estimate shape in adverse conditions. There is some merit then in testing shape-from-shading in reduced scenes.

Sun and Schofield [32] took this reductionist approach close to the limit by presenting repetitive grating stimuli. These stimuli were not rendered but were rather simple sine wave, square wave and sawtooth gratings drawn onto the stimulus. There were no surface markings to produce contours, nor any bounding contours, occlusion edges, specular highlights, or cast shadows. These stimuli contained luminance edges only where the grating stimuli gave way to the mean luminance background or where the shading itself underwent sharp transitions (square wave and sawtooth gratings), and (arguably) at the zero crossings of the sine wave gratings. Sun and Schofield manipulated the number and polarity of the luminance edges in the image by manipulating the number of grating cycles presented and the phase of the gratings.

Using such stimuli Sun and Schofield identified two principle modes of operation for shape-from-shading. Further, the visual system seems to switch between these modes on the basis of the polarity of edges within the shading patterns. When multiple cycles of grating were present, each cycle was bounded by edges of the same polarity. In this case perceived slant was set proportional to luminance such that sine waves were seen as sinusoidal surfaces with an approximately 90 degree offset between surface peaks and luminance peaks (see also [25]). Square wave gratings were seen as triangular wave surfaces with the light section sloping in one direction (typically upward) and the dark section sloping in the other direction. Sawtooth gratings were seen as either sharp ridges with broad valleys or broad mounds with sharp valleys. All these interpretations are consistent with slant being proportional to luminance, with Pentland's [25] model, and also with the assumption of a collimated, directional, oblique light source.

Next, single cycles (actually 1.2 cycles) of the sine and square wave stimuli were presented with a central bright region flanked by two darker regions of just over half the width of the central region. Excluding the edges at the extent of the cropping zones these stimuli contain only two edges and they are of opposite polarity. Here people set surface height (not slant) proportional to luminance as is consistent with the dark-is-deep rule and either diffuse or frontal lighting.

The most intriguing aspect of Sun & Schofield's data was the transition between the linear shading model (slant proportional to luminance) and the dark-is-deep model following relatively simple image manipulations. These two models are both candidates for the computation of shape-from-shading, and both are known to operate in human vision [16]. It is clear that some mechanism must exist to mediate between the two modes of operation. Sun and Schofield's results suggest that such a switch might be mediated by relatively low level cues rather than an estimate of the light field derived from a well-articulated scene. Sun & Schofield show that edges are important whereas Schofield et al. [29] suggest that stimulus orientation may also mediate between the two methods for estimating shape-from-shading.

Finally, Schofield, et al. suggest an outline model in which both 'dark-is-deep' and 'slant proportional to luminance' are computed with the final perceived surface being a weighted sum of the two solutions; the weights being determined by low level stimulus properties. However, this model has not been tested on complex/natural stimuli. It is also not clear if such shifts should best be viewed as a change in the mechanisms by which shape-from-shading is calculated or a change in the lighting assumptions employed, because the shift between the two operational modes can equally be seen as a shift in the composition of the assumed illuminant from point-like to diffuse.

Summary   When highly reduced stimuli are used, estimates of surface shape seem to be derived from rather simple linear relationships between luminance variations in the image and either surface slant (gradient) or height. Pentland's [24, 25] linear transformations of luminance to gradient and Langer and Bülthoff's [16] modified dark-is-deep rule would be sufficient to explain each mode of operation. Some combination of the two processes, arbitrated by low level cues, might explain shape-from-shading in reduced scenes.

8.9 Conclusion

Humans are clearly able to estimate surface shape from shading/luminance even in the most reduced images where there is insufficient information to constrain the ill-posed mathematical problem presented by such shading patterns. In such cases humans would seem to employ relatively simple linear mechanisms to convert luminance to shape estimates so that either surface slant or surface height are set proportional to luminance. Such mechanisms can operate without boundary conditions or knowledge of the light field. At this level, the choice of setting slant or height proportional to luminance would seem to be governed by simple image features such as luminance edges and orientation. Shape-from-shading in such reduced scenes seems also to benefit from a number of default assumptions such as the convexity and lighting from above priors although the default light source has a strong diffuse component. Although the perceived shape produced from such reduced stimuli is often not veridical to the ground truth, it may nonetheless provide a useful working hypothesis for further processing. Such estimates may be idiosyncratic and vary with task demands.

When scenes are better articulated cues to the light field composition will aid in the estimation of the light sources illuminating the scene and such information may improve shape-from-shading making it less reliant on default lighting assumptions. Bounding contours and surface markings will provide key constraints on perceived surface shape, disambiguating the luminance signal. At this level shape-from-shading is likely to produce percepts that are stable across observers and tasks up to an affine transformation of some common surface shape. However, perceived shape may not be veridical to the generating surface.

The addition of further cues such as edges contours, cast shadows, texture gradients, stereopsis, and motion will further constrain and may override solutions to shape-from-shading and so it may be more appropriate to use rich, complex, scenes for the study of shape perception as a whole and more reduced scenes for studying shape-from-shading in isolation.

References

1. Adams WJ, Graf EW, Ernst MO (2004) Experience can change the 'light-from-above' prior. Nat Neurosci 7:1057–1058
2. Belhumeur PN, Kriegman DJ, Yuille AL (1999) The bas-relief ambiguity. Int J Comput Vis 35:33–44
3. Curran W, Johnston A (1996) The effect of illuminant position on perceived curvature. Vis Res 36(10):1399–1410
4. Christou CG, Koenderink JJ (1997) Light source dependence in shape from shading. Vis Res 37(11):1441–1449
5. Erens RGF, Kappers AML, Koenderink JJ (1993) Perception of local shape from shading. Percept Psychophys 54:145–156
6. Gerardin P, Kourtzi Z, Mamassian P (2010) Prior knowledge of illumination for 3d perception in the human brain. Proc Natl Acad Sci USA 107:16309–16314
7. Hill H, Bruce V (1994) A comparison between the hollow-face and "hollow-potato" illusions. Perception 23:1335–1337
8. Ikeuchi K, Horn BKP (1981) Numerical shape from shading and occluding boundaries. Artif Intell 17(1–3):141–184
9. Johnston A, Passmore PJ (1994) Independent encoding of surface orientation and surface curvature. Vis Res 34:3005–3012
10. Johnston A, Passmore PJ (1994) Shape from shading: surface curvature and orientation. Perception 23:169–189
11. Knill DC (1992) The perception of surface contours and surface shape: from computation to psychophysics. J Opt Soc Am A 9:1449–1464
12. Koenderink JJ, Pont SC, van Doorn AJ, Kappers AML, Todd JT (2007) The visual light field. Perception 36:1595–1610
13. Koenderink JJ, van Doorn AJ, Kappers AML (1992) Surface perception in pictures. Percept Psychophys 52:487–496
14. Koenderink JJ, van Doorn AJ, Kappers AML (2001) Ambiguity and the 'mental eye' in pictorial relief. Perception 30:431–448
15. Koenderink JJ, van Doorn AJ, Pont SC (2007) Perception of illuminance flow in the case of anisotropic rough surfaces. Atten Percept Psychophys 69:895–903
16. Langer MS, Bülthoff HH (2000) Depth discrimination from shading under diffuse lighting. Perception 29(6):649–660
17. Langer MS, Bülthoff HH (2001) A prior for local convexity in local shape from shading. Perception 30:403–410
18. Liu B, Todd JT (2004) Perceptual biases in the interpretation of 3d shape from shading. Vis Res 44:2135–2145
19. Mamassian P, Goutcher R (2001) Prior knowledge on the illumination position. Cognition 81:B1–B9
20. Marr D (1982) Vision. Freedman, New York
21. Mingolla E, Todd JT (1986) Perception of solid shape from shading. Biol Cybern 53:137–151
22. Morgenstern Y, Murray RF, Harris LR (2011) The human visual system's assumption that light comes from above is weak. Proc Natl Acad Sci USA 108(30):12551–12553
23. Pentland A (1982) Finding the illuminant direction. J Opt Soc Am 72:448–455
24. Pentland A (1984) Local shading analysis. IEEE Trans Pattern Anal Mach Intell 6:170–187
25. Pentland A (1989) Shape information from shading: a theory about human perception. Spat Vis 4:165–182
26. Pizlo Z (2008) 3D shape: its unique place in visual perception. MIT Press, Cambridge
27. Ramachandran VS (1988) Perception of shape-from-shading. Nature 331:163–165
28. Rittenhouse D (1786) Explanation of an optical deception. Trans Am Philos Soc 2:37–42
29. Schofield AJ, Rock PB, Georgeson MA (2011) Sun and sky: does human vision assume a mixture of point and diffuse illumination when interpreting shape-from-shading? Vis Res 51:2317–2330

30. Seyama J, Sato T (1998) Shape from shading: estimation of reflectance map. Vis Res 38:3805–3815
31. Sun J, Perona P (1998) Where is the Sun? Nat Neurosci 1:183–184
32. Sun P, Schofield AJ (2012) Two operational modes in the perception of shape from shading revealed by the effects of edge information in slant settings. J Vis 12(1):12
33. Todd JT, Mingolla E (1983) Perception of surface curvature and direction of illumination from patterns of shading. J Exp Psychol Hum Percept Perform 9:583–595
34. Tyler CW (1998) Diffuse illumination as a default assumption for shape-from-shading in graded images. J Image Sci Technol 42:319–325

Chapter 9
Deformations and Lighting

David Jacobs, Anne Jorstad, and Alain Trouvé

9.1 Introduction

One of the most basic problems in vision is to formulate an effective distance between two images. This should account for two effects. First, pixels can change their position as viewpoint or the shape of objects change. Second, pixels may change their intensity as lighting changes. A good distance should capture both of these transformations. Further, it should allow us to unwind them, so that we can determine correspondences between the two images that we compare.

In many vision problems, intensity changes are primarily due to lighting variation. In this chapter we sketch a general approach to this problem, and then describe some initial results that implement components of this approach. Our work rests on a new approach to modeling lighting effects, which yields a new image distance, with many appealing properties. We will also focus on combining this with both existing and new models of image deformation.

Our image distance aims to capture three ubiquitous properties of real world images. *Geometric* variations have the effect of *deforming* the 2D appearance of an object. For example, a 3D object might deform or have parts that articulate, causing its image to deform. Or, if we view even a rigid 3D object from a new viewpoint, this can have the effect of deforming the resulting image. Also, different instances of objects within the same class can vary considerably in shape; we can treat some of the effects of this shape variation as a deformation. Therefore, we can model a significant number of geometric variations as image deformations.

D. Jacobs (✉) · A. Jorstad
Department of Computer Science, University of Maryland, College Park, MD, USA
e-mail: djacobs@cs.umd.edu

A. Jorstad
e-mail: jorstad@math.umd.edu

A. Trouvé
CMLA, École normale supérieure de Cachan, Cachan, France
e-mail: trouve@cmla.ens-cachan.fr

S.J. Dickinson, Z. Pizlo (eds.), *Shape Perception in Human and Computer Vision*,
Advances in Computer Vision and Pattern Recognition,
DOI 10.1007/978-1-4471-5195-1_9, © Springer-Verlag London 2013

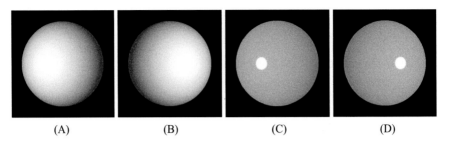

(A)   (B)   (C)   (D)

Fig. 9.1 A simple illustration of some problems that arise in image matching. (**A**) and (**B**) are images of a sphere illuminated from different directions. (**C**) is identical to (**A**), with a change in its histogram to create higher contrast. (**D**) is similarly derived from (**B**). We would like to judge the similarity of each image pair, and the extent to which they should be matched by deforming the image or by positing a lighting change. Our proposed algorithm has the following properties: when intensities with smooth shading shift position, as between (**A**) and (**B**), the metric tends to view this as a lighting change, whereas when high contrast intensity patterns shift position, as between (**C**) and (**D**), the metric tends to interpret this as an image deformation. Also, changes in contrast that do not affect image gradient directions but that do introduce high contrast edges, as between (**A**) and (**C**), can be costly

Usually, the effects of image deformations are complicated by simultaneous variations due to changes in *lighting*. As an object articulates, deforms or moves relative to a camera, it also moves relative to the light. When we view two similar objects, we rarely view them under identical lighting. These changes in lighting can have a dramatic effect on the appearance of objects. Moreover, deformations and lighting changes will occur in the presence of *noise*, *occlusions* and other unmodeled image variations that require *robust* matching. Therefore, *our primary goal is to develop robust image matching methods that can simultaneously handle changes in lighting and geometry.*

We model deformations as continuous one-to-one transformations of the image that affect the position of pixels but not their intensity. Lighting, on the other hand, affects the intensity of pixels, but not their position. These effects can be difficult to separate because of the ambiguity that occurs in finding a correspondence between two images. Figure 9.1 illustrates this problem. We can match each pair of images using a pure deformation that warps the bright pixels in one image to the position they occupy in a second image. Or we can explain the image change with a change in lighting position that alters the intensity of all pixels (we show in [5] that any two images can be explained with a single, Lambertian scene and a lighting change). In general, any possible deformation can be combined with alteration in intensities to match two images; our problem is to select the combination of deformation and intensity change that provides the best explanation. For object recognition, it is also important that we assign a cost to this interpretation, so we can judge its validity.

We will approach this problem by first developing a Riemannian metric for images that captures deformations and lighting change. This kind of metric is appropriate for image transformations that can be modeled as the result of a continuous sequence of small transformations. That is, it is appropriate when it makes sense to continuously morph from one shape to another, or one lighting condition to another.

Therefore, we can build a distance between images by constructing a metric on any infinitesimal change in the image, and then stitching these together to provide a geodesic distance between any two images.

There is much work already on constructing Riemannian metrics that capture image deformations. Though we have some proposed enhancements to these, our main focus is on developing comparable metrics for intensity variation that capture lighting effects, so that these may be effectively combined. We first propose such a metric, and show that it has many of the properties of existing, successful approaches to lighting change, and also has some desirable properties not possessed by these representations. As an additional benefit, this metric also robustly captures variations in image intensity due to occlusion and clutter.

This metric will provide a theory of computation for deformation and lighting, that encodes our notion of image similarity. However, it is still a considerable challenge to find ways to effectively compute with such an image metric. To address this, we first show that our local metric can be incorporated into an optical flow framework to produce an image distance that performs face recognition effectively. Then, we show that for the intensity component of our metric alone, geodesic distances can be computed extremely efficiently in the wavelet domain. Most of the results in this chapter and further developments are described in greater detail in [13].

9.2 Background

There is a vast amount of work on image matching. First, we note that many approaches have been suggested for comparing images in ways that are insensitive to illumination, typically through a process of locally normalizing the image intensities. Osadchy et al. [19] reviews these methods and proves that several are essentially equivalent. Gopalan and Jacobs [9] performs an experimental comparison of many of these approaches and finds that comparison using simple gradient directions works best. Representing an image in terms of the gradient direction is equivalent to a local normalization that is invariant to additive or multiplicative changes in intensity. We conclude that a good lighting metric can be expected to bear some resemblance to image comparison using gradient direction, as a prototypical example of local normalization.

There is also a great deal of prior work on non-rigid image matching. Much of this has been done in the context of tracking, in which image changes are assumed to be small ([1, 2] provide some entry points to this vast literature). Much work that handles larger deformations has been done, especially in the domain of medical imaging, in which body structures from different individuals are non-rigidly aligned (e.g., [6, 8]), although often these ideas are applied to other domains, such as faces. Riemannian metrics for deformable matching have been developed, (e.g., [3, 17, 22]), as well as novel image descriptors that are invariant to deformations [14]. In general, all these approaches typically find a deformation by combining some penalty on the deformation, to encourage smoothness, with some image term that encourages the aligned images to have similar intensities. Our proposal fits into this framework; however we propose that the image term should be designed to robustly compare intensities in a way that captures the effects of lighting variation.

Finally, there has been much work on image matching when there is both geometrical and lighting variation, primarily in the context of motion tracking. These approaches attempt to deal with the fact that a moving object deforms in the image and moves relative to the lighting (e.g., [2, 10]). There is also a huge literature on optical flow, some of which explicitly focuses on matching with lighting variation [4, 15, 18].

9.3 Robust Image Metrics for Lighting and Deformation

Our approach will make use of the theory of image metamorphosis as a framework that allows us to embed the notion of simultaneous deformation and lighting change into a proper Riemannian formulation. Prior developments of this framework are summarized in [23]. Intuitively, in this approach we proceed by first defining a cost on infinitesimal image changes. This defines a tangent space for each image. This tangent space spans the image space; that is, any small change to the image is possible. But the cost of these local changes may be quite different from Euclidean distances in the image space. Together, these tangent spaces define a manifold that fills the space of all images. The distance between any two images, then, is a *geodesic* path on this manifold. We can think of this geodesic as the lowest cost metamorphosis from the first image to the second, in which the image is simultaneously deforming and changing intensity.

More precisely, we can express a small change, δI, to an image I, through a deformation, as:

$$\delta I(x) = \partial_t I\big(x - tv(x)\big)\big|_{t=0} = -\langle \nabla I(x), v(x) \rangle$$

Here t represents time, $\langle , \rangle$ denotes the inner product, and v is a vector field that encodes the instantaneous deformation. This equation is essentially the equation of optical flow. Alternately, we can express the image change as a change in the intensity of pixels, with no deformations, as: $\delta I = h$, where $h(x)$ represents the change in intensity at x. More realistically, we should describe the image change as the sum of these two processes, $\delta I(x) = -\langle \nabla I(x), v(x) \rangle + h(x)$, each of which might explain image changes. Given a metric $|v|_V$ on the deformation, and a metric $|h|_H$ on the intensity change, one can define a combined metric:

$$\|\delta I\|_I^2 = \inf_{v \in V} \big(|v|_V^2 + \lambda |\delta I + \langle \nabla I, v \rangle|_H^2 \big) \tag{9.1}$$

This gives the cost of an image change as the minimum possible cost of a deformation and intensity change, where λ weights the costs. Note that any specific deformation implies a specific intensity change. Most of the work on metamorphosis of images concerns the simplest case in which the metric on intensity change, $|h|_H$, is just the L^2 metric.

9.3.1 Intensity Variation

We now present two new, related metrics for intensity variation, and describe some of their mathematical properties. The analysis in this section concerns intensity variation only, and does not consider deformations. These metrics are closely related to image comparison based on the direction of the image gradient, which has proven to be very robust to lighting changes. At the same time, these metrics also measure contrast variations in a way that fits some intuitive notions about intensity change. Finally, these metrics also produce a robust image comparison method for occlusions, related to L^1 norms.

Intuitively, we want to develop an intensity metric that is related to the likelihood that two images come from the same 3D scene, and that the difference between the two images is due to a lighting variation. Because we are constructing a general metric for images, this distance cannot be based on specific knowledge of the 3D structure of the current scene, but rather should depend on general considerations about the effect of lighting variation on image intensities.

We begin with a simplified, intuitive description of some key issues posed by lighting. The intensity of a pixel mainly depends on the lighting conditions at the corresponding scene point, on the direction of the surface normal at that point, and on the albedo, that is, the fraction of light reflected at that point. When there is a small change in lighting, an image, I, will change by some amount δI. First, we note that as lighting changes, the intensity at a single pixel can change in almost any way. That is, $\delta I(x)$ is not very constrained for any point x. However, δI is often correlated at nearby points, so we will consider the properties of δI as it varies spatially, that is the properties of $\nabla \delta I$. Usually, lighting conditions vary slowly within a scene, so $\nabla \delta I$ is primarily the result of the differential effect that lighting variation has as surface normals and albedos vary throughout a scene. We consider three situations.

First, consider the case of regions of smooth or planar surfaces with nearly uniform albedo. In this case, $\nabla \delta I(x)$ tends to be small, and also the initial image gradient, $\nabla I(x)$ tends to be small. Second, suppose the albedo changes in this region, but the surface normal is constant or changes slowly. In this case, lighting tends to uniformly scale the intensities of pixels in a region, so $\nabla \delta I(x)$ tends to be proportional to $\nabla I(x)$, and $\nabla \delta I(x)$ is large only when $\nabla I(x)$ is large. Finally, consider surfaces with high curvature or curvature discontinuities, in which nearby points have very different surface normals. In this case, nearby points are exposed to different lighting, and affected quite differently even by the same lights. So changing lighting can affect nearby pixels in a way that is almost uncorrelated. Therefore, $\nabla \delta I(x)$ tends to be quite unpredictable, it might be low or high. However, usually (but not always) in this situation $\nabla I(x)$ tends to be high.

As an example to illustrate these situations, consider a v-shaped roof with two sides, facing in two different directions. If a region is on one side of the roof and has uniform albedo, it will tend to have uniform intensity. As the sun moves, the whole region may get brighter or darker, but it will continue to be uniform. So $\nabla I(x)$ and $\nabla \delta I(x)$ will both be low. Suppose, now, the roof is striped, and consider a region that is still on one side of the roof, but that crosses this stripe. The gradient across this stripe will get stronger when the sun faces the roof more directly, and the whole side of the roof gets brighter. Therefore, the image gradient produced by the stripe changes in proportion to the overall intensity, i.e., $\nabla \delta I(x)$ is proportional to $\nabla I(x)$. Finally, consider a region of the images that crosses the two sides of the roof. As the sun moves, or the light otherwise changes, the intensity on the two sides of the roof also changes. The relationship between these two intensities cannot be predicted without specific knowledge of the geometry and lighting. So, $\nabla \delta I(x)$ is unpredictable across the edge separating the two sides of the roof. However, most of the time this edge will have a strong gradient itself. Therefore, we see that when $\nabla I(x)$ is large, this may signal that $\nabla \delta I(x)$ can also be large, or at least its value is hard to predict from the image alone. The following metric on intensity changes captures these properties:

$$C(\delta I) = \left(\int_{\Omega} \left(\frac{|\nabla \delta I(x)|}{|\nabla I(x)| + \varepsilon} \right)^2 dx \right)^{1/2} \tag{9.2}$$

Here $C(\delta I)$ denotes the cost of a small change to the intensities, and the integral is over the image. This cost has the desired properties: (1) When $\nabla I(x)$ is low, large values of $\nabla \delta I(x)$ are very expensive; (2) When $\nabla \delta I(x)$ is proportional to $\nabla I(x)$ the cost is fairly constant; (3) When $\nabla I(x)$ is high, the value of $\nabla \delta I(x)$ is not important in determining the overall cost. Note that ε is a small constant. This prevents division by zero, and adds other useful properties, as we will see later.

We can also consider a somewhat more complex metric that bases the cost of a change not only on the magnitude of its gradient but also on its direction, with a lower cost for changes in the direction of the image gradient. This cost has interesting theoretical properties, though we have not yet evaluated it experimentally.

$$C(\delta I) = \left(\int_{\Omega} \frac{((1 + \rho(|\nabla I|)) \langle \frac{\nabla \delta I}{|\nabla I| + \varepsilon}, \frac{\nabla I^\perp}{|\nabla I^\perp|} \rangle^2 + \langle \frac{\nabla \delta I}{|\nabla I| + \varepsilon}, \frac{\nabla I}{|\nabla I|} \rangle^2)}{(2 + \rho(|\nabla I|))} \right)^{1/2} \tag{9.3}$$

ρ is a function that serves as a weight between the two terms. $\rho(|\nabla I|)$ goes to 0 as $|\nabla I|$ goes to 0, and becomes large as $|\nabla I|$ goes to infinity. One natural choice for ρ would be $\rho(|\nabla I|) = \log(1 + |\nabla I|)$. $\nabla I^\perp/|\nabla I^\perp|$ is a unit vector orthogonal to the image gradient, while $\nabla I/|\nabla I|$ is a unit vector in the direction of the gradient. Equation (9.3) becomes identical to (9.2) as $|\nabla I|$ goes to 0.

Intuitively, this metric divides the change in the image into two parts, one orthogonal to the image gradient, and one in the direction of the image gradient. The first type of change is more costly than the second. This allows us to also express the fact that typically the direction of $\nabla \delta I(x)$ is the same as the direction of $\nabla I(x)$, because the direction of $\nabla I(x)$ is more likely to be the direction in which scene properties are changing rapidly. Note that this is true in our roof example.

We have been able to analytically determine the distance between pairs of images for some simple cases that show that our metric has a number of favorable properties. We will summarize these properties here, while omitting derivations:

1. *Relation to direction of gradient comparisons:* Let us consider the above metrics for the case in which $\nabla \delta I(x)$ is always in the direction perpendicular to $\nabla I(x)$. In this case, we can show that the cost of a local change in image intensities is approximately proportional to the change in the direction of the image gradient. That is, if we denote the change in the direction of the image gradient by: $\delta\theta(x)$, the cost in (9.2) reduces to:

$$C(\delta I) = \left(\int_\Omega \left(\frac{|\nabla I(x)|}{|\nabla I(x)| + \varepsilon} \right)^2 (\delta\theta(x))^2 \, dx \right)^{1/2}$$

For (9.3), we can select a parameter ρ so that $\rho(|\nabla I|)$ is always high. This assigns minimal cost to all intensity changes in which $\nabla \delta I(x)$ is parallel to $\nabla I(x)$. So, by proper parameter selection we can make our metric reduce to one that measures the change in the direction of the image gradients. As noted above, many current approaches to lighting insensitive image comparison use representations like this, so this assures us that we can achieve good performance with this metric.

2. *Contrast change:* When $\nabla \delta I(x)$ is in the same direction as $\nabla I(x)$, this alters the contrast in an image, without changing the direction of the image gradient. For this case, we can derive a closed form solution for the total cost of the geodesic path between two images, which we denote $d(I_0, I_1)$. We can show that when the magnitude of the gradient in an image changes from $|\nabla I_0|$ to $|\nabla I_1|$ then our metric assigns this a cost proportional to:

$$d(I_0, I_1) = \left(\int_\Omega \left(\log \frac{|\nabla I_1(x)| + \varepsilon}{|\nabla I_0(x)| + \varepsilon} \right)^2 dx \right)^{1/2}$$

That is, the cost at each point is generally proportional to the log of the ratio of the change, though it becomes linear when the gradient magnitude is near zero. This means that when there is a strong image gradient, such as an edge, changing the contrast has little cost. However, changing a low contrast region of the image into a strong edge can have a high cost, even if the direction of the image gradient does not change. This cost is not captured by most current lighting insensitive representations, and seems useful.

3. *Robustness:* Our proposed metrics accounts for occlusions robustly. We can analytically determine the cost of transforming a region of uniform intensity into an arbitrary image pattern caused by occlusion. This cost is similar to, and bounded by, a constant times the bounded variation norm (BV-norm) of the image gradient of the new image pattern. That is, when I_0 is a constant image, and I_1 is not, for the geodesic distance we have:

$$d(I_0, I_1) \leq \frac{1}{\varepsilon} \int_\Omega |\nabla I_1(x)| \, dx$$

This implies that the cost of transforming one image pattern into a totally different pattern is bounded by the sum of the BV-norms of the two patterns. This is a type of L^1-norm on the image gradients, and is known to be much more robust than L^2-norms.

9.3.2 Interaction Between Deformations and Intensity Change

We can combine our metric for intensity variation with standard metrics for deformation using (9.1). With this formulation, deformations and intensity changes compete to explain image changes. We have analyzed some simple cases of this, in order to gain intuitions. We will consider here the case of an image pattern undergoing a small translation. The cost of explaining such a change through a deformation cost is always low, and is independent of the image content. However, this change can also be explained through intensity variation. We have shown that for a smoothed edge, this cost will vary linearly with the sharpness of the edge. So a small translation of a sharp, high contrast edge is very expensive to explain with an intensity variation. Translation of a smooth, gradual edge is more easily modeled as an intensity variation with our metric (Fig. 9.1).

When there is a more complicated deformation of image intensities, the cost of explaining this with deformations rises, while the cost of explaining this through intensity variations will be the aggregate of a collection of local translations, and depend on the number and sharpness of edges that are shifting.

Consequently, explaining the motion of a number of sharp edges in an image as an intensity variation is very expensive. If a set of sharp edges are deformed, even quite a lot, we will tend to interpret this as a deformation. However, when there are fewer, more gradual edges in the image, we will be more inclined to interpret a complex deformation of these patterns as an intensity variation.

9.4 Using These Metrics for Image Comparison

The metrics we have described form the basis for several algorithms that we have created. First, we have used the local image metric described in Eqs. (9.1) and (9.2) to build an optical flow algorithm. Our goal is not motion understanding, the traditional focus of optical flow research, but to apply this algorithm to compare images with changes in lighting and shape. Second, we show that if we only consider the intensity component of our local metric, given in Eq. (9.2), we can compute an approximation to geodesic distances on a Riemannian manifold constructed with this local metric using a very efficient algorithm that works in the wavelet domain. Finally, an initial foray into the computation of geodesic costs that take account of intensity changes and deformations can be found in [13].

9.4.1 A Deformation and Lighting Insensitive Metric for Face Recognition

Our primary goal is to create a Riemannian manifold of images, in which geodesic distances represent image similarity. However, our local image metric can be more

Table 9.1 Face recognition experiments, comparing our new methods with top previous methods. Run time is given on common hardware, when available. Results shown on recognition with changes in expression, lighting, or both

Method	Time (sec)	Expression	Lighting	Overall
Image Differencing	3.1×10^{-5}	83.0 %	9.0 %	46.0 %
Normalized Cross-Correlation	7.2×10^{-3}	84.0 %	59.3 %	71.7 %
Significant Jet Point [24]	–	80.8 %	91.7 %	86.3 %
Binary Edge and MI [21]	–	78.5 %	97.0 %	87.8 %
Gradient Direction	3.8×10^{-4}	85.0 %	95.3 %	90.2 %
Our Optical Flow Approach	1.0	89.6 %	98.9 %	94.3 %
Our Wavelet Approach	1.3×10^{-3}	93.7 %	96.7 %	95.2 %
Pixel Level Decisions [11]	5.6×10^{-4}	98.0 %	94.0 %	96.0 %
Our Wavelets Thresholded	1.3×10^{-3}	97.3 %	97.0 %	97.2 %

easily evaluated by using it as the cost function in an optical flow algorithm. We then use the correspondences from optical flow to judge similarity, evaluating our results quantitatively on a Face Recognition task. For reasons of space, we only briefly summarize our algorithm here; a full description may be found in [12].

- The intensity component of our local metric is given in Eq. (9.2). To measure deformations, we introduce a new regularization term: $E_r(\alpha) = \frac{1}{2}\langle \alpha, k * \alpha \rangle_G$. Here G denotes a generalized inner product on vector fields, and the flow field is $k * \alpha$, where k is a smooth kernel, such as a Gaussian, and $*$ denotes convolution. α can be considered to represent the dual elements of the flow field. This results in smoother gradients and superior rates of convergence.
- The kernel, k, is a combination of fine and coarse scale Gaussians. This allows the method to converge accurately to a solution that is effective at a fine scale, while avoiding convergence to local minima.
- Optimization over correspondence fields is performed using a modified gradient descent. Convolutions are calculated using the fast Fourier Transform, for efficiency.

We experiment by applying this algorithm to face recognition. To compare two face images, we compute the optical flow between them. At each pixel, this provides us with four values: a flow vector and an intensity gradient change. We use a naïve Bayes classifier to determine whether the resulting values are more consistent with two images of the same person, or of two different people. Results of experiments with the Martinez data set [16] are shown in Table 9.1. This data set contains images of 100 individuals taken with variations in lighting and facial expression. Recognition based on our local metric performs competitively.

9.4.2 Geodesics for Image Comparison with a Lighting-Insensitive Metric

Using Eq. (9.2) as a local metric, we can define an image manifold in which distances will tend to be low when intensity changes are due to lighting variation. It turns out that we can compute approximate geodesic distances on this manifold very efficiently by working in the wavelet domain. While this metric does not explicitly account for deformations, there is a close relationship with an approximate algorithm for computing the Earth Mover's Distance [20], which suggests that this metric will also be insensitive to small deformations. Using this local metric, we must solve the following:

$$I_{\text{geod}}(t) = \arg\min_{I(t)} \frac{1}{2} \int_0^1 \sum_{x,y} \frac{\|\nabla \delta I(x,y,t)\|^2}{\|\nabla I(x,y,t)\|^2 + \varepsilon^2} \, dt$$

Here, t parameterizes the images along a geodesic path traveled starting at $t = 0$, and ending at $t = 1$. We then rewrite the image in the wavelet domain, using orthonormal wavelets whose horizontal and vertical components, H, and V, are approximations to horizontal and vertical first derivative operators. This gives us a local cost:

$$E_{\text{wav}}(I) = \frac{1}{2} \sum_{m,n} \frac{\delta H^2 + \delta V^2}{H^2 + V^2 + \varepsilon^2}$$

In the wavelet domain, each wavelet basis location is now independent of its neighbors, as the local descriptions of the gradients are handled during the wavelet filtering, a result of the orthogonality of the wavelets. This allows us to rewrite the geodesic computation as:

$$I_{\text{geod}}(t) = \frac{1}{2} \sum_{m,n} \arg\min_{H(t),V(t)} \int_0^1 \frac{H'^2 + V'^2}{H^2 + V^2 + \varepsilon^2} \, dt$$

where H' and V' denote derivatives taken with respect to t. Note that $H(t)$ and $V(t)$, the horizontal and vertical components of the images that lie on the geodesic path, can be computed independently for each location. Each of these minimization problems can be converted to a differential equation using the Euler-Lagrange equations, and solved numerically. The boundary conditions of these equations are $H(0)$, $H(1)$, $V(0)$ and $V(1)$, two corresponding wavelet coefficients in each image. Because the geodesic cost is invariant when both images are rotated together, there are three degrees of freedom in these conditions, allowing us to construct a look-up table for the geodesic cost at a single image location. Computing the geodesic distance between two images, then, can be done by adding together the results of a table look-up for each image location, which can be done in about a millisecond.

When taken at a single scale, this metric is closely linked to our original metric on intensity changes. We then combine information over many scales (see [13, 20]), building a metric on the $(H, V)_{(m,n)}$ space which is a direct product of the metric on each (H, V) fiber. Mapping to the wavelet domain creates greater stability to deformations.

We show the results of using this distance in Table 9.1. Although it doesn't explicitly account for deformations, this cost, based on geodesic distances, slightly outperforms our method based on optical flow. When combined with a thresholding technique developed in [11], this method produces the best current results on this data set.

9.5 Conclusions

In this chapter, we describe a new, local image distance. Our overall goal is to use this local metric to define an image manifold, in which geodesic distances measure the similarity of images in which shape and lighting may have changed. We have argued analytically that our local metric has some intuitive properties, and begun to evaluate it experimentally. First, we have shown that by integrating our local metric into an optical flow framework we can achieve strong performance on a face recognition task. Second, we have shown that using our new, lighting insensitive metric on intensity changes, we can compute geodesics very efficiently in the wavelet domain, and also achieve excellent face recognition results. Further work remains to develop a complete approach to image comparison in the presence of lighting and shape changes, but these initial results encourage us to believe that this problem can be profitably addressed using Riemannian manifolds.

References

1. Aggarwal JK, Cai Q (1999) Human motion analysis: a review. Comput Vis Image Underst 73:90–102
2. Baker S, Matthews I (2004) Lucas-Kanade 20 years on: a unifying framework. Int J Comput Vis 56(3):221–255
3. Beg MF, Miller MI, Trouvé A, Younes L (2005) Computing large deformation metric mappings via geodesic flows of diffeomorphisms. Int J Comput Vis 61(2):139–157
4. Brox T, Bruhn A, Papenberg N, Weickert J (2004) High accuracy optical flow estimation based on a theory for time warping. In: ECCV, vol 4, pp 25–36
5. Chen H, Belhumeur P, Jacobs D (2000) In search of illumination invariants. In: IEEE proc comp vis and pattern recognition, vol I, pp 254–261
6. Cootes TF, Taylor CJ (2001) Statistical models of appearance for medical image analysis and computer vision. In: Proc. SPIE medical imaging, pp 236–248
7. Criminisi A, Blake A, Rother C, Shotton J, Torr PHS (2007) Efficient dense stereo with occlusions for new view-synthesis by four-state dynamic programming. Int J Comput Vis 71(1):89–110
8. Durrleman S, Pennec X, Trouvé A, Thompson P, Ayache N (2008, in press) Inferring brain variability from diffeomorphic deformations of currents: an integrative approach. Med Image Anal

9. Gopalan R, Jacobs D (2010) Comparing and combining lighting insensitive approaches for face recognition. Comput Vis Image Underst 114:135–145
10. Hager G, Belhumeur P (1998) Efficient region tracking with parametric models of geometry and illumination. IEEE Trans Pattern Anal Mach Intell 20(10):1125–1139
11. James AP (2010) Pixel-level decisions based robust face image recognition. In: Oravec M (ed) Face Recognition, chap 5. INTECH, pp 65–86
12. Jorstad A, Jacobs D, Trouvé A (2011) A deformation and lighting insensitive metric for face recognition based on dense correspondence. In: IEEE conference on computer vision and pattern recognition (CVPR)
13. Jorstad A (2012) Measuring deformations and illumination changes in images with applications to face recognition. PhD thesis, University of Maryland
14. Ling H, Jacobs D (2005) Deformation invariant image matching. In: IEEE international conference on computer vision, vol II, pp 1466–1473
15. Martinez A (2003) Recognizing expression variant faces from a single sample image per class. In: CVPR, vol 1, pp 353–358
16. Martinez A, Benavente R (1998) The AR face database. CVC technical report #24
17. Miller MI, Trouvé A, Younes L (2006) Geodesic shooting for computational anatomy. J Math Imaging Vis 24(2):209–228
18. Negahdaripour S (1998) Revised definition of optical flow: integration of radiometric and geometric cues for dynamic scene analysis. IEEE Trans Pattern Anal Mach Intell 20:961–979
19. Osadchy M, Jacobs D, Lindenbaum M (2007) Surface dependent representations for illumination insensitive image comparison. IEEE Trans Pattern Anal Mach Intell 29(1):98–111
20. Shirdhonkar S, Jacobs D (2008) Approximate earth movers distance in linear time. In: CVPR
21. Song J, Chen B, Wang W, Ren X (2008) Face recognition by fusing binary edge feature and second-order mutual information. In: IEEE conf on cybernetics and intelligent systems, pp 1046–1050
22. Trouvé A, Younes L (2005) Local geometry of deformable templates. SIAM J Math Anal 37(1):17–59
23. Trouvé A, Younes L (2005) Metamorphoses through Lie group action. Found Comput Math 5(2):173–198
24. Zhao S, Gao Y (2008) Significant jet point for facial image representation and recognition. In: ICIP, pp 1664–1667

Chapter 10
The Shape of Space

Jan Koenderink and Andrea van Doorn

10.1 The Shape of Space

Does space have a shape? The question might sound slightly odd to the naive addressee. The answer has to be evidently *yes* though. In mathematics, the notion that space has a shape became common during the course of the nineteenth century, when the familiar space of Euclid of Alexandria (ca. 300 BCE) was finally seen as just one of infinitely many possible geometries [4]. Gauss (1777–1855) famously attempted to measure the shape of the space we move in by geodesical methods. This was comparable to the first estimate of the radius of the (then generally considered flat) earth by Erathostenes of Cyrene (276–194 BCE). In the twentieth century, the zoo of possible space forms really exploded [9]. Perhaps more importantly, it became clear that the space we physically exist in, has a shape that is determined by the distribution of matter in it. Space became just another physical object.

The notion that the space of perceptual awareness does not have the familiar Euclidean shape is comparatively recent. Psychophysical data became available from the late nineteenth century to the present. Formal, conceptual developments started with Helmholtz [8], Riemann [28] and Mach [24]. However, it would be too optimistic to say that we are dealing with a well understood topic here. On the contrary,

J. Koenderink (✉)
Laboratory of Experimental Psychology, University of Leuven (K.U. Leuven), Tiensestraat 102, box 3711, 3000 Leuven, Belgium
e-mail: jan.koenderink@ppw.kuleuven.be

J. Koenderink
Faculteit Sociale Wetenschappen, Afdeling Psychologische Functieleer, Utrecht University, Willem C. van Unnikgebouw 17.24.C, Heidelberglaan 2, 3584 CS Utrecht, The Netherlands

A. van Doorn
Industrial Design, Delft University of Technology, Landbergstraat 15, 2628 CE Delft, The Netherlands
e-mail: A.J.vanDoorn@tudelft.nl

S.J. Dickinson, Z. Pizlo (eds.), *Shape Perception in Human and Computer Vision*, Advances in Computer Vision and Pattern Recognition,
DOI 10.1007/978-1-4471-5195-1_10, © Springer-Verlag London 2013

the field of "visual space" is a mess, with many unresolved problems. Many of such problems occur as apparent conflicts between various data sets.

There are a number of reasons for this unfortunate state of affairs. In this chapter, we discuss some of these. We also suggest alternatives that might be empirically addressed.

10.2 Some Spaces of Interest

Some spaces of immediate interest are the space we move in, henceforth denoted "physical space", and what is often called "visual space". The latter is a space of visual awareness. One problem is that there are many of these, almost certainly not all identical or equivalent. Consider some important instances.

First distinctions of basic importance are enactive[1] versus contemplative[2] vision, and optically guided behavior versus visual awareness [10]. It makes a major difference in the available optical structure whether the observer moves or is stationary [6].

Even with a stationary observer, and an emphasis on visual awareness, the full state of the observer is not fully determined. What does "stationary" mean? One thing we require is monocular vision, binocular vision implying a momentary shift of view point. (For distances that are large with respect to the interocular segment binocular disparity just contributes another, minor depth cue, and the present discussion applies.) But it makes a huge difference whether one fixes the location of the body, the skull, or the eyeball. In each case one obtains a distinct "shape of visual space".

The situation is actually more complicated than that. For example, Helmholtz's "subjective curvatures" [26] of objectively straight lines in the visual field (e.g., the images of taut wires) are "explained" by Helmholtz [8] on the basis of the kinematics of eyeball rotations (especially Listing's law). However, in the experiment the observer fixates a point, thus does not make eye movements at all. The movements are of crucial importance for Helmholtz's theory, even when the eye is stationary!

A categorically different space is that experienced when looking "into" a picture. This is so called "pictorial space" [11]. The shape of pictorial space is quite unlike the shape of the picture, which (in generic cases) will be a planar surface covered with pigments in some simultaneous order. Pictorial space, and the visual

---

[1]"Enaction" was introduced by Jerome Bruner [2, 3] who distinguished between iconic and symbolic knowledge. It is presently (also by us) used for knowledge that comes through action. It is acquired through motor skilled motor actions, such as handling objects and locomotion. Enactive vision is not necessarily accompanied by any acute *visual* awareness.

[2]"Contemplation" is commonly defined as "to admire something and think about it". It typically involves no motor action, but acute awareness, and is akin to *meditation*. Contemplative vision is also akin to *artistic* vision, and is so described in Hildebrand [10] with the notion of "far image" (G. *Fernbild*), and "serenely viewing eye" (G. *das ruhig schauende Auge*).

space experienced by a stationary observer in front of some physical space, are similar, though often different. Looking out of a window, or into a mirror, is clearly different from looking into a painting. However, there appears to be a continuous spectrum here, ranging from essential identity, to categorical difference. The differences have to do with minor deviations from strict "stationarity", say the monocular, physiological cues. Pictorial space—as indeed visual space with minimal cues—is rather volatile, as is well known from many common phenomena [1, 25].

In the remainder of this section, we discuss a few characteristic cases. In many real life situations, one is likely to meet with some in between case, of course.

10.2.1 The Pinned down Observer

With the "pinned down observer" we indicate a fixed view point. Otherwise the spatial attitude of the body, head, and eye ball are fully arbitrary. In such a case, the shape of visual space should be spherically symmetric. This is a case we have analyzed in some detail before [12].

The key point is that rotations about the viewpoint have no effect on the available optical structure. Eye movements will never reveal anything new, their effect is purely interospecific.[3] Likewise, magnifications of the world about the viewpoint have no effect on the available optical structure. Lilliput looks the same as Brobdignac, it requires a common currency like Gulliver in order for the difference to become visible. This means that the shape of space should be invariant with respect to these transformations. It implies the Riemannian metric

$$ds^2 = \frac{dx^2 + dy^2 + dz^2}{x^2 + y^2 + z^2} = d\mu^2 + d\vartheta^2 + \sin^2 \vartheta \, d\varphi^2, \qquad (10.1)$$

where $\{x, y, z\}$ are Cartesian coordinates of physical space with the origin at the view point. In polar form $\mu = \log \sqrt{x^2 + y^2 + z^2}$, and $\{\vartheta, \varphi\}$ the usual angular coordinates. The geodesics of this space are planar logarithmic spirals about the origin (as seen immediately when specializing to constant φ). (See Fig. 10.1.) The space has constant, elliptic curvature.

Notice that this is a model that suggests a rigid relation between physical space and visual space. This is perhaps odd, because the pinned down observer is not able to gain experience with the structure of physical space. What is really going on here is that the model purports to describe the visual space of a pinned down observer with plenty of experience in enactive vision.

---

[3]One distinguishes "interospecific" and "exterospecific" information. We don't use the origin of the terms, but they were used by Gibson [7] to differentiate between information that relates to the observer and to the external world. For an ideal camera–eye eye–movements do not reveal any novel information about the scene, since no novel perspectives are gained. They lead to pure interospecific information. (E.g., the optic nerve activity may be used to monitor eye movements.)

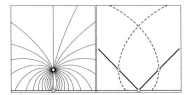

Fig. 10.1 At *left* bundles of geodesics through a point in the forward direction, according to Eq. (10.1). These geodesics are logarithmic spirals that even exist behind the observer (although we have clipped them at the fronto-parallel). At *right* parallel geodesics through two symmetrically located *points*. The *drawn lines* are "railway tracks" (in terms of the metric), whereas the *dashed geodesics* are launched in (Euclidean) parallel directions

10.2.2 The Pinned down Observer, Fixating the Forward Direction

In this case the observer's body scheme, defined by the body's bilateral symmetry and the direction of gravity, as well as a fixed spatial attitude of the eye ball, limit the observer's freedom to the utmost extent. Visual space can hardly be assumed spherically symmetric, since only (about) a half-space in front of the observer is optically effective. The frontal plane through the view point acts as a hard limit, and may be assumed to play an important role in settling the shape of space.

If we assume visual space to be homogeneous, and the limiting plane to be at infinity in terms of the metric, then the obvious model is a Riemann space with metric

$$ds^2 = \frac{dx^2 + dy^2 + dz^2}{z^2}, \tag{10.2}$$

where Z is the forward direction, Y the vertically upward direction, and X the right-left direction. (See Fig. 10.2.) This is a well-known metric of hyperbolic geometry. (For $x = 0$, or $y = 0$, one has the Poincaré half-plane model of the hyperbolic plane.) The geodesics are semicircles in planes orthogonal to the frontal ($z = 0$) plane. (See Fig. 10.3.) This space has constant, hyperbolic curvature.

This shape of space is essentially identical (except for some minor adjustments) to Luneburg's model of visual space [23]. Indeed, the argument of homogeneity used here was exactly Luneburg's argument. (Although Luneburg purports to deal with binocular space, his key argument has nothing to do with that.)

Notice that this model has much in common with the previous one. For instance, in either case visual rays are mutually parallel geodesics (in the sense of a fixed distance between the two geodesics, like the rails of a railway track), and spheres concentric with the view point appear as "fronto-parallel" geodesic surfaces. There are important differences too. For instance, the model from the previous subsection does not allow a projective structure, whereas the present one does.

The fact that the visual rays in either model appear as bundles of parallel directions is interesting. It appears to capture at least one important phenomenological property of visual space.

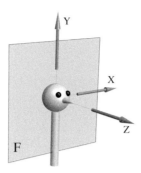

Fig. 10.2 The canonical coordinate system used throughout the text. The plane F is the "frontal plane", it passes through the view point, and is orthogonal to the viewing direction (which coincides with the anterior direction of the body). The Z-axis is the anterior direction, the Y-axis the cranial (up) direction, and the X-axis the left to right direction

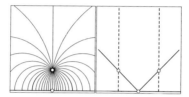

Fig. 10.3 At *left* bundles of geodesics (semicircles with center in the frontal plane) through a point in the forward direction, according to Eq. (10.2). These geodesics stop at the fronto-parallel through the view point, they meet the fronto-parallel at right angles. At *right*, parallel geodesics through two symmetrically located points. The *drawn lines* are "railway tracks" (in terms of the metric), whereas the *dashed lines* are launched in (Euclidean) parallel directions

10.2.3 The Pictorial Observer

In the case of the pictorial observer, there is no notion of any "physical space". There is no such a thing as "range" (distance as measured from the view point), whereas "depth" is a purely mental entity that is (in many cases) defined up to an origin and a scaling. Depths in different directions cannot necessarily be compared, except for some idiosyncratic gauge transformation. The shape of pictorial space is that of a fiber bundle [13, 22], in simple cases equivalent to a singly isotropic space.

We understand pictorial space well enough that we can apply geometric transformations to compare various observers quantitatively, even if their responses might appear very different to a naive analysis.

In the simplest instances, pictorial space is described by a semi-metric

$$\mathrm{d}s^2 = \mathrm{d}\xi^2 + \mathrm{d}\eta^2, \tag{10.3}$$

where $\{\xi, \eta\}$ are picture plane coordinates, and ζ denotes the depth [11]. Notice that the depth dimension does not occur in the semi-metric. It is an "isotropic dimension". In this way, the metric captures the basic fiber bundle structure.

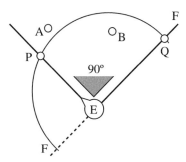

Fig. 10.4 The "cone of sight" is a right angle. The observer at E views a point P, thus the frontal plane is FF. The point Q at $90°$ from P is just visible. (The *circular arc* is the geodesic PQ, its center is on FF.) Any points like the points A, B, inside the right angled cone are simultaneously visible

10.3 The "Polarized" Pinned down Observer

With "polarized" we mean that the observer is pinned down, but will typically orient body, head, and eyes according to need. Different from the general pinned down observer (Eq. (10.1)), this means that the observer has only access to a half-space at any time (Eq. (10.2), but with unspecified frontal plane). This observer is free to rotate (body, head, or eyes, as the case may be) in order to "look around", and change the frontal plane.

This has a number of important consequences. For instance, given two locations (say a pointer and a target), it is not necessarily the case that the observer is able to see both at the same time. Only within a right circular cone of top-angle ninety degrees can the observer simultaneously see any point pair *wherever she happens to be looking*. This reminds one of the fact that the ancients—who failed to distinguish between the visual field and the field of view—considered the cone of vision to be limited to a right angled cone. (See Fig. 10.4.)

As the observer compares two points $\mathscr{A}$ and $\mathscr{B}$ (say), it is likely that she fixates one of the two at a time, perhaps sequentially. As the observer changes fixation, the "effective fronto-parallel plane" moves too, staying at right angles to the primary viewing direction. Thus the metric is view direction dependent, and may be written

$$ds^2 = \frac{dx^2 + dy^2 + dz^2}{(\mathbf{r} \cdot \mathbf{d})^2}, \qquad (10.4)$$

where $\mathbf{d}$ (with $\mathbf{d} \cdot \mathbf{d} = 1$) denotes the primary direction of view, and $\mathbf{r} = \{x, y, z\}$. (The simple case of Eq. (10.2) is regained by setting $\mathbf{d} = \{0, 0, 1\}$.)

In the case the two points $\mathscr{A}$ and $\mathscr{B}$ do not occur in a single view, there is no metric relation, and we have to do something special. Such cases occurred in prior experiments. We analyzed the data in terms of a general pinned down observer model (Eq. (10.1)), but the present discussion suggests that this was perhaps not the right way to proceed.

The case of the polarized pinned down observer (Eq. (10.4)) has far reaching consequences. For instance, it implies that in many cases the geometrical relation of

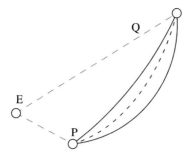

Fig. 10.5 As the eye E fixates either location P, or location Q, one obtains (according to Eq. (10.4)) the *drawn* geodesics PQ (both circular arcs, but with different centers and radii), which are clearly distinct. Equation (10.1) yields the *dashed* geodesic (a logarithmic spiral) in either case. Of course, one might fit an inflected, cubic arc to match the direction of the appropriate drawn geodesic at either end point. However, this would be really contrived, and corresponds to no reasonable geometry

a point $\mathscr{A}$ with respect to a point $\mathscr{B}$ is not simply the reverse of the geometrical relation of a point $\mathscr{B}$ with respect to a point $\mathscr{A}$. (See Fig. 10.5.) For instance, pointings from each point to the other are not guaranteed to "mesh". This is a phenomenon that we have encountered in previous experiments [5, 18], and that caused us much reasons for concern, because it indicated the impossibility of *any* "geometry of visual space" to account for the data.

10.4 Reanalysis of Some Pertinent Empirical Data

In this section, we consider a few pertinent cases. We concentrate upon data collected by ourselves because in each case we know the experimental setting in intimate detail. It would be quite hard to analyze arbitrary literature data this way. Moreover, our reanalysis will often cause us to criticize the original analysis, and we prefer to do that to ourselves, rather than to a colleague scientist.

External local sign   In each of the models, visual rays are mutually parallel. This is perhaps most obvious from Eq. (10.1) in polar form, specialized to a meridional plane (thus $d\varphi = 0$, for instance by setting $\varphi \to 0$). The interpretation is that observers should experience their visual rays, which diverge from the anterior nodal point, as mutually parallel. Thus, they have no access to an external local sign.

This surprising prediction, that seems to be largely unknown to the vision community, has been amply verified in a number of experiments [19, 20, 27]. It has far reaching consequences, both for optical spatial recognition, and for pictorial perception.

Failures of "simple geodesic arcs"   In several experiments we found indications that simple geodesic arcs (similar to parabolic arcs) failed to fit the data [5, 18].

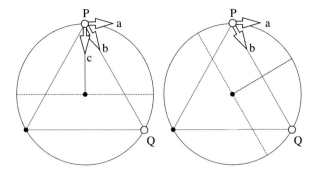

Fig. 10.6 Pointing from one vertex of an equilateral triangle to the next, the observer being at the center. At *left* the observer fixates *P*, at *right* the middle of the arc *PQ*. In both cases pointing *b* would be veridical, whereas Eq. (10.4) would predict the pointing direction *a*. However, in the case at *left* the points *P* and *Q* are not simultaneously visible. While fixating the pointer at *P*, the point *Q* is behind the observer. A default "behind" pointing would yield *c*, whereas a "memory pointing" might yield *b*. One expects perhaps a result between *b* and *c*

This is serious, because it suggests that it might be nonsense to speak of a "shape of space" at all. There seems to be no single arc that explains both pointing from $\mathscr{P}$ to $\mathscr{Q}$, and pointing from $\mathscr{Q}$ to $\mathscr{P}$. (Fig. 10.5.)

In these experiments, we did not constrain the fixation of the observer. In an exocentric pointing task, they often end up (after a period of looking back and forth) looking at the pointer, rather than the target. If that is the case, we would indeed predict exactly the asymmetry found in the experiments. There would not be a single "shape of space", but the shape would depend upon where the observer happened to be looking. This is only a mild complication, but it greatly influences the way such experiments should be analyzed.

Pointing in circles   In a basic experiment on the nature of visual space, we had observers stand at the center of equilateral triangles of various sizes, and had them perform exocentric pointing between vertices [14]. (Fig. 10.6.) We reported large systematic deviations from the Euclidean prediction, depending upon triangle size. These experiments were analyzed in terms of a pinned down, but otherwise free observer model. It appeared that space curvature changed from elliptic to hyperbolic with increasing range.

The vertices are 120° apart in the visual field. When fixating one vertex, the observer cannot see the other. If we assume that the observer will look at the mid point of the vertices, thus seeing both simultaneously, we predict an error of 60° *away* from the observer (Fig. 10.6 arrow *a*). If we assume that the observer fixates a vertex, we are in a quandary, because the other vertex cannot be seen. Since it is behind the observer, it is perhaps reasonable to assume that the pointing will be at the observer, implying a 30° error *toward* the observer (Fig. 10.6 arrow *c*).

In these experiments, the pointer was of constant size. This implies that observers are indeed able to see both vertices by fixating the midpoint if pointer and target are close, but not when the pointer is far away, its angular size then becoming too small.

Thus, one expects the observer to fixate the pointer in the latter case. This at least qualitatively predicts the results that were actually obtained.

The conclusion is that these results may well be explained with a homogeneous space shape. The explanation by way of varying space curvature is not forced upon us.

Pointing to opposite sides   What happens if an observer has to perform exocentric pointing between mutually opposite locations? Only one location can be seen in any case. If the observer fixates one location, one expects the pointing to be toward the observer. If the observer fixates a direction orthogonal to the connecting line of the two locations, and makes minor left and right head movements to see one or the other location in alternation, one predicts that the pointing will be at right angles to the connecting line. Depending on various additional assumptions, we predict errors between 0° and 90° away from the observer.

In the experiment [17], we find a rather small value of about 6° away from the observer. It was interpreted in terms of a pinned down, spherically symmetric setting. From the present discussion, it is clear that alternative "explanations" cannot be ignored off hand.

The existence of planes   The issue of whether visual space admits of planes is conceptually important because it relates to the (possible) projective structure of visual space. In a recent experiment [21], we found that visual space in general does not admit of a projective structure. However, the data were hard to interpret due to very significant individual differences.

The main task in the experiment was to set the mid point of a geodesic arc in depth (the direction being given). In the present interpretation, this task will depend critically on the viewing direction. The locations were about a right angle apart, so the observer is almost forced to look at the mid point. If not, then we predict different settings according to which point is fixated.

In the experiment we had three target points, in mutually orthogonal directions, and ranges in the ratios $1 : 2 : 4$. The observer set the mid points of the sides of this triangle, then the barycenter, a point on the arc between a vertex and the opposite mid point. One obtains three estimates for the barycenter, in the same direction (by design), but with different ranges. We define the ratio of the largest to the smallest range as the "discrepancy". In the present setting (Eq. (10.4)), we predict a discrepancy of $1.414\ldots$, different from the original prediction (based on Eq. (10.1)), which was $1.129\ldots$. Neither prediction is well borne out by the results, though both are within the range of the data.

Given the many possibilities of variation (in the numerous subtasks the observers are free to pick idiosyncratic fixation directions), it is not very surprising that the results of the study turned out to be confusing.

The curvature of large fronto-parallels   Given the basic model of the pinned down observer, one would expect the curvature of large scale fronto-parallels to be very significant. In reality, they are found to be significantly curved, but perhaps less so then naively expected [15, 16].

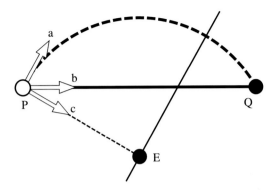

Fig. 10.7 *PQ* is a fronto-parallel of 120°. When the observer fixates the midpoint of *PQ*, one predicts the *curved, dashed* geodesic. Thus, with the pointer at *P*, target at *Q*, one predicts the pointing direction *a*. When the observer fixates the pointer at *P*, the target at *Q* is invisible, it is behind the observer. One perhaps expects the default "behind" pointing direction *c*. A "memory pointing" might yield pointing direction *b*. In reality, one perhaps expects something between *b* and *c*. Notice that the sign of curvature in the cases of fixating the mid point, and fixating an end point are opposite. In experiments we obtained instances of either case, depending upon the observer

This is easily understood from the model of the forward looking observer. The naive prediction uses the spherically symmetric, pinned down observer. In this case one would expect the fronto-parallels to be almost semi-circles. (Fig. 10.7.) However, if the observer fixates an end point, then the prediction would change to an almost straight line. In the actual experiments, various points were set on the fronto-parallels, and it is very likely that the viewing direction changed systematically with the current task. Thus, it becomes very difficult to interpret the results as reflecting some integral geometrical object. Rather, it is likely that the actual "object" changed from setting to setting.

Pointing in pictorial space   In pointing tasks in pictorial space, we find clear evidence that observers "point by curved arcs", instead of straight lines [29]. This is perhaps more remarkable than the analogous case in physical space, because the pointing occurs fully in pictorial space, which is already a mental entity.

We did not find evidence of failures of the pointings to "mesh", thus a single parabolic arc always accounted for two-way pointing. In the case of pictorial space it is hard to motivate the metric of Eq. (10.4). Moreover, it is not clear how to interpret the singular plane $\mathbf{d} \cdot \mathbf{r} = 0$: is it the plane orthogonal to the line of sight, or rather the picture plane? Whereas the semi-metric equation (10.3) accounts very well for numerous aspects of the shape of pictorial space, it predicts straight geodesics. There evidently remains much to clear up here. Unfortunately, there is hardly any empirical data to start from (except from our study referred to above).

10.5 Conclusion

We have contrasted mainly two very simple models of human visual space. Either model is capable of almost limitless refinement. However, we have refrained from even the obvious refinements, because we wanted to show the most elementary properties instead of attempting any data fitting.

One important omission is that we (except in the case of pictorial space) considered only transformations of physical space. In any reasonable model, the metrics as used here would be applied to an intermediary space, in which at least the physical range (distance from the eye) would be replaced with a subjective representation. Such a transformation would depend upon the exact setting of the experiments, that is to say, on the available depth cues.

In typical experiments, memory will play an important role if only part of the configuration is visible at any given time. This suggests, perhaps, that in many cases predictions should be some compromise between the spherically symmetric, and the forward looking case.

One important message is that experiments like the ones considered in the analysis should be replicated with explicit emphasis on the viewing directions (as evident from body, head, and eye movements) of the observer. There is no doubt that the free observer will adjust posture, head attitude, and eye direction according to the task, and the constraints imposed by the experimenter. The present analysis shows that this has important consequences for the predictions of even the simplest of models of visual space.

In conclusion, we find that the "shape of space" in the context of human visual perception remains an entity that is only very partially understood, both from a phenomenological and from a formal, conceptual perspective.

Acknowledgement   This work was supported by the Methusalem program by the Flemish Government (METH/08/02), awarded to Johan Wagemans.

References

1. Berkeley G An essay towards a new theory of vision. Printed by Aaron Rhames, at the Back of Dick's Coffee-House, for Jeremy Pepyat, Bookseller Skinner-Rows Dublin, MDCCIX
2. Bruner J (1966) Toward a theory of instruction. Belknap Press of Harvard University Press, Cambridge
3. Bruner J (1968) Processes of cognitive growth: infancy. Clark University Press, Worcester
4. Coxeter HSM (1989) Introduction to geometry. Wiley classics library Series. Wiley, New York
5. Doumen MJA, Kappers AML, Koenderink JJ (2005) Visual space under free viewing conditions. Percept Psychophys 67:1177–1189
6. Gibson DJJ (1950) The perception of the visual world. Houghton Mifflin, Boston
7. Gibson JJ (1986) The ecological approach to visual perception. Houghton Mifflin, Boston
8. von Helmholtz H (1892) Handbuch der physiologischen Optik. Voss, Hamburg
9. Hilbert D, Cohn-Vossen S (1952) Geometry and the imagination, 2nd edn. Chelsea, New York
10. Hildebrand A (1893) In: Das Problem der Form in der bildenden Kunst. Heitz, Strassburg

11. Koenderink JJ (2011) Geometry of imaginary spaces. J Physiol (Paris). doi:10.1016/j. jphysparis.2011.11.002
12. Koenderink JJ, van Doorn AJ (2008) The structure of visual spaces. J Math Imaging Vis 31:171–187
13. Koenderink JJ, van Doorn AJ (2012) Gauge fields in pictorial space. SIAM J Imaging Sci 5(4):1213–1233
14. Koenderink JJ, van Doorn AJ, Lappin JS (2000) Direct measurement of the curvature of visual space. Perception 29:69–80
15. Koenderink JJ, van Doorn AJ, Kappers AML, Todd JT (2002) Pappus in optical space. Percept Psychophys 64:380–391
16. Koenderink JJ, van Doorn AJ, Kappers AML, Lappin JS (2002) Large-scale visual frontoparallels under full-cue conditions. Perception 31:1467–1476
17. Koenderink JJ, van Doorn AJ, Lappin JS (2003) Exocentric pointing to opposite targets. Acta Psychol 112:71–87
18. Koenderink JJ, van Doorn AJ, Kappers AML, Doumen MJA, Todd JT (2008) Exocentric pointing in depth. Vis Res 48:716–723
19. Koenderink JJ, van Doorn AJ, Todd JT (2009) Wide distribution of external local sign in the normal population. Psychol Res 73:14–22
20. Koenderink JJ, van Doorn AJ, de Ridder H, Oomes AHJ (2010) Visual rays are parallel. Perception 39:1163–1171
21. Koenderink JJ, Albertazzi L, van Doorn AJ, van Ee R, van de Grind WA, Kappers AML, Lappin JS, Norman JF, Oomes AHJ, te Pas SF, Phillips F, Pont SC, Richards WA, Todd JT, Verstraten FAJ, de Vries S (2010) Does monocular visual space contain planes? Acta Psychol 134:40–47
22. Koenderink JJ, van Doorn AJ, Wagemans J (2011) Depth. i-Perception 2:541–564
23. Luneburg RK (1950) The metric of binocular visual space. J Opt Soc Am 50:637–642
24. Mach E (1906) Space and geometry. Open Court Publishing, Chicago
25. Necker LA (1832) Observations on some remarkable optical phaenomena seen in Switzerland; and on an optical phænomenon which occurs on viewing a figure of a crystal or geometrical solids. Lond Edinburgh Philos Mag J Sci 1(5):329–337
26. Oomes AHJ, Koenderink JJ, van Doorn AJ, de Ridder H (2009) What are the uncurved lines in our visual field? A fresh look at Helmholtz's checkerboard. Perception 38:1284–1294
27. Pont SC, Nefs HT, van Doorn AJ, Wijntjes MWA, te Pas SF, de Ridder H, Koenderink JJ (2012) Depth in box spaces. Seeing Perceiving 25:339–349
28. Riemann B (1854) Über die Hypothesen, welche der Geometrie zu Grunde liegen. Aus dem dreizehnten Bande der Abhandlungen der Königlichen Gesellschaft der Wissenschaften zu Göttingen, 10 June 1854
29. Wagemans J, van Doorn AJ, Koenderink JJ (2011) Measuring 3D point configurations in pictorial space. i-Perception 2:77–111

Chapter 11
The Visual Hierarchy Mirage: Seeing Trees in a Graph

Steven W. Zucker

11.1 Introduction

In everyday language, and in much of computer and human vision, we speak about early or low-level vision and about high-level vision. Early vision is about the first stages of visual processing, and spans much of the processing anchored by the sensor. While this includes communication and signal processing, for our argument we center on feature detection. Calculating edge and color maps, typical low-level tasks, differs from high-level vision, which includes object recognition and other "cognitive" tasks.

Early vision has a very natural expression in neurobiological terms. A cornerstone of visual physiology is the concept of *receptive field*, or the locus of positions to which a neuron responds, weighted by the response. Loosely speaking, receptive fields are filters. There is an elegant linear theory of filtering and it is popular to interpret receptive fields in terms of the statistics (e.g., co-occurrence probabilities of nearby pixels) in image datasets [1]. Nonlinearities are occasionally considered, but these are limited in (spatial) scope. Pooling, squaring [2], and "winner take all" are common examples. Although these non-linearities are less well understood statistically, in effect this view of processing is one in which neurons with early visual receptive fields "summarize" a local region of visual space via a template. As above, some templates are thought to correspond to edge and line elements, for example.

High-level vision is often described in very different terms. First, it is inherently not local. Shape representations are global and object detection is global; all of the relevant information must be used. Decisions are completely nonlinear. The tasks are typically general, such as detection of a face, tracking an object or tracing a contour. We can be aware of high-level processing [3] and can actively control parts of it with attention [4]. As present practice puts it, early and high-level vision are rather different beasts.

S.W. Zucker (✉)
Yale University, New Haven, CT, USA
e-mail: steven.zucker@yale.edu

S.J. Dickinson, Z. Pizlo (eds.), *Shape Perception in Human and Computer Vision*,
Advances in Computer Vision and Pattern Recognition,
DOI 10.1007/978-1-4471-5195-1_11, © Springer-Verlag London 2013

157

But what lies in between, and how is the transition achieved? Does early vision proceed, well, "half-way" up the processing stream and high-level vision take over after that? Algorithmically one could make a distinction that early vision consists of a hierarchy of template-like computations, which summarize the high-dimensional image data, effectively putting it into a proper space for making decisions; the high-level computation is this final decision making apparatus (say, a support vector machine).

Taken crudely, this view seems to be supported by biology, pushed almost to the limit. Nearly half of the primate brain consists of a collection of visual areas that parcellate cortex, each enjoying a rather similar anatomy. This suggests a view of the visual machine consisting of iterated layers of processors. Since there are many projection neurons (in a given visual area) that synapse with a given target neuron (in the next area), the machine is postulated to have fan-in, or a contraction mapping, between layers. The contraction map has very local support, and suggests a natural story line for processing information in an incremental, step-like development. To illustrate, consider this metaphor as an account: local edge elements are agglomerated into curves; curves into clusters (e.g., the eyes, nose and mouth); clusters into superclusters (e.g., a face), and positions of the face into a person in an automobile and *voila*, Uncle Jack is recognized. (Something close to this is achieved, for a few examples, in [5, 6].) The gap between low-level and high-level processing is gone—the feedforward network is almost complete—except perhaps for a support vector machine or classifier at the very end. A natural abstraction hierarchy has emerged, and can perhaps even be learned. It looks like it's all about trees, or summaries of summaries of . . . summaries. Of course, this is the simplest form; many models are slightly more general and involve partial orderings or directed acyclic graphs (DAGs). Convolutional networks [7] and deep learning networks are of this form [8].

This story-line is hard to resist. The performance of deep learning networks is driving commercial applications, and DAGs and trees are elegant data structures. In various forms this model has become the dominant architecture for visual recognition systems today. It has a rich history, which is briefly outlined after the next section.

There is a basic concern about whether the story line from the Introduction suffices. Are low-level and high-level vision truly decoupled in this way, with feedforward architectures dominating until the end? Basically the question boils down to whether this simple contraction mapping exists. I shall argue that more is required.

11.2 What Is Intermediate-Level Vision?

Our argument about architectures for vision systems, both computer and biological, centers on the question of intermediate-level processing: why is it required, what might it be, and how can it illuminate the overall system. We begin with evidence for its existence.

The first pillar of the argument is the actual experience in computer vision. Although segmentation is seen as a goal for early vision, and recognition as a goal for high-level vision, separating them has been problematic. The original argument was that recognition is difficult, so a good segmentation could provide clues about where to deploy expensive computational resources; this thinking still survives [9], although now it is thought by many that segmentation and recognition cannot be separated; they must be solved together [10]. One cannot be confident in a segmentation until recognition is complete, and one cannot be confident in a recognition until the segmentation is complete. There are no shortcuts, which makes it theoretically questionable about how to proceed.

One possibility for how to proceed, then, is to appeal to neuroanatomy, the second pillar of our argument. Most emphatically, cortical neuroanatomy is much more complex than a simple feedforward architecture. As reviewed shortly, there are both *long-range* horizontal connections within an area, and feedback connections between areas. If simpler architectures sufficed, wouldn't mother nature have preferred them? Or making this point in the other direction, since only a small portion of V1 can be viewed a filters: "what is the other 85 % of V1" doing [11]? An answer to this could provide insight into intermediate-level processing.

A third pillar for the argument is that, for the so-called "natural" imagery currently being used to evaluate object recognition systems, little more than simple filtering models for V1 are required [12]. This suggests that either (i) the processing beyond V1 is not necessary, which seems unlikely from an evolutionary perspective, or (ii) something fundamental has taken place in the selection of these datasets. After all, in the natural habitats occupied by non-human primates there is no social web on which to collect "natural" images.

Thus, we need to understand the difference between "natural" images (from web collections) and natural images. One way this could be realized is asking which tasks are relevant. Lots of web images are from birthday parties and car photographs. Again, an answer to this could also provide insight into intermediate-level processing.

Another view of imagery derives from the tasks and behaviors it supports, and this brings up a different heuristic from neuroscience: seek pathways rather than layers. Perhaps the most popular of this other type of decomposition derives from studying lesions and perceptual deficits, and two basic pathways have been identified: one related to identifying objects—the *what* or ventral pathway—and another related to judgements about *where* these objects were—the dorsay pathway [13, 14]. The object recognition task is often assumed to live in the *what* pathway, and some researchers put the distinction between low-level and high-level somewhere around the fourth visual area, V4, [15]; research on visual attention further supports this [4]. But what about the parietal—*where*—pathway? What might the distinction be between early and high-level place tasks? That eye movements are driven by both types of information suggests this is something of a problem.

The what/where processing stream heuristic [13] is, in a sense, orthogonal to the low-level/high-level distinction. As we delve deeper into different schemes for processing (e.g., color vs. contrast; motion vs. static; etc.) we end up with a patchwork quilt of visual processes, with little organization, little predictive power, and little guidance about how to build computer vision systems. Putting it all together, it now seems that visual processing takes place in a machine organized as a graph, or perhaps even a hypergraph, rather than a tree or a DAG. But this is now too general a view, so the question for vision researchers is how to constrain this graph. (A view of this graph is provided in the next section.)

My sense is that hierarchies are too restricted a model to achieve the rich processing capabilities exhibited by advanced biological vision systems because of a kind of local/global problem. There are many situations in which global information is required to make local decisions, and many of these occur rather early in the visual processing stream. A classical example of this is the figure/ground distinction, and I return to this problem later in the chapter.

To my knowledge there is no "segmentation machine" in primate neurobiology; there is perceptual organization machinery. They are not equivalent. Perceptual organization is not about partitioning the image (which is a side-effect, sometimes, available behaviorally), but rather is about good continuation [16], figure/ground and border ownership [17] , and the beginnings of inferences about surfaces [18]; in other words, about the early universals in descriptions inferred from the image. It follows from this that hierarchies are too restricted a model to achieve the rich processing capabilities exhibited by advanced biological vision systems. Significantly, these systems are organized (at least) as graphs of processing units, and not trees. But not arbitrary graphs. And perhaps there is a continuous (rather than discrete) aspect to this organization as well.

Of course there are many different ways (Cayley's formula) in which trees can approximate graphs, and each has different properties. However, without the full processing capabilities of the graphical machine, something is missing. I focus on the border ownership problem because it illustrates several points about what is missing. First, the global information needed locally is the type used in shape description, but is more regularized (in a technical sense). This breaks the need to solve the full segmentation and the full recognition problems together. Second, general processing architectures are needed to implement it. It is not a feedforward, hierarchical construct. Finally, recent mathematical ideas suggest that (at least for biological systems) there could be continua of processing, and not just graphs of interconnected neurons. While this last point is still speculative, it severely underlines the limitations of feedforward processing.

In summary of the paper, I argue that perceptual organization comprises the intermediate-levels of processing necessary to cope with the large variations in natural imagery in support of the diversity of visually-mediated behaviors, and that important aspects of perceptual organization are realized only when global information is fed back to influence local decisions. It is in this sense that I claim the visual processing hierarchy is illusory: it works well when designed within a highly constrained image space, but collapses when true natural imagery is used. We are now ready to explain the title to this Chapter: Just as the desert, the atmosphere, and the heat conspire to create an imaginary pool of water, the problems being considered within—and architectures of—computer vision conspire to create the mirage that feedforward, visual hierarchies suffice.

11.3 Hierarchies and Trees

Informally hierarchies are layered structures with a contraction mapping. Historically, the word *hierarchy* arose in connection with the church, an application in which the flow of information can be thought of as progressing across levels: the views of parishioners are summarized by priests, whose views are (in turn) summarized by bishops, and so on. Locality follows from the parish membership, and information can be viewed as flowing "up" the tree from the leaves to the root. Conceptually one thinks of abstraction increasing as one moves up the tree.

Trees provide a fundamental data representation for, for example, organizing efficient search, which works naturally in the other direction. Logarithmic complexity algorithms arise because, working from the root of the tree, decisions are made at nodes and each decision eliminates a significant portion of the data from being searched. In binary search, for example, each node in the search tree has two children and half of the possibilities are eliminated at each step. Now, abstraction decreases as one moves down the tree.

A basic tenet of complexity theory is that, when the proper data structure is build, processing can be most efficient. In vision systems, the processing architecture provides the framework for learning these "data structures." Because these aspects of trees are so fundamental, many different contraction maps and data abstractions have been used in computer vision and in neurobiology. Here is a brief listing, in which examples from both domains are described. I organize them into four time epochs, to emphasize the recurrent presence of these ideas.

1. *Classical Period*
   MYSTICAL IDEAS MIXED WITH AN INTUITION ABOUT HOW COMPLEX THE INFERENCE PROCESS CAN BE.

   a. *Visual Spirits* "How the image or picture is composed by the visual spirits that reside in the retina and the [optic] nerve, and whether it is made to appear before the tribunal of the visual faculty, like a magistrate sent by the soul ... Kepler, p. 202 [20]. da Vinci's early anatomical experiments suggested a processing sequence across the ventricles. See Fig. 11.1(a).

2. *Early Period*
   TWO FOCI EMERGING: (I) EFFICIENCY (SPEND RESOURCES WHERE RESULTS ARE LIKELY TO BE FOUND) AND (II) BUILDING ABSTRACTIONS.

   a. *Pandemonium* [21] Oliver Selfridge's inspired proposal for computational *daemons* arranged in layers, each "shouting" for attention but moderated by stochastic search and hill climbing. Paradigm foundational for AI; strictly a heterarchy rather than a hierarchy, but set the stage.

   b. *Hubel/Wiesel* Original model for the hierarchical, mechanistic view. The lateral geniculate contains cells with circular surround receptive fields, which can be combined into simples cells, which can be combined into complex cells, and then hypercomplex cells. [22]. Are grandmother cells [23] at the top of the abstraction pyramid?

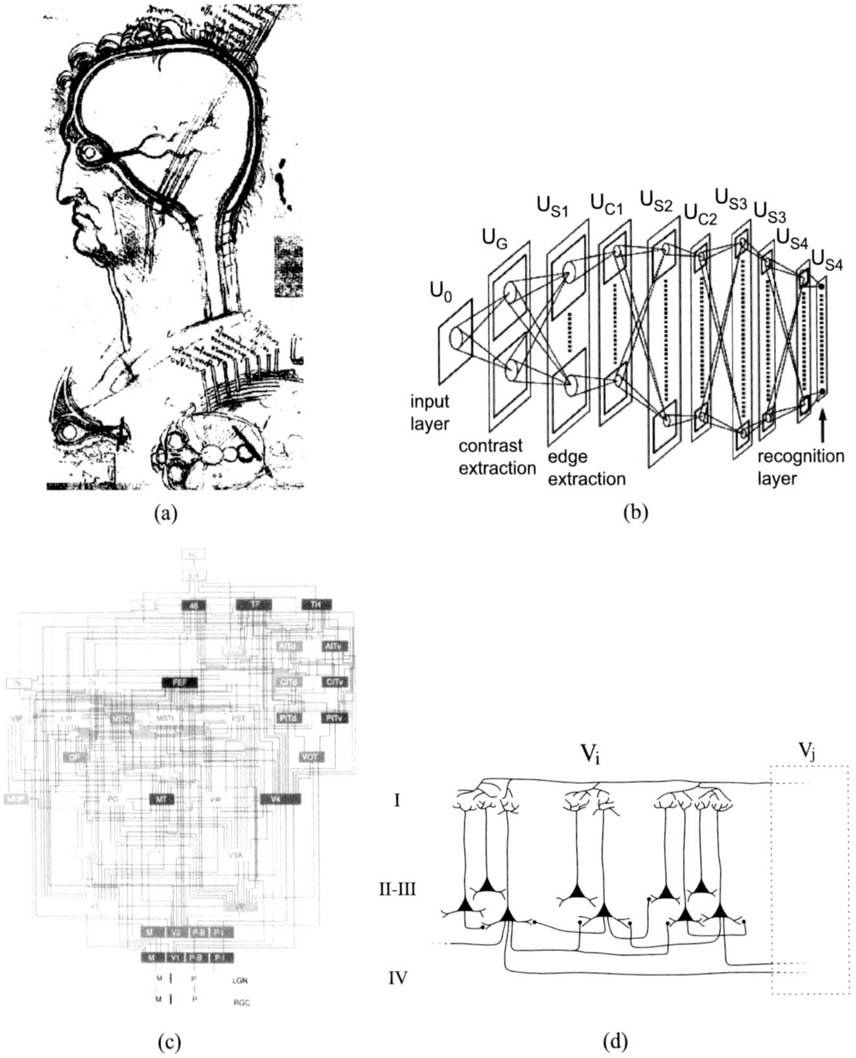

Fig. 11.1 Developing views of the primate brain, with the standard, feedforward view on the top and the rich biological complexity on the bottom. (**a**) Da Vinci's (c. 1490) drawing of the scalp, skull and "visual system", which we now know to be the ventricles. It clearly shows a feedforward progression from the eye through a series of three (ventricle) stages. (**b**) Fukishima's Neocognitron. Notice the layered organization and the feedforward projections. (**c**) A rough "wiring diagram" of the brain, showing the connections between areas. For every forward connection there is a back projection. This suggests a much richer graphical model than the tree structure common in feedforward systems. Although there is an attempt to layer the different areas, with height corresponding roughly to abstraction, this is at best only partial. This diagram, or portions of it, are often summarized as describing the hierarchical organization of the visual system. (**d**) A finer-scale view, in which neurons within a typical visual area are shown to form networks. These involve circuits both within the area and between areas. The neurons comprising the visual system define a graph, not a tree. Credits: fig. (**b**) after Scholarpedia; fig. (**c**) after David van Essen, Washington University, [19]

    c. *Neocognitron* Early computational model that placed the Hubel/Wiesel hierarchy in a pattern recognition framework [24]. See Fig. 11.1(b).

    d. *Image pyramids and coarse-fine analysis* Efficient search in the early days of computer vision. An example was Rosenfeld's coarse-fine approach to edge detection [25]. Connections to multiple-size receptive fields and to more recent edge detection algorithms [26].

3. *Intermediate Period*
MATURATION OF IDEAS, PLUS DEEPER UNDERSTANDING OF MATHEMATICAL AND ANATOMICAL FOUNDATIONS.

    a. *Scale Spaces* Evolution of the idea of coarse-fine, but placing a mathematical structure on it. Central idea: group formed by for example, Gaussians under the heat operator [27–30].

    b. *Hierarchy of Visual Areas* [19] This diagram of the organization of the visual system codified an enormous amount of anatomical information, and became central to thinking about layers of abstraction. Central idea: one function per visual area [31]; this is essential for the abstraction notion to persist.

4. *Modern Period*
REALIZING THE POTENTIAL OF EARLIER MODELS SCALED UP IN SIZE; FACILITATED BY THE ENORMOUS GROWTH IN COMPUTATIONAL RESOURCES AND THE POTENTIAL OF MACHINE LEARNING METHODS.

    a. *Decision Trees* Statistical version of: ask the right question at the right time for recognition [32]. Since trees are limited, sometimes more general structures (e.g., forests [33]) or richer statistical ideas (e.g., boosting [34]) are required.

    b. *Hierarchical Networks* Key idea: takes the Hubel-Wiesel idea above and pushes it to its limit, with only mild non-linearities [5]. Feedforward only.

    c. *Deep Networks* Feedforward convolutional networks with learning algorithms [7]. Opens the door to understanding learning across layers. Highly successful for a number of applied problems [35].

    d. *Bi-Directional Networks* Early attempts to integrate top-down with bottom-up information flows [36]. There is even some evidence that intermediate fragments help recognition [37], although the tests were done with image fragments and not intermediate representations.

Above I concentrate on feedforward and sequential aspect of visual processing. Hierarchies and DAGs arise within other parts of computer vision as well, and these provide a somewhat expanded role for them. Shape hierarchies (fingers, hands, arms/legs, torso, person) [38] articulate the natural partial ordering over parts, and these hierarchies have much in common with memory hierarchies as deployed in computer systems and in biological systems. These partial orders are relevant for searching and matching, because they often provide an efficient organization for structuring complex problems. Constructing the right tree is key to algorithm design [39].

A second major source for DAGs are probabilistic inference nets, Bayesian networks, and belief propagation (expanding 4(a) above). These are also applied widely in computer vision systems (e.g., [40]). They are completely global, but involve very different issues from those on which we are concentrating. In particular, the goal is often to find an approximation (e.g., difference functionals for stereo) that can be efficiently computed. These approaches do not illuminate the intermediate-structure question.

Complexity analysis also illustrates the limitations of trees; or at least their special nature. The traveling saleman problem (TSP), for example, is normally defined on a graph but enjoys a certain advantage when the points are in a Euclidean space. This Euclidean TSP admits an approximation, enjoys a relationship to Steiner trees [41], highlighting how metrics and locality, when assumed, can help.

In vision problems, we do not always have a metric locality structure to fall back upon; as neurobiology teaches us, sometimes we need to look some distance away.

11.4 Neuroanatomy is a Graph

As is clear from Fig. 11.1, the visual system is a graph of neurons and not a tree. The Felleman-Van-Essen diagram (Fig. 11.1(c)) summarizes the large scale organization among visual areas; we stress that there are both feedforward and feedback connections. Understanding the role of feedback connections remains something of an open problem, whose subtlety is amplified by looking at a finer scale drawing (Fig. 11.1(d)). Within each area neurons form circuits with inputs from feedforward projections, local connections, long-range horizontal connections, and feedback connections. The visual areas are not homogeneous structures, but are layered organizations themselves with rich circuits within and between them. The complexity of this graph of connections is daunting. Which tree approximates it? The very question now seems naive.

Rather than address it, researchers in computer vision have addressed the practicalities of the segmentation problem. An incredible range of techniques have been stitched together: local edge signals, global region information, spectal theory, and hierarchical image regions; some systems even attempt to use all of these techniques at once (for recent examples, see, e.g., [42, 43]).

I believe that a deep connection exists between the functional architecture of cortical areas and the computational abstractions they support. For early vision, visual cortex is organized largely around orientation; that is, around selective responses to local oriented bars. In a classical observation, Hubel and Wiesel made [22] recordings along different penetrations of cortex. Tangential penetrations (roughly, parallel to the cortical surface) revealed groups of cells with regular shifts in orientation preference, while normal penetrations (normal to cortical surface) revealed cells with similar orientation and position preferences but different receptive field sizes. (This is the receptive field scale variation that supported the early attempts at image pyramids and coarse/fine edge detection discussed earlier.) Together they define an array of orientation columns, and combined with eye of origin, these columns provide a representation for visual information processing. In effect these columns represent an instance of the cortical columnar machine specialized for problems in vision. It is not a tree and can support many forms of Gestalt good continuation for curves, textures, and colors; see [44–46]. But more is required, as we describe next.

11.5 Border Ownership as Visual Inference

Computer vision is focused largely on detection and recognition problems, driven by applications in the automotive, security, advertising, and biomedical domains. A defining characteristic of these applications is that images are highly constrained and the problem is well specified a priori. But for animate vision it is not just recognition. Primates must infer the three-dimensional structure of trees before leaping, while searching for food and avoiding predators. Missing a branch could mean falling to the ground, and missing fruits and nourishing leaves could have metabolic consequences.

The Gestalt psychologists recognized the importance of perceptual organization in natural environments by observing how camouflage worked. The evidence is that it relates to intermediate levels. Kanizsa [47] provides some of the most compelling modern examples relating to surface organization, material properties, and lighting. The myriad of coupled visual inferences is extensive, and well beyond this short position paper. Instead, we concentrate on an aspect of border detection that goes well beyond standard models. Most importantly, it illustrates distant influences on local events.

Border ownership is the property that borders belong to figure, and not to background [48]. It is illustrated by Rubin's classical demonstration (Fig. 11.3). Most importantly, we now know that there are border ownership influences on the firing of neurons in the first and (extensively) second cortical visual areas [49]; see Fig. 11.3(b,c). Two stimuli are used, the first shows a dark square on a white background (Fig. 11.3(b)), and the second (c) a white square on a dark background. Recordings were made from a neuron whose receptive field is shown as the small ellipse, and the stimuli were aligned so that the receptive field was optimally situated. Notice that, in both cases the neuron "sees" a dark (left)/bright (right) edge pattern. However, for some neurons, the response is more vigorous to pattern (b) than to (c); for others it might be the reverse; and for still others it responds equally to both configurations. In other words, the neuron is responding in a manner that complements geometric good continuation (as in Fig. 11.2 which depends differentially to the global arrangement of edges (or brightnesses).

How might such border-ownership responses be computed? They are clearly related to Gestalt notions of perceptual closure, and several models have been proposed. In effect, they all provide a means of estimating properties of the shape of the enclosed region. Most importantly, this shape estimate has to regularize over different possible shapes, such as straight or wiggly edges (Fig. 11.3(d–f)). Thus,

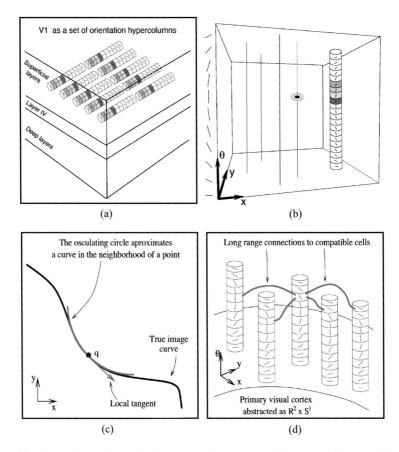

Fig. 11.2 A first view of circuits in the superficial layer of visual cortex. (**a**) A tangential pene-
tration reveals neurons whose receptive fields are at about the same location in visual space, but
whose orientations differ. These can be rearranged into columns, in which the orientation changes
progressively and then (**b**) viewed in an geometrically abstracted view of cortex. The geometric
view embodies the idea that orientation changes smoothly along boundaries, as indicated (**c**) by
the curvature approximation. (**d**) Long-range horizontal connections realize these geometric connection patterns

we have a global to local problem (estimate the boundary response at a point as
a function of whether it bounds a shape) but one in which details have to be integrated away. Building detailed wiring diagrams such as those suggested in Fig. 11.2
are daunting in the combinatorics: how are all of the different edge arrangements
organized into equivalence classes of figures?

We have suggested a very different type of solution to this problem, based on
field-theoretic notions [50]. Briefly, edge responses (in a lower area) are integrated
into contour fragments based on geometric good continuation (long-range connections in that area) and grouping, and are summarized in a higher visual area. The
arrangement of these boundary fragments is then fed back to the lower area via pro-

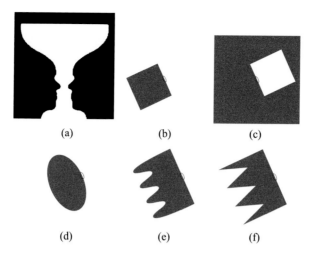

(a)   (b)   (c)

(d)   (e)   (f)

Fig. 11.3 (**a**) The concept of border ownership is illustrated by Rubin's classical vase. Perceptually a closed figure alternates with a pair of "faces," and the border appears to switch; it always belongs to the figure. (**b, c**) Border ownership is signaled by the response of certain neurons. Consider two stimuli, the first of which is a dark square on a white background (**b**), and the second (**c**) a white square on a dark background. Recordings were made from a neuron whose receptive field is shown as the small ellipse, aligned to see identical local stimulation in both configurations. The interpretation is that this neuron prefers for example, "light" figures against a dark background, as in (**c**), and is providing a border and a border-ownership response; that is, that the global boundary defines a light figure. (Individual responses not shown.) Note that the light-dark pattern within the receptive field does not change, only the global arrangement of which it is a part. Figure after [49]. (**d, e, f**) Border ownership must somehow regularize over different shape completions; from the perspective of the neuron whose receptive field is shown, it should be about constant regardless of the figure's exact shape

jections ending in the most superficial layers. But these feedback connections also set up a local potential field in the earlier area, and it is this local field potential that gates the boundary neuron's firing (Fig. 11.4). Most significantly, the gradient of this potential (when evaluated at a boundary point) provides information about global shape by being proportional to properties of the distance map. Thus the loop is closed, and global shape information is available locally.

How might these field-theoretic techniques be used in computer vision? Airports are examples of complex image features that so far have defied standard approaches. Templates are impossible to specify, because airports are defined more by their syntax than by their actual layout. Nevertheless, humans are quite good at recognizing airports from imagery. We suggest that this is because the problem of specifying airports (and other complex features, such as industrial complexes, hospital complexes, etc) is given at an abstract level. Some preliminary experiments have shown that the enclosure field notion can be used for these types of recognition problems; See Fig. 11.5 [50]; in effect they provide a measure of edge element density, alignment, and overall, global arrangement.

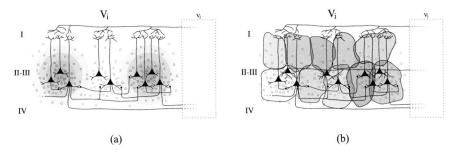

(a)   (b)

Fig. 11.4 Neural substrates that could support border ownership computations. We continue the circuitry outlined in Fig. 11.2, by showing (**a**) the local field potential (*in gray*) built up around neurons from the superficial layer feedback signal. This field-theoretic model carries global information about a kind of "enclosure field." (**b**) Each neuron is surrounded by networks of glial cells, which further participate in setting up local fields (glia also have channels) and provide an active context for learning. If correct, models such as this suggest that a much richer perspective is required in neural modeling, and also suggests that field-theoretic mechanisms could also be relevant to computer vision. For more details, see [50]

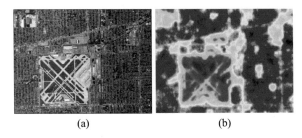

(a)   (b)

Fig. 11.5 Airports are complex features whose description may exist at a "distance map" level. (**a**) Original image. (**b**) Enclosure field as a particular scale. Notice how different edge densities and arrangements are summarized into the potential. *Blue values* correspond to enclosed regions in this implementation. After [51]

11.6 Summary

The current practice in computer vision is to view the processing machine as a layered architecture, with local contraction mappings between layers. This view also pervades visual neuroscience. In computer vision, however, the problem is often limited to a feed-forward network. This raises big problems around segmentation and recognition for natural (unlimited) imagery.

A deeper view of the neuroscience reveals much richer processing architectures. These are required for tasks in perceptual organization, or the inference of intermediate-level structures from images that can support high-level tasks. One of the more subtle aspects of perceptual organization is the manner in which global information can effect local decisions. We illustrate this with the problem of border ownership.

Border ownership illustrates how general properties of shape (namely, figure) can influence border detection. Thus, it serves to illustrate in a concrete fashion how neurobiology may first be solving the segmentation (i.e., perceptual organization) and recognition problems as formulated in computer vision by organizing contours into figures while putative (generalized) figures select from among possible contours. Their coupling comes not in a tree-structured machine, but though beautifully structured feedback connections. Discovery of such roles for feedback in computer vision could be a rich extension of current paradigms.

References

1. Simoncelli E, Olshausen BA (2001) Annu Rev Neurosci 24:1193
2. Schwartz O, Pillow JW, Rust NC, Simoncelli EP (2006) J Vis 6:484
3. Lamme VA (2003) Trends Cogn Sci 7(1):12
4. Itti L, Rees G, Tsotsos J (eds) (2005) Elsevier/Academic Press
5. Serre T, Wolf L, Bileschi S, Riesenhuber M, Poggio T (2007) IEEE Trans Pattern Anal Mach Intell 29(3):411
6. Fidler S, Boben M, Leonardis A (2009) In: Object categorization: computer and human vision perspectives. Cambridge University Press, Cambridge. http://vicos.fri.uni-lj.si/data/alesl/chapterLeonardis.pdf
7. Lecun Y, Bengio Y (1995) In: Arbib MA (ed) The handbook of brain theory and neural networks. MIT Press, Cambridge
8. Hinton GE, Osindero S, Teh YW (2006) Neural Comput 18:1527
9. Mori G, Ren X, Efros A, Malik J (2004) In: Proceedings of the 2004 IEEE computer society conference on computer vision and pattern recognition, 2004, CVPR 2004, vol 2, pp II-326–II-333. doi:10.1109/CVPR.2004.1315182
10. Yao BZ, Yang X, Lin L, Lee MW, Zhu SC (2010) Proc IEEE 98(8):1485
11. Olshausen BA, Field D (2006) In: van Hemmen J, Sejnowski T (eds) 23 problems in systems neuroscience. Oxford University Press, Oxford. doi:10.1093/acprof:oso/9780195148220.001.0001
12. Pinto N, Cox DD, DiCarlo JJ (2008) PLoS Comput Biol 4(1):e27. doi:10.1371/journal.pcbi.0040027
13. Ungerleider LG, Mishkin M (1982) In: Ingle D, Goodale MA, Mansfield R (eds) Analysis of visual behavior. MIT Press, Cambridge
14. Goodale M, Milner AD (1992) Trends Neurosci 15(1):20
15. Desimone R, Schein S (1987) J Neurophysiol 57(3):835
16. Wertheimer M (1923) Psychol Forsch 4:301
17. Koffka K (1935) Principles of Gestalt psychology. Harcourt, Brace & World, New York
18. Nakayama K, Shimojo S (1992) Science 257(5075):1357
19. Felleman D, Essen DV (1991) Cereb Cortex 1:1
20. Lindberg DC (1996) Theories of vision from Al-kindi to Kepler. University of Chicago Press, Chicago
21. Selfridge O (1959) In: Laboratory NP (ed) Symposium on the mechanization of thought processes. H. M. Stationary Office, London
22. Hubel DH, Wiesel TN (1977) Proc R Soc Lond B 198:1
23. Gross CG (2002) Neuroscientist 8(5):512. doi:10.1177/107385802237175
24. Fukushima K (1980) Biol Cybern 36:193
25. Rosenfeld A, Thurston M (1971) IEEE Trans Comput C-20:562
26. Marr D, Hildreth E (1979) Theory of edge detection. Tech. Rep. MIT AI Memo 518, MIT AI Lab

27. Koenderink JJ (1984) Biol Cybern 50:363
28. Witkin AP (1983) In: Proceedings of the 8th international joint conference on artificial intel-
     ligence, Karlsruhe, West Germany, pp 1019–1022
29. Lindeberg T (1994) Scale-space theory in computer vision. Kluwer Academic, Norwell
30. Caselles V, Morel JM, Sbert C (1998) IEEE Trans Image Process 7(3):376
31. Zeki S, Shipp S (1988) Nature 335:311
32. Geman D, Jedynak B (1996) An active testing model for tracking roads in satellite images.
     Tech. Rep. 2757, INRIA
33. Amit Y, Geman D (1997) Neural Comput 9(7):1545
34. Viola P, Jones M (2001) Rapid object detection using a boosted cascade of simple features
35. Lee H, Grosse R, Ranganath R, Ng AY (2009) In: International conference on machine learn-
     ing
36. Ullman S (1994) In: Koch C, Davis J (eds) Large-scale neuronal theories of the brain. MIT
     Press, Cambridge, pp 257–270
37. Ullman S, Vidal-Naquet M, Sali E (2002) Nat Neurosci 5:682
38. Pelillo M, Siddiqi K, Zucker SW (1998) IEEE Trans Pattern Anal Mach Intell 21:1105
39. Sivic J, Russell BC, Zisserman A, Freeman WT, Efros AA (2008) In: IEEE conference on
     computer vision and pattern recognition
40. Tappen MF, Freeman WT (2003) In: International conference on computer vision
41. Arora S (1998) J ACM 45(5):753. doi:10.1145/290179.290180
42. Arbeláez P, Maire M, Fowlkes C, Malik J (2011) IEEE Trans Pattern Anal Mach Intell
     33(5):898. doi:10.1109/TPAMI.2010.161
43. Ullman S, Epshtein B (2006) In: Ponce J, Hebert M, Schmid C, Zisserman A (eds) To-
     ward category-level object recognition. Lecture notes in computer science, vol 4170. Springer,
     Berlin, pp 321–344
44. Ben-Shahar O, Zucker SW (2003) Neural Comput 16:445
45. Ben-Shahar O, Huggins P, Izo T, Zucker SW (2003) J Physiol (Paris) 97:191
46. Ben-Shahar O, Zucker SW (2004) Neural Netw 17:753
47. Kanizsa G (1979) Organization in vision: essays on Gestalt perception. Praeger, New York
48. Koffka K (1935) Principles of Gestalt psychology. Harcourt Brace and Co., New York
49. Zhou H, Friedman H, von der Heydt R (2000) J Neurosci 20:6594
50. Zucker SW (2012) J Physiol (Paris) 106:297
51. Dimitrov P, Lawlor M, Zucker SW (2011) In: Third international conference on scale space
     and variational methods in computer vision, Israel

Chapter 12
Natural Selection and Shape Perception

Manish Singh and Donald D. Hoffman

12.1 Introduction

Our perception of shape is, like all of our perceptions, a product of evolution by natural selection. This entails that our perception of shape is a satisficing solution to certain problems faced by our ancestors, e.g., the need to stalk prey, secure mates, elude predators, and predict outcomes of actions. Natural selection produces *satisficing* solutions, rather than *optimizing* solutions, because selection favors survival of the *fitter,* not of the *fittest*: A gene need confer only a slight edge over the competition—a standard far lower than optimality—to proliferate in later generations.

It is standard in vision research to assume that more accurate perceptions are fitter perceptions, and that therefore natural selection tunes our perceptions to be veridical, i.e., to be accurate reflections of the objective world. For instance, Palmer argues that "Evolutionarily speaking, visual perception is useful only if it is reasonably accurate ... This is almost always the case with vision" [29]. Geisler and Diehl argue that "In general, (perceptual) estimates that are nearer the truth have greater utility than those that are wide of the mark" [12].

If perception is indeed veridical, then the world of our visual experience shares the attributes of the objective world. Our visual world has three spatial dimensions, a temporal dimension, and contains 3D objects with shapes, colors, textures and motions. Vision researchers standardly assume that the objective world does also. In other words, they standardly assume that the language of our visual representations is the correct language for describing objective reality.

M. Singh (✉)
Department of Psychology and Center for Cognitive Science, Rutgers University,
New Brunswick, NJ, USA
e-mail: manish.singh@rutgers.edu

D.D. Hoffman
Department of Cognitive Science, University of California, Irvine, CA, USA
e-mail: ddhoff@uci.edu

S.J. Dickinson, Z. Pizlo (eds.), *Shape Perception in Human and Computer Vision,*
Advances in Computer Vision and Pattern Recognition,
DOI 10.1007/978-1-4471-5195-1_12, © Springer-Verlag London 2013

In this chapter we propose, contrary to standard assumptions, that natural selection does not in general favor veridical perceptions. The reason, in short, is that fitness is distinct from truth; it depends not only on the objective world, but also on the organism, its state, and the action class in question. A gazelle, for instance, offers lots of "fitness points" to a hungry cheetah seeking to eat, but none to a cheetah seeking to mate. Natural selection favors fitness, not truth. It is straightforward to produce evolutionary games in which true perceptions are driven to extinction by nonveridical perceptions that simply report fitness [26].

The consequences of this for shape perception are profound. If our perceptions of 3D shape are not veridical reconstructions of objective 3D shapes, then a new framework, entirely different from the standard, is required to properly understand shape perception. In this chapter, we sketch such a formal framework that incorporates the role of evolution in a fundamental way, and in which perceived shape is an adaptive guide to behavior, not a reflection of objective reality. This framework is consistent with the *interface* theory of perception [16].

Because natural selection has tuned our perception of shape to be an adaptive guide to behavior, our perception of shape has evolved to be tightly coupled with our actions, a coupling that we formalize here with a commuting diagram that we call the "perception-decision-action" loop, or PDA loop. Thus the detailed properties of perceived shapes, such as their symmetries and parts, are not depictions of the true properties of shapes in an objective world, but simply guides to adaptive action.[1]

12.2 Bayesian Decision Theory

A common framework for modeling vision in general, and the "recovery" of 3D shape from 2D images in particular, is Bayesian decision theory (BDT) [13, 18, 19, 22, 24, 25]. BDT provides a probabilistic framework at the computational (or competence) level [27], at which visual problems are analyzed in terms input-output relations (e.g., the formal constraints needed to derive desired outputs from given inputs)—independently of performance considerations involving specific algorithms or their implementations.

Given the basic inductive problem that any image is consistent with many different 3D interpretations, the visual system can resolve this ambiguity only by bringing additional constraints (or biases) to bear—based on regularities observed in the terrestrial environment in which our species evolved—and comparing the relative probabilities of different scene interpretations. For example, in estimating 3D shape from shading, human vision appears to assume that light comes from above (e.g., [20, 25]). Similarly, theories of shape-from-contours often assume that the 3D shapes are symmetric, or maximally compact (e.g., [31]).

---

[1]We use "action" in the broadest sense of the word—to include not only visually-guided manipulation of objects ("dorsal stream"), but also visual categorizations ("ventral stream") that inform subsequent behavior, e.g., whether or not to eat a fruit that has some probability of being poisonous.

Formally, given an image y_0, the visual system must compare the posterior probability $p(x|y_0)$ for different scene interpretations x. By Bayes' theorem, this posterior probability is proportional to the product of the likelihood of the scene $p(y_0|x)$ and its prior probability $p(x)$. The likelihood term captures the extent to which the scene interpretation x is consistent with—and hence can "explain"—the image y_0. In theories of shape-from-X, it is usually taken to be a projective mapping from 3D to 2D (orthographic or perspective), plus some model of noise. Because many different 3D interpretations are typically consistent with any given image, the likelihood cannot generally resolve the ambiguity by itself (i.e., the likelihood may be equally high for a large number of 3D interpretations). The other source of information—the prior probability—reflects the observer's internalized beliefs about fact that certain scenes, shapes, or states of the world are more likely than others—e.g., light tends to come from above, objects tend to be compact, there is a prevalence of symmetric objects, etc. [20, 25, 31].

The combined use of the prior and likelihood—via Bayes—yields a posterior distribution on the space of scene interpretations. It is common to use the maximum-a-posteriori (MAP) estimate as one's "best" interpretation. More generally, however, the choice of a "best" point estimate depends on the loss function one assumes—namely, the consequences of errors, or deviations from the "true" (but unknown) interpretation. If the loss function is essentially a Dirac-delta function (i.e., no loss for the correct answer, equal loss for every other answer) the value that minimizes expected loss is the mode of the posterior distribution, i.e., the MAP estimate. However, if the loss function is quadratic (i.e., squared-error), the value that minimizes expected loss is the mean of the posterior distribution. Hence, different choices of loss functions lead to different strategies for picking a single "best" scene interpretation from the posterior distribution (e.g., [25]).

12.3 A General Framework for Perception and Its Evolution

Bayes' theorem provides a provably optimal way of combining the two probabilistic sources of information embodied in the likelihood and prior [18]. Hence there is strong, principled justification for using Bayes, once a likelihood model and a prior have been specified on a particular space of possible interpretations. However, the Bayesian framework as it is standardly applied to vision involves important assumptions about the choice of interpretation space that we will argue are too restrictive.

Consider the standard Bayesian setup for vision shown in Fig. 12.1a. X is the space of scene interpretations (say, 3D shapes), with prior probability distribution μ_X. Y is the space of 2D images. The likelihood mapping L is the projective map from 3D to 2D (possibly with noise). B is the Bayesian posterior map from Y to X. Technically, L and B are both Markovian kernels [32]. Thus, for each $x \in X$, the projective map L specifies a probability distribution on Y (in the noise-free case, this distribution is supported on a single point). And for each $y \in Y$, the Bayesian posterior B gives a probability distribution on the space X of 3D shapes.

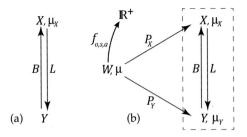

Fig. 12.1 (a) The standard Bayesian framework for vision. (b) The computational evolutionary perception (CEP) framework. In CEP, the objective world W lies outside of the probabilistic inferential apparatus for vision. There are perceptual channels P_X and P_Y to the two representational spaces X and Y, respectively. And there are specific fitness functions on W that assign, for a given organism o, its state s, and the type of action a in question, "fitness points" to each $w \in W$

Importantly, note that in this setup the space X plays two distinct roles: (i) it corresponds to the space of objective world states; and (ii) it corresponds to the space of possible perceptual interpretations from which the visual system must "choose." This dual role is entirely consistent with the *inverse optics* approach to vision— according to which the goal of vision is essentially to invert or "undo" the effects of optical projection (e.g., [1, 28, 30]). It is also consistent with the historical roots of Bayesian methods, namely, as techniques for computing "inverse probability"— a prototypical case being to infer the relative probabilities of possible underlying causes $p(C|E)$ given some observed event E, when what one actually knows are the probabilities of obtaining various events $p(E|C)$ from particular causes C [23].

This dual role played by X makes it clear how BDT embodies the common assumption that human vision has evolved to see the truth. It is *not* the case, of course, that a BDT observer always makes veridical perceptual inferences. Indeed, it cannot. Because a BDT observer embodies specific assumptions about regularities in the world ("light tends to come from above," "objects tend to be mostly convex," etc.) it is always possible to place it within a context where its assumptions are violated. At a more fundamental level, however, BDT makes the basic assumption that the *language* of scene interpretations X is the correct language for describing objective reality. In other words, BDT assumes that the representational space X contains somewhere within it a true description of the objective world—even if the observer's estimate misses it in any given instance. It is in this more fundamental sense that BDT assumes that human vision has evolved to see the truth.

Consideration of vision in other species, especially those with simpler visual systems, suggests that this implicit identification of the representational space X with the objective world is too simplistic. As we will see, it is also too restrictive if one wants a formal framework that is general enough to encompass the evolution of visual systems.

In discussing simpler visual systems, such as those of the fly and the frog, Marr [27] noted that they "... serve adequately and with speed and precision the needs of their owners, but they are not very complicated; very little objective information about the world is obtained. The information is all very subjective ..."; and that "... it is extremely unlikely that the fly has any explicit representation of the visual world around him—no true conception of a surface, for example, but just a few triggers and some specifically fly-centered parameters..." (p. 34). Thus, Marr seemed to acknowledge that visual systems that do not compute objective properties of the world can serve the needs of their owners well enough for them to survive, even thrive, in their respective niches. This should not be surprising; after all, what matters in evolution is fitness, not truth, and even visual systems that compute only simple, purely "subjective," properties can confer sufficient fitness. Despite this, Marr held that the properties computed by *human* vision—such as object shape— are objective properties of the world that exist independently of any observer. There is no reason to believe, however, that the representational spaces that evolved in the species *Homo sapiens* must correspond to objective reality. The evolution of *Homo sapiens* is guided no less by fitness than the evolution of any other species. And fitness is clearly distinct from objective truth because it depends not only on the objective world, but also on the *organism* (fly vs. elephant), its *state* (hungry vs. satiated), and the *type of action* under consideration (eating vs. mating). Therefore, one's formal framework must be broad enough to include the possibility that *human* visual representations also do not capture objective truth.

Thus, rather than simply assuming, or postulating, that the space of interpretations X is identical to (or in one-to-one correspondence with) the objective world— let's call it W—one's formal framework must consider different possible relationships between X and W. We make no assumptions about W, except that it is meaningful to talk about probabilities in W, governed by some (unknown) probability measure μ on an event space $\mathcal{W}$. We define a *perceptual strategy* as a measurable function $P : W \rightarrow X$. One can think of P as a channel between W and X, that allows information to flow from the objective world to the organism. In the general case, P is a Markovian kernel which specifies, for each $w \in W$ [7], a probability distribution on X.[2] One can then consider four classes of perceptual strategies corresponding to different relationships between X and W (see [17, 26]): (i) the *naïve realist* strategy assumes that $X = W$ and that P preserves all structures on W; (ii) the *strong critical realist* strategy assumes only that $X \subset W$ but requires that P projects all structures of W onto X; (iii) the *weak critical realist* strategy allows that $X \not\subset W$ but requires that P projects all structures of W onto X; and (iv) an *interface strategy* allows that $X \not\subset W$ and does not require that P projects all structures of W onto X. The interface strategy *need not see the truth* in the more fundamental sense that the very language of the space X may be the wrong language to capture the structure of the objective world W.

Most vision researchers today are weak critical realists. They recognize— contrary to the claim of naive realism and strong critical realism—that perceptual

---

[2]Hence, formally, P is a mapping $P : W \times \mathcal{X} \rightarrow [0, 1]$, where $\mathcal{X}$ is the event space on X. One can view P as a linear operator that maps probability measures on W to probability measures on X. In the discrete case, it would be represented by a stochastic matrix whose rows add up to 1. For more on Markovian kernels, see [3, 32].

representations are distinct from objective reality, but assume that perceptual representations are isomorphic, or at least homomorphic, to objective reality. We call these two versions "isomorphic realism" and "homomorphic realism."

We generalize BDT to a framework we call Computational Evolutionary Perception (CEP; [17]). In CEP, the objective world W lies outside of the Bayesian inferential apparatus (see Fig. 12.1b). X and Y are simply two representational spaces—neither corresponds to the objective world W (nor are they assumed to be isomorphic to W). For example, Y may be a lower-level representation (say, a 2D representation of image structure) that evolved earlier, whereas X may be a higher-level representation, involving some 3D structure, that evolved later. There are perceptual channels P_X and P_Y from the world W to X and Y, respectively. As noted above, in the general case, P_X and P_Y are also Markovian kernels. Thus, for each $w \in W$, P_X specifies a probability measure on X, and P_Y specifies a probability measure on Y. In particular, the measure μ on W yields, via P_X, a pushdown measure μ_X on X, and similarly via P_Y, a measure μ_Y on Y.[3] In the diagram in Fig. 12.1b, therefore, all four mappings shown (L, B, P_X and P_Y) are Markovian kernels. It is therefore meaningful to take their compositions, which are also Markovian kernels (such as the composition $P_X L : W \rightarrow Y$).[4] An important constraint in the CEP framework is that the diagram in Fig. 12.1b must commute. As a result, for example, $P_Y = P_X L$. This is a coherence constraint on perceptual representations that allows observers to predict the perceptual consequences of their actions, despite the fact that they are ignorant about the objective world itself (see also Sect. 12.4).

What shapes the evolution of perception is, of course, fitness. We therefore expect that natural selection tunes perceptual channels (and their corresponding representational spaces) to the only signal that matters for evolution, namely, fitness. In order to bring fitness into our formalism, we view organisms as gathering "fitness points" as they interact with the world. As we noted, fitness depends not only on the objective world, but also on the organism, its current state, and the type of action in question. Thus, we define a *global fitness function* $f : W \times O \times S \times A \rightarrow \mathbb{R}^+$, where O is the set of organisms, S of their possible states, and A of possible action classes. Once we fix a particular organism $o \in O$, state $s \in S$, and action class $a \in A$, the *specific fitness function* $f_{o,s,a} : W \rightarrow \mathbb{R}^+$ assigns fitness points to each possible $w \in W$ (say, of a starving lion eating a gazelle).

Given a specific fitness function $f_{o,s,a}$, evolution shapes a source message about fitness and a channel to communicate that message, that results in hill-climbing toward greater expected-fitness payout to the organism. This means that a perceptual channel P_X from W to X may be expressed as the composition of two Markovian kernels: a message construction kernel P_{C_X} from W to a set of messages M,

---

[3]Thus, whereas in BDT μ_X is taken to be the world prior, in CEP μ_X is the pushdown, via the perceptual channel P_X, of the prior μ on the objective world.

[4]Kernel composition is defined as follows: let M be a kernel from $(X, \mathscr{X})$ to $(Y, \mathscr{Y})$, and N be a kernel from $(Y, \mathscr{Y})$ to $(Z, \mathscr{Z})$. Then the composition kernel MN from $(X, \mathscr{X})$ to $(Z, \mathscr{Z})$ is defined, $\forall x \in X$ and $A \in \mathscr{Z}$, by $MN(x, A) = \int_Y M(x, dy) N(y, A)$. This is simply a generalization to the continuous case of the familiar multiplication of (stochastic) matrices. For details, see [32].

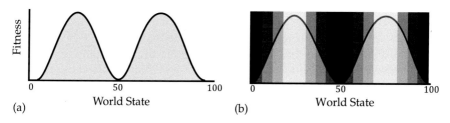

Fig. 12.2 (**a**) A specific fitness function defined on a world containing a resource that varies in quantity from 0 to 100. Resource quantities around 25 and 75 confer the greatest fitness, whereas resource values around 0, 50, and 100 confer the least fitness. (**b**) The construction of a message set with 4 messages, based on a simple clustering of fitness values into four categories: "very high" (*white*), "somewhat high" (*light gray*), "somewhat low" (*dark gray*) and "very low" (*black*)

and a transfer kernel P_{T_X} from M to X [7]. The message *construction* kernel P_{C_X} is needed because the messages to be transmitted depend not only on the world W, but also on the fitness values associated with elements of W (for a particular organism o, its state s, and action class a). Hence, given the same W, but a different specific fitness function $f_{o,s,a}$, the set of messages to be transmitted may be different. Consider an example of a simple world with multiple territories, each of which contains a resource whose quantity varies from 0 to 100. Thus, each value from 0 to 100 may be considered to be a different world state. Now consider the specific fitness function $f_{o,s,a}$ shown in Fig. 12.2a. As shown, resource quantities around 25 and 75 confer the greatest fitness, whereas resource values around 0, 50, and 100 confer the least fitness. Assume that the representational space X contains 4 elements, say, $X = \{A, B, C, D\}$. Then an efficient way to construct a message set might be to have four messages, obtained by clustering the fitness values into four categories: "very high" (white), "somewhat high" (light gray), "somewhat low" (dark gray) and "very low" (red) (see Fig. 12.2b). The received messages are then highly informative about fitness, and would allow the organism to choose between territories in a manner that will result in high expected-fitness payout (e.g., given a choice between a "white" territory vs. a "light gray" one).[5] (Note that this occurs despite the fact that the received messages carry little information about the actual number of resources.) We use the term *Darwinian Observer* to refer to a perceptual channel P_X that has been shaped by natural selection as a satisficing solution for a specific fitness function.

The above analysis assumed that the representational space X was fixed, and the perceptual channel P_X was being tuned to increase expected-fitness payout. Another way, however, to increase expected-fitness payout is to evolve the representational space itself: $X_1 \to X_2 \to \cdots$. Presumably, there would be selection pressure to evolve a more complex representational space (e.g., a representation that captures some 3D structure) when the expected-fitness payout with the current space is insuf-

---

[5]In this example, a simple clustering based on fitness values was sufficient. More generally, however, multi-dimensional scaling may be required. Indeed, MDS-type solutions may also provide an explanation of how dimensional structure can arise in perceptual representations.

ficient to survive or compete, and going to the more complex representational space would allow a substantial increase in expected-fitness payout.

The CEP framework is thus more general than the BDT framework for vision. First, while incorporating the fundamental role of probabilistic inference, it allows us to consider different possible relationships between the space of interpretations X and the objective world W (rather than simply assuming that $X = W$, or that X is isomorphic to W). Second, it explicitly incorporates the role of fitness into the formal framework, in a way that does not simply reduce fitness to the gain/loss function of BDT. And third, by using Markovian kernels to map the relationship between W and X, it allows us to articulate precisely different ways in which perceptual evolution can proceed (e.g., by tuning a perceptual channel to a fixed representational space, or evolving the representational space itself).

12.4 Shape as a Code for Fitness

12.4.1 Implications for Shape Perception

With our general framework in place, the implications for shape perception now follow straightforwardly. First, our framework makes it clear that we really have no basis for assuming—as is standardly done—that shape is an objective property of the world. For example, it is fairly standard among shape researchers to speak of "shape recovery" when referring to the computation of 3D shape from different 2D cues. This nomenclature reflects the identification of the representational space X with the objective world W that is assumed in the *inverse optics* approach to vision (and, as noted above, is commonly made in Bayesian approaches to vision). When one sees the 3D shape of an object, the undulations in its surface, etc., one sees, according to the inverse optics approach, geometric properties that correspond to objective properties of the world[6]—properties that exist independently of any observer. However, as we noted above, this is too simplistic. It is certainly much more than can be claimed based on available facts. There is surely an objective world W, but there is no basis for saying that *shape* is a property of that world. Rather, shape is simply a representational format used by our visual systems to guide interactions with the objective world. It is part of the representational space X, not W. It should be clear from this that our position is strictly weaker—not stronger—than the standard *inverse optics* or *shape recovery* approach. Whereas the standard approach assumes, or postulates, that $X = W$ or that X is isomorphic to W, we are open to different possible relations between X and W.

---

[6]The inverse optics approach allows for misperceptions—e.g., that observers tend to perceive an object from a certain viewpoint as being less elongated in depth than physical measurements of the object tell us it is. But the inverse optics approach nevertheless assumes that *one* of the shapes in X is the "correct" one in the objective world W. In other words, at a more fundamental level, the inverse optics approach assumes that the very property we call *shape* is an intrinsic property of the objective world W itself.

Second, our framework entails that *shape*, as a representational format, most likely evolved because it made possible the development of a perceptual channel with high expected-fitness payout. Thus the property we call *shape* is essentially an effective coding scheme that has been tuned by natural selection: it conveys to an organism—in a compact and efficient format—the various ways in which the organism could interact with objects in the world to gain more "fitness points." Therefore when we perceive the 3D shape of an object—the undulations on its surface, its symmetries, its part structure—all of these are different aspects of a representational format that natural selection has fashioned, one which compactly summarizes the different possible actions that we could take, and that allows us to predict the perceptual consequences of those actions (e.g., how the perception of a 3D object would change were we to rotate it slightly to left, pick it up in a certain way, etc.), and what the fitness consequences would be (e.g., would we successfully eat that apple or evade that tiger).

This last point raises a natural question: How is it possible for us to interact successfully with the objective world if we are fundamentally ignorant of it, and can assume no simple correspondence between our perceptions and that objective world? This is where the third implication of our framework comes in, namely, that action (broadly construed) plays a central role in the evolution of shape perception. In brief, it is perfectly possible to interact successfully with a fundamentally unknown objective world because (i) there is a regularity in the perceptual mapping; (ii) there is regularity in the consequences of our actions in the objective world; and (iii) these mappings are linked in a coherent manner. This is a fundamental point for our framework and, to develop it fully, we need to introduce some more formalism, namely that of the *perception-decision-action* (or PDA) loop. Before we do this in the next subsection, however, we provide an example that should help fix intuitions.

Consider the desktop interface of a PC. A file's icon on the desktop might be green, rectangular and in the middle of the screen. Does this entail that the file itself is green, rectangular and in the middle of the computer? Of course not. The shape, position and color of the icon are merely conventions that allow the user to interact with the computer despite being ignorant of the complex details of its diodes, resistors, software, voltages and magnetic fields. The desktop interface is useful not because it reveals the truth about the computer, but because it hides the complex truth, and instead provides simple symbols that guide useful interactions with the computer. In like manner, natural selection has shaped our perceptions to be an interface that hides the true nature of the objective world, and guides adaptive behavior [15, 16, 21]. Spacetime is the desktop, and objects with their shapes, colors, textures and motions are icons in the desktop. Spacetime and objects are not the objective truth, and do not resemble the truth. Instead, they are a species-specific adaptation shaped by natural selection to guide adaptive behaviors and to allow us to survive long enough to reproduce. Perception has been shaped by the imperative to produce offspring, not to see truth.

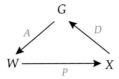

Fig. 12.3 The Perception-Decision-Action (PDA) loop. W denotes the objective world, X a space of perceptual representations of an organism, and G the related set of actions the organism can take. P is a perception kernel, D a decision kernel, and A an action kernel. All kernels are Markovian

12.4.2 The Role of Action in the Evolution of Shape Perception

In this section, we incorporate action and decision into our formalism, and draw out implications for shape perception. Natural selection necessarily couples perception and action because fitness, to which perception is tuned, depends crucially on the actions of the observer. Different classes of action are, in general, coupled with different expected fitnesses. The fitness points gleaned from an apple for the action of eating is greater than for the action of mating. Since natural selection tunes perceptual channels to convey information about fitness, one expects tight coupling between perceptual channels and the actions they inform.

When an observer receives a perceptual experience $x \in X$, it must decide what action to take. We will denote the set of available actions by a set G, where we think of G as including a group that acts on W. Recall that if a group G acts on W, then for every $g \in G$ the mapping $w \mapsto gw$ is a bijective map from W to W. Common examples are the actions of translation and rotation on Euclidean spaces. We also allow there to be actions in G other than group actions.

Thus, given a perceptual experience $x \in X$ the observer must decide which action $g \in G$ to take. The natural formalism to describe such a decision is again a Markovian kernel, D, from $(X, \mathcal{X})$ to $(G, \mathcal{G})$. We call D the decision kernel.

Once an action g is chosen, the observer must then act on the objective world W. We model this action by a Markovian kernel A from $(G, \mathcal{G})$ to $(W, \mathcal{W})$, which we call the action kernel. Given this formalism, we can think of action as sending a message from the observer to the objective world.

Thus, we have three kernels: P, D, and A. P maps from W to X; D maps from X to G; A maps from G back to W (see Fig. 12.3). So together they form a loop, which we call the PDA loop. We have a PDA loop for each perceptual representation space X. So, in the CEP example discussed in Sect. 12.3, there is a PDA loop for the 2D image space Y and another PDA loop for the 3D space X.

However, just as we assume that the observer does not know the objective world W, and therefore does not know the perception kernel P, so also the observer does not know the action kernel A. Informally, this means that when we act, we don't really know what effects we are having in the objective world W itself; however we do know the results of those effects back in our perceptual experiences X. Formally, even though the observer cannot know the kernels P and A, it can know the kernel AP from $(G, \mathcal{G})$ to $(X, \mathcal{X})$, which is formed by the kernel composition of A and

P. It can also know the kernel DAP from $(X, \mathscr{X})$ to $(X, \mathscr{X})$ (i.e., from X back to itself). This allows the observer to learn how to interact with W, even while being ignorant of W. The observer can try different actions $g \in G$ and note their consequences for perceptual experiences in X. If the consequences are unexpected, the observer can update its decision kernel D to correct this.

This applies to actions with objects and shapes. If, for instance, the observer acts in a way that leads it to perceive that its body moves through space via an element of the Galilean group, or that its hand is grasping an object and rotating it, then, given its perceptions of the relative position of an object, and the symmetries and parts of that object, it can predict what the consequences of its action should be for changes in the relative position and perceived shape of that object.

This also applies to object categorization. Such categorization allows the observer to predict the fitness consequences of various current and future interactions with the object (such as eating it). We are thus using the word "action" broadly to include not only "dorsal stream" visually-guided motor behavior, but also "ventral stream" perception and categorization that inform future behavior.

Let's return to the desktop metaphor discussed above. A new generation of desktops now employs 3D interfaces [4]. In such a desktop, if the icon of a file has a particular 3D shape, say the shape of a book, and the desktop contains a 3D bookshelf with a book-shaped gap, then the user can be guided by the shape and position of the 3D icon to grasp it and place it in the bookshelf. In one sense, this is unremarkable. But the key concept here is that the file itself in the computer has no 3D shape, and in particular is not shaped like a book. Moreover, the directory system in the computer has no 3D shape, and in particular is not shaped like a bookshelf. These 3D shapes are mere conveniences for guiding effective interactions of the user, not insights into the true nature of files and directories—and certainly not of the myriads of voltages and magnetic fields in the computer.

12.4.3 Perceptual Organization of Shape

Apart from computing 3D shape from 2D image cues, another fundamental aspect of shape perception is the perceptual organization of shape. A great deal of psychophysical work indicates that human vision organizes complex shapes hierarchically in terms of parts and their spatial relationships (e.g., [6, 8, 14, 33]). This "structural" approach to shape separates the representation of individual parts from that of their spatial relationships—thereby allowing a shape to be identified as comprising the same parts, but in somewhat different spatial relations (e.g., a sleeping cat vs. a standing cat). It is also closely related to the axis or skeleton-based approach, which provides a compact "stick-figure" representation of a complex shape that captures its structural aspects (e.g., its branching structure) [5]. A recent probabilistic approach to the computation of shape skeletons yields a one-to-one correspondence between parts and skeletal branches—indicating that parts and skeletons are indeed complementary aspects of the perceptual organization of shape [9].

They key point, for current purposes, is that the perceptual organization of shape in terms of parts and axes has no natural interpretation in terms of inverse optics. There is no objective "ground truth" regarding whether an object "really" has one part or two, or whether an axis that continues from one portion of a shape to another is "really" the same or a different axial branch (e.g., consider a U-shape vs. a V-shape, and a morphing sequence between them). The organization of shape in terms of segmented parts, or in terms of axes, is something that the visual system *imposes* on perceptual objects—it is not an objective property of the world. This does not mean that a Bayesian analysis of the problem is not possible. However, the likelihood or the "forward" mapping in that case has a different interpretation; it is not a projective or rendering map, but the visual system's own *generative model* concerning how objects are formed [9]. This is easily accommodated within the current framework, since for us the space of interpretations X is distinct from the world W. Hence, in this case, the space X would consist of all possible interpretations of a shape as a hierarchical organization using segmented parts (e.g., different partitions of a shape, and different tree structures capturing possible part hierarchies). In the context of perceptual organization of shape, it is therefore especially clear that elements of X have no simple correspondence to the objective world W.

A natural question is: Why have shape representations based on parts and axes evolved, if they have no simple correspondence to the objective world W? The answer, as expected, has to do with fitness. Organisms that can predict, upon seeing an object at one time, what that object might look like on other occasions, are likely to interact with it much more successfully—and thus have greater fitness—than those that cannot. And a shape representation based on parts and axes goes a long way in conferring this ability: Upon seeing an animal in one particular articulated pose (configuration of limbs), for example, it is much easier to predict other possible (unseen) articulated poses if one's shape representation is part-based than, say, if one's representation consists simply of an unstructured template of the shape as a whole. In sum, a framework that allows X and W to be distinct, and incorporates the role of fitness, makes it much easier to understand the perceptual organization of shape.

12.5 Discussion

We sketched a formal framework—Computational Evolutionary Perception—that subsumes and generalizes the standard Bayesian framework for vision. While incorporating the role of probabilistic inference, CEP also incorporates fitness in a fundamental way, and it allows us to consider different possible relationships between the objective world and perceptual representational spaces. In our framework, shape is not an objective property of the world. It is simply a representational format employed by our visual systems to guide adaptive interactions with the world. This representational format evolved because it allows a high-capacity channel for fitness. In other words, *shape is an effective code for expected fitness that has been tuned by natural selection.* Because fitness depends crucially on the actions of an organism, shape representations in our framework are closely tied to actions. Thus when we perceive the 3D shape of an object—the undulations of its surface, its local and global symmetries, its part and skeletal structure—these are various aspects of a code that compactly summarizes the possible actions that one could take (including future actions based on current categorization), and to predict the fitness consequences of those actions. To model this formally, we introduced the perception-decision-action (PDA) loop. Among other things, the PDA loop clarifies how, even though one cannot know the effects of one's actions in the objective world itself, one can nevertheless know (because of the coherent coupling between perception and action) the results of those effects back in our perceptual experience. This explains how organisms can interact effectively with a fundamentally unknown objective world. Finally, CEP and the PDA loop provide a new framework for understanding the perceptual organization of shape using parts and skeletons—something that is difficult to accommodate within a standard inverse-optics approach to shape.

Acknowledgements   For helpful discussions, we thank Jacob Feldman, Pete Foley, Brian Marion, Justin Mark, Darren Peshek, and Kyle Stevens. MS was supported by NIH EY021494 (joint with Jacob Feldman); DH was supported by a grant from Procter & Gamble.

Appendix: Relation to Quantum Bayesianism

One possible objection to the framework proposed in this chapter might be: "It is naive for vision scientists to propose that our perceptions are not veridical, and that therefore the objective world need not be spatiotemporal and need not contain 3D objects with shapes. Surely physicists know otherwise, and would dismiss such a proposal out of hand."

Although some physicists might dismiss such a proposal, there are others who, in trying to best interpret the formalism of quantum theory, have been led to a view about quantum states that comports well with our proposal. These physicists, who call their approach "quantum Bayesianism," or QBism for short, claim that quantum states are not objective representations of the external world, but rather are compendia of beliefs about possible outcomes of measurements [2, 10, 11]. As Fuchs [10] puts it, "... there is no sense in which the quantum state itself represents (pictures, copies, corresponds to, correlates with) a part or a whole of the external world, much less a world that *just is*" and "... a quantum state is a *state of belief* about what will come about as a consequence of ... actions upon the system." So, for instance, according to QBism a state function of a quantum system, represented say in the basis of the position operator, has a particular shape in space that can be used to predict the consequences of actions on that system.

This is entirely consistent with the view we propose about our perceptual experiences in general, and our experiences of shape in particular. There is no sense in which the objects in our perceptual experiences picture, copy, correspond to, or correlate with a part or a whole of the external world. Instead such objects and their shapes, and perceived space-time itself, are states of belief about what will come about as a consequence of our actions (which could include measurement). The reason is that natural selection, which has tuned our perceptions, rewards fitness and nothing else. Therefore our perceptions have been tuned to inform us of the fitness consequences of our possible actions, not to copy or picture the objective world.

References

1. Adelson EH, Pentland A (1996) The perception of shading and reflectance. In: Knill D, Richards W (eds) Perception as Bayesian inference. Cambridge University Press, Cambridge, pp 409–423
2. Appleby D, Ericsson A, Fuchs C (2011) Properties of QBist state spaces. Found Phys 41:564–579
3. Bauer H (1996) Probability theory. de Gruyter, Berlin
4. Bowman D, Kruijff E, Laviola J Jr., Poupyrev I (eds) (2004) 3D user interfaces: theory and practice. Addison-Wesley, Boston
5. Blum H (1973) Biological shape and visual science: part I. J Theor Biol 38:205–287
6. Cohen EH, Singh M (2006) Perceived orientation of complex shape reflects graded part decomposition. J Vis 6:805–821
7. Cover T, Thomas J (2006) Elements of information theory. Wiley, New York
8. De Winter J, Wagemans J (2006) Segmentation of object outlines into parts: a large-scale integrative study. Cognition 99:275–325
9. Feldman J, Singh M (2006) Bayesian estimation of the shape skeleton. Proc Natl Acad Sci 103(47):18014–18019
10. Fuchs C (2010) QBism, the perimeter of quantum Bayesianism. arXiv:1003.5209v1
11. Fuchs C, Schack R (2010) Quantum-Bayesian coherence. arXiv:0906.2187v1
12. Geisler W, Diehl R (2003) A Bayesian approach to the evolution of perceptual and cognitive systems. Cogn Sci 27:379–402
13. Geisler W, Kersten D (2002) Illusions, perception and Bayes. Nat Neurosci 5:508–510
14. Hayworth K, Biederman I (2006) Neural evidence for intermediate representations in object recognition. Vis Res 46:4024–4031
15. Hoffman D (1998) Visual intelligence: how we create what we see. Norton, New York
16. Hoffman D (2009) The interface theory of perception. In: Dickinson S, Tarr M, Leonardis A, Schiele B (eds) Object categorization: computer and human vision perspectives. Cambridge University Press, Cambridge, pp 148–165
17. Hoffman D, Singh M (2012) Computational evolutionary perception. Perception 41:1073–1091
18. Jaynes E (2003) Probability theory: the logic of science. Cambridge University Press, Cambridge
19. Kersten D, Mamassian P, Yuille A (2004) Object perception as Bayesian inference. Annu Rev Psychol 555:271–304
20. Kleffner D, Ramachandran V (1992) On the perception of shape from shading. Percept Psychophys 52:18–36
21. Koenderink J (2011) Vision and information. In: Albertazzi L, Tonder G, Vishnawath D (eds) Perception beyond inference: the information content of visual processes. Cambridge University Press, Cambridge
22. Knill D, Richards W (1996) Perception as Bayesian inference. Cambridge University Press, Cambridge
23. Laplace PS (1986) Memoir on the probability of the causes of events. Stat Sci 1:364–378. (English translation by S.M. Stigler. Original work published in 1774)
24. Maloney L, Zhang H (2010) Decision-theoretic models of perception and action. Vis Res 50:2362–2374

25. Mamassian P, Landy M, Maloney L (2002) Bayesian modeling of visual perception. In: Rao R, Olshausen B, Lewicki M (eds) Probabilistic models of the brain: perception and neural function. MIT Press, Cambridge, pp 13–36
26. Mark J, Marion B, Hoffman D (2010) Natural selection and veridical perception. J Theor Biol 266:504–515
27. Marr D (1982) Vision: a computational investigation into the human representation and processing of visual information. Freeman, San Francisco
28. Mausfeld R (2002) The physicalist trap in perception theory. In: Heyer D, Mausfeld R (eds) Perception and the physical world: psychological and philosophical issues in perception. Wiley, New York, pp 75–112
29. Palmer S (1999) Vision science. MIT Press, Cambridge
30. Pizlo Z (2001) Perception viewed as an inverse problem. Vis Res 41:3145–3161
31. Pizlo Z, Sawada T, Li Y, Kropatsch W, Steinman RM (2010) New approach to the perception of 3d shape based on veridicality, complexity, symmetry and volume. Vis Res 50:1–11
32. Revuz D (1984) Markov chains. North-Holland, Amsterdam
33. Singh M, Hoffman D (2001) Part-based representations of visual shape and implications for visual cognition. In: Shipley T, Kellman P (eds) From fragments to objects: segmentation and grouping in vision. Elsevier, New York, pp 401–459

Chapter 13
Shape as an Emergent Property

Ian H. Jermyn

13.1 Shape Inference

Changes in the properties of matter with position in space, on a scale small enough relative to our own that they can be treated as discontinuities, are ubiquitous in our world. The discontinuities define surfaces, which have geometric properties, which we call 'shape'. The omnipresence of such surfaces, and the distinctive physical properties of the matter that they surround, means that shape is frequently informative about matters of importance to us and to other biological systems, and so inferences involving shape become useful. In particular, because the reflective properties of matter often change along with the properties that define shape surfaces, measurements of light intensity, whether by retina or CCD, can be used to make inferences about shape. Image formation can be approximated in geometric terms, meaning that inferences about two-dimensional shape become relevant too.

What is required to make such inferences? To solve an inference problem, we should construct a probability distribution describing our knowledge of the unknown quantity of interest given the known information. For inferences involving shape, this will involve probability distributions $P(R|K)$, where $R \in \mathscr{R}$ is, in general, an element of a suitable set $\mathscr{R} \subset 2^{\mathscr{D}}$ of subsets of a space $\mathscr{D}$ possessing sufficient geometric structure to render the idea of shape meaningful. In any specific case, R will parameterize a set of propositions whose probabilities we wish to calculate, for example, "region R in the image domain $\mathscr{D}$ contains entity X" (where X is 'human being', 'Ian', 'road network', 'car', etc.). The quantity K denotes all the knowledge we have of the situation (or anyway all the information that we choose, or are able, to express). In particular, this will include all the information we have about the shape of R, perhaps arising from knowledge of X.

In order to make inferences involving shape, then, we need to understand how to construct distributions $P(R|K)$ for given knowledge K: that is, how to encode

I.H. Jermyn (✉)
Department of Mathematical Sciences, Durham University, Durham, UK
e-mail: i.h.jermyn@durham.ac.uk

S.J. Dickinson, Z. Pizlo (eds.), *Shape Perception in Human and Computer Vision*,
Advances in Computer Vision and Pattern Recognition,
DOI 10.1007/978-1-4471-5195-1_13, © Springer-Verlag London 2013

Fig. 13.1 An example of an element of the space of 'regions', $\mathcal{R}$, showing the complicated nature of such elements

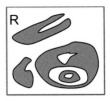

information about shape into the probability distribution. We will look at the properties probability distributions must have to be regarded as shape models, and then at how these properties have typically been implemented in machine vision. After looking at the drawbacks of this 'classical' approach, we then discuss an alternative, inspired by classes of shapes arising in certain image processing problems. In the resulting framework, shape becomes an emergent property of interactions in a network of simple nodes. It may therefore be of some biological relevance. We conclude with a discussion of this approach, and of what remains to be done to turn it into a complete shape modelling framework.

13.2 Modelling Shape

The key task, then, is to construct probability distributions $P(R|K)$ on a suitable space of shapes $\mathcal{R}$.[1] We will focus attention on a space $\mathcal{R} \subset 2^{\mathcal{D}}$, where $\mathcal{D} \subset \mathbb{R}^2$ is a relevant domain (often the support of an image), although much of the discussion applies to other spaces and other dimensions. 'Regions' $R \in \mathcal{R}$ are open sets, but we do not specify them further; we assume they possess whatever properties are needed to render the models well defined. Note that the space $\mathcal{R}$ is complicated: regions can have arbitrarily many connected components; connected components can contain holes; and these in their turn can contain connected components; and so on. Figure 13.1 shows an element of this space.

Now we need a category of mathematical objects to represent the elements of $\mathcal{R}$, a 'representation space' $\mathcal{S}$. Many such spaces have been used in the literature. Some are isomorphic to $\mathcal{R}$ (indicator functions, distance functions [16]). This seems good, but leaves the complexity of $\mathcal{R}$ intact: $\mathcal{S}$ still contains infinitely many connected components, for example. For others ('many-to-one'), there is a non-injective map from $\mathcal{R}$ to $\mathcal{S}$ (landmark points [6, 12], various Fourier descriptors [20], medial axis [2, 8]). Such representations are often low-dimensional, and can be intrinsically invariant to transformations. However, a region cannot be reconstructed from

---

[1]A continuum description of regions involves spaces of infinite dimension. The task of constructing probability measures on such spaces, once we move beyond Gaussians, is difficult, and we will not address it. The details are anyway usually irrelevant because they concern infinitely small distances; it is enough to imagine some kind of frequency cut-off imposed at a scale too fine to matter. There may be strong dependence on the scale of the cut-off unless the model parameters are made cut-off dependent, but in practice, since the parameters are determined experimentally for a known cut-off, this is of little importance.

Fig. 13.2 Predicting one part
of a boundary from another.
Left: a sample from the Ising
model, where accurate
prediction is not possible.
Right: a case where accurate
prediction is possible

its representation, and so there is no probability distribution on shapes; we do not
consider them further. Finally, there are representations ('one-to-many') for which
there is a non-injective map $\sigma : \mathscr{S} \to \mathscr{R}$ (parameterized closed curves, phase field).
The advantage is that $\mathscr{S}$ may have a much simpler structure than $\mathscr{R}$; however, we
have to think about the distribution induced on $\mathscr{R}$ by a distribution on $\mathscr{S}$:

$$P(R) = \int_{\mathscr{S}} \delta\bigl(R, \rho(S)\bigr) P(S) = \int_{\mathscr{S}_R} P(S), \qquad (13.1)$$

where $\mathscr{S}_R = \{S \in \mathscr{S} : R = \sigma(S)\}$. Often one uses a saddle point approximation: $P(R) \propto P(S_R)$, where $S_R = \arg\max_{S \in \mathscr{S}_R} \rho(S)$, with $\rho(\cdot)$ a suitable density
for $P(S)$.

Next, we have to construct probability distributions on $\mathscr{S}$ expressing shape information. Do all distributions on $\mathscr{S}$ count? The only precise answer is yes, but
this is not very useful. The standard Ising model on $\mathbb{Z}^2$ can be viewed as a probability distribution on regions in $\mathbb{R}^2$ by associating the indicator function of a square
with each vertex, but while this distribution undoubtedly contains information about
region geometry, because regions with greater boundary length have lower probability, it cannot really be called a 'shape model'. This can be seen by looking at distant
parts of the sample in Fig. 13.2: high probability regions do not have any properties
in common that we would normally call 'shape'.

Why do we say that the Ising model does not contain shape information? The
reason is that the set of high probability regions is too large, that is, the entropy is
too high. In order to reduce the entropy, we have to create more dependence in the
distribution. Indeed, it is clear that what we normally refer to as 'shape', involves
the ability to make quite precise inferences about the overall region give only partial information about its boundary. For example, most people could make a good
estimate of the part of the object boundary that is concealed in the image on the
right-hand side of Fig. 13.2, given the part that is revealed: the conditional entropy
is small. The same is not true of the left-hand side. In other words, the probability
distribution induced by our knowledge of the object's identity and behavior contains
strong, long-range dependencies between parts of the region boundary. Such dependencies, then, are key to the construction of non-trivial shape models. We now turn
to how to build probability distributions that incorporate such dependencies.

13.3 The Classical Approach

We will first look at what we will call the 'classical approach' to shape modelling. The focus here is on defining a 'dissimilarity measure' $d : \mathscr{S} \times \mathscr{S} \to \mathbb{R}_{\geq 0}$ between points in $\mathscr{S}$. Usually, although not always, this measure is metric [3, 4, 10, 14, 15, 18, 19]. Once defined, the metric can be used to define a probability distributions on $\mathscr{S}$ as a function of distance to a 'template' shape S_0. The most common form of distribution is 'pseudo-Gaussian', taking the form:

$$P(S|S_0) \propto dS \, e^{-\frac{1}{2}d^2(S,S_0)}, \tag{13.2}$$

where S_0 is the 'template', and dS is an underlying measure on $\mathscr{S}$. (Mixtures of such distributions over a set of templates have also been used [5].)

The distribution (13.2) encourages S to be close to the region S_0, but this is rarely what is required. Typically, there will be uncertainty about the position, orientation, and perhaps scale of the shape. To incorporate such uncertainty in the classical approach, one must create mixture models over these transformations. Let G be the transformation group acting on $\mathscr{S}$, with the action denoted gS. Then the distribution one is really interested in is

$$P(S|S_0) = \int_G P(S|g, S_0)P(g|S_0) \propto dS \int_G dg \, \rho(g)e^{-\frac{1}{2}d^2(S,gS_0)}, \tag{13.3}$$

with $P(g|S_0) = dg \, \rho(g)$, where dg is an invariant measure on G. Often complete invariance to G is needed. This requires dS to be G-invariant, $\rho \equiv 1$, and G to act by isometries on $\mathscr{S}$: $d^2(gS, S_0) = d^2(S, g^{-1}S_0)$. In practice, the integral in Eq. (13.3) is rarely evaluated. Rather a saddle point approximation is made in which $g^* = \arg\min_{g \in G} d^2(S, gS_0)$ is substituted, giving $P(S|S_0) \propto dS \, e^{-\frac{1}{2}d^2(S,g^*S_0)}$, that is, pose is estimated. Although easier than performing the integral, this still requires significant computational effort.

How do the long-range dependencies necessary for nontrivial shape modelling arise in the classical approach based on templates? The answer is that the template itself, or rather its parameters, such as the group elements just discussed, act as hidden variables. Once they are integrated out, they introduce long-range dependencies between boundary points. A trivial example, in one dimension, is the following. In 1-d, regions are unions of intervals; we consider only connected regions. Let the template region be an interval of length 1, with center at c. Let the probability of a region $[x, y]$ be $P(x, y|c) = \delta(x - (c - \frac{1}{2}))\delta(y - (c + \frac{1}{2}))$. Thus, given c, x and y are independent. If we now add a uniform prior on c (suppose $c, x, y \in S^1$ so this is normalized), we can integrate out c to obtain $P(x, y) = \delta(y - x - 1)$. Thus not knowing c, x and y are dependent: in this singular case, x determines y completely. In the general case, integration over a group as above, or integrations over other unknown template parameters, play exactly the same role as in this simple example, introducing the long-range dependencies that contain nontrivial shape information.

Fig. 13.3 *Left*: multiple instances of an entity ('gas of near-circles'). *Right*: a 'network' region

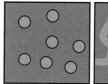

13.3.1 Drawbacks of the Classical Approach

While the classical approach to creating long-range dependencies using templates and a metric is useful and efficient in many applications, it does not apply, or is inefficient, in many important cases. In particular, the use of templates and metrics means that high probability shapes only occur 'close' to one or more points in the space of shapes. There are entities, however, for which our knowledge of their shape cannot be expressed in terms of small variations around a template shape or shapes. In particular, when the entity involved has an extent or a topology that is in some way unconstrained, the use of templates fails to allow sufficient variability.

Perhaps the most commonly occurring example is when multiple instances of an entity can be present: see Fig. 13.3 left. In this case, although each entity might be well described by a template and small variations, the whole may have any number of connected components, and hence is not amenable to a template/metric description. Although in principle this situation can be dealt with by using object point processes [13], in practice the large number of degrees of freedom per object, together with the necessity to estimate transformation group parameters for each instance, mean that such methods are very inefficient.

Another example is provided by 'network' regions: see Fig. 13.3 right. The set of network regions can be divided into topologically distinct subsets classified by the graph of which they are a fattened version. It is thus clear that such shapes cannot be described as variations around a finite number of templates.

To overcome these drawbacks, a new modelling framework is needed that allows the incorporation of strong constraints on region shape, without necessarily constraining region topology, and that provides intrinsic invariance. To achieve this, the long-range dependencies necessary for shape modelling will be encoded in the distribution in a new way. This turns out to be of interest in its own right, independently of the examples that inspired it.

13.4 Nonlocal Interactions

In this section, we will look at an alternative method for introducing the long-range dependencies needed in order to encode non-trivial shape information. Rather than using a template to introduce such dependencies, explicit nonlocal interactions between region boundary points will be introduced. These interactions generate long-range dependencies strong enough to constrain region shape, but because no template is used, they need not constrain region extent or topology. In addition, the models will be intrinsically invariant to Euclidean transformations, meaning that these transformations do not have to be estimated for each instance of an entity. Multiple instances thus become easier to handle. We first describe these models in terms of the 'contour representation', but then go on to reformulate them in terms of nonlocal interactions in networks of simple real- and binary-valued nodes.

The contour representation represents $R \in \mathscr{R}$ by its boundary ∂R, which consists of a set of oriented, closed curves. (The dark lines bounding the region in Fig. 13.1 show an example of a region boundary; the boundary orientation is not shown in the figure.) The contour representation space $\mathscr{S} = \Gamma$, is thus the space of multiple, oriented, closed curves, subject to certain constraints, to which we return later. In fact, it is often convenient to write probability distributions in terms of circle embeddings $S^1 \to \mathbb{R}^2$: making a distribution invariant to the action of $\mathrm{Diff}(S^1)$ then ensures that it is well-defined on Γ, and hence on $\mathscr{R}$.

We now introduce a class of models, expressed in the contour representation and known as 'higher-order active contours' [17], that encode nontrivial shape information via explicit nonlocal interactions.[2]

13.4.1 Higher-Order Active Contours

The simplest Euclidean invariant model one can place on Γ is

$$E_{C,0}(\partial R) = \lambda_C L(\partial R) + \alpha_C A(\partial R), \tag{13.4}$$

where L and A are region boundary length and region area respectively; and $\lambda_C, \alpha_C \in \mathbb{R}_{\geq 0}$. This model, or minor variants of it, has been much used as a region model in the literature, starting with [11]. Indeed, it is essentially the Ising model in a constant external field, expressed in the contour representation. As such, although this model contains important information about the (low-resolution) smoothness of region boundaries, it contains no real shape information. Indeed, both L and A can be expressed as single integrals over ∂R involving only tangent vectors, meaning that only 'infinitesimally nearest neighbor' points on the boundary interact: the model does not contain the long-range dependencies necessary to incorporate nontrivial shape information.

To incorporate nonlocal interactions, and hence long-range dependencies, one must move from single integrals to multiple integrals, thereby incorporating information from more than one contour point at a time. Two integrals is the simplest case: pairs of points on the boundary then interact. The idea is illustrated in Fig. 13.4. One possibility among many for such a 'higher-order active contour' energy is

$$E_{C,\mathrm{NL}}(\partial R) = -\beta_C \iint_{S^1 \times S^1} dt \, dt' \, n \cdot \mathbf{G}(\gamma, \gamma') \cdot n', \tag{13.5}$$

---

[2]We will not talk about probability distributions directly from now on, but rather about their energies E, defined, up to an additive constant, by $P(R|K) \propto \exp(-E(R|K))$.

Fig. 13.4 *Left*: the 'nearest-neighbor' interactions induced by first derivatives. *Right*: nonlocal interactions

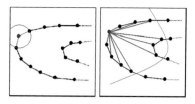

where γ is an embedding of a circle (or multiple circles, if the region has more than one connected component or is multiply-connected), whose image is ∂R; t, t' are coordinates on S^1; n indicates the un-normalized normal vector field to γ (i.e., $\dot{\gamma}$ rotated by $\pi/2$); (un)primed quantities are evaluated at $(t)t'$; and $\mathbf{G} : \mathbb{R}^2 \times \mathbb{R}^2 \rightarrow T^*\mathbb{R}^2 \boxtimes T^*\mathbb{R}^2$, where $\boxtimes$ indicates the outer tensor product, is a bitensor field. Note that it is easy to make $E_{C,\mathrm{NL}}$ intrinsically Euclidean invariant, for example by taking $\mathbf{G}(x, x') = \Psi(|x - x'|)\mathbb{I}$.

Summing the nonlocal term (13.5) with Eq. (13.4) gives an energy $E_C = E_{C,0} + E_{C,\mathrm{NL}}$ with interesting properties, documented in [9, 17]. In particular, for certain parameter ranges, calculable via stability analyses [7, 9], E_C has local minima corresponding to 'network' regions or to 'gas of near-circles' regions. Examples of such local minima of E_C, generated by gradient descent, are shown in Fig. 13.5. Network regions consist of a number of branches joining together at junctions, and can be thought of an 'fattened embedded graphs', as in Fig. 13.3. 'Gas of near-circles' regions consist of any number of connected components, each of which has infinitely many degrees of freedom, but which with high probability is 'close' to being a circle of a given radius. Note that 'gas of near-circles' regions represent multiple instances of a shape, with different interaction functions Ψ favoring different perturbations of the circle, and hence different shapes. Intrinsic Euclidean invariance of E_C means that no pose estimation is required.

Higher-order active contours demonstrate that non-trivial shape information can be encoded using explicit nonlocal interactions between boundary points, and they have been used successfully in a number of image processing applications [9, 17]. Nevertheless, the contour representation in which they are expressed suffers from a number of drawbacks arising from the fact that not all sets of oriented, closed curves are boundaries: constraints are needed to prevent (self-)intersections; curve orientations, which describe 'inside' and 'outside', have to be mutually consistent; and the space Γ is not connected, having one component for each topologically distinct set of regions (connected region components, holes, nested regions, ...). These difficulties can all be alleviated by changing the shape representation. In the

Fig. 13.5 Local minima under E_C. *Left*: network regions; *right*: gas of near-circles regions

process, we will see that shape information can be encoded in terms of nonlocal interactions in a network of simple binary- or real-valued nodes.

13.4.2 Reformulation as a Network of Nodes

A region can be represented by a binary-valued function $\phi : \mathscr{D} \to \{\pm 1\}$, with $R = \zeta(\phi) = \{x \in \mathscr{D} : \phi(x) > 0\}$. It turns out to be convenient to relax this to a real-valued 'phase field' function $\phi : \mathscr{D} \to \mathbb{R}$ (we will use the same symbol) controlled by an energy that encourages it to take on the values ± 1. Perhaps the simplest such energy is the Ginzburg-Landau energy:

$$E_0 = \int_{\mathscr{D}} dx \left\{ \frac{D}{2} |\partial \phi|^2 + \lambda \left(\frac{\phi(x)^4}{4} - \frac{\phi(x)^2}{2} \right) + \alpha \left(\phi(x) - \frac{\phi(x)^3}{3} \right) \right\}, \quad (13.6)$$

where all ϕ are evaluated at x. The ultralocal part of the integrand has minima at ± 1. This means that if $D = 0$, $\phi_R = \arg\min_{\phi: \zeta(\phi)=R} E_0(\phi)$ will take the value $+1$ inside, and -1 outside R, that is, will be binary. It is then easy to see that $E(\phi_R) = \frac{2}{3}\alpha A(R)$ up to an additive constant. Nonzero D has the effect of smoothing the discontinuity, and also measures the boundary length. Indeed it can be shown that

$$E_0(\phi_R) \simeq \lambda_C L(R) + \alpha_C A(R), \quad (13.7)$$

where λ_C and α_C are functions of λ, α, and D. The energy E_0 is thus $E_{C,0}$ reformulated in terms of the phase field representation.

It is now natural to ask whether it is possible to create a phase field energy that is equivalent to $E_C = E_{C,0} + E_{C,\mathrm{NL}}$. This is indeed the case. The equivalent of the nonlocal energy $E_{C,\mathrm{NL}}$ in Eq. (13.5) is

$$E_{\mathrm{NL}}(\phi) = -\frac{\beta}{2} \iint_{\mathscr{D}^2} dx \, dx' \, \partial \phi(x) \cdot \mathbf{G}(x, x') \cdot \partial \phi(x'). \quad (13.8)$$

It can then be shown that

$$E(\phi_R) = E_0(\phi_R) + E_{\mathrm{NL}}(\phi_R) \simeq E_{C,0}(R) + F_{C,\mathrm{NL}}(R) = E_C(R). \quad (13.9)$$

The phase field representation $\mathscr{S} = \Phi$ is a one-to-many representation. Equation (13.9) shows that in a saddle-point approximation to Eq. (13.1), the phase field model E is equivalent to the contour model E_C. (The same is true in the Gaussian approximation also.) In particular, for different parameter ranges, the phase field model has local energy minima corresponding to networks and a gas of near-circles; the ranges can be found by translating the results of the stability analyses performed in the contour representation to the phase field representation, and are well verified numerically. This is useful because the phase field representation turns out to have multiple advantages. First, unlike the contour representation, there are no difficult constraints to implement: ϕ lives in a linear space Φ. Second, regions of arbitrary

Fig. 13.6 Diagram of the
network interactions in the
spatially-discretized phase
field model

topological complexity are all represented in a single, connected space, so that no
special methods are needed to deal with multiple connected components, handles,
etc. Coupled with the intrinsic Euclidean invariance of the energy, this means that
multiple instances of an entity are modeled at essentially no extra cost. Third, in the
contour representation, γ appears as an argument to $\mathbf{G}$, which makes the nonlocal
term complicated. In the phase field representation, the nonlocal term is quadratic,
and when translation invariant, is diagonal in the Fourier basis. This greatly simpli-
fies any computations involving it.

The continuum form of the phase field energy is easy to manipulate, but computations, whether in a machine or biological visual system, will inevitably involve discretization of some sort. If we spatially discretize Eq. (13.6), the result is a Markov
random field ψ, consisting of a set of real-valued nodes, interacting (see Fig. 13.6):
with themselves via the potential (red); with their nearest neighbors via the derivative term (green); and also with the large number of nodes that lie within the support
of the nonlocal interaction (blue). We thus see that nontrivial shape information can
be encoded as nonlocal interactions in a network of real-valued nodes.

We can simplify things even further, at the cost of losing some geometric accuracy, as follows. On most of its domain, the phase field takes values very close to the
set $\{-1, 1\}$. This suggests replacing ψ by a field taking values *only* in the set $\{-1, 1\}$,
that is, by a binary-valued Markov random field ω. By definition, the distribution for
ω is given in terms of that for ψ by $P(\omega) = \int_{\psi} P(\omega|\psi) P(\psi)$. Binarization means
that $P(\omega|\psi) = \delta(\omega, \text{sgn}(\psi))$. In the saddle point approximation, the energy U of
the binarized field is given by $U(\omega) = E(\psi_{\omega})$, where $\psi_{\omega} = \arg\min_{\psi:\,\text{sgn}\,\psi=\omega} E(\psi)$.
Computing ψ_{ω} is a difficult task in itself. A crude but practically effective approxi-
mation gives rise to the energy [1]:

$$U(\omega) = \frac{D_b}{2} \sum_{i,j:\,i\sim j} (\omega_i - \omega_j)^2 + \alpha_b \sum_i \omega_i + \frac{\beta_b}{2} \sum_{i,j} \omega_i F_{ij} \omega_j, \qquad (13.10)$$

where $\alpha_b = \frac{2\alpha}{3}$, $\beta_b = \beta$, $D_b = \frac{D}{4}$, and F is related to $\partial^2 \mathbf{G}$. Gibbs sampling from this
distribution, with appropriate temperature and parameter ranges (again derived from
stability analyses performed in the contour representation) shows convergence to gas
of near-circles or network regions. These then fluctuate, but remain stable, under
further sampling. As with the other two representations, the probability distribution
can have local maxima at these shape families. Thus, the same nontrivial shape
information can be encoded as nonlocal interactions in a network of binary nodes.

13.4.3 Nonlocality via Local Interactions

Nonlocal interactions have so far been introduced explicitly. However, explicit non-locality may not be plausible in some contexts, for example the biological, so it is important to note that nonlocality can arise from purely local energies. We introduce a vector field $v : \mathbb{R}^2 \to \mathbb{R}^2$, and define a joint distribution with Gibbs energy

$$\hat{E}(\phi, v) = E_0(\phi) + a\langle v|\partial\phi\rangle + \frac{1}{2}\langle v|F|v\rangle, \qquad (13.11)$$

where $\langle|\rangle$ is the L^2 inner product on $\mathscr{D}$; F is a positive operator; and $a \in \mathbb{R}$. Notice that v couples to the gradient of ϕ, that is, to the boundary. At the same time v is spatially correlated (e.g., smoothed) by the interaction represented by F. It therefore induces an interaction between points on the boundary. To find this interaction, we marginalize over v. The resulting Gibbs energy is

$$\tilde{E}(\phi) = E_0(\phi) - \frac{1}{2}\beta\langle\partial\phi|F^{-1}|\partial\phi\rangle, \qquad (13.12)$$

where $\beta = a^2$. This has the same form as the nonlocal phase field energy E defined in Eqs. (13.7), (13.8), and (13.9). A similar procedure works for the binary MRF model. Thus rather than encoding shape information via nonlocal interactions, it can instead be encoded by allowing the network to have several 'layers'.

13.5 Discussion

Thus, we reach the end of the story. Shape information can be encoded via non-local interactions in a network of binary- or real-valued nodes. In turn, these non-local interactions can be re-encoded as local interactions in a network with multiple 'layers'. Control of these interactions then allows different shape families to be modeled. Shape, therefore, does not have to be described by exogenous templates, or constructed from arbitrary building blocks. Instead, it can arise naturally, as an emergent property of the connections in a network of simple nodes.

The fact that shape information is encoded as interactions in a network means that shape processing can be inherently parallel. The domain $\mathscr{D}$ can be separated into subdomains that can be processed simultaneously, with some communication overheads. Note that to search for a shape in multiple subdomains using a template would be equivalent to searching for multiple instances, requiring separate pose estimations for each subdomain.

For image processing applications, the nodes are usually generated by spatial discretization onto a square lattice, but any discretization is possible, for example, using a hexagonal lattice. The nodes need not even correspond to spatial elements: one of the strengths of the phase field representation is that it can be written in any basis, and so a discretization could be generated by imposing a frequency cut-off

Fig. 13.7 A Fourier
component, quadratically
unstable at zero but stabilized
at a finite value by quartic
behavior, added to an
otherwise stable circle

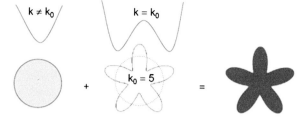

in Fourier space, or a scale cut-off in wavelet space. The local and non-local terms
(but not the potential) are diagonal in the Fourier basis, while the potential term is
diagonal in the spatial point basis. This suggests that a wavelet basis, which is intermediate between these two extremes, might simplify the interactions in the model.
This would also have the advantage of providing a naturally multiscale representation of shape.

Despite all its promising aspects, however, the framework cannot yet be called a
complete shape modelling method. Only simple shapes have been modeled so far,
and the natural question is whether one can model more complex shapes.

One possible direction is suggested by observations in numerical experiments.
Shapes have been seen that were neither circles nor bars, but instead were star-
shaped: circles plus a sinusoidal perturbation of their radius. These appeared to be
stable. While it is possible that this was an artefact of the numerical method, it is also
possible that the chosen parameter values produced a new type of local minimum.
A simple explanation is as follows. To second order in a small perturbation of a circle, only two behaviors are possible for each Fourier component of the perturbation:
stable or unstable, corresponding to positive or negative second-order coefficient
in the expansion. To fourth order, however, more complex behaviors can occur. In
particular, if the second-order coefficient is negative but the fourth-order coefficient
is positive, then although the zero amplitude state is unstable, there will be some
finite amplitude that *is* stable. Now imagine that all Fourier components are stable quadratically except for one, which is unstable quadratically but stabilized by a
fourth-order term. The circle itself is now a saddle-point of the energy, while a circle
perturbed by a sinusoid of the correct frequency and amplitude is a local minimum.
This is illustrated in Fig. 13.7.

This picture suggests that by adjusting the interaction function of the model, one
might be able to assign different stable amplitudes to each Fourier component. Were
this possible, it would be mean that any star domain could be modeled.

An alternative approach to the modelling of more complex shapes involves the
introduction of higher-order interactions. There are two issues with such interactions. The first is learning the interactions necessary to model a given family of
shapes. In order for an energy to model such a family, it should have local minima
at the appropriate points in $\mathscr{R}$, and this involves difficult analysis. It could perhaps
be achieved using standard statistical estimation techniques verified a posteriori for
local minimality, or by placing constraints on the parameters during estimation. The
first seems wasteful, while the second is complex, and its theoretical basis is not

clear. The second issue is algorithmic complexity. Simply evaluating higher-order terms is expensive, and although there are algorithms available for certain types of higher-order term in the binary MRF case, it is not likely that they would apply to the types of term needed. Nevertheless, some promising progress is being made in these areas, and there is good reason to hope that the picture of shape as an emergent property of interactions between network nodes can be fully realized.

Acknowledgements Most of the work described herein was carried out while the author was working in the Ariana group at INRIA. Many people contributed, and continue to contribute to this work. The author would like to acknowledge and thank: J. Zerubia, Z. Kato, M. Rochery, P. Horváth, A. El Ghoul, T. Blaskovics, J. Nemeth, C. Molnar, and I. Bechar.

References

1. Blaskovics T, Kato Z, Jermyn IH (2009) A Markov random field model for extracting near-circular shapes. In: Proc IEEE international conference on image processing (ICIP), Cairo, Egypt, November 2009
2. Blum H (1973) Biological shape and visual science. J Theor Biol 38:20–287
3. Bronstein A, Bronstein M, Kimmel R (2006) Efficient computation of isometry-invariant distances between surfaces. SIAM J Sci Comput 28(5):1812–1836
4. Cremers D, Soatto S (2003) A pseudo-distance for shape priors in level set segmentation. In: Paragios N (ed) Proc IEEE workshop variational, geometric and level set methods in computer vision, Nice, France, October 2003, pp 169–176
5. Cremers D, Osher SJ, Soatto S (2006) Kernel density estimation and intrinsic alignment for shape priors in level set segmentation. Int J Comput Vis 69(3):335–351
6. Dryden IL, Mardia KV (1998) Statistical shape analysis. Wiley series in probability and statistics: probability and statistics. Wiley, New York. ISBN 9780471958161
7. El Ghoul A, Jermyn IH, Zerubia J (2008) Phase diagram of a long bar under a higher-order active contour energy: application to hydrographic network extraction from VHR satellite images. In: Proc international conference on pattern recognition (ICPR), Tampa, Florida, December 2008
8. Geiger D, Liu T-L, Kohn RV (2003) Representation and self-similarity of shapes. IEEE Trans Pattern Anal Mach Intell 25(1):86–99
9. Horvath P, Jermyn IH, Kato Z, Zerubia J (2009) A higher-order active contour model of a 'gas of circles' and its application to tree crown extraction. Pattern Recognit 42(5):699–709
10. Joshi SH, Klassen E, Liu W, Jermyn IH, Srivastava A (2011) Shape analysis of elastic curves in Euclidean spaces. IEEE Trans Pattern Anal Mach Intell 33(7):1415–1428
11. Kass M, Witkin A, Terzopoulos D (1988) Snakes: active contour models. Int J Comput Vis 1(4):321–331
12. Kendall DG (1984) Shape manifolds, procrustean metrics, and complex projective spaces. Bull Lond Math Soc 16:81–121
13. Kulikova MS, Jermyn IH, Descombes X, Zhizhina E, Zerubia J (2011) A marked point process model including strong prior shape information applied to multiple object extraction from images. Int J Comput Vis Image Process 1(2):1–12
14. Leventon ME, Grimson WEL, Faugeras O (2000) Statistical shape influence in geodesic active contours. In: Proc IEEE computer vision and pattern recognition (CVPR), vol 1, Hilton Head Island, South Carolina, USA, June 2000, pp 316–322
15. Michor PW, Mumford D, Shah J, Younes L (2008) A metric on shape space with explicit geodesics. Rend Lincei, Mat Appl 9:25–57
16. Osher S, Sethian JA (1988) Fronts propagating with curvature dependent speed: algorithms based on Hamilton-Jacobi formulations. J Comput Phys 79(1):12–49

17. Rochery M, Jermyn IH, Zerubia J (2006) Higher-order active contours. Int J Comput Vis 69(1):27–42
18. Srivastava A, Joshi S, Mio W, Liu X (2005) Statistical shape analysis: clustering, learning, and testing. IEEE Trans Pattern Anal Mach Intell 27(4):590–602
19. van Kaick O, Zhang H, Hamarneh G, Cohen-Or D (2011) A survey on shape correspondence. Comput Graph Forum 30(6):1681–1707. ISSN 1467-8659
20. Zahn CT, Roskies RZ (1972) Fourier descriptors for plane close curves. IEEE Trans Comput, C 21(3):269–281

Chapter 14
Representing 3D Shape and Location

Andrew Glennerster

14.1 A Primal Sketch That Survives Eye Rotation

Many of the chapters in this book are concerned with 2D shape whereas this chapter discusses the representation of 3D shape. However, I will argue that there is a strong link between these. 3D shape may be better understood in terms of the 2D image changes that occur when an observer moves than 3D ego-centered or world-centered coordinates frames. The same applies to representations of 3D location. 3D shape and 3D location are properties that remain the same as an observer moves through a static world, despite rapidly changing images. Two different conceptions for visual stability emerge. One relies on generating a representation that is like the world and is stable in the face of observer movements. The other relies only on an ability to predict the sensory consequences of a movement. The implications for representation of 3D shape (and location) are quite different under these two frameworks.

Most of the literature on visual stability focuses on a situation that is relatively straightforward from a computational perspective, namely that of a camera (or the eye) rotating around its optic center [3–7]. In this case, all the light rays we wish to consider arrive at a single optic center from all possible directions (a panoramic view, what Gibson called the 'optic array' at a single point). In computer vision, the process of 'mosaicing' a set of such images is now standard [8, 9]. In principle, it requires only that the rays corresponding to each pixel in each image to be registered in a common 2D coordinate frame, or sphere, of visual directions from the optic center. Nevertheless, this is a sensible starting point for considering visual stability in general. If points in the scene are all very distant (take, as an extreme example, the stars at night), the optic array remains unchanged wherever you move. If these points are stable in the representation, we have a sound foundation for explaining visual stability in general.

A. Glennerster (✉)
School of Psychology and Clinical Language Sciences, University of Reading,
Reading RG6 6AL, UK
e-mail: a.glennerster@reading.ac.uk

S.J. Dickinson, Z. Pizlo (eds.), *Shape Perception in Human and Computer Vision*,
Advances in Computer Vision and Pattern Recognition,
DOI 10.1007/978-1-4471-5195-1_14, © Springer-Verlag London 2013

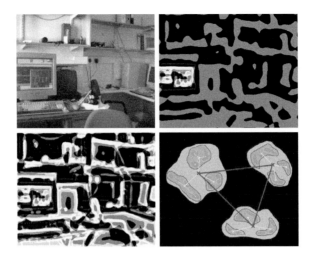

Fig. 14.1 Hierarchical encoding of position. An image (*top left*) is bandpass-filtered to show regions that are darker than the local mean luminance, including finer scale features in one part of the image, such as the fovea (*top right* image) or across the whole scene, e.g., after many saccades (*bottom left*). Because the combination of filter outputs follows the MIRAGE algorithm [1], there is a natural hierarchical encoding of position as shown schematically in the *bottom right* image (see also Fig. 14.3)

We are now in a position to consider translation of the optic center, either for a moving observer or the case of binocular vision. Translation of the optic center causes a change in the optic array. Two aspects of this change can be examined separately: first, the image change generated by a small patch in the scene and, second, the changes in the relative visual direction of objects that are separated by wide visual angles. The first is relevant for the representation of 3D surface shape; the second is relevant for encoding object location.

14.2 Translation of the Optic Center

14.2.1 Representing Surface Slant and Depth Relief

When viewing a small surface patch, the rays reaching the eye can be considered to be parallel (orthographic projection). This means that the ways the image of the surface deforms when the optic center translates are relatively simple. For example, the component of eye translation along the line of sight causes expansion (or contraction) while the orthogonal component causes 1D shear or stretch. The *axis* of the shear/stretch depends on the tilt of the surface, corresponding to the intersection of the plane perpendicular to the line of sight with the plane of the surface. The *direction* of the shear/stretch depends on the direction of the observer translation. The *magnitude* of the shear/stretch is influenced by the slant of the surface away from

Fig. 14.2 A representation of visual direction. (**a**) An eye that rotates about its optic center (which is an approximation to the truth in most cases) provides information about the relative visual direction of objects. Fixating different objects provides different sets of relative visual directions (e.g., *blue and red arcs*) which can be combined across the entire sphere to provide a single, stable representation of relative visual directions. (**b**) An illustration of forming this type of representation from images taken using a camera that rotates about its optic center, including the same image and primitives as used in Fig. 14.1. Features *J* and *n* appear in two of the images allowing them to be registered with the correct orientation (adapted, with permission, from Glennerster et al. [2])

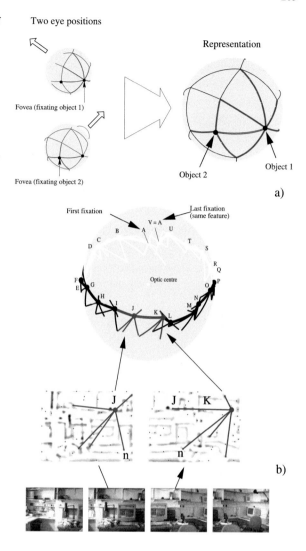

fronto-parallel. Figure 14.3 shows one 'patch' or blob that has been stretched as a result of observer translation. It also shows how a hierarchical encoding of spatial location could help to implement a method of recording image changes. Koenderink and van Doorn [10] have proposed that surface structure could be represented using an image-based coordinate frame that would not require the generation of a 3D object-based representation. Because the three basis vectors of the frame are image based, the coordinates of all points on a rigid object remain unaffected by changes in viewpoint, rather like the coordinates of points on a deformable rubber sheet. A similar approach can be applied to the deformation of the blob shown in Fig. 14.3. The centroids of the blobs at each scale are recorded in relation to the centroid of the

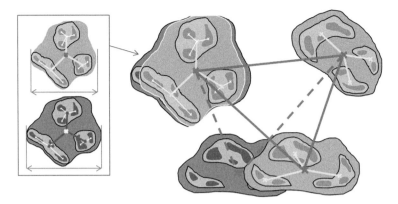

Fig. 14.3 Consequences of translating the optic center. The 'blobs' shown in Fig. 14.1 are repeated here with, in *grey*, the changes that would be caused by a movement of the observer or a change from the left to right eye's view. The lower blob has shifted to the *left* without any change in width, size or the configuration of the finer scale blobs within it. This is compatible with the surface being fronto-parallel and at a different depth from the other blobs. The centroid location of the *top left blob* has not changed so it is at the same depth as the *top right blob*. However, the width of the blob has changed, compatible with these features being on a slanted surface. The *inset* shows that in this case all the relative visual directions of the features (*yellow and white lines*) have changed together, as if drawn on a rubber sheet. These features all lie in the same slanted plane

blob at a larger scale. If the coordinate frame for measuring these relative positions is inherited from the scale above, that is, the distance metric is not measured in minutes of arc at the eye but relative to the width and height of the blob at the next coarsest scale, this would lead to a representation of location with similar properties to those advocated by Koenderink and van Doorn [10]. Shear, stretch or expansion of an image region caused by moving laterally or closer to a planar surface patch (as shown in Fig. 14.3) would yield no change in the relative position of the finer scale features if positions are measured in this locally-defined, hierarchical coordinate frame. Similarly, any depth relief of points relative to the surface plane would give rise to a change in hierarchical position when the viewpoint changes but this would be independent of the slant of the surface and signal only the relief relative to the surface [11, 12].

One difference between this hierarchical scale-based scheme and that of Koenderink and van Doorn [10] concerns the basis vectors used. In Koenderink and van Doorn's scheme, provided that the points defining the three basis vectors are not co-planar, the coordinate of every point on a rigid object is recorded using the same basis vectors. But in the hierarchical system illustrated in Fig. 14.3, the coordinate frame is local and scale-based. This means that the representation amounts to something like a set of planar patches at each scale, each patch having a location, depth, tilt and slant defined relative to the 'parent' patch at the scale above. With this proviso, the scale-based hierarchy is very similar to the object-based representation Koenderink and van Doorn proposed and has the advantage of avoiding an explicit 3D coordinate frame.

A series of psychophysical studies support the hypothesis that the visual system may use a surface-based coding system of this sort. Mainly, these studies have investigated the processing of binocular disparity but there is also some evidence from structure from motion experiments [13]. Mitchison and McKee [14] showed that binocular correspondences in an ambiguous stereogram were determined not by a nearest-neighbor rule using retinal coordinates to define proximity, as had always been supposed, but by proximity to an invisible 'interpolation' surface drawn between the edges of the patch. This is equivalent to the prediction of the hierarchical 'rubber sheet' representation outlined above, in which the metric for measuring the location of dots in the left and right eyes is determined by the shear/stretch of the patch in that eye. Like correspondence, perceived depth relief is also determined by the disparity of a point relative to a local surface even when observers are remarkably insensitive to the slant of the surface [15–17]. Finally, sensitivity to depth perturbations are determined not by the disparity of a point relative to neighboring points but instead by its disparity relative to an invisible interpolation plane [12, 18, 19], as a 'rubber sheet' model would predict.

As an aside, it is worth noting that the hierarchical encoding of blob location proposed here (following Watt and Morgan [1, 20]) brings some theoretical disadvantages but there is experimental evidence to suggest that the visual system may be prepared to pay this cost. In the coarse-to-fine stereo correspondence algorithm proposed by Marr and Poggio [21], the 'coarse scale' version of an image is always sparse, with large spacing between features (in their case, 'zero-crossings'). This means that there will always be relatively wide gaps between true and false matches along any given epipolar line and hence a nearest-neighbor rule will yield correct correspondences over a wide range of disparities. In Watt and Morgan's MIRAGE scheme, however, the 'coarse scale' representation is generated by summing the 'on' responses of filters at all spatial scales and, separately, the 'off'-responses. While this has the merit that the fine scale features *always* lie within the boundary of coarse-scale blobs, the disadvantage is that in certain situations the 'coarse scale' representation can be much more densely packed with features than the pure low frequency channel output envisaged by Marr and Poggio. Figure 14.4 shows such a situation: a dense random dot pattern with, on the right, a MIRAGE 'coarse scale' output and a schematic version to illustrate how the 'sea' between the low frequency blobs have been 'filled in'. A random dot pattern has much greater power at high frequencies than natural images and perceptually it appears far more crowded than most images. Glennerster [22] measured the ability of the visual system to find matches when random dot patterns were shifted (either in motion or by adding disparity) and showed that MIRAGE primitives predicted well the magnitude of shift that the visual system could tolerate before the perception of motion or stereo depth broke down. This price (a small D_{max} for high density patterns) appears to be an acceptable sacrifice for the visual system. The positive benefit is that fine scale features always have a simple, hierarchical 'address' to define their location.

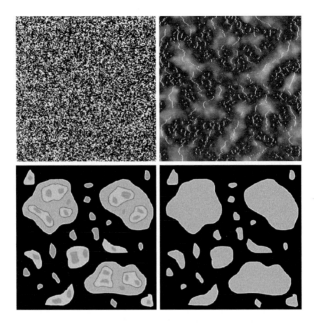

Fig. 14.4 A penalty for hierarchical encoding. If fine scale features are always to lie within the boundaries of coarse scale features, as they do in the MIRAGE algorithm [1] and illustrated in Figs. 14.1 and 14.3, then the 'coarse scale' representation must inevitably be more crowded than a low-pass version of the image. This is particularly evident in white noise images such as the random dot pattern shown here. In a $D_{\max}$ task (see text), observers behave as if their representation of this type of image is quite crowded with features, as shown on the *top right* (reproduced, with permission, from [22]). The *white dots* mark the centroids of each blob measured along horizontal raster lines. The 'coarse scale' representation is crowded, as shown schematically in the *bottom right panel*, because blobs originating from different low, medium and high spatial frequency filters all contribute to the representation (see *bottom left panel*) and 'fill in the sea' between low spatial frequency 'islands'

14.2.2 Representing Location

Having considered the effect of observer translation on a small patch of the visual field, we now turn to the consequences for widely separated features. There are strong similarities between these two scales but also important differences. In particular, disparity and motion of a small patch provide useful information about surface shape while changes in relative position of widely separated features, such those shown in Fig. 14.2a, provide information about object location.

Unlike the image changes in a small region of the visual field, the changes in relative visual direction of widely separated features do not suffer from the 'bas relief ambiguity'. This refers to the fact that a small disparity or motion can be due either to the depth relief being small or to the patch being far away. By contrast, for two widely separated features, if the angle separating them does not change when the observer moves (or there is no change between the left and right eye's view) then, in general, the points are distant: the bas relief ambiguity has disappeared (discussed in detail by Glennerster et al. [2]). The tendency for the relative visual direction of two features to change as the observer moves gives useful information about whether those features belong to near or distant objects. The most distant points in a scene form a set whose relative visual directions (the angles separating each pair and triple of points) are the most stable when the observer translates. Against the background of these distant objects, nearer objects 'slide around' as the observer moves [8]. One could turn this around and propose, in Gibsonian fashion, that an observer moves themselves from one place to another by 'grabbing' an object (visually, by fixating it) and 'pushing it' one way or another against the background (by walking, say) until it is in the desired place relative to the background.

The advantage of this representation is that the 3D origin of the coordinate frame is never defined. This makes sense. If you are star-gazing and see only stars, their relative visual directions do not change as you move and hence they provide no information about where you are on earth. The location of the 3D origin is impossible to define. Distant mountains allow your location to be defined more precisely, nearby trees even more so. The closer the objects in view, the more it becomes possible to pinpoint the location of the origin. Only with near objects in view would it make sense to distinguish between the origin of a coordinate system being at the eye, head, body or hand. If, however, the goal is not to build a 3D coordinate frame at all but instead to build an image-based representation, then the stars, the mountains, trees and very near objects provide a hierarchical method of locating the current image in that representation. These ideas are discussed in detail by Glennerster, Hansard and Fitzgibbon [2, 23].

In summary, both 3D shape and 3D location can be considered as properties derived from the changes in relative visual direction of features produced by observer translation. The way that each of these are encoded in the visual system should leave traces when we test psychophysical performance, as we have discussed. Two further examples are described in the final section (Sect. 14.4).

14.3 Implementation of a Universal Primal Sketch

There is no pretence that the suggestions raised in this chapter are anything like a recipe for implementation, but they do provide some useful pointers. The case of a camera rotating around its center is an exception. In that case, a solution was described by Watt 25 years ago [1, 24], with the location (visual direction) of features defined hierarchically across scale space for the entire optic array. But once the optic center of the camera or observer translates, practical issues emerge that are considerably more tricky.

One example is the matching process that must link data structures describing the same surface seen from different view points. For example, if a surface is viewed from two distances, the spatial frequency of the filters responding to features on the surface will be higher for the farther viewing distance but if scales, like positions, are defined relative to one another, then the data structure recording fine scale features and a coarse scale outline of the object might be relatively unchanged by this alteration in viewing distance. Relative measures are likely to be a prominent aspect of the primal sketch. Of course, in the real world, with real images, complex changes occur with changes in viewpoint due to cast shadows, occlusions and specularities. The suggestions made in this chapter provide no quick fix for these problems.

It is also worth questioning the extent to which a view-based representation could underlie *all* visual tasks, not just the ones described here. One particularly problematic class of tasks involves imagining you are at a different location and making responses as if you were there. In a familiar environment, the observer may have visited that location in the past, in which case it is possible that an observer could 'run the tape' instead of actually walking to the new location and solve the task that way. But people are able to imagine being on the other side of a room that they have never seen before and to make judgements as if from that location. In our lab, we are currently exploring ways to model behaviors of this type using view-based methods, without relying on the assumption that the brain generates a Cartesian representation of the scene. In general, it is not yet clear what the limits will be to the set of tasks that could be carried out using a primal sketch or view-based framework.

14.4 Apparent Paradoxes in the Representation of 3D Shape and Location

The primal sketch outlined in this chapter is a source of 'raw' visual information that could be used for many different tasks. We discuss here two experiments that show how participants' performance appears paradoxical if we assume the visual system uses a 3D representation but both experiments are readily explained if we suppose that the visual system extracts 'raw' visual information once the task is defined [25]. In one case, the task is a judgement of object shape and in the other it is a judgement of object location.

Figure 14.5 illustrates the shape task. We know that under rich-cue conditions, people show good size constancy and good depth constancy when they compare the size or depths of similar objects across different distances [26, 27] but exhibit large biases when asked to make a judgement of the metric shape of a surface such as comparing the depth to the half-height of a horizontal cylinder [27–29]. In the case shown in Fig. 14.5, the visual system must apparently estimate four values, namely the depths and half-heights of two semi-cylinders presented at two distances: d_1, h_1 and d_2, h_2. If these values were all available to the visual system, independent of the task the participant was set, then it would not be possible for participants to judge $d_1 \approx d_2$, $h_1 \approx h_2$ and yet, under the same viewing conditions, $d_1 > h_1$, $d_2 < h_2$ (i.e. d_1 judged as reliably larger than h_1 but d_2 judged to be reliably smaller that h_2). Yet, this is what observers see. If they built a single consistent representation of the scene and accessed the values d_1, h_1, d_2 and h_2 from this representation for all tasks, then the data would present a paradox. However, comparisons of height (h_1 versus h_2) can be done with other short-cuts, such as comparing the retinal size of test objects to other objects in the scene and the same is true of the comparisons of

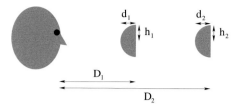

Fig. 14.5 Paradoxical representations of shape. Observers are good at size constancy ($h_1 = h_2$) and depth constancy ($d_1 = d_2$) but, under essentially identical viewing conditions, they make systematic errors when judging the shape of objects ($d_1 > h_1$ while at the same time $d_2 < h_2$). The solution to the apparent paradox is to assume that in each case, once the task is defined, the visual system acquires the relevant information and computes the solution. One task depends on an estimate of viewing distance (e.g., D_1) while the other requires only an estimate of the ratio of viewing distances to the two objects (D_1/D_2) [27]

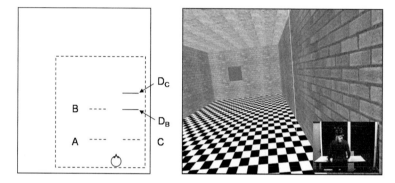

Fig. 14.6 Paradoxical representation of location. In virtual reality, observers judged the relative depth of two squares presented in separate intervals. Sometimes the room expanded between intervals (A to B and C to D), although the participants never noticed a change in room size [30]. On the other trials, the room stayed still (small room: A to C or large room B to D). It is impossible to determine a single location of D relative to A that is compatible with all the pairwise settings observers make. However, similar to Fig. 14.5, there is no paradox if the visual system acquires the relevant information for any given comparison once the task is defined

depths. By contrast, comparing d_1 to h_1 or d_2 to h_2 requires an estimate of absolute (not relative) viewing distance which means that these estimates are open to a source of bias that does not affect the other judgements [27]. The important point is that these data provide compelling evidence that the visual system uses information in a more 'raw' form than the metric values d_1, h_1, d_2 and h_2 when carrying out these judgements of 3D shape.

For 3D location, a good example of an apparent paradox is the case illustrated in Fig. 14.6 from Svarverud et al. [30]. Several experiments using immersive virtual reality have shown that moving observers fail to see a room changing in size around them, by as much as a factor of four in all directions, provided that looming cues are eliminated [31–33]. This is compatible with earlier evidence on observers' poor sensitivity to change in disparity in the absence of looming cues [34] and raises interesting questions about the type of representation that observers must be building of the scene. Svarverud et al. [30] measured subject's biases when they judged the relative depth of objects either with or without an expansion of the room between the presentation of the two objects. Observers did not notice any difference between these two types of trial. As Fig. 14.6 illustrates, although their perception of the room was stable throughout, their pairwise depth matches cannot be explained by a single, consistent 3D representation. There is, therefore, no one-to-one mapping between a participant's internal representation of the room and a single static 3D room. It does not matter that the stimulus is an unusual one. The point is that the observer's perception is one of an ordinary, stable room so the conclusions we draw from probing the representation underlying that perception should apply to other ordinary, stable scenes.

These examples raise questions about what the minimum requirements are for a useful representation of the scene. It is no use claiming, as Gibson often appeared to [35], that an internal representation is unnecessary. More recent accounts emphasise the importance of information stored 'out in the world' rather than in the head [25], but these still require a coherent set of rules that will allow the information 'out there' to be accessed. The stored information must remain useful even if the object or visual information is not within the current field of view. This chapter outlines a possible primal sketch of blob location that is an example of a representation of 'raw' visual information. Something like this might, with further elaboration, fulfil the criteria for a store that could be used to access information 'out there'. Such a representation must store sufficient information to allow the observer to turn their gaze to any object they remember and, if necessary, walk in the right direction until the object comes into view. It must also contain information about the slant of surfaces and the depth relief of points compared to local surfaces. These requirements fall short of the attributes of a full 3D reconstruction, but psychophysical evidence suggests the same is true of human vision.

Acknowledgement   Supported by the Wellcome Trust.

References

1. Watt RJ (1987) Scanning from coarse to fine spatial scales in the human visual system after the onset of a stimulus. J Opt Soc Am A 4:2006–2021
2. Glennerster A, Hansard ME, Fitzgibbon AW (2001) Fixation could simplify, not complicate, the interpretation of retinal flow. Vis Res 41:815–834
3. Duhamel JR, Colby CL, Goldberg ME (1992) The updating of the representation of visual space in parietal cortex by intended eye-movements. Science 255:90–92
4. Zipser D, Andersen RA (1988) A back-propagation programmed network that simulates response properties of a subset of posterior parietal neurons. Nature 331:679–684
5. Bridgeman B, van der Heijden AHC, Velichovsky BM (1994) A theory of visual stability across saccadic eye movements. Behav Brain Sci 17:247–292

6. Melcher D (2007) Predictive remapping of visual features precedes saccadic eye movements. Nat Neurosci 10(7):903–907
7. Burr DC, Morrone MC (2011) Spatiotopic coding and remapping in humans. Philos Trans R Soc Lond B, Biol Sci 366(1564):504–515
8. Irani M, Anandan P (1998) Video indexing based on mosaic representation. Proc IEEE 86:905–921
9. Brown M, Lowe DG (2007) Automatic panoramic image stitching using invariant features. Int J Comput Vis 74(1):59–73
10. Koenderink JJ, van Doorn AJ (1991) Affine structure from motion. J Opt Soc Am A 8:377–385
11. Mitchison G (1988) Planarity and segmentation in stereoscopic matching. Perception 17(6):753–782
12. Glennerster A, McKee SP (2004) Sensitivity to depth relief on slanted surfaces. J Vis 4:378–387
13. Hogervorst MA, Glennerster A, Eagle RA (2003) Pooling speed information in complex tasks: estimation of average speed and detection of non-planarity. J Vis 3:464–485
14. Mitchison GJ, McKee SP (1987) The resolution of ambiguous stereoscopic matches by interpolation. Vis Res 27:285–294
15. Mitchison GJ, McKee SP (1990) Mechanisms underlying the anisotropy of stereoscopic tilt perception. Vis Res 30:1781–1791
16. Cagenello R, Rogers BJ (1993) Anisotropies in the perception of stereoscopic surfaces—the role of orientation disparity. Vis Res 33:2189–2201
17. Bradshaw MF, Rogers BJ (1999) Sensitivity to horizontal and vertical corrugations defined by binocular disparity. Vis Res 39:3049–3056
18. Glennerster A, McKee SP, Birch MD (2002) Evidence of surface-based processing of binocular disparity. Curr Biol 12:825–828
19. Petrov Y, Glennerster A (2004) The role of a local reference in stereoscopic detection of depth relief. Vis Res 44:367–376
20. Watt R, Morgan M (1983) Mechanisms responsible for the assessment of visual location: theory and evidence. Vis Res 23:97–109
21. Marr D, Poggio T (1979) A computational theory of human stereo vision. Proc R Soc Lond B, Biol Sci 204:301–328
22. Glennerster A (1998) $D_{\max}$ for stereopsis and motion in random dot displays. Vis Res 38:925–935
23. Glennerster A, Hansard ME, Fitzgibbon AW (2009) View-based approaches to spatial representation in human vision. Lect Notes Comput Sci 5064:193–208
24. Watt RJ (1988) Visual processing: computational, psychophysical and cognitive research. Erlbaum, Hove
25. O'Regan JK, Noë A (2001) A sensori-motor account of vision and visual consciousness. Behav Brain Sci 24:939–1031
26. Burbeck CA (1987) Position and spatial frequency in large scale localisation judgements. Vis Res 27:417–427
27. Glennerster A, Rogers BJ, Bradshaw MF (1996) Stereoscopic depth constancy depends on the subject's task. Vis Res 36:3441–3456
28. Johnston EB (1991) Systematic distortions of shape from stereopsis. Vis Res 31:1351–1360
29. Tittle JS, Todd JT, Perotti VJ, Norman JF (1995) A hierarchical analysis of alternative representations in the perception of 3-d structure from motion and stereopsis. J Exp Psychol Hum Percept Perform 21:663–678
30. Svarverud E, Gilson S, Glennerster A (2012) A demonstration of 'broken' visual space. PLoS ONE 7:e33782. doi:10.1371/journal.pone.0033782
31. Glennerster A, Tcheang L, Gilson SJ, Fitzgibbon AW, Parker AJ (2006) Humans ignore motion and stereo cues in favour of a fictional stable world. Curr Biol 16:428–443
32. Rauschecker AM, Solomon SG, Glennerster A (2006) Stereo and motion parallax cues in human 3d vision: can they vanish without trace? J Vis 6:1471–1485

33. Svarverud E, Gilson SJ, Glennerster A (2010) Cue combination for 3d location judgements. J Vis 10:1–13. doi:10.1167/10.1.5
34. Erkelens CJ, Collewijn H (1985) Motion perception during dichoptic viewing of moving random-dot stereograms. Vis Res 25:583–588
35. Gibson JJ (1950) The perception of the visual world. Houghton Mifflin, Boston

Chapter 15
Joint Registration and Shape Analysis of Curves and Surfaces

Jingyong Su, Sebastian Kurtek, and Anuj Srivastava

15.1 Introduction

There are several meanings of the word *shape*. Although the use of words *shape* or *shape analysis* is very common in computer vision, its definition is seldom made precise in a mathematical sense. According to the Oxford English Dictionary, it means "the external form or appearance of someone or something as produced by their outline". Kendall [8] described shape as a mathematical property that remains unchanged under certain transformations such as rotation, translation, and global scaling. Shape analysis seeks to represent shapes as mathematical quantities, such as vectors or functions, that can be manipulated using appropriate rules and metrics. *Statistical* shape analysis is concerned with quantifying shape as a random quantity and developing tools for generating shape registrations, comparisons, averages, probability models, hypothesis tests, Bayesian estimates, and other statistical procedures on shape spaces.

Shape is an important physical property of objects that characterizes their appearances, and can play an important role in their detection, tracking, and recognition in images and videos. A significant part has been restricted to "landmark-based" analysis, where shapes are represented by a coarse, discrete sampling of the object contours [1, 16]. This approach is limited in that automatic detection of landmarks is not straightforward, and the ensuing shape analysis depends heavily on the choice of landmarks. One usually restricts to the boundaries of objects, rather than the whole objects, for shape analysis and that leads to a shape analysis of curves (for 2D images) and surfaces (for 3D images). Figure 15.1 suggests that shapes of boundaries can help characterize objects present in images.

To understand the issues and challenges in shape analysis, one has to look at the imaging process since that is a major source of shape data. A picture can be taken

J. Su (✉) · S. Kurtek · A. Srivastava
Department of Statistics, Florida State University, Tallahassee, FL, USA
e-mail: jingyong@stat.fsu.edu

S.J. Dickinson, Z. Pizlo (eds.), *Shape Perception in Human and Computer Vision*,
Advances in Computer Vision and Pattern Recognition,
DOI 10.1007/978-1-4471-5195-1_15, © Springer-Verlag London 2013

Fig. 15.1 Shapes of boundary curves are useful in object characterizations

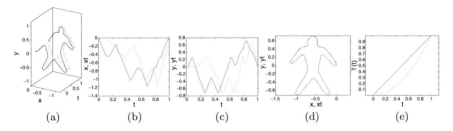

Fig. 15.2 Re-parameterized curve has different coordinate functions but same shape as the original curve. (**a**) curves $(t, \beta_x(t), \beta_y(t))$ and $(t, \tilde{\beta}_x(t), \tilde{\beta}_y(t))$; (**b**) $\beta_x(t)$ and $\tilde{\beta}_x(t)$; (**c**): $\beta_y(t)$ and $\tilde{\beta}_y(t)$; (**d**): curves $(\beta_x(t), \beta_y(t))$ and $(\tilde{\beta}_x(t), \tilde{\beta}_y(t))$; (**e**): $\gamma(t)$

from an arbitrary pose (arbitrary distance and orientation of the camera relative to the imaged object), and this introduces a random rotation, translation, and scaling of boundaries in the image plane. Therefore, any proper metric for shape analysis should be independent of the pose and scale of the boundaries. A visual inspection also confirms that any rotation, translation, or scaling of a boundary, while changing its coordinates, does not change its shape.

In case of parameterized curves and surfaces, an additional challenge arises when it comes to invariance. Let $\beta : [0, 1] \to \mathbb{R}^2$ represent a parameterized curve and let $\gamma : [0, 1] \to [0, 1]$ be a smooth, invertible function such that $\gamma(0) = 0$ and $\gamma(1) = 1$. Then, the composition $\tilde{\beta}(t) \equiv (\beta \circ \gamma)(t)$ represents a curve with coordinate functions that are different from those of $\beta(t)$ but have the same shape. $\tilde{\beta}$ is called a *re-parameterization* of β. Figure 15.2 illustrates this issue with a simple example. It shows that the coordinate functions of the re-parameterized curve, $\tilde{\beta}_x(t)$ and $\tilde{\beta}_y(t)$, as functions of t, are different from the original coordinate functions $\beta_x(t)$ and $\beta_y(t)$. But when $\tilde{\beta}_x(t)$ is plotted versus $\tilde{\beta}_y(t)$, it traces out the same sequence of points, that is, the same shape, as that traced by $\beta_x(t)$ versus $\beta_y(t)$. This results in an additional invariance requirement in shape analysis of parameterized curves (and similarly for surfaces). That is, the shape metrics should be invariant to how the curves are parameterized. Similarly, for parameterized surfaces, a change of parameterization does not change the shape of the object. Figure 15.3 shows three

Fig. 15.3 The same surface
with different
parameterizations

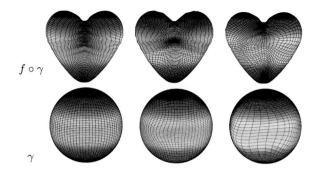

$f \circ \gamma$

γ

different parameterizations of a surface but the overall shape of the objects remains
the same. We will treat a closed surface as an embedding of unit sphere in $\mathbb{R}^3$, that
is, $f : \mathbb{S}^2 \to \mathbb{R}^3$. If γ is an arbitrary diffeomorphism of $\mathbb{S}^2$, then $f \circ \gamma$ is nothing
but a re-parameterization of the surface. We seek shape metrics and techniques for
analysis which will be invariant to the introduction of arbitrary γ in shape representations. For example, a parameterization-invariant metric between the three surfaces
shown in Fig. 15.3 should be zero.

Another important issue in comparing shapes is registration, that is, matching of
points across objects. Any shape metric requires a registration component to help
decide which point on one shape is compared to which point on the other. A registration is good when it matches points across shapes that have similar geometric
features. A majority of current techniques in shape analysis need registration as an
input or they perform registration-shape analysis in a sequential fashion. These two
steps are often performed under two different criteria. Even if one can achieve optimal solutions under the individual steps, the overall system will be suboptimal due
to these differing criteria. A better strategy is to solve the two problems simultaneously under the same objective function. This is accomplished in a Riemannian
framework by forming quotient spaces under the re-parameterization group. To un-
derstand this important idea, let us take two curves $\beta_1, \beta_2 : [0, 1] \to \mathbb{R}^n$. By default,
the point $\beta_1(t)$ is matched with the point $\beta_2(t)$, for any $t \in [0, 1]$. However, if we
re-parameterize one of the curves, say β_2 using $\beta_2 \circ \gamma$, then the registration of points
depends on γ. Thus, optimal registrations between curves and surfaces can be controlled using re-parameterizations. The key point is to find metrics that serve two
purposes: (1) form an objective function for finding optimal re-parameterizations
and (2) lead to proper parameterization-invariant metrics for comparing shapes.

There are several papers in the literature that consider the problem of registering curves [2–4, 15]. While this literature represented a major progress in that the
authors recognized the importance of curve registration, the proposed criteria for
registration had certain major limitations. We elaborate the main limitation next.
Once again consider any two curves β_1 and β_2. It is easy to show that an iden-
tical re-parameterization of β_1 and β_2 ($\beta_1 \circ \gamma, \beta_2 \circ \gamma$) does not change the correspondence. Thus, any criterion (a cost function or a metric) used for determin-
ing optimal correspondences between curves should satisfy the isometry property:
$d(\beta_1, \beta_2) = d(\beta_1 \circ \gamma, \beta_2 \circ \gamma)$. Note that under the standard $\mathbb{L}^2$ metric, we have

$\|\beta_1 - \beta_2\| \neq \|\beta_1 \circ \gamma - \beta_2 \circ \gamma\|$, in general. Most criteria used in the current literature (including [2–4, 15]) do not satisfy this fundamental property. In other words, the quantity for registration of curves is not invariant to the re-parameterization action. Many criteria, such as minimum description length, mutual information, relative entropy, etc, are not even proper metrics on representation spaces. One exception is the framework used in [19], but it only applies to curves in $\mathbb{R}^2$. In addition, isometry is needed for subsequent statistical analysis of shapes such as defining geodesic paths, distances, and summary statistics such as means and covariances.

In this paper, we summarize recent progress in using Riemannian methods for shape analysis of curves and surfaces. The advantages of these methods are as follows: (1) they allow for a joint solution to the problem of shape registration and analysis, (2) the criterion used for registration and analysis is based on an elastic Riemannian metric, (3) the analysis is fully invariant to translation, scale, rotation and re-parameterization, and (4) they allow one to define geodesic paths between shapes, sample means and covariances and other statistics on manifolds containing curves and surfaces. (These sample statistics can be further used for deriving probability models.) Furthermore, because of these desirable properties, the use of these methods in pattern recognition tasks such as shape classification and tracking significantly improves performance over existing methods. We will consider shape analysis of curves and surfaces separately in the next two sections.

15.2 Shape Analysis of Curves

Although the framework described here is valid for curves in any Euclidean space $\mathbb{R}^n$, we will focus primarily on planar closed curves. These curves originate as boundaries of imaged objects in 2D images and their shapes form an important feature in object classification and recognition. While many current techniques, such as the active shape model and Kendall's shape analysis (KSA) [1, 8] use discrete points (or landmarks) sampled from the curves for analyzing their shapes, we will work with full parameterized curves. As mentioned earlier, an important aspect of this framework is that shape distances, geodesics, and statistics should be invariant to how the curves are parameterized. For details, please refer to the papers [6, 17, 18].

Mathematical Representation   We start by describing the mathematical framework for the elastic shape analysis of curves. Let a parameterized closed curve be denoted as $\beta : \mathbb{S}^1 \to \mathbb{R}^2$. (The domain of parameterization for closed curves is naturally chosen to be $\mathbb{S}^1$ rather than an interval.) In order to analyze its shape, β is represented by its square-root velocity function (SRVF): $q(t) = \frac{\dot{\beta}(t)}{\sqrt{\|\dot{\beta}(t)\|}} \in \mathbb{R}^2$. The SRVF q includes both the instantaneous speed and the direction of the curve β at time t. The use of the time derivative makes the SRVF invariant to any translation of curve β. In order for the shape analysis to be invariant to scale, one can rescale each curve to be unit length. The set of all unit length, closed curves in $\mathbb{R}^2$, represented by their SRVFs, is called the *preshape space* $\mathcal{C}$. If q is the SRVF of a curve β, then the

SRVF of $\beta \circ \gamma$ is $(q, \gamma) = (q \circ \gamma)\sqrt{\dot{\gamma}}$. An important property of SRVFs is that for any two curves, the corresponding SRVFs satisfy $\|q_1 - q_2\| = \|(q_1, \gamma) - (q_2, \gamma)\|$ for any re-parameterization function γ.

There are four shape-preserving transformations for curves: translation, scale, rotation, and re-parameterization. Of these, the first two have already been eliminated from the representations, but the other two remain. Curves that are within a rotation and/or a re-parameterization of each other result in different elements of $\mathcal{C}$ despite having the same shape. Let $SO(2)$ be the group of 2×2 rotation matrices and Γ be the group of all re-parameterizations (they are actually orientation-preserving diffeomorphisms of the unit circle $\mathbb{S}^1$). In order to unify all elements in $\mathcal{C}$ that denote the same shape, one can define equivalence classes of the type: $[q] = \{O(q \circ \gamma)\sqrt{\dot{\gamma}} | O \in SO(2), \gamma \in \Gamma\}$. Each such equivalence class $[q]$ is associated with a shape uniquely and vice versa. The set of all these equivalence classes is called the shape space $\mathcal{S}$; mathematically, it is a quotient space of the preshape space: $\mathcal{S} = \mathcal{C}/(SO(2) \times \Gamma)$.

An important advantage of the SRVF representation is that the elastic Riemannian metric defined by Mio et al. [14], turns into the standard $\mathbb{L}^2$ metric, as shown by Joshi et al. [6], Srivastava et al. [18]. That is, one can alternatively compute the path lengths, or the sizes of deformations between curves, using the cumulative norms of the differences between successive curves along the paths in the SRVF space. This turns out to be much simpler and a very effective strategy for comparing shapes of curves, by finding the paths with least amounts of deformations between them, where the amount of deformation is measured by an elastic metric. This gives a proper distance d_c for comparing elements of $\mathcal{C}$. Another distinct advantage of using SRVFs is that the distance between any two curves remains same if they are rotated and re-parameterized in the same way, that is, $d_c(q_1, q_2) = d_c((q_1, \gamma), (q_2, \gamma))$ and $d_c(q_1, q_2) = d_c(Oq_1, Oq_2)$ for all $O \in SO(2)$ and $\gamma \in \Gamma$. Consequently, a shape distance between any two curves is given by:

$$d_s([q_1], [q_2]) = \inf_{\gamma \in \Gamma, O \in SO(2)} d_c(q_1, O(q_2 \circ \gamma)\sqrt{\dot{\gamma}}). \tag{15.1}$$

Shape Matching and Geodesics   According to Eq. (15.1), the distance between any two shapes is given by the length of the shortest path, called a *geodesic*, connecting them in that manifold. An interesting feature of this framework is that it not only provides a distance between shapes of two curves, but also a geodesic path between them in $\mathcal{S}$. The geodesics are actually computed using the differential geometry of the underlying space $\mathcal{S}$. One technique for finding geodesics is called *path straightening* [9]. It is an iterative technique that initializes an arbitrary path and then iteratively "straightens" it by updating it along the negative gradient of the cost function. This gives a geodesic and a geodesic distance between SRVFs in $\mathcal{C}$ but the goal is to compute geodesic paths in $\mathcal{S}$. In other words, geodesic paths between the equivalence classes $[q_1]$ and $[q_2]$ are needed, not just between q_1 and q_2. This desired geodesic is obtained by finding the shortest geodesic amongst all pairs $(\tilde{q}_1, \tilde{q}_2) \in ([q_1] \times [q_2])$. This search is further simplified by fixing an arbitrary element of $[q_1]$, say q_1, and searching over all rotations and re-parameterizations of

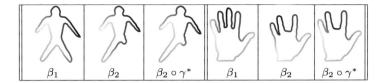

Fig. 15.4 Comparison of initial matching and matching after optimization over Γ

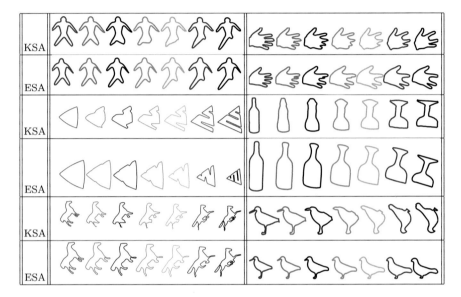

Fig. 15.5 Examples of geodesic paths between shapes using KSA and ESA

q_2 to minimize the geodesic length, as stated in Eq. (15.1). The minimization over $SO(2)$ is in conventional way and the optimization over Γ is accomplished using the dynamic programming algorithm or a gradient-type approach [18].

We present two examples of optimization over Γ in Fig. 15.4. The parametrization of a curve is displayed using colors, that is, same color implies the same value of t. It can be seen that the matching after the optimization over Γ is better in matching similar geometric features. Several examples of geodesic paths in the shape space S are shown in Fig. 15.5; these geodesics are compared with the geodesics obtained by KSA, for the same shapes. KSA is a method that only considers rigid transformation and scaling. It is easy to see that the geodesics resulting from our elastic shape analysis (ESA) appear to have more natural deformations as they are better in matching features across shapes.

Shape Statistics of Curves   The richness of this framework comes from its ability to provide shape statistics, such as sample mean or sample PCA, under proper shape metrics. The notion of a mean on a nonlinear manifold is typically established using the Karcher mean [7]. For a given set of curves $\beta_1, \beta_2, \ldots, \beta_n$, repre-

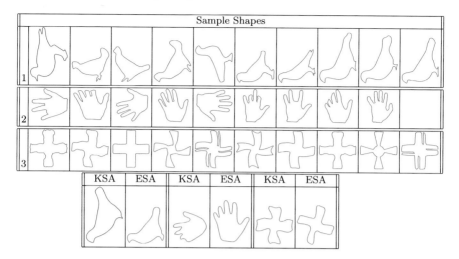

Fig. 15.6 Examples of mean shapes under two different methods

sented by their SRVFs $q_1, q_2, \ldots, q_n$, their Karcher mean is defined as the quantity that satisfies: $[\mu] = \arg\min_{[q] \in \mathcal{S}} \sum_{i=1}^{n} d_s([q], [q_i])^2$. There is a gradient-based iterative algorithm for finding the minimizer of this cost function that can be found in [7, 13, 17]. Shown in Fig. 15.6 are some examples of mean shapes. The top three rows show a set of given curves and bottom rows display their means computed using the two methods discussed here: KSA and ESA.

For computing and analyzing the second and higher moments of a shape sample, the tangent space to the shape manifold $\mathcal{S}$ at the point μ is used. This space, denoted by $T_\mu(\mathcal{S})$, is convenient because it is a vector space and one can apply more traditional methods here. The details are omitted for brevity. Figure 15.7 shows the principal geodesic paths along two different dominant directions, respectively. The middle points in each row are the mean shapes.

One important use of means and covariances of shape families is in devising "Gaussian"-type probability densities on the shape space $\mathcal{S}$. In order to tackle the nonlinearity of the shape space, a common approach is to impose a Gaussian distribution on the tangent space $T_\mu(\mathcal{S})$ since that is a vector space. In case of ESA this space is infinite-dimensional, so the Gaussian model is actually imposed on a finite-dimensional subspace, for example, a principal subspace, of $T_\mu(\mathcal{S})$. Shown in Fig. 15.8 are examples of random samples from $\mathcal{S}$ using means and covariances estimated from data shown in Fig. 15.6. For comparison, this figure also shows random samples from similar Gaussian models but using KSA.

It is easy to observe the superiority of the results obtained using ESA. Consider the example of hand, the mean using ESA is much more representative. In the principle geodesic paths, using ESA, the last finger shrinks and the fourth one grows in the first principle direction and both fingers shrink in the second principle direction. The shapes obtained by KSA are distorted, including the mean, the principle

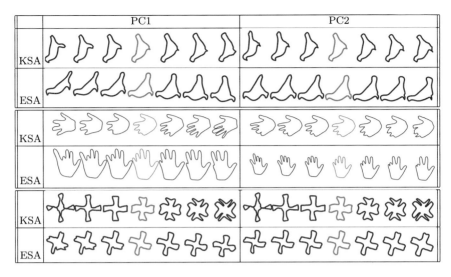

Fig. 15.7 Two principal directions of variability in shapes shown in Fig. 15.6

Method	"Gaussian" Random Samples		
KSA			
ESA			

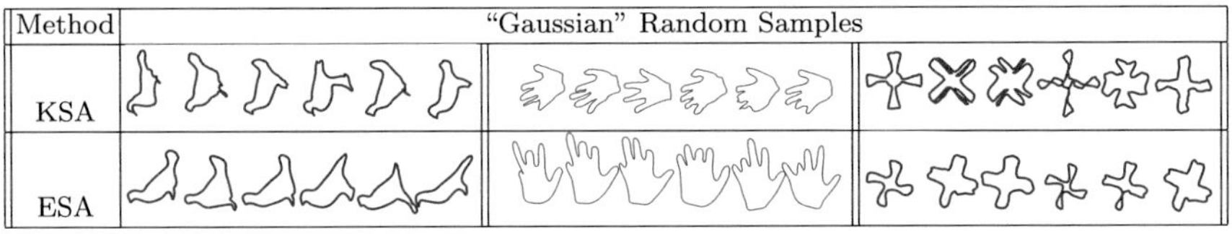

Fig. 15.8 Random samples from "Gaussian"-type distributions under the two methods: KSA, and ESA, for parameters estimated from the given shapes shown in Fig. 15.6

geodesic paths and random samples. The same distortion can be observed in another two cases using KSA.

15.3 Shape Analysis of Parameterized Surfaces

In this section, we describe a similar framework for studying shapes of parameterized surfaces using novel mathematical representations. For details of this approach, please refer to the papers by Kurtek et al. [10–12]. We assume that the surfaces are closed and have genus zero, so they can be represented as embeddings of $\mathbb{S}^2$ in $\mathbb{R}^3$, that is, $f : \mathbb{S}^2 \to \mathbb{R}^3$. The function f also denotes a *parameterization* of $\mathbb{S}^2$. Let the set of parameterized surfaces be $\mathcal{F} = \{f : \mathbb{S}^2 \mapsto \mathbb{R}^3 | \int_{\mathbb{S}^2} \|f(s)\|^2 ds < \infty$ and f is smooth$\}$, where ds is the standard Lebesgue measure on $\mathbb{S}^2$. A re-parameterization γ of a surface is given by a diffeomorphism of $\mathbb{S}^2$ to itself; let Γ be the set of all re-parameterizations. The re-parameterization of a surface f is then given by the composition $f \circ \gamma$.

Mathematical Representation   To endow $\mathcal{F}$ with a Riemannian metric, we begin by defining a new representation of surfaces, called q-maps, defined as $q(s) = \sqrt{\kappa(s)} f(s)$, where $\kappa(s)$ is the area-multiplication factor at the point $s \in \mathbb{S}^2$. (An alternative mathematical representation using the normal vector field on a surface is described in a recent paper [5].) If a surface f is re-parameterized as $f \circ \gamma$, then its q-map is given by $(q, \gamma) \equiv (q \circ \gamma)\sqrt{J_\gamma}$, where J_γ is the determinant of Jacobian of γ. For comparing shapes, we choose the natural $\mathbb{L}^2$ metric on the space of q-maps. Similar to SRVFs for curves, an important advantage of using these q-maps is that a simultaneous re-parameterization of any two surfaces does not change the distance between them. That is, for any two surfaces f_1 and f_2, represented by their q-maps, q_1 and q_2 respectively, we have that $\|q_1 - q_2\| = \|(q_1, \gamma) - (q_2, \gamma)\|$. Actually, the Riemannian metric that we will use on $\mathcal{F}$ is the pullback of the $\mathbb{L}^2$ metric from the space of q-maps. With this induced metric, $\mathcal{F}$ becomes a Riemannian manifold.

Shape analysis of surfaces can be made invariant to translation and scaling by normalizing. With a slight abuse of notation, we define the space of normalized surfaces as $\mathcal{F}$. $\mathcal{F}$ forms the pre-shape space in our analysis. The remaining groups— rotation and re-parameterization—are dealt with differently, by removing them algebraically from the representation space. The equivalence class of a surface f is given by $[f] = \{O(f \circ \gamma) | O \in SO(3), \gamma \in \Gamma\}$ and the set of all such equivalence classes is defined to be $\mathcal{S}$.

Shape Matching and Geodesics   The next step is to define geodesic paths in $\mathcal{S}$. Similar to the curve case, a path-straightening approach is used to find geodesics in $\mathcal{F}$ [12]. Once we have an algorithm for finding geodesics in $\mathcal{F}$, we can obtain geodesics and geodesic lengths in $\mathcal{S}$ by solving an additional minimization problem over $SO(3) \times \Gamma$. Let f_1 and f_2 denote two surfaces and let $\langle\langle \cdot, \cdot \rangle\rangle$ be the inherited Riemannian metric on $\mathcal{F}$. Then, the geodesic distance between shapes of f_1 and f_2 will be given by quantity of the following type:

$$\min_{\gamma, O} \left(\min_{\substack{F:[0,1] \to \mathcal{F} \\ F(0)=f_1, F(1)=O(f_2 \circ \gamma)}} \left(\int_0^1 \langle\langle F_t(t), F_t(t) \rangle\rangle^{(1/2)} \, dt \right) \right). \qquad (15.2)$$

Here $F(t)$ is a path in $\mathcal{F}$ indexed by t, and the quantity $\int_0^1 \langle\langle F_t(t), F_t(t) \rangle\rangle^{(1/2)} dt$ denotes the length of F where F_t is used for $\frac{dF}{dt}$. The minimization inside the brackets, thus, denotes the problem of finding a geodesic path between the surfaces f_1 and $O(f_2 \circ \gamma)$, where O and γ stand for an arbitrary rotation and re-parameterization of f_2, respectively. The minimization outside the bracket seeks the optimal rotation and re-parameterization of the second surface so as to best match it with the first surface. In simple words, the outside optimization solves the registration or matching problem while the inside optimization solves for both an optimal deformation (geodesic, F^*) and a formal distance (geodesic distance) between shapes.

We demonstrate these ideas using some examples in Fig. 15.9. These examples also highlight improvements in registration of surfaces during the optimization over

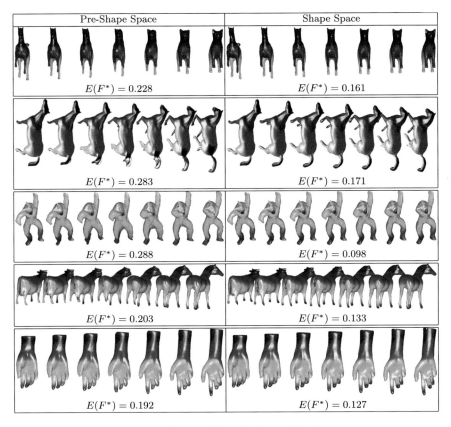

Pre-Shape Space	Shape Space
$E(F^*) = 0.228$	$E(F^*) = 0.161$
$E(F^*) = 0.283$	$E(F^*) = 0.171$
$E(F^*) = 0.288$	$E(F^*) = 0.098$
$E(F^*) = 0.203$	$E(F^*) = 0.133$
$E(F^*) = 0.192$	$E(F^*) = 0.127$

Fig. 15.9 Comparison of geodesics in $\mathcal{F}$ and $\mathcal{S}$, and their geodesic distances

$SO(3) \times \Gamma$, by comparing corresponding geodesic paths between the same pairs of surfaces in $\mathcal{F}$ and $\mathcal{S}$. In all of these experiments, we notice that the geodesic distances in $\mathcal{S}$ are much smaller than the geodesic distances in $\mathcal{F}$.

Shape Statistics of Surfaces   Here we briefly present some examples for computing the Karcher mean for a set of surfaces using the method similar to planar closed curves.

We present some examples of Karcher mean shapes using toy objects. For comparison, we also display $\tilde{f} = (1/n) \sum_{i=1}^{n} f_i$, that is, without any rotational or re-parameterizational alignment. For each example we show the decrease in the gradient of the cost function during the computation of the Karcher mean. In the top part of Fig. 15.10, we present means for ten unimodal surfaces with random peak placements on a sphere. The $\tilde{f}$ surface has ten very small peaks at the locations of the peaks in the sample. On the other hand, the mean in $\mathcal{S}$ has one peak, which is of the same size as all of the peaks in the sample. In this simple example one can clearly see the effect of feature preservation due to rotational and re-parameterizational alignment. In the bottom part of Fig. 15.10, we present mean shapes of nine surfaces with

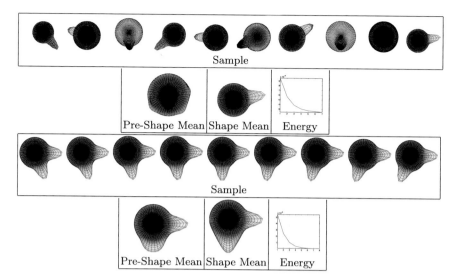

Fig. 15.10 Mean computation for a sample of surfaces with one peak (*top*) and dual peaks (*bottom*). The figures compare mean computations in $\mathcal{F}$ and $\mathcal{S}$

dual peaks. We note that the mean in $\mathcal{F}$ has one peak aligned (at the location of the common peak in the sample) and one very wide and small peak, which could be considered as a failure mode. The very wide peak happens due to averaging out of features. The mean in $\mathcal{S}$ has two peaks due to a crisp alignment and thus is a much better representative of the sample.

15.4 Conclusion

In this paper, we have described recent progress in using Riemannian methods in shape analysis of curves and surfaces. An important attribute of this framework is that it performs shape comparison and registration jointly under the same metric. The choice of elastic metric and novel mathematical representations (SRVFs for curves and q-maps for surfaces) enable us to use $\mathbb{L}^2$ norms and standard optimization tools. This framework provides geodesics—optimal deformations—between shapes, and tools for computing statistical summaries of sets of shapes.

References

1. Dryden IL, Mardia KV (1998) Statistical shape analysis. Wiley, New York
2. Frenkel M, Basri R (2003) Curve matching using the fast marching method. In: Proceedings of energy minimization methods in CVPR, pp 35–51

3. Gdalyahu Y, Weinshall D (1999) Flexible syntactic matching of curves and its application to automatic hierarchical classification of silhouettes. IEEE Trans Pattern Anal Mach Intell 21(12):1312–1328
4. Geiger D, Gupta A, Costa LA, Vlontzos J (1995) Dynamic programming for detecting, tracking, and matching deformable contours. IEEE Trans Pattern Anal Mach Intell 17(3):294–302
5. Jermyn IH, Kurtek S, Klassen E, Srivastava A (2012) Elastic shape matching of parameterized surfaces using square root normal fields. In: Proceedings of ECCV
6. Joshi SH, Klassen E, Srivastava A, Jermyn IH (2007) A novel representation for Riemannian analysis of elastic curves in $\mathbb{R}^n$. In: Proceedings of CVPR, pp 1–7
7. Karcher H (1977) Riemannian center of mass and mollifier smoothing. Commun Pure Appl Math 30(5):509–541
8. Kendall DG (1984) Shape manifolds, Procrustean metrics and complex projective spaces. Bull Lond Math Soc 16:81–121
9. Klassen E, Srivastava A (2006) Geodesics between 3d closed curves using path-straightening. In: Proceedings of ECCV. Lecture notes in computer science, pp 95–106
10. Kurtek S, Klassen E, Ding Z, Jacobson SW, Jacobson JL, Avison MJ, Srivastava A (2011) Parameterization-invariant shape comparisons of anatomical surfaces. IEEE Trans Med Imaging 30(3):849–858
11. Kurtek S, Klassen E, Ding Z, Srivastava A (2010) A novel Riemannian framework for shape analysis of 3d objects. In: Proceedings of CVPR, pp 1625–1632
12. Kurtek S, Klassen E, Gore JC, Ding Z, Srivastava A (2012) Elastic geodesic paths in shape space of parameterized surfaces. IEEE Trans Pattern Anal Mach Recogn 34(9):1717–1730
13. Le HL, Kendall DG (1993) The Riemannian structure of Euclidean shape spaces: a novel environment for statistics. Ann Stat 21(3):1225–1271
14. Mio W, Srivastava A, Joshi SH (2007) On shape of plane elastic curves. Int J Comput Vis 73(3):307–324
15. Sebastian TB, Klein PN, Kimia BB (2003) On aligning curves. IEEE Trans Pattern Anal Mach Recogn 25(1):116–125
16. Small CG (1996) The statistical theory of shape. Springer, Berlin
17. Srivastava A, Joshi SH, Mio W, Liu X (2005) Statistical shape analysis: clustering, learning and testing. IEEE Trans Pattern Anal Mach Intell 27(4):590–602
18. Srivastava A, Klassen E, Joshi SH, Jermyn IH (2011) Shape analysis of elastic curves in Euclidean spaces. IEEE Trans Pattern Anal Mach Intell 33:1415–1428
19. Younes L, Michor PW, Shah J, Mumford D, Lincei R (2008) A metric on shape spaces with explicit geodesics. Mat E Appl 19(1):25–57

Chapter 16
The Statistics of Shape, Reflectance, and Lighting in Real-World Scenes

Richard F. Murray

16.1 Introduction

Visual perception is a statistical problem *par excellence*. If the goal of vision is to give a reliable reconstruction of the scenes and objects in the external world from 2D images on the retinas, then in one sense it is an impossible problem: there is simply not enough information in retinal images alone to infer what is being seen. Put differently, there are many combinations of lighting, surface shapes, and surface colors that could have given rise to any particular 2D retinal image. Accordingly, a visual system can only reconstruct a 3D scene if it has criteria for choosing a particular 3D interpretation of a 2D retinal image out of the wide range of interpretations that are physically consistent with the image.

The generalized bas-relief (GBR) ambiguity illustrates this problem vividly [9]. Suppose we have a Lambertian object, with an arbitrary shape and an arbitrary surface reflectance pattern, under arbitrary lighting. The GBR ambiguity shows that we can drastically change the shape and reflectance pattern of the object, without changing the retinal image that it generates. Specifically, we can compress and shear the object along the viewer's line of sight; then adjust the lighting so that the positions of cast shadows on the object are unchanged; and finally adjust the surface reflectance at each point on the object (now with a new surface normal and new lighting conditions) so that it creates the same image luminance as before. The GBR ambiguity shows constructively that images are not ambiguous just in special cases, or to some small degree, but that they are consistently and deeply ambiguous.

R.F. Murray (✉)
Centre for Vision Research, York University, Toronto, Canada
e-mail: rfm@yorku.ca

S.J. Dickinson, Z. Pizlo (eds.), *Shape Perception in Human and Computer Vision*,
Advances in Computer Vision and Pattern Recognition,
DOI 10.1007/978-1-4471-5195-1_16, © Springer-Verlag London 2013

Furthermore, the GBR ambiguity is a lower limit; images are much more ambiguous than the GBR ambiguity alone suggests.[1] The strategy of distorting the shape of an object, and then adjusting lighting conditions and reflectance so that the resulting image is unchanged, is obviously a very general one. We can make many kinds of local, nonlinear deformations in an object's shape, and compensate for their effect on the image by adjusting lighting and reflectance accordingly. At the extreme, we can relight and repaint practically any scene so that it generates the same image as practically any other scene. Thus a visual system cannot simply live with the ambiguity in 2D images. The ambiguity is too great, and without some way of at least partly overcoming it, visual stimuli are all but useless.

The objects created by GBR and GBR-like transformations of real objects are, in some sense, odd. A highly transformed object (e.g., greatly stretched or compressed along the viewer's line of sight) does not usually correspond to our percept of what is shown in the image, and it surprises us that these distorted objects create the same images as the more familiar, untransformed objects. But in what sense are the transformed objects odd? The answer I will explore in this chapter is that there are statistical regularities in the shapes, reflectance patterns, and lighting conditions of real world scenes that allow observers to rule out implausible interpretations, and thereby overcome image ambiguity. On this view, transformed scenes are odd because they have shapes, reflectance patterns, or lighting conditions that are unlikely to occur in the real world.

This answer seems so natural, even obvious, that it is worth pointing out that it is not the only possible answer. The generic viewpoint assumption, for instance, is a reasonable principle that suggests we should prefer 3D interpretations of 2D images that are stable across small changes in viewpoint, instead of interpretations that assume the scene is being viewed from a tightly constrained 'accidental' viewpoint [17]. This principle makes only weak assumptions about shape, reflectance, and lighting (e.g., that lighting is equally likely from all directions), and yet it gives a criterion for preferring some 3D interpretations over others. The generic viewpoint assumption resolves the GBR ambiguity by preferring planar interpretations over interpretations with depth [38], so it is not, by itself, a good way of completely overcoming image ambiguity. Nevertheless, it demonstrates that approaches other than relying on the most obvious scene statistics are possible.

These issues have long been understood in broad terms, and yet remarkably little is known about exactly what statistical regularities in real world scenes can support perception of shape and reflectance, or which of these regularities human observers rely on. Here I selectively review and evaluate recent work on these problems.

---

[1] Belhumeur et al. showed that image ambiguity is limited to the GBR ambiguity for an observer who has images of an object under all possible distant point lighting conditions. This is important for understanding the limits of methods such as photometric stereo, but the ambiguity is much greater when the observer sees an object under just one lighting condition. This has sometimes not been understood, e.g., Todd [36] suggests that work on the GBR ambiguity shows that the ambiguity of 2D images is highly constrained.

(a)   (b)

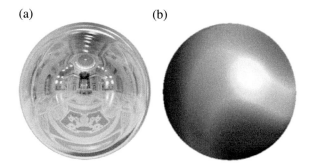

Fig. 16.1 A light probe is a spherical representation of the illumination incident from all directions at a single point in space, i.e., an omnidirectional luminance snapshot. (**a**) A spherical, globe-like representation of a high-resolution light probe assembled from photographs of a mirrored sphere (from [13]). This light probe includes color as well as luminance. (**b**) A similar representation of a low-resolution light probe measured with a multidirectional photometer. *White* represents high luminance, and *black* represents low luminance (from [22])

I will use "scene" to mean a 3D arrangement of surfaces, reflectance patterns, and lights, and "image" to mean the 2D retinal luminance pattern that a scene gives rise to.

16.2 Lighting

16.2.1 Lighting: Scene Statistics

The direction, diffuseness, and complexity of lighting can have an enormous effect on the appearance of a scene. Many studies have examined real world lighting conditions, and have found that despite the great variability in lighting, there are also strong regularities. Most interesting for our purpose are the relatively few studies of 'light probes', omnidirectional snapshots of the pattern of light incident from all directions at a single point in space (Fig. 16.1). A light probe captures the lighting that would illuminate an object at the light probe's measurement location, so an understanding of the statistical regularities in real world light probes is useful for understanding the relationship between 3D scenes and 2D images.

Dror, Willsky, and Adelson [14] examined around 100 high-resolution light probes, and found that they had some of the same statistical properties as conventional images: a pink-noise-like power spectrum, kurtotic wavelet coefficient distributions, and statistical dependencies between wavelet coefficients at adjacent scales, orientations, and positions. They also found that, unlike conventional images, the luminance distribution of light probes peaks at low luminances, with a few very high luminance values due to small, bright sources such as the sun.

Fig. 16.2 GBR transformations change a diffuse light probe (*center*) so that its luminance is concentrated either along a great circle (*left*) or in two opposite directions (*right*)

Mury, Pont, and Koenderink [28] used a similar approach, but they paid special attention to the low-pass components of natural lighting that are relevant to shading of convex Lambertian objects [8, 32]. They found that although high frequency components of light probes vary rapidly as one moves through a scene, the low frequency components are much more stable. They examined a few different types of scenes, such as open-sky scenes and forests, and showed that the pattern of changes in low-frequency lighting structure through a scene is largely determined by the scene's coarse geometry.

Mury, Pont, and Koenderink [29, 30] built a multidirectional photometer to measure low-pass light probes. Mury et al. [30] measured light probes in several environments, and consistent with their previous work [28], they found that a lighting model based on a coarse description of the scene layout accounted for the structure of the measured light probes.

Morgenstern [22, 23] used a multidirectional photometer to measure several hundred low-pass light probes in diverse environments. He examined the diffuseness of natural lighting, that is, the extent to which light comes mainly from one direction, as on a sunny day, or from all directions, as on a cloudy day. He found that the diffuseness levels in different environments (e.g., sunny, cloudy, indoors), span a fairly limited range, and that across all environments the diffuseness levels cluster in the lower-middle region of the physically possible range of diffuseness.

Morgenstern also found that some low-pass lighting patterns were much more likely than others. He showed that natural low-pass lighting can be approximated reasonably well using a classic computer graphics lighting model, in which light is the sum of a distant point source and uniform ambient source (e.g., [31]). Consistent with this, he found that ring-like lighting patterns, where light is weak in two opposite directions and strong along the great circle halfway between them, are rare. Interestingly, GBR transformations can create just such ring-like lighting patterns (Fig. 16.2): some GBR transformations shift uniform (i.e., very diffuse) light distributions so that they are concentrated either along a great circle of directions, or in two directly opposed directions. This is one sense in which GBR-transformed scenes are unusual, and it gives one possible criterion for choosing the most likely 3D interpretations of 2D images.

16.2.2 Lighting: Psychophysics

Whether an observer's 3D interpretation of an image is accurate often depends on whether they have an accurate estimate of the scene's lighting. For human observers, this estimate is a compromise between the observer's prior on lighting conditions, and cues to lighting conditions in individual scenes. We know more about the human visual system's priors on lighting than about any other perceptual prior.

Metzger [21] first suggested that in order to perceive the 3D shapes depicted in 2D images, we rely on an assumption that light comes from above and slightly to the left, an assumption that has come to be known as the light-from-above prior[2] Metzger based this suggestion on informal observations of the appearance of images at different orientations, and more quantitative psychophysics has supported his notion of a preferred lighting direction above and to the left [35]. (One cannot say more *careful* psychophysics, since it is remarkable that Metzger was able to conclude that we prefer a lighting direction to the left of vertical, based only on his own qualitative observations.) Interestingly, there are large individual differences in the precise direction of the prior [2], and the direction of the prior can be modified by just an hour or two of experience in an environment with oblique lighting [1].

Even if light comes from some direction on average (e.g., directly above, or above and to the left), it does not come from that direction in every scene, leading to the question of what happens when lighting direction cues like shading and shadows indicate a lighting direction different from the direction suggested by the light-from-above prior. Morgenstern, Murray, and Harris [24] showed that instead of the prior overriding lighting direction cues or vice versa, information about lighting direction from the prior and from lighting direction cues is combined, so that the perceived lighting direction that guides shape from shading is a compromise between the prior and direction cues. They also found that the light-from-above prior is remarkably weak, in the sense that even very faint cues to lighting direction have a greater effect in this compromise. This suggests that the light-from-above prior has little influence in everyday perception.

Recent psychophysical work suggests that human vision also relies on assumptions about the diffuseness of lighting. Boyaci et al. [11] and Bloj et al. [10] examined lightness constancy as a function of the orientation of the test patch being judged. They found that constancy was quite good when the patch was within $\pm 60°$ of frontoparallel to the dominant light source, but that reflectances were consistently underestimated when the test patch was more oblique than this. They noted that this unusual pattern of success and failure in judging surface reflectance is what one would expect from observers who overestimate lighting diffuseness in the scene

---

[2]Brewster [12] is often credited with discovering the light-from-above prior. In fact, he mostly elaborated Rittenhouse's [33] observation that we perceive ambiguous shaded patterns as having a 3D shape that is consistent with whatever we believe about the lighting direction in the scene being viewed. Neither Rittenhouse nor Brewster suggested that we have a default assumption that light comes from overhead.

being viewed. Boyaci et al. and Bloj et al. calculated the level of assumed diffuseness that would explain each observer's performance, and they found that observers consistently behaved as if lighting was much more diffuse than it actually was in the experimental apparatus. This suggests that observers' diffuseness estimates may have been biased by a prior for high levels of diffuseness. It is also possible, though, that observers simply always overestimate lighting diffuseness; it would be interesting to see whether experiments similar to Boyaci et al.'s and Bloj et al.'s, but with very diffuse light, find that observers underestimate diffuseness, as would occur if their errors were due to a lighting prior that favored high but not maximal levels of diffuseness.

Schofield, Rock, and Georgeson [34] used very different methods than Bloj and Boyaci, and reached similar conclusions. They noted that observers tend to see sinusoidal luminance gratings as corrugated surfaces that are sinusoidal in depth, and that the phase difference between the luminance grating and the perceived depth grating changes with the orientation of the luminance grating. They showed that this is what one would expect from an observer who has a prior on lighting direction, and they showed that, under certain modelling assumptions, the magnitude of the phase change across luminance grating orientations is a signature of the observer's assumptions about lighting diffuseness: a smaller phase change corresponds to an assumption of more diffuse light. They calculated the level of diffuseness that explained each observer's shape percepts, and their results were quantitatively very similar to Bloj et al.'s. Furthermore, Morgenstern [22, 23] showed that the diffuseness levels that Bloj et al. and Schofield et al. arrived at match the range of lighting diffuseness found in real world environments. This suggests that just as observers have a prior on lighting direction that matches the average lighting direction in real world scenes, they also have a prior on lighting diffuseness that matches real world lighting. Boyaci et al.'s observers seem to have been guided by much higher levels of diffuseness, but Morgenstern argues that Boyaci et al.'s results were probably biased by partial failures of lightness constancy in perceiving computer-generated stimuli.

Fleming, Dror, and Adelson [15] found that human vision also relies on higher-order properties of natural lighting, beyond its direction and diffuseness. They examined material perception under real and synthetic lighting, and they found that natural lighting is important for accurate perception of material properties, in particular for perception of gloss. They concluded that one of the most important properties of natural lighting, for human observers, is that it contains point-like light sources and spatially extended light sources with edges.

16.3 Shape and Reflectance

16.3.1 Shape and Reflectance: Scene Statistics

Torreão [37] developed a Markov random field (MRF) approach to shape from shading, that used mathematically convenient assumptions about object shape to arrive

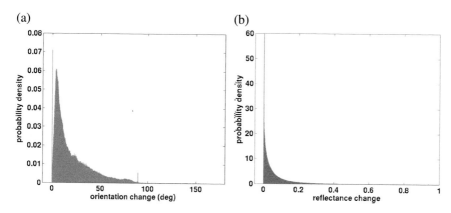

Fig. 16.3 (a) Orientation and (b) reflectance changes across real-world objects [26]. These histograms were created by viewing digital scans of real objects of various sizes through a virtual 100×100 grid, and measuring the changes in orientation or reflectance between adjacent grid elements. Here reflectance is measured on the interval [0,1]

at maximum a priori (MAP) shape interpretations of shaded images. Freeman, Pasztor, and Carmichael [18] used a similar approach to the problem of recovering both shape and reflectance from shading, but with some important innovations. For our purpose, the most interesting development was that instead of using convenient assumptions about shape and an assumption of uniform reflectance, Freeman et al.'s algorithm learned the statistical distribution of shape and reflectance patches in a computer-rendered virtual world. The algorithm built up a library of surface patches from the virtual world, with both shape and reflectance information represented, and interpreted new images by assembling a grid of surface patches from the library that best accounted for the luminance patterns in the shaded image.

Murray [26] examined the shape and reflectance distribution in real objects. He used 3D digital scans of 80 natural and man-made objects. From random viewpoints, he examined how surface orientation and reflectance changed across the surface of the objects. The histograms of surface and reflectance changes were highly regular (Fig. 16.3). One of the most noteworthy findings was that reflectance changes were much more narrowly peaked around zero than surface orientation changes, suggesting that a rational visual system will tend to attribute shading changes to surface orientation changes instead of reflectance changes whenever possible.

Barron and Malik [6, 7] developed an MRF algorithm to recover shape and reflectance from shading, but unlike Torreão and Freeman et al. they incorporated shape and reflectance statistics of real objects. They used parametric models of shape and reflectance gradients, and they fit these models to digital scans of ten real world objects. They found that the MAP estimates from the resulting algorithm were able to recover shape and reflectance from shaded images, and that scene statistics learned from a set of training objects worked well with a new set of test objects.

These studies support the notion that natural scene statistics can overcome the ambiguity inherent in 2D images. Murray, and Attewell and Baddeley [5], show that scene statistics are sufficiently stable that they can be measured with a reasonable number of samples. Torreão, Freeman et al., and Barron and Malik show that probabilistic algorithms that incorporate assumptions about scene statistics can recover shape and reflectance from shaded images. One shortcoming of work to date is that it has not given us a good theoretical understanding of what statistical regularities in 3D scenes are important for recovering shape and reflectance. For instance, is it enough to assume in some way, as Murray suggests, that reflectance changes are rare compared to shape changes, or is the specific parametric form that Barron and Malik assume for reflectance changes also important? Is there any role for correlations between shape and reflectance? Researchers have developed algorithms that learn to infer shape and reflectance, demonstrating that scene statistics can overcome image ambiguity, but there has been less progress in determining what the key properties of natural scenes are, that such algorithms learn.

One possibility that has been overlooked in previous work is that measuring the precise distribution of shape and orientation in real world scenes might be less important than using statistical properties that one can predict from first principles. For instance, in GBR and GBR-like transformations, an object's shape, reflectance, and lighting are put through changes that cancel one another precisely, e.g., if the shape and lighting transformations result in a lower image luminance for a given surface patch, then the surface patch's reflectance is increased in order to undo the change in image luminance. This introduces statistical dependencies between surface orientation, illuminance, and reflectance. Some of these dependencies might be very unnatural. In natural objects, for instance, we expect illuminance and reflectance to be statistically independent across surface patches. Such almost-a-priori constraints may be useful for finding correct 3D interpretations of shaded images.

16.3.2 Shape and Reflectance: Psychophysics

Very little is known about the assumptions that human observers make about shape and reflectance. One of the most successful approaches to lightness perception is Gilchrist's anchoring theory, a set of rules for predicting human lightness percepts under a wide range of conditions [19, 20]. Gilchrist [19] argues that Bayesian theories of lightness perception are unlikely to be successful, because they are normative theories, and will not account for the systematic errors in human lightness perception that are observed empirically and that form an important part of anchoring theory.

Adelson [3] proposes an alternative, Bayesian theory of lightness perception. He suggests that human observers assume that real world reflectances follow some statistical distribution, and that observers also assume that reflectances r and image luminances l are related by an affine transformation, $l = mr + b$. From observed luminances l, observers make statistical estimates of the reflectances r and the lighting condition parameters m and b.

Recent work in my laboratory has shown that a Bayesian theory along these lines accounts for much of anchoring theory [27]. The Bayesian theory assumes that

(a) reflectances follow a broad, asymmetric normal distribution, (b) lighting consists of multiplicative and additive components, so luminance and reflectance are related by $l = mr + b$, and (c) the proportion of additive light $b/(m + b)$ tends to be low. This simple theory predicts many of the rules of anchoring theory, thereby showing that some systematic errors in human lightness perception are actually rational consequences of simple assumptions about lighting and reflectance.

One obstacle to understanding the human visual system's assumptions about real world scenes is that we know little about how the visual system represents scenes. I have spoken, for instance, of the human visual system's assumptions about reflectance, but reflectance is a notion that is most useful in a Lambertian imaging model. The image luminance of a non-Lambertian surface varies as a function of incident lighting and/or viewing direction, so to describe such surfaces we need more information than the proportion of light reflected. Few real world surfaces are truly Lambertian, and this fact along with recent work on material perception (e.g., [4, 25]) suggests that the human visual system does not rely on a purely Lambertian model. Without knowing more about the human visual system's model of surfaces, though, it is difficult to know what properties of real world surfaces we should try to characterize statistically. Similar comments apply to the perceptual representation of surface shape and lighting conditions. For instance, Fleming, Holtmann-Rice, and Bülthoff [16] suggest that the human visual system infers 3D shape from the local orientation field of the retinal image, in which case an important goal for studies of 3D scene statistics would be to examine the statistical relationship between local image orientation and 3D shape in real world scenes.

16.4 Conclusion

There has been important progress on understanding statistical properties of 3D natural scenes and how they guide human vision. Nevertheless, the most fundamental problems are still almost completely open.

What assumptions about 3D scenes guide human perception of shape and reflectance? Consider assumptions about lighting. Human observers certainly have a prior that light comes from above, but Morgenstern et al. [24] have shown that this prior is very weak, and probably unimportant in everyday perception. Bloj et al., Boyaci et al., and Schofield et al. report intriguing evidence that human observers have a prior on lighting diffuseness, but these results are highly model-dependent, and further work is needed before we can say with confidence exactly what assumptions human observers make about diffuseness, and how these assumptions guide visual perception.

Our understanding of assumptions about shape and reflectance is even more tentative. Work in computer vision has shown that assumptions about shape, reflectance, and lighting can be used to estimate 3D scene properties. These studies provide functioning algorithms, but they leave many basic questions unanswered. For instance, what types of image luminance patterns are best attributed to shape patterns, and what types are best attributed to reflectance patterns? Are any general principles possible, such as that changes in reflectance are less likely than changes in surface orientation? Furthermore, what scene properties does the human visual system have priors on, e.g., reflectance, or the gradient of reflectance, or both? And how strong are the various priors that the human visual system relies on, e.g., priors on shape vs. priors on reflectance? It is remarkable, when there is such broad support for the notion that assumptions about natural scenes play a crucial role in perception of 3D scenes, that these fundamental questions are still largely unanswered.

References

1. Adams WJ, Graf EW, Ernst MO (2004) Experience can change the 'light-from-above' prior. Nat Neurosci 7:1057–1058
2. Adams WJ (2007) A common light-prior for visual search, shape, and reflectance judgments. J Vis 7(11):1–7
3. Adelson EH (2000) Lightness perception and lightness illusions. In: Gazzaniga M (ed) The new cognitive neurosciences, 2nd edn. MIT Press, Cambridge, pp 339–351
4. Anderson BL, Kim J (2009) Image statistics do not explain the perception of gloss and lightness. J Vis 9(11):10, 1–17
5. Attewell D, Baddeley RJ (2007) The distribution of reflectances within the visual environment. Vis Res 47:548–554
6. Barron JT, Malik J (2011) High-frequency shape and albedo from shading using natural images. In: IEEE conference on computer vision and pattern recognition, Colorado Springs, Colorado, June 20–25, pp 2521–2528
7. Barron JT, Malik J (2012) Shape, albedo, and illumination from a single image of an unknown object. In: IEEE conference on computer vision and pattern recognition, Providence, Rhode Island, June 16–21, pp 334–341
8. Basri R, Jacobs DW (2002) Lambertian reflectance and linear subspaces. IEEE Trans Pattern Anal Mach Intell 25:218–233
9. Belhumeur PN, Kriegman DJ, Yuille AL (1999) The bas-relief ambiguity. Int J Comput Vis 35:33–44
10. Bloj M, Ripamonti C, Mitha K, Hauck R, Greenwald S, Brainard DH (2004) An equivalent illuminant model for the effect of surface slant on perceived lightness. J Vis 4:735–746
11. Boyaci H, Maloney LT, Hersh S (2003) The effect of perceived surface orientation on perceived surface albedo in binocularly-viewed scenes. J Vis 3:541–553
12. Brewster D (1826) On the optical illusion of the conversion of cameos into intaglios, and of intaglios into cameos, with an account of other analogous phenomena. Edinb J Sci 4:99–108
13. Debevec P (1998) Rendering synthetic objects into real scenes: bridging traditional and image-based graphics with global illumination and high dynamic range photography. In: Proceedings of SIGGRAPH 98. Annual conference series, pp 189–198
14. Dror RO, Willsky AS, Adelson EH (2004) Statistical characterization of real-world illumination. J Vis 4:821–837
15. Fleming RW, Dror RO, Adelson EH (2003) Real-world illumination and the perception of surface reflectance properties. J Vis 3:347–368
16. Fleming RW, Holtmann-Rice D, Bülthoff HH (2011) Estimation of 3D shape from image orientations. In: Proceedings of the National Academy of Sciences of the USA, vol 108, pp 20438–20443
17. Freeman WT (1994) The generic viewpoint assumption in a framework for visual perception. Nature 368:542–545
18. Freeman WT, Pasztor EC, Carmichael OT (2000) Learning low-level vision. Int J Comput Vis 40:25–47

19. Gilchrist A (2006) Seeing black and white. Oxford University Press, New York
20. Gilchrist A, Kossyfidis C, Bonato F, Agostini T, Cataliotti J, Li X, Spehar B, Annan V, Economou E (1999) An anchoring theory of lightness perception. Psychol Rev 106:795–834
21. Metzger W (2006) The laws of seeing. The MIT Press, Cambridge. (Original work published 1936)
22. Morgenstern Y (2011) The role of low-pass natural lighting regularities in human visual perception. Ph.D. thesis, York University
23. Morgenstern Y, Murray RF, Geisler WS (submitted) Human vision is attuned to the diffuseness of natural light
24. Morgenstern Y, Murray RF, Harris LR (2011) The human visual system's assumption that light comes from above is weak. Proc Natl Acad Sci USA 108:12551–12553
25. Motoyoshi I, Nishida S, Sharan L, Adelson EH (2007) Image statistics and the perception of surface qualities. Nature 447:206–209
26. Murray RF (2006) Local 3D shape and orientation statistics of natural surfaces. In: Vision sciences society annual meeting, Sarasota, Florida, May 5–10
27. Murray RF (2013) Human lightness perception is guided by simple assumptions about reflectance and lighting. In: Human vision and electronic imaging XVII, San Francisco, California, February 4–7, 2013
28. Mury AA, Pont SC, Koenderink JJ (2007) Light field constancy within natural scenes. Appl Opt 46:7308–7316
29. Mury AA, Pont SC, Koenderink JJ (2009) Representing the light field in finite three-dimensional spaces from sparse discrete samples. Appl Opt 48:450–457
30. Mury AA, Pont SC, Koenderink JJ (2009) Structure of light fields in natural scenes. Appl Opt 48:5386–5395
31. Phong BT (1975) Illumination for computer generated pictures. Commun ACM 18:311–317
32. Ramamoorthi R, Hanrahan P (2001) On the relationship between radiance and irradiance: determining the illumination from images of a convex Lambertian object. J Opt Soc Am A 18:2448–2459
33. Rittenhouse D (1786) Explanation of an optical deception. Trans Am Philos Soc 2:37–42
34. Schofield AJ, Rock PB, Georgeson MA (2011) Sun and sky: does human vision assume a mixture of point and diffuse illumination when interpreting shape-from-shading? Vis Res 51:2317–2330
35. Sun J, Perona P (1998) Where is the Sun? Nat Neurosci 1:183–184
36. Todd J (2004) The visual perception of 3d shape. Trends Cogn Sci 8:115–121
37. Torreão JRA (1995) Bayesian shape estimation: shape-from-shading and photometric stereo revisited. Mach Vis Appl 8:163–172
38. Yuille AL, Coughlan JM, Konishi S (2003) The generic viewpoint assumption and planar bias. IEEE Trans Pattern Anal Mach Intell 25:775–778

Chapter 17
Structure vs. Appearance and 3D vs. 2D? A Numeric Answer

Wenze Hu, Zhangzhang Si, and Song-Chun Zhu

17.1 Introduction

It has been widely acknowledged that while humans are quite good at extracting structures from images, that is, the edges [4], textons [10] etc. which are concepts hidden in pixel intensities, the notion of structure does not lend itself to its precise detection by computer programs. As a result, there now exist appearance based image representations [6, 14] which directly express the image using statistics or histograms of image operator (filter) responses. Structure based and appearance based image representations are advocated by different researchers, whose reasons for endorsement range from the practical benefits in building simple vision applications to the faith that computer vision would ultimately stick to human vision.

When different views of objects are taken into account, a similar dichotomy happens in describing the image structures. The intrinsic 3D shape of objects suggests that object-centered representation using volumetric primitives [1, 2, 15] should be simple yet capable of representing the observed image structure changes. But again the difficulty of extracting these 3D hidden concepts from images make the viewer-centered representation [11, 12, 17, 21] a competing alternative, which uses a collections of 2D representations each covering a small portion of the modeled views. Over the two representations, researchers showed various cases where one representation prevailed [3, 8, 20], but there is no clear winner.

In our view, these competing representations are points lying in different positions of representation spectrum, and they should be combined to better represent

W. Hu (✉) · Z. Si · S.-C. Zhu
University of California, Los Angeles, CA, USA
e-mail: wzhu@stat.ucla.edu

Z. Si
e-mail: zzsi@stat.ucla.edu

S.-C. Zhu
e-mail: sczhu@stat.ucla.edu

S.J. Dickinson, Z. Pizlo (eds.), *Shape Perception in Human and Computer Vision*,
Advances in Computer Vision and Pattern Recognition,
DOI 10.1007/978-1-4471-5195-1_17, © Springer-Verlag London 2013

Fig. 17.1 Images of leaves at different scales. From left to right, our description of the image gradually changes from exact structure to the overall appearance of the leaves

Fig. 17.2 (**a**) Hybrid image template mixing sketch (*dark bar*) and texture (*red disk*) representations. (**b**) Templates mixing 2D primitives (*dark bar*) and 3D primitives (*red bar*) to describe the desktop globe images over different views. Image in (**b**) is adopted from [9]

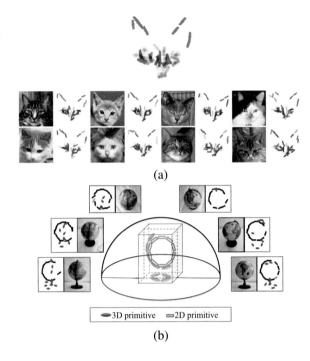

images. For example, consider the images of leaves at different scales shown in Fig. 17.1, one can easily identify the structures inside the first image, but quickly give up and change to appearance based description for the last image. By gradually zooming the camera, images in between must combine some portion of both structure and appearance. A similar spectrum for the 2D and 3D case is suggested in [7].

In this chapter, we want to evaluate and combine these representations on purely intrinsic and quantitative measurements. The idea behind this work is that elements (primitives) in competing representations should be weighted by their information contribution. Borrowing from information theory, we take information gain as a quantitative measure of this contribution. We further introduce a mathematical framework called information projection, which evaluates and sequentially selects elements from both competing representations, so that the best representation of a given set of images can be learned automatically.

As a result of using a combined pool of representational elements, we find that the learned result almost always mixes the competing representations. Figure 17.2

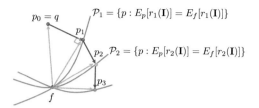

Fig. 17.3 Learning by information projection, illustrated in the model space. Each point in this space represents a possible model or a distribution over the target images. The series of models $p_0, p_1, \ldots, p_K$ converge to the target probability f monotonically by sequentially matching the constraints. Image adopted from [19]

shows two typical examples for the structure vs. appearance case and 3D vs. 2D case in our study. In the structure vs. appearance case, we take deformable Gabor filters [16] as primitives for structure representation, and oriented histograms of Gabor responses as those for appearance. On cat face images shown in Fig. 17.2(a), Gabor filters (dark bars) are automatically selected to describe the boundary of cat ears, eyes and mouth etc., while the histograms (red disks) are used to encode the texture of fur on the cat face. Similarly, in the 2D vs. 3D case, we take 2D Gabor filters and 3D stick-like elements as primitives for object-centered representation and viewer-centered representation respectively. Given the set of desktop globe images shown in Fig. 17.2(b), the algorithm selects 3D primitives (red bars) for the handle and the base as their appearance change drastically across views, and uses 2D primitives (dark bars) for the much more view invariant circular shape of the globe. More experiments on various image classes reveal that the representation spectrum exist, which further shows the importance of having a numerical solution to the representation integration problem.

In the rest of this chapter, we will first introduce the information projection framework along with our information gain criterion, followed by detailed case studies over the above two pairs of competing representations.

17.2 Information Projection

We treat the set of images we want to model as samples from a target image distribution $f(\mathbf{I})$:

$$\left\{\mathbf{I}_m^{\text{obs}}; m = 1, 2, \ldots, M\right\} \sim f(\mathbf{I}). \tag{17.1}$$

Our objective is to learn a sequence of models p starting from an initial reference model q, which would incrementally approach the target distribution f by minimizing the Kullback-Leibler divergence $KL(f \| p)$:

$$q = p_0 \to p_1 \to \cdots p_k \text{ to } f. \tag{17.2}$$

The approach can be explained in the space of probability distributions shown in Fig. 17.3, where each point is a model describing a probability distribution over target images. Our true model f and the initial model q are two points in the space with a large divergence $KL(f\|q)$.

The learning proceeds iteratively. In each iteration, we augment the current model p_{k-1} to p_k, by adding one statistical constraint so that p_k matches a new marginal statistics $E_f[r_k(\mathbf{I})]$, where $r_k(\mathbf{I})$ is a scalar or vector valued function of images, denoting the response of an element (such as a Gabor filter) in image representations. Specifically, an iteration is composed of the following two steps:

1. *Min-step.* Given an unobserved image statistics $E_f[r_k(\mathbf{I})]$, we want to find the model p_k^* in the set of models $\mathcal{P}_k$ having the same statistics as f while as close to p_{k-1} as possible:

$$\mathcal{P}_k = \{p : E_p[r_k(\mathbf{I})] = E_f[r_k(\mathbf{I})]\}. \tag{17.3}$$

The closeness is evaluated by $KL(p_k\|p_{k-1})$. Intuitively, this is to enforce that on the element k our model should produce the same image statistics as the true model f. In Fig. 17.3, this set of models $\mathcal{P}_k$ can be shown as the corresponding gray curve passing through f. According to the Pythagorean theorem [5] in information theory, the new model p^* is the perpendicular projection of p_{k-1} on $\mathcal{P}_k$, and the three points f, p_k^*, p_{k-1} form a right triangle.

The step above actually solves the constrained optimization problem of

$$p_k^* = \underset{p \in \mathcal{P}_k}{\arg\min}\, KL(p\|p_{k-1}). \tag{17.4}$$

By using Lagrange multiplier, we have

$$p_k(\mathbf{I}; \Theta_k) = \frac{1}{z_k} p_{k-1}(\mathbf{I}; \Theta_{k-1}) e^{-\lambda_k r_k(\mathbf{I})} \tag{17.5}$$

where λ_k is the parameter satisfying the constraint in Eq. (17.3), z_k is the partition function that normalize the probability to 1, and $\Theta_k = \{\lambda_1, \lambda_2, \ldots, \lambda_k\}$.

2. *Max-step.* Among all the candidate elements $r(\mathbf{I})$ and their statistics, choose the one that reveals the largest difference between p_k and p_{k-1}.

$$r_k^* = \arg\max\, KL(p_k\|p_{k-1}). \tag{17.6}$$

As the KL divergence is non-negative and

$$KL(p_k\|p_{k-1}) = KL(f\|p_{k-1}) - KL(f\|p_k), \tag{17.7}$$

this step greedily minimize the KL-divergence between f and our final model p. Intuitively, this step chooses a curve in Fig. 17.3 which is farthest away from the current model p_{k-1}.

After K iterations, we obtain a model

$$p(\mathbf{I}|\Theta) = q(\mathbf{I}) \prod_{k=1}^{K} \frac{1}{z_k} e^{-\lambda_k r_k}, \tag{17.8}$$

and the information gain of each step k is:

$$Ig_k = E_{p_k}\left[\log \frac{p_k(\mathbf{I}|\Theta)}{p_{k-1}(\mathbf{I})}\right] = KL(p_k \| p_{k-1}). \tag{17.9}$$

As the information gain in step k is equal to $KL(p_k \| p_{k-1})$, each of the training iterations above actually selects the representation element which achieves maximum information gain over the current model p_{k-1}. This learning process sequentially projects the current model to a number of constrained spaces, and thus is called information projection.

As the only assumption in the above model is that the candidate element should have a scalar or vector valued response, the information projection framework can be used in many feature or pattern learning problems, provided that the goal of learning is to construct the target image distribution, and the candidate element pool is fixed before learning. In the following, we discuss in detail the candidate element pools and implementation details in studying the two groups of competing representations introduced Sect. 17.1.

17.3 Case I: Combining Sketch and Texture

In the first case study, we illustrate the integration of structure and appearance as hybrid image templates (HIT) for object image modelling. More discussion about this hybrid image template can be seen in [19].

We assume the training images $\{\mathbf{I}_m^{\mathrm{obs}} : m = 1, 2, \ldots, M\}$ are instances of an object category and are roughly aligned in position, orientation and scale with arbitrary background, such as the ones shown in Fig. 17.2(a). While a single template suffices for the cat examples here, when there is large pose variations on the objects in training images, multiple templates can be learned through an EM-like clustering procedure.

Given the set of training image, the lattice of the image Λ is decomposed into a set of K non-overlapping patches $\{\Lambda_i\}_{i=1}^{K}$ selected from a large pool of candidate patches. Note that these patches do not necessary compose the full lattice Λ as some pixels in Λ may correspond to object background which have inconsistent feature responses.

By enumerating all possible patch candidates, and assuming each patch can be represented either by its structure or appearance, we are able to construct a large pool of candidate representation elements. It is worth noting that although the final selected set of patches are assumed to be non-overlapping, patches in the candidate pool are not subject to this restriction.

Currently, we limit the structure elements to be sketches only, such as those shown on the boundary of the hedgehog template in Fig. 17.4(b). If an image patch $\mathbf{I}_{\Lambda_k}$ is represented as a sketch, we define its element response $r^{\mathrm{skt}}(\mathbf{I}_{\Lambda_k})$ by

$$r^{\mathrm{skt}}(\mathbf{I}_{\Lambda_k}) = \max_{\mathrm{d}x \in \partial x, \mathrm{d}o \in \partial o} S\left(\left|\langle \mathbf{I}, B_{x_k+\mathrm{d}x, o_k+\mathrm{d}o}\rangle\right|^2\right) \tag{17.10}$$

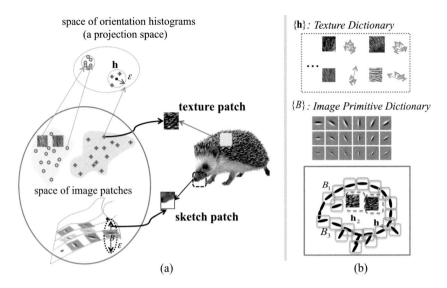

space of orientation histograms
(a projection space)

{**h**}: *Texture Dictionary*

texture patch

{*B*}: *Image Primitive Dictionary*

space of image patches

sketch patch

(a)   (b)

Fig. 17.4 (**a**) A hedgehog image may be seen as a bunch of local image patches, being either sketches or textures. (**b**) Quantization in the image space and histogram feature space provides candidate pools for sketches {*B*} and textures {**h**}, respectively. A hybrid template of hedgehog $T = \{B_1, \mathbf{h}_2, B_3, \mathbf{h}_4, \ldots\}$ is composed of sketches and histogram prototypes explaining local image patches at different locations. Image adopted from [19]

which is a transformed local maximum response of a image primitive B around a local neighborhood of a specific position x and orientation o indexed by k. Here we choose the primitives to be Gabor filters at a set of discrete orientations, such as the ones shown in Fig. 17.4(b), $\langle \cdot, \cdot \rangle$ denotes the inner product between the image and the filter, and $S(\cdot)$ is the sigmoid transform that saturates large filter responses.

Similarly, we limit the appearance elements to be those for texture only, and define the element response as:

$$r^{\mathrm{app}}(\mathbf{I}_{\Lambda_k}) = S\big(\big\| H(\mathbf{I}_{\Lambda_k}) - \mathbf{h} \big\|^2\big) \qquad (17.11)$$

where $H(\mathbf{I}_{\Lambda_k})$ is the histogram of the responses from Gabor filters at different orientations pooled within $\mathbf{I}_{\Lambda_k}$ and $\mathbf{h}$ is a pre-computed histogram prototype (one may consider it as a cluster center of similar texture patches). In practice, $\mathbf{h}$ is obtained by averaging the histograms at the same position over all the observed training examples.

By constructing this candidate pool, we derive a large set of constraints as in Eq. (17.3) on the individual response of patch representations, where $E_f[r(\mathbf{I}_{\Lambda_k})]$ is estimated by the average response on observed images

$$E_f\big[r(\mathbf{I}_{\Lambda_k})\big] \approx \frac{1}{M} \sum_{m=1}^{M} r(\mathbf{I}_{m, \Lambda_k}). \qquad (17.12)$$

Fig. 17.5 Learned HITs of several object categories. *Bold black bars* denote sketches, while *gray blobs* denote texture patches. For illustration purpose, we only show sketches/textures of a single scale and vary the (relative) Gabor scales for different categories

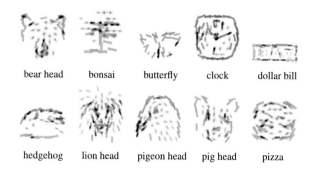

bear head   bonsai   butterfly   clock   dollar bill

hedgehog   lion head   pigeon head   pig head   pizza

Because we assume the selected patches are non-overlapping,

$$Ig_k = KL\big[p_k(\mathbf{I}) \| p_{k-1}(\mathbf{I})\big] = KL\big[p(\mathbf{I}_{\Lambda_k}) \| q(\mathbf{I}_{\Lambda_k})\big], \qquad (17.13)$$

thus the information gain of each candidate element can be computed ahead of time by matching $E_p[r_k(\mathbf{I})] = E_f[r_k(\mathbf{I})]$. During learning, the patch non-overlapping assumption is enforced by inhibiting (removing) candidate patches with significant overlap with selected ones.

Figure 17.5 shows the hybrid templates learned from several categories. The sketches usually outlines the rough shape of the target object category, with the appearance patches fill in the furs on animal head or leaves on the tree.

We also study how the structure and appearance patches are ordered by their information gains. We choose four categories ranging from structured to textured: head-shoulder, hedgehog, pizza, and wavy water. In Fig. 17.6 we plot the information gains of the selected patches in decreasing order: the hollow bars are for structure patches and the solid bars are for texture patches. For image categories with regular shape, for example, head/shoulder, sketches dominate the information gain. For the wavy water, textures makes the most contributions. The two categories in the middle contains different degrees of mix of sketch and texture.

Learned templates can be used for image classification. Quantitative experiments in [19] show that our method performances on-par with HoG+SVM approach [6] on several public datasets, while using far shorter (at least 1/10) feature dimensions.

17.4 Case II: Mixing 3D and 2D Primitives

In the second case study, we illustrate the automatic selection of viewer-centered and object-centered representations, which build object templates composed of 3D and 2D primitives. The observed images are those of an object category captured from different views $\{\mathbf{I}_m, \omega_m\}_{m=1}^{M}$, where ω denotes the view of the image parameterized by the pan and tilt angle of camera. For simplicity, we assume the camera roll angle is zero, and object images are captured at the same scale. More discussion about this case study can be found in [9].

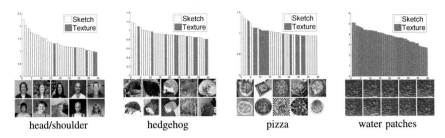

head/shoulder   hedgehog   pizza   water patches

Fig. 17.6 Transition from structure based to appearance based representation. For each image category, the top 40 selected patches are ordered by their information gains in decreasing order. Image adopted from [19]

Similar to the structure vs. appearance case, we have two types of image primitives to build our pool of constraints.

The first type is the primitive for object-centered representation, which we call 3D primitives. The 3D primitives are stick like primitives with position X and orientation O in 3D space, such as the ones shown in the center of Fig. 17.8. On object images, primitives are realized by Gabor filters at their projected positions and orientations, and primitive responses can be defined similar to the sketch responses in the previous case study:

$$r_k^{3D}(\mathbf{I}; \omega) = \max_{dx \in \partial x, do \in \partial o} \mathrm{S}\left(\left|\langle \mathbf{I}, G_{P(X_k,\omega)+dx, P(O_k,\omega)+do}\rangle\right|^2\right) \qquad (17.14)$$

where $P(\cdot, \cdot)$ denotes the camera projection function.

Our 3D primitive pool is created by enumerating combinations of 3D positions X and orientations O as in Fig. 17.7(a). To avoid an excessive enumeration of 3D primitives, we quantize the 3D object volume into non-overlapping cuboids, and inside each cuboid, we sample primitive orientations uniformly.

We illustrate how the proposed 3D primitives pool information from images in Fig. 17.8. For each hypothesized 3D primitive, we project it on to observed images from different views, compute its primitive responses on images and estimate its statistics. Primitive responses of meaningful ones will be consistently high across views and will contribute significant information gains.

The 2D primitives we choose for viewer-based image representation are the same as the sketches in case study I, and thus are not further explained.

Compared with learning the hybrid image templates model in Sect. 17.3, one key difference in mixing 3D and 2D primitives is that the primitives might occlude each other, such as in the desktop globe example. Also, as a viewer-centered representation, the 2D primitives should be allowed to be view specific, thus individual 2D sketches may only explain some of the observed images whose views are in a specific range.

To model these effects, we introduce another auxiliary variable Ω to describe the visible range of a primitive, which is defined as a set of N views on which the corresponding primitive is visible: $\Omega = \{\omega_1, \omega_2, \ldots, \omega_N\}$.

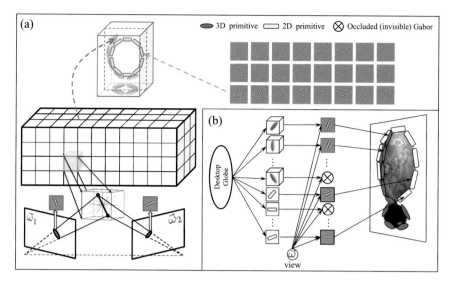

Fig. 17.7 (**a**) Illustration of 3D and 2D primitives and how they are used to compose mixed representations. The 3D primitives can be viewed as sticks with selected 3D positions and orientations, while 2D primitive are Gabor filters located at selected 2D positions and orientations. (**b**) When generating object images at a particular view ω, we project the 3D primitives and superimpose the 2D primitives. A primitive is not instantiated if it is not visible in the particular view. Image adopted from [9]

Fig. 17.8 Illustration of how 3D primitives are learned from images in different views. The learning step can be interpreted as trying all possible locations and orientations of 3D primitives and incrementally select ones with high overall responses. Image from [9]

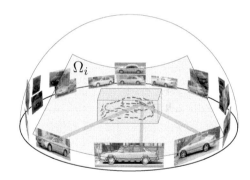

Adding this auxiliary variable leads to the following changes in *Min-step* and *Max-step*:

In *Min-step*, the estimation of $E_f[r(\mathbf{I})]$ is changed to the sample mean of the primitive response on visible images:

$$E_f\big[r(\mathbf{I})\big] \approx \frac{1}{N} \sum_{m=1}^{M} r_k(\mathbf{I}_m) \cdot \mathbf{1}(\omega_m \in \Omega_k) \tag{17.15}$$

where $\mathbf{1}(\cdot)$ is an indicator function that equals 1 if ω_m is in set Ω_k, and 0 otherwise. In Eq. (17.15), $N = \sum_{m=1}^{M} \mathbf{1}(\omega_m \in \Omega_k)$.

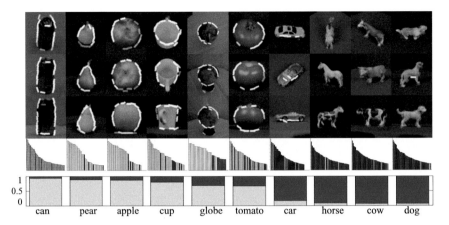

Fig. 17.9 Spectrum of image representations in 2D/3D case. *Row 1–3*: Learned templates for each object category. The *white bars* represent 2D primitives and red ellipses are 3D primitives. *Row 4*: The selection order of 2D and 3D primitives in each object class and their information gains. *Row 5*: The ratio on the information contribution of 3D and 2D primitives. Image from [9]

In *Max-step*, the constraint selection criterion is also updated to

$$\left(r_k^*, \Omega_k^*\right) = \arg\max KL(p_k \| p_{k-1}). \tag{17.16}$$

Conceptually, adding auxiliary variable Ω will dramatically increase the computational complexity, since for each primitive, we need to search through 2^M possible different view ranges. However, since we only care about the pair which leads to maximum information gain, these 2^M evaluations would be reduced to less than M evaluations. Details of this simplification can be found in [9].

For experiments, we use the ETH80 dataset [13], and further augment it by adding images of soda cans and desktop globes to have 10 categories of object images, where each one is captured from different views and with a few instances. Due to the difficulty in illustrating the 3D elements in mixed templates, we directly show their projections on sample training images in the first three rows of Fig. 17.9.

From the figure, we can see that our method automatically finds suitable representations for different object categories, which spans a spectrum from nearly pure 2D to pure 3D. For object categories with stable 2D shapes, the algorithm automatically selects 2D primitives to form the rough shape of that category. For parts such as the tip of tomatoes, and handle of cups, it selects 3D primitives, because these details are view specific and only appear in part of the view sphere. For categories with complex shapes, coding the projected shape for each single view will be less efficient than coding the general 3D shape using 3D primitives. So, the algorithm automatically transit to mostly selecting 3D primitives.

Row 4 and 5 of Fig. 17.9 shows the selection order of the 3D (red) and 2D (gray) primitives, their information gains, and their proportion of information contribution in each template. By sorting these categories according to this proportion, Fig. 17.9

Fig. 17.10 The confusion matrix over 8 poses in the 3D car dataset [18], and sample car pose estimation results. 3D and 2D primitives are all showed using white bars. Image adopted from [9]

clearly shows that the learned representations reside in different positions of the spectrum, and their positions are related to the complexity of the object shape.

The learned model can be used for image classification and object pose estimation. Figure 17.10 shows sample pose estimation results and the confusion matrix over the 8 views in 3D car dataset [18]. More experiment results can be found in [9].

17.5 Discussion

This chapter introduces a general learning framework that automatically mixes different representations to find the best representation for a given set of images. By using images of different object classes, we show that there are representation spectrum where images are best represented by mixing different proportions of competing representations. Although only particular cases are illustrated, the framework we describe permits the exploration of this approach to general representations and we hope it will prove to be useful for researchers in the vision community.

Acknowledgements This work is supported by DARPA grant FA 8650-11-1-7149, NSF IIS1018751 and MURI grant ONR N00014-10-1-0933.

References

1. Barr AH (1981) Superquadrics and angle-preserving transformations. IEEE Comput Graph Appl 1(1):11–23
2. Biederman I (1987) Recognition-by-components: a theory of human image understanding. Psychol Rev 94:115–117
3. Biederman I, Gerhardstein PC (1995) Viewpoint-dependent mechanisms in visual object recognition: reply to Tarr and Bülthoff (1995). J Exp Psychol Hum Percept Perform 21(6):1506–1514
4. Canny J (1986) A computational approach to edge detection. IEEE Trans Pattern Anal Mach Intell 8:679–698
5. Csiszár I, Shields PC (2004) Information theory and statistics: a tutorial. Now Publishers, Hanover

6. Dalal N, Triggs B (2005) Histograms of oriented gradients for human detection. In: CVPR, pp 886–893

7. Dickinson SJ, Pentland AP, Rosenfeld A (1991) From volumes to views: an approach to 3-d object recognition. In: Workshop on directions in automated CAD-based vision, pp 85–96

8. Hayward WG, Tarr MJ (1997) Testing conditions for viewpoint invariance in object recognition. J Exp Psychol Hum Percept Perform 23(5):1511–1521

9. Hu W, Zhu S-C (2010) Learning a probabilistic model mixing 3D and 2D primitives for view invariant object recognition. In: Computer vision and pattern recognition, pp 2273–2280

10. Julesz B (1981) Textons, the elements of texture perception, and their interactions. Nature 290(5802):91–97

11. Koenderink JJ, Doorn AJ (1976) The singularities of the visual mapping. Biol Cybern 24(1):51–59

12. Koenderink JJ, Doorn AJ (1979) The internal representation of solid shape with respect to vision. Biol Cybern 32(4):211–216

13. Leibe B, Schiele B (2003) Analyzing appearance and contour based methods for object categorization. In: CVPR

14. Lowe DG (2004) Distinctive image features from scale-invariant keypoints. Int J Comput Vis 60(2):91–110

15. Marr D (1982) Vision. A computational investigation into the human representation and processing of visual information. Freeman, New York

16. Olshausen BA, Field DJ (1996) Emergence of simple-cell receptive field properties by learning a sparse code for natural images. Nature 381:607–609

17. Poggio T, Edelman S (1990) A network that learns to recognize three-dimensional objects. Nature 343(6255):263–266

18. Savarese S, Fei-Fei L (2007) 3d generic object categorization, localization and pose estimation. In: ICCV

19. Si Z, Zhu S-C (2012) Learning hybrid image templates (hit) by information projection. IEEE Trans Pattern Anal Mach Intell 34(7):1354–1367

20. Tarr MJ, Bülthoff HH (1995) Is human object recognition better described by geon structural descriptions or by multiple views? Comment on Biederman and Gerhardstein (1993). J Exp Psychol Hum Percept Perform 21(6):1494–1505

21. Ullman S, Basri R (1991) Recognition by linear combinations of models. IEEE Trans Pattern Anal Mach Intell 13(10):992–1006

Chapter 18
Challenges in Understanding Visual Shape Perception and Representation: Bridging Subsymbolic and Symbolic Coding

Philip J. Kellman, Patrick Garrigan, and Gennady Erlikhman

18.1 Introduction

Our everyday perceptual experience is of a world populated by objects and surfaces arrayed in space, as well as of events that produce changes in these arrangements over time. Successful perception, thought and action depend on processes that produce accurate descriptions of these objects and events. Often, object contours are only partially visible as we move or as they move around us. Nevertheless, we experience a unified, stable world: the squirrel running through the tree branches appears as a single animal, not as dissociated squirrel-bits, and the house seen through the slats of a fence is one house, not a collection of independent house fragments. These perceptual outcomes depend on a number of segmentation, grouping, and interpolation processes, which, taken together, perform some of the most crucial and remarkable tasks in allowing us to perceive the world visually. They also pose some of the greatest challenges in understanding the underlying processes and mechanisms of vision.

Researchers in the past several decades have made considerable progress on a number of important components of these perceptual capabilities. Much is known about early cortical processing of visual information. At a more abstract level, experimental data and computational models have revealed a great deal about contour, object, and shape perception. Neurophysiological and imaging methods have provided evidence for functional specificity in areas of cortex for animate and inanimate objects, tools, faces, and places. However, between the initial encodings by spatially localized units and higher level descriptions of contours, surfaces, objects and their properties lies a considerable gap. To use a chess analogy, we do not understand

P.J. Kellman (✉) · G. Erlikhman
Department of Psychology, University of California, Los Angeles, USA
e-mail: kellman@cognet.ucla.edu

P. Garrigan
Department of Psychology, St. Joseph's University, Philadelphia, PA, USA

S.J. Dickinson, Z. Pizlo (eds.), *Shape Perception in Human and Computer Vision*,
Advances in Computer Vision and Pattern Recognition,
DOI 10.1007/978-1-4471-5195-1_18, © Springer-Verlag London 2013

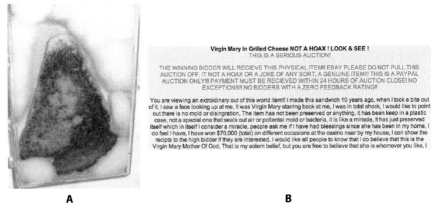

Fig. 18.1 Spiritual, culinary, and commercial aspects of shape perception. (**A**) This 10-year-old, partially eaten cheese sandwich sold for $28,000 on Ebay; the owner claimed to see the face of the Virgin Mary in it. (**B**) Description from the Ebay ad. (See text.) (From http://www.slate.com/articles/news_and_politics/explainer/2004/11/the_28k_sandwich_that_grew_no_mold.html)

much about the "middle game." The study of shape perception and representation is important in its own right but also because it gives us a sharp focus on some of the biggest unsolved general issues in the computational and neural understanding of perception.

Early cortical encodings (e.g., responses of neural units in V1) are spatially local, retinally specific, and modulated by oriented contrast. The functionally important outputs of perceiving are constancy-based descriptions of bounded objects, their contours, surfaces, and shapes, and their arrangements in space. Our goal in this chapter is to shed light on shape perception, but also to use it as a vehicle to focus on major issues that must be addressed in order to understand how early visual processes connect to high-level representations. We describe (1) the dependence of shape perception on segmentation and grouping processes, and (2) properties that (some) shape representations must have and how they might be assembled from lower level encodings. In both discussions, we end with thoughts and efforts on a crucial frontier of work in these areas, which we might call "modeling the middle."

18.2 Some Useful Examples

To begin, we offer two demonstrations that illustrate the flexible and abstract nature of shape representations and the important issue of what gets assigned a shape representation.

What is shown in Fig. 18.1? It is perhaps the most famous cheese sandwich in history. The story, in the owner's own words in an E-bay advertisement, is given in Fig. 18.1B. The image and description may relate to several different scientific mysteries. Given that this cheese sandwich has had "no disingration [sic]" in 10 years, one of the mysteries is, obviously: What are they in putting in the bread?!

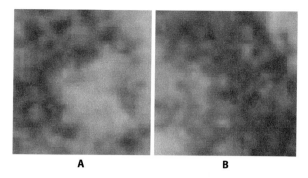

Fig. 18.2 Which region was part of the display in Fig. 18.1A? The difficulty of answering provides a simple demonstration that we encode simplified and abstract descriptions of displays, not pixel maps or records of feature activations

For us, the more important fact is that humans spontaneously see a face in the toast. This reveals more than one interesting fact about shape representations. A key observation is that such representations are flexible enough to be matched to new input that is markedly different from previously experienced faces. Putting aside whether the image is in fact the Virgin Mary, or bears, as others have suggested, a resemblance to Greta Garbo or a young Shirley Temple, the striking fact is that any recognition here is not a match at the pixel level. Presumably, if you have seen Garbo before, she was not impersonating a cheese sandwich. More formally, our encoding of this display is both much less and much more than a literal copy of the stimulus. Consider Fig. 18.2. Suppose we tell you that one of the panels shows a region of Fig. 18.1A. Without looking at Fig. 18.1A, which is it—Fig. 18.2A or 18.2B? We doubt anyone can answer correctly with confidence. Now, compare the regions to Fig. 18.1A. With serious effort, you can see that the region in Fig. 18.2A matches an area near the left eye, and the region in Fig. 18.2B also matches, around the right eye. Even with all images visible, verification of the match is an effortful task. This kind of demonstration, and many ordinary observations, indicate that we preserve very little of the point-by-point stimulus in encoding shape information.

This should not be seen as a shortcoming of our visual processing. The ability to see a face here and to detect similarities to previously seen faces implicates extraction of relevant structure while ignoring irrelevant variation. The structure extracted must be encoded in some abstract form sufficient to trigger activation of previously encoded structure. Two other notable points here are that we are able to see a face while still encoding the entire object as a cheese sandwich, and that we spontaneously see the face despite the low expectations (and low prior odds, in Bayesian frameworks) for seeing faces in partially eaten cheese sandwiches. Most important, however, is the suggestion of an abstract, flexible representational format that allows matching of selected structure to categorical shape information encoded or formed earlier.

Our second demonstration leads more directly into the connection between shape perception and visual segmentation and grouping processes. Glance at the picture in

Fig. 18.3 Illustration of the dependence of shape descriptions on object formation. (See text.) (Reprinted with permission from fotosearch.com)

Fig. 18.3 and then cover it up. Looking at Fig. 18.4, which panel, A or B, shows a shape that was present in the original figure? The question is difficult to answer.

Now uncover Fig. 18.3. Both regions turn out to be part of the picture. The region in Fig. 18.4A is part of the cow's head, and the shape in Fig. 18.4B is part of the fence post. Both of the regions shown in Fig. 18.4 are fairly well delineated by contrast boundaries in the image.[1] Naively, we might expect that bounded regions in the visual input comprise the objects to which we assign shape descriptions. Examples such as these demonstrate that such an expectation is often incorrect.

We assign shape descriptions to *objects*. The detection of objects in a visual scene, if it is to correspond to actual physical objects in the world, must overcome a number of obstacles. Perhaps most important is occlusion. A single object in the world may project to the retinae of our eyes in multiple, spatially separated regions, as illustrated by the cow in Fig. 18.3. A single object may have a variety of colors, such that lightness and color boundaries are incomplete indicators of object boundaries. Fortunately, our visual processing includes sophisticated mechanisms

Fig. 18.4 Which region is part of the display in Fig. 18.3? (See text)

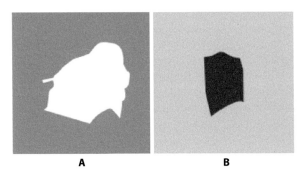

A   B

---

[1]These are mostly, but not fully, delineated by contrast boundaries. The difficulty in using contrast boundaries alone to find the functionally important shapes in the environment is another important aspect of the relation between processes that accomplish segmentation and shape representation.

for perceiving coherent objects from information that is fragmentary in space (and also in time, although we do not consider spatiotemporal fragmentation here; see [37] for relevant research and [32] for a review).

Shape perception in biological vision, then, means something more than finding regions of roughly homogeneous lightness and/or color. Rather, shape encoding appears to be reserved for functional units delivered by segmentation and grouping processes. In the next section, we describe processes of interpolation that connect visible regions across gaps to furnish the objects that receive shape descriptions. Introducing these will show their relevance to shape perception and also highlight the issue of "modeling the middle" in vision science.

18.3 Interpolation Processes Underlying Object Perception

From the perspective of an organism that needs to see, the projection of objects and scenes in the world onto the sensitive surfaces of our eyes is beset by several chronic problems. The world has three spatial dimensions, but information is lost as it is projected onto the essentially two-dimensional surface of each retina. Light moves in straight lines, and objects are usually opaque; these facts dictate that in ordinary environments nearer objects will often partly occlude farther ones, meaning the projections of farther objects will be interrupted by the projections of nearer ones. Commonly, a single object may project to multiple, spatially separated retinal regions.

When motion of objects or observers is involved, these patterns of occlusion become more complex, changing over time. Different parts of a single object may be visible at different times, while some parts of objects may never project to the eyes at all. Such problems of occlusion are not exclusively products of modern, cluttered environments; some of the richest and most complex patterns of occlusion occur when we view objects and scenes through foliage, a situation that has likely been important in human behavior over evolutionary time.

Perhaps these enduring constraints on seeing are responsible for the sophisticated and elegant visual processes that serve to overcome occlusion. The human visual system possesses remarkable mechanisms for recovering coherent objects and surface representations from fragmentary input. Specifically, object and surface perception depends on interpolation processes that overcome gaps in contours and surfaces in 2-D, 3-D, and spatiotemporal displays. Recent research suggests that the mechanisms for doing so are deeply related in that they exploit common geometric regularities.

18.4 Contour and Surface Processes

Evidence suggests that there are two kinds of mechanisms for connecting visible areas across gaps: contour and surface interpolation. These processes can be distinguished because they operate in different circumstances and depend on different

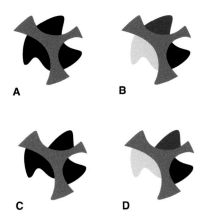

Fig. 18.5 Contour and surface interpolation. (**A**) Both contour and surface interpolation processes contribute to perceived unity of the three black regions behind the gray occluder. (**B**) Contour interpolation alone. (**C**) Surface interpolation alone. (**D**) Both contour and surface interpolation have been disrupted, causing the *blue, yellow, and black regions* to appear as three separate objects. (See text)

variables. Contour interpolation depends on geometric relations of visible contour segments that lead into contour junctions. These geometric constraints have been most frequently studied in 2-D displays, but they have been shown to govern contour interpolation in 3-D scenes as well [33]. Surface interpolation in 2-D displays can occur in the absence of contour segments or junctions; it depends on the similarity of lightness, color, and/or texture of visible surface patches. In 3-D scenes, it also depends on the orientations and positions of visible fragments [9]. For simplicity, we describe interpolation processes in 2-D displays here.

Figure 18.5 illustrates distinguishable contour and surface interpolation processes, as well as some of their interactions. In Fig. 18.5A, the three black regions appear as one object connecting behind the gray occluder. Both the contour relationships of the black regions and their surface similarity contribute to this percept. In Fig. 18.5B, the surface colors of the visible regions have been altered to block surface interpolation. However, the relations of the contours still engage contour interpolation, leading to an impression of a unified object despite the color differences. Figure 18.5C shows the converse arrangement. Here, the geometry of *contour relatability* (see below) has been disrupted blocking contour interpolation. Due to surface interpolation (included by the matching surface color of the fragments), however, there is still some impression that the three fragments connect behind the occluder. Finally, Fig. 18.5D shows both contour and surface interpolation disrupted. Here, the blue, yellow, and black regions appear as three separate objects.

Figure 18.6 further illustrates the action of surface interpolation. Surface interpolation in Fig. 18.6B causes the same black objects that appear separate in Fig. 18.6A to appear connected. Surface interpolation also causes the circle within the gray area to appear as a hole, rather than a spot on top of a surface [54]. In this display, con-

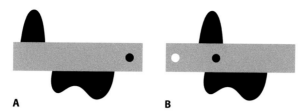

Fig. 18.6 Rules of surface interpolation under occlusion. Contour relations in both displays are arranged so as not to produce contour interpolation behind the occluder. (**A**) The three black regions appear as separate objects; the *circle on the right* appears as a spot on top of the gray background. (**B**) The three black regions have been positioned so that surface spreading within extended tangents of edge orientations at points of occlusion allows areas to connect behind the occluder. A bloblike single object, whose contours behind the occluder are vague, is perceived. The *black circle* is now seen as a *hole* in the occluder. The *white circle* also illustrates surface spreading; it appears as a hole through which the white background is seen

tour interpolation is blocked due to misalignment of the edges. It has been shown that the surface interpolation process under occlusion integrates areas of similar surface quality (1) when they fall within edges connected by contour interpolation, (2) when they fall within the extended tangents of nonrelatable edges, or (3) when the fall within a fully surrounding area (as in the case of the white dot in Fig. 18.6B) [55]. Whereas contour interpolation processes are relatively insensitive to relations of lightness or color, the surface process depends crucially on these.

18.5 Contour Interpolation

Central to establishing perceived shape is the process of contour interpolation, which unifies visible regions across gaps (for reviews, see [31, 33]). Perhaps the most basic question in understanding visual object and surface formation is what stimulus relationships cause it to occur. This question is fundamental because it allows us to understand the nature of visual interpolation. For contour interpolation, certain relations of visible contours lead the visual system to fill in connections between visible regions whereas other contour relationships do not. Discovering the geometric relations and related stimulus conditions that lead to object formation is analogous to understanding the grammar of a language (e.g., what constitutes a well-formed sentence). This level of understanding is also most crucial for appreciating the deepest links between the physical world and our mental representations of it. While these efforts are at first descriptive, as unifying principles are revealed, they allow us to relate the information used by the visual system to the physical laws governing how objects and surfaces project to the eyes, in the form of deep constraints about the way the world works (e.g., [16, 36]) or as natural scene statistics (e.g., [14]).

18.6 Triggering Contour Interpolation

A general fact about contour interpolation is that interpolated contours begin and end at junctions or corners in visible contours (tangent discontinuities). These are locations at which contours have no unique orientation [44, 46]. Most typically in vision, they are intersections of two oriented contours, such as "T" junctions that form when the boundary of an occluding object interrupts that of an occluded object. Whereas a zero-order discontinuity would be a spatial gap in a contour, a first-order or tangent discontinuity is a point at which the direction of the contour changes abruptly. Besides first-order discontinuities, some have suggested that second-order discontinuities (as where a straight segment joins a constant curvature segment, with the slopes matching at the join point) might also play a role in triggering interpolation ([2–4, 46]; for discussion see [33]). The importance of tangent discontinuities in visual processes coping with occlusion stems from an ecological invariant: Shipley and Kellman [46] observed that in general, interpolated contours begin and end at tangent discontinuities and showed that their removal eliminated or markedly reduced contour interpolation. In the patterns that induce illusory contour formation, "L" junctions, rather than T junctions, are most common. In these displays, the presence or absence of tangent discontinuities can be manipulated by rounding the corners of inducing elements, a manipulation that experimental evidence shows reduces or eliminates contour interpolation (e.g., [3, 33, 37, 46]).

18.7 Contour Relatability

What determines which visible contour fragments get connected to form objects? Although tangent discontinuities are ordinarily necessary conditions for contour interpolation, they are not sufficient. After all, many corners in images are corners of objects, not points at which some contour passes behind an intervening surface (or in front, as in illusory contours).

Empirical research shows that contour interpolation depends crucially on geometric relations of visible contour fragments, specifically the relative positions and orientations of pairs of edges leading into points of tangent discontinuity [11, 26, 29–31, 33, 37, 44, 46]. These relations have been described formally in terms of *contour relatability* [29, 49]. Relatability is a mathematical notion that defines a categorical distinction between edges that can connect by interpolation and those that cannot (see [29]). The key idea in contour relatability is smoothness (e.g., interpolated contours are differentiable at least once), but it also incorporates monotonicity (interpolated contours bend in only one direction) and a 90° limit (interpolated contours bend through no more than 90°). Figure 18.7 shows a construction that is useful in defining contour relatability. Formally, if E_1 and E_2 are surface edges, and R and r are perpendicular to these edges at points of tangent discontinuity, then E_1 and E_2 are relatable if and only if:

$$0 \leq R\cos\theta \leq r.$$

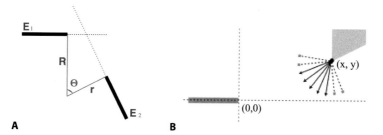

Fig. 18.7 Contour relatability. Contour relatability describes formally a categorical distinction between edges that can be connected by visual interpolation and those that cannot. (**A**) Geometric construction defining contour relatability (see text). (**B**) Alternative expression of relatability. Given one visible contour fragment terminating in a contour junction at $(0, 0)$ and having orientation 0 deg, those orientations Θ that satisfy the equation $\tan^{-1}(y/x) \leq \Theta \leq \pi/2$ are relatable. In the diagram, these are shown with *solid lines*, whereas nonrelatable orientations are shown with *dotted lines*. (Adapted from [23]. A unified model of illusory and occluded contour interpolation. *Vision Research, 50,* 284–299. Reprinted with permission)

Although the precise shape of interpolated contours is a matter of some disagreement, there are two properties of relatability that cohere naturally with a particular class of contour shapes. First, it can be shown that interpolated edges meeting the relatability criteria can always be comprised of one constant curvature segment and one zero curvature segment. Second, it appears that this shape of interpolated edges has the property of being a minimum curvature solution in that it has lowest maximum curvature: any other first-order continuous curve will have at least one point of greater curvature [29]. This is a slightly different minimum curvature notion than minimum energy.

Relatability is primarily a categorical distinction, indicating which edges can be connected by contour interpolation. Object perception often involves a discrete determination of whether two visible fragments are or are not part of the same object. Figure 18.8 shows examples of relatable and nonrelatable edges, in both perception of partly occluded objects and perception of illusory objects. Complete objects are formed in the top row but not in the bottom row. In general, object formation has profound effects on further processing, such as generation of a representation of missing areas, generation of an overall shape description, and comparison with items or categories in memory. Research indicates that the representation of visual areas as part of a single object or different objects has many important effects on information processing [6, 33, 56].

Relatability is a mathematical formulation that accounts for empirical findings on the geometric relations that support contour interpolation. It incorporates several separable claims, all of which have received substantial confirmation in empirical research. These include the requirements that the edge fragments that participate in interpolation are those terminating in tangent discontinuities [18, 33, 44, 46], the requirements that interpolated edges have orientations matching their inducing edges at the points of tangent discontinuity, are smooth (differentiable at least once), and monotonic (i.e., they do not doubly inflect) [10, 11, 29, 33, 37, 48]. Most evidence

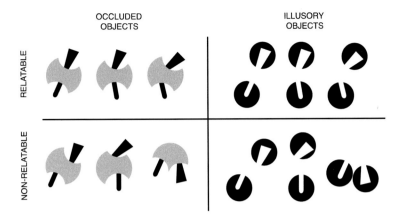

Fig. 18.8 Examples of relatable and nonrelatable contours. (See text)

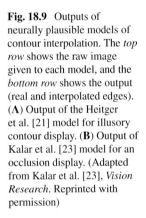

Fig. 18.9 Outputs of
neurally plausible models of
contour interpolation. The *top
row* shows the raw image
given to each model, and the
bottom row shows the output
(real and interpolated edges).
(**A**) Output of the Heitger
et al. [21] model for illusory
contour display. (**B**) Output of
Kalar et al. [23] model for an
occlusion display. (Adapted
from Kalar et al. [23], *Vision
Research.* Reprinted with
permission)

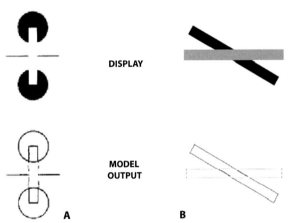

also supports the idea that interpolation is weak or absent for Θ greater than 90 deg
in Fig. 18.9B [10, 11, 14, 26, 33, 49], although data also suggests that the cutoff may
not be abrupt [11, 19]. Although discrete classification of visible areas as connected
or not is important, there is also evidence that quantitative variation exists within the
category of relatable edges [5, 10, 29, 47–49]. Singh and Hoffman [49] proposed an
expression for quantitative decline of relatability with angular change.

Some work based on scene statistics has been interpreted as showing some deviations from the predictions of relatability. Geisler & Perry [13] reported statistics
about the probabilities of arbitrary contour segments being connected in a variety
of scenes. In the same paper, the authors reported that observers' subjective judgments of contour connectedness conformed reasonably well to the scene statistics.
Compared to relatability, the most systematic deviation appeared to be that relatability allows connections between edge fragments of opposite contrast polarity, a
phenomenon that has been confirmed experimentally [10, 15, 24, 28], whereas the
collected scene statistics indicate that such connections are highly improbable. The

authors' data also indicates that an ideal observer using the natural priors they obtained would interpolate only between very nearly collinear edge fragments and primarily those within one deg of separation. These outcomes are surprising, in that they markedly differ from considerable evidence obtained from a variety of paradigms about human contour interpolation [11, 18, 33, 42, 48].

The discrepancies are not difficult to understand, however. The scene statistics gathered by Geisler & Perry [13] involved the probabilities of any arbitrary edge fragments in scenes being connected. A key geometric invariant in contour interpolation is that occlusion produces tangent discontinuities in the optical projection [29] and evidence indicates that this information is influential in contour interpolation (e.g., [44, 46]). Sampling edge fragments terminating in tangent discontinuities would involve a more restricted set of edge pairs and these may produce different scene statistics. The conditional probability of a pair of edge fragments being part of the same contour in the world, given their relative orientation, position, and separation may differ from the conditional probability of a pair of edge fragments being part of the same contour given those spatial relations *and* the fact that each terminates in a contour junction (typically a T junction, for potential cases of amodal completion). The latter seems more relevant to understanding the relations of environmental regularities to contour interpolation. We do not know whether these two conceptually different conditional probabilities would differ in their empirical distributions, but intuitively, the locations, orientations, sizes, etc. of occluders seems unlikely to be uniformly distributed across images.

Also difficult to interpret is the empirical study reported by Geisler & Perry [13], which involved subjective judgments of 7 observers, two of whom were not naïve. Observers were instructed that half of edge pairs presented in the study would be connected. Such instructions seem incompatible with an attempt to assess participants' natural perceptions of whether two edges appear to be connected under occlusion or not. These instructions also did *not* reflect the priors derived from scene statistics, so observers' results were compared to arbitrarily revised scene statistics incorporating a 0.5 prior on edges being connected, a prior that far exceeded the "natural priors" obtained from Geisler & Perry's scene statistics. Unlike many studies that have used objective performance methods [10, 30, 33, 37], the subjective report methods employed by Geisler & Perry [13] in combination with the prompting of participants to judge 50 % of edge pairs as connected make the task fraught with demand characteristics, as well as difficult to relate either to scene statistics or to other data on interpolation performance. One other major difference from both prior research and ordinary perception of natural scenes is that each "edge" presented in the experiment was a tiny Gabor element (with length roughly 6–7 arc min), and pairs of elements had comparatively large separations (occluders had diameters of 40, 80, and 180 arc min). It is known that strength of interpolation between pairs of inducers is a roughly linear function of support ratio [5, 48, 50], defined as the length of interpolated edge as a fraction of total (real plus interpolated) edge length. Relatively little or very weak interpolation would be expected with support ratios ranging from 0.07–0.25, as in this study, and the scene statistics in this study did not incorporate inducing edge lengths in any manner. It would be interesting to study the relationship of contour relatability to richer scene statistics in future research. Existing data support the geometric relations encompassed by relatability as a formal account of human contour interpolation, and the value of this particular geometry might indeed bear close relations to relevant statistical regularities in natural scenes.

18.8 Neural Models of Contour Interpolation

The model of object formation from fragmentary information, as we have sketched it here, as well as in more elaborate treatments [23, 25, 26, 33], assumes that certain kinds of inputs have been identified in prior visual processing. The inputs to contour interpolation, for example, are oriented edges of surface regions. The contour orientations that matter are those leading into tangent discontinuities, which we assume can be located by earlier visual processing. Whether such contour inputs connect depends on geometric relations of their orientations, which we assume are also encoded. Once a contour segment is interpolated, it, along with the physically given parts of the contour, become a continuous contour that closes, defining the boundary of some object. To these closed contour tokens, we assign a perceived shape.[2]

A variety of neural-style models have been proposed as giving the underlying, neurally plausible mechanisms by which the above computations are performed [17, 21, 23, 31]. Therefore, it would seem that the general issues we raised at the start of this paper have been addressed: High-level information processing accounts of visual object completion have been connected to plausible neural mechanisms, providing not necessarily final or correct explanations, but at least explanations that show how we can go from initial registration of visual information to high-level scene descriptions.

This impression, however, would be as illusory as many of the contours perceived in the visual completion literature. Although neural-style models of visual completion exist, in general, they illustrate, rather than solve, the problem of bridging low-level visual coding and higher level, symbolic representations. Figure 18.9 helps to illustrate the issues.

In the figure are displays presented to two contour interpolation models (Fig. 18.9A) as well as the outputs of those models (Fig. 18.9B). The display and output on the left are from Heitger et al. [21] and those on the right are from Kalar et al. [23]. It is evident that the models fill in illusory and occluded contours based on the input contours. These models use local oriented edge detectors and grouping

---

[2]Obviously, this brief description leaves out many additional specifics. For example, our treatment here has been confined to 2-D interpolation and the "object" formed by completing the boundary would be a planar (2-D) object. Consideration of 3-D and spatiotemporal object formation is discussed in more detail elsewhere [33, 37], but the current treatment is sufficient to raise the general issues about modeling that are the focus of this section.

operators that examine the relations of activated units to determine interpolated activation in the space in between. Each pixel in the interpolated area is the output of a grouping operator that was positioned at that location.

These models and others (e.g., [17]) show that an early stage of interpolation can be done by sets of local operators that look at relations of contour activation in nearby regions and produce activation maps for regions in between. The input operators (edge detectors) and grouping operators are consistent with known characteristics of early visual cortical areas [20, 21], and their outputs likely approximate an important early stage in object formation [23]. However, it is crucial to understand what these models do and do not do. Specifically, the models have indicated points of interpolation in areas with no stimulus contrast, but they don't do much else. When we look at the output images, we see complete contours that span between input edges, but the models do not connect the interpolation points into contour tokens, nor do they connect the interpolated and real contours into contour tokens. They also do not certify whether these contours close, assign shapes to either the contour parts or the enclosed regions, determine what the objects are, or indicate which object is closer in the display. For example, in the display in Fig. 18.9B, we see two rectangles, with the gray rectangle partly occluding the black one. Given edge orientations and positions, the computational interpolation model of Kellman & Shipley [29] would interpolate the edges as shown. The model of Kalar et al. [23], intended as a neurally plausible implementation of the Kellman & Shipley model that operates on raw images, produced the image in Fig. 18.9B. The model's output, however, and the predecessor model of Heitger et al. [21], consists of a collection of points of "interpolation activation": it marks where interpolated edges would occur, but it does not produce a representation of connected edges, closed objects or depth relations. The apparent continuity of contours and shapes of closed figures are generated by the viewer when they look at the model's output image. The model itself does not "know" what is connected to what. We might call these "subsymbolic" models. Thus, "local" interpolation models leave a lot of work to be done. They build from the kinds of spatially localized neural units that exist in cortex, but they stop short of giving contour and object descriptions needed for higher level representations. Those descriptions need to be much more abstract, symbolic representations, as we discuss in the next section.

18.9 Shape Perception

Modern work in computational vision has typically addressed shape with a variety of sophisticated mathematical techniques (for a review, see [8]). These techniques allow great precision. For contour shape, having even a few data points allows, for example, polynomial approximation that specifies all of the contour's derivatives at all points. Yet neither these computational techniques nor neurophysiological data about the functions of cortical neurons has yet produced a real understanding of shape perception in biological vision.

Fig. 18.10 Examples of
shape invariance. Which of
the figures in **B**, **C**, or **D**, has
the same shape as the figure
in **A**? (See text)

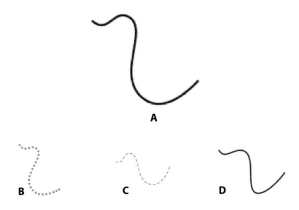

To understand some of the key issues in shape perception, we first specify some properties that human shape representations must have. These will help us to understand the central problem of bridging between early visual encoding (e.g., by local, orientation-sensitive units) and higher-level notions of shape. On one hand, it is clear that human perceptual abilities to see shape and shape similarities implicate more abstract symbolic coding than can be accomplished by sets of local orientations. On the other hand, it seems doubtful that our brains represent shapes with the arbitrary level of precision possible with mathematical techniques common in computer vision. For example, for the shapes of occluded contours, it has been argued [11] that experimental data is fit best by quintic (5th order) polynomials. This is no doubt a faithful description of curve-fitting results; however, one may wonder whether we should take seriously the idea that the brain really uses such a complex representation for shape and how it might generate quintic polynomials. Certainly no brain mechanism for generating them has yet been proposed. Moreover, such a representation, in a given case, would suggest a highly precise contour description, whereas psychophysical tests on human representations would likely show that our shape memory, at least, is substantially more vague.

For simplicity, we focus primarily, but not exclusively, on contour shape [12, 27]. Even the relatively basic shape notions we will consider evoke the issues of abstraction and simplification in shape representations that we wish to illustrate. Figure 18.10 illustrates some properties that seem to characterize human contour shape representations.

A shape representation for the contour given in Fig. 18.10A is sufficient to allow a shape match with one or more of the shapes in Figs. 18.10B, C, and D. This is possible despite changes in size, orientation, or even the elements comprising the figure. In terms of the lines or elements making up the figure, the display in 18.10C is most like 18.10A, yet inspection readily reveals that it is the only figure whose overall shape is different from 18.10A. Some of the key properties indicated by these simple shape-matching capabilities are that shape representations have some degree of scale invariance, orientation invariance, and that a common shape can be extracted despite differing constituent elements. These points were made long ago by the Gestalt psychologists (e.g., [34]), who emphasized that the simple summation

Fig. 18.11 Illustration of gist and similarity relations in shape representation. (See text.) (From http://lolyard. com/3448/cloud-fish)

A

B

C   D

of sensory elements did not comprise form; indeed, form consists of relations, which can be conveyed by many different kinds of sensory elements.

The modern version of the Gestalt point is fully relevant to primary issues in understanding shape and the connection between early visual coding and symbolic representations. We know that the patterns in Fig. 18.10 stimulate sets of spatially localized, orientation-sensitive units in the visual cortex (in V1 and V2). Yet human shape-matching performance clearly indicates that seeing the same or similar shape is not a matter of activating the same local orientation-sensitive units. The transformation of size changes the spatial frequency of the relevant units; changing orientation of the shape alters the relevant local orientations that are detected; and various elements can be used such that there is little or no overlap in populations of basic detectors that are activated and lead to perception of the same shape. How do we get from the stage of local orientation encoding to more abstract percepts and representations of shape?

Figure 18.11 illustrates two other crucial properties of human shape perception and representation. One we might call "gist." The cloud shown in Fig. 18.11A has quite ragged edges, including various protrusions and "frayed edges" in various places. A fully precise contour representation that matched all of the visible boundary points (e.g., what one might get by doing a precise, higher-order polynomial fit) would give a very jagged and complicated boundary contour representation. It is doubtful that, after looking briefly at such an image, we possess any such fully detailed representation. As a thought experiment, if we showed observers such images, took them away, and then presented new images in which the perturbations along the edges had been moved or changed, it is unlikely that observers would be good at detecting these changes (for a more detailed example, see [12]). Our representations encode the overall shape at a level that is likely to be relevant to our functioning in the world. Encoding all of the little wisps and deviations along the edges in this case are unlikely to be of functional importance (although given specialized tasks, this could change).

The other property illustrated in Fig. 18.11 is closely related to gist. It is that our shape representations support similarity relations in a constrained but flexible manner. The shape similarity of the cloud and the fish are obvious. Slightly more demanding is the question of which of two aircraft more closely matches the cloud shape. Pretty clearly it is the aircraft in Fig. 18.11D (the one on the right). These shape matching feats are remarkable because the matching images are far from a match at the pixel level or at the level of sets of local orientation detectors activated by the two patterns.

In summary, the visual system must somehow get from early local encodings of oriented contrast to more global and abstract shape representations. These representations are unlikely to be precise polynomial approximations to detailed boundaries, but are likely to be simplifications in some way. And these simplifications are likely to be the very properties that allow approximate matching to similar forms that are by no means identical, either at the one extreme of activating the same population of oriented units or at the other extreme of matching a precise mathematical description of a bounding contour.

18.10 Constant Curvature Coding: An Example of a Bridge Between Subsymbolic and Symbolic Shape Coding

The foregoing discussion of requirements of human contour shape representation may be useful in indicating important constraints on theories of biological shape representation, but they also represent a set of daunting challenges. Much of the point of this discussion is that we do not currently have suitable theories of shape that meet these requirements. There is no doubt, of course, that mathematical approaches for specifying shape are flexible enough such that we could specify symbolic representations that meet the requirements, but that would leave open the question of how such representations are acquired from the initial encoding of visual information. We do not offer a comprehensive answer to these problems, but we propose a scheme that addresses some particular issues, and, more generally, offers an existence proof of how more symbolic tokens might be acquired from subsymbolic precursors.

18.11 Early Symbolic Encoding of Contours: Arclets

Based on considerations of simplicity, coding efficiency, and some existing psychophysical and neurophysiological data, we have developed a scheme that uses the simplicity of the circle as the link between low- and higher-level vision [12, 27]. We propose that neural circuits exist that combine small groups of oriented units that are linked by constant turning angles, e.g., they encode constant curvature segments (including zero curvature) of contour shape. We call these *arclets*. Any open contour (including a part of the bounding contour of an object) may be described in terms of segments of constant curvature. In recent work, we have proposed two computational models of how this encoding could work, with the models differing in the tradeoff between the load in terms of number of segments and the fidelity of getting a near exact match to a viewed contour [12]. We refer the reader to that work for details.

For present purposes, the more important point is how arclets can operate as a bridge between subsymbolic and symbolic encoding. In their application to interpolation, activation initiated by real contours spreads along restricted paths in a network of oriented units; these paths consist of arclets. Because of this restriction, there is a unique path of interpolation connecting any relatable edges [29, Appendix A]. In their application to shape coding, arclets are symbolic tokens that are activated by signals in chains of several oriented units. This allows a natural means of handing off the information encoded by local oriented units to higher-level shape representations.

The central idea is that an important basic level of abstract shape encoding consists of contour representations comprised of one or more constant curvature segments. These middle-level shape representations result from detectors that are activated by sets of oriented units in particular relations to each other (cf., [10]). As illustrated in Fig. 18.12, a given arclet is activated if a chain of oriented units forming a collinear or co-circular path are simultaneously activated. At the bottom of this figure is the viewed object. The object activates sets of oriented units (shown as Gabor patches) in early cortical areas. Arclet detectors respond to chains of these units having a constant angular relation (turn angle).

This is the locus of the transition from local, contrast-sensitive elements to the first symbolic representation. The activated arclet token contains three pieces of information: the scale (spatial frequency) of the oriented units, the turn angle relating them (20 deg in the example given), and the number of oriented units (encoding segment length). We assume some system of competition to find the best-fitting arclet for any segment, as arclets of different scales and turn angles may fit to differing degrees.

Different arclets code different curvatures. Activation of a single arclet indicates the presence of that curvature at a certain position and orientation. The encoding of a constant curvature segment extends along a contour until a transition zone, at which arclets of that curvature exceed some threshold of accurately matching the contour (or are less well activated than some arclet having a different curvature value). A shape representation consists of a set of constant curvature values characterizing

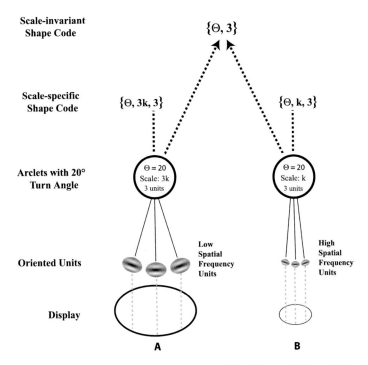

Fig. 18.12 Illustration of constant curvature segment encoding. (See text.) (From [27]. In M.A. Peterson, B. Gillam, & H.A. Sedgwick, (Eds.) *In the Mind's Eye: Julian Hochberg on the Perception
of Pictures, Film, and the World.* New York: Oxford University Press. Reprinted with permission)

segments along a contour, along with some marking of transition zones between
constant curvature segments. (For working models of this scheme, see [12]).

As shown in Fig. 18.12, arclets have the interesting property of permitting con-
current scale-variant and scale-invariant coding of contours. A problem for understanding invariance in human perception is that standard mathematical notions of
curvature do not capture shape invariance. A large circle and a small circle obviously have the same shape, but they have very different curvatures (where curvature is given by the change in contour orientation per unit arc length). Typically,
use of relative curvatures or normalization by some overall object size measurement is used to compare shapes in computer vision and some biological vision work
[8, 22].

Arclets offer a means of achieving scale invariance in a more natural way. Because orientation-sensitive units in early visual areas exist across a range of spatial
scales, arclets would similarly span this range. An interesting invariant characterizes
arclets made of differently sized elements that are related by the same turn angle.
As long as all elements within each arclet are of equal size, all arclets based on
the same turn angle between oriented elements represent the *same scale-invariant
shape*, i.e., shape pieces that differ only by a scalar. This is shown in Fig. 18.12,
in which two arclets at different scales both encode segment lengths including the

same number of oriented units in a chain having the same turn angle. Activating a best-fitting arclet at any scale therefore signals a unique number (based on the turn angle) that specifies scale-invariant shape for that part of the contour. Two circles of different sizes, for example, will have contours that best match arclets at different scales, but both arclets will have the same turn angle.

Remarkably, this property of obtaining size invariance for free comes from the use of oriented segments of finite lengths to encode curvature. Mathematically, a perfect description of a curve would have infinitesimal segments; orientation is constantly *changing* along a curve! Approximating curvature using units sensitive to orientations that are constant along their lengths would seem a necessary but regrettable compromise in encoding. It is, however, this characteristic that allows a scale-invariant curvature property to emerge automatically. Our analysis is consistent with the fact that the size of oriented units in human vision co-varies with their spatial frequency.

In Fig. 18.12, the two ellipses, having the same shape but different sizes, each have a constant curvature segment that is shown as encoded by arclets with the same turn angle and the same number of participating units (length). At the level of a scale-specific representation (allowing us to see that the two ellipses are different in size), the scale-specific arclet representation preserves the turn angle information and the scale of the elements in the best fitting arclet. At this level, the large ellipse is shown as having scale $3k$ and the smaller ellipse as having scale k. The scale invariant representation, in which the shape of the corresponding segment of each ellipse is encoded identically, simply drops out the scale term. Curved segments having the same turn angle and comprised of the same number of units specify the same perceived shape (relative curvature).

Because the arclets are encoding change information (turn angles), orientation invariance also comes naturally with this form of representation. Orientation invariance has limits in human form perception [43]. Analogous to the concurrent scale-variant and scale-invariant encoding, absolute orientation information of segments is likely preserved for some purposes, including form coding that has privileged reference axes.

Garrigan & Kellman [12] discuss alternative versions of an arclet-based code that trades off between complexity (in terms of number of parts) and fidelity (in terms of how faithfully the code represents the contour). Most contours in the world do not consist of constant curvature segments (as is true of the ellipse in Fig. 18.12), but they could be approximated to any level of precision by many small constant curvature pieces. A simpler code in terms of constant curvature segments would have fewer segments but more distortion. It seems likely that the precision of contour coding varies with attention and task demands.

There are alternative possibilities for early symbolic encoding of contours. Codes that utilize more complicated primitives, e.g., any spline fitting model, will outperform the arclet-based approach in some cases, but also have a number of shortcomings when considered as a model of contour shape representation that can handle the shape-related problems the human visual system encounters under normal viewing conditions. Consider, e.g., recognizing that one contour segment is part of another contour. More simple shape primitives (like the arclets) are less sensitive to long-range relationships along the contour, a characteristic that may be critical for matching the representation of a smaller contour segment to part of the representation of a larger contour.

The simplicity of the arclet representation is also an advantage as the problem of shape representation is scaled up to more ecological shapes. Contour shape representation likely precedes intermediate representations (e.g., surface shape) and the representation of the shapes of behaviorally important objects that may have additional complexities (e.g., an animal with articulating parts). A simpler code that does not leverage some of the more complicated, perhaps distal relationships among the features of a contour may be more robust when these additional complexities are included. Consider the problem of articulating parts. A shape code that represents the bounding contour of an object with a very small set of relatively complicated contour shape primitives will have little relationship to the representation of the bounding contour of that same object if one part of the object unexpectedly moves. In sum, besides the tradeoff between fidelity and complexity, there is likely a tradeoff between efficiency and stability. The arclets are not the most efficient representation of contour shape, but they may lead to a more stable representation than more sophisticated primitives that leverage regularities that do not persist across viewing conditions.

18.12 Evidence for Constant Curvature Coding in Human Shape Perception

The arclets approach to constant curvature encoding of contours offers an example of how subsymbolic encoding might lead to more abstract shape codes. This specific proposal of constant curvature coding is also consistent with a variety of evidence in human vision, including results of recent research.

Pizlo, Salach-Golyska, & Rosenfeld [41] compared detection performance for a curve formed from dots arranged in straight lines, dots arranged in circular arcs, and dots arranged in various types of irregular paths. They found that straight lines were easiest to detect, but that circular arcs were easier to detect than irregular paths (provided the change in curvature along the irregular path was not too small). Pizlo, et al. also found that circular arcs were significantly easier than all the irregular paths they tested when the subject was given prior information about the shape of the target. These results are consistent with the importance of constant curvature extraction and memory in shape perception.

More recently, Achtman, Hess, & Wang [1] used a Gabor-path detection paradigm and showed that circular paths were more easily detected than radial or spiral paths. Similar detection threshold advantages for circles have been found using Glass patterns [35, 45, 53]. Other evidence, however, suggests that the primitives for form perception may include both circular and spiral pooling mechanisms [52].

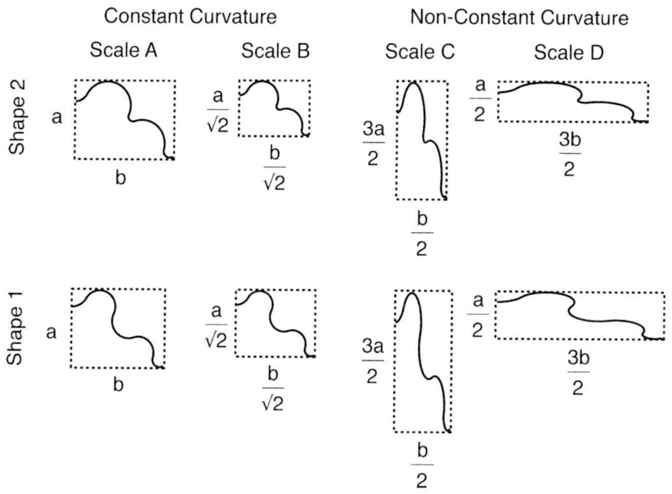

Fig. 18.13 Stimuli in experiments on constant curvature segment coding. Shape 1 is composed of five circular segments with differing radii. Each segment has constant curvature. Scaling horizontally and vertically by the same amount preserved the constant curvature (scale B), whereas scaling along the two dimensions by different amounts produces regions of non-constant curvature (scales C and D). These are all "matching" shapes. Shape 2 is created by changing the curvature of one of the circular segments of Shape 1 and is a "non-match" shape. (From P. Garrigan and P.J. Kellman, 2011, *Perception*, *40*(11), p. 1297. Reprinted with permission)

Neurophysiological evidence also supports a special role for constant-curvature encoding in shape perception. Single cell recordings in macaque monkeys are consistent with the idea that intermediate visual areas such as V4 may be representing object-oriented contour curvature [38–40]. These investigators suggest that representations of overall shapes can be derived from the collective output of such cells.

In recent psychophysical work, Garrigan and Kellman [12] used open contours to investigate the role of constant curvature in shape representations. Subjects judged whether two sequentially presented contour segments were the same or not, allowing for scale, rotation and translation transformations. The stimuli were created by combining five circular segments of differing radii and spans (Fig. 18.13). Because they were constructed from circles, each segment had a constant curvature. Scaling the shape by an equal amount horizontally and vertically preserved the constant curvature, while scaling by different amounts along each dimension produced non-constant curvature segments. Non-matching shapes were created by changing the curvature of one of the circular segments (see Shape 2, Fig. 18.13).

Subjects were reliably more accurate in matching constant curvature shapes than non-constant curvature shapes. Even when all transformations were removed so that the two stimuli were exactly identical, subjects were more accurate in matching constant curvature shapes, when shapes had to be compared across a retention interval of 1000 ms. Similar recognition performance was observed for both shape types, however, when they were compared at the same size and viewpoint and the retention interval was reduced to 500 ms. These findings are consistent with a symbolic encoding of 2-D contour shapes into constant curvature parts when the retention intervals over which shapes must be stored exceeds the duration of initial, transient, visual representations.

These experiments and the arclets model provide a plausible proposal for the how a location-specific, subsymbolic representation might transition to an abstract, symbolic one. Local edge information may be integrated into a scale and rotation invariant representation of contour curvature. They represent modest steps, as efforts to understand abstraction in perceptual representations is a multifaceted, challenging, and ongoing effort. These proposals do, however, offer an existence proof related to some of the most open-ended questions in understanding perceptual representations: How does the visual system construct abstract, flexible, functionally useful shape representations from the early encoding of local, literal image properties? Constant curvature representations of contours are computationally possible, and consistent with both properties of early cortical units in vision and some results suggesting curvature coding in visual area V4.

18.13 Connecting Contour Interpolation and Shape Descriptions

Consistent with the complexity of problems of contour, object, and shape perception, even this short overview has covered a lot of ground. We noted the relevance of interpolation processes to shape, in that shape descriptions typically encompass not image fragments, but the outputs of object formation processes. We then focused on representations of contour shape, which the visual system may obtain in symbolic form by recoding object contours in terms of constant curvature parts. Figure 18.14 provides an example pulling together these themes, using the picture of a cow from Fig. 18.3. The cow's partially occluded head in the original image (Fig. 18.14A) is shown represented as a completed, constant-curvature based shape representation (Fig. 18.14B). Primary edges were found using a version of the Canny edge detector [7]. (This approach was used for simplicity here, although its outputs are highly consistent with some models that utilize neutrally plausible local units to do initial edge finding (e.g., [23]).) In Fig. 18.14B, the edges of the cow's head are shown after recoding as constant curvature segments, consistent with the contour curvature model of Garrigan & Kellman [12]. Dotted lines indicate amodally completed contours; these have been interpolated following the rules of contour relatability, with the resulting interpolated contours also represented with constant curvature parts. The interpolation model and the contour shape model are guaranteed to be consistent, as any interpolated contour consistent with relatability can be described uniquely as consisting of one zero curvature and one constant curvature segment ([29], cf., [51]).

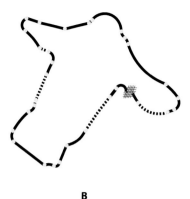

A   **B**

Fig. 18.14 Example of interpolation and constant curvature coding in shape perception. The cow's partially occluded head in the original image (**A**) is shown represented as a completed, constant-curvature based shape representation (**B**). Primary edges were obtained from the raw image using a common edge-detection operator. Edges of the cow's head in the image on the right have been recoded as constant curvature segments, consistent with the contour curvature model of Garrigan & Kellman [12]. *Dotted lines* indicate amodally completed contours following the rules of contour relatability, with the resulting interpolated contours also represented with constant curvature parts. The *cross-hatched area in the display on the right* indicates an area where edges and textures are ambiguous and do not permit clear interpolation. (See text)

This example is not meant to minimize challenging problems that remain in understanding the transition from subsymbolic to symbolic coding, even in the relatively simple domain of contour perception. As we have discussed elsewhere, although some extant interpolation models can use raw images as their input, they will be improved when certain symbolic encoding is added, such as representing a unique edge orientation at each contour junction rather than a distribution of orientation activations (for discussion, see Kalar et al. [23]). Natural scenes may also have areas for which the outputs of edge finding and/or interpolation models are indeterminate, as in the cross-hatched area indicated in Fig. 18.14B. Sometimes these outputs are likely consistent with some indeterminacy in actual perception, but in other cases they likely indicate limitations of current models. Regarding the recoding of contours into segments of constant curvature, the model of Garrigan & Kellman [12] is a working algorithm that takes a contour specified in terms of local orientation values and produces constant curvature segments as outputs, but no full implementation yet exists in terms of attaining each local orientation value from the outputs of separate, local, orientation-sensitive units at multiple scales. Moreover, versions of the model vary in their tradeoff of fidelity (minimizing differences from the input image, but requiring greater numbers of segments in the approximation) and economy (accepting limits in fidelity due to some capacity or complexity limit). We have proposed that the visual system may similarly adjust contour shape coding for greater fidelity or greater economy [12], depending on task demands and attention, but the specifics are not known.

18.14 Summary

Shape perception and representation pose fascinating challenges in vision science. In this article, we have focused on perhaps the greatest theoretical chasm in understanding shape: the origin of abstract, symbolic representations. Perceived shape is not a readout of image characteristics, nor is it a collection of activations of early orientation-sensitive units. Image regions do not receive shape descriptions in human perception; rather, the shapes we record relate to objects formed by interpolation processes that may connect various separated regions. Both the shapes of interpolated contours and of real contours share representational formats that make possible invariant shape recognition despite certain scale and orientation changes, matching of shapes despite different constituent elements, and extraction of gist in shape encoding, allowing detection of shape similarities. Understanding the nature of these symbolic representations, and how they are constructed from earlier encodings, is a complex task. Vision science is fortunate in having some understanding of initial subsymbolic encoding by neural units, and having also a number of middle or high-level vision models that begin with representations that are already abstract. The challenge is to discover how these meet in the middle—how we attain more global, symbolic, interpreted descriptions from local, non-symbolic encodings. For contour and object boundary representations, extraction of constant curvature segments as basic tokens of early symbolic representations may comprise an important step, one consistent with psychophysical and neurophysiological data, and one that illustrates how the visual system may approach "the middle game."

Acknowledgements   We thank Brian Keane, Evan Palmer, and Hongjing Lu for helpful discussions and Rachel Older for general assistance. Portions of the research reported here were supported by National Eye Institute Grant EY 13518 to PJK.

References

1. Achtman RL, Hess RF, Wang Y-Z (2003) Sensitivity for global shape detection. J Vis 3:616–624
2. Albert MK (2001) Surface perception and the generic view principle. Trends Cogn Sci 5(5):197–203
3. Albert MK, Hoffman DD (2000) The generic-viewpoint assumption and illusory contours. Perception 29(3):303–312
4. Albert MK, Tse P (2000) The role of surface attraction in perceiving volumetric shape. Perception 29:409–420
5. Banton T, Levi DM (1992) The perceived strength of illusory contours. Percept Psychophys 52(6):676–684
6. Baylis GC, Driver J (1993) Visual attention and objects: evidence for hierarchical coding of location. J Exp Psychol Hum Percept Perform 19(3):451–470
7. Canny J (1986) A computational approach to edge detection. IEEE Trans Pattern Anal Mach Intell 8(6):679–698
8. Costa LF, Cesar RM (2001) Shape analysis and classification: theory and practice. CRC Press, Boca Raton

9. Fantoni C, Hilger J, Gerbino W, Kellman PJ (2008) Surface interpolation and 3d relatability. J Vis 8(7):1–19
10. Field DJ, Hayes A, Hess RF (1993) Contour integration by the human visual system: evidence for a local "Association field". Vis Res 33(2):173–193
11. Fulvio JM, Singh M, Maloney LT (2009) An experimental criterion for consistency in interpolation of partly occluded contours. J Vis 9(4):1–19
12. Garrigan P, Kellman PJ (2011) The role of constant curvature in 2-d contour shape representations. Perception 40(11):1290–1308
13. Geisler WS, Perry JS (2009) Contour statistics in natural images: grouping across occlusions. Vis Neurosci 26:109–121
14. Geisler WS, Perry JS, Super BJ, Gallogly DP (2001) Edge co-occurrence in natural images predicts contour performance. Vis Res 41:711–724
15. Ghose T, Erlikhman G, Kellman PJ (2011) Spatiotemporal object formation: contour vs surface interpolation. Perception 40 ECVP Abstract Supplement, p 59
16. Gibson JJ (1979) The ecological approach to visual perception. Houghton Mifflin, Boston
17. Grossberg S, Mingolla E (1985) Neural dynamics of form perception: boundary completion, illusory figures, and neon color spreading. Psychol Rev 92:173–211
18. Guttman SE, Kellman PJ (2004) Contour interpolation revealed by a dot localization paradigm. Vis Res 44:1799–1815
19. Guttman SE, Sekuler AB, Kellman PJ (2003) Temporal variations in visual completion: a reflection of spatial limits? J Exp Psychol Hum Percept Perform 29(6):1211–1227
20. Heitger F, Rosenthaler L, von der Heydt R, Peterhans E, Kübler O (1992) Simulation of neural contour mechanisms: from simple to end-stopped cells. Vis Res 32(5):963–981
21. Heitger F, von der Heydt R, Peterhans E, Rosenthaler L, Kübler O (1998) Simulation of neural contour mechanisms: representing anomalous contours. Image Vis Comput 16(6–7):407–421
22. Hoffman DD, Singh M (1997) Salience of visual parts. Cognition 63:29–78
23. Kalar DJ, Garrigan P, Wickens TD, Hilger JD, Kellman PJ (2010) A unified model of illusory and occluded contour interpolation. Vis Res 50:284–299
24. Keane BP, Lu H, Papathomas TV, Silverstein SM, Kellman PJ Reinterpreting behavioral receptive fields: lightness induction alters visually completed shape, accepted pending minor revision. PLoS ONE
25. Kellman PJ (2003) Interpolation processes in the visual perception of objects. Neural Netw 16:915–923
26. Kellman PJ (2003) Segmentation and grouping in object perception: a 4-dimensional approach. In: Behrmann M, Kimchi R (eds) Perceptual organization in vision: behavioral and neural perspectives: the 31st Carnegie symposium on cognition. Erlbaum, Hillsdale
27. Kellman PJ, Garrigan P (2007) Segmentation, grouping, and shape: some Hochbergian questions. In: Peterson MA, Gillam B, Sedgwick HA (eds) In the mind's eye: Julian Hochberg on the perception of pictures, film, and the world. Oxford University Press, New York
28. Kellman PJ, Loukides MG (1987) An object perception approach to static and kinetic subjective contours. In: Meyer G, Petry G (eds) The perception of illusory contours. Springer, New York, pp 151–164
29. Kellman PJ, Shipley TF (1991) A theory of visual interpolation in object perception. Cogn Psychol 23:141–221
30. Kellman PJ, Yin C, Shipley TF (1998) A common mechanism for illusory and occluded object completion. J Exp Psychol Hum Percept Perform 24(3):859–869
31. Kellman PJ, Guttman SE, Wickens TD (2001) Geometric and neural models of object completion. In: Shipley TF, Kellman PJ (eds) From fragments to objects: segmentation and grouping in vision. Elsevier, Oxford
32. Kellman PJ, Garrigan P, Shipley TF (2005) Object interpolation in three dimensions. Psychol Rev 112(3):586–609
33. Kellman PJ, Garrigan P, Shipley TF, Yin C, Machado L (2005) J Exp Psychol Hum Percept Perform 31(3):558–583
34. Koffka K (1935) Principles of Gestalt psychology. Harcourt Brace, New York

35. Kurki I, Saarinen J (2004) Shape perception in human vision: specialized detectors for concentric spatial structures? Neurosci Lett 360(1–2):100–102
36. Marr D (1982) Vision. Freeman, New York
37. Palmer EM, Kellman PJ, Shipley TF (2006) A theory of dynamic occluded and illusory object perception. J Exp Psychol Gen 135:513–541
38. Pasupathy A, Conner CE (1999) Responses of contour features in macaque area V4. J Neurophysiol 82:2490–2502
39. Pasupathy A, Conner CE (2001) Shape representation in area V4: position-specific tuning for boundary conformation. J Neurophysiol 86:2505–2519
40. Pasupathy A, Conner CE (2002) Population coding of shape in area V4. Nat Neurosci 5:1332–1338
41. Pizlo Z, Salach-Golyska M, Roenfeld A (1997) Curve detection in a noisy image. Vis Res 37(9):1217–1241
42. Ringach DL, Shapley R (1996) Spatial and temporal properties of illusory contours and amodal boundary completion. Vis Res 36:3037–3050
43. Rock I (1973) Orientation and form. Academic Press, San Diego
44. Rubin N (2001) The role of junctions in surface completion and contour matching. Perception 30:339–366
45. Seu L, Ferrera VP (2001) Detection thresholds for spiral glass patters. Vis Res 41(28):3785–3790
46. Shipley TF, Kellman PJ (1990) The role of discontinuities in the perception of subjective contours. Percept Psychophys 48(3):259–270
47. Shipley TF, Kellman PJ (1992) Perception of partly occluded objects and illusory figures: evidence for an identity hypothesis. J Exp Psychol Hum Percept Perform 18(1):106–120
48. Shipley TF, Kellman PJ (1992) Strength of visual interpolation depends on the ratio of physically-specified to total edge length. Percept Psychophys 52(1):97–106
49. Singh M, Hoffman DD (1999) Completing visual contours: the relationship between relatability and minimizing inflections. Percept Psychophys 61(5):943–951
50. Singh M, Hoffman DD, Albert MK (1999) Contour completion and relative depth: Petter's rule and support ratio. Psychol Sci 10:423–428
51. Ullmann S (1979) The shape of subjective contours and a model for their generation. Biol Cybern
52. Webb BS, Roach NW, Peirce JW (2008) Masking exposes multiple global form mechanisms. J Vis 8(9):1–10
53. Wilson HR, Wilkinson F, Asaad W (1997) Concentric orientation summation in human form vision. Vis Res 37(17):2325–2330
54. Yin C, Kellman PJ, Shipley TF (1997) Surface completion complements boundary interpolation in the visual integration of partly occluded objects. Perception 26:1459–1479
55. Yin C, Kellman PJ, Shipley TF (2000) Surface integration influences depth discrimination. Vis Res 40:1969–1978
56. Zemel R, Behrmann M, Mozer M, Bavelier D (2002) Experience-dependent perceptual grouping and object-based attention. J Exp Psychol Hum Percept Perform 28:202–217

Chapter 19
3D Face Reconstruction from Single Two-Tone and Color Images

Ira Kemelmacher-Shlizerman, Ronen Basri, and Boaz Nadler

19.1 Introduction

This chapter addresses the problem of reconstructing the three-dimensional shape of faces from single images. We present an algorithm that uses prior knowledge of faces—a single shape model of a face—to eliminate the ambiguities in the reconstruction [13, 14]. The algorithm achieves veridical reconstruction results on images taken under a wide range of viewing conditions. In addition, it can reconstruct the shape of a face from two-tone ("Mooney") images of faces [15]. Our algorithm demonstrates the importance of "top-down" information in 3D shape reconstruction.

The extent to which internal representations affect perception is fundamental to the understanding of cognitive processes. Perceiving the appearance of a 3D shape in an image can be complicated as shapes are distorted by projection and their appearance is affected by lighting as well as by their color and texture. Yet people can readily perceive shape (perhaps qualitatively) merely from one image. A fundamental question therefore is whether the perception of shape is guided primarily by bottom-up processes, in which only image intensities are used along with generic assumptions regarding the statistics of natural scenes, or, alternatively, if it is dictated by top-down processes, which may be driven by memory and attention and

I. Kemelmacher-Shlizerman (✉)
Department of Computer Science and Engineering, University of Washington, Seattle, WA, USA
e-mail: kemelmi@cs.washington.edu

R. Basri · B. Nadler
Department of Computer Science and Applied Mathematics, Weizmann Institute of Science, Rehovot, Israel

R. Basri
e-mail: ronen.basri@weizmann.ac.il

B. Nadler
e-mail: boaz.nadler@weizmann.ac.il

S.J. Dickinson, Z. Pizlo (eds.), *Shape Perception in Human and Computer Vision*,
Advances in Computer Vision and Pattern Recognition,
DOI 10.1007/978-1-4471-5195-1_19, © Springer-Verlag London 2013

Fig. 19.1 Two-tone
("Mooney") face images [1].
These images may initially
seem difficult to interpret due
to poor visual detail, but
eventually lead to a rich and
stable percept of a face

preceded by a preliminary recognition process. The example of random dot stereograms [12] suggests that the perception of 3D shape in stereo vision is governed by bottom-up processes. In contrast, two-tone images (see Fig. 19.1) suggest that familiarity with an object can enhance the perception of its shape.

Two-tone images were introduced in the 1950s by Craig Mooney [20] to investigate the development of shape perception in children [20, 28]. A number of recent studies suggest that the perception of Mooney images is driven by memory and attention and preceded by a preliminary recognition process. In particular, it was shown that people usually fail to perceive upside-down faces in two-tone images, arguably due to their unfamiliarity [8, 23], and that pre-exposure to original gray level (or color) image facilitates their recognition [6, 9]. Moreover, Moore and Cavanagh [21] showed that shape primitives (e.g., generalized cones) are rarely perceivable in two-tone images, both in isolation and in novel configuration with other primitives, even when the image contains explicit hints about the direction of the light source. These shapes, however, can readily be interpreted from gray level images and even from degraded line drawings. Familiar classes of objects, in contrast, are much more often perceivable in two-tone images. Even volumetric primitives of faces, if rearranged, cease to be perceived as coherent 3D objects. These findings support the view that the interpretation of Mooney images is guided by top-down processes. Here we provide further support for this claim by showing from a mathematical standpoint that, in the absence of a model, the interpretation of Mooney images is highly ambiguous.

Our further aim in this chapter is to provide an example of how top-down processing can play a role in the reconstruction of 3D faces. We focus on faces, as the overall similarity of faces [11] can provide a strong prior for reconstruction. Yet despite this similarity the reconstruction task is hard, since people are sensitive to minute shape differences across different individuals. 3D reconstruction of faces from single images can potentially be achieved by applying shape-from-shading (SFS) algorithms [10]. However, SFS requires knowledge of the lighting, albedo, and boundary conditions and is ill-posed in the absence of this information. The approach presented in this chapter uses prior knowledge about faces to achieve a well-posed formulation in which this missing information can be inferred. For a prior, we use a single 3D reference face model of either a different individual or a generic face. Our method assumes Lambertian reflectance (indeed, most face reconstruction methods assume that faces can be modeled accurately as Lambertian [19]), light sources at infinity, and rough alignment between the input image and the reference model. To model reflectance, we use a spherical harmonic approximation (following [3, 22]), which allows for multiple unknown light sources and attached shadows. We note that other work used face priors (although not in the context of Mooney images), by combining information from hundreds of faces (e.g., [4, 5]). We find it interesting that veridical reconstructions can be obtained with just one model.

19.2 Reconstruction Ambiguities in Two-Tone Images

In this chapter, we ask whether a unique 3D shape can be recovered from a single Mooney image. We examine this question under typical SFS settings. We assume a single point light source of known magnitude and direction, the observed surface is Lambertian, and albedo is uniform (or otherwise known). Our formulation also accounts for boundary conditions. We focus on the *Mooney transition curve*, i.e., the boundary between bright and dark regions in the image, as the information contained in a Mooney image is captured almost entirely in this curve. We show that reconstruction is not unique even along this curve, indicating that top-down information is essential for shape perception.

Consider a gray level image $I(x, y)$ of a smooth Lambertian surface $z(x, y)$ with uniform albedo obtained with a directional illuminant $\mathbf{l} \in \Re^3$. The intensities $I(x, y)$ is given by $I = \mathbf{l}^T \mathbf{n}$, where $\mathbf{n} = n(x, y)$ denotes the surface normal at (x, y), $\mathbf{n} = (1/\sqrt{z_x^2 + z_y^2 + 1})(-z_x, -z_y, 1)$. A two-tone image is obtained from I by thresholding the image $I \geq T$ by some constant $T > 0$. Without loss of generality, we assume below that T is known, and that the light source direction coincides with the viewing direction, so that $\mathbf{l} = (0, 0, 1)$. Note however that our analysis can be applied to any directional source by a change of coordinates, as in [17], and the magnitude of the light can be scaled by appropriately scaling T. With these assumptions, we obtain

$$I(x, y) = \frac{1}{\sqrt{z_x^2 + z_y^2 + 1}}, \tag{19.1}$$

which can be expressed in the form of an Eikonal equation

$$|\nabla z|^2 = E(x, y) \tag{19.2}$$

on some closed domain $\Omega \subset \Re^2$, $E = (1/I^2) - 1$. Such an Eikonal equation can be solved for example by applying an upwind update scheme using a Dijkstra-like algorithm [17, 24, 27]. In general, such solutions require Dirichlet boundary conditions so that z needs to be specified at every local minimum of E (maximum of I) in Ω. These may include minimal points in Ω, as well as points along the boundaries of Ω. Our analysis therefore considers the introduction of boundary conditions.

Consider two surfaces z and z' that respectively produce two images I and I' (and hence E and E') which are "Mooney equivalent." By this we mean that $|\nabla z|^2 = E(x, y)$ and $|\nabla z'|^2 = E'(x, y)$ and $I = I' = \text{const}$ along an isoluminance curve γ. Some boundary conditions may also be specified, so that $z = z'$ (and at internal points also $|\nabla z|^2 = |\nabla z'|^2 = 0$) in a set $\mathcal{B} \subset \Omega$. Let $\alpha(x, y) = z' - z$, our goal is given z to characterize the possible assignments of α along γ.

Subtracting the two eikonal equations for z and z' results in a new eikonal equation in α

$$|\nabla \alpha|^2 + 2\nabla \alpha \cdot \nabla z = E' - E. \qquad (19.3)$$

To solve for α, we introduce a (local) change of coordinates $(x, y) \rightarrow (t, s)$ such that $\alpha_s = 0$ and $\alpha_t \neq 0$. In this coordinate frame, t points in the direction of the gradient of α, which is also the characteristic direction of (19.3). Consequently, (19.3) becomes

$$\alpha_t^2 + 2z_t\alpha_t - \left(E' - E\right) = 0. \qquad (19.4)$$

This equation is quadratic in α_t and can have up to two real solutions,

$$\alpha_t = -z_t \pm \sqrt{z_t^2 + E' - E}. \qquad (19.5)$$

We can use this equation to derive a general solution for α in the entire domain Ω by integrating (19.5) with respect to t along the characteristic directions as follows

$$\alpha(t, s) = -z(t, s) + z(t_0, s) \pm \int_{t_0}^{t} \sqrt{z_t^2 + E' - E} \, dt, \qquad (19.6)$$

where the point $(t_0, s) \in \mathcal{B}$. One can readily verify that indeed $\alpha(t_0, s) = 0$.

Clearly, given a Mooney image we cannot use (19.6) to recover α, since in general neither E nor E' are known. However, along the transition curve, γ, we know that $E = E'$, and so (19.5) implies that $\alpha_t|_\gamma = -z_t \pm z_t \in \{0, -2z_t\}$. In general, we are interested here in the negative solution $\alpha_t|_\gamma = -2z_t$ since only this solution can produce a nontrivial ambiguity. We next use this solution to derive an explicit solution for α along the transition curve γ. Denote the arclength parameterization of γ by σ, and the angle between the tangent to γ and the t direction by $\theta(\sigma)$. Then

$$\alpha|_\gamma = -2\int_\gamma z_t \cos\theta \, d\sigma + \alpha(\sigma_0). \qquad (19.7)$$

This solution implies that if we choose a set of characteristic directions for α along the transition curve γ then there can be exactly two shapes along this curve that are consistent with the input two-tone image, namely z and $z' = z + \alpha$. In general, however, we are free to choose any set of smoothly varying characteristic directions along γ and this way produce many additional solutions. A valid solution for α therefore must be consistent with the boundary conditions in $\mathcal{B}$, if such conditions are provided, and its gradients must coincide with *some* smoothly varying directional derivatives at points along γ. This implies in general that many ambiguities exist even if we only restrict our attention to the Mooney transition curve.

19.3 Shape Reconstruction with a Prior Model

In the remainder of this chapter, we introduce an algorithm for reconstructing the 3D shape of a face from a single image by exploiting our familiarity with faces as a class. Previous methods attempted to learn the set of allowable reconstructions from a large number of 3D laser-scanned faces. This was achieved by embedding all 3D faces in a linear space [2, 4, 26, 30] or by using a training set to determine a density function for faces [25, 29]. Similarly, Active Shape Models [5, 7, 18] seek to construct image-based, linear 2D representations of faces by exploiting large datasets of prototype faces for face recognition and image coding. In contrast to this work our method uses only a *single* reference model, and by that avoids the need to establish pointwise correspondence between many face models in a database.

Consider an image $I(x, y)$ of a face whose shape $z(x, y)$ is defined on a compact domain $\Omega \subset \Re^2$. We assume that the face is Lambertian with albedo $\rho(x, y)$, and that lighting can be an arbitrary combination of point sources, extended sources and diffuse lighting that need not be known ahead of time. Under these assumptions, Lambertian surfaces reflect only the low frequencies of lighting [3, 22], and so the reflectance function can be expressed in terms of spherical harmonics as

$$R\big(\mathbf{n}(x, y); \mathbf{l}\big) \approx \sum_{n=0}^{N} \sum_{m=-n}^{n} l_{nm} \alpha_n Y_{nm}\big(\mathbf{n}(x, y)\big), \qquad (19.8)$$

where l_{nm} are the coefficients of the harmonic expansion of the lighting, α_n are factors that depend only on n and capture the effect of the Lambertian kernel acting as a low pass filter, so α_n becomes very small for large values of N, and $Y_{nm}(x, y)$ are the surface spherical harmonic functions evaluated at the surface normal. Because the reflectance of Lambertian objects under arbitrary lighting is in general very smooth, this approximation is highly accurate already when a low order (first or second) harmonic approximation is used.

For simplicity, we model the reflectance function using a first order harmonic approximation. In [14] we present a more general formulation using also the second order harmonics. We write the reflectance function in vector notation as

$$R\big(\mathbf{n}(x, y); \mathbf{l}\big) \approx \mathbf{l}^T \mathbf{Y}\big(\mathbf{n}(x, y)\big), \qquad (19.9)$$

with $\mathbf{Y}(\mathbf{n}) = (1, n_x, n_y, n_z)^T$, where n_x, n_y, n_z are the components of the surface normal $\mathbf{n}$ and $\mathbf{l}$ is a four vector. The image irradiance equation is then expressed as $I(x, y) = \rho(x, y) R(x, y)$.

We are further given a reference face model and denote respectively by $z_{\mathrm{ref}}(x, y)$, $\mathbf{n}_{\mathrm{ref}}(x, y)$, and $\rho_{\mathrm{ref}}(x, y)$ the surface, the normals, and the albedo of the reference face. We use the reference model to regularize the reconstruction problem. To that end, we define the difference shape and albedo as $d_z(x, y) = z(x, y) - z_{\mathrm{ref}}(x, y)$ and $d_\rho(x, y) = \rho(x, y) - \rho_{\mathrm{ref}}(x, y)$ respectively and require these differences to be smooth. We are now ready to define our optimization function:

$$\min_{\mathbf{l}, \rho, z} \int_\Omega \big(I - \rho\,\mathbf{l}^T \mathbf{Y}(\mathbf{n})\big)^2 + \lambda_1 (\triangle G * d_z)^2 + \lambda_2 (\triangle G * d_\rho)^2 \, dx\, dy, \qquad (19.10)$$

where $\triangle G*$ denotes convolution with the Laplacian of a Gaussian, and λ_1 and λ_2 are positive constants. Below, we refer to the first term in this integral as the "data term" and the other two terms as the "regularization terms". Evidently, without regularization the optimization functional (19.10) is ill-posed. Specifically, for every choice of depth $z(x, y)$ and lighting vector $\mathbf{l}$ it is possible to prescribe albedo $\rho(x, y)$ to make the data term vanish. With regularization and appropriate boundary conditions, the problem becomes well-posed. Note that we chose to regularize d_z and d_ρ rather than z and ρ in order to preserve the discontinuities in z_{ref} and ρ_{ref}.

We assume the input image is roughly aligned to the reference model and approach this optimization by solving for lighting, depth, and albedo separately.

Step 1: Recovery of Lighting Coefficients   In the first step, we attempt to recover the lighting coefficients $\mathbf{l}$, by fitting the reference model to the image. To this end, we substitute in (19.10) $\rho \to \rho_{\text{ref}}$ and $z \to z_{\text{ref}}$ (and consequently $\mathbf{n} \to \mathbf{n}_{\text{ref}}$). At this stage both regularization terms vanish, and only the data term remains:

$$\min_{\mathbf{l}} \int_{\Omega} \left(I - \rho_{\text{ref}} \mathbf{l}^T \mathbf{Y}(\mathbf{n}_{\text{ref}})\right)^2 dx\, dy. \tag{19.11}$$

In discrete form this produces a highly over-constrained linear least squares optimization system with only four unknowns, the components of $\mathbf{l}$, and can be solved simply using the pseudo-inverse. Our experiments indicate that, in practice, the error of recovering lighting using the face of a different individual is sufficiently small (around 4–6°).

Step 2: Depth Recovery   We continue using $\rho_{\text{ref}}(x, y)$ for the albedo and turn to recovering $z(x, y)$. Below we exploit the reference face to further simplify the data term. The data term thus minimizes the squared difference between the two sides of the following system of equations

$$I = \rho_{\text{ref}} l_0 + \frac{\rho_{\text{ref}}}{N_{\text{ref}}} (l_1 z_x + l_2 z_y - l_3), \tag{19.12}$$

where $\mathbf{Y}(\mathbf{n}) = (1, z_x/N, z_y/N, -1/N)^T$ and we use $N_{\text{ref}}(x, y)$ to approximate $N(x, y) = \sqrt{z_x^2 + z_y^2 + 1}$. Replacing z_x and z_y, for example, by forward differences, the data term thus provides one equation for every unknown $z(x, y)$ (except for the pixels on the boundary of Ω). Note that by solving directly for $z(x, y)$ we in fact enforce consistency of the surface normals ("integrability"). Clearly, (19.12) is linear in $z(x, y)$ and so it can be solved using linear least squares optimization.

Next, we consider the regularization term $\lambda_1 \triangle G * d_z$. We implement this term as the difference between $d_z(x, y)$ and the average of d_z around (x, y) obtained by applying a Gaussian function to d_z. Consequently, this term minimizes the difference between the two sides of the following system of equations

$$\lambda_1 \big(z(x, y) - G * z(x, y)\big) = \lambda_1 \big(z_{\text{ref}}(x, y) - G * z_{\text{ref}}(x, y)\big). \tag{19.13}$$

This system too is linear in $z(x, y)$. The second regularization term vanishes since we have substituted ρ_{ref} for ρ.

Boundary Conditions for Depth Recovery   For boundary conditions, we assume in our algorithm that the gradient of the surface in the direction perpendicular to the exterior boundary vanishes (i.e., the surface is planar near the boundaries; note that this does not imply that the entire bounding contour is planar). Specifically, we add for each boundary point the following constraint

$$\nabla z(x, y) \cdot \mathbf{n_c}(x, y) = 0. \qquad (19.14)$$

where $\mathbf{n_c}(x, y)$ is a two-dimensional vector representing the normal to the bounding contour. These constraints will be roughly satisfied if the boundaries are placed in slowly changing parts of the face. They will be satisfied for example when the boundaries are placed along the cheeks and the forehead, but will not be satisfied when the boundaries are placed along the eyebrows, where the surface orientation changes rapidly.

Finally, since the obtained equation system involves only partial derivatives of $z(x, y)$, while $z(x, y)$ itself is absent from these equations, the solution can be obtained only up to an additive factor. We remedy this by arbitrarily setting one point to $z(x_0, y_0) = z_{\text{ref}}(x_0, y_0)$.

Step 3: Estimating Albedo   Using the data term the albedo $\rho(x, y)$ is found by solving the following equation

$$I(x, y) = \rho(x, y)\mathbf{l}^T \mathbf{Y}(\mathbf{n}). \qquad (19.15)$$

The first regularization term in (19.10) is independent of ρ, and so it can be ignored. The second term optimizes the following set of equations

$$\lambda_2 \triangle G * \rho = \lambda_2 \triangle G * \rho_{\text{ref}}. \qquad (19.16)$$

These provide a linear set of equations, in which the first set determines the albedo values, and the second set smoothes these values. We avoid the need for boundary conditions simply by terminating the smoothing process at the boundaries.

19.4 Experiments

We demonstrate our algorithm on photographs taken under uncontrolled viewing conditions. Additional experiments and quantitative comparisons can be found in [14, 15]. We align the input image to the reference model by manually marking five points (the two centers of the eyes, the tip of the nose, the center of the mouth and the bottom of the chin), and then determine a 2×4 affine transformation, which aligns 3D points on the reference model to marked 2D points in the input image. After the alignment procedure the images are of typical size of 360×480 pixels. Our MATLAB implementation of the algorithm takes about 9 seconds on a quad-core AMD processor 2354 1100 MHz Linux workstation.

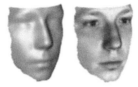

Fig. 19.2 A face model from the USF dataset used as a reference model in our experiments. The model is shown with uniform texture (*left*) and with an image overlay on the model (*right*)

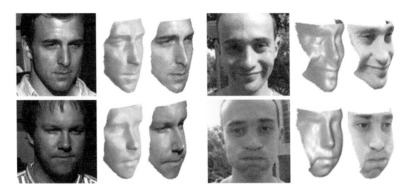

Fig. 19.3 Reconstruction results on images from the YaleB dataset (*left column*) and images photographed by us (*right column*). In each example we present the input image, our 3D shape reconstruction, and an image overlay on the reconstructed shape

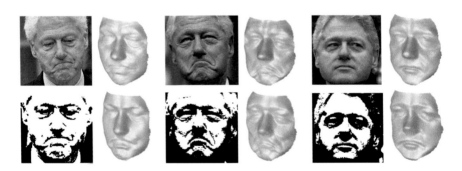

Fig. 19.4 Reconstruction from color (*top*) and two-tone (*bottom*) images. Each pair shows an input image and a reconstruction result

In Figs. 19.2–19.4, we show a few illustrative results obtained with our algorithm. The reference model used in our experiments is shown in Fig. 19.2. Figure 19.3 shows results on two images from the YaleB dataset and two more that were photographed by us. Figure 19.4 shows reconstruction results from three color images and from three two-tone images obtained by thresholding the intensity values.

We can see that convincing reconstructions are obtained for these images despite differences in identity, head orientation and facial expressions relative to the reference model. In addition, our reconstruction results for the two-tone images are similar to those obtained for the color images. These results are encouraging given the ill-posedness of the single view reconstruction problem and particularly reconstruction from two-tone images.

19.5 Conclusion

In this chapter, we explored the role of top-down information in the 3D reconstruction of faces from single images. We provided mathematical evidence that two-tone images provide ambiguous shape information and presented a novel method for reconstruction of faces from single image by using only a single reference model. Our results demonstrate that familiarity with faces as a class can help overcoming the difficulties in applying SFS algorithms and achieve veridical reconstructions even for Mooney images in which only two-tone intensity information is available.

We can foresee a number of potential directions to further extend over our method. One natural extension is to incorporate information from several images of the same individual, as in [16]; this could also address degeneracies of the current approach occurring under particular lighting conditions (see more details in [14]). Additionally, while facial expression is captured in the reconstruction, this is not directly targeted by the method and pixel-wise correspondence is not established. Establishing such correspondence can be useful also if we wish to generalize our ideas and apply them to other classes of objects. Finally, it will be interesting to further explore to what extent our algorithmic objectives are indeed achieved by the visual cortex.

Acknowledgement   Research was supported in part by the Israel Science Foundation grant number 266/02 and by the European Commission Project IST-2002-506766 Aim Shape. The vision group at the Weizmann Institute is supported in part by the Moross Laboratory for Vision Research and Robotics.

References

1. http://www.princeton.edu/artofscience/gallery/view.php%3fid=77.html
2. Atick JJ, Griffin PA, Redlich AN (1996) Statistical approach to shape from shading: reconstruction of 3d face surfaces from single 2d images. Neural Comput 8(6):1321–1340
3. Basri R, Jacobs DW (2003) Lambertian reflectance and linear subspaces. PAMI 25(2)
4. Blanz V, Vetter TA (1999) A morphable model for the synthesis of 3d faces. Comput Graph I:187–194
5. Cootes TF, Edwards GJ, Taylor CJ (1998) Active appearance models. In: ECCV, vol 2
6. Dolan RJ, Fink GR, Rolls E, Booth M, Holmes A, Frackowiak RSJ, Friston KJ (1997) How the brain learns to see objects and faces in an impoverished context. Nature 389
7. Edwards GJ, Lanitis A, Taylor CJ, Cootes TF (1996) Modelling the variability in face images. In: Proc of the 2nd int conf on automatic face and gesture recognition, vol 2

8. George N, Jemel B, Fiori N, Renault B (1997) Face and shape repetition effects in humans: a spatio-temporal ERP study. NeuroReport 8(6):1417–1423
9. Hegde J, Thompson S, Kersten D (2007) Identifying faces in two-tone ('mooney') images: a psychophysical and fMRI study. J Vis 7(9):624
10. Horn BKP, Brooks MJ (eds) (1989) Shape from shading. MIT Press, Cambridge
11. Hursh TM (1976) The study of cranial form: measurement techniques and analytical methods. In: Giles E, Fiedlaender J (eds) The measures of man
12. Julesz B (1971) Foundations of cyclopean perception. The University of Chicago Press, Chicago
13. Kemelmacher I, Basri R (2006) Molding face shapes by example. In: ECCV, vol 1, pp 277–288
14. Kemelmacher I, Basri R (2011) 3d face reconstruction from a single image using a single reference face shape. IEEE Trans Pattern Anal Mach Intell 33(2):394–405
15. Kemelmacher-Shlizerman I, Basri R, Nadler B (2008) 3d shape reconstruction of mooney faces. In: CVPR
16. Kemelmacher-Shlizerman I, Seitz SM (2011) Face reconstruction in the wild. In: ICCV
17. Kimmel R, Sethian JA (2001) Optimal algorithm for SFS and path planning. J Math Imaging Vis 14(3):237–244
18. Lanitis A, Taylor CJ, Cootes TF (1997) Automatic interpretation and coding of face images using flexible models. IEEE Trans Pattern Anal Mach Intell 19(7):743–756
19. Marschner SR, Westin SH, Lafortune EPF, Torrance KE, Greenberg DP (1999) Image-based brdf measurement including human skin. In: 10th eurographics workshop on rendering, pp 139–152
20. Mooney CM (1957) Age in the development of closure ability in children. Can J Psychol 11:219–226
21. Moore C, Cavanagh P (1998) Recovery of 3d volume from 2-tone images of novel objects. Cognition 67:45–71
22. Ramamoorthi R, Hanrahan P (2001) On the relationship between radiance and irradiance: Determining the illumination from images of a convex Lambertian object. J Opt Soc Am 18(10):2448–2459
23. Rodriguez E, George N, Lachaux JP, Martinerie J, Renault B, Varela FJ (1999) Perception's shadow: long-distance synchronization of human brain activity. Nature 397:430–433
24. Sethian JA (1996) A fast marching level set method for monotonically advancing fronts. Proc Natl Acad Sci USA 93:1591–1595
25. Sim T, Kanade T (2001) Combining models and exemplars for face recognition: an illuminating example. In: CVPR workshop on models versus exemplars
26. Smith WAP, Hancock ER (2005) Recovering facial shape and albedo using a statistical model of surface normal direction. In: ICCV
27. Tsitsiklis JN (1994) Efficient algorithms for globally optimal trajectories. In: Proc conf on decision and control
28. Yoon J, Winawer J, Wittoft N, Markman E (2007) Mooney image perception in preschool-aged children. J Vis 7(9):548
29. Zhang L, Samaras D (2003) Face recognition under variable lighting using harmonic image exemplars. In: CVPR
30. Zhou SK, Chellappa R, Jacobs DW (2004) Characterization of human faces under illumination variations using rank, integrability, and symmetry constraints. In: ECCV

Chapter 20
Perception and Action Without Veridical Metric Reconstruction: An Affine Approach

Fulvio Domini and Corrado Caudek

The variety of motor tasks we often carry out effortlessly and unconsciously are the result of very complex mechanisms that utilize visual information. These motor tasks depend on decisions that are based on perceptual judgments. Both perception and action require efficient and robust encoding of visual information, the nature of which is still debated. The large majority of researchers postulate that the visual system derives a veridical metric representation of the environment from retinal images. According to this approach, it is the veridical metric representation that allows the correct execution of motor actions and accurate perceptual judgments.

We argue, however, that the visual system does not aim at a veridical metric analysis of the visual scene. Our main claim, instead, is that the brain extracts from retinal signals the local affine information of environmental objects. This information lacks the specification of metric properties, but is a sufficiently rich description of the 3D shape of objects to serve the requirements of a robust and functional perceptual experience. Most importantly, this information is sufficient for enabling the correct execution of motor actions.

In support of our claim, after a brief description of what metric reconstruction entails (Sect. 20.1), we will present empirical evidence from published studies that clearly shows the fallibility of both perceptual and motor systems in metric tasks

F. Domini (✉)
Center for Neuroscience and Cognitive Systems@UniTn, Istituto Italiano di Tecnologia, Rovereto, Italy
e-mail: fulvio.domini@iit.it

F. Domini
Department of Cognitive, Linguistic and Psychological Sciences, Brown University, Providence, RI, USA
e-mail: fulvio_domini@brown.edu

C. Caudek
Department of Psychology, Università degli Studi di Firenze, Firenze, Italy
e-mail: corrado.caudek@unitn.it

S.J. Dickinson, Z. Pizlo (eds.), *Shape Perception in Human and Computer Vision*,
Advances in Computer Vision and Pattern Recognition,
DOI 10.1007/978-1-4471-5195-1_20, © Springer-Verlag London 2013

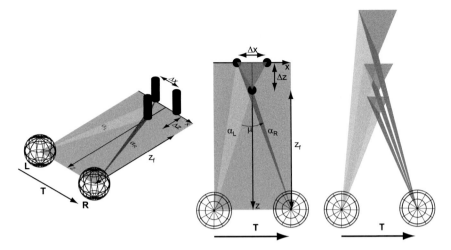

Fig. 20.1 *Left*: Information about the 3D structure of the three-rod configuration can be provided by binocular disparities, specified by the two different views of the left (L) and right (R) eyes. The same information can also be specified by the change in the monocular retinal projection of the three-rod configuration induced by a change in viewpoint from L to R. *Center*: Binocular disparities and retinal velocities can be defined as the difference between the visual angles at R (α_R) and at L (α_L). *Right*: If the vergence angle of the eyes (μ) or the lateral motion of the observer (T) are unknown then the same binocular disparities and retinal velocities are compatible with the projection of an infinite family of 3D structures

(Sect. 20.2). We will then describe a recent theory of 3D shape reconstruction that is based on a non-metric analysis of visual information and redescribe the results of Sect. 20.2 in light of this novel account (Sect. 20.3).

In all three sections, we will be considering the example of perceiving and interacting with an object as the three-rod configuration in Fig. 20.1 and will limit our discussion to two sources of 3D information: binocular disparities and retinal velocities.

20.1 Veridical Metric Structure from Binocular Disparities and Retinal Velocities

Metric properties are not directly specified by retinal information. Binocular disparities and retinal velocities must be scaled to yield a veridical representation of the scene in Fig. 20.1, such as the correct estimate of the egocentric distance of the object (z_f), depth extent (Δz) and size (Δx). In Fig. 20.1 (left and center) the relative disparity (d) between the front rod and one of the two flanking rods is defined as the difference $\alpha_R - \alpha_L$, where α_R and α_L are the visual angles subtended by the two rods on the right and left eye, respectively. d is related to the depth Δz of the object, but the same disparity can be produced by larger objects that are further away

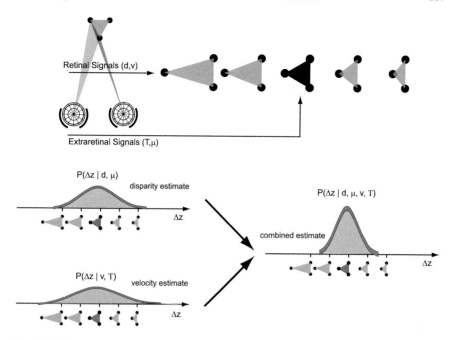

Fig. 20.2 *Top:* Retinal signals (d or v) specify an infinite family of 3D structures (*gray*). The precise estimate of retinal signals in conjunction with the precise estimate of extra-retinal signals (μ or T) allows the computation of the veridical metric structure (*black*). *Bottom left:* The precision of a depth estimate is hindered by the measurement noise of retinal and extra-retinal signals. In this example, depth-from-disparity (*top*) is more precise than depth-from-velocities (*bottom*). *Bottom right:* Combining the depth estimates from multiple signals in a statistically optimal fashion yields a more precise depth estimate

from the observer or smaller objects that are closer to the observer (Fig. 20.1, right). Without a specification of the distance to the object (z_f), Δz cannot be inferred from d. Retinal velocities are very similar to binocular disparities in the way they specify metric depth. In Fig. 20.1, the positions **L** and **R** can be thought of as the locations of one eye at two different instants of time (t_L and t_R), resulting from a lateral movement of size **T**. The relative velocity between the front rod and a flanking rod, defined as $v = \frac{\alpha_R - \alpha_L}{t_R - t_L}$, specifies Δz only up to a scaling factor that depends again on the distance z_f and the observer's motion T.

The correct scaling factors for metric depth estimates are determined by extraretinal information. z_f can be estimated by the vergence angle μ, encoded by the efferent signals related to the eyes' rotation and by ocular accommodation. Assuming stationarity of the object, T could in principle be obtained via an efferent copy of the motor commands sent by the central nervous system to the muscles responsible for the observer's lateral movement.

In Fig. 20.2 (top), the depicted 3D configurations of the three rods correspond to some, among infinite, different scalings; however, only one scaling is veridical (black triangle). In an ideal world, where measurements of retinal and extra-retinal signals are accurate and infinitely precise the scaling of disparities and velocities yields the veridical solution. In reality, both the measurement of retinal signals and the estimates of scaling factors are subject to measurement noise. This in turn leads to uncertain estimation of the veridical metric depth Δz, whose likelihood is usually modeled as a Gaussian distribution centered at the true depth (Fig. 20.2, bottom panels). Depending on the specific viewing conditions, different signals are subject to different levels of uncertainties. The most popular theory of cue integration postulates that the visual system combines separate estimates in a way that takes into account the reliability of each estimate; this gives rise to a more reliable combined estimate. This theory now belongs to a more general framework: modeling perception as a Bayesian inference. This framework postulates that vision deals with uncertainty in a statistically optimal fashion, with the goal of maximizing both the accuracy and the precision of metric estimates ([1] for a review).

According to this framework, veridical metric reconstruction is the basic requirement for perception and action. Once a scene, or parts of a scene that are directly relevant to a specific task, are represented in a metric fashion, an agent can make accurate perceptual judgments or plan a motor action.

The assumption of veridical metric estimates underlies most studies on 3D shape perception and it is believed to be true at least for mechanisms involving motor actions. According to the *dual visual system theory*, precise metric judgments are not fundamental for a functional perceptual system. Perception can be thought of as the conscious representation of objects and their relationships, that allows us to make decisions about our future actions. Since this representation must be robust and invariant in many viewing conditions, it may be more general and abstract than a metric representation. Once we perform an action like grasping, however, we have to be able to match our finger grip configuration to that of the object we intend to grasp. The *dual visual system theory* of perception and action therefore postulates the existence of two dedicated sub visual systems [2]. The perceptual system delivers a non-metric representation of the environment, whereas the action system performs a precise metric reconstruction of objects in the scene.

20.2 Is Veridical Metric Structure Used or Needed?

We argue that neither perceptual judgments nor motor actions are based on a veridical metric analysis of the visual scene. This claim stems from a series of empirical studies showing a systematic failure in perceptual and motor tasks that *do* in fact require a veridical metric representation of environmental objects. Thus, perceptual distortions in metric tasks are the norm and not the exception. Large biases are found, for example, when observers are asked to judge the distance between pairs of points, the orientation, or the curvature of smooth surfaces [3–6]. These biases persist regardless of the number of cues present that specify the 3D shape of an object [7]. Distortions are found for virtual as well as real objects [8, 9]. Motor actions, as described in the following sections, are not immune to large biases either. Instead, they follow a pattern of systematic errors, that cannot be reconciled with a theory postulating a veridical reconstruction of metric properties for the purpose of an effective interaction with the environment. In the next paragraphs, we will provide examples of these perceptual and motor failures in the specific case of stereo and motion cues. We will then present an alternate theory of depth processing which postulates a non metric analysis of visual information. The specific assumptions characterizing this theory lead to a new model of 3D processing; this can then predict the systematic biases found in the empirical studies.

20.2.1 Perceived 3D Structure from Stereo and Motion Signals

Perceived metric properties from binocular disparities and retinal motion are not only inaccurate, but also largely sensitive to specific viewing conditions. Depth from stereo varies with viewing distance, revealing a systematic failure of depth constancy. Objects appear increasingly shallow as their distance from the viewer increases; furthermore, their depth is overestimated at close distances and underestimated at larger distances [10]. Depth from retinal velocities is largely dependent on the relative motion between the observer and the distal object [11–14]. Whereas in the case of passive viewing of moving objects it may be less surprising, (since observers do not have access to extraretinal information), it is most striking that it holds true in the more natural case when the observer's self motion generates the retinal optic flow. Indeed our recent studies indicate that extraretinal information about the observer's egomotion is mostly ignored by the visual system, in spite of its potential availability [15–17].

To establish whether binocular disparities and retinal velocities undergo veridical metric scaling, we tested depth perception on visual stimuli that were created to simulate the viewing condition depicted in Fig. 20.1. The task was to compare the perceived depth of a stimulus specified by only motion information with that of a stimulus specified by only stereo information [18]. The simulated depth of the motion stimulus was kept fixed (z_v) whereas that of the stereo stimulus was varied through a staircase procedure so to find the point (PSE_d) at which stereo and motion stimuli were perceived to have the same depth. The graph on Fig. 20.3 (left panel) shows the PSEs of individual observers for simulated motion depths of 2.5 mm (small symbols) and 5 mm (large symbols), and viewing distances (z_f) of 0.5 m (circles) and 1 m (squares). The data clearly shows a lack of accuracy and a very large variability across observers.

In further studies, we investigated whether inaccuracy of depth judgments diminishes when the visual system has access to more sources of 3D information [7, 19]. From a computational stand point, the joint analysis of binocular disparities and retinal velocities allows the estimation of missing scaling parameters like the viewing distance (z_f) and the relative motion between the observer and the distal object (T) [20]. This is especially important in the absence of efferent motor information about the observer's ego-motion. In a recent experiment, we tested whether the visual system exploits a similar mechanism [21]. Observers judged the depth of the

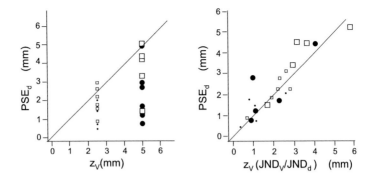

Fig. 20.3 *Left:* Binocular depth values (PSE_d) perceptually matched to motion specified depths (z_v) of 2.5 mm (*small symbols*) and 5 mm (*large symbols*) simulated at two viewing distances (50 cm—*circles* and 100 cm—*squares*) for individual observers. The *oblique line* represents veridical performance. *Right:* The same values re-plotted as function of a predictor based on the assumption that a perceptual match is obtained when the SNR of the two signals is the same (see text)

three-rod configuration depicted in Fig. 20.1; they were asked to make judgments in three conditions, in which only stereo, only motion or both signals specified the 3D structure. The results plotted in Fig. 20.4 (left panel) show systematic biases of metric depth estimates. As in the previous example, we found a very large inter-subject variability. Most notably, the combined-cue stimuli were systematically overestimated, showing that perceived metric depth from multiple-cues is also inaccurate. Another important characteristic of this pattern of results is that the combined-cue stimuli were perceived as deeper than the single-cue stimuli. This finding is incompatible with theories of cue-integration predicting that combined-cue estimates are the result of a weighted sum of single-cue estimates. We replicated this basic finding in other studies with different methodologies [19] and even with "real" 3D structures [9].

20.2.2 Reach-to-Grasp Without Visual or Haptic Feedback

The *dual visual system theory* postulates the existence of two separate processes for perception and motor action. Any distortions found in perceptual judgments should disappear when action is involved, since precise metric estimates are required for the correct execution of motor tasks. The results described in the next two examples, however, clearly contradict this claim.

In a recent study observers were requested to reach for and grasp the virtual three-rod configuration depicted in Fig. 20.1 [22]. They could view the object (which was specified by stereo information) but not their hand. Moreover, they could not feel the object at the end of their grasping action. We recorded both the Final Hand Position (FHP) and the index-thumb Final Grip Aperture (FGA), with which the observers mimicked a potential grasp. A correct FHP would indicate an accurate assessment

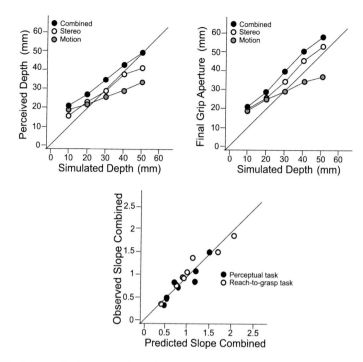

Fig. 20.4 *Left panels:* Mean perceived depth (*left*) and mean Final Grip Aperture (FGA) of a reach-to-grasp task (*center*) as function of simulated depth in three stimulus conditions: motion-only (*grey*), stereo-only (*white*) and combined (*black*). The *oblique line* indicates accurate performance. For each subject and in each stimulus condition we estimated the slope of the linear function relating perceived depth and FGA values to the simulated values. *Right panel:* Observed slopes of the combined-cue condition as function of the slopes predicted by our model. The predictions are based on the assumption that depth scaling depends on the SNR of single and multiple signals (see text) and not on the metric structure of the simulated object. Data from the perceptual and motor tasks are represented by *black* and *white circles*, respectively

of the egocentric distance from the observer, whereas a correct FGA would reveal an appropriate scaling of stereo information. The graphs in Fig. 20.5 show the results of individual observers for both measures of performance. It is important to note the large deviations from veridicality and the large inter-subject variability. Without any feedback about the final position of hand and fingers, the target configuration was largely missed by most observers.

Identical stimuli used in the experiment described in Sect. 20.2.1 [21] were also used in a reach-to-grasp task. This task investigated the accuracy of grasping when only stereo information, only motion information or a combination of motion and stereo information specified the 3D structure. The pattern of results (Fig. 20.4, middle panel) is very similar to that of the perceptual task (Fig. 20.4, left panel). First, FGAs were inaccurate and varied by a large amount among observers. Second, FGAs for the combined-cue stimuli were larger than those for the single-cue stimuli; furthermore, they indicated a large depth overestimation.

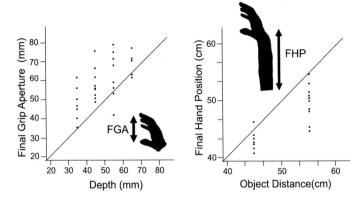

Fig. 20.5 Final Grip Aperture (FGA, *left panel*) and Final Hand Position (FHP, *right panel*) of a reach-to-grasp task as function of simulated depth (*left*) and distance (*right*) for each individual subject. The *oblique line* represents accurate performance

20.2.3 Is Veridical Metric Reconstruction Needed?

The few examples given in the previous sections and the results of several other studies show that accurate metric estimates are not a priority for the visual system, neither for perception nor for action. Perhaps the most surprising findings are those that show a systematic failure of motor tasks, casting doubt on the notion of a "metric dorsal stream". But how is it possible that we can successfully interact with the environment without metric knowledge? The answer may be that we do not need accurate metric knowledge at all. There are at least two strategies that could be adopted by the brain to execute motor tasks without a veridical representation of objects in the world. Both strategies capitalize on the use of visual or haptic feedback (both of which were unavailable to the subjects in the previously described experiments).

Vision of both hand and target has been shown to play a major role in the control of reaching movements [23]. Of particular relevance is evidence that vision of the hand is also important for very fast movements, indicating that the process of motor control requires continuous visual feedback of the effectors, even for tasks that were thought to be entirely preplanned. This means that within a split second, the visual system monitors the relative position of the hand and the target; subsequently, it uses this information to update the motor commands. What is relevant for the present discussion is that if both hand and fingers are visible while a grasping action unfolds, then metric information is in theory unnecessary for a correct execution of the movement. It is sufficient that the *relative distances* between the fingers and the object grasp points are nulled. In this case the scene could be scaled by any arbitrary factors, as long as both hand and object are scaled in the same way (see Fig. 20.6).

Another important component of each motor action is the presence of the final haptic feedback the brain receives when a grasping action is completed. As discussed before, when subjects reach for objects within a new visual scene without

Fig. 20.6 A precise grasping action can take place without veridical metric reconstruction, only precise affine information about hand and object is required

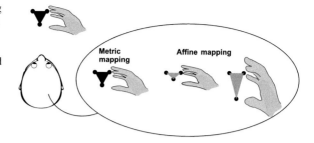

vision of their hand they make large errors. However, it has been shown that after only a few trials where they can feel some objects in the scene, reaching errors are reduced or nulled [24]. The explanation for this effect is that when vision of the hand is unavailable, haptic feedback allows the *calibration* of the visuomotor system: after feeling an object an appropriate scaling of the scene can be applied in order to re-adjust the motor commands.

20.3 Local Affine Information and Heuristic Scaling

In Sect. 20.1 we saw that, in addition to retinal signals, veridical metric scaling requires precise extraretinal information about the egocentric location of objects in the scene or the relative movement between the object and the observer. Retinal signals, however, directly specify non-metric 3D properties. Consider again Fig. 20.2 (top-right panel): binocular disparities and retinal velocities identify an infinite class of possible 3D shapes that could have generated the retinal signals. All these shapes have a similar structure but they differ in their metric properties. The structure that is common to all the shapes is defined as the *affine structure*. In words: "*two rods at the same depth plane and one in front in the middle*". From a geometric perspective, all the structures in Fig. 20.2 (top-right panel) have the same affine structure since they are related to each other through a linear transformation: a linear stretching along the depth dimension [25–27].

As previously discussed, a successful interaction with the environment does not necessarily require accurate metric knowledge: affine information suffices. This concept is illustrated in Fig. 20.6, where we sketched three different visual reconstructions of a scene representing a grasping action. In one case, hand and object are mapped onto a veridical metric representation. In the other two, *both* hand and object are wrongly scaled, but the relationship between them (i.e., the affine structure) is preserved. Thus, imprecise and inaccurate estimates of metric properties do not prevent precise grasping as long as *the local affine information* about object and hand is accurately preserved.

Since the affine structure of distal objects is directly specified by optical information, it is reasonable to speculate that the visual system has evolved to pick up this information. In contrast, accurate metric scaling requires the fine tuning of extraretinal information, which is mostly unreliable and specific to the retinal signal

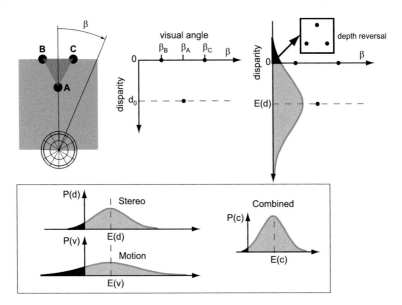

Fig. 20.7 *Top left panels:* Disparity of each element of a the three-rod configuration as function of the cyclopean visual direction β. Disparity alone specifies the correct depth order of the configuration. *Top right panel:* When corrupted by Gaussian noise the measured disparity signal can jump to negative values and therefore lead to perceived depth reversals. *Bottom panels:* The precision of the depth order estimate (i.e., the affine structure) depends on the retinal Signal to Noise Ratio (SNR). The SNR can be improved by directly combining multiple image signals *before* any metric scaling

being scaled. Hence, a veridical metric mapping requires a more complex visual system that would also be less robust to extraretinal noise perturbations.

If the goal of the visual system is to pick up local affine information, then it must also have evolved to carry out this goal with the maximum precision allowed by the optical apparatus. This implies that metric information (via extraretinal signals) is ignored in the process and that different image signals (e.g., disparity and velocity) are combined before any metric scaling is applied. This is our general assumption:

> ***Affine Hypothesis:*** *(a) Local affine information is derived from multiple image signals at the earliest stage of 3D processing. (b) The combination of signals into a single affine estimate is optimal insofar as it maximizes precision. Metric knowledge is ignored, the only information carried on to further processing being affine.*

(a) Local Affine Information In order to understand how disparities (and by analogy retinal velocities) directly specify the affine structure of the three-rod configuration, consider Fig. 20.7 (top-left panels) where we plotted the disparities of the rods as a function of their visual direction β.[1] It is simple to visualize how relative disparities specify the affine structure of the three-rod configuration. When both the visual directions (β_A, β_B, β_C) and the sign of the relative disparities (d) of the rods are known, the depth order of the rods is perfectly specified. In Fig. 20.7, the central rod has a positive disparity d_0, which indicates that it is in front of the flankers.

(b) Maximizing Precision of Affine Estimates This example describes the ideal case of infinitely precise measurements of retinal information. In reality, measurement noise affects the estimate of both binocular disparities and retinal velocities. Figure 20.7 (top-right panel) shows how Gaussian noise can corrupt the estimation of the affine structure. In this case, whenever the measured value of disparity (or velocity) jumps to a negative value, it defines a different affine structure, where the depth order of central and flanking rods is reversed. It follows that the precision of affine structure estimation depends on both the true value of disparity (d_0) or velocity (v_0) and the standard deviation of the measurement noise of the retinal signals (σ_d and σ_v). Since the noise is considered to be Gaussian, the true values d_0 and v_0 correspond to the expected values $E(d)$ and $E(v)$. A measure of the precision of the affine estimates is therefore given by the Signal to Noise Ratios (SNRs): $\frac{E(d)}{\sigma_d}$ and $\frac{E(v)}{\sigma_v}$.

Image signals can be directly combined for a more precise estimate of the affine property (Fig. 20.7, bottom panel). The optimal combination rule, which guaranties the maximum precision, yields an estimate whose SNR is larger than that of each individual signal[2] (see [7] and [28] for a detailed description of the combination rule).

20.3.1 Metric Tasks and Heuristic Scaling

Most tasks in laboratory experiments investigating 3D perception involve metric judgements. The experiments described above, for example, require observers to judge the perceived depth of the three-rod configuration or shape their grasp without vision of their hand. These tasks, therefore, require some sort of metric scaling.

According to the *Affine Hypothesis*, at the initial stage of 3D processing only affine information is extracted from image signals. Hence, whatever metric scaling takes place *after* this early stage, it is based on affine information. Our theory does not specify the exact mechanisms of this scaling, but we can be certain that (1) it depends on viewing parameters (e.g., vergence angle) and global scene information (e.g., perspective) specifying egocentric distance and (2) it is heuristic, since in general it cannot lead to veridical metric information.

---

[1] We arbitrarily chose a zero disparity value for the flankers, as if the observers were fixating the plane identified by the two flanking rods.

[2] In the specific case of disparity and velocity $SNR_c = \sqrt{SNR_d^2 + SNR_v^2}$.

To understand this second point consider again disparities and velocities: In order to obtain veridical metric information, disparities and velocities must be scaled separately, through an accurate estimate of viewing distance in the former and the relative motion between object and observer in the latter. If these signals are combined *before* each of these scalings can take place, as the *Affine Hypothesis* postulates, then the veridical metric knowledge carried by each signal is lost. Hence, we can formulate the following:

> **Heuristic Scaling Hypothesis** *Performance in metric tasks is heuristically determined by (1) affine information of image signals and (2) egocentric distance information (e.g. vergence angle, observer motion, perspective information, etc.).*

Thus, assuming the egocentric distance information remains constant, two signals will give rise to the same metric judgement if they specify the same affine structure with the same precision (i.e., same SNRs), regardless of the actual metric properties of the configuration that has generated them. Going back to the three-rod configuration of Fig. 20.1, whenever disparities and velocities specify the same affine structure with the same SNRs, they will generate the same perceptual (and motor) response, even if their simulated depths are different.

We have previously shown that when asked to set the depth of a stereo stimulus so to appear as deep as that of a motion stimulus of simulated depth z_v, observers are highly inaccurate ($PSE_d \neq z_v$; Fig. 20.3 left panel). The *Heuristic Scaling Hypothesis* predicts that a perceptual match should occur when the SNRs of the two signals are the same. In order to test this assumption, we measured the discrimination thresholds of disparities (JND_d) at PSE_d and velocities (JND_v) at z_v[18]. It can be shown that $SNR_v = \frac{E(v)}{\sigma_v} = \frac{z_v}{JND_v}$ and that $SNR_d = \frac{E(d)}{\sigma_d} = \frac{PSE_d}{JND_d}$. By equating the two SNRs it follows that $PSE_d = z_v \frac{JND_d}{JND_v}$, which provides an alternative prediction to the metric account ($PSE_d = z_v$). Figure 20.3 (right panel), where we re-plotted the results of Fig. 20.3 (left panel) as a function of $z_v \frac{JND_d}{JND_v}$, clearly shows the good agreement between data and the prediction of the *Heuristic Scaling Hypotheses*. This means that we do scale signals based on affine information, not metric properties.

What if the precision of two affine estimates is different (i.e., SNRs are different)? From a statistical point of view, deeper objects are more likely to produce larger SNRs since they generate, "on average", image signals with larger magnitudes.[3] We can thus formulate the following hypothesis:

> **SNR Hypothesis:** *The magnitude of heuristic metric estimates is an increasing function of the Signal-to-Noise Ratio of the affine estimate, as long as the factors that affect heuristic scaling (e.g. vergence angle, observer motion, etc.) are kept constant.*

---

[3]Consider binocular disparities: The relative disparity d is proportional to the depth Δz of the distal object through a scaling factor k_d, related to the egocentric distance of the object ($d = k_d \Delta z$) and, therefore, to the Signal to Noise Ratio ($SNR_d = \frac{k_d}{\sigma_d} \Delta z$). For a fixed value of k_d, SNR_d increases with Δz. Thus, "on average", larger values of SNR correspond to larger values of Δz.

A corollary of this hypothesis is that the scaled depth of combined-cue stimuli is larger than the scaled depth of single-cue stimuli, since the SNR of combined-cue stimuli is larger than the SNR of single-cue stimuli. This is exactly what we found in the experiment described in the previous section for both perceptual judgments and reach-to-grasp actions (Fig. 20.4, left panels) [21]. If it is assumed that the function relating scaled depth and SNR is linear within the range of simulated depths, then it is possible to predict its slope for the combined-cue results from the slopes of the single-cue results [21]. In Fig. 20.4 (right panel), we plotted the predicted slope vs. the observed slope of the combined-stimulus estimates for both perceptual (filled circles) and motor (open circle) tasks for each individual observer. The good agreement between predictions and data suggests that for both tasks depth estimates are based on the local affine information.

These empirical results constitute strong evidence for the validity of the *Affine Hypothesis* and, at the same time, cast serious doubts on previous theories postulating a veridical metric analysis of the visual scene, for both perception and action. Several other studies provide additional converging evidence since they test the *Affine Hypothesis* with different sets of 3D cues (e.g., texture and shading) and in natural 3D settings, where cues-to-flatness are not present [7, 9].

20.4 Conclusion

A biological system has a successful interaction with the environment when sufficient information about the physical world is channeled through its sensory organs. While metric reconstruction is certainly sufficient for the achievement of this goal, its necessity has never been proven. Instead, empirical work and theoretical considerations indicate that metric reconstruction may not have been the ultimate result of evolutionary pressure.

We argue that local affine information directly available at the retinal level determines both our conscious perception of the world and the basic input for the control of motor actions. Image signals are combined at the very first stage of 3D processing through mechanisms that maximize the reliability of affine information, while disregarding metric information. Thus, only relational properties of object structures (e.g., depth order of feature points) are accurately carried on to further processing, yet enabling sufficient information about the world to be perceived and motor actions to be correctly executed.

References

1. Trommershauser J, Kording K, Landy M (2011) Sensory cue integration. Oxford University Press, New York
2. Goodale MA (2011) Transforming vision into action. Vis Res 51:1567–1587
3. Todd JT, Bressan P (1990) The perception of 3-dimensional affine structure from minimal apparent motion sequences. Percept Psychophys 48:419–430

4. Todd JT, Norman JF (2003) The visual perception of 3-d shape from multiple cues: are observers capable of perceiving metric structure? Percept Psychophys 65:31–47
5. Todd JT, Oomes AHJ, Koenderink JJ, Kappers AML (2001) On the affine structure of perceptual space. Psychol Sci 12:191–196
6. Norman JF, Lappin JS, Norman HF (2000) The perception of length on curved and flat surfaces. Percept Psychophys 62:1133–1145
7. Di Luca M, Domini F, Caudek C (2010) Inconsistency of perceived 3D shape. Vis Res 50:1519–1531
8. Norman JF, Crabtree CE, Clayton AM, Norman HF (2005) The perception of distances and spatial relationships in natural outdoor environments. Perception 34:1315–1324
9. Domini F, Shah R, Caudek C (2011) Do we perceive a flattened world on the monitor screen? Acta Psychol 138:359–366
10. Johnston EB (1991) Systematic distortions of shape from stereopsis. Vis Res 31:1351–1360
11. Domini F, Braunstein ML (1998) Recovery of 3-d structure from motion is neither Euclidean nor affine. J Exp Psychol Hum Percept Perform 24:1273–1295
12. Domini F, Caudek C (1999) Perceiving surface slant from deformation of optic flow. J Exp Psychol Hum Percept Perform 25:426–444
13. Domini F, Caudek C (2003) 3D structure perceived from dynamic information: a new theory. Trends Cogn Sci 7:444–449
14. Domini F, Caudek C (2003) Recovering slant and angular velocity from a linear velocity field: modeling and psychophysics. Vis Res 43:1753–1764
15. Fantoni C, Caudek C, Domini F (2010) Systematic distortions of perceived planar surface motion in active vision. J Vis 10:1–20. doi:10.1167/10.5.12
16. Caudek C, Fantoni C, Domini F (2011) Bayesian modeling of perceived surface slant from actively-generated and passively-observed optic flow. PLoS ONE. doi:10.1371/journal.pone. 0018731
17. Fantoni C, Caudek C, Domini F (2012) Perceived surface slant is systematically biased in the actively-generated optic flow. PLoS ONE. doi:10.1371/journal.pone.0033911
18. Domini F, Caudek C (2010) Matching perceived depth from disparity and velocity: modeling and psychophysics. Acta Psychol 133:81–89
19. Domini F, Caudek C, Tassinari H (2006) Stereo and motion information are not independently processed by the visual system. Vis Res 46:1707–1723
20. Richards W (1985) Structure from stereo and motion. J Opt Soc Am 2:343–349
21. Foster R, Fantoni C, Caudek C, Domini F (2011) Integration of disparity and velocity information for haptic and perceptual judgments of object depth. Acta Psychol 136:300–310
22. Campagnoli C, Volcic R, Domini F (2012) The same object and at least three different grip apertures. J Vis. doi:10.1167/12.9.429
23. Saunders JA, Knill DC (2003) Humans use continuous visual feedback from the hand to control fast reaching movements. Exp Brain Res 152:341–352
24. Bingham G, Coats R, Mon-Williams M (2007) Natural prehension in trials without haptic feedback but only when calibration is allowed. Neuropsychologia 45:288–294
25. Chen M, Chen K (1982) A transformational analysis of form recognition under plane isometries. J Math Psychol 26:237–251
26. Van Gool M, Moons T, Pauwels E, Wagemans J Invariance from the Euclidean geometer's perspective. Perception 23:547–561
27. Wagemans J, Van Gool L, Lamote C, Foster DH (2000) Minimal information to determine affine shape equivalence. J Exp Psychol Hum Percept Perform 26:443–468
28. Domini F, Caudek C (2011) Combining image signals before 3D reconstruction: the intrinsic constraint model of cue integration. In: Trommershauser J, Kording K, Landy M (eds) Sensory cue integration. Oxford University Press, New York, pp 120–143

Chapter 21
A Stochastic Grammar for Natural Shapes

Pedro F. Felzenszwalb

21.1 Introduction

In this chapter, we consider the problem of detecting objects using a generic model for natural shapes. A common approach for object recognition involves matching object models directly to images. Another approach involves building intermediate representations via a generic grouping processes. One of the ideas behind the work described here is that these two processes (model-based recognition and grouping) are not necessarily different. By using a generic object model, we can use model-based techniques to perform category-independent object detection. This leads to a grouping mechanism that is guided by a generic model for objects.

It is generally accepted that the shapes of natural objects have certain regularities and that these regularities can be used to guide visual perception. For example, the Gestalt grouping laws explain how the human visual system favors the perception of some objects over others. Intuitively, the tokens in an image should be grouped into regular shapes because these groupings are more likely to correspond to the actual objects in the scene. This idea has been studied in computer vision over several decades (see [6–10, 12]).

We propose a method in which a generic process searches the image for regular shapes to generate object hypotheses. These hypotheses should then be processed further in a way that depends on the perceptual task at hand. For example, each hypothesis could be matched against a database of known objects to establish their identities. Our algorithm works by sampling shapes from a conditional distribution defined by an input image. The distribution is constructed so that shapes with high probability look natural, and their boundaries align with areas of the image that have high gradient magnitude.

Our method simply generates a number of potential object hypothesis. Two hypothesis might overlap in the image, and some image areas might not be in any

P.F. Felzenszwalb (✉)
Department of Engineering, Brown University, Providence, RI, USA
e-mail: pff@brown.edu

S.J. Dickinson, Z. Pizlo (eds.), *Shape Perception in Human and Computer Vision*,
Advances in Computer Vision and Pattern Recognition,
DOI 10.1007/978-1-4471-5195-1_21, © Springer-Verlag London 2013

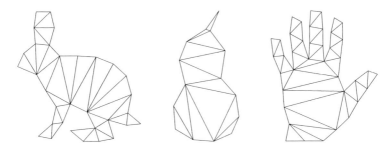

Fig. 21.1 Rabbit, pear, and hand represented by triangulated polygons. The polygonal boundaries represent the outlines, while the triangulations decompose the objects into parts

hypothesis. A consequence of this approach is that the low-level processing doesn't commit to any particular interpretation of the scene.

We start by defining a stochastic grammar that generates random triangulated polygons. This grammar can be tuned to capture regularities of natural shapes. For example, with certain choice of parameters the random shapes generated tend to have piecewise smooth boundaries and a natural decomposition into elongated parts. We combine this prior model with a likelihood model that defines the probability of observing an image given the presence of a particular shape in the scene. This leads to a posterior distribution over shapes in a scene. Samples from the posterior provide hypotheses for the objects in an image.

Our approach is related to [13] who also build a stochastic model for natural shapes. One important difference is that our approach leads to polynomial time inference algorithms, while [13] relied on MCMC methods.

The ideas described here are based on the author's PhD thesis [3].

21.2 Shape Grammar

We represent objects using triangulated polygons. Intuitively, a polygonal curve is used to approximate the object boundary, and a triangulation provides a decomposition of the objects into parts. Some examples are shown in Fig. 21.1.

There is a natural graph structure associated with a triangulated polygon, where the nodes of the graph are the polygon vertices and the edges include the polygon boundary and the diagonals in the triangulation. Figure 21.2 shows a triangulated polygon T and its dual graph G_T.

Here we consider only objects that are represented by *simple* polygons (polygons without holes). If T is a triangulated simple polygon, then its dual graph G_T is a tree [1]. There are three possible types of triangles in T, corresponding to nodes of different degrees in G_T. The three triangle types are shown in Fig. 21.3, where solid edges are part of the polygon boundary, and dashed edges are diagonals in the triangulation. Sequences of triangles of type 1 form branches, or necks of a shape. Triangles of the type 0 correspond to ends of branches, and triangles of the type 2

Fig. 21.2 A triangulated
polygon T and its dual graph
G_T. If the polygon is simple
the dual graph is a tree where
each node has degree 1, 2 or 3

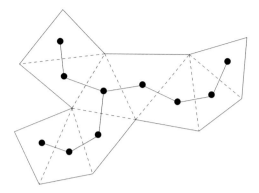

form junctions connecting multiple branches together. For the rest of this chapter, we
will use a particular labeling of the triangle vertices shown in Fig. 21.3. A triangle
will be defined by its type (0, 1 or 2) and the location of its vertices x_0, x_1 and x_2.

A procedure to generate triangulated polygons is given by the following growth
process. Initially a seed triangle is selected from one of the three possible types.
Then each dashed edge "grows" into a new triangle. Growth continues along newly
created dashed edges until all branches end by growing a triangle of the first type.
Figure 21.4 illustrates the growth of a polygon. A similar process for growing com-

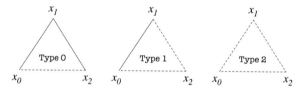

Fig. 21.3 Different triangle types in a triangulated polygon. The types corresponds to nodes of
different degrees in the dual graph. *Solid edges* correspond to the polygon boundary while *dashed
edges* are diagonals in the triangulation

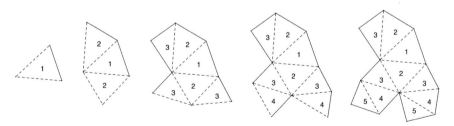

Fig. 21.4 Growth of a triangulated polygon. The *label in each triangle* indicates the stage at which
it was created. Initially we select a triangle (stage 1) from one of three possible types. Then each
dashed edge grows into a new triangle (stage 2) and growth continues along newly created *dashed
edges* (stages 3, 4, 5). New branches appear whenever a triangle of type 2 is created. All branches
end by growing a triangle of type 0

Fig. 21.5 In principle our
growth process can generate
objects with overlapping parts

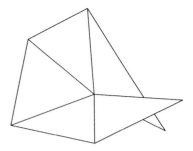

binatorial structures known as n-clusters is described in [5]. The growth process can
be made stochastic as follows. Let a triangle of type i be selected initially or during
growth with probability t_i. As an example, imagine picking t_i such that t_1 is large
relative to t_0 and t_2. This would encourage growth of shapes with long branches.
Similarly, t_2 will control the number of branches in the shape.

The three parameters t_0, t_1, t_2 control the structure of the object generated by
the stochastic process. The shape of the object is determined by its structure and
distributions that control the shape of each triangle. Let $X = (x_0, x_1, x_2)$ be the
locations of the vertices in a triangle. We use $[X]$ to denote the equivalence class of
configurations that are equal up to translations, scales and rotations. The probability
that a shape $[X]$ is selected for a triangle of type i is given by $s_i([X])$. We assume
the triangle shapes are independent.[1]

The growth process described above can be characterized by a stochastic grammar. We note however that this grammar will not only generate triangulated polygons, but will also generate objects with overlapping parts as illustrated in Fig. 21.5.

There are two types of symbols in the grammar, corresponding to triangles cre-
ated during growth $\mathcal{T}$ and dashed edges that still need to grow $\mathcal{E}$. Triangles cre-
ated during growth are elements of $\mathcal{T} = \{0, 1, 2\} \times \mathbb{R}^2 \times \mathbb{R}^2 \times \mathbb{R}^2$. The element
$(i, a, b, c) \in \mathcal{T}$ specifies a triangle of type i with vertices $x_0 = a$, $x_1 = b$, $x_3 = c$
following the labeling in Fig. 21.3. Edges that still need to grow are elements of
$\mathcal{E} = \mathbb{R}^2 \times \mathbb{R}^2$. The element $(a, b) \in \mathcal{E}$ specifies an internal edge of the triangulated
polygon from point a to point b. The edges are oriented from a to b so the system
can "remember" the direction of growth. Figure 21.6 illustrates the production rules
for the grammar. Note that there are two different rules to grow a triangle of type
1, corresponding to a choice of how the new triangle is glued to the edge that is
growing. We simply let both choices have equal probability, $t_1/2$.

To understand the effect of the parameters t_0, t_1, t_2, consider the dual graph of
a triangulated polygon generated by our stochastic process. The growth of the dual
graph starts in a root node that has one, two or three children with probability t_0, t_1
and t_2 respectively. Now each child of the root grows according to a Galton–Watson
process [4], where each node has i children with probability t_i.

---

[1]The fact that we can safely assume that triangle shapes are independent in a triangulated polygon
and get a sensible model follows from Theorem 2.1 in [3].

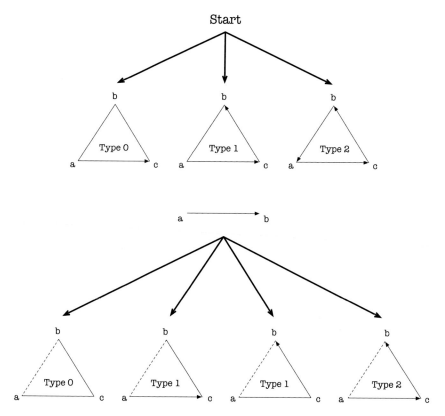

Fig. 21.6 Production rules for the shape grammar. The grammar generates triangles and oriented edges. The variables a, b and c correspond to locations in the plane. The three variables are selected in a production from the start symbol, but only c is selected in a production from an edge. Note that edges are oriented carefully so that growth continues along a particular direction

An important parameter of a Galton–Watson process is the expected number of children for each node, or Malthusian parameter, that we denote by m. In our process, $m = t_1 + 2t_2$. When $m < 1$ the probability that the growth process eventually terminates is one. From now on, we will always assume that $m < 1$, which is equivalent to requiring that $t_2 < t_0$ (here we use that $t_0 + t_1 + t_2 = 1$).

Let e, b and j be random variables corresponding to the number of end, branch and junction triangles in a random shape. Let $n = e + b + j$ be the total number of triangles in a shape. For our Galton–Watson process (corresponding to growth from each child of the root of the dual graph), we can compute the expected number of nodes generated, which we denote by x,

$$x = 1 + (x)t_1 + (2x)t_2 \quad \Rightarrow \quad x = 1/(t_0 - t_2).$$

The total number of triangles in a shape is obtained as one node for the root of the dual graph plus the number of nodes in the subtrees rooted at each child of the root.

So the expected value of n is,

$$E(n) = 1 + (x)t_0 + (2x)t_1 + (3x)t_2.$$

Substituting for x we get,

$$E(n) = \frac{2}{t_0 - t_2}. \tag{21.1}$$

Similarly we can compute the expected value of j, the number of junction triangles in a shape. This quantity is interesting because it gives a measure of the complexity of the shape. In particular it is a measure of the number of parts (limbs, necks, etc.). For the Galton–Watson process, let y be the expected number of nodes with degree 3 (two children),

$$y = (y)t_1 + (1 + 2y)t_2 \quad \Rightarrow \quad y = t_2/(t_0 - t_2).$$

The number of junction triangles in a shape equals the number of such triangles in each subtree of the root plus one if the root itself is a junction triangle,

$$E(j) = (y)t_0 + (2y)t_1 + (1 + 3y)t_2.$$

Substituting for y we get,

$$E(j) = \frac{2t_2}{t_0 - t_2}. \tag{21.2}$$

Equations (21.1) and (21.2) provide intuition to the effect of the parameters t_0, t_1, t_2. The equations also show that the parameters are uniquely defined by the expected number of triangles and the expected number of junction triangles in a random shape. We can compute the t_i corresponding to any pair $E(n)$ and $E(j)$ such that $E(n) \geq 2$ and $E(n) \geq 2E(j) + 2$. These requirements are necessary since the growth process always creates at least two triangles and the number of triangles is always at least twice the number of junction triangles plus two.

$$t_0 = \left(2 + E(j)\right)/E(n),$$
$$t_1 = 1 - \left(2E(j) + 2\right)/E(n),$$
$$t_2 = E(j)/E(n).$$

While the t_i control the combinatorial structure of the random shapes we generate, their geometry is highly dependent on the choice of shape for each triangle. The triangle shapes are chosen according to distributions that depend on the triangle type. As an example we can define,

$$s_i\left([X]\right) \propto e^{-k_i \, \mathrm{def}(X_i, X)^2},$$

where X_i is an ideal triangle of type i and $\mathrm{def}(X_i, X)$ is the log-anisotropy of the affine map taking X_i to X (see [2, 3]). The constant k_i controls how much the individual triangle shapes are allowed to vary. For the experiments in this chapter,

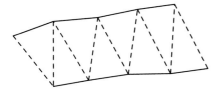 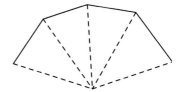

Fig. 21.7 Connecting multiple type 1 triangles in alternating orientations to form an elongated branch, and with the same orientation to form a bend. If the neck triangles tend to be isosceles and thin than the shape boundary tends to be smooth

we chose both X_0 and X_2 to be equilateral triangles and X_1 to be isosceles, with a smaller side corresponding to the polygon boundary edge. This choice for X_1 generates shapes that tend to have smooth boundaries. Figure 21.7 shows what happens when we connect multiple triangles of this type with alternating or similar orientations.

Figure 21.8 shows some random shapes generated by the random process with $E(n) = 20$, $E(j) = 1$, and the choice for $s_i([X])$ described above. Note how the shapes have natural decompositions into parts, and each part has an elongated structure, with smooth boundaries almost everywhere. These examples illustrate some of the regularities captured by our stochastic shape grammar. In the next section, we will show how the grammar can be used for object detection.

21.3 Sampling Shapes from Images

Now we describe how our model for random shapes can be combined with a likelihood function to yield a posterior distribution $p(T|I)$ over triangulated polygons in an image. We then show how to sample from the posterior using a dynamic programming procedure. The approach is similar to sampling from the posterior distribution of a hidden Markov model using weights computed by the forward-backward algorithm [11]. Our experiments in the next section illustrate how samples from $p(T|I)$ provide hypotheses for the objects in an image.

Recall that each triangle created during growth is an element of $\mathcal{T}$, specifying a triangle type and the location of its vertices. We assume that the likelihood $p(I|T)$ factors into a product of terms, with one term for each triangle,

$$p(I|T) \propto \prod_{(i,x_0,x_1,x_2)\in T} \pi_i(x_0, x_1, x_2, I). \tag{21.3}$$

This factorization allows for an efficient inference algorithm to be developed to generate samples from the posterior $p(T|I) \propto p(I|T)p(T)$.

We expect the image to have high gradient at the boundary of objects, with orientation perpendicular to the boundary. In practice, we have used a likelihood function

Fig. 21.8 Examples of random shapes generated by the stochastic grammar

of the form,

$$P(I|T) \propto \exp\left(\lambda \int \|(\nabla I \circ f)(s) \times f'(s)\| \, ds \right).$$

Here $f(s)$ is a parametrization of the boundary of T by arclength. The term $\|(\nabla I \circ f)(s) \times f'(s)\|$ is the component of the image gradient that is perpendicular to the

Fig. 21.9 A partial shape
generated from the edge
(a, b)

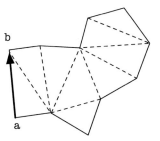

object boundary at $f(s)$. The integral above can be broken up into a sum of terms, with one term for each boundary edge in the triangulated polygon. This allows us to write the likelihood in the form of Eq. (21.3) where $\pi_i(x_0, x_1, x_2, I)$ evaluates the contribution to the integral due to the boundary terms (solid edges) of a triangle of type i with vertices (x_0, x_1, x_2).

Let T_r denote a triangulated polygon rooted at a triangle r. Using Bayes' law, we can write the posterior distribution for rooted shapes given an observed image as,

$$p(T_r|I) \propto p(T_r)p(I|T).$$

There are two approximations we make to sample from this posterior efficiently. We consider only shapes where the depth of the dual graph is bounded by a constant d (the depth of a rooted graph is the maximum distance from a leaf to the root). This should not be a significant problem since shapes with too many triangles have low prior probability anyway. Moreover, the running time of our sampling algorithm is linear in d, so we can let this constant be relatively large. We also only consider shapes where the location of each vertex is constrained to lie on a finite grid $\mathscr{G}$, as opposed to an arbitrary location in the plane. The running time of our algorithm for sampling from $p(T|I)$ is $O(d|\mathscr{G}|^3)$.

To sample from the posterior we first pick a root triangle, then pick the triangles connected to the root and so on. The root triangle r should be selected according to its marginal conditional distribution,

$$p(r|I) = \sum_{T_r} p(T_r|I). \qquad (21.4)$$

Note that the sum is over all shapes rooted at r, and with the depth of the dual graph bounded by d. We can compute this marginal distribution in polynomial time because the triangles in a shape are connected together in a tree structure.

Let $T_{(a,b)}$ denote a partial shape generated from an edge (a, b). Figure 21.9 shows an example of a partial shape. We denote the probability that the grammar would generate $T_{(a,b)}$ starting from the edge (a, b) by $p(T_{(a,b)})$. The posterior probability of a partial shape $T_{(a,b)}$ given an image I is given by,

$$p(T_{(a,b)}|I) \propto p(T_{(a,b)}) \prod_{(i,x_0,x_1,x_2)\in T_{(a,b)}} \pi_i(x_0, x_1, x_2, I).$$

We define the following quantities in analogy to the backward weights of a hidden Markov model (see [11]),

$$V_j(a, b) = \sum_{T_{(a,b)}} p(T_{(a,b)} | I),$$

where the sum is taken over all partial shapes with depth at most j. Here we measure depth by imagining the root to be a triangle that would be immediately before the edge (a, b). The quantities $V_j(a, b)$ can be computed recursively using a dynamic programming procedure,

$$V_0(a, b) = 0,$$

$$V_j(a, b) = t_0 \sum_c s_0([b, c, a]) \pi_0(b, c, a, I)$$

$$+ (t_1/2) \sum_c s_1([b, c, a]) \pi_1(b, c, a, I) V_{j-1}(a, c)$$

$$+ (t_1/2) \sum_c s_1([c, a, b]) \pi_1(c, a, b, I) V_{j-1}(c, b)$$

$$+ t_2 \sum_c s_2([b, c, a]) \pi_2(b, c, a, I) V_{j-1}(a, c) V_{i-1}(c, b).$$

Now, depending on the type of the root triangle we can rewrite the marginal distribution in Eq. (21.4) as,

$$p((0, a, b, c) | I) \propto t_0 s_0([a, b, c]) V_d(a, c),$$

$$p((1, a, b, c) | I) \propto t_1 s_1([a, b, c]) V_d(a, c) V_d(c, b),$$

$$p((2, a, b, c) | I) \propto t_2 s_2([a, b, c]) V_d(a, c) V_d(c, b) V_d(b, a).$$

The equations above provide a way to sample the root triangle from its marginal distribution. The running time for computing all the $V_j(a, b)$ and the marginal distribution for the root triangle is $O(d|\mathscr{G}|^3)$. Once we compute these quantities we can obtain samples for the root by sampling from a discrete distribution. After choosing $r = (i, x_0, x_1, x_2)$ we need to sample the triangles connected to the root. We then sample the triangles that are at distance two from the root, and so on. When sampling a triangle at distance j from the root, we have an edge (a, b) that is growing. We need to sample a triangle by selecting the location c of a new vertex and a triangle type according to

$$p((0, b, c, a) | I, (a, b)) \propto t_0 s_0([b, c, a]),$$

$$p((1, b, c, a) | I, (a, b)) \propto (t_1/2) s_1([b, c, a]) V_{d-j}(a, c),$$

$$p((1, c, a, b) | I, (a, b)) \propto (t_1/2) s_1([c, a, b]) V_{d-j}(c, b),$$

$$p((2, b, c, a) | I, (a, b)) \propto t_2 s_2([b, c, a]) V_{d-j}(a, c) V_{d-j}(c, b).$$

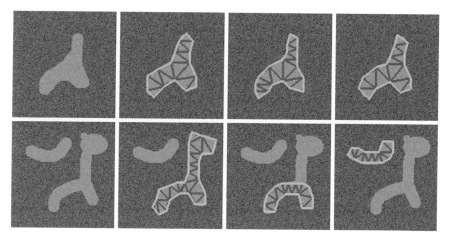

Fig. 21.10 Samples from $p(T|I)$ for two synthetic images I. Note how in the second image we get multiple potential objects among the samples

We evaluate these probabilities using the precomputed V_j quantities and then sample a triangle type and location c from the corresponding discrete distribution. Note that for a triangle at depth d the only choices with nonzero probability will have type zero, as $V_0(a,b) = 0$.

21.4 Experimental Results

For the experiments in this section, we used a grid $\mathcal{G}$ of 40×40 locations for the vertices of the shapes. We used the likelihood model defined in the last section, and the same grammar parameters used to generate the random shapes in Fig. 21.8.

Figure 21.10 shows some of the samples generated from the posterior distribution $p(T|I)$ for two different synthetic images. The first image has a single object and each sample from $p(T|I)$ gives a slightly different representation for that object. The second image has two objects and the samples from $p(T|I)$ are split between the two objects. Note that we obtain samples that correspond to each object and also to a part of one object that can be naturally interpreted as a single object. Overall the samples in both cases give reasonable interpretations of the objects in the images.

Figures 21.11 and 21.12 show samples from the posterior distribution $p(T|I)$ for two natural images. In practice we obtain groups of samples that are only slightly different from each other, and here we show representatives from each group. For the mushroom image, we obtained different samples corresponding to competing interpretations. In one case the whole mushroom is considered as an object, while in another case the stem comes out on its own.

Fig. 21.11 Sample from $p(T|I)$ for an image with a bird

Fig. 21.12 Samples from $p(T|I)$ for an image with a mushroom

References

1. De Berg M, Cheong O, Van Kreveld M, Overmars M (2008) Computational geometry: algorithms and applications. Springer, Berlin
2. Dryden IL, Mardia KV (1998) Statistical shape analysis. Wiley, New York
3. Felzenszwalb PF (2003) Representation and detection of shapes in images. PhD thesis, MIT, September 2003
4. Habib M, McDiarmid C, Ramirez-Alfonsin J, Reed B (1998) Probabilistic methods for algorithmic discrete mathematics. Springer, Berlin
5. Harary F, Palmer EM, Read RC (1975) On the cell-growth problem for arbitrary polygons. Discrete Math 11:371–389
6. Jacobs DW (1996) Robust and efficient detection of salient convex groups. IEEE Trans Pattern Anal Mach Intell 18(1):23–37
7. Jermyn IH, Ishikawa H (2001) Globally optimal regions and boundaries as minimum ratio weight cycles. IEEE Trans Pattern Anal Mach Intell 23(10):1075–1088
8. Lee MS, Medioni G (1999) Grouping ., -, ->, 0, into regions, curves, and junctions. Comput Vis Image Underst 76(1):54–69
9. Mumford D (1994) Elastica and computer vision. In: Algebraic geometry and its applications. Springer, Berlin, pp 491–506
10. Nitzberg M, Mumford D (1990) The 2.1-d sketch. In: ICCV, pp 138–144
11. Rabiner LR (1989) A tutorial on hidden Markov models and selected applications in speech recognition. Proceedings of the IEEE 77(2)
12. Shashua A, Ullman S (1988) Structural saliency: the detection of globally salient structures using a locally connected network. In: ICCV, pp 321–327
13. Zhu SC (1999) Embedding gestalt laws in Markov random fields. IEEE Trans Pattern Anal Mach Intell 21(11):1170–1187

Chapter 22
Hard-Wired and Plastic Mechanisms in 3-D Shape Perception

Qasim Zaidi, Andrea Li, Carson Wong, Elias H. Cohen, and Xin Meng

22.1 Introduction

Learning has intrigued scientists and scholars for as long as we know, for example, Plato's *Meno*, in part because the ability to learn confers plasticity to an organism in dealing with a variable environment. It has also been understood that learning specific knowledge requires biological structures that facilitate the learning [20, 21, 100]. The evolution of such hard-wired structures can be considered long-term genetic learning of capacities to deal with the environment. The two processes have interesting similarities, such that genetic algorithms form a major stream in machine learning [47], the equations for population genetics (especially for selection at a single locus) can be formally identical to those for Bayesian inference [16], and Bayesian adaptation has been used as a model for the evolution of neural mechanisms [38, 39]. Functionally, one would expect hard-wired and plastic mechanisms to be matched to long and short-term invariants of the environment, sometimes captured in the pithy statement, "The mean is in the genes, the variance in the synapses". In this paper, by combining the results presented by Li and Zaidi [57, 58], Wong and Zaidi [101], Cohen and Zaidi [24], and Meng and Zaidi [73], we examine how the interplay of hard-wired and plastic neural mechanisms enables humans to perceive generally informative 3-D shapes from textures/patterns.

22.2 Orientation and Frequency Cues for 3-D Shape Perception

In the retinal image of a curved 3-D surface, the statistics of the texture pattern change with the curvature of the surface. (We follow convention in using the term

Q. Zaidi (✉) · A. Li · C. Wong · E.H. Cohen · X. Meng
SUNY College of Optometry, Graduate Center for Vision Research, State University of New York, 33 West 42nd St, New York, NY 10036, USA
e-mail: qz@sunyopt.edu

S.J. Dickinson, Z. Pizlo (eds.), *Shape Perception in Human and Computer Vision*, Advances in Computer Vision and Pattern Recognition, DOI 10.1007/978-1-4471-5195-1_22, © Springer-Verlag London 2013

texture for surface markings that form a repetitive pattern.) Almost all shape-from-texture models assume that the texture on the surface is statistically homogeneous (i.e. stochastically stationary and invariant to translation), so inhomogeneities in the image arise from the projection of segments of the surface that are not fronto-parallel with respect to the observer [22, 36, 65]. This assumption is true for developable surfaces that can be unfolded into a flat plane without stretching or cutting, for example, cylinders, cones, and sinusoidal corrugations. However, developable surfaces only have zero Gaussian curvatures (maximum curvature x minimum curvature), whereas erosion, accumulation, carving, or stretching can generate complex surfaces with positive and negative Gaussian curvatures. Whereas it is possible to carefully paint any surface with homogeneous texture [22], under generic conditions the texture on a saddle, ellipsoid, or any varying Gaussian curvature surface is not homogeneous. For patterned animal skin, the inhomogeneity may change as the surface deforms. Thus, for most complex shapes, texture inhomogeneities in an image are not caused solely by the projection. Therefore, estimating the projective transform and reversing it, as in Garding [36], Malik and Rosenholtz [65], Clerc and Mallat [22], is not always sufficient to infer the 3-D shape of the surface.

We show that the assumption of homogeneity is not necessary for extracting 3-D shape because observers correctly perceive 3-D curvatures and slants when signature patterns of orientation modulations are visible, irrespective of whether the texture on the surface is homogeneous or not (Note: Throughout this paper, correct percepts explicitly mean that the perceived signs of curvatures and directions of slants are identical to those of the simulated 3-D surface). In the generic case, these orientation modulations appear in perspective images of carved, stretched and developable surfaces only at the locations of the correct curvatures or slants. Shape from texture can thus rely on hardwired neural modules that extract signature orientation modulations. We also show that these neural templates take advantage of cross-orientation inhibition, and that cortical anisotropies in orientation tuning can explain constancy failures of some 2-D and 3-D shapes.

When signature patterns of orientation modulations are not visible, observers infer shape using spatial frequency gradients as cues to distance. This leads to correct percepts for images where spatial frequency varies with distance from the observer, but incorrect percepts where the spatial frequency varies because of the varying slant of the surface. Using haptic feedback on virtual 3-D surfaces, we tested the function of touch in such cases. We found that in the perception of 3-D shapes from texture cues, haptic information can dominate vision in some cases, changing percepts qualitatively from convex to concave and concave to slant. The effects take time to develop, do not outlive the cessation of the feedback, are attenuated by distance, and drastically reduced by gaps in the surface.

We discuss 3-D sinusoidal corrugations because they can form a set of basis shapes, that is, shapes that in combination could generate a wide variety of shapes [12]. In addition, these shapes contain a large range of local slants so that our results can be generalized to a large range of surface views. We consider sinusoidally carved and developable corrugations (Fig. 22.1). The signals that are used in both feed-forward and feed-back models of shape perception depend on the receptive

Fig. 22.1 Developable (folded) and carved solid surfaces with identical sinusoidally corrugated shapes from the observer's viewpoint

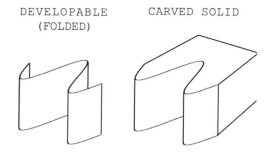

field properties of V1 cells [75, 76]. Since V1 neurons are tuned for orientation and spatial frequency, it is useful to parse texture variations in an image into orientation and frequency modulations. We first discuss two classes of texture patterns to separate the contributions of orientation and frequency modulations to shape perception.

The first set of patterns were composed of oriented sinusoidal gratings and are shown with their amplitude spectra in the left column of Fig. 22.2: a horizontal–vertical plaid, an octotropic plaid consisting of 8 gratings of the same spatial frequency equally spaced in orientation, and the octotropic plaid minus the horizontal grating. The second set, shown in the right column of Fig. 22.2, consisted of patterns made of circular dots: a pattern consisting of uniformly sized dots that were randomly positioned (with a minimal overlap constraint), a pattern in which the uniformly sized dots were horizontally and vertically aligned, and a pattern in which the size of the aligned dots was randomly varied. While the elements of all three of the patterns are isotropic, the first pattern is the only one that is also globally isotropic as shown by its amplitude spectrum. The other two patterns contain concentrations of energy at discrete orientations. When larger versions of these textures are folded into a developable surface, the texture on the surface remains statistically homogeneous. The texture on the surface, however, is not homogeneous when solids containing these patterns are carved, or when elastic versions of these patterns are stretched over curved surfaces. The surface markings on carved or stretched surfaces are locally affine transformations of these homogeneous patterns, depending on the local curvature. Texture distortions in perspective images are therefore due to a combination of shape-based and projective transformations.

22.3 Folded Surfaces

When any of the patterns in Fig. 22.2 is folded into a corrugation, the texture on the surface remains unchanged, but appears distorted in perspective images. (Fig. 22.3 top: centrally concave; bottom: centrally convex.) For both the horizontal–vertical plaid and the octotropic plaid, it is easy to identify right and left slants, and thus concavities and convexities. Slants are not easily distinguished, however, in the third column where the texture pattern is missing the horizontal grating. For this pattern, observers confuse left and right slants, and often classify both as flat [56]. This

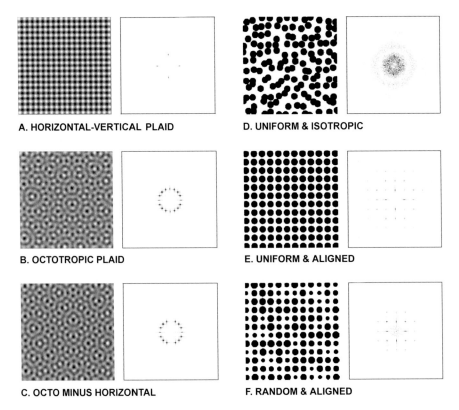

Fig. 22.2 Two groups of texture patterns with their amplitude spectra: Composites of sinusoidal gratings (**A–C**) and locally isotropic dot patterns (**E–F**). **A**. Horizontal–vertical plaid. **B**. Octotropic plaid consisting of 8 gratings of the same frequency as those in **A**, equally spaced in orientation (see next figure). **C**. Octotropic plaid without the horizontal component. **D**. Uniformly sized, randomly positioned dot pattern. **E**. Uniformly sized, horizontally and vertically aligned dot pattern. **F**. Randomly sized, horizontal and vertically aligned dot pattern

demonstrates the critical information supplied by the grating parallel to the axis of maximum curvature, visible as contours that bow inward towards the center of the image at local concavities, bow outward at local convexities, and converge rightward or leftward respectively at rightward and leftward slants. These contour flows occur generically in retinal images at the locations of the 3-D shape features simply as a result of perspective projection (Fig. 22.4a).

It is easy to show why the horizontal grating uniquely carries the shape information in these images. For the corrugated surfaces in concave phase, Fig. 22.4b shows the perspective projections of the eight oriented components of the octotropic plaid (see [58], for mathematical derivations of projected orientations and frequencies). The image of the horizontal component ($0°$) is the only one that shows patterns of orientation modulations that are different for different signs of curvature. The image of the vertical grating ($90°$) shows frequency modulation but no changes in orientation. For all the oblique components, the local orientation and frequency at fronto-

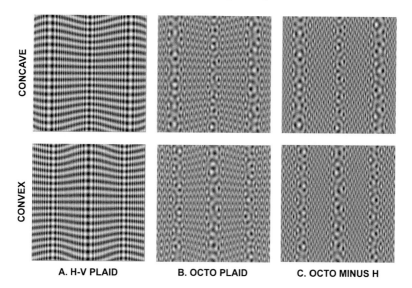

Fig. 22.3 Perspective images of developable surfaces containing central concavities (*top*) and convexities (*bottom*) overlaid with the three grating composite patterns. Signature orientation modulations of the horizontal component in both plaid patterns (**A**–**B**) contain sufficient information to correctly convey concavities, convexities, right slants and left slants. Subtracting the horizontal component (**C**) eliminates these orientation modulations, and the surface shapes are not correctly perceived

parallel portions of the surface equal the original orientation and frequency, and increase with increasing slant. When all eight components are added, the horizontal component is visible. The other seven components do not convey shape individually or summed together. Li and Zaidi [58] show that the pattern of critical orientation modulations is universal for texture patterns containing discrete energy parallel to the axis of maximum curvature.

Frequency modulations in the image, however, vary as a function of how the surface is formed. Frequency modulations in perspective images of developable surfaces are caused largely by changes in surface slant. Figure 22.5a shows an aerial view of a patterned surface slanted at two different angles with respect to the observer's eye. Since the frequency of the pattern on the surface is constant, as slant increases, the projected width of the pattern in the image plane decreases, and the frequency in the image increases. In images of textured objects whose internal depth is substantially less than their distance from the observer, spatial frequency modulations are due more to changes in slants than to changes in distance from the observer. Consequently, images of rightward and leftward slants exhibit similarly increased frequency because of the slant. As a result, images of concave and convex portions of the corrugation exhibit similar high-low-high frequency gradients. Observers do not resolve this ambiguity and perceive convex and concave curvatures both as convexities. This percept is consistent with the frequency gradient functioning as a cue to relative distance from the eye since the effect of distance is to increase the spatial

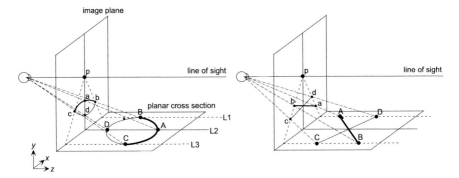

Fig. 22.4a Perspective images of horizontal 3-D contours below eye-height, bowed away or towards, or slanted away to right or left, project as bowed up or down, or slanted up to right or left respectively. The opposite is true for contours above eye-height

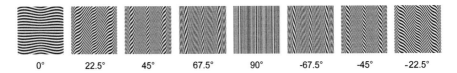

Fig. 22.4b Perspective images of the developable surface (with a central concavity) overlaid with each of the eight grating components of the octotropic plaid. The horizontal component exhibits the signature orientation modulations. All other components exhibit lowest frequencies at frontoparallel segments, and higher frequencies at slants. Orientation modulations of these components are all steeper than those exhibited by the horizontal component

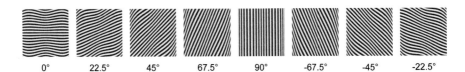

Fig. 22.4c Perspective images of carved solids (with central concavity) with each of the eight grating patterns of the octotropic plaid. The orientation modulations of the horizontal component are the same as those for developable surfaces. The orientation modulations of the ±22.5° components overlap in range with those of the horizontal component

frequencies in the image of a pattern [55]. It is worth noting that in cases where the observer is navigating through a textured environment, distances to the observer vary over a large range. Consequently the frequency modulations in the retinal image would be mainly due to changes in distance, and thus provide veridical cues.

Images of the developable corrugations overlaid with the three dot patterns are shown in Fig. 22.6. The images of the corrugations with the isotropic dot pattern exhibit slant-caused frequency modulations along the horizontal axis with high-low-high frequency gradients at both concavities and convexities. For this pattern, observers confused left and right slants. Li and Zaidi [55] showed that for glob-

Fig. 22.5a Frequency modulations in images of developable surfaces are largely slant-caused. Aerial view of a vertical grating on a flat surface at two different slants. As slant increases, frequency in the perspective image increases

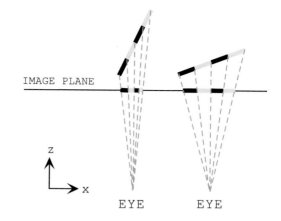

Fig. 22.5b Frequency modulations for carved depth-invariant textures. Aerial view of a depth-invariant texture solid formed by vertical grating planar patterns. As the angle of the cut is increased, the frequency on the surface of the cut decreases, however projection increases the frequency in the image plane. As a result there is little frequency modulation in the image

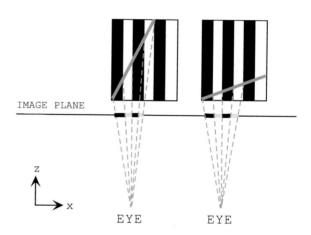

ally isotropic patterns, observers report that concavities and convexities both appear convex, indicating that, rather than attribute these modulations to changes in surface slant, observers attribute them to changes in distance. This is done despite the fact that frequency changes due solely to distance would be isotropic, whereas these frequency gradients are pre-dominantly along the axis of maximum curvature, suggesting that shape changes of texture elements are less potent cues to 3-D shape. Orientation modulations are difficult to perceive for the isotropic dot pattern, but the modulations are apparent when the dots are horizontally and vertically aligned in the texture. These modulations are similar to those of the horizontal gratings. Concavities, convexities, right slants, and left slants are all identifiable. Randomizing the size of the aligned dots, may compromise the ability to extract frequency modulations but it does not affect the shape percepts much, the different surface shapes are easily distinguishable.

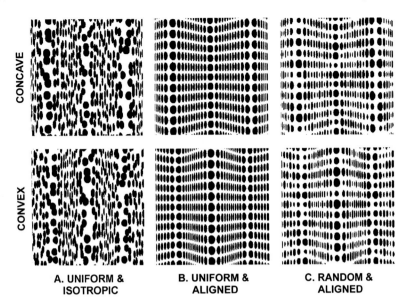

CONCAVE

CONVEX

A. UNIFORM &
ISOTROPIC

B. UNIFORM &
ALIGNED

C. RANDOM &
ALIGNED

Fig. 22.6 Perspective images of the developable surfaces overlaid with the three dot patterns. Slant-caused frequency modulations in the globally isotropic dot pattern (**A**) are misinterpreted as changes in distance and as a result concavities are misperceived as convex. Horizontal and vertical alignment of the dots (**B**) adds the signature orientation modulations of the horizontal component and concavities become distinguishable from convexities. Randomizing the size of the aligned dots (**C**) makes little difference in the percepts

22.4 Carved Surfaces

Surface textures were homogeneous for all the developable examples, but that is often not the case for carved surfaces. Figure 22.7 shows perspective images of corrugations carved from solids formed by repeating a single texture pattern along the depth-axis. In the images of the solids patterned with the horizontal–vertical plaid (Fig. 22.7A), concavities, convexities, right and left slants can all be correctly identified. The orientation modulations of the horizontal component are identical to those of the horizontal component on the developable surface. Despite identical orientation modulations, the shapes of the carved surfaces appear more gradually curved than their developable counterparts. This is because the frequency of the vertical component modulates much less than for the developable surface. Figure 22.5b shows an aerial view of a solid formed by repeated vertical-grating planar patterns carved at two different angles (indicated by the thick dark grey lines). Unlike for the developable surface, the frequency on the surface of the cut decreases with increasing slant angle. However, as slant angle increases, the projected width of a unit length of solid decreases in the image. These two tendencies counteract each other, so that in the perspective image, the frequency is little affected by slant. Gradients in the image are thus mainly due to changes in distance from the observer. Consequently, the frequency gradients around concavities and convexities are distinct

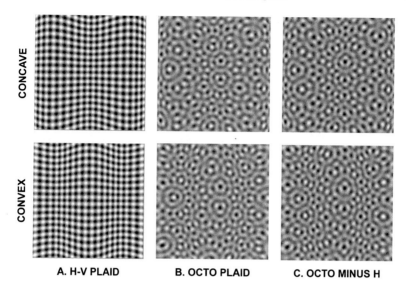

Fig. 22.7 Perspective images of the sinusoidal surfaces carved from depth-invariant textures with the three grating component planar patterns. The horizontal component in the HV plaid exhibits the same signature orientation modulations that convey concavities and convexities, however the surfaces appear more gradually curved than their developable counterparts. These orientation modulations are invisible in the octotropic plaid patterns (**B–C**) which both appear flat

from one another: low-high-low for concavities and high-low-high for convexities. Variations in spatial frequency on the carved surface show that the texture is not homogeneous on a surface carved with multiple slants.

The images in Figs. 22.7B and C appear flat. This is particularly surprising for Fig. 22.7B, where the horizontal component of the octotropic plaid could be expected to contribute the signature orientation modulations. The reason is revealed by Fig. 22.4c, which shows the images of the eight components for the carved solid. As expected, the horizontal component exhibits the signature orientation modulations that observers use to perceive shape correctly for the horizontal–vertical plaid. However, the images of the ±22.5° components contain orientations and frequencies that are similar to those of the horizontal component and mask the orientation modulations of the horizontal component in the summed image. In Fig. 22.8, these two components are subtracted from the octotropic plaid, the signature orientation modulations of the horizontal component become visible, and concavities, convexities, and right and left slants become distinguishable. It is interesting that the distance caused frequency modulations of the seven other components in Fig. 22.4c are consistent with correct percepts of the central concavity, but the perceived shape is essentially flat when all seven components are combined in Fig. 22.7C.

Images of the carved corrugations with the dot patterns are shown in Fig. 22.9. All the images for the dot patterns contain frequency modulations determined by distance. Orientation modulations are visible in the aligned dot patterns, but not in the isotropic pattern. In Fig. 22.9A, concavities and convexities are discernible, but

Fig. 22.8 Octotropic plaid
from Fig. 22.7B without the
±22.5° components. The
signature orientation
modulations of the horizontal
component are revealed and
concavities and convexities
become distinguishable

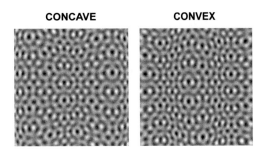

just barely, from the frequency cue to distance. While observers make some correct
slant judgments for this pattern, a large proportion of the slants are classified as flat.
Signs of curvature and slant are easily identifiable when signature orientation modulations are visible. The addition of random frequency modulations hardly affects
the shape percepts.

It is worth pointing out that all six of the patterns are inhomogeneous on the
carved surface, but that frequency and orientation modulations signal correct locations and signs of curvature. The orientation modulations, in particular, are identical
for the developable and carved surfaces, and provide unambiguous cues to the signs
of curvature and slant. Parsing the perspective image in terms of orientation and
frequency modulations thus obviates a need to restrict shape-from-texture models
to homogeneous textures.

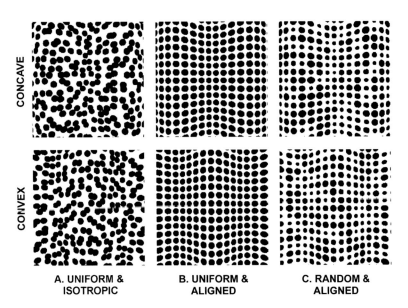

Fig. 22.9 Perspective images of carved solids with the three dot planar patterns. Distance-caused
frequency modulations in the random dot pattern (**A**) roughly convey concavities and convexities,
however they are much more compelling when the dots are aligned in the solid (**B**). Randomizing
the size of the aligned dots (**C**) makes little difference in the percept

22.5 Perceptual Strategies

All the projected images shown previously are flat surfaces containing repeating but statistically non-homogeneous patterns. When these are viewed monocularly, even without access to stereo or motion, 3-D shape percepts are extremely vivid if the signature orientation modulations are visible. This suggests that the visual system automatically creates percepts of curvature corresponding to signature orientation modulations. Given that signature orientation modulations automatically evoke corresponding shape percepts, the question of whether these percepts are correct reduces to whether these modulations occur in the correct locations in perspective images of real surfaces. Li and Zaidi [58] show that this is true for developable, carved, and stretched surfaces under many different conditions, which suggests that the same neural mechanisms of extracting orientation modulations from images will suffice for all of these conditions. Similarly, a discrete number of mechanisms tuned to extract frequency modulations can provide information about distances to different parts of the surface. In other words, rather than perform the reverse optics operations of assuming texture properties, estimating texture distortions from the image, and then reversing the projection transform to infer the 3-D shape, the visual system might instead signal the presence of 3-D shape features automatically from the outputs of a discrete number of matched filters configured for particular orientation and frequency patterns.

This perceptual strategy differs from other computational approaches in the way that we have characterized the information present in retinal images of texture surfaces. There are an infinite number of ways to parse this information. Some of the ways that have been shown to be useful are deformation gradients [36], local affine deformations of the spectrum of a pattern [65], and deformations of wavelets [22]. We have parsed the information in terms of orientation and frequency modulations [8]. This has been useful because orientation modulations are generically different for concavities, convexities, right slants and left slants, whereas frequency modulations are not. The corollary is that unless the texture pattern contains discretely oriented energy that distorts into signature orientation flows, the textured image will not contain in-formation that is different for different signs of curvatures and slants. Consequently, to identify 3-D shapes from texture cues, the minimum requirement for a visual system, machine or natural, is that it be able to extract orientation modulations and be able to differentiate between orientation modulations that are signatures for distinct 3-D features. Further, as shown by the carved octotropic plaid pattern, only those visual systems will identify 3-D shapes correctly that can extract the signature orientation modulations in the presence of distractor orientations. Thus, correct shape perception relies both on the information contained in the image, and on the capacity of the visual system to extract the relevant information.

The figures above use only limited classes of texture patterns and upright corrugated solids, but these results generalize to naturally occurring texture patterns, and other 3-D shapes. For the case of homogeneous textures on upright developable shapes, we have previously examined the Brodatz [14] set of natural and man-made textures [59]. For these texture patterns, we found that similar to synthetic patterns, visibility of the signature orientation modulations, and the perception of correct curvatures and slants can be predicted by the discreteness of energy in the critical Fourier component. For example, for certain natural textures, like wood with fairly parallel grain, shapes are perceived correctly or incorrectly depending on whether the axis of 3-D curvature is parallel or orthogonal to the grain. These results are likely to generalize to non-developable surfaces because the oriented components that distort into the signature orientation modulations are the same as for developable surfaces. We have also shown that whereas the Fourier component parallel to the axis of maximum curvature is critical for upright corrugations, other components provide the signature modulations for pitched corrugations [103], and that this is the reason why texture patterns can convey more varied shapes than the parallel contours explored by Stevens [97]. In addition, shape percepts are also correct for two non-generic but theoretically important classes of images. First, if signature orientation modulations are defined solely by contrast variations (that is, without Fourier energy) [33, 56], and second if the orientation modulations are created by illusions [60]. Finally, perceived shapes of sinusoidal depth plaids can be predicted from the perceived shapes of the constituent corrugations [58].

These results that patterns of orientation modulations obviate the need to calculate texture gradients or assume homogeneity have implications for neural and computational models of shape from texture. The results suggest that a neural implementation of the extraction of 3-D shape-from-texture would require only a small number of mechanisms, each receiving input from local orientation sensitive operators configured in signature patterns of orientation modulations that represent individual 3-D shapes. Other mechanisms receiving input from frequency sensitive operators would contribute supplementary inferences about relative distance along the surface.

22.6 Cross-Orientation Inhibition

In the perspective image of a slanted textured surface, when oriented components of the texture that are aligned with the 3-D slant converge to form orientation flows, the horizontal component appears perceptually more salient than other components when a surface is slanted (Fig. 22.10A, top left and right), to a greater extent than it does when the surface is fronto-parallel (Fig. 22.10A, top center). The increase in saliency is more pronounced in complex texture patterns, for example, the octotropic plaid (Fig. 22.10A bottom). Since these converging orientation flows play a critical role in conveying the perceived 3-D slant and shape of the surface, an increase in their saliency should enhance the 3-D perceived slant. In this section, we examine the neural mechanisms that enhance the visibility of orientation flows.

Many surface textures contain components of roughly the same frequencies at many different orientations, with most of the frequencies in the higher-frequency declining segment of the human CSF [17]. Slanting the surface increases the frequencies of components not aligned with the slant [54], thus leading to a reduction in visibility. If different oriented components were processed independently by the

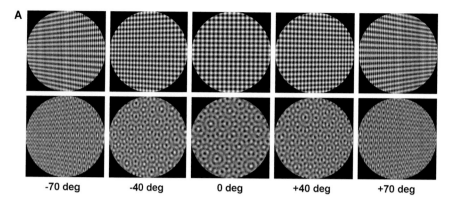

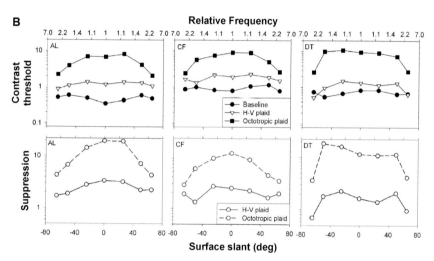

Fig. 22.10 Suppression of the test grating as a function of surface slant. **A**. Planar surfaces at different slants patterned with horizontal–vertical (h–v) (*top*) and octotropic (*bottom*) plaids. **B**. *Top*: Contrast thresholds for three observers for the horizontal component alone (*filled circles*), with a vertical component (*open triangles*), and with seven non-horizontal components (*filled squares*) as a function of surface slant. The *top axis of each panel* represents the frequency of the vertical component relative to the frequency of the test in the image. *Bottom*: Suppression factor as a function of surface slant

visual system, the increase in saliency of the components parallel to the slant could be due just to the reduced visibility of the other components. However, the response of oriented neurons in cat and primate striate cortex, to a stimulus at a preferred orientation, is suppressed by the superposition of a stimulus at the null orientation [9]. Parallel to these results, psychophysical studies have reported that the contrast threshold of an oriented stimulus is increased in the presence of a superimposed orthogonal stimulus [19]. Physiologically measured cross-orientation suppression (COS) is broadband for orientation and occurs over a wide range of spatial frequencies [10, 26, 74]. Psychophysically measured COS appears to be broadband for orientation [87], but with mixed evidence for frequency-selectivity [71, 72, 81, 88, 89]. Thus, it is possible that psychophysically measured COS has components that are distinct from the COS measured in V1 neurons.

Li & Zaidi [57] showed that the visibility of orientation flows increases as a function of surface slant, and that the increased salience results from the frequency-selectivity of COS and not the frequency dependent visibility of the masking components. We used planar surfaces projected in perspective, patterned with horizontal–vertical (h–v) and octotropic plaid patterns, and measured contrast-thresholds for detecting the horizontal component with a 2IFC method, in a variety of configurations. First, of the horizontal grating alone at left and right slants of 25, 50, and 65 deg, and then in the presence of the non-horizontal components. Contrast thresholds of the horizontal components in the different conditions are shown for the three observers in Fig. 22.10. Thresholds of the grating alone were relatively unchanged by surface slant, reflecting the fact that the spatial frequency of this component was relatively unchanged. The presence of the vertical grating, increased thresholds for all surface slants, reflecting an overall decrease in visibility of the horizontal component. Thresholds increased even more in the presence of the seven non-horizontal components of the octotropic plaid. We quantified the suppression induced by non-horizontal components by dividing thresholds of the horizontal grating in the presence of other components by thresholds in the absence of other components. Suppression for both patterns decreased as surface slant increased, with substantially greater and steeper changes in suppression for the octotropic plaid.

It is clear from these results that contrast-thresholds are raised by orthogonal masks, which is a signature of COS. We used four conditions to provide two independent comparisons of whether the peak suppression is a function of the similarity of frequencies between the test and mask, or of the salience of the mask. Fronto-parallel surfaces were patterned with an iso-frequency h–v plaid (Fig. 22.11A) or an h–v plaid consisting of a vertical grating of half the frequency of the horizontal grating (Fig. 22.11C). The same surfaces were also presented slanted at left or right at 60 deg which approximately doubles the vertical frequency in the image, thus making the frequencies in the image of the originally 2:1 frequency plaid approximately equal (Fig. 22.11D). In Fig. 22.11 (bottom), mean suppression factors averaged across the three observers are plotted for all conditions. First, the similarity hypothesis predicts that thresholds should be higher in the iso-frequency fronto-parallel plaid (Fig. 22.11A) than for the unequal frequency fronto-parallel plaid (Fig. 22.11C), whereas the salience hypothesis predicts the opposite. Thresholds were raised more by the iso-frequency mask than the more salient unequal frequency mask. Second, the increase in suppression when the unequal frequency plaid (Fig. 22.11C) is slanted also supports the similarity hypothesis over the salience hypothesis. In addition, in comparing the two slanted plaids, suppression was greater when the image pattern was iso-frequency (Fig. 22.11D) than when the surface pattern was iso-frequency (Fig. 22.11B). These results indicate that the COS from the vertical grating is greatest when the frequency in the projected image is equal to that of the horizontal grating, even when the frequency is one to which we are less sensitive. Previous measurements of the spatial frequency tuning of COS [15] showed

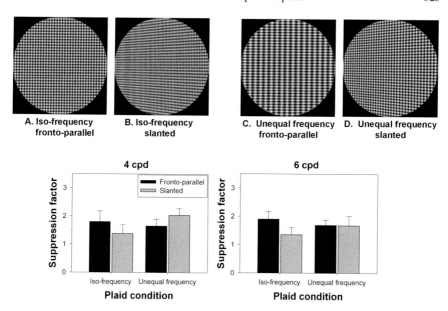

Fig. 22.11 Suppression of the test grating from iso-frequency vs. unequal frequency masks. *Top*: An iso-frequency plaid (**A**), and an unequal frequency plaid (**C**) consisting of a horizontal grating and a vertical grating at half the frequency. At slants of 60 deg, the components in the image of the iso-frequency plaid are unequal in frequency (**B**), and the components in the image of the unequal frequency plaid are equal in frequency (**D**). *Bottom*: Suppression factors averaged across three observers (*left*: 4 cpd test frequency, *right*: 6 cpd test frequency). *Error bars* represent one standard error of the mean. *Black bars* represent suppression factors in the fronto-parallel conditions, and *grey bars* represent suppression factors in the slanted conditions

a decrease in masking for a 4 cpd test when the mask frequency increased from 4 to 8 cpd, but did not determine whether spatial-frequency mismatch or a decrease in mask saliency was the cause.

COS is well-documented in cortical area V1, the first site in the visual pathway containing orientation tuned cells. COS has been attributed to compressive contrast nonlinearities in LGN [62, 84], but a cortical component has also been revealed [64]. Although several electrophysiological studies examining the frequency selectivity of COS suggest that suppression mechanisms are broadly tuned [11, 26, 78], it is unclear whether this kind of tuning plays out psychophysically. It would be remarkable if the facilitation of 3-D shape perception occurs automatically through the neural processes that lead to COS, so to ascertain its locus, we explored the possibility of frequency selectivity in an LGN based model.

Although intra-cortical inhibition was the original suggestion for COS, the fact that suppression is not reduced by prior monocular or binocular adaptation to the masking stimulus, that suppression is robust for masks at temporal frequencies beyond the limits of cortical neurons, and that COS has an early onset led to the suggestion that the suppression results from the depression of thalamo-cortical synapses [35, 72, 95]. More recent papers quantifying the fast recovery times of COS [62] and the suppression of both synaptic inhibition and excitation by orthogonal masks [84] challenge the notion of synaptic depression. Instead these models suggest that COS results from contrast saturation and rectifying nonlinearities in the LGN, and expansive spike threshold nonlinearities in the cortex [62, 84].

To test the frequency-selectivity of COS in the models of Li et al. [62] and Priebe and Ferster [84], Li and Zaidi [57] computed cortical responses to a vertical test grating in the presence of superimposed horizontal masks of the same or different frequency. All combinations of receptive fields and nonlinearities led to frequency selectivity, with suppression greatest when the frequency of the mask matched that of the test. The suggested roles of COS in visual encoding have included orientation tuning [10, 92, 93], contrast gain control [2, 18, 26, 37, 43], and redundancy reduction in the coding of natural images [32, 79, 91]. Here, we present a potential role for COS in the decoding of 3-D slant [85].

22.7 Hebbian Learning of Matched Filters

The results above show that folding or carving patterned surfaces creates signature orientation flows in the retinal image, and 3-D shape is conveyed by these orientation flows. Since many textures contain multiple orientations, flows have to be extracted in the presence of other orientations. The parallel extraction of multiple orientations at every retinotopic location by the striate cortex is perfectly matched to the demands of this task, especially when critical orientations are enhanced by frequency-dependent cross-orientation inhibition. Wong and Zaidi [101] asked whether extra-striate neural filters matched to orientation flows could extract 3-D shapes? Could neural matched filters for specific flows evolve through supervised learning from another modality or sense? Would this require Cross Orientation Inhibition? Since the critical orientation information occurs at different locations for different textures, image-based procedures require augmentation. We sorted a large number of textured images into shape categories, filtered them with oriented pyramids similar to V1 receptive fields [94], and implemented a Hebbian learning procedure on the filter outputs. As Fig. 22.12 shows, Hebbian learning gave matched filters that resembled the ideal filter, but this required frequency-specific COI. Normalization [43] of V1 responses, led to denser but less continuous filters. Similar results were obtained for other shape categories and orientations and locations. This exercise points out the critical role of V1 parallel processing in the decoding of 3-D shapes from texture cues [44].

22.8 Hardwired Cortical Anisotropies

Shape is the attribute of an object that is mathematically invariant to location, rotation and scale effects [49, 67–69, 82]. The ability to perceive the shape of a rigid object as constant, despite differences in the viewing angle, has been considered an

With un-normalized responses as input   Ideal Orientation Flows   With normalized responses as input

Fig. 22.12 (*Center*) Orientation structure of an ideal matched-filter for a vertical concavity. (*Left & right*) Matched filters from Hebbian Learning using cross-orientation inhibition, without and with normalized responses

Fig. 22.13a Convex and concave wedges oriented vertically and obliquely

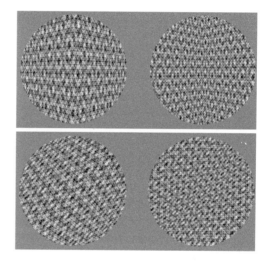

essential component of representing objects in the visual world accurately. Because the visual system cannot generally discount perspective distortions, shapes of certain classes of 3-D objects are not perceived as constant across viewpoints [40, 41, 83], but shape constancy is expected to hold for simple shapes under 2-D rotations of the image plane [53]. In striate cortex, cells tuned to orientation are sampled unevenly, with greater concentration, as well as narrower tuning, near horizontal and vertical [61, 66]. These anisotropies raise questions about whether shape constancy can survive image rotations [25].

Figure 22.13a depicts four shapes that appear triangular in depth due to texture cues. The concave and convex 3-D wedges with vertical axes (top) appear deeper than the corresponding wedges with oblique axes (bottom), especially when viewed monocularly. However, when the page is rotated 45°, the bottom shapes appear deeper than the top. The bottom images are simply rotated copies of the top images, revealing that perceived depth depends on shape orientation. To quantify the orientation dependence of depth percepts, two 3-D wedges (one oriented at 45° and

Fig. 22.13b (**a**) Highlights
2-D angles in the image of a
3-D convex shape. (**b**) and (**c**)
Display vertical and oblique
obtuse angles similar to those
used in the experiment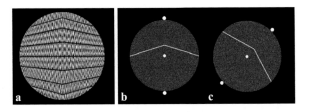

the other at 90°) were viewed successively in random order, and observers identified which appeared greater in depth. The average ratios of subjectively equivalent vertical to oblique depths for convex and concave shapes were 0.766 (SE = 0.006) and 0.781 (SE = 0.010), respectively. Physically identical shapes were perceived as deeper when oriented vertically than when oriented obliquely, consequently, 3-D shapes are not perceived as constant even across rotations in the image plane.

Since the perception of 3-D shapes from texture cues depends critically on the orientation modulations around the axis of maximum curvature, we tested whether the 3-D inconstancy results from anisotropy in perception of 2-D image features. The critical orientation flows, form obtuse angles that bow inward in the center of the perspective image of the concave wedge, and bow outwards in the center of the image of the convex wedge (Fig. 22.13b). Changes in the magnitudes of angles above and below eye-height determine the perceived depth. We tested whether there is a corresponding anisotropy in the perception of obtuse 2-D angles when angles symmetric around 90° are compared to angles symmetric around 45° (Fig. 22.13b). All 2-D angles were perceived to be sharper at vertical than at 45°. The average subjectively equivalent vertical angle was 4.5° (SE = 0.38°) shallower than the oblique angle. Consequently, 2-D angles are not perceived as constant across plane rotations. In addition, the 3-D depth inconstancy could be quantitatively explained by anisotropy in perception of 2-D features.

Having traced 3-D perceptual anisotropy to an oblique bias for 2-D angles, Cohen & Zaidi [25] used a probabilistic stimulus decoding model [90] to test whether this 2-D bias could be explained by anisotropies in numbers or tuning widths of cortical cells tuned to different orientations [61], or the anisotropic distribution of oriented energy in images of natural scenes [42]. COS was a necessary part of this model. The decoded oblique angles were wider than the decoded vertical angles by magnitudes similar to the empirically measured bias. In numerous simulations, as long as the anisotropy in the excitatory bandwidths and a constant ratio of excitatory to inhibitory tuning-widths was maintained, the oblique angle was decoded as broader than the vertical angle. The anisotropy in numbers of cells, maximum at horizontal and less at oblique [61] tended to pull the posterior estimates of the arms of the angles toward the horizontal, creating a bias in perceived angles that is opposite to the empirical results, but weaker than the bias due to tuning width anisotropy. The decoded difference was insensitive to the prior probability of image angles, that is, a uniform prior led to the same predictions as the empirical frequency distribution. The model thus showed that the combination of narrower tuning of cells for horizontal orientations with cross-orientation inhibitory effects, explains the orientation dependent angle misperception and hence the 3-D shape inconstancy.

Perhaps because investigations of oblique effects concentrated on detection and discrimination (e.g., [4, 25, 99]) or memory of oriented information [31], the oblique bias for angles remained undiscovered. The oblique bias has direct consequences for a variety of shape and space constancies. First, it suggests that 2-D shapes defined by contours will also not be perceived as constant across axis orientations. In addition, contour curvature is known to be fundamental to uncovering depth [51] as well as representation of the part-structure of 2-D and 3-D shapes [23, 46], and cells in area V4 have been shown to be selective for angles and curves in particular orientations [80]. Our finding that perception of even a simple angle is dependent upon image orientation thus has broad implications for object-shape perception.

22.9   Plastic Processes in Shape from Texture

Perceiving the correct shapes of objects is necessary for inferring object qualities, manipulating tools, avoiding obstacles, and other aspects of functioning successfully in the world. Since observers can estimate object properties from larger distances using vision than they can from touch, generally vision makes predictions that touch relies on, such as the shape of a handle or chair. Visual percepts are often used to make predictions for tactile properties like soft, stiff, brittle, sharp, dull, sticky, or slippery, whereas touch is rarely used to make predictions for visual percepts [104]. However, since the information in retinal images is inherently under-determined, the inferential power of vision arises from employing intelligent heuristics, assumptions, or priors, such as shown in this paper, but this inevitably leads to illusory percepts in some cases. What are the possible functions of touch in such cases? Observers could rely entirely on the haptic percept and ignore the erroneous visual percept, or touch could temporarily correct the visual percept, or there could be longer lasting effects if observers learn to change their visual prior assumptions [1] and/or weights for different visual cues [29]. Meng & Zaidi [73] tested these possibilities by measuring the effects of various types of haptic feedback on the perception of images that evoke incorrect visual percepts despite being proper perspective projections of 3-D surfaces.

Figure 22.14A demonstrates that observers perceive veridical 3-D shapes when looking at perspective projections of half-cycles of a sinusoidal corrugation covered with a plaid texture, but identical shapes covered by a random-dot texture evoke qualitatively incorrect percepts (Fig. 22.14B). The images of the random-dot textured surfaces do not exhibit the orientation flows, but contain spatial-frequency gradients similar to the gradients of the vertical component of the plaid. Spatial-frequency gradients in an image can result from variations in surface distance or slant. In the absence of orientation flows, the perceived 3-D shapes are consistent with the prior assumption that low and high frequencies result solely from closer and more remote regions: in Fig. 22.14B, concave and convex surfaces are seen as convex (high-low-high horizontal gradients of spatial frequency), while right and

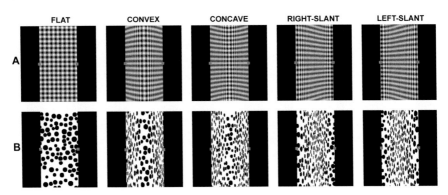

Fig. 22.14 Veridical and non-veridical percepts of 3-D shapes conveyed by surface textures:
(**A**) Flat fronto-parallel surface and half-cycles of a 3-D vertical sinusoidal corrugation covered
with horizontal–vertical plaid textures. (**B**) Identical surfaces covered with random-dot textures

left slants are seen as concave (low-high-low gradients) [55]. In other words, despite the stimuli in Fig. 22.14B being ecologically valid, observers do not perceive
veridical shapes.

Meng & Zaidi [73] tested whether touch can "correct" the visual percepts [6]
in Fig. 22.14B, and if observers can learn to dissociate spatial-frequency gradients
from distance, after repeatedly touching the surfaces. Observers viewed each of the
images in Fig. 22.14B at the proper distance through a monocular aperture, while
actively "touching" the virtual 3-D surface with a SensAble PHANTOM Omni sty-
lus. A mirror was used to locate the visual image and the haptic feedback in the
same plane. The PHANTOM was set to one of three conditions: (i) No haptic feedback; (ii) haptic feedback consistent with simulated 3-D shape; (iii) haptic feedback
opposite to simulated 3-D shape (concave, convex; r-slant, l-slant). Each trial was
100 sec. Every 10 sec there was a beep to prompt the observers to say whether they
saw the shape as convex, concave, right-slant, left-slant, or flat, and either deep or
shallow. Each session contained every trial condition randomly interleaved. In the
absence of a visual stimulus, when observers were instructed to touch each virtual
surface between two landmarks for 40 secs, they reported veridical percepts on 97
to 100 % of the trials (10 trials per shape for each of 3 observers), so we know that
the haptic feedback conveys the intended shapes.

Results from 20 trials (5 observers × 4 trials) per shape-feedback condition,
are summarized in Fig. 22.15. For each response interval, the shape of the symbol
represents the most frequently reported shape, and the size of the symbol represents the proportion of the 20 trials on which observers reported the majority shape
(Fig. 22.15A). In the trials without haptic feedback (Fig. 22.15B), on the majority
of the trials, observers perceived concavities and convexities as convex, and both
slants as concave. In the trials that provided continuous haptic feedback consistent
with the simulated shape (Fig. 22.15C), observers' visual percepts were already different from the no-feedback condition after 10 secs of touching, and as the trial pro-
gressed, they started perceiving the concave and slanted surfaces "correctly" with

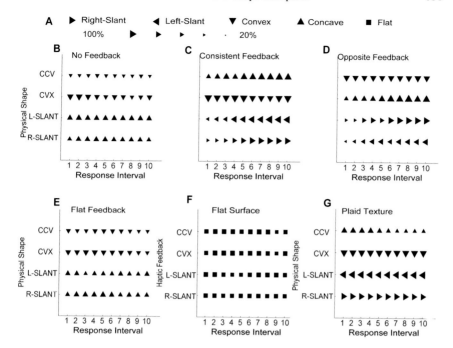

Fig. 22.15 Effects of haptic feedback: (**A**) Symbols: Most frequently reported shape (4 trials × 5 observers). Size: Proportion of majority responses per condition. Data panels show majority shape reported at each prompt after a 10 sec interval when viewing sinusoidal corrugations covered by random-dot texture without haptic feedback (**B**), with haptic feedback consistent with simulated 3-D shape (**C**), and with haptic feedback opposite to 3-D shape (**D**). Without haptic feedback, the observers generally perceived concavities and convexities as convex, and both slants as concave; With haptic feedback consistent with the simulated surface, observers gradually started perceiving the concave and slanted surfaces "correctly". With the haptic feedback opposite to the simulated surface, the observers gradually perceived the surface indicated by the haptic feedback. (**E**) Shapes reported when viewing sinusoidal corrugations covered by random-dot texture with flat fronto-parallel haptic feedback. This feedback failed to modify the pre-training percept. (**F**) A flat fronto-parallel surface textured with random dots was tested with convex, concave, right-slant and left-slant haptic feedback. The curved or slanted haptic feedback did not alter the percept of the flat stimulus. (**G**) When the simulated surfaces were covered by a plaid texture, the observers could perceive the shape correctly, and haptic feedback opposite to the shape did not alter the visual percept

increasing frequency. In the trials that provided haptic feedback opposite to the simulated surface (Fig. 22.15D), the observers' percepts changed to the shape indicated by the haptic feedback, = that is, opposite to the previous condition. It is interesting that visual percepts developed with similar time-courses in the two haptic-feedback conditions.

To test whether haptic feedback could create visual percepts at odds with visual cues, we used three additional conditions: (i) flat fronto-parallel haptic feedback was combined with the images of the random-dot curved and slanted surfaces, (ii) a random-dot flat fronto-parallel surface was coupled with convex, concave, right-slant, and left-slant haptic feedback, (iii) Convex, Concave, Right-slant, and

Left-slant corrugations covered by plaid textures, which observers perceive as correct 3-D shapes, were presented with haptic feedback opposite to each simulated shape. The summary figures, show that in all of these conditions the feedback failed to modify the initial visual percept prior to haptic feedback. The shape reports under flat haptic feedback (Fig. 22.15E) were essentially the same as under no haptic feedback, and the curved haptic feedback did not change the flat percept of the images simulating flat surfaces (Fig. 22.15F). Finally, the "opposite" haptic feedback did not change the percepts of the images with plaid textures that contain orientation cues to the veridical shapes (Fig. 22.15G).

All of the shape-feedback conditions were randomly mixed in each session, so we presume that observers were using the same criteria to report what they saw in all the trials. The results showed that haptic feedback reliably altered the visual percept in some of the conditions (Figs. 22.15C, D), but in others the reported shapes were different from those simulated by haptic feedback (Figs. 22.15E–G), confirming that observers' reports reflected not the shape that they touched, but rather the shape they saw as per the instructions. Could the effects of haptic feedback be understood in terms of statistically optimal cue combination [28]? In the absence of haptic feedback, Fig. 22.15A shows that observers perceive the random-dot concave surface predominantly as convex, but only on about 54 % of the trials, and the two slants as concave on about 73 % of the trials, whereas in the absence of visual stimulation, haptic feedback evoked the intended percept on 97–100 % of the trials. A Bayesian observer would give greater weight to the lower variance (more reliable) percepts [52], so in the case of conflict between visual and haptic percepts, haptic information would be more likely to modify the less reliable visual percept. In the case of the flat feedback with the curved visual surfaces (Fig. 22.15F), these surfaces were never reported as flat without feedback, so the feedback did not modify the visual percept from 3-D to flat. Similarly, since there was almost no variance in the initial visual percepts prior to haptic feedback of the flat surfaces (Fig. 22.15G) and the non-concave surfaces with plaid textures (Fig. 22.15H), haptic feedback had little effect.

While running the experiment, we noticed that even after 100 sec of continuous touching, as soon as we stopped touching the virtual surface, the effect of the feedback vanished. To quantify this effect, we used the L-slant and R-slant stimuli with random-dot textures. Observers were asked to first report the perceived shape after looking at it for 5 secs. They then touched the virtual surface for 40 secs with veridical haptic feedback (consistent with the simulated 3-D shapes but inconsistent with the initial percepts of concavity), and reported the perceived shape 0, 5, 10, and 15 secs after cessation of feedback (i.e., 45, 50, 55 & 60 secs after the beginning of each trial). The results plotted in Fig. 22.16, show that before haptic feedback, both slanted surfaces were perceived as concave. After 40 secs of veridical haptic feedback, each slant was perceived correctly on over 90 % of the trials, but 5 secs after cessation of feedback, the percept started to change, and after 15 secs the reported shape had reverted to the pre-feedback percept. We had hoped that visual system would use the haptic feedback to learn that the frequency gradients in the images actually signaled slant rather than distance, and would learn to correlate the elliptical shapes of the texture elements with the surface angle indicated by touch, so

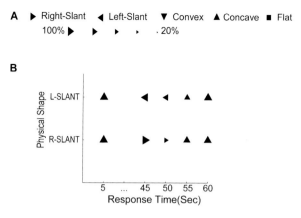

Fig. 22.16 Temporary nature of haptic feedback: (**A**) Symbols: Most frequently reported shape (5 trials × 3 observers). Size: Proportion of majority responses per condition. (**B**) Data panel shows majority shape reported when viewing L-slant and R-slant sinusoidal corrugations covered by random-dot texture with haptic feedback consistent with simulated 3-D shape. Observers viewed the stimulus for 5 sec without haptic-feedback, reported the shape, then touched the stimulus for 40 sec, reported the shape, and then made reports every 5 secs without any additional haptic feedback

the temporary nature of the effect was disappointing, and suggested an absence of perceptual learning or other lasting neural modification.

These results are related to earlier results showing statistically significant effects of haptic feedback on the weighting of texture versus disparity cues [29], and on the "light from above" prior assumption [1], in perception of 3-D shape from static images. The light prior study showed that proportion of observers' percepts reported as convex or concave spheres, changed as their assumptions about light position were altered by haptic feedback. Our results are compatible with observers giving greater weight to the haptic information where it was more reliable than the visual information, but the temporary nature of the perceptual modification, makes it unlikely that observers changed their prior assumption that spatial frequency is a cue to distance not slant, or learned to increase the weight of the change in element shape from circular to elliptical as a cue to slant. The lack of a substantial lasting effect in our experiments, may also explain why the effects of haptic learning on the weighting of different visual cues were extremely small when measured after cessation of feedback [29].

Since vision functions over longer distances than touch, during everyday activities, vision generally provides predictions for touching, grasping, stepping, sitting down etc. Consequently, vision is sometimes claimed to dominate touch [86], but our experiments show that haptic feedback can substantially alter visual percepts when the visual percepts are less reliable than the haptic percepts. On the other hand, our demonstrations of the temporary nature of haptic dominance, and the lack of substantial visual learning from haptic feedback, argue against Berkeley's notion of the primacy of touch for spatial awareness [6]. Instead, it seems that the nervous system dynamically weighs the reliability of disparate signals in reaching a percept.

An increasing number of intriguing interactions between touch and vision have been documented recently [30, 45, 77]. Parallel to our work are demonstrations of perceiving two flashes from a single flash presented concurrently with two brief tactile stimuli [98], resolving the perceived rotation of a motion defined sphere by touching a real rotating sphere [7] and resolving binocular rivalry between oriented Gabors by touching a real grooved stimulus [63]. The importance of co-ordination between visual and haptic percepts has generated a search for neural substrates in single-cells [70, 96] and cortical areas [3, 27, 48]. Shape analysis is a necessary pre-semantic component of object recognition. Given these robust and specific changes in qualitative 3-D shapes, it would be interesting to decipher whether the dynamic shifts from perceived convexity to concavity are due just to shifts in activation of individual neurons in population coding analyses, or whether they involve changes in shape-tuning of neurons selective for 3-D object shapes [102].

22.10 Conclusion

Signature orientation flows [50, 56, 58] arise generically in perspective images of patterned 3-D shapes. It would thus be adaptive for a visual system to evolve hardwired mechanisms sensitive to each of these patterns to identify the shapes present in front of the observer. These mechanisms should ideally take advantage of lower-level mechanisms, such as cross-orientation inhibition, that enhance the critical information. We show that Hebbian learning could evolve such hardwired matched filters if shape information was available form other sensory modalities, for example, touch, or other visual modalities, for example, stereo. One disadvantage of being hardwired, however, is that the decoding of shapes from such mechanisms would be susceptible to any biases in lower-level orientation processing. Consistent with these ideas, we show the oblique bias for 3-D depths, and that conflicting haptic feedback does not modify the link between perceived 3-D shapes and signature orientation patterns. Since orientation flows have also been implicated in 3-D shape perception from reflections and shading [5, 13, 34], it is likely that shapes defined by these cues also show the characteristics of being processed by similar hard-wired mechanisms. Frequency gradients in images, however, can arise from at least two different causes. Since they are more likely to occur because of changes in distance than because of surface slant, an observer is well-served by generally using them as a cue to distance, but revising the percept to slanted when provided with veridical haptic information. We show that this effect of haptic information is strong, but temporary, and unlikely to lead to long-term learning. Hardwired and plastic mechanisms thus serve complementary purposes for the visual system in judging 3-D shapes from texture cues.

Acknowledgements   This work was supported by NEI grants EY07556 and EY 13312 to QZ.

References

1. Adams W, Graf E, Ernst M (2004) Experience can change the "light-from-above" prior. Nat Neurosci 7:1057–1058
2. Albrecht D, Geisler W (1991) Motion selectivity and the contrast-response function of simple cells in the visual cortex. Vis Neurosci 7:531–546
3. Amedi A, Malach R, Hendler T, Peled S, Zohary E (2001) Visuo-haptic object-related activation in the ventral visual pathway. Nat Neurosci 4:324–330
4. Appelle S (1972) Perception and discrimination as a function of stimulus orientation: the "oblique effect" in man and animals. Psychol Bull 78:266–278
5. Ben-Shahar O, Huggins P, Zucker S (2002) On computing visual flows with boundaries: the case of shading and edges. In: Biologically motivated computer vision. LNCS, vol 2525, pp 189–198
6. Berkeley G (1702) An essay towards a new theory of vision. Dublin & London: 1732
7. Blake R, Sobel K, James T (2004) Neural synergy between kinetic vision and touch. Psychol Sci 15:397–402
8. Blakemore C, Campbell F (1969) On the existence of neurones in the human visual system selectively sensitive to the orientation and size of retinal images. J Physiol 203(1):237–260
9. Blakemore C, Carpenter R, Georgeson M (1970) Lateral inhibition between orientation detectors in the human visual system. Nature 228(5266):37–39
10. Bonds A (1989) Role of inhibition in the specification of orientation selectivity of cells in the cat striate cortex. Vis Neurosci 2:41–55
11. Bonin V, Mante V, Carandini M (2005) The suppressive field of neurons in lateral geniculate nucleus. J Neurosci 25:10844–10856
12. Bracewell RN (1995) Two-dimensional imaging. Prentice Hall, Englewood Cliffs
13. Breton P, Zucker S (1996) Shadows and shading flow fields. In: IEEE conf on computer vision and pattern recognition, pp 782–789
14. Brodatz P (1966) Textures: a photographic album for artists and designers. Dover, New York
15. Burbeck C, Kelly D (1981) Contrast gain measurements and the transient/sustained. J Opt Soc Am 71:1335–1342
16. Bürger R (2000) The mathematical theory of selection, recombination and mutation. Wiley, West Sussex
17. Campbell F, Robson J (1968) Application of Fourier analysis to the visibility of gratings. J Physiol 197:551–566
18. Carandini M, Heeger D, Movshon J (1997) Linearity and normalization in simple cells of the macaque primary visual cortex. J Neurosci 17:8621–8644
19. Carpenter R, Blakemore C (1973) Interactions between orientations in human vision. Exp Brain Res 18(3):287–303
20. Chomsky N (1968) Language and mind. Harcourt Brace & World, New York
21. Chomsky N (1984) Modular approaches to the study of the mind. San Diego State University Press, San Diego
22. Clerc M, Mallat S (2002) The texture gradient equation for recovering shape from texture. IEEE Trans. Pattern Anal. Mach. Intell. 24(4):536–549
23. Cohen E, Singh M (2006) Perceived orientation of complex shape reflects graded part decomposition. J Vis 6:805–821
24. Cohen E, Zaidi Q (2007) Fundamental failures of shape constancy resulting from cortical anisotropy. J Neurosci 27:12540–12545
25. Cohen E, Zaidi Q (2007) Salience of mirror symmetry in natural patterns [Abstract]. J Vis 7(9):970
26. DeAngelis G, Robson J, Ohzawa I, Freeman R (1992) Organization of suppression in receptive fields of neurons in cat visual cortex. J Neurophysiol 68:144–163
27. Driver J, Noesselt T (2008) Multisensory interplay reveals crossmodal influences on 'sensory-specific' brain regions, neural responses, and judgments. Neuron 57:11–23

28. Ernst M, Banks M (2002) Humans integrate visual and haptic information in a statistically optimal fashion. Nature 415:429–433
29. Ernst M, Banks M, Bülthoff H (2000) Touch can change visual slant perception. Nat Neurosci 3:69–73
30. Ernst M, Bülthoff H (2004) Merging the senses into a robust percept. Trends Cogn Sci 8:162–169
31. Essock E (1980) The oblique effect of stimulus identification considered with respect to two classes of oblique effects. Perception 9:37–46
32. Field D, Wu M (2004) An attempt towards a unifying account of non-linearities in visual neurons. J Vis 4:283a
33. Filangieri C, Li A (2009) Three-dimensional shape from second-order orientation flows. Vis Res 49:1465–1471
34. Fleming R, Torralba A, Adelson E (2004) Specular reflections and the perception of shape. J Vis 4(9):798–820
35. Freeman T, Durand S, Kiper D, Carandini M (2002) Suppression without inhibition in visual cortex. Neuron 35:759–771
36. Garding J (1992) Shape from texture for smooth curved surfaces in perspective projection. J Math Imaging Vis 2:327–350
37. Geisler W, Albrecht D, Salvi R, Saunders S (1991) Discrimination performance of single neurons: rate and temporal-pattern information. J Neurophysiol 66:334–362
38. Geisler W, Diehl R (2002) Bayesian natural selection and the evolution of perceptual systems. Philos Trans R Soc Lond B, Biol Sci 357:419–448
39. Girshick A, Landy M, Simoncelli E (2011) Cardinal rules: visual orientation perception reflects knowledge of environmental statistics. Nat Neurosci 14:926–932
40. Griffiths A, Zaidi Q (2000) Perceptual assumptions and projective distortions in a three-dimensional shape illusion. Perception 29:171–200
41. Griffiths A, Zaidi Q (1998) Rigid objects that appear to bend. Perception 27:799–802
42. Hansen B, Essock A (2004) A horizontal bias in human visual processing of orientation and its correspondence to the structural components of natural scenes. J Vis 4:1044–1060
43. Heeger D (1992) Normalization of cell responses in cat striate cortex. Vis Neurosci 9:181–198
44. Hel Or Y, Zucker S (1989) Texture fields and texture flows. Spat Vis 4:131–139
45. Heller M (1992) Haptic dominance in form perception: vision versus proprioception. Perception 21:655–660
46. Hoffman D, Richards W (1984) Parts of recognition. Cognition 18:65–96
47. Holland J (1975) Adaptation in natural and artificial systems: an introductory analysis with applications to biology, control, and artificial intelligence. University of Michigan Press, Ann Arbor
48. James T, Humphrey G, Gati J, Servos P, Menon R et al (2002) Haptic study of three-dimensional objects activates extrastriate visual areas. Neuropsychologia 40:1706–1714
49. Kendall D, Barden D, Carne T, Le H (1999) Shape and shape theory, Wiley, Hoboken
50. Knill D (2001) Contour into texture: information content of surface contours and texture flow. J Opt Soc Am A 18(1):12–35
51. Koenderink J (1984) What the occluding contour tells us about solid shape. Perception 13:321–330
52. Landy M, Maloney L, Johnston E, Young M (1995) Measurement and modeling of depth cue combination: in defense of weak fusion. Vis Res 35:389–412
53. Lawson R (1999) Achieving visual object constancy across plane rotation and depth rotation. Acta Psychol 102:221–245
54. Li A, Zaidi Q (2001) Erratum to "Information limitations in perception of shape from texture". [Vis Res 41 (2001) 1519–1534]. Vis Res 41: 2927–2942
55. Li A, Zaidi Q (2003) Observer strategies in perception of 3-d shape from isotropic textures: developable surfaces. Vis Res 43:2741–2758

56. Li A, Zaidi Q (2000) Perception of three-dimensional shape from texture is based on patterns of oriented energy. Vis Res 40:217–242
57. Li A, Zaidi Q (2009) Release from cross-orientation suppression facilitates 3d shape perception. PLoS ONE 4(12):e8333
58. Li A, Zaidi Q (2004) Three-dimensional shape from non-homogeneous textures: carved and stretched surfaces. J Vis 4:860–878
59. Li A, Zaidi Q (2001) Veridicality of three dimensional shape perception predicted from amplitude spectra of natural textures. J Opt Soc Am A 18(10):2430–2447
60. Li A, Tzen B, Yadgarova A, Zaidi Q (2008) Neural basis of 3-d shape aftereffects. Vis Res 48:244–252
61. Li B, Peterson M, Freeman R (2003) Oblique effect: a neural basis in the visual cortex. J Neurophysiol 90:204–217
62. Li B, Thompson J, Duong T, Peterson M, Freeman R (2006) Origins of cross-orientation suppression in the visual cortex. J Neurophysiol 96:1755–1764
63. Lunghi C, Binda P, Morrone M (2010) Touch disambiguates rivalrous perception at early stages of visual analysis. Curr Biol 20:R143–R144
64. MacEvoy S, Tucker T, Fitzpatrick D (2009) A precise form of divisive suppression supports population coding in the primary visual cortex. Nat Neurosci 12:637–645
65. Malik J, Rosenholtz R (1997) Computing local surface orientation and shape from texture for curved surfaces. Int J Comput Vis 23(2):149–168
66. Mansfield R (1974) Neural basis of orientation perception in primate vision. Science 186:1133–1135
67. Mardia K, Dryden I (1989) The statistical analysis of shape data. Biometrika 76:271–281
68. Marr D (1982) Vision: a computational investigation into the human representation and processing of visual information. Freeman, San Francisco
69. Marr D, Nishihara H (1978) Representation and recognition of the spatial organization of three-dimensional shapes. Proc R Soc Lond B, Biol Sci 200:269–294
70. Maunsell J, Sclar G, Nealey T, DePriest D (1991) Extraretinal representations in area V4 in the macaque monkey. Vis Neurosci 7:561–573
71. Meese T, Holmes D (2007) Spatial and temporal dependencies of cross-orientation suppression in human vision. Proc Biol Sci 274:127–136
72. Meier L, Carandini M (2002) Masking by fast gratings. J Vis 2:293–301
73. Meng X, Zaidi Q (2011) Visual effects of haptic feedback are large but local. PLoS ONE 6(5):e19877. doi:10.1371/journal.pone.0019877
74. Morrone M, Burr D, Maffei L (1982) Functional implications of cross-orientation inhibition of cortical visual cells. I. Neurophysiological evidence. Proc R Soc Lond B, Biol Sci 216:335–354
75. Mumford D (1992) On the computational architecture of the neocortex II. The role of cortico-cortical loops. Biol Cybern 66:241–251
76. Murray S, Kersten D, Olshausen B, Schrater P, Woods D (2002) Shape perception reduces activity in human primary visual cortex. Proc Natl Acad Sci USA 99:15164–15169
77. Newell F, Ernst M, Tjan B, Bülthoff H (2001) Viewpoint dependence in visual and haptic object recognition. Psychol Sci 12:37–42
78. Nolt M, Kumbhani R, Palmer L (2007) Suppression at high spatial frequencies in the lateral geniculate nucleus of the cat. J Neurophysiol 98:1167–1180
79. Olshausen B, Field D (2005) How close are we to understanding v1? Neural Comput 17:1665–1699
80. Pasupathy A, Connor C (1999) Responses to contour features in macaque area V4. J Neurophysiol 82:2490–2502
81. Petrov Y, Carandini M, McKee S (2005) Two distinct mechanisms of suppression in human vision. J Neurosci 25:8704–8707
82. Pizlo Z (2008) 3D shape: its unique place in visual perception. MIT Press, Cambridge
83. Pizlo Z, Stevenson A (1999) Shape constancy from novel views. Percept Psychophys 61:1299–1307

84. Priebe N, Ferster D (2006) Mechanisms underlying cross-orientation suppression in cat visual cortex. Nat Neurosci 9:552–561
85. Purpura K, Mechler F, Schmid A, Ohiorhenuan I, Hu Q et al (2007) Monocular correlates of 3d shape reduce suppression in V1 and V2 of macaques. Soc Neurosci Abstr 33:229.226
86. Rock I, Victor J (1964) Vision and touch: an experimentally created conflict between the two senses. Science 143:594–596
87. Roeber U, Wong E, Freeman A (2008) Cross-orientation interactions in human vision. J Vis 8(3):15 (11 pp)
88. Ross J, Speed H (1991) Contrast adaptation and contrast masking in human vision. Proc Biol Sci 246:61–69
89. Ross J, Speed H, Morgan M (1993) The effects of adaptation and masking on incremental thresholds for contrast. Vis Res 33:2051–2056
90. Sanger T (1996) Probability density estimation for the interpretation of neural population codes. J Neurophysiol 76:2790–2793
91. Schwartz O, Simoncelli E (2001) Natural signal statistics and sensory gain control. Nat Neurosci 4:819–825
92. Series P, Latham P, Pouget A (2004) Tuning curve sharpening for orientation selectivity: coding efficiency and the impact of correlations. Nat Neurosci 7:1129–1135
93. Sillito A (1979) Inhibitory mechanisms influencing complex cell orientation selectivity and their modification at high resting discharge levels. J Physiol 289:33–53
94. Simoncelli EP, Freeman WT (1995) The steerable pyramid: a flexible architecture for multiscale derivative computation. In: IEEE second int'l conf on image processing, Washington DC
95. Smith M, Bair W, Movshon J (2006) Dynamics of suppression in macaque primary visual cortex. J Neurosci 26:4826–4834
96. Stein B, Stanford T (2008) Multisensory integration: current issues from the perspective of the single neuron. Nat Rev Neurosci 9:255–266
97. Stevens KA (1981) The visual interpretation of surface contours. Artif Intell 17:47–73
98. Violentyev A, Shimojo S, Shams L (2005) Touch-induced visual illusion. NeuroReport 16:1107–1110
99. Westheimer G (2003) Meridional anisotropia in visual processing: implications for the neural site of the oblique effect. Vis Res 43:2281–2289
100. Wittgenstein L (1953) Philosophical investigations. Blackwell, Hoboken
101. Wong C, Zaidi Q (2008) Matched filters for 3-d shape from Kernel-Based image analysis. Vision Sciences Society, annual meeting 2008
102. Yamane Y, Carlson E, Bowman K, Wang Z, Connor C (2008) A neural code for three-dimensional object shape in macaque inferotemporal cortex. Nat Neurosci 11:1352–1360
103. Zaidi Q, Li A (2002) Limitations on shape information provided by texture cues. Vis Res 42:815–835
104. Zaidi Q (2011) Visual inferences of material changes: color as clue and distraction. Cogn Sci 2(6):686–700

Chapter 23
Holistic Shape Recognition: Where-to-Look and How-to-Look

Jianbo Shi

23.1 Introduction

Shape is an expressive abstraction of visual patterns in natural images, in body movements, even in abstract paintings. In computer vision, different applications that can benefit from accurate shape recognition, including robot navigation, image search, video analysis and medical image understanding. Shape is a critical cue for recognition, as it is sufficiently invariant to represent commonalities of different instances of a particular object category, while preserving enough detail about objects in order to differentiate them from each other or the background. It also varies systematically with 3D viewpoint, enabling estimation of the object pose. While there are many different approaches to using object shape for recognition, there are two difficulties faced by nearly all approaches: object deformation and the presence of background clutter.

Shape is a vast topic. We have focused on the three important sub-tasks of object recognition (Fig. 23.1) which are detection, alignment and segmentation:

- Detection: indicating the presence or absence of an object at a particular location in the image.
- Alignment: determining the pose of an object by corresponding it to a shape model.
- Segmentation: determining the boundaries of the object, necessary for manipulating it and interacting with it.

J. Shi (✉)
Department of Computer and Information Science, University of Pennsylvania, Philadelphia, USA
e-mail: jshi@cis.upenn.edu

S.J. Dickinson, Z. Pizlo (eds.), *Shape Perception in Human and Computer Vision*,
Advances in Computer Vision and Pattern Recognition,
DOI 10.1007/978-1-4471-5195-1_23, © Springer-Verlag London 2013

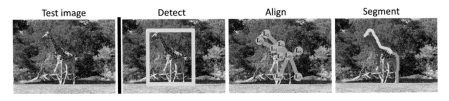

Fig. 23.1 Three goals of recognition: detection, alignment and segmenting object boundaries

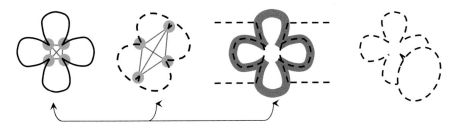

Fig. 23.2 A set of line figures illustrating shape as a global abstraction of visual patterns. The *two left figures* are visually very dissimilar. They share similar local patches, but have different structure as a whole. The *third figure* has a large overlap with the *figure on the right* at detail level, while their shapes are completely different. The *right-most figure* shows that occlusion and missing edges do not alter shape perception

23.1.1 What Have We Learned?

To see shape, we need to know not only *where* to look, but also *how* to look. We can think *where-to-look* as a detection task, and *how-to-look* as a perceptual grouping/segmentation task.

The fundamental difficulty is that *where-to-look* and *how-to-look* need to be tight integrated, one does not always precedes the other (Fig. 23.2). The *how-to-look* question is especially difficult, and distinguishes shape recognition from more generic deformable object recognition problem.

From computational perceptive, shape perception is all about deformation and de-cluttering. A straight line is not much to look at. It is only when the line starts to turn, bend, and twist, that the shape emerges. A crowded group of lines are not much to look at either. It is only when the lines stand out from clutter that we perceive their shape.

23.1.2 What Were the Challenges We Faced

If an image is uncluttered, for example a giraffe standing against a blue sky, the task of recognizing the giraffe is a simple one: no matter how the giraffe bends its neck or lifts its feet off the ground, perception of its shape can be achieved through precise geometrical analysis of its boundary contours. If the object shape category is rigid, no matter how complex is its shape, recognizing it is not hard even in cluttered environments. This task reduces to a typical problem in statistical learning. Using supervised learning, a statistical classifier can be used to detect such objects reliably in the image.

The key challenge is when both deformation and clutter are present in the image and object category. These two quantities (two ratios) affect our ability to see shape:

1. *Deformation ratio*: for a category of object shape, it is the ratio between (a) the range of deformation between the *rigidly detectable* parts and (b) the *size* of these parts. The uncertainties of the deformation can be un-isotropic. For 'shape' objects, such uncertainties of deformation are often very large in an unknown 1D space. Most of the success we have seen on object detection has been on objects with small "deformation ratio", and with uncertainties of deformation well constrained in a 2D domain isotropically.

2. *Clutter ratio*: for an image, it is the ratio between (a) size of the object, and (b) size of the segmentable region on object. We can allow sampling in the segmentation space, to produce multiple segmentations, so long it is not too large. For semantic scene recognition, we have seen success when large object shapes can be segmented using bottom-up cues.

The challenge is dealing with an object category with large deformation ratio (related to detectable parts), and an image with large clutter ratio (large uncertainties in segmentation due to clutter).

23.1.3 How Has Our Thinking on the Problem Changed over the Course of Research? What's Worked and What Hasn't?

Shape as an abstract mathematical object has been extensively studied. Algebra is a perfect and powerful tool to encode geometrical concepts. However, to compute and encode geometrical properties on images, which live in the signal space, remains a mystery. The shape story we will explore makes this link between geometry and signal.

Deformation has to do with geometry and topology. Geometry, the study of distance and angle, provides a mathematical foundation for shape analysis. The limitation is that we have to start with a clean set of lines (not necessarily limited to occluding boundaries). De-cluttering has to do with perceptual organization of the visual elements. A strong statement to make is that no shape can be perceived unless the underlying structure can be segmented. There are external de-cluttering and internal de-cluttering. The internal one has to do with simplification of the shape (medial axis for example), while the external de-cluttering has to do with separation of background and foreground.

Deformable Graphical Model and Co-segmentation-Recognition

Our initial focus was on deformable graphical models for computing shape deformation. Pair-wise attributes are important for reasoning geometric relationship, and can be conveniently encoded using an attributed graph. Furthermore, probabilistic graphical models (such as MRFs) seem to be a perfect tool for dealing with uncertainties in the data: using local features to set up graph node matching, and use pairwise geometric attributes to add contextual constraints.

Accidental alignment is important issue to deal with, and that requires segmentation. Motivated by a line of work by Ullman, we combined segmentation as a parallel process, where the parts provide bias to the segmentation. Those segmentation/parts constraints are combined in a con-current graph partitioning framework. We build on Spectral graph theory, and produced several solutions for efficient attribute graph matching for object detection and segmentation.

This deformable graphical model did not work well, particularly for free form objects. The biggest lesson we learned is that pair-wise relationship are unreliable and uninformative when the distance between the parts are much larger than the part size. The useful graph connections are mostly short range (distance equal to roughly the part size). If the patches are about 30 pixels wide, the pairwise relationship are only reliable up to 30 pixels away.

Shape Jigsaw Model

The second approach is to iteratively construct bottom-up structures into recognizable shape using grammatical rules. Starting from too small elements, such as isolated edges, is not a good idea. While we can recursively group them into larger structure, the exponential grouping hypothesis expansion leads to huge uncertainties of detected structure. Instead, we start from more salient region segmentation or long salient contours grouping. We formulated our problem as a "shape jigsaw" fitting problem where the image segments are the jigsaw parts. The jigsaw problem can be described as *'many-to-one'* matching of image segments to an object model, specifically for articulated body pose estimation.

For the human body, different shape exemplars were specified for different regions of the body. Because the body is compositional in nature, proposals for a particular body region were created by combining proposals from subregions (Fig. 23.3). For example, to form a proposal for the lower body, a single segment could be taken, two proposals for legs could be combined, or a proposal for three-fourths of the lower body and a lower leg (the remaining one-fourth) could be combined. Because these proposals consist of image segments, a region of the body could be formed by combining one or more image segments together.

A key insight is to separate the cost function of "proposal" from the one for "evaluation". The proposals are generated by merging segments based on geometrical grammar. The evaluation process uses "deformable" Inner Distance Shape Context

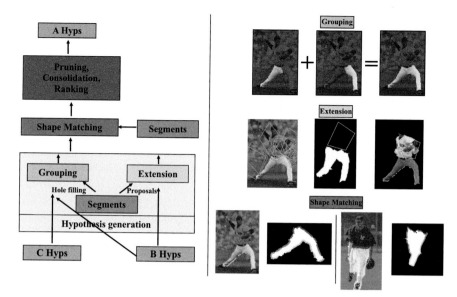

Fig. 23.3 Shape Jigsaw fitting. *Left*: parse rule application procedure. Using a set of binary merging rules, a pair of parses (segments) that are within 10 pixels of each other are composed via grouping, with hole filling provided by segments if needed. For unary rules, the child parses undergo extension using projected quadrilaterals and segment proposals. Shape matching is performed on both the original segments as well as the composed parses. For leaf nodes, shape matching is performed only on the segments. After shape matching, the parses are consolidated, pruned and ranked. *Right*: Grouping: two legs, on the *left*, are grouped into a lower body parse, on the *right*. Extension: the leftmost image shows a lower body parse with multiple different torso quadrilaterals projected from exemplars on to the image using the correspondence between the lower body parse and the lower body exemplars; the *center image* shows the exemplar with its torso quadrilateral that yielded the best torso parse, seen in the *right image*. Shape matching: two examples of shape matching. The lower body on the *right* was detected directly from the segments S, underscoring the importance of injecting the shapes from S into all levels of the parse tree

(IDSC) to achieve articulation invariant matching. Using large segments helps us to avoid accidental alignment in clutter, using IDSC allow us to deal with deformation.

We demonstrated our results in ETH Horse dataset, and Baseball set. We learned holistic shape features are much better in describing and discriminating deformable shape. However, the biggest drawback is that the deformable proposal generation can be very fragile, due in part the large search space.

Many-to-Many Shape Packing Model

Saliency of the parts, and holistic deformable matching are two important ingredients for robust shape detection. Bottom-up image segmentation can yield important image structures that are useful for object recognition. However, these image structures may fragment in unpredictable ways (depending on pose and context) result-

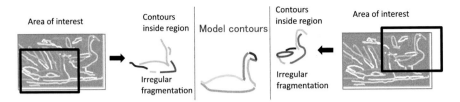

Fig. 23.4 In this image, we have two different swans. Despite being the same object, the Fragmentation of the contours that comprise the swans are very different. Therefore, one-to-one matching of image contours to model is unlikely to succeed, and would likely require an exponential fragmentation of the swan shape model to accommodate all the possible fragmentations that occur in real images

ing in no possible one-to-one correspondence between image structures and object parts.

The work of [1] highlights the concept of *many-to-many* matching as a way of dealing with this fragmentation problem. The work of Demirci et al. [2] formulated the many-to-many matching problem between two graphs by first finding an embedding of nodes of each graph using a low-distortion graph embedding technique, followed by solving an Earth Mover's Distance (EMD; [3]) problem where the flows between nodes were interpreted as the many-to-many matching. They applied their method to match shock graphs of silhouette images for shape matching. Some of these ideas can be traced to an earlier work of [4].

We [5] developed an alternative approach for *many-to-many* matching formulated as a 'Packing' problem (Fig. 23.4). Given two sets of contours (or segments), the goal was to find a subset of contours (or segments) that had similar *holistic shape*. Shape similarity was measured by comparing shape contexts computed over the selected subsets of contours, and a computationally efficient approximation to this combinatorial problem was formulated as a linear program 'Packing' problem. The many-to-many matching was used to detect object parts in the image, which were then combined via a voting scheme to provide object detection scores. The approach was evaluated on the ETHZ Shape Classes dataset from [6], and showed good detection performance.

The key innovation is to construct a holistic shape descriptor that is an *algebraic* function of the latent selection variable of foreground and background contours. As such, we can use computational tools for the combinatorial Packing problem as a robust computational solution. A drawback of this approach is dependence on precise segmentation boundary, or long contour grouping.

23.1.4 What Are the Obstacles to the Community's Success?

The three big areas for shape recognition are: representation of the shape model, shape features used for matching, and the method of matching the shape features to the image. All of these choices come with different trade-offs among computational efficiency, tractability of good approximate or exact inference, and learnability of good cost functions for recognition.

Shape Model Representation

On the model side, there are many different methods for representing object shape. Broadly speaking, representations in the early history of computer vision research tended towards greater abstraction, representing objects in terms of high-level concepts, such as geometric shapes, such as *Generalized cylinders:* proposed by Binford ([7]), and *Geons* by Biederman ([8]). More recently, semantic category based representations (e.g., an airport is composed of a runway and a terminal building), such as *AND-OR Graphs* [25] have been proposed. Unfortunately, the semantic gap between these abstract representations and the image pixels has proven to be difficult to bridge directly. As a result, vision research since 1990 has focused on much simpler template representations of objects. Templates do not capture the same general properties of object shape, but are much easier to compare against image features than abstract representations.

Model Obstacles   Most of the algorithms today proceed in a pre-set path for shape detection, which does not know to take advantage of the opportunities presented by the image itself (images are not trying to hide shape patterns). I wish for a shape model that knows how to 'opportunistically' take advantage of the structures in the image, explain the plausible bottom-up patterns, and guide them to complete the shape.

We also need more detailed shape models, that are able to understand the physical functionality of the shape.

Shape Features

Shape features are statistics about the shape that can be compared with the image in order to find shape matches in the image. These image features allow us to compare the template models of objects against bottom-up image structures.

The most successful features are texture histogram features such as *HOG feature* [9] and *Shape context* [10], both are histogram over gradient orientations in a particular region of the image. However, clutter may corrupt the descriptors in complex scenes, resulting in poor match scores despite the actual object of interest being present. For this reason, the descriptor support is typically very small relative to the overall object size, limiting the scale of shape features that can be represented. The descriptors are often scored using a set of linear weights learned discriminatively, e.g. from a support vector machine (SVM), that emphasize the important local features of object shape for good detection performance.

Related to the shape context, the inner-distance shape context (IDSC) proposed by Ling et al. ([11]) is a histogram over the locations of object boundary points, but is computed in a way as to be invariant to articulation using shortest paths between two points on the boundary of the shape through the interior. The length of this path and the local orientation of the object shape at each of the boundary points are used to compute an articulation-invariant descriptor. The IDSC was used for shape matching of silhouette images for shape retrieval in [11].

While most recent works have focused on boundary base shape feature, earlier works such as [12] have developed volumetric medial axis based shape feature and shape similarity function.

Feature Obstacles   We need shape features that can pick up small subtitle shape variations that are functionally important, while tolerating deformation and clutter. We need image features that extract more abstract concepts of topological as well as physical functionality of the shape elements.

Shape Matching

Given shape features in the image, these features must be matched against the object shape model in order to achieve recognition. This typically involves at least alignment of the model to the image, and may also include segmentation of the object. Many different methods for shape matching have been developed, implementing a variety of different cost functions with corresponding trade-offs in computational complexity and detection accuracy.

Template Matching Using Local Features can be done using Chamfer matching/Distance transform, which can be generalized and computed efficiently [13]. *Abstract Representation Matching* can be achieved via the interpretation tree, introduced by Gatson and Lozano-Perez in [14]. Local features + pairwise geometric constraints, can be achieved by graph matching methods. Multiple object parts can be detected in the image using this method and their scores can be combined via voting for the object center using the known spatial relationships of the parts relative to the object center, as in [15]. Arbitrary pair-wise relationships can also be incorporated, as did Coughlan and Ferreira ([16]), using loopy belief propagation for inference.

Matching Obstacles   The key missing piece is understanding uncertainties in the matching process, and a computational mechanism to mediate the uncertainties in both the top-down and bottom-up path. Another key element is turning this matching process to gain discriminative power.

Above, we see the shape recognition task is ultimately about building up a parametrization of the image shape, such that geometrical measures can be made. Recognizing this underlying image structure is what allows us to answer the "how-to-look" question, which is crucial for shape measurement.

23.2 Many-to-Many Shape Packing

Given a set of image structures, discovered by bottom-up grouping, recognition typically requires matching these structures against an object model. Because one-to-one matching is insufficiently flexible to handle the matching of bottom-up structures that fragment unpredictably, we need methods for many-to-many matching, which maps subsets of a set A to subsets of a set B.

23.2.1 Many-to-Many Matching as a Packing Problem

We formulate in [5, 17], the *many-to-many* matching task for matching object shape as a combinatorial Packing problem. We are given a set of model contours M and image contours C, and wish to find a subset of each such that the overall shapes of the two subsets is similar. In the case where model is made of one deformable contour, $|M| = 1$, this reduces to *many-to-one* matching.

The advantage of many-to-many matching is that groups of image structures can be holistically matched to the object model without regard to their specific fragmentation. The contours corresponding to the outline of the object in the image could be fragmented arbitrarily, yet *many-to-many* matching would be able to match them to the object shape model with the same cost.

To characterize the shape of the subsets, we can use any spatial histogram, such as one or more shape contexts [18], or a grid histogram. During matching, we must find both the subsets of contours in the model and the image as well as an aligning transformation that aligns the image contours to the object shape model so that shape similarity can be measured accurately. These quantities can be defined as:

- $\mathbf{T} \in \mathbb{R}^2$: a transformation that describes the alignment of the image contours to the model contours.
- $\mathbf{x}^{sel} \in \{0, 1\}^{|C|}$: an indicator vector that defines which image contours are *selected* for matching to the model. Contour C_i is selected if and only if $\mathbf{x}_i^{sel} == 1$.
- $\mathbf{y}^{sel} \in \{0, 1\}^{|M|}$: an indicator vector that defines which model contours are *selected* for matching to the image. Contour M_i is selected if and only if $\mathbf{y}_i^{sel} == 1$.

Figure 23.5, left, shows a set of contours in two images as input to the matching; an aligning transformation $\mathbf{T}$ aligns the two sets of contours. We define a spatial histogram of dimension d_m over the edge points of image contours selected by $\mathbf{x}^{sel}$ and transformed by $\mathbf{T}$ as: $h_{\mathbf{T}(C),\mathbf{x}^{sel}}$. Any type of spatial histogram is allowed, including grid histograms (as used in [9]) or log-polar radial histograms (as in [18]). We encapsulate this property via a histogram function H, which maps a point in $\mathbb{R}^2$ to a vector in $\mathbb{R}^{d_m}$, or $H : \mathbb{R}^2 \to \mathbb{R}^{d_m}$. In general, any possible histogram is permitted as long as it satisfies the following property: given two sets R and S and the histogram function H, we require: $H(R \cup S) + H(R \cap S) == H(R) + H(S)$. Specifically in this case, a histogram over the points of several contours is equivalent to summing the histograms computed for each contour individually, first noted in [5], and also

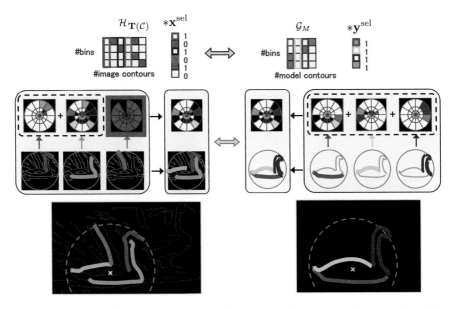

Fig. 23.5 Overview of the many-to-many matching process. *Top*: two sets of contours M and C are provided as input. An aligning transformation $\mathbf{T}$ transforms contours C such that some object(s) align between the two sets of contours. A histogram function H operates on the contours M and transformed contours $T(C)$, producing a histogram for each contour, which appears as a column of matrices $\mathcal{G}_M$ and $\mathcal{H}_{\mathbf{T}(C)}$. *Middle*: our goal is to infer indicator vectors x^{sel}, y^{sel} that specify a specific subset of contours in the two sets such that the two subsets have similar histograms (and hence shape). To compare histograms, we use histogram comparison features $K(\mathbf{T}, x^{\text{sel}}, y^{\text{sel}})$, a function of the transformation $\mathbf{T}$ and the contour subsets. *Bottom*: our goal is to maximize the similarity of the two histograms over the choices of subsets of contours to match the contours of the common aligned object (a car in this instance). The two quantities $\mathbf{x}^{\text{sel}}_*$ and $\mathbf{y}^{\text{sel}}_*$ together are the optimal solution (subsets of image contours) to the many-to-many matching problem

depicted in Fig. 23.5. This means that histogram $h_{\mathbf{T}(C),\mathbf{x}^{\text{sel}}}$ can be represented as a linear function of $\mathbf{x}^{\text{sel}}$ as shown in Fig. 23.5. We introduce the per-contour histogram matrix $\mathcal{H}_{\mathbf{T}(C)}$ and write the histogram over selected-contours $h_{\mathbf{T}(C),\mathbf{x}^{\text{sel}}}$ as a linear function of $\mathbf{x}^{\text{sel}}$:

$$\mathcal{H}_{\mathbf{T}(C)} \in \mathbb{R}^{d_m \times |C|} \; h_{\mathbf{T}(C),\mathbf{x}^{\text{sel}}} \Longleftrightarrow \mathcal{H}_{\mathbf{T}(C)} \mathbf{x}^{\text{sel}} \tag{23.1}$$

The k-th column of $\mathcal{H}_{\mathbf{T}(C)}$ is a histogram over the points in contour C_k. Similarly, we can also represent the model contour shape contexts with a matrix $\mathcal{G}_M$, where each column is a shape context for a model contour. To compare the histograms that result from selecting only a subset of the image and model contours, we measure two types of features: bin-wise difference features $-|\mathcal{H}_{\mathbf{T}(C)}\mathbf{x}^{\text{sel}} - \mathcal{G}_M \mathbf{y}^{\text{sel}}|$ and intersection features $\min(\mathcal{H}_{\mathbf{T}(C)}\mathbf{x}^{\text{sel}}, \mathcal{G}_M \mathbf{y}^{\text{sel}})$:

$$K\left(\mathbf{T}, \mathbf{x}^{\text{sel}}, \mathbf{y}^{\text{sel}}\right) = \begin{bmatrix} -|\mathcal{H}_{\mathbf{T}(C)}\mathbf{x}^{\text{sel}} - \mathcal{G}_M \mathbf{y}^{\text{sel}}| \\ \min(\mathcal{H}_{\mathbf{T}(C)}\mathbf{x}^{\text{sel}}, \mathcal{G}_M \mathbf{y}^{\text{sel}}) \end{bmatrix} \tag{23.2}$$

Figure 23.5, middle, shows the comparison of the two histograms resulting from choosing a subset of contours in both the model and image, and the features used for histogram comparison. Given a weighting on these features $w^{app} \geq 0$, our goal is to solve the maximization problem:

$$\max_{\substack{\mathbf{x}^{sel} \in \{0,1\}^{|C|} \\ \mathbf{y}^{sel} \in \{0,1\}^{|M|}}} w^{app\top} K\left(\mathbf{T}, \mathbf{x}^{sel}, \mathbf{y}^{sel}\right) \qquad (23.3)$$

An important question is how to perform the above maximization over $\mathbf{T}, \mathbf{x}^{sel}, \mathbf{y}^{sel}$. For fixed $\mathbf{T}$, the resulting optimization problem is an integer linear program; if we can solve (or approximate) this integer linear program, we can directly search over different possible choices of $\mathbf{T}$, solving a separate optimization problem for each one. Instead of trying to solve the integer linear program exactly, we can relax $\mathbf{x}^{sel} \in [0, 1]^{|C|}$ and $\mathbf{y}^{sel} \in [0, 1]^{|M|}$, resulting in a linear program. This optimization problem is an instance of the combinatorial *Packing* problem, as all the variables take on positive values. An efficient computational solution using Prime-Dual methods is shown in [5].

Many-to-One Matching   An important special case of the many-to-many matching problem is the many-to-one matching problem. In this setting, instead of having multiple model contours, there is just one, which must always be matched (cannot be de-selected). The variables for model contour selection $\mathbf{y}^{sel}$ can be eliminated, and the term $\mathcal{G}\mathbf{y}^{sel}$ can be replaced with a single model histogram $h_{\mathcal{M}}$.

23.3 Shape Detection and Segmentation

For object detection, we use the building block of many-to-one matching of image contours to a shape model (learned or given by hand drawing), but with a matching score tuned for discrimination. To accommodate object deformation, we extend to model to have $N + 1$ parts: Parts: $P_0, P_1, \ldots, P_N$. Our parts are typically large and locally deformed. Parts may deform relative to the root part, P_0, that represents the center of the object. In the model, parts $P_1, \ldots, P_N$ are located at points of high curvature on the model shape contours: $P'_1, \ldots, P'_N$. We use the discrete curve evolution method of [19] to find these points P'_i from the model shape contours, and P'_0 on the model is computed as simply the mean of $P'_1, \ldots, P'_N$ in the model. Part appearances for parts P_i, $i = 1, \ldots, N$ are represented with model part histograms $h^i_{\mathcal{M}}$ centered at P'_i computed over the model shape (P_0 has no appearance term, although our formulation can accommodate one); we use shape context histograms.

For an image I_j with contours C^j, a detection of consists of a many-to-one matching for each part: transformations $\mathbf{T}_i$ for each part (which align placement of the part in the image back to the location of the part on the model), and selected contours for matching to each part P_i, $i = 1, \ldots, N$, $\mathbf{x}^{sel}_i$ (with the exception of the

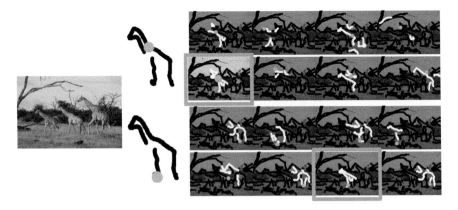

Fig. 23.6 Examples of many-to-one matching. *Left*: input image; *center*: two different points on model to be matched in the image; *right*: different many-to-one matchings of model to image. A single shape context was used as the histogram, centered at the highlighted points on the model; the transformation **T** relating the image to the model was simply a translation of image contours derived from the relative locations of the model part point and the corresponding image point. Correct correspondences are highlighted in *green*; matched image contours are shown in *white*, and unmatched contours are *black*

root part, which only serves to spatially relate the other parts):

$$\mathbf{T}_i \ : P_i \rightarrow \mathbb{R}^2$$
$$\mathbf{x}_i^{\text{sel}} : C^j \rightarrow \{0, 1\}^{|C^j|}$$

(23.4)

We define a detection as $D = \{\mathbf{T}_0, \mathbf{T}_1, \mathbf{x}_1^{\text{sel}}, \mathbf{T}_2, \mathbf{x}_2^{\text{sel}}, \ldots, \mathbf{T}_N, \mathbf{x}_N^{\text{sel}}\}$. For simplicity, we abuse notation and refer to the correspondence of model point P_i' in the image using T_i. Following the terminology of [15], we also call T_i a *placement* of part P_i, since it refers to the location in the image where part P_i is hypothesized to lie. Figure 23.7 describes a detection.

Placement Score   For each part P_i, we need to be able to score a placement $\mathbf{T}_i$ of the part in the image along with matching contours $\mathbf{x}_i^{\text{sel}}$. We use the same many-to-one shape matching features K, with a part-specific weight vector $w_i^{\text{app}} \geq 0$: $w_i^{\text{app}\mathsf{T}} K(\mathbf{T}_i, \mathbf{x}_i^{\text{sel}})$. The corresponding model part shape histogram is $h_{\mathcal{M}}^i$.

Deformation Score   For each part $i = 1, \ldots, N$ we use a part offset $O_i = (O_i^x, O_i^y)$ that describes the expected spatial position of P_i in the image, $\mathbf{T}_i$, relative to $\mathbf{T}_0$, the position of the root part in the image: $\mathbf{T}_0 + O_i$. O_i is computed as the difference between the locations of parts P_i and P_0 in the model: $P_i' - P_0'$. The deviation of a part P_i from its expected position relative to the root provides part deformation features G:

$$G(\mathbf{T}_0, \mathbf{T}_i) = \begin{bmatrix} -(\mathbf{T}_i^x - (\mathbf{T}_0^x + O_i^x))^2 \\ -(\mathbf{T}_i^y - (\mathbf{T}_0^y + O_i^y))^2 \end{bmatrix}$$

(23.5)

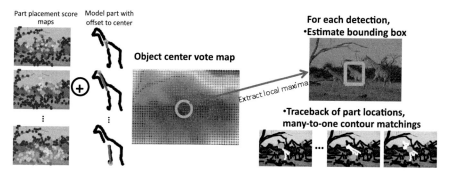

Part placement score maps Model part with offset to center

$\oplus$

Object center vote map

Extract local maxima

For each detection,
•Estimate bounding box

•Traceback of part locations, many-to-one contour matchings

...

Fig. 23.7 Step of detection: first for each model part, we try many-to-one matching at multiple image locations. Figure 23.6 shows the resulting score map and selection of contours for different placement of each part. The score maps for different parts are combined via center voting using the known offset of the model part to the center of the object model, to produce an object center vote map. Local maxima of the object center vote map can be extracted to provide multiple detectors. For each detection, we can do a simple traceback to find the location of the object parts for that detection, as well as matching of image contours to each object part. The bounding box can be estimated by computing the bounding box of the part locations for that detection

A set of parameters w_i^{def}, $i = 1, \ldots, N$ (to be learned, along with w_i^{app}) penalizes deviation of part P_i from its expected position relative to P_0. The overall score function for a particular detection D is:

$$\text{DetScore}(D) = \sum_{i=1}^{N} \begin{bmatrix} w_i^{\text{def}} \\ w_i^{\text{app}} \end{bmatrix}^{\mathsf{T}} \begin{bmatrix} G(\mathbf{T}_0, \mathbf{T}_i) \\ K(\mathbf{T}_i, \mathbf{x}_i^{\text{sel}}) \end{bmatrix} \tag{23.6}$$

In contrast to [15], our appearance term does not depend simply on the placement $\mathbf{T}_i$ of part P_i, but also on the contours chosen for matching, $\mathbf{x}_i^{\text{sel}}$.

Inference for Detection The space of possible detections is exponential in the number of possible placements for each part and number of image contours. To cope, we create a regular grid of possible root part locations $\mathcal{R}$ in the image and only keep the highest scoring detection per root part location $R_j \in \mathcal{R}$, as in [15]. For each possible root location R_j, we fix $\mathbf{T}_0 = R_j$, and then maximize the detection score subject to this root constraint to obtain score $S(R_j, w)$:

$$S(R_j, w) = \max_{D|\mathbf{T}_0 = R_j} \text{DetScore}(D) \implies$$
$$\max_{\{\mathbf{T}_1, \ldots, \mathbf{T}_N, \mathbf{x}_1^{\text{sel}}, \ldots, \mathbf{x}_N^{\text{sel}}\}} \sum_{i=1}^{N} \begin{bmatrix} w_i^{\text{def}} \\ w_i^{\text{app}} \end{bmatrix}^{\mathsf{T}} \begin{bmatrix} G(R_j, \mathbf{T}_i) \\ K(\mathbf{T}_i, \mathbf{x}_i^{\text{sel}}) \end{bmatrix} \tag{23.7}$$

We note that $w_i^{\text{app}\mathsf{T}} K(\mathbf{T}_i, \mathbf{x}_i^{\text{sel}})$ does not depend on $\mathbf{T}_0$, and hence for each part P_i the maximization over $\mathbf{x}_i^{\text{sel}}$ can be pre-computed for each possible placement $\mathbf{T}_i$.

In [15], this step corresponds to convolving the image with the filter associated with a part. In our case, we use the previously described linear programming relaxation to efficiently and accurately approximate the many-to-one matching score.

Given $w_i^{app\top} K(\mathbf{T}_i, \mathbf{x}_i^{sel})$ for each possible placement $\mathbf{T}_i$ of each part P_i, $\max_{D|\mathbf{T}_0=R_j} DetScore(D)$ can be computed easily by picking the best part placement for each part P_i individually. For fixed $\mathbf{T}_0$, the scores for parts $P_1, \ldots, P_N$ are independent. The set of possible placements are sampled from points of high curvature along image contours, following the method of [19]. We take as a bounding box the bounding box of the part locations. A detection with center R_j can be labeled as a true or false positive (label $y_j = \pm 1$) according the overlap of its bounding box with a ground truth bounding box. Non-maximum suppression allows us to eliminate many redundant/overlapping detections, reducing the complexity of learning.

Latent SVM for Discriminative Detector Learning   Given detections centered at $R_j \in \mathcal{R}$ with labels $y_j = \pm 1$ from the training images, we learn discriminative model parameters $w = [w_1^{def\top} w_1^{app\top} \cdots w_N^{def\top} w_N^{app\top}]^\top$ to optimize detection performance. We in [17] adapt the "coordinate descent" method from [15] for minimizing a hinge- loss function associated with the above score function in Eq. (23.7).

Joint Many-to-One Matching   For a fixed set of part placements, we can solve the many-to-one matching problem simultaneously for all parts. In essence, this is like treating the shape contexts of all the object parts as a single large histogram, and solving the many-to-one matching problem with this unified histogram. The result is a single $\mathbf{x}^{sel}$ that encodes which contours are matched to the object as a whole. Given an existing detection $D = \{\mathbf{T}_0, \ldots, \mathbf{T}_n, \mathbf{x}_1^{sel}, \ldots, \mathbf{x}_n^{sel}\}$, we can write the maximization problem as:

$$\max_{\mathbf{x}^{sel}} \sum_{i=1}^{N} w_i^{app\top} K\left(\mathbf{T}_i, \mathbf{x}^{sel}\right) = \max_{\mathbf{x}^{sel}} \begin{bmatrix} w_1^{app} \\ w_2^{app} \\ \vdots \\ w_N^{app} \end{bmatrix}^\top \begin{bmatrix} K(\mathbf{T}_1, \mathbf{x}^{sel}) \\ K(\mathbf{T}_2, \mathbf{x}^{sel}) \\ \vdots \\ K(\mathbf{T}_N, \mathbf{x}^{sel}) \end{bmatrix} \tag{23.8}$$

This can also be approximated via the same linear program (considering of all the shape contexts together forming a single large histogram) as the usual single-part many-to-one matching.

Joint Matching and Final Evaluation   Given the final part placements, we can again perform joint matching of image contours to all the object parts. On the histogram comparison features and the geometric relationships of parts to the object center, we can train an SVM classifier to provide a final detection score.

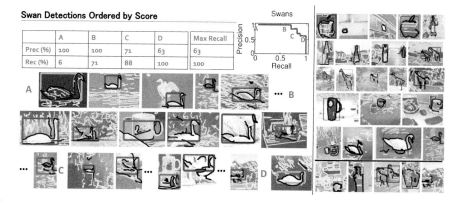

Fig. 23.8 *Left*: listing of detection results for the swans class. In the *upper right* is the precision-recall curve, annotated at several different points with letters "A", "B", etc… Shown below are detections in descending order of detection score, along with the locations on the curve indicated by the letters. *Green bounding boxes* indicate true positives, while *red bounding boxes* indicate false positives. Selected contours for each detection are highlighted in black. *Right*: Some of our detection results on the ETHZ Shape Classes dataset. Each image shows segmented object contours and bounding boxes for one or more detections. *Bottom row* shows false positives for Applelogos, Bottles, Giraffes, Mugs and 82 Swans (l-to-r); rest are true positives

23.4 Experiments on ETHZ Shape

We tested our method on the ETHZ Shape Classes dataset ([20]; freely available online), with five classes: Applelogos, Bottles, Giraffes, Mugs and Swans. We follow the train/test split described in [21]; for training for each category we used the first half of the images from that category as positive examples, and an equal number of negative images chosen equally from the remaining classes. Each category had 32 to 86 training images.

During detection, images were searched at 6 different scales, 2 per octave. Each part had up to 200 different possible placements in the image; for each part/placement/scale tuple, a separate linear program was solved, taking a few minutes per image. Latent SVM parameters w were initialized uniformly as in model shape learning, and convergence took 3–7 iterations. After training the initial detector, learning was done for part placement refinement, affine transformation estimation and joint selection using high-scoring detections from voting (<200 detections). All our results used 0.5 overlap score threshold for determining if a detection bounding box overlaps with a ground truth bounding box (PASCAL criterion). Each detector was tested on remaining 169 (Giraffe) to 223 (Swan) test images.

We compare our approach against the reported results from [21] and the method of [15] with the same train/test split. Our APs for the five classes are (0.845/0.916/0.787/0.888/0.922; mean: **0.872**), much better than the next best result at (mean: 0.771; [21]). Our method is comparable in Applelogos/Bottles and substantially outperforms on Mugs/Giraffes/Swans which have large deformation comparing to [15]. Our detection rates at 0.3/0.4 FPPI of (0.95/0.95; 1/1; 0.872/0.896;

Table 23.1 Ablative analysis of different components of our method on the ETHZ Shape Classes dataset. We can see that the additional steps of joint selection (joint sel.) and training produce significant improvements in performance. Removing discriminative training produces substantially worse results, and removing both training as well as joint selection severely impacts performance

Components	Avg. AP	Avg. Rec. at 0.3/0.4 FPPI
Many-to-one Voting (training)	0.822	0.877/0.883
Many-to-one matching (training and joint sel.)	**0.872**	**0.952/0.956**
Same as above (no training)	0.712	0.852/0.856
No training, and joint sel.	0.574	0.765/0.790

0.936/0.936; 1/1) and mean across classes of **0.952/0.956**, are a substantial improvement over the results of [21], 0.919/0.932 and [22], 0.930/0.952 (hand-drawn models). We also outperform methods using hand-drawn models [5, 22, 23]. Figure 23.8 shows detections/segmentations from our method. Both internal and external contours (e.g., mug handle/outline) are segmented out.

To gain further insight into the results, we display selected detections (ordered by detection score in decreasing order) from the ETHZ test data for each category in Fig. 23.8 along with the positions on the PR curve of those detections. We can see that the false positives tend to have the shape of the object we are looking for, while some true positives have low score due to object deformation (e.g., articulation of the Giraffe or out of plane rotation of Applelogos) or missing contours.

We also performed an ablative analysis of the different steps of the method: many-to-one matching and voting, joint selection, and supervised learning as seen in Table 23.1. While voting with discriminative training is itself effective, the additional of joint selection also produce substantial increases in performance. By contrast, removing learning drastically worsens the results.

23.5 Comments

Our main theme is that shape perception involves both detection (where-to-look) and segmentation/perceptual organization (how-to-look). The fundamental challenges are *object* deformation and *image* de-cluttering. We focused on objects with large deformation ratio (related to detectable parts), and on images with large clutter ratio (large uncertainties in segmentation due to clutter).

Our approach of Contour Packing shows that salient long contours can de-clutter the image and be organized into a deformable object shape. It specifically addresses the problem that every image has highly unpredictable bottom-up contour groupings. We further conjuncture that this approach would require far fewer training examples.

The experimental analysis of our algorithm shows that three shape recognition subtasks, (1) detection (via discriminative pattern matching), (2) alignment (of parts and local orientation of features), and (3) segmentation (of figure-ground), all need to work together for improving shape detection performance. Building on this theme of integrated detection-alignment-segmentation, we recently developed a joint combinatorial optimization solution in [24] which achieved the average AP of 91.1 % on the ETHZ Shape Classes.

The importance of each subtask varies case-by-case depending on the type of image clutter and amount of object deformation. This points to the need of better shape recognition benchmarks, which will measure more precisely how an algorithm performs under different image/object conditions. This is important as our community moves towards a more experimental science.

Acknowledgement The Contour Packing algorithm described here are based on Ph.D. thesis works of Qihui Zhu and Praveen Srinivasan.

References

1. Keselman Y, Dickinson S (2005) Generic model abstraction from examples. IEEE Trans Pattern Anal Mach Intell 22(7):1141–1156
2. Demirci MF, Shokoufandeh A, Keselman Y, Bretzner L, Dickinson S (2006) Object recognition as many-to-many feature matching. Int J Comput Vis 69(2):203–222
3. Rubner Y, Tomasi C, Guibas LJ (2000) The earth mover's distance as a metric for image retrieval. Int J Comput Vis 40(2):99–121
4. Pelillo M, Siddiqi K, Zucker SW (1998) Matching hierarchical structures using association graphs. IEEE Trans Pattern Anal Mach Intell 21:1105–1120
5. Zhu Q, Wang L, Wu Y, Shi J (2008) Contour context selection for object detection: a set-to-set contour matching approach. In: ECCV (2), pp 774–787
6. Ferrari V, Jurie F, Schmid C (2007) Accurate object detection with deformable shape models learnt from images. In: CVPR
7. Binford TO (1971) Visual perception by computer. In: IEEE conf on systems and controls
8. Biederman I (1987) Recognition-by-components: a theory of human image understanding. Psychol Rev 94:115–147
9. Dalal N, Triggs B (2005) Histograms of oriented gradients for human detection. In: CVPR
10. Belongie S, Malik J, Puzicha J (2002) Shape matching and object recognition using shape contexts. IEEE Trans Pattern Anal Mach Intell 24(4):509–522
11. Ling H, Jacobs DW (2005) Using the inner-distance for classification of articulated shapes. In: CVPR
12. Siddiqi K, Kimia BB, Tannenbaum A, Zucker SW (2001) On the psychophysics of the shape triangle. Vis Res 41(9):1153–1178
13. Felzenszwalb PF, Huttenlocher DP (2004) Distance transforms of sampled functions. Technical report, Cornell Computing and Information Science
14. Gaston PC, Lozano-Prez T (1983) Tactile recognition and localization using object models: the case of polyhedra on a plane. IEEE Trans Pattern Anal Mach Intell 6:257–265
15. Felzenszwalb P, McAllester D, Ramanan D (2008) A discriminatively trained, multiscale, deformable part model. In: CVPR
16. Coughlan JM, Ferreira SJ (2002) Finding deformable shapes using loopy belief propagation. In: ECCV, vol 3, pp 453–468
17. Srinivasan P, Zhu Q, Shi J (2010) Many-to-one contour matching for describing and discriminating object shape. In: 2010 IEEE conference on computer vision and pattern recognition (CVPR). IEEE, New York, pp 1673–1680
18. Belongie S, Malik J, Puzicha J (2002) Shape matching and object recognition using shape contexts. IEEE Trans Pattern Anal Mach Intell 24:509–521

19. Latecki LJ, Lakamper R (1999) Polygon evolution by vertex deletion. In: Scale-space
20. Ferrari V, Jurie F, Schmid C (2009) From images to shape models for object detection. In: PAMI
21. Maji S, Malik J (2009) A max-margin hough transform for object detection. In: CVPR
22. Ravishankar S, Jain A, Mittal A (2008) Multi-stage contour based detection of deformable objects. In: ECCV
23. Lu C, Latecki LJ, Adluru N, Ling H, Yang X (2009) Shape guided contour grouping with particle filters. In: ICCV
24. Zhang W, Srinivasan P, Shi J (2011) Discriminative image warping with attribute flow. In: 2011 IEEE conference on computer vision and pattern recognition (CVPR). IEEE, New York, pp 2393–2400
25. Zhu CS, Mumford D (2006) A stochastic grammar of images. In: Foundations and trends in computer graphics and vision. Now Publishers, Hanover, pp 259–362

Chapter 24
Shape Processing as Inherently Three-Dimensional

Christopher W. Tyler

24.1 The Inherently Three-Dimensional Demand Characteristics of Visual Encoding

In order to plan and coordinate actions for foraging, procreation and self-preservation, organisms need a functional representation of the three-dimensional scene layout and of the spatial configuration and dynamics of the objects within it, both in the 2D visual field and in depth. A primary goal of visual encoding is, therefore, to determine the inherently three-dimensional shape structure and motion trajectories of the objects in the surrounding environment.

These demand characteristics pose a problem, however, in relation to the properties of the visual array, such as edge contours, binocular disparity, color, shading, texture, and motion vector fields, which have an entirely different metric structure from that of the spatial configuration of the objects. The laws governing the spatial relationships within these two domains, the physical array and the visual array, are strikingly incompatible. Physically, objects consist of aggregates of particles that cohere together, with empty space (or non-coherent media, such as air or water) between them. Objects may be rigid or flexible, but in either case, a given object is formed from a particular set of particles with invariant connectivity. The visual cues that convey the presence of objects to the brain or to artificial sensing systems, however, share none of these properties. The visual cues may change in luminance or color, and they may be disrupted by reflections or disappear entirely from occlusion by intervening objects. Moreover, the information carried by the multiplicity of visual cues about different aspects of an object may even be non-coherent or disjunctive across the different cues.

In particular, any of these cues may be sparse, with missing information about the object structure across gaps where there are no edge or texture cues to carry

C.W. Tyler (✉)
Brain Imaging Center, Smith-Kettlewell Institute, San Francisco, CA, USA
e-mail: cwt@ski.org

S.J. Dickinson, Z. Pizlo (eds.), *Shape Perception in Human and Computer Vision*,
Advances in Computer Vision and Pattern Recognition,
DOI 10.1007/978-1-4471-5195-1_24, © Springer-Verlag London 2013

Fig. 24.1 Extension of shape
completion by illusory
contours to illusory 3D shape
in the undefined white region

information about the object shape; or ambiguous, where the cue information is consistent with multiple interpretations of the object shape. Nevertheless, despite the sparse, inconsistent, and variable nature of the local cues, we perceive the shape of solid, three-dimensional (3D) objects by interpolating the sparse depth cues into coherent spatial structures generally matching the physical nature of the objects.

In the more restricted domain of the surface structure of objects in the world, surfaces are perceived not just as flat planes in two dimensions, but also as complex manifolds in three dimensions. Here "manifold" is used in the sense of a continuous two-dimensional (2D) subspace of the 3D Euclidean space. A striking example of 3D shape completion is the tetrahedral pyramid that can be seen in the occluded white space in Fig. 24.1. Within the enclosed white area in this figure, there is no information, either monocular (shading, texture gradient, etc.) or binocular (disparity gradient) about the object structure. Yet our perceptual system performs a compelling reconstruction of the 3D shape of the pyramid, based on the monocular cues of the spherical border shapes. This example illustrates the flexibility of the surface-completion mechanism in adapting to the variety of unexpected demands for shape reconstruction. Developing a means of representing the proliferation of 3D object shapes in the world around us is therefore a key stage in the neural representation of the object structure.

It is important to stress that the 3D shape reconstruction of Fig. 24.1 provides a perceptually valid sense of depth and encourages the view that the 3D surface representation is the primary cue to object structure [13, 25]. Objects in the world are typically defined by contours and local features separated by featureless regions (such as the gores, or sectors, of a beach ball, or the smooth skin between facial features). Surface representation is an important stage in the visual coding of shape. The concept of 3D shape representation requires a surface interpolation mechanism to represent the surface shape in regions of the field where the information is undefined. Such interpolation is analogous to the "shrink-wrapping" of a protective membrane around an irregular object such as an item of food or domestic hardware. It takes the information available at defined points and extends a membrane across the regions of empty space between these anchor points. This is the natural way to overcome the sparseness of the representation of object shape on the basis of the available cues to its depth.

24.2 Theoretical Analysis of Shape Representation as Surface Manifolds

It may seem self-evident that the shape of objects is three-dimensional, but it is striking that current computational analysis is largely limited to the 2D projection of object outlines for shape recognition (e.g., [1, 16]). This may be somewhat understandable in applications involving the recognition of static 2D images, such as Internet image search algorithms, but it is even the case for 3D applications in robotics, such as object manipulation routines. Even in these inherently 3D tasks, the requirement to grasp arbitrary object shapes is often addressed by the brute-force approach of storing large numbers of possible 2D views of the likely forms of objects for viewpoint recognition.

With a sufficiently large number of 2D profile representations of the shape, it may seem that they amount to an effective 3D representation, but this is not the case. Each profile is treated as an independent sample of the object and the one best fitting the current image is the sole current representation, with no formal means of combining it with past best fits. This is very different from a full 3D representation of the object form, which would involve an understanding of the dihedral-angle relationships among the surfaces, not just their cross-sectional cuts. Indeed, the truly complete 3D representation would include the array of values of material density at every point in space, as in an MRI scan. However, although this voxel array provides the full 3D data representing the object structure, it does not do so in a form that could be considered a *shape* representation. 'Shape' is some abstracted subset of this full 3D array of structure information, since shape is largely defined by the surface boundary of the structure, which inherently forms a 2D manifold in 3D.

In general, then, the primary meaning of the term 'shape' may thus be conceptualized as the properties of a manifold embedded in a higher-dimensional space. In common usage, it is applied either to one-dimensional manifolds (or loop structures) in two- or higher-dimensional spaces, or to 2D surface manifolds in three or higher-dimensional spaces. In more complex or metaphorical informational representations, such as in the phrase "the shape of things to come", it may be extended to higher dimensional manifolds in the full space of the cultural domain that we inhabit.

24.3 Neural Aspects of 3D Shape Representation

We have seen that the sparse nature of depth cues requires interpolation to determine the surface structure, but what is the nature of interpolation? Although it involves a form of spatial integration, interpolation should be distinguished from the standard

(2D) receptive-field *summation* mechanism, which shows a decreasing response as the amount of stimulus information is reduced. The characteristic of an *interpolation* mechanism, however, is to *increase* its response as stimulus information is reduced, because more extended interpolation is required to cover the empty spaces with defined surface information. In particular, depth interpolation of the 2D surface manifold in 3-space is an essential prerequisite of a full object representation, and one that cannot be replaced by 2D luminance or color interpolation mechanisms [5], since such mechanisms are, by definition, restricted to the frontoparallel plane. Such frontoparallel interpolation cannot represent even slanted surfaces, let alone curved surfaces, which can be either developable or intrinsically curved. These aspects of object structure are inaccessible to traditional surface propagation or 'filling-in' mechanisms [2, 4, 18]. Some neural mechanism is needed for completing the surface manifold on the basis of the depth structure implied by the cues around the edge of the empty regions. Once the 3D interpolation has been used to generate the complex object surfaces from the sparse depth cue information, specification of the 3D object shape requires the relevant shape features to be identified and to be localized relative to each other. Only when the shape features have been both identified and localized can the shape be said to have been encoded.

24.4 Need for the Surface Representation of 3D Shape

If the neural shape representation takes the form of representing shapes in terms of their surface structure, surfaces should play a key role in organizing the perceptual inputs into a coherent shape representation. Such shape recognition is particularly challenging under conditions where the objects could be considered as "sampled" by overlapping noise or partial occlusion—the tiger behind the trees, the face behind the window-curtain. Similarly, the edge features of typical objects, such as the form of a face or the edges of a computer monitor, may be separated by blank regions of many degrees of visual angle. These situations require interpolation, and low-level filter integration can only account for interpolation behavior up to the tiny range of 2–3 arc min in foveal vision [15], scaling proportionately with eccentricity. This limitation raises the "long-range depth interpolation problem" that is still largely unrecognized, although there has been much recent interest in relation to the position coding for extended stimuli, such as Gaussian blobs and Gabor patches [6, 12, 13, 15]. Thus, the interpolation required for specifying the shape of most objects is well beyond the range of the available filters.

To address this problem, Likova and Tyler [13] used a sampling paradigm for object location in which the objects were defined by sampled luminance profiles in the form shown in Fig. 24.2. (Sample positions were randomized to prevent them from being used as the position cue.) This sampled paradigm is a powerful means for probing the properties of the luminance information contributing to shape perception. Surprisingly, the accuracy of localization by humans is almost independent of the sample spacing [11]. In the case of the depth task, the Gaussian profile information is carried both (a) by the luminance of the sample lines (b) the disparity in

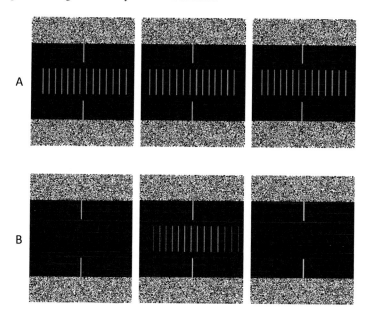

Fig. 24.2 Free-fusion stereogram (three-panel) depicting the sampled Gaussian bulge used by Likova and Tyler [13] to study the depth surface interpolation process. The panels are defined for stereoscopic viewing across pairs of panels, providing both crossed and uncrossed disparity for either a crossed or an uncrossed vergence angle. **A.** Disparity-defined bulge, seen as forward in one panel and recessed in the other, depending on whether vergence is crossed or uncrossed. **B.** Luminance-defined (non-stereoscopic) bulge, arranged for monocular viewing with a black field in the non-viewing eye. Note the strong perceived depth despite the lack of disparity information (or even in the presence of zero-disparity information when viewed directly)

their positions in the two eyes, allowing the separate luminance and disparity depth cues to be combined or segregated as needed. It should be noticeable in Fig. 24.2 that the luminance profile evokes a strong sense of depth as the luminance fades into the black background. Both luminance and disparity profiles were identical Gaussians, and the two types of profiles were always congruent in both peak position and width.

The localization task is depicted in Fig. 24.3. The bars depict the local depth information in the sample bars, and the continuous curve depicts the Bayesian model of the interpolated Gaussian surface that needs to be localized by access to the local depth information, relative to the fiducial markers. (Inspection of Fig. 24.2 should make it clear that the depth is experienced as a floating surface interpolation. Note that this is effectively a cyclopean stimulus [10], in the sense that the bars contain no visible information as to the form of the Gaussian bulge when viewed monocularly. It is only when they are viewed stereoscopically that the form and its depth sign become apparent.)

The task was to assess whether, on any given trial, the interpolated surface peaked to the left or right of the fiducial marker (regardless of the position of the samples). Localization accuracy from disparity alone was as fine as 1–2 arc min, requiring ac-

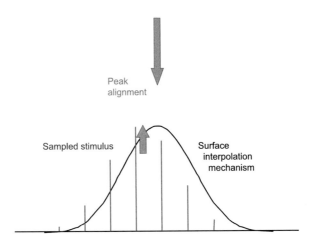

Fig. 24.3 Schematic of the surface interpolation task. The *vertical bars* represent the sampled depth information (luminance, disparity, or both). The *Gaussian curve* represents the perceptual model of the expected surface to be interpolated onto the stimulus. The *up arrow* represents the optimal interpolated location for the peak of the Gaussian, and the *down arrow* represents the fiducial marker against which the peak location needs to be judged

curate interpolation to localize the peak of the function between the samples spaced 16 arc min apart. This performance contrasted with that for pure luminance profiles, which was about ten times worse [13].

The implication to be drawn from these basic results is that some long-range interpolation mechanism is required to determine the 3D shape of extended objects before us. The ability to encode shape is degraded once the details fall outside the range of the local filters. However, the location was still specifiable to a much finer resolution than the sample spacing, implying the operation of an interpolation mechanism to determine the location of the peak of the Gaussian despite the fact that it was not consistently represented within the samples.

Perhaps the most startling aspect of the results was that position discrimination in sampled profiles could be completely nulled by the addition of a slight disparity profile to null the perceived depth from the luminance variation. It should be emphasized that the position information from disparity was identical to the position information from luminance on each trial, so addition of the second cue would be expected to reinforce the ability to discriminate position if the two cues were processed independently. Instead, the nulling of the luminance-based position information by the depth signal implies that the luminance target is processed exclusively through the *depth* interpretation. Once the depth interpretation is nulled by the disparity signal, neither the luminance nor the disparity information supported position discrimination.

This evidence suggests that depth surface reconstruction is the key process in the accuracy of the localization process. It appears that visual patterns defined by different depth cues are interpreted as objects in the process of determining their location. Only an interpolation mechanism operating at the level of a generic depth representation can account for the data. Specifically, a depth interpolation mechanism accounts for the impossibility of position discrimination at the cancellation point and the asymmetric shift of the cancellation point by the luminance cue (Fig. 24.2). The fine resolution of the performance when disparity information is present clearly implies that an interpolation process is involved in the performance, because it is about eight times better than could be supported by the location of the samples alone (even assuming that the sample nearest the peak could be identified from the luminance information; see [13]).

Evidently, the full specification of objects in general requires extensive interpolation to take place, even though some textured objects may be well defined by local information alone. The interpolated position task may therefore be regarded as more representative of real-world localization of objects than the typical Vernier acuity or other line-based localization tasks of the classic literature. It consequently seems remarkable that luminance information, per se, is unable to support localization for objects requiring interpolation. The data indicate that it is only through the interpolated depth representation that the position of the features can be recognized. One might have expected that positional localization would be a spatial form task depending on the primary form processes [14]. The dominance of a depth representation in the performance of such tasks indicates that the depth information is not just an overlay to the 2D sketch of the positional information. Instead, it seems that a full 3D depth reconstruction of the surfaces in the scene must be completed before the position of the object is known.

24.5 Hypercyclopean Form Analysis

The concept of 'hypercyclopean analysis' refers to the level of processing of stereoscopic images defined as cyclopean, and therefore containing no monocular information about the depth form. It is intended to emphasize the need for specific mechanisms for shape encoding once the depth map of the visual scene has been established (as opposed to the cyclopean processes required to establish the depth map). By analogy with the cortical neurons with receptive fields selective for particular properties of the retinal image, there must be higher-level processes in cortex operating as 'receptive fields' encoding the depth structure at the level of the 'cleaned' cyclopean depth image. These receptive fields would have a cyclopean basis, in the sense of having properties specific to the disparity-selective neurons in the cyclopean retina, but would perform a hypercyclopean analysis of the spatial and temporal form of the depth image. Hypercyclopean receptive fields would have characteristics defined in terms of the figural properties of the cyclopean image, but independent of its specific disparity characteristics, i.e., which particular disparity is stimulated at any given retinal location.

A simple example of a cyclopean stimulus is provided in Fig. 24.4, which is an autostereogram of a sinusoidal stereograting originally published by Tyler [24]. Free-fusion of the red dots give the percept of one binocular dot flanked by two

Fig. 24.4 Cyclopean autostereogram of depicting sinusoidal furrows in depth (from [24]). Fuse the *two large central dots* to see one binocular dot flanked by two monocular dots and allow visual processing to operate on the rest of the field while maintaining fixation on the binocular dot

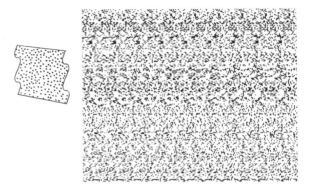

monocular dots will reveal the stereograting embedded in the repeated dot pattern. For those experiencing difficulty with free fusion, a couple of cycles of the stereograting are depicted graphically at left. Again, note that the stereograting is cyclopean in the sense that there is no information defining it in the non-fused dot array. The furrows could be of any orientation or spatial pitch with no visible trace in the dot array when directly viewed.

The existence of a hypercyclopean level of processing can be demonstrated by means of a stereograting adaptation paradigm in which the stereograting is moved continuously across the retina, so as to avoid any stereoscopic depth afterimage. The obtained threshold elevation, which is specific to both spatial frequency and orientation of the adapting grating, therefore must be occurring at a higher level of form processing beyond that of the cyclopean processing for depth per se. Hypercyclopean specificity for adaptation to the spatial frequency content of the cyclopean image was demonstrated by Tyler [23] and Schumer and Ganz [21], for orientation specificity in a cyclopean tilt aftereffect by Tyler [23] and for motion specificity in the form of a motion aftereffect to motion of the purely cyclopean depth image by Papert [17].

The structure of the hypercyclopean form processing channels was measured directly by Tyler and Kontsevich [28] by means of a spatial summation paradigm. They were found to be well-approximated by one-cycle Gabor functions that were generally elongated along the orientation of the cyclopean stimulus (Fig. 24.5), although the summation was isotropic for vertical oriented cyclopean bar stimuli. The detection functions were tuned to the peak frequency of about half a cycle per degree (as expected from the range of sensitivity to cyclopean stimuli; [22]). This depth processing capability was evaluated by Hibbard [7], who used notch cyclopean noise to determine the hypercyclopean orientation bandwidths and found them to be isotropic, implying that the elongated summation fields must follow a (high-level) processing nonlinearity of some kind. These few studies represent only the beginning of the exploration of the hypercyclopean processing domain, which can form the basis for a full paradigm of extended high-level processing investigations.

Another approach to the 2D organization of hypercyclopean processing is to measure stereoscopic (2D) shape discrimination in the form of the just-noticeable difference in aspect ratio for cyclopean rectangles defined entirely by disparity. With

Fig. 24.5 Hypercyclopean processing field in the form of a horizontally-oriented single-cycle Gabor function operating on the cyclopean depth image

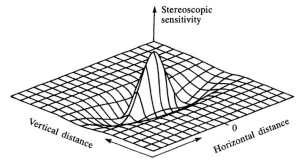

this paradigm, Regan and Hamstra [19] found that aspect ratio discrimination was different for crossed and uncrossed disparities, first decreasing and then leveling out as its disparity increased from zero, while the perceived depth of the rectangle increased smoothly and approximately linearly. The lowest value of aspect ratio discrimination threshold (3 %) was the same for both crossed and uncrossed disparities, and occurred at the disparity limit for the onset of diplopia. The implication here is that larger disparities improved the signal/noise ratio for the shape cue but hit an upper depth limit beyond which it no longer improved. Interestingly, the shape discrimination threshold had a precision better than 1 arc min—an order of magnitude better than the (cyclopean) stereograting resolution. This performance seems to reflect the fact that stereoscopic vision can integrate over long edges to determine detailed shape information even though the local form processing is relatively coarse.

24.6 Metric Constraints on 3D Shape Perception

In generalizing from 2D to 3D shape perception, there are two main issues that need to be considered. One is the issue of the 3D perceptual metric and its distortions in the third dimension relative to two primary dimensions of the visual field, which forms the topic of this section. The other is the core encoding of 3D shape as such, which will be addressed in the next section. The metric issues are commonly discussed in terms of shape judgment, but they are really a precondition for shape perception rather than being an intrinsic property of shape coding. For example, the study by Johnston [9] of the perceived shapes of cylinders at a range of viewing distances showed that the depth form was perceived as remarkably distorted away from the 'sweet spot' of the optimal viewing distance. Johnston interpreted these distortions as a unidimensional failure of the distance encoding metric, an interpretation extended to the depth motion of stereoscopic objects by Scarfe and Hibbard [20]. If the perceived distances in space are non-veridical, the implied distortion of the space metric would translate to a distortion of the 3D shape of the cylinders, being seen as having an elliptical cross-section either flattened or extended relative to the true circular cross-section. This metric distortion hypothesis accounted for the distortions that she measured.

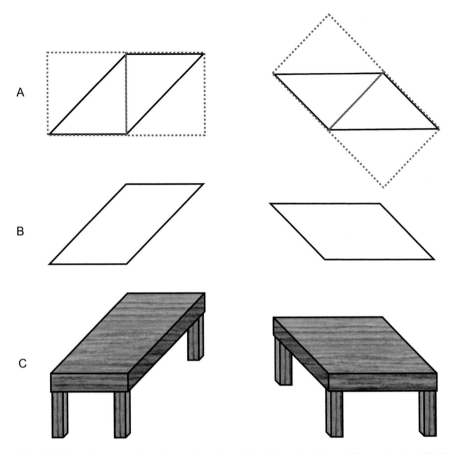

Fig. 24.6 Development of an enhanced version of the Shepard table-top illustration (modified from [26]). The metric structure of the identical parallelograms is maintained throughout the figure, as can be verified with a ruler, despite the strong perceived distortion when incorporated as table tops. The distortion illustrates the power of the depth interpretation to modify perceived shape

In terms of the perceptual shape, a 3D interpretation can give rise to marked illusions in the perceived 2D shape of even simple figures. A striking example is the Shepard table-top illusion analyzed in Fig. 24.6 (modified from [26]). Two parallelograms of the identical 2D shape are shown with a relative 45 deg rotation. Figure 24.6A illustrates the construction geometry of each parallelogram from two right triangles with hypotenuse-to-side ratios of $\sqrt{2} : 1$. When viewed rotated, there is already some shape distortion (Fig. 24.6B), but when the identical shapes are given strong 3D depth cues in the form of box sides and table legs (Fig. 24.6C), the depth illusion generates perceived distortion of the order of $\sqrt{2}$ (~40 %), such that the left-hand tabletop seems to be rectangular with about a 2 : 1 aspect ratio while the right-hand one looks like an oblique square (rhombus). The illustration can be checked with a ruler to ensure that this is a fully perceptual effect and not some fakery in the illustration.

Quantitatively, the two tabletops would need to be slanted in depth by a 45° dihedral angle relative to the orientation of the page (or monitor surface) in order to generate the observed degree of shape distortion. The implication is that the 45° angle of the parallelogram sides would need to translate to the same angle in depth in order to account for the strength of the illusion. Moreover, the shape has to be assessed as if viewed from directly above the surface, as though we had rotated our position in space by the same angle as the surface rotation to assess the intrinsic shape of the two tabletops independent of their physical orientation.

Note all these depth compensation processes are taking place despite the fact that the tabletop images have conflicted perspective cues, in that the receding sides remain parallel rather than converging, as should be expected by the rules of linear perspective. The tabletops are thus subject to the 'Chinese perspective' distortion that the rear edges appear wider than the front edges. It might be expected that the perceived aspect-ratio distortion would be even stronger if perspective were introduced, but this would violate the format requirement that the two shapes remain identical. (Note, conversely, that the legs seem to be subject to the *opposite* illusion of seeming shorter in the back, a novel effect analyzed by Tyler [26]).

The general point is that this illusion is a strong example of what Gregory [3] termed 'inappropriate constancy scaling'. It is 'inappropriate' in the sense that the explicit task is a 2D shape evaluation, while the depth cues force a slanted 3D interpretation that intrudes into the process to scale the perceived shape as though it were slanted in 3D. What is surprising is that we do not see the image as having much of an explicitly 3D slant. It is very clearly being displayed in a flat, 2D format on the printed page (or computer monitor). Even if asked to suspend the knowledge that the image is displayed on the printed page, most viewers would say that they look like cardboard cutouts with a depth of about a quarter of the height, not nearly enough to account for the illusory slant. Unlike the Johnston [9] 3D shape experiment, therefore, the perceived depth does not appear to be sufficient to account for the strength of the illusory shape distortion. The implication is that there is some intermediate stage of 'pictorial depth' at which the depth structure of images is understood but not perceived. This pictorial depth structure is not the same process as the cognitive assessment of the physical depth of the display being viewed, or as the perceptual assessment of the local depth actually invoked in the region of the image being queried.

This triple conceptualization of human depth processing is encapsulated in the diagram of Fig. 24.7. The diagram begins with the early processing modules for five types of depth cue, which are treated as feeding with differential weights into mid-level modules for three types of depth processing: the perceived depth experienced by the viewer, the pictorial depth understanding in viewing pictures and photographs, and the cognitive understanding of the physical depth of flatness (or otherwise) of the image support medium (the paper, wall, canvas or screen displaying the image). Under optimal viewing conditions, the cognitive understanding of flatness may be overcome by the strength of the depth cues such that the image

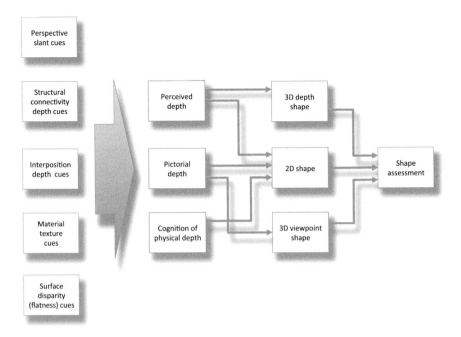

Fig. 24.7 Schematic of the three-level processing scheme required to account for the perceptual experience of illusions such as that in Fig. 24.6. Differential weights from the array of depth cues (*large arrow*) form the input to three types of depth processing: perceived depth, pictorial depth and the cognition of physical depth (or physical distance structure). These depth encoding processes in turn feed the estimation of three aspects of 3D shape processing: depth shape, 2D frontal shape and projected perpendicular viewpoint shape, each of which can be quantitatively assessed for the requisite psychophysical task

is experienced as having physical depth. This achievement is termed *trompe l'oeil* (fooling the eye), and is usually followed by some probe action such as moving to see if the perceived scene undergoes the corresponding transformation. If it does not, the cognitive interpretation of flatness is reinstated even though the vivid depth impression remains.

In terms of the shape assessment task that is the explicit processing goal, three types are identified in the above discussion. (1) One is the assessment 3D depth shape, as for the cylinders of Johnston [9], which depends purely on the perceived depth derived from the concatenation of the various depth cues (and perhaps others not mentioned). (2) The effects of depth variables on the assessment of 2D shape is an old issue going back to at least the Holway and Boring [8] study of the perceived (projected, or retinal) shape of an obliquely-viewed circle. There the emphasis was on the fact that this assessment is affected not only by the perceived depth and the knowledge of the physical depth (i.e., that it is lying on a physically flat floor), but is also influenced by the perspective and other pictorial depth cues even when the perceived depth is relatively nullified by various cues to flatness, as in the case of the Shepard illusion in Fig. 24.6. Note that this interpretation implies that the same array of initial depth cues may be processed with different weights into the perceived depth and pictorial depth components of the system.

(3) The final form of shape assessment is of the 3D viewpoint shape, i.e., the 'true' physical shape assessed from a viewpoint perpendicular to its surface. To determine this shape from the optic array requires a veridical assessment of its depth, and is often considered characteristic of children's drawings and the Cubist approach to 20th century painting, depicting shapes "as you know they are rather than as you see them". This is shown in Fig. 24.7 as having input from the pictorial depth component only, since it requires this level of reconstruction of the viewpoint shape, disregarding the physical form of the surface and the net perceived shape, but in practice it may have distorting influences from either or both of them. Overall, this scheme implies an extended array of quantitative studies to verify the existence of this triple scheme and the proposed interactions between them.

24.7 Cortical Organization of 3D Shape Representation

A key question is which part of the visual hierarchy houses the neural apparatus for the various aspects of depth processing? One part of the answer is the representation of depth structure, which was provided by the results of a study of cyclopean disparity structure by Tyler et al. [29]. An example of the activation to static bars of disparity (presented in a dynamic noise field, with a flat disparity plane in the same dynamic noise as the null stimulus) is shown in Fig. 24.8. Notice that the early retinotopic hierarchy delineated by the red, green and blue outlines is not differentially activated at all by this stimulus contrast, implying that it is equally activated by both the test and null noise fields, regardless of the presence of disparity structure. The only patches of coherent activation (at the required statistical criterion level) are in the dorsal retinotopic areas V3A and V3B and in lateral cortex posterior to V5, in a cortical region identified as KO by the standard localizer for kinetic borders [30]. Not shown here is the control stimuli for several kinds of luminance-defined borders, which did not activate KO but did activate the V3AB complex.

Why should the same area be activated by both motion-defined borders and (static) disparity-defined borders, but not luminance-defined borders? If it were responsive to border structure per se, it should respond to all three types of borders, but that is the role played by the V3AB complex (as was also the case for purely dynamic texture-defined borders [13]. The KO region, on the other hand, was only activated by the motion- and disparity-defined borders, which have neither motion nor disparity in common between them. However, the factor that they do have in common is perceived depth structure, since the motion-defined borders usually elicit a strong percept of depth separation between the two directions of motion. We are justified in concluding that this particular region of the lateral occipital complex is specialized for the processing of perceived depth structure per se (as distinct from motion structure, disparity structure or luminance structure). For this reason, we have proposed renaming it the Occipital Depth Structure (ODS) region. What role it plays in 3D shape processing, and how it relates to the stages delineated in Fig. 24.6, however, remain to be determined.

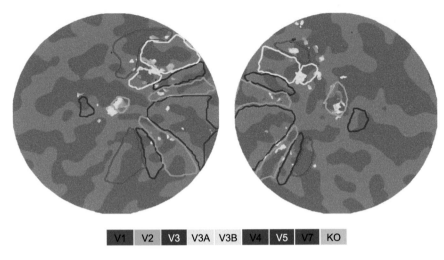

V1 V2 V3 V3A V3B V4 V5 V7 KO

Fig. 24.8 Functional MRI flatmaps of the posterior pole of the two hemispheres of a typical subject showing the synchronized response to stereoscopic structure (*yellowish phases*) localized to fovealV3A/B (*yellow outlines*) and area KO (*cyan outlines*) (From [29])

24.8 Conclusion

This brief overview of the components of the human processing of 3D shape has attempted to lay the groundwork for a fuller investigation of the topic, and to provide a framework for further conceptualization of the various processing modules that need to be considered in accounting for the range of perceptual phenomena involved. In doing so, I have been motivated by the underlying question of how to think about the nature of 3D shape. As laid out in Tyler and Kontsevich [27], the key to thinking about any perceptual domain is first to identify the cardinal dimensions of its representational space and then to identify the channel structure (or 'primitives') of the processing throughout the representational space. In the case of 3D shape, this space is not the easily conceptualized 3D space that the shapes inhabit, but the much larger configurational space of all recognizable 3D shapes. In this context, 'shape' is obviously a conceptual abstraction to fit within the relatively limited cognitive window. When thinking about a hedge, one does not speak of the 'shape' of the concatenation of all the leaves in a hedge, which would be far too complex to attempt to describe. To be accessible within our cognitive capacities, the concept of 'shape' is restricted to the hedge as a whole. Marr [14], for example, proposed to restrict it to the concatenation of generalized cylinders. But the variety of 3D shape configurations seems endless, and one can always think of counterexamples to any given representational scheme. In fact, the universe of 3D shapes could be considered to be coextensive with the universe of actual and imaginable objects, since every object must have a shape. On the other hand, since we can talk of spheres, cubes, and so on, independently of the specific objects exhibiting those shapes, there must be some level of coding of shape into superordinate categories, and we can also extend this to metric deformation of the shapes, as into ellipsoids, cuboids, and so on, which incorporate many different proportions into the same shape descriptor. It is not the goal of the present remarks to attempt to resolve either the dimensionality or the neural processing structure of the domain of '3D shape', but to point out that it seems to be a large-scale problem that few have attempted to address, and perhaps to stimulate further efforts in this direction.

Acknowledgement   Supported by FA9550-09-1-0678.

References

1. Chum O, Philbin J, Sivic J, Isard M, Zisserman A (2007) Total recall: automatic query expansion with a generative feature model for object retrieval. In: Proc ICCV 07, Rio de Janeiro, Brazil, pp 1–8
2. Gerrits HJ, Vendrik AJ (1970) Simultaneous contrast, filling-in process and information processing in man's visual system. Exp Brain Res 11:411–430
3. Gregory RL (1963) Distortion of visual space as inappropriate constancy scaling. Nature 199:678–680
4. Grossberg S, Kuhlmann L, Mingolla E (2007) A neural model of 3D shape-from-texture: multiple-scale filtering, boundary grouping, and surface filling-in. Vis Res 47:634–672
5. Grossberg S, Yazdanbakhsh A (2005) Laminar cortical dynamics of 3D surface perception: stratification, transparency, and neon color spreading. Vis Res 45:1725–1743
6. Hess RF, Holliday IE (1992) The coding of spatial position by the human visual system: effects of spatial scale and contrast. Vis Res 32:1085–1097
7. Hibbard PB (2005) The orientation bandwidth of cyclopean channels. Vis Res 45:2780–2785
8. Holway AE, Boring EG (1941) Determinants of apparent visual size with distance variant. Am Psychol 51:21–37
9. Johnston EB (1991) Systematic distortions of shape from stereopsis. Vis Res 31:1351–1360
10. Julesz B (1971) Foundations of cyclopean perception. University of Chicago Press, Chicago
11. Kontsevich LK, Tyler CW (1998) How much of the visual object is used in estimating its position? Vis Res 38:3025–3029
12. Levi DM, Klein SA, Wang H (1994) Discrimination of position and contrast in amblyopic and peripheral vision. Vis Res 34:3293–3313
13. Likova LT, Tyler CW (2003) Peak localization of sparsely sampled luminance patterns is based on interpolated 3D surface representation. Vis Res 43:2649–2657
14. Marr D (1982) Vision: a computational investigation into the human representation and processing of visual information. Freeman, New York
15. Morgan MJ, Watt RJ (1982) Mechanisms of interpolation in human spatial vision. Vis Res 25:1661–1674
16. Ovsjanikov M, Bronstein AM, Bronstein MM, Guibas LJ (2009) ShapeGoogle: a computer vision approach for invariant shape retrieval. In: Proc workshop on nonrigid shape analysis and deformable image alignment NORDIA, Kyoto, Japan, pp 320–327
17. Papert S (1964) Stereoscopic synthesis as a technique for locating visual mechanisms. MIT Q Pro Rep 73:239–243
18. Paradiso MA, Nakayama K (1991) Brightness perception and filling-in. Vis Res 31:1221–1236
19. Regan D, Hamstra SJ (1994) Shape discrimination for rectangles defined by disparity alone, by disparity plus luminance and by disparity plus motion. Vis Res 34:2277–2291
20. Scarfe P, Hibbard PB (2006) Disparity-defined objects moving in depth do not elicit three-dimensional shape constancy. Vis Res 46:1599–1610
21. Schumer RD, Ganz L (1979) Independent stereoscopic channels for different extents of spatial pooling. Vis Res 19:1303–1314

22. Tyler CW (1974) Depth perception in disparity gratings. Nature 251:140–142
23. Tyler CW (1975) Stereoscopic tilt and size aftereffects. Perception 4:187–192
24. Tyler CW (1983) Sensory processing of binocular disparity. In: Schor CM, Ciuffreda KJ (eds) Basic and clinical aspects of binocular vergence eye movements. Butterworth, Stoneham, pp 199–295
25. Tyler CW (2006) Spatial form as inherently three-dimensional. In: Jenkin MRM, Harris LR (eds) Seeing spatial form. Oxford University Press, Oxford, pp 67–88
26. Tyler CW (2011) Paradoxical perception of surfaces in the Shepard tabletop illusion. i-Perception 2:137–141
27. Tyler CW, Kontsevich LL (1995) Mechanisms of stereoscopic processing: stereoattention and surface perception in depth reconstruction. Perception 24:127–153
28. Tyler CW, Kontsevich LL (2001) Stereoprocessing of cyclopean depth images: horizontally elongated summation fields. Vis Res 41:2235–2243
29. Tyler CW, Likova LT, Kontsevich LL, Wade AR (2006) The specificity of cortical area KO to depth structure. NeuroImage 30:228–238
30. Van Oostende S, Sunaert S, Van Hecke P, Marchal G, Orban GA (1997) The kinetic occipital (KO) region in man: an fMRI study. Cereb Cortex 7:690–701

Chapter 25
The Role of Shape in Visual Recognition

Björn Ommer

25.1 Regularity, Structure, and Form

Our interaction with the world is constantly defined by the structure and characteristics of the objects around us, in particular by their form. This is only possible
since our world exhibits an astounding degree of regularity. Let us now survey the
prevalence of structure and the implications this has on cognition. Regardless, what
scale we observe our universe on, order and regularity are evident everywhere. On
a large scale, orderless clouds of matter condense due to gravitational attraction to
form stars, stellar systems, and eventually galaxies consisting of billions of stars.
On a scale that is directly accessible with our eyes we can, for instance, observe the
complex, ordered patterns and forms exhibited by animals, plants, and non-living
matter on earth. Examples are the symmetry and self-similarity featured by ferns,
sea stars, or snowflakes. Finally, on an even smaller scale, the highly complex structure of DNA controls the development, functioning, and eventually the form of all
living organisms. Moreover, the temporal domain features periodical structures such
as the hydrologic cycle, the ever repeating seasons of the year, or our heartbeat.

It is astonishing that such complex, highly ordered structure even exists, since
the second law of thermodynamics implies that the entropy (the degree of "disor-
der") of an isolated system—the universe in the most general case—is monotonically increasing. Moreover, not only the mere existence of order and structure, but
its robustness to disrupting factors is as striking as it is necessary for the existence of
life and our world as we know it. Consequently, it is self-evident that regularity and
structure also play an important role in human thinking. Man has always been striv-
ing for a limited set of simple rules, laws, or relationships that, together with some
simple physical entities, would explain complex entities and thereby make the world
comprehensible. When investigating these laws of nature, the scientific method has

B. Ommer (✉)
Heidelberg Collaboratory for Image Processing (HCI) & Interdisciplinary Center for Scientific
Computing (IWR), University of Heidelberg, Heidelberg, Germany
e-mail: ommer@uni-heidelberg.de

S.J. Dickinson, Z. Pizlo (eds.), *Shape Perception in Human and Computer Vision*,
Advances in Computer Vision and Pattern Recognition,
DOI 10.1007/978-1-4471-5195-1_25, © Springer-Verlag London 2013

always exploited the regularity and order of our world. Seminal examples are the discovery of Newton's law of universal gravitation, which applies to apples as it does to extraterrestrial bodies like the moon and the prediction of the periodic table of (then mostly unknown) elements by Mendeleev. Consequently, only the regularity and order of our world makes it possible to learn from the past about the future, thus rendering learning and inference feasible.

25.1.1 The Nature of Shape

Recognizing objects and dealing with them depends on their structure and characteristics. With our different senses we observe different modalities and, thus, different properties of objects. For visual perception the most important features are appearance and shape. Whereas appearance comprises aspects such as the reflectivity, color, and texture, shape represents the form or Gestalt of objects. Commonly shape is thought of as a feature of the object silhouette, e.g., the form of a boundary contour [25, 44, 57] or region [3], whereas appearance describes the properties of the face of the surface surrounded by the boundary. Thus, both can be seen as dual characteristics of an object, one being based on contour shape, the other on region appearance. Nevertheless, other notions of shape beyond the form of boundary contours have been utilized as well, such as the spatial configuration of patches in part-based models, for example, [21, 22, 33, 42], or the spatial layout of landmark points in procrustes analysis [17]. Given a set of image patches or coordinates of landmark points, we need to combine all these distributed observations to obtain a representation of the object (this is the *binding problem* in perception [45]) and segregate them from spurious clutter. Individual local features typically do not contain sufficient information about an object and, thus, there is a large *semantic gap* [51] between local measurements and semantic concepts such as object categories. In this context, shape can be thought of as the "glue" that combines all local features by ensuring a sound overall spatial layout and thereby capturing the co-occurrence of all features. This spatial structure or geometric configuration of an object is commonly referred to as its *shape* [8, 17, 29, 50, 52]). Kendall [29] has given an informal definition of shape that has been aptly paraphrased by Dryden and Mardia [17]:

> *Shape* is all the geometrical information that remains when location, scale and rotational effects are filtered out from an object.

Visual object recognition requires then to solve the *correspondence problem*— features of a test image have to be matched against the descriptors of a learned representation, for example, the complete boundary contour, patches, or keypoints. For an optimal assignment of query features to model features, local descriptor correspondences as well as the global spatial structure need to be handled at the same time [5]. The matching process is based on the assumption that objects do not scatter features arbitrarily in an image. This assumption is in turn founded on the structure and regularity of the visual world.

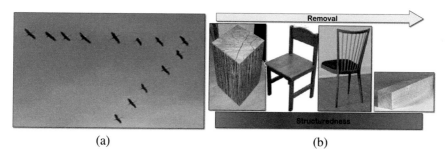

(a)   (b)

Fig. 25.1 The emergence of shape. (**a**) The triangular shape of the flock of birds is an emergent property that is not inherent in any of its components, i.e., no individual bird exhibits the characteristic of the triangle, only their ensemble does. (**b**) When removing parts of the block of wood, structure starts to emerge and it persists even when individual parts such as the leg of the chair are lost. A further removal, however, destroys the structure again

The Special Role of Shape: Invariance and Emergence   Among all visual characteristics, shape plays a special role. As indicated by Kendall's definition, shape is not only invariant to geometric transformations such as translation, rotation, and scaling. It is also invariant to changes of appearance, that is, varying illumination, reflectivity, color, or texture. Therefore, shape is crucial for rendering vision robust to our ever-changing environment and it is key to enable recognition in adverse situations such as under low light.

Shape is, however, special in another respect. Whereas appearance can be directly perceived or measured by (semi-)locally observing brightness, color, or texture, shape cannot be captured directly. The shape of a hand is not immanent in any image pixel or edge; neither is it captured by individual photoreceptors or the receptive fields of retinal ganglion cells. Similarly, the triangular form of the flock of birds in Fig. 25.1(a) is not inherent in any single bird. So how can we represent shape, if it cannot be measured directly? Shape is an *emergent* property that only evolves from the ensemble of foreground stimuli once background clutter has been suppressed. Therefore, perception and modeling of shape directly depend on several other processes that are mutually interlinked. A *grouping* of foreground parts is needed to obtain object shape and *segmentation* segregates foreground from distractors. Grouping again consists of a data-driven bottom-up process and a top-down registration based on learned object models. As argued by Gestalt psychology [55], there exist cognitive processes of perceptual organization that follow the law of *Prägnanz* thereby seeking simple, robust groupings. Gestalt laws such as *good continuation* or *closure* yield a purely data-driven grouping that is directly based on the visual stimulus (Fig. 25.2 left). However, there are also complex grouping processes that require object knowledge and reasoning about them such as Fig. 25.2 right. These processes are in the spirit of cognitivism and they present a correspondence problem, that is, registering parts of the stimulus to previously learned object models.

Finally, shape is robust with respect to missing parts and clutter. As can be seen in Fig. 25.1(b), the operation of part removal creates structure and eventually annihi-

Fig. 25.2 *Left*: Kaizsa
triangle, illusionary contours
due to data-driven, bottom-up
perceptual grouping. *Right*:
young/old lady, ambiguous
optical illusion due to
top-down reasoning

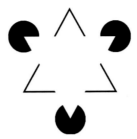

lates it. Removing clutter lets structure (the shape of a chair) emerge. This structure
is robust to further removal of object parts, but eventually it disappears and we are
again left with a mere block of wood. Robustness with respect to missing parts
depends on the content of the parts. As argued by Attneave [2], points of high curvature are especially informative. [6] has proposed psychophysical experiments that
underline this claim and Fig. 25.3 demonstrates how the recognition system of [47]
approximates shape using a sparse representation with variable degree of detail.

25.2 Shape Representation for Visual Recognition

Computer-based object recognition has been actively pursued for half a century and
a wide range of shape representations have been investigated. Over these years of
research on shape models for visual recognition, several major trends evolved, disappeared, and reappeared again. Let us now review these broad movements and the
influence they had on vision research.

25.2.1 The Days of Geometry: Blocks, Cylinders, and Acronyms

The first artificial object recognition systems entered the stage in the late 1950s,
adopting ideas from signal processing, formal logic, and statistics and being tightly
linked to the then newly proposed theme of artificial intelligence coined by John Mc-
Carthy and Marvin Minsky at the Dartmouth conference of 1956. 1963 can then be

Fig. 25.3 Shape is robust with respect to missing parts and shape information is predominantly
concentrated at points of high curvature. Example sparse shape representation taken from [47]

viewed as the real advent of the field when L.G. Roberts [46] presented his recognition system and proposed an edge detector, a line fitting, and a feature grouping procedure. To facilitate these first big steps into computer vision with the limited hardware resources of the day, significant simplifying assumptions were made. Systems were confined to a *blocks world* consisting of only polyhedral shapes on uniform background. While these restrictions enabled a sound theoretical investigation, they lead to vision algorithms that were founded on numerous unrealistic assumptions. Thus, later research tried to alleviate these restrictions by allowing for more and more complex scenes. Examples are Guzman's system [25] for recognizing 2-D curved object line drawings and Binford's *generalized cylinders* [7] that were taking curved shapes to 3-D. Based on the generalized cylinders, Brooks [10] constructed the symbolic reasoning system *ACRONYM* that utilized geometric constraints to prove the existence of parameterized configurations. Biederman [6] then proposed *geons*, a universally applicable dictionary of volumetric primitives for compositional recognition. To bridge the gap between 2-D images and the 3-D world, Marr [37] introduced the primal sketch and the $2\frac{1}{2}$-D sketch. While many of these early systems were limited by requiring bottom-up extraction of object boundaries, Lowe's *SCERPO* system [35] directly searches for non-accidental combinations of edgels. A main theme of research in these days was model-based vision by posing recognition as a correspondence problem between a model and contours in the image, e.g., [27]. However, with *aspect graphs* the orthogonal movement of view-based approaches started in the 1970s (e.g., [30] and see [16] for a later bridge between aspect graphs and geons) although it was later discovered that this framework suffers from severe complexity issues. Moreover, *moment invariants* [26] received considerable interest in this era, but later this theme lost momentum due to limited representational power in case of only a single view.

All in all a main theme of the 1960s–1980s was geometry especially based on the shape of boundary contours. Moreover, representations were typically hierarchical and object centered.

25.2.2 *The Dawn of Appearance*

As a response to setbacks of geometric approaches based on object boundary shape and with improvements in computational resources, the 1990s saw the rise of appearance methods. By applying principle component analysis to the intensity image, Turk and Pentland removed noisy dimensions and obtained *eigenfaces* [53]. More general eigenspace representations were analyzed by [39] and in the comparison by [11] template matching was superior to keypoint geometry. However, global image transformations such as translation, scaling, or illumination changes have to be removed in a preprocessing stage before applying appearance models such as the PCA-based approach. Therefore, sliding window procedures [48] or cascaded evaluation [54] are typically used. Moreover, the holistic object representation (the complete object is represented as one appearance patch of intensity values) leads to models of high complexity and renders them fragile with regard to variability in spatial structure as is the case for articulated objects. To address the latter problem, *deformable template matching* has been introduced [58] and prototypical deformations have been captured by *active appearance models* [12]. This approach compensates for variations in the spatial structure by applying a global transformation when matching templates. Another solution that is currently very popular are *part-based models* in spirit of the approach by Fischler and Elschlager [24]. These models represent an object as consisting of a number of specific parts that feature characteristic spatial structure which can be modeled using a graph [31], a joint constellation model of all parts [22], or with probabilistic Hough voting [33].

In retrospective it can be observed how early contributions in the era of appearance models have abandoned spatial structure and shape only to see it reappear a few years later to handle articulation. Nevertheless, the main focus has been on appearance and compared to the previous geometric period, shape representation has become significantly more coarse, e.g., part-based models sampled at few interest points. Moreover, the view-based paradigm and shallow structures have dominated.

25.2.3 Textons Everywhere

The turn of the millennium clearly marks the advent of powerful semi-local feature descriptors and interest point detectors. Compared to appearance patches that represent objects as a matrix of intensities or colors, these features gained invariance to geometric deformations, illumination changes, and noise by histogramming over edge pixels and their orientations, thereby again picking up the idea of *textons* [28]. The influential *SIFT* features introduced by David Lowe in [34] were followed by numerous other descriptors such as *shape context* [4] and *histograms of oriented gradients (HOG)* [14]. Popular object representations built upon these descriptors were *bag-of-feature models* [13], and models based on probabilistic latent semantic analysis such as [49]. These approaches model only feature co-occurrence and completely disregard spatial structure. By evaluating separate bag-of-features in cells of a regular grid, spatial pyramid kernels were used in [32] to add rigid grid-like structure to this framework. In effect, this led again to a classical rigid template matching approach—this time however with bag-of-features over image sites replacing the intensity values of image pixels. To obtain additional flexibility to geometric deformations, Felzenszwalb et al. [20] combined rigid, regular-grid-like templates with part-based models. All of these template-based approaches utilize sliding windows. However, scanning over all locations and scales and evaluating a classifier is not only computationally costly but also lacks psychophysical motivation. These issues are tackled by voting methods such as [36, 43].

Texton features have successfully addressed the invariance issues of appearance patches. The potential of these powerful descriptors inspired early models like bag-of-features that abandoned spatial structure altogether, which returned later on again. However, compared to the geometric era, the spatial models were fairly simple, that is, rigid templates, subsequently extended by star-shaped part models in the currently popular approach of [20]. All in all the root filter of the currently successful approach of [20] is a mere texton template—the whole object is represented as a spatially varying texture (cf. Fig. 25.4(b)), same being true for the parts as well.

25.2.4 Half a Century of Evolution—A Critique

Looking back on the development of shape models for visual recognition, some interesting trends become apparent. There have obviously been orthogonal movements as well, but these could be seen as the mainstream developments of the field.

Complexity of Shape Models   Whereas the early years saw a focus on rich object shape and scene models [40], currently popular representations such as [20] describe objects as a mere texton. After only a few years of development, Roberts [46] had invented many of the key components of modern recognition systems in 1963. Some 15 years later, models that contained almost anything up to a complete scene interpretation had been proposed [40], Fig. 25.4(a). Moving another 30 years forward in time and comparing these rich models of the 1970s with the currently popular, template-like texton models (e.g., Fig. 25.4(b)) this could be seen as a great setback. However, the judgment depends on the vantage point and requires further discussion. So what went wrong, what right, and why?

Real World Benchmarks and Performance   Although the representation of shape has become less intricate, there has been a dramatic improvement in performance. Whereas blocks world (Fig. 25.4(c)) and other early scenarios used for system evaluation were artificial and simplistic, present day benchmarks made significant steps towards the real world recognition challenge, cf. Fig. 25.4(d). Rather than detecting blocks in front of uniform background, multi-scale detection of diverse object categories in cluttered natural scenes [19] has become a main theme, thus dealing with difficult problems such as large intra-class variability, many categories, segmentation of clutter, and multi-scale detection. Despite this positive development it should however be noted that several of the simpler problems in less realistic scenes are still unsolved, that benchmarks such as [19] are also only caricatures of reality, and, most importantly, they are blending numerous unsolved problems of vision and do not allow to evaluate the progress on individual subproblems.

Dimensionality and Flexibility   While there has been a trend towards less complex shape models, the complexity of the low-level descriptors has increased enormously. Simple parametrized surfaces were followed by PCA applied to appearance templates before texton features became popular and increased dimensionality from 128-D (SIFT) over 10 000-D [20] to over 160 000-D in [15]. Dealing with this high

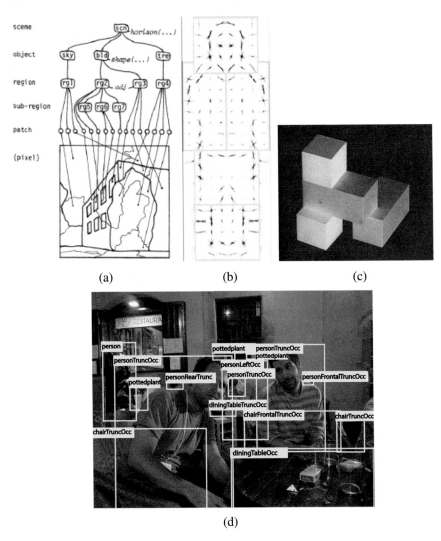

Fig. 25.4 (a) Full-up scene interpretation from the 1970s, [40] and (b) currently popular, template-like texton models [20]. (c) Benchmark problems of the early days, e.g., blocks world and (d) present day recognition benchmarks such as PASCAL VOC [19]

dimensionality became only possible by adopting landmark contributions from machine learning and pattern recognition such as kernel methods. However, given the limited amount of training and test data, curse of dimensionality is a serious concern in light of these developments. Nevertheless, there are also very promising developments. Compared to simple condition-action-rules such as the production rules of [40], machine learning has lead to flexible systems that automatically adapt to training data.

25.3 Quo Vadis?

Visual object recognition has made great progress, especially in terms of the realism of its benchmark problems, the flexibility of the developed systems, and the retrieval performance. However, there has been a shift in mainstream research to focus on much coarser and less accurate shape representations than in the early days and on high-dimensional low-level descriptors. Many reasons including practicability (complex low-level features are readily available), universality (coarse structure models make less restricting assumptions), and feasibility (simpler structure models can be easily adapted from the literature) have led to this trend. Nevertheless, using textons to represent complete objects and their shape is obviously only a very crude approximation. In effect the rich spatial structure of shape is basically treated as a mere texton, cf. Fig. 25.4(b).

25.3.1 Shape: Representing Statistical Dependencies Between Parts

We have seen that shape is an emergent property that captures statistical dependencies between local features by aggregating descriptors, for example, those that lie along object boundaries. However, commonly used part-based methods such as propabilistic Hough voting [33, 36] fail to model these dependencies and simply treat heavily overlapping features that are sampled close to another as being independent. Voting then sums over the mutually dependent feature votes. The same critique also applies to sliding windows based on texton templates such as the popular approach [20]. By utilizing a linear classifier to combine the cells of the rootfilter (nonlinear classification is not feasible due to complexity), mutual dependencies cannot be learned. Consequently, the two most common approaches to visual object detection—voting and sliding window texton templates—are treating objects to be a mere sum of their parts, cf. [56]. This assumption is against the fundamental conviction of Gestalt theory that the whole object is different from the sum of its parts [55] and that shape emerges from all constituents by explicitly capturing mutual part relationships.

Compositionality   We cannot measure shape directly in an image. Neither are joint models of all parts such as constellation models [22] feasible for the usually large quantities of parts. How can we then model part dependencies effectively in a way that lets shape emerge? To bridge the large gap between local features and holistic object shape, hierarchical approaches have been proposed. These were highly popular in the early days when only weak features such as edges or geometric primitives were used. Hierarchies then lost momentum with the arrival of powerful features when some vision problems could be addressed on the level of features without reasoning about more complex object structure (e.g., bag-of-features). Recently, however, compositional methods have shown to be effective in combining local descriptors in hierarchies that culminate in a holistic representation of object structure with all its flexibility. *Compositionality* refers to the prominent ability of human cognition to represent entities as hierarchies of meaningful and generic parts. As demonstrated by Biederman [6], the atomic constituents are usually much simpler than the scenarios described by their compositions. Moreover, these parts are generic so that they can be used for representing numerous object categories, thus being essential for the flexibility of human cognition. The power of compositionality is not rooted in the atomic parts but stems from modeling the dependencies between the parts. In particular, seeking *non-accidental* [35] part relationships renders vision robust with regard to clutter and object variability. Written language can for instance be represented with just a mere 26 letters, where meaning is not inherent in individual characters but only results from their compositions, i.e., words and sentences.

Based on these ideas, a compositional system for category-level recognition has been presented in [41]. Using the Gestalt laws of perceptual organization, candidate compositions are formed. Then a discriminative strategy is employed to retain only characteristic compositions. This unsupervised discovery of mid-level discriminative compositions [41, 42] establishes a layer of intermediate abstractions in the resulting hierarchy. In [42] a graphical model combines multiple layers of compositions and scene context while learning follows a Bayesian approach and is based on cross-validation. Whereas these methods learn the compositional structure without supervision, poselets [9] have followed-up on these ideas by requiring additional supervision information for labeling object specific compositions. Fidler et al. [23] have build a hierarchy of constellation models to speed-up multi-class classification.

A Compositional Shortcut   Compositional hierarchies are ideal for representing object structure by modeling relationships between parts. However, we cannot merely stack an arbitrary number of layers on top of each other and expect a functioning hierarchy. Noise and other disturbances at the feature level can be amplified by successive representation layers. Consequently, a recent development has been to avoid arbitrarily deep hierarchies by iteratively optimizing a single layer of compositions. In [56], this is achieved by integrating compositionality into Hough voting. Rather than incorrectly assuming parts to be independent, dependent parts are grouped while solving the correspondence problem and forcing all parts within the resulting compositions to agree on a concerted object hypothesis, Fig. 25.5(a). As a result three key problems of vision are addressed jointly, (i) grouping object parts into meaningful compositions, (ii) establishing correspondences between query object and training samples, and (iii) foreground/background segregation. To avoid bottom-up grouping altogether, [57] applies maximum margin multiple instance learning to obtain a dictionary of meaningful contours. Shape is then represented by learning the consistent joint placement of all these contours, Fig. 25.5(b). Object detection and the assembling of their shape are addressed simultaneously. Contour co-activation captures part dependencies and a discriminative approach yields consistent joint placements of all model contours. The dual problem of shape-based compositional region grouping has been addressed in [38]. Finally, compositionality and shape are not limited to representing individual objects. [1] has presented

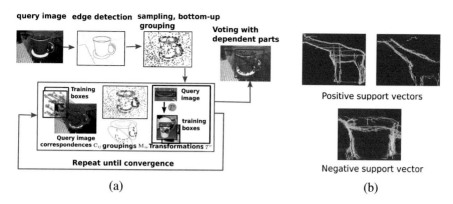

query image   edge detection   sampling, bottom-up grouping

Voting with dependent parts

Positive support vectors

Negative support vector

(a)   (b)

Fig. 25.5 (**a**) Compositions by grouping dependent parts and solving the correspondence problem [56]. (**b**) Learning discriminative joint placements of contours yields object shape (sample support vectors for giraffes) [57]

a video parsing approach to abnormality detection. They parse complete scenes by establishing a set of shapes that jointly represent all the foreground, thereby taking interactions between object shapes into account.

25.4 Conclusion and Outlook

Among all visual characteristics, shape is of crucial importance. Shape exhibits important invariance properties, unites heterogeneous scattered features, and captures the holistic structure of objects. Being an emergent property, shape cannot be measured directly, thus rendering its representation challenging. Consequently, a large body of vision research has focused on modeling object structure during the last half century. Broad trends during this time were (i) a geometric era with an emphasis on spatial structure, boundary contours, hierarchies, and model-based approaches, (ii) appearance models with comparably coarse shape representation, shallow structures, and a view-based paradigm, and recently (iii) an era of powerful texton-based features with bag-of-features, part-based models, and texton templates. Over the years the performance of vision systems, the complexity of recognition benchmarks, and the flexibility of the learning algorithms has increased, significantly. Compared to the early days there is, however, an emphasis on relatively coarse models of object shape (to the point of treating shape as a spatially varying texture) and a trend towards ever increasing dimensionality (addressed in [18]). Moreover, there has been a back and forth of interest in and complexity of shape models. The arrival of new features has typically first led to an increased interest in low-level representation followed by a later reemphasis of shape. Finally, hierarchical models based on compositionality have recently shown great potential for bridging the gap between local features and holistic shape. They capture non-accidental part dependencies to model structure and they have addressed key problems of vision such as top-down grouping, foreground/background segregation, and the correspondence problem.

References

1. Antic B, Ommer B (2011) Video parsing for abnormality detection. In: ICCV
2. Attneave F (1954) Some informational aspects of visual perception. Psych Rev 61(3)
3. Basri R, Jacobs D (1995) Recognition using region correspondences. Int J Comput Vis 25:8–13
4. Belongie S, Malik J, Puzicha J (2002) Shape matching and object recognition using shape contexts. IEEE Trans Pattern Anal Mach Intell 24(4):509–522
5. Berg AC, Berg TL, Malik J (2005) Shape matching and object recognition using low distortion correspondence. In: CVPR, pp 26–33
6. Biederman I (1987) Recognition-by-components: a theory of human image understanding. Psychol Rev 94(2):115–147
7. Binford TO (1971) Visual perception by computer. In: IEEE conf on systems and control
8. Bookstein FL (1986) Size and shape spaces for landmark data in two dimensions. Stat Sci 1(2):181–222
9. Bourdev L, Malik J (2009) Poselets: body part detectors trained using 3d human pose annotations. In: ICCV
10. Brooks RA (1981) Symbolic reasoning among 3-d models and 2-d images. Artif Intell 17(1–3):285–348
11. Brunelli R, Poggio T (1993) Face recognition: features versus templates. IEEE Trans Pattern Anal Mach Intell 15(10):1042–1052. http://doi.ieeecomputersociety.org/10.1109/34.254061
12. Cootes TF, Edwards GJ, Taylor CJ (1998) Active appearance models. In: ECCV
13. Csurka G, Dance CR, Fan L, Willamowski J, Bray C (2004) Visual categorization with bags of keypoints. In: ECCV. Workshop on statistical learning in computer vision
14. Dalal N, Triggs B (2005) Histograms of oriented gradients for human detection. In: CVPR, pp 886–893
15. Deselaers T, Ferrari V (2010) Global and efficient self-similarity for object classification and detection. In: CVPR, pp 1633–1640
16. Dickinson SJ, Pentland A, Rosenfeld A (1992) 3-D shape recovery using distributed aspect matching. IEEE Trans Pattern Anal Mach Intell 14(2):174–198
17. Dryden IL, Mardia KV (1998) Statistical shape analysis. Wiley, New York
18. Eigenstetter A, Ommer B (2012) Visual recognition using embedded feature selection for curvature self-similarity. In: NIPS
19. Everingham M, Zisserman A, Williams CKI, Van Gool L (2006) PASCAL VOC'06
20. Felzenszwalb P, Mcallester D, Ramanan D (2008) A discriminatively trained, multiscale, deformable part model. In: CVPR
21. Felzenszwalb PF, Huttenlocher DP (2005) Pictorial structures for object recognition. Int J Comput Vis 61(1):55–79
22. Fergus R, Perona P, Zisserman A (2003) Object class recognition by unsupervised scale-invariant learning. In: CVPR, pp 264–271
23. Fidler S, Boben M, Leonardis A (2010) A coarse-to-fine taxonomy of constellations for fast multi-class object detection. In: ECCV
24. Fischler MA, Elschlager RA (1973) The representation and matching of pictorial structures. IEEE Trans Comput c-22(1):67–92
25. Guzman A (1971) Analysis of curved line drawings using context and global information. Mach Intell 6:325–376
26. Hu MK (1962) Visual pattern recognition by moment invariants. Trans Inf Theory 8(2)
27. Huttenlocher DP, Ullman S (1987) Object recognition using alignment. In: ICCV
28. Julesz B (1981) Textons, the elements of texture perception, and their interactions. Nature 290(5802):91–97
29. Kendall D (1984) Shape manifolds, procrustean metrics and complex projective spaces. Bull Lond Math Soc 16(2):81–121
30. Koenderink JJ, van Doorn AJ (1976) The singularities of the visual mapping. Biol Cybern 24:51–59

31. Lades M, Vorbrüggen JC, Buhmann JM, Lange J, von der Malsburg C, Würtz RP, Konen W (1993) Distortion invariant object recognition in the dynamic link architecture. IEEE Trans Comput 42:300–311
32. Lazebnik S, Schmid C, Ponce J (2006) Beyond bags of features: spatial pyramid matching for recognizing natural scene categories. In: CVPR, pp 2169–2178
33. Leibe B, Leonardis A, Schiele B (2004) Combined object categorization and segmentation with an implicit shape model. In: ECCV. Workshop on stat learn in comp vision
34. Lowe D (1999) Object recognition from local scale-invariant features. In: ICCV
35. Lowe DG (1985) Perceptual organization and visual recognition. Kluwer, Amsterdam
36. Maji S, Malik J (2009) Object detection using a max-margin hough transform. In: CVPR
37. Marr D (1982) Vision. Freeman, San Francisco
38. Monroy A, Ommer B (2012) Beyond bounding-boxes: learning object shape by model-driven grouping. In: ECCV, pp 580–593
39. Murase H, Nayar SK (1995) Visual learning and recognition of 3-d objects from appearance. Int J Comput Vis 14(1):5–24
40. Ohta Y, Kanade T, Sakai T (1978) An analysis system for scenes containing objects with substructures. In: Intl joint conf on pattern recognition, pp 752–754
41. Ommer B, Buhmann JM (2006) Learning compositional categorization models. In: ECCV. LNCS, vol 3953, pp 316–329
42. Ommer B, Buhmann JM (2010) Learning the compositional nature of visual object categories for recognition. IEEE Trans Pattern Anal Mach Intell 32(3):501–516
43. Ommer B, Malik J (2009) Multi-scale object detection by clustering lines. In: ICCV
44. Opelt A, Pinz A, Zisserman A (2006) Incremental learning of object detectors using a visual shape alphabet. In: CVPR, pp 3–10
45. Revonsuo A, Newman J (1999) Binding and consciousness. Conscious Cogn 8:123–127
46. Roberts LG (1963) Machine perception of three-dimensional solids. PhD thesis, MIT
47. Schlecht J, Ommer B (2011) Contour-based object detection. In: BMVC
48. Schneiderman H, Kanade T (1998) Probabilistic modeling of local appearance and spatial relationships for object recognition. In: CVPR, pp 45–51
49. Sivic J, Russell BC, Efros AA, Zisserman A, Freeman WT (2005) Discovering objects and their localization in images. In: ICCV, pp 370–377
50. Small CG (1996) The statistical theory of shape. Springer, New York
51. Smeulders AWM, Worring M, Santini S, Gupta A, Jain R (2000) Content-based image retrieval at the end of the early years. IEEE Trans Pattern Anal Mach Intell 22:1349–1380
52. Thompson DW (1917) On growth and form. Dover, New York
53. Turk M, Pentland A (1991) Eigenfaces for recognition. J Cogn Neurosci 3(1):71–86
54. Viola PA, Jones MJ (2001) Rapid object detection using a boosted cascade of simple features. In: CVPR, pp 511–518
55. Wertheimer M (1922) Untersuchungen zur Lehre von der Gestalt I. Prinzipielle Bemerkungen. Psychol Forsch 1:47–58
56. Yarlagadda P, Monroy A, Ommer B (2010) Voting by grouping dependent parts. In: ECCV, pp 197–210
57. Yarlagadda P, Ommer B (2012) From meaningful contours to discriminative object shape. In: ECCV
58. Yuille AL, Hallinan PW, Cohen DS (1992) Feature extraction from faces using deformable templates. Int J Comput Vis 8(2):99–111

Chapter 26
Human Object Recognition: Appearance vs. Shape

Irving Biederman

26.1 Cortical Pathways for Visual Processing

High-resolution visual information is conveyed from the retina to the cortex via the lateral geniculate nucleus of the thalamus. The first cortical stage, V1, performs, essentially, a multiscale, multiorientation, Gabor filtering of the local contrast in the image through cells with small, local receptive fields (~0.5–$2°$). Activation is then fed forward through two major pathways. The *ventral pathway*, which we will focus on in this chapter, mediates *recognition*—how we know *what* we are looking at. This pathway extends from V1, through a series of stages, V2, V3, V4, and, in the macaque, the inferior temporal (IT) region (Fig. 26.1). The human homologue to IT—the final visual stage in the ventral pathway—in the macaque appears to be a region termed the lateral occipital complex (LOC), which will be discussed in detail below. A *dorsal pathway* mediates vision for purposes of motor interaction (or "how to") and extends from V1 (and V3 and V4) to the parietal cortex, which has extensive connections to the premotor cortex in the frontal lobe. This pathway specifies where objects are and their characteristics for, say, reaching and grasping. Another visual function is that of motion perception, with a region termed MT critical for its specification. MT is often considered to be a dorsal function but a case can be made that it be considered independently of its role in motor interaction.

I. Biederman (✉)
Department of Psychology and Neuroscience Program, University of Southern California,
Los Angeles, CA, USA
e-mail: bieder@usc.edu

S.J. Dickinson, Z. Pizlo (eds.), *Shape Perception in Human and Computer Vision*,
Advances in Computer Vision and Pattern Recognition,
DOI 10.1007/978-1-4471-5195-1_26, © Springer-Verlag London 2013

Fig. 26.1 Dorsal and ventral
cortical visual pathways

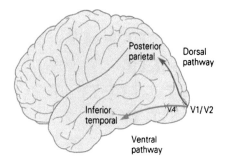

26.2 The Ventral Pathway

26.2.1 The Lateral Occipital Complex (LOC): An Area Critical for Perceiving Shape

LOC is operationally defined as the difference in the fMRI BOLD response to those regions of the cortex that show a heightened BOLD response to intact images of objects compared to their scrambled counterparts. In a typical study to localize LOC, subjects view 12 s blocks of images of 24 intact objects, with each image shown for 500 msec. After a 10 s blank period during which nothing is shown (to allow the BOLD signal to return to its resting state), the same objects can be shown, except that they are scrambled so that they resemble texture. (For another participant, the textured block would precede the intact block.) This procedure, when repeated for several cycles, yields a greater BOLD response in the lateral occipital cortex and the posterior portion of the fusiform gyrus (Fig. 26.2), which collectively comprise LOC [22]. LOC is functionally equivalent to the anterior inferior temporal area (IT) in the macaque in that it is considered the final stage in the ventral cortical pathway mediating shape recognition. Evidence for this equivalence derives, in part, from the similarity in the coding of object classes in IT and LOC. Kriegeskorte et al. [20] showed that the tuning of cells in IT of the macaque revealed the same similarity structure as fMRI-defined voxels in LOC. For example, if a cell responded strongly to a face it tended to respond strongly to other faces but not household appliances, a voxel could be found in human LOC that showed the same similarity relations.

That LOC is not just responsive to images of objects but is critical for their recognition is documented by studies of patient DF, who suffered bilateral lesions to LOC, with sparing of other cortical areas, as a consequence of carbon monoxide poisoning at the age of 34 [23]. DF does not report seeing objects yet she shows normal motor interaction with them in that her hand normally conforms to an object prior to its grasping. Specifically, when picking up an object, the span of her pre grip is accurately tuned to the position and width of the object that she is about to grasp and her grasping points are optimal in that they pass through the center of mass of the object, in a manner that is virtually indistinguishable from normal control subjects [11]. She is normal or near normal in perceiving the color and texture of an object and whether it is moving or stationary.

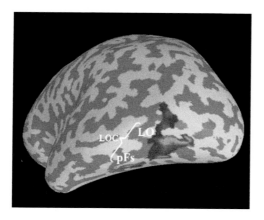

Fig. 26.2 Location of the lateral occipital cortex (LO) and the posterior fusiform gyrus which, together, constitute the lateral occipital cortex (LOC). A left hemisphere of an inflated brain is shown. *Darker regions* are sulci. This is the region that shows greater fMRI BOLD activation to intact objects compared to their scrambled counterparts resembling texture. From Malach, Levi, & Polat [21] TICS, v. 6, p. 177, Fig. 26.1

DF cannot copy line drawings of simple common objects such as an apple or a house yet she can draw them reasonably well from memory, as we would if we had to draw the object in the dark. Her visual memory is excellent and she can process previously learned shape information in novel tasks, such as judging which capital letters of the alphabet have vertical lines on their left side and which have curved segments or whether particular objects are taller than they are wide. In all cases she is unable to visually recognize the letters or objects that she is judging.

It is possible to get the complementary deficit from a lesion in the parietal cortex that affects the dorsal pathway. Such individuals have no difficulty in recognizing objects but they are unable to achieve the fluid and efficient motor interactions of normal subjects. In picking up an object, they grope for it with open hand, the way we would when attempting to pick up an object in the dark.

26.2.2 Coding for Shape vs. Surface in LOC

Objects vary in shape, color, texture, and the luminance pattern over their surface depends on the direction of illumination. LOC represents the object as a line drawing that codes the orientation and depth discontinuities of an object—that is, its shape— to the exclusion of the surface features of the original image, such as color, texture, and direction of illumination. An fMRI experiment by Grill-Spector, Kourtzi, & Kanwisher [12] used an *adaptation design* in which subjects viewed a number of presentations of a sequence of two images. If the images were identical (Cup → Cup) then the BOLD response was smaller than if the images were different (Cup → Violin). The repetition of the identical images is said to produce adaptation and the different images are said to produce a release from adaptation, indicating that the underlying neural representations of the two images differ. (Exactly why repetition of the identical image reduces the BOLD response, that is, adaptation, is still a subject of debate with non-exclusive interpretations including fatigue, narrowing of tuning, and competitive coding.) But what happens if, say, the first image is a photograph of a cup and the second is a line drawing of the same cup? Remarkably, the adaptation is unaffected, that is, there is no release of adaptation. Despite the drastic alteration of the image by the removal of its surface properties, the absence of an effect on adaption indicates that the coding of LOC is independent of surface properties.

When we look at the tuning of single units in macaque IT, we can witness the same equivalence in the coding of line drawings and photographs. Given the preferences, i.e., spike rate, of a neuron over a set of colored photos of objects, that preference ordering is maintained over line drawings of the objects (e.g., [16, 18]). That is, if the cells fired at a higher rate to a color photograph of a chair over a lamp, that ordering was maintained for line drawings of those objects.

The representation of objects in terms of their orientation and depth discontinuities renders them invariant in terms of recognition performance to the direction of illumination [24]. This invariance to direction of illumination is also witnessed in the tuning of macaque cells in IT [29].

Although there is no question that humans can readily determine an object's orientation and depth discontinuities, that is, they can produce an excellent line drawing by depicting those discontinuities, this capacity still remains a great challenge to the computer vision community. The design of a system for determining those discontinuities and distinguishing them from shadows, texture, surface markings, reflection highlights, etc. is still an unsolved problem. In fact, the major motivation for appearance-based approaches in the computer vision community may arise out of the inability to model how a line drawing can be extracted from an image of an object. This challenge is not restricted to those designing computer vision systems. Vision scientists do not know how line drawings of 3D shape are achieved by the visual system.

26.2.3 Different Subregions for the Processing Different Stimulus Dimensions

If LOC does not code for surface properties, where are they coded? Within the ventral pathway, different regions appear to be maximally activated when we attend to an object's shape, color, or texture. Consider the unfamiliar shaped-objects that vary in shape, texture, and color in Fig. 26.3 [8]. Cant and Goodale had subjects view sequences of these objects and in separate blocks of trials, the subjects had to press a key if the object on the current trial matched the shape of the object in the prior trial. In such blocks, the color and texture could be ignored. In other blocks subjects judged if the prior object matched in texture and in still other blocks of trials,

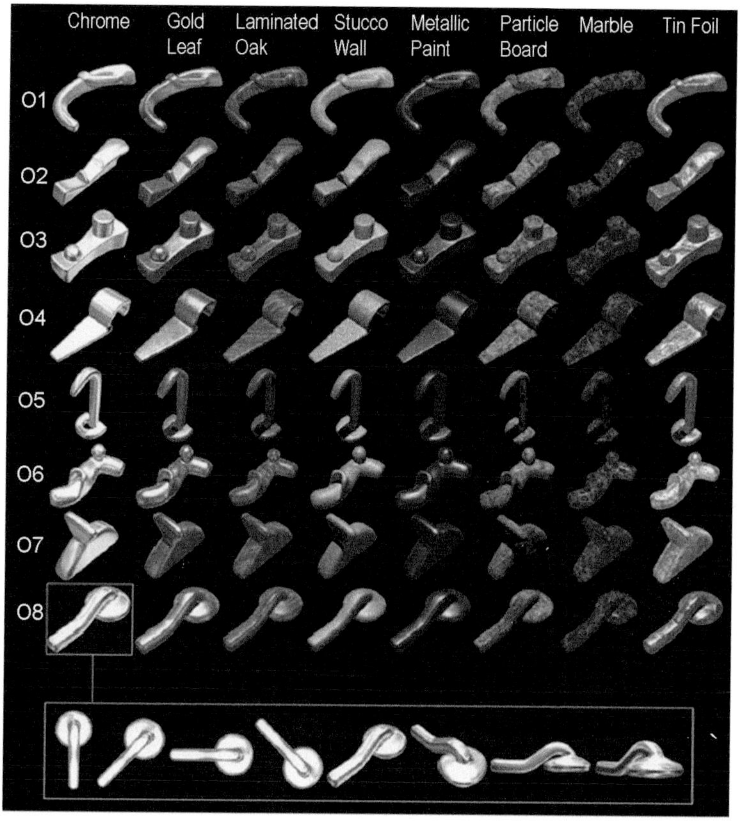

Fig. 26.3 Stimuli from the Cant & Goodale [8] experiment that varied in shape, color, texture, and orientation. From *Cerebral Cortex*, v. 17 Fig. 26.2

in color (which was varied within textures, although not shown in Fig. 26.3), each time ignoring the other dimensions of stimulus variation. As noted previously, attention to shape maximally activated LOC. Attention to texture (or material properties) activated the collateral sulcus. Attention to color overlapped the collateral sulcus and LOC. One doesn't have to give an explicit task to induce attention to a stimulus dimension. Merely passively viewing objects, such as those shown in Fig. 26.3, that vary in only one attribute, say texture, while shape and color are held constant, will be enough to differentially activate the collateral sulcus, the cortical area tuned to texture.

We should not be surprised to learn that there is independent coding of texture, color, and shape. Certainly we can look for our car in a parking lot or a garment in the laundry basket on the basis of its color, ignoring the variations in shape. It has been known for some time that people can demonstrate perfectly efficient selective attention to shape and ignore surface color or luminance and vice versa. For example, Fitts and Biederman [10] showed that the speed and accuracy in discriminating all black or all white circles and squares by human subjects was unaffected when the shapes varied irrelevantly in luminance. The discrimination of luminance was similarly unaffected by irrelevant variation in shape. Biederman [1] demonstrated selective attention between dimensions of color, size, and orientation. Combinations of stimulus dimensions that can be selectively attended, such as luminance and shape, are said to be *analyzable*. In contrast, some dimensions, such as hue and saturation, cannot be efficiently selectively attended. Such dimensions are said to be *integral*. The neuroimaging work of Cant and Goodale suggest that efficient (i.e., fast and accurate) selective attention to a particular stimulus attribute in the presence of other varying attributes may be dependent on the coding these attributes at different cortical loci.

26.2.4 How Efficient are Line Drawings for Object Recognition?

Biederman and Ju [7] investigated the speed and accuracy of naming, in one experiment, and verification, in another, of briefly presented line drawings and photographs of common objects. In the naming tasks, an image with a common basic-level name is briefly presented followed by a mask and the subject has to name the object as quickly as possible. The time from the onset of the presentation to the onset of naming is measured. In a verification task, following the presentation of a target name, for example, "chair," on half the trials a subsequently presented image matches the target and the subject is to press a key that indicates a match. In the other half of the trials, the image is not of a chair and the subject presses a non-match key. Both basic-level naming and verification were as fast and as accurate for line drawings as they were for color photography of the same instances. That is, the availability of surface cues—color, texture, luminosity gradients—added *nothing* to the recognition speed and accuracy of a line drawing of an object that specified well its orientation and depth discontinuities.

Some additional results confirmed the dominance of shape over surface for object classification/recognition. Some objects have diagnostic colors, such as a fish, a banana, or a fork, all familiar to human subjects. Other objects, such as a chair, pen, or a mitten do not. In both naming and verification the objects with the diagnostic colors showed the same equivalence with their line drawing counterparts as did the objects with non-diagnostic colors.

The equivalence of line drawings and colored photos only holds for concrete objects with definite boundaries. Linguistically, these tend to be *count* nouns for which, as the term implies, we can apply number and the indefinite article, so we can say three chairs or *a* chicken. Visual entities specified by *mass* nouns, such as sand or water, tend to be identified through their surface properties, for which we cannot apply number or the indefinite article. Perhaps predictably, the identification of objects dependent on their surface properties, including the case where an object's characteristic shape is altered, as occurs with a balled up shirt in the laundry basket, is markedly slower and more error prone than object classes with well-defined discontinuities that can be conveyed by a line drawing [6].

Table 26.1 Six characteristics of human object recognition supported by behavioral and neural experiments

1. Objects are represented by a *structural description* that specifies the *parts*, and the *relations* between the parts.

2. The representation is largely *edge-based*—specifically, those edges specifying orientation and depth discontinuities—rather than surface-based (i.e., color, texture).

3. The representation is of simple *parts*, rather than local features, templates, or concepts.

4. The parts, which can be modeled as generalized cylinders (GCs), are distinguished by *nonaccidental properties* (NAPs) of their GC attributes, e.g., whether the axis is straight or curved or the sides parallel or not, rendering them *geons*.

5. There is *low sensitivity* for discriminating complex, irregular shapes (= texture?) compared to simple shapes but high sensitivity for distinguishing texture from shape.

6. The representation is largely invariant to translation, size, reflection, source of illumination, and rotation in depth, as long as the originally viewed parts and their relations can be readily discerned.

26.3 What Aspects of Shape are Coded in LOC?

To pose the above question in a principled manner, we have to first understand what aspects of shape are apparent in object recognition behavior. There are six results (Table 26.1) motivated from Geon Theory (also termed Recognition-by-Components), Biederman's [2] account of human object recognition that have received strong behavioral and neural support but are not expressed by appearance-based theories of object recognition.

We have previously considered the sufficiency of a line-drawing representation (#2) Space precludes an extensive account of all six characteristics of human object recognition so I will just provide a brief overview of the evidence for a parts-based representation (#3) as well as the evidence for explicit coding of the relations between object parts (and objects) (#1).

26.3.1 Evidence for the Representation of Objects in Terms of Parts Rather than Local Features, Templates or Concepts

An object's shape is coded in terms of its simple parts—its geons—rather than templates of the whole object or the local features. There are considerable advantages in coding an object in terms of its parts. Under the most common causes of image variation, namely partial occlusion or rotation in depth, a template (such as the silhouette) can change markedly but only minimal costs in recognition are observed as long as two or three of the parts remain in view. If an object is missing a part, human subjects—even young children—can readily describe what it is that is missing.

It is important to note that the invariance to rotation in depth, as well as to changes in size, position, reflection, and direction of illumination can be witnessed with a "one shot" brief presentation of a novel object [3]. That is, a single 100 msec view

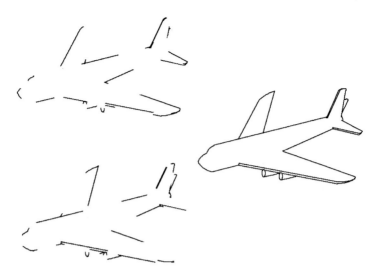

Fig. 26.4 Illustration of local feature-deleted stimuli from [5]. From each part, every other line and vertex was deleted forming a complementary pair of images such that if the two members of a complementary pair were superimposed they would produce an intact object without any overlap in contour

of an object never seen previously is sufficient to achieve an invariant representation of that object so that the gain in speed and accuracy in identifying a subsequent presentation of the object is unaffected by a change in the viewing conditions. There is, however, an episodic *memory*, of the viewing parameters of the object so that we can remember where the object was, its size, and its orientation (e.g., [4]).

Biederman and Cooper [5] tested whether the representation was indeed parts-based by employing complementary, contour-deleted line drawings of familiar objects (Fig. 26.4) to assess the presentation that mediated *repetition priming* of objects. Repetition priming, as the name implies, is the increase in the speed and accuracy of recognizing briefly presented, masked images of objects on their second presentation compared to their first. In their experiment, subjects named the objects, all of which had a common basic-level name, for example, "elephant," "piano," as quickly and as accurately as possible. In the first of two experiments, the contour deletion was of every other line and vertex of each part (Fig. 26.4) so that when both members of a complementary pair were combined they would make for the original intact object without any overlap in contour. Subjects named the objects in two blocks separated by approximately 10 minutes. The images in the second block could be classified into three conditions: (a) images that were identical to those on the first block, (b) complementary images which had the deleted contour of those for that object on the first block, and (c) a same name, different exemplar, such as an upright piano on the first block and a grand on the second.

The Different Exemplar condition was designed to rule out non-visual sources of facilitation, such as lexical access or basic-level priming. That is, if all the facilitation was just from repetition of the basic-level name or concept, then the Different

Exemplar condition should have been equivalent to the Identical condition. This was not the case. The different exemplar condition showed minimal facilitation from the first to the second presentation compared to the identical condition and most, if not all, that facilitation was because different exemplars of the same basic level class share some of the parts and relations, for example, airplanes will have wings emerging from their bodies and dogs will have four legs. Thus almost all the facilitation on this task could be considered *visual* priming and not conceptual or lexical priming. The remarkable result was the equivalence in the Identical and Complementary conditions. This indicates that *none* of the visual priming can be attributed to local features, as there was zero overlap of the contours and vertices between members of the same exemplar.

Although the results excluded that repetition of local features or basic level concepts or names accounted for the priming, the possibility remained that the priming was accounted for by repetition of *subordinate-level* concepts, that is, that it was the *idea* that one had seen a grand piano and not an upright piano or an elephant in a particular pose that mediated the priming. A complementary-priming experiment was then executed in which the complements were composed of different *parts*. Here complex objects were used each requiring at least six parts to look complete. The contour deletion was not of local features but of complete parts so that each member of a complementary pair had half the parts (and about half the total contour) of the other member. In this experiment there was absolutely *no* visual priming; performance in the Complementary condition was now equivalent to the Different Exemplar condition with the Identical condition showing a sizable advantage (lower RTs and error rates) compared to the Complementary Condition. These behavioral results have received confirmation in fast, event-related fMRI-adaptation experiments [13]. In these experiments, subjects viewed two images of contour-deleted objects, each presented for 300 msec separated by a blank frame. When the two images were identical, the BOLD response in LOC was minimal, an indicant of adaptation. When the images were of local feature-deleted complementary versions of the same objects, there also was no release from adaptation. However, when the two images were complements with different parts, there was a significant release of adaption—a higher BOLD response—indicating that they were coded as different representations in LOC even though they were of the same exemplar. In brief, the fMRI-adaptation experiment was completely consistent with the behavioral priming experiment in indicating that objects are coded in terms of their parts rather than in their local features or subordinate level concepts.

26.3.2 Relations Between Parts and Between Objects

Just as different orderings of the same set of letters can form different words, different relations among the same set of parts can form different objects [2]. People have ready access to these relations and not only can describe them verbally but can quickly judge whether different novel objects composed of different geons, say, are in the same or different arrangements in terms of their medial axis structure. Moreover, even when classifying which set of geons makes up a novel object while, presumably, ignoring axis structure, the pattern of fMRI activation nevertheless shows sensitivity to the axis structure [19]. This neural sensitivity to the relations among object parts is also witnessed when viewing minimal scenes composed of different objects [14, 17]. When subjects view two frames of a novel scene, say a bus above a turtle, separated by a brief interval, there is a marked release from adaptation (greater BOLD response) if the second frame is that of a turtle above a bus, and virtually no release if the objects are simply translated by an equal extent but maintain the same relation. Appearance models posit that local features between the objects specify the relations but direct tests of such a proposal found no evidence for such coding [14]. A structural description representation explicitly specifying parts and relations can be argued to be a necessary prerequisite to support true 'understanding' of visual structure. By rendering neither parts nor relations explicit, this prerequisite is not achieved by "bag of features" appearance models, e.g., [27].

To incorporate explicit relations into representations of objects and scenes, it is necessary to solve the binding problem, minimally, that the bus is ABOVE the turtle. So the relation of ABOVE is bound to bus and BELOW is bound to turtle. Although some have claimed that vision can solved without solution to the binding problem, e.g., [26], it is not clear that image *understanding* (vs. classification into familiar categories) can be so achieved, e.g., [15].

26.4 Coda

Probably the greatest challenge to machine vision efforts to achieve object recognition is the extraction of orientation and depth discontinuities and distinguishing such discontinuities from shadows, reflection edges, texture and color differences, etc. A secondary challenge is whether machine-based attempts at object recognition that do not achieve a structural description, as well as capturing the other characteristics listed in Table 26.1, can rival recognition performance readily evidenced by humans.

References

1. Biederman I (1972) Human performance in contingent information processing tasks. J Exp Psychol 93:219–238
2. Biederman I (1987) Recognition-by-components: a theory of human image understanding. Psychol Rev 94:115–147
3. Biederman I, Bar M (1999) One-shot viewpoint invariance in matching novel objects. Vis Res 39:2885–2899
4. Biederman I, Cooper EE (1992) Size invariance in visual object priming. J Exp Psychol Hum Percept Perform 18:121–133
5. Biederman I, Cooper EE (1991) Priming contour-deleted images: evidence for intermediate representations in visual object recognition. Cogn Psychol 23:393–419

6. Biederman I, Hilton HJ, Hummel JE (1991) Pattern goodness and pattern recognition. In: Pomerantz JR, Lockhead GR (eds) The perception of structure, APA Washington, pp 73–95. Chap. 5

7. Biederman I, Ju G (1988) Surface vs. edge-based determinants of visual recognition. Cogn Psychol 20:38–64

8. Cant J, Goodale M (2007) Attention to form or surface properties modulates different regions of human occipitotemporal cortex. Cereb Cortex 17:713–731

9. Epshtein B, Ullman S (2005) Hierarchical features for object classification. In: ICCV, pp 220–227

10. Fitts PM, Biederman I (1965) S-R Compatibility and information reduction. J Exp Psychol 69:408–412

11. Goodale MA, Meenan JP, Bulthoff HH, Nicolle DA, Murphy KJ, Racicot CI (1994) Separate neural pathways for the visual analysis of object shape in perception and prehension. Curr Biol 4:604–610

12. Grill-Spector K, Kourtzi Z, Kanwisher N (2001) The lateral occipital complex and its role in object recognition. Vis Res 41:1409–1422

13. Hayworth KJ, Biederman I (2006) Neural evidence for intermediate representations in object recognition. Vis Res 46:4024–4031

14. Hayworth KJ, Lescroart MD, Biederman I (2011) Neural encoding of relative position. J Exp Psychol Hum Percept Perform. doi:10.1037/a0022338

15. Hummel JE, Biederman I (1992) Dynamic binding in a neural network for shape recognition. Psychol Rev 99:480–517

16. Kayaert G, Biederman I, Vogels R (2003) Shape tuning in macaque inferior temporal cortex. J Neurosci 23:3016–3027

17. Kim JG, Biederman I (2011) Where do objects become scenes? Cereb Cortex 21:1738–1746. doi:10.1093/cercor/bhq240

18. Kovacs G, Chadaide Z, Koteles K, Sary G, Tompa T, Fiser J, Biederman I, Benedek G (2000) Processing of contours in the macaque inferior temporal cortex. J Physiol 526:26S

19. Lescroart MD, Biederman I (2012) Cortical representation of medial axis structure. Cereb Cortex. doi:10.1093/cercor/bhs046

20. Kriegeskorte N, Mur M, Ruff DA, Kiani R, Bodurka J, Esteky H, Tanaka K, Bandettini PA (2008) Matching categorical object representations in inferior temporal cortex of man and monkey. Neuron 60:1126–1141

21. Malach R, Levy I, Hasson U (2002) The topography of high order human object areas. Trends Cogn Sci 6:176–184

22. Malach R, Reppas JB, Benson RR, Kwong KK, Jlang H, Kennedy WA et al (1995) Object-related activity revealed by functional magnetic resonance imaging in human occipital cortex. Proc Natl Acad Sci USA 92:8135–8139

23. Milner AD, Goodale MA (1995) The visual brain in action. Oxford University Press, New York

24. Nederhouser M, Mangini MC, Subramaniam S, Biederman I (2001) Translation between S1 and S2 eliminates costs of changes in the direction of illumination. J Vis. http://journalofvision.org/1/3/92/

25. Oliva A, Torralba A (2006) Building the gist of a scene: the role of global image features in recognition. Prog Brain Res Vis Percept 155:23–36

26. Riesenhuber M, Poggio T (1999) Are cortical models really bound by the 'binding problem'? Neuron 24:87–93

27. Serre T, Oliva A, Poggio T (2007) A feedforward architecture accounts for rapid categorization. Proc Natl Acad Sci 104:6424–6429

28. Ullman S (2007) Object recognition and segmentation by a fragment-based hierarchy. Trends Cogn Sci 11:58–64

29. Vogels R, Biederman I (2002) Effects of illumination intensity and direction on object coding in macaque inferior temporal cortex. Cereb Cortex 12:756–766

Chapter 27
Shape-Based Object Discovery in Images

Sinisa Todorovic and Nadia Payet

27.1 Introduction

This paper presents an overview of the shape-based approach to object discovery and related problems that we have developed over the last several years [1–3]. We briefly describe the major components of our work, and explain its advantages over the more common methods based on point features (e.g., [4–11]).

The role of shape in representing and recognizing objects in images is a long-standing question in computer vision. In psychophysics, it is widely recognized that shape is one of the most categorical object properties [12]. Yet, most recent work on object recognition exclusively resorts to appearance features (e.g., color, textured patches), arguing that they are more stable to variations in imaging conditions (e.g., illumination, viewpoint). However, there are a number of unsatisfying aspects associated with point features. They are usually defined only in terms of local disconti-nuities in brightness. The inherent locality of points cannot represent the full spatial extent of objects in the image. As a direct consequence, point-based object detection requires the use of scanning windows of pre-specified size and shape, resulting in overlapping candidate detections that need to be resolved in a postprocessing step (e.g., non-maxima suppression). This postprocessing is usually based on heuristic assumptions about the numbers, sizes, and shapes of objects present. Since the final result of this is identification of the points associated with detected objects, it leads to only approximate object localization.

A number of approaches, including our previous work, use image contours as features [11, 13–25]. These methods argue that contours are in general richer de-scriptors, more discriminative, and more noise-tolerant than interest points. Con-tours make various constraints, frequently used in object recognition—such as those dealing with continuation, smoothness, containment, and adjacency—implicit and

S. Todorovic (✉) · N. Payet
School of Electrical Engineering and Computer Science, Oregon State University, Corvallis, OR 97331, USA
e-mail: sinisa@eecs.oregonstate.edu

S.J. Dickinson, Z. Pizlo (eds.), *Shape Perception in Human and Computer Vision*, Advances in Computer Vision and Pattern Recognition, DOI 10.1007/978-1-4471-5195-1_27, © Springer-Verlag London 2013

easier to incorporate than points. Contours often coincide with the boundaries of objects and their subparts. This allows simultaneous object detection and segmentation. Shape-based recognition typically requires a manually specified shape template [21, 22], or manually segmented training images to learn the object shape [26]. Such a high level of supervision in training can be relaxed by combining shape with point features [27, 28].

It is worth noting that the impact of any shortcomings of a contour detection algorithm should not be confused with the weaknesses of shape-based representation. For example, oversimplifying assumptions made by some edge detection algorithms about shape, curvature, size, gray-level contrast, and topological context of objects to be expected in an image may lead to various errors [29–31]. From our experience, these errors could be addressed by a higher-level recognition algorithms, as presented here.

In this paper, we study the role of object shape in the problem of discovering instances of frequently occurring object categories (e.g., faces, bikes, giraffes, etc.) in an unlabeled set of images. Object discovery is arguably a more difficult problem than learning visual properties of objects from labeled images, since the former additionally requires identifying a meaningful image content in the background clutter, whereas the latter exploits human annotation for directly accessing the image content of interest. Object discovery brings together most recognition related problems of interest here, and serves well to highlight the strengths and shortcomings of using shape as object features for recognition. In particular, for object discovery, we deliberately disregard appearance features, and use only the geometric properties of image contours. In this way, we are in a position to empirically evaluate if shape is expressive and discriminative enough to provide robust detection and segmentation of common objects in the midst of background clutter. Also, we can empirically show advantages of using only shape-based cues over photometric features for object discovery.

Most previous work on unsupervised object discovery exploits photometric properties of objects. For example, color of image regions is used in [32, 33], and texture properties of image patches are used in [34, 35]. In our experiments, we outperform these appearance-based approaches to object discovery in both object detection and segmentation on benchmark datasets.

The remainder of this paper is organized as follows. Section 27.2 briefly reviews our approach to object discovery and points out our contributions. Section 27.3 specifics our shape representation. Section 27.4 describes how to build a graph from all pairs of image contours to capture shape properties of objects. Section 27.5 presents our graph multicoloring algorithm for object discovery. Section 27.5 presents our experimental evaluation. Finally, Sect. 27.7 presents our concluding remarks.

27.2 A Brief Review of Our Approach

This section reviews our approach, originally presented in [2]. It consists of three steps, illustrated in Fig. 27.1. *Step 1:* Given a set of unlabeled images, we extract

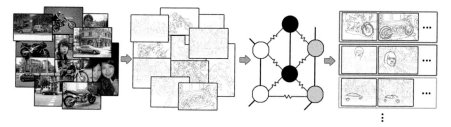

Fig. 27.1 Overview: Given a set of unlabeled images (*left*), we extract their contours (*middle left*), and then build a graph of pairs of matching contours. Contour pairs are viewed as collaborating (straight graph edges), if they similarly deform from one image to another, or conflicting (zigzag graph edges), otherwise. Such coupling of contour pairs facilitates their clustering with the Coordinate Ascent Swendsen-Wang cut (CASW). The resulting clusters represent shapes of discovered objects (*right*). (Best viewed in color)

their contours by the minimum-cover algorithm of [36]. Each contour is characterized as a sequence of beam-angle histograms, computed at points sampled along the contour. Similarity between two contours is estimated by the dynamic time warping (DTW) of the corresponding sequences of beam-angle descriptors. *Step 2* builds a weighted graph of matching contours, aimed at facilitating a separation of the background from object shapes in Step 3. We expect that there will be many similarly shaped curves, belonging to the background. Since the backgrounds vary, by definition, similar background curves will most likely have different spatial layouts across the image set. In contrast, object contours (e.g., curves delineating a giraffe's neck) are more likely to preserve both shape and layout similarity in the set. Therefore, for object discovery, it is critical that we capture similar configurations of contours. We build a graph, where nodes correspond to pairs of matching contours, and graph edges capture spatial layouts of quadruples of contours. *Step 3* conducts a probabilistic, iterative multicoloring of the graph using the Coordinate-Ascent Swendsen-Wang (CASW) cut. In each iteration, CASW cut probabilistically samples graph edges, and then assigns colors to the resulting groups of connected nodes. The assignments are accepted by the Metropolis-Hastings (MH) mechanism. After convergence, the resulting clusters represent shapes of objects that are discovered in the image set.

27.3 Image Representation Using Shapes and Shape Description

This section presents Step 1 of our approach. In each image, we extract relatively long, open contours using the minimum-cover algorithm of [36], referred to as gPb+ [36]. Similarity between two contours is estimated by aligning their sequences of points by the Dynamic Time Warping (DTW). Each contour point is characterized by the weighted Beam Angle Histogram (BAH), illustrated in Fig. 27.2. BAH is a weighted version of the standard unweighted BAH, aimed at mitigating the uncertainty in contour extraction. BAH down-weights the interaction of distant contour

Fig. 27.2 BAH is a weighted histogram of beam angles θ_{ij} at contour points P_i, $i = 1, 2, \ldots$

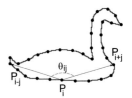

Table 27.1 Contour matching on the ETHZ image dataset [28]. Top is *Precision*, bottom is *Recall*. The rightmost column shows matching results of Oriented Chamfer Distance [27], and other columns show DTW results. Descriptors (left to right): our BAH, unweighted BAH, Shape Context [37], and SIFT [38]

Contour detectors	**BAH**	BAH-U	[37]	[38]	[27]
Canny	**0.23 ± 0.01**	0.21	0.18	0.15	0.21
	0.59 ± 0.02	0.57	0.48	0.48	0.52
[28]	**0.32 ± 0.03**	0.30	0.25	0.18	0.29
	0.78 ± 0.03	0.75	0.62	0.61	0.72
gPb+ [36]	**0.37 ± 0.02**	0.34	0.26	0.20	0.34
	0.81 ± 0.03	0.78	0.63	0.61	0.74

parts, as they are more likely to belong to distinct objects in the scene, rather than to the same objects. BAH is invariant to translation, in-plane rotation, and scale. Experimentally, we find that BAH with 12 bins gives optimal and stable results, and seems more robust to errors in contour extraction than some alternative shape descriptors, as reported in Table 27.1.

27.4 Constructing the Graph of Pairs of Image Contours

This section presents Step 2 that constructs a weighted graph, $G = (V, E, \rho)$, from contours extracted from all images in the set. Nodes of G represent candidate matches of contours, $(u, u') \in V$, where u and u' belong to two different images. Similarity of two contours is estimated by DTW. We keep only the best 5 % of contour matches as nodes of G. The graph is instrumental in capturing both intrinsic geometric properties of shape parts, and relative layout relationships between shape parts. This facilitates generating hypotheses of frequently occurring objects in the image set as similar contours repeating in similar layouts in the images.

Edges of G, $e = ((u, u'), (v, v')) \in E$, capture spatial relations of corresponding image contours. If contours u and v in image 1, and their matches u' and v' in image 2 have similar spatial layout, then they are less likely to belong to the background clutter. All such contour pairs will have a high probability to become positively coupled in G. Otherwise, matches (u, u') and (v, v') will have a high probability to become negatively coupled in G, so that they could be placed in distinct clusters. This probabilistic coupling of nodes in G is encoded by edge weights,

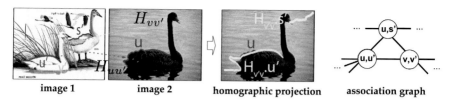

Fig. 27.3 Estimating layout difference $\delta_{(u,u',v,v')}$ when contours u and v are in image 1, and their matches u' and v' are in image 2. We use the affine-homography projection of u' and v' to image 1, $u'' = H_{vv'}u'$ and $v'' = H_{uu'}v'$, and compute δ as the average distance between u and u'', and v and v''. The figure with projections shows that the contours (u, s', v, v') have different layouts in image 1 and image 2, whereas the contours (u, u', v, v') have a similar layout

ρ_e, defined as the likelihood $\rho_e^+ \propto \exp(-w_\delta^+ \delta_e)$, given the positive polarity of e, and $\rho_e^- \propto \exp(-w_\delta^- (1-\delta_e))$, given the negative polarity of e. w_δ^+ and w_δ^- are the parameters of the exponential distribution, and $\delta_e \in [0, 1]$ measures a difference in spatial layouts of u and v in image 1, and their matches u' and v' in image 2.

We specify δ_e so as to account for small object pose and camera viewpoint differences across the images. From our experiments, this is critical for enabling robustness in the face of noise in contour extraction and representation. We make a distinction between the following two cases.

Case 1 (u, u') and (v, v') come from *two* images, where u and v are in image 1, and u' and v' are in image 2, as illustrated in Fig. 27.3. We estimate δ_e in terms of affine homographies between the matching contours, denoted as $H_{uu'}$, and $H_{vv'}$, as follows. From the DTW alignment of points along u and u', we estimate their affine homography $H_{uu'}$. Similarly, for v and v', we estimate $H_{vv'}$. Then, we project u' to image 1, as $u'' = H_{vv'}u'$, and, similarly, project v' to image 1 as $v'' = H_{uu'}v'$ (Fig. 27.3 right). Next, in image 1, we measure distances between corresponding points of u and u'', where the point correspondence is obtained from DTW of u and u'. Similarly, we measure distances between corresponding points of v and v''. δ_e is defined as the average point distance between u and u'', and v and v''.

Case 2 (u, u') and (v, v') come from *three* images, where u and v belong to image 1, u' is in image 2, and v' is in image 3, as illustrated in Fig. 27.4. In this case, we can neither use $H_{vv'}$ to project u' from image 2 to image 1, nor $H_{uu'}$ to project v' from image 3 to image 1. Instead, we resort to context provided by auxiliary contours s' in a vicinity of u', and auxiliary contours t' in a vicinity of v'. For every neighbor s' of u' in image 2, we find its best DTW match s in image 1, and compute homography $H_{ss'}$. Similarly, for every neighbor t' of v' in image 3, we find its best DTW match t in image 1, and compute homography $H_{tt'}$. Then, we use all these homographies to project u' to image 1, multiple times, as $u_s'' = H_{ss'}u'$, for each neighboring contour s. Similarly, we project v' to image 1, multiple times, as $v_t'' = H_{tt'}v'$, for each neighboring contour t. Next, as in Case 1, we measure distances between corresponding points of all u and $\{u_s''\}$ pairs, and all v and $\{v_t''\}$ pairs. δ_e is defined as the average point distance.

| image 1 | image 2 | image 3 | homographic projection |

Fig. 27.4 Estimating layout difference $\delta_{(u,u',v,v')}$ when contours u and v are in image 1, and their matches u' and v' are in image 2 and image 3, respectively. We use auxiliary contours s in the neighborhood of u to estimate multiple affine-homography projections of u' to image 1, $u''_s = H_{ss'}u'$, where s' is the best matching contour of s in image 2. Also, we use auxiliary contours t in the neighborhood of v to estimate multiple projection of v' to image 1, $v''_t = \sum_s H_{tt'}v'$, where t' is the best matching contour of t in image 3. On the right, we show example projections $u''_s = H_{ss'}u'$ and $v''_t = H_{tt'}v'$. Finally, we compute δ as the average distance between u and $\{u''_s\}$, and v and $\{v''_t\}$

27.5 Coordinate-Ascent Swendsen-Wang Cut

This section presents Step 3. Our goal is to perform multicoloring of the graph of contour matches, $G = (V, E, \rho)$, specified in the previous section. The multicoloring partitions G into two subgraphs. One subgraph will represent a composite cluster of nodes, consisting of a number of connected components (CCPs), receiving distinct colors. This composite cluster contains contours of the discovered object categories. Nodes outside of the composite cluster are interpreted as the background. An edge, $e \in E$, can be negative or positive. A negative edge indicates that the nodes are conflicting, and thus should not be assigned the same color. A positive edge indicates that the nodes are collaborative, and thus should be favored to get the same color. If nodes are connected by positive edges, they form a CCP, and receive the same color. A CCP cannot contain a negative edge. CCPs connected by negative edges form a composite cluster. The amount of conflict and collaboration between two nodes is defined by the likelihood ρ, defined in Sect. 27.4.

For multicoloring of G, we use the Coordinate Ascent Swendsen-Wang cut (CASW) that iterates the following three steps: (1) Sample a composite cluster from G, by probabilistically cutting and sampling positive and negative edges between nodes of G. This results in splitting and merging nodes into a new configuration of CCPs. (2) Assign new colors to the resulting CCPs within the selected composite cluster, and use the Metropolis-Hastings (MH) algorithm [39] to estimate whether to accept this new multicoloring assignment of G, or to keep the previous state. (3) If the new state is accepted, go to step (1); otherwise, if the algorithm converged, re-estimate parameters of the pdf's controlling the MH iterations, and go to step (1), until the pdf re-estimation does not affect convergence. CASW is characterized by large MH moves, involving many strongly-coupled graph nodes. This typically helps avoid local minima, and allows fast convergence, unlike other related MCMC methods (e.g., [40]). In the following, we present our Bayesian formulation of the CASW cut.

27.5.1 Bayesian Formulation

Multi-coloring of G amounts to associating labels l_i to nodes in V, $i = 1, \ldots, |V|$, where $l_i \in \{0, 1, \ldots, K\}$. K denotes the total number of target objects, which is a priori unknown, and $(K + 1)$th label is the background. The multicoloring can be formalized as $\mathcal{M} = (K, \{l_i\}_{i=1,\ldots,|V|})$. To find $\mathcal{M}$, we maximize the posterior $p(\mathcal{M}|G)$, as

$$\mathcal{M}^* = \arg\max_{\mathcal{M}} p(\mathcal{M}|G) = \arg\max_{\mathcal{M}} p(\mathcal{M})p(G|\mathcal{M}). \tag{27.1}$$

We define the prior as $p(\mathcal{M}) \propto \exp(-w_K K) \exp(-w_N N)$, where N is the number of nodes that are labeled as background, and w_K and w_N are the parameters of the exponential distribution. $p(\mathcal{M})$ penalizes large K and N.

We specify the likelihood, $p(G|\mathcal{M})$, in terms of independent Bernoulli edges of G. We define binary functions $\mathbb{1}_{l_i \neq l_j}$ and $\mathbb{1}_{l_i = l_j}$, which indicate whether node labels l_i and l_j are different, or the same. Then we have

$$p(G|\mathcal{M}) \propto \prod_{e \in \mathbb{E}^+} \rho_e^+ \prod_{e \in \mathbb{E}^-} \rho_e^- \prod_{e \in \mathbb{E}^0} \left(1 - \rho_e^+\right) \mathbb{1}_{l_i \neq l_j} \cdot \left(1 - \rho_e^-\right) \mathbb{1}_{l_i = l_j}, \tag{27.2}$$

where $\mathbb{E}^+$ and $\mathbb{E}^-$ are the sets of positive and negative edges present in the composite cluster, and $\mathbb{E}^0$ is the set of edges that are probabilistically cut.

27.5.2 Inference Using the CASW Cut

The CASW cut iterates the following two steps in inference. In step (1), edges of G are probabilistically sampled. If two nodes have the same label, their positive edge is sampled, with likelihood ρ_e^+. Otherwise, if the nodes have different labels, their negative edge is sampled, with likelihood ρ_e^-. This re-connects all nodes into new connected components (CCPs). The negative edges that are sampled will connect CCPs into a number of composite clusters, denoted by V_{cc}. This configuration is referred to state A. In step (2), we choose at random one composite cluster, V_{cc}, and probabilistically reassign new colors to the CCPs within V_{cc}, resulting in a new state B.

The CASW accepts the new state B as follows. Let $q(A \to B)$ be the proposal probability for moving from state A to B, and let $q(B \to A)$ denote the reverse. The acceptance rate, $\alpha(A \to B)$, of the move from A to B is defined as

$$\alpha(A \to B) = \min\left(1, \frac{q(B \to A)p(\mathcal{M} = \mathcal{B}|\mathcal{G})}{q(A \to B)p(\mathcal{M} = \mathcal{A}|\mathcal{G})}\right). \tag{27.3}$$

If $\alpha(A \to B)$ is low, state B cannot be accepted, and CASW remains in state A.

$q(A \to B)$ is defined as a product of two probabilities: (i) the probability of generating V_{cc} in state A, $q(V_{cc}|A)$; and (ii) the probability of recoloring the CCPs within V_{cc} in state B, where V_{cc} is obtained in state A, $q(B(V_{cc})|V_{cc}, A)$. Thus, we have

$$\frac{q(B \to A)}{q(A \to B)} = \frac{q(V_{cc}|B)}{q(V_{cc}|A)} = \frac{\prod_{e \in \mathrm{Cut}_B^+}(1-\rho_e^+)\prod_{e \in \mathrm{Cut}_B^-}(1-\rho_e^-)}{\prod_{e \in \mathrm{Cut}_A^+}(1-\rho_e^+)\prod_{e \in \mathrm{Cut}_A^-}(1-\rho_e^-)}. \tag{27.4}$$

Note that complexity of each move is relatively low, since computing $\frac{q(B \to A)}{q(A \to B)}$ involves only those edges that are probabilistically cut around V_{cc} in states A and B—not all edges. Also, $\frac{p(\mathcal{M}=B|\mathcal{G})}{p(\mathcal{M}=A|\mathcal{G})} = \frac{p(\mathcal{M}=B)p(G|\mathcal{M}=B)}{p(\mathcal{M}=A)p(G|\mathcal{M}=A)}$ can be efficiently computed. $p(\mathcal{M}=B)$ can be directly computed from the new coloring in state B, and $\frac{p(G|\mathcal{M}=B)}{p(G|\mathcal{M}=A)}$ depends only on those edges that have changed their polarity.

27.6 Results

This section reviews the empirical validation of our approach, presented in [2]. The experiments demonstrate advantages of using shape-based representations and modeling of objects for recognition versus alternative approaches.

Given a set of images, we perform object discovery in two stages, as in [34, 35, 41]. We first coarsely cluster images based on their contours using CASW cut, and then again use CASW to cluster contours from only those images that belong to the same coarse cluster. The first stage serves to discover different object categories in the image set. The second, fine-resolution stage serves to separate object contours from the background, and identify characteristic parts of each discovered object category.

We use the following benchmark datasets: Caltech-101 [42], ETHZ [28], LabelMe [43], and Weizmann Horses [44]. In the experiments on Caltech-101, we use all Caltech images showing the same categories as those used in [34]. Evaluation on ETHZ and Weizmann Horses uses the entire datasets. For LabelMe, we keep the 15 first images retrieved by keywords *car side*, *car rear*, *face*, *airplane* and *motorbike*. ETHZ and LabelMe increase complexity over Caltech-101, since their images contain multiple object instances, which may: (a) appear at different resolutions, (b) have low contrasts with textured background, and (c) be partially occluded. The Weizmann Horses are suitable to evaluate performance on articulated, non-rigid objects.

In the first stage of object discovery, CASW finds clusters of images. This is evaluated by *purity*. Purity measures the extent to which a cluster contains images of a single dominant object category. In the second stage, on each of these image clusters, we use *Bounding Box Hit Rate* (BBHR) to verify whether contours detected by CASW fall within the true foreground regions. The ground truth is defined as all pixels of the extracted image contours that fall in the bounding boxes or segments of target objects. A contour detected by CASW is counted as "hit" whenever the contour covers 50 % or more of the ground-truth pixels. Since we discard contours that are less than 50 pixels, this means that at least 25 ground-truth pixels need to

Table 27.2 Mean purity of category discovery for Caltech-101 (A: Airplanes, C: Cars, F: Faces, M: Motorbikes, W: Watches, K: Ketches), and ETHZ dataset (A: Applelogos, B: Bottles, G: Giraffes, M: Mugs, S: Swans)

Caltech categories	Our method	[35]	[34]	[41]	ETHZ categories	Our method	[35]
					A,B,G,M,S (bbox)	96.16 ± 0.41	95.85
A,C,F,M	98.62 ± 0.51	98.03	98.55	88.82	A,B,G,M,S (expanded)	87.35 ± 0.37	76.47
A,C,F,M,W	97.57 ± 0.46	96.92	97.30	N/A	A,B,G,M,S (entire image)	85.49 ± 0.33	N/A
A,C,F,M,W,K	97.13 ± 0.42	96.15	95.42	N/A			

be detected within the bounding box. Our accuracy in the second clustering stage depends on the initial set of pairs of matching contours (i.e., nodes of graph G) input to CASW. This is evaluated by plotting the ROC curve, parameterized by a threshold on the minimum DTW similarity between pairs of matching contours which are included in G.

We evaluate the first and second stages of object discovery. *First Stage:* We build a weighted graph whose nodes represent entire images. Edges between images in the graph are characterized by weights, defined as an average of DTW similarities of contour matches from the corresponding pair of images. A similar characterization of graph edges is used in [34, 35]. For object discovery, we apply CASW to the graph, resulting in image clusters. Each cluster is taken to consist of images showing a unique object category. Unlike [34, 35], we do not have to specify the number of categories present in the image set, as an input parameter, since it is automatically inferred by CASW. Evaluation is done on Caltech-101 and the ETHZ dataset. Table 27.2 shows that our mean purity is superior to that of [34, 35, 41]. On Caltech-101, CASW successively finds $K = 4, 5, 6$ clusters of images, as we gradually increase the true number of categories from 4 to 6. This demonstrates that we are able to automatically find the number of categories present, with no supervision. On ETHZ, CASW again correctly finds $K = 5$ categories. As in [35], we evaluate purity when similarity between the images (i.e., weights of edges in the graph) is estimated based on contours falling within: (a) the bounding boxes of target objects, (b) twice the size of the original bounding boxes (called expanded in Table 27.2), and (c) the entire images. On ETHZ, CASW does not suffer a major performance degradation when moving from the bounding boxes, to the challenging case of using all contours from the entire images. Overall, our purity rates are high, which enables accurate clustering of contours in the second stage. *Second Stage:* We use contours from all images grouped within one cluster, found in the first stage, to build our graph G, and then conduct CASW. This is repeated for all image clusters. The clustering of contours by CASW amounts to foreground detection, since the identified contour clusters are taken to represent parts of the discovered object category. We evaluate BBHR and FPR on Caltech-101, ETHZ, LabelMe, and Weizmann Horses. Figure 27.5 shows that our BBHR and FPR values are higher than those of [34, 35] on the Caltech and ETHZ. CASW finds $K = 1$ for *Airplanes, Cars Rear, Faces, Ketches, Watches* in Caltech-101, *Apples, Bottles, Mugs* in ETHZ, and *Car rear, Face, Airplane* in LabelMe. These objects do not have articulated parts that

	CASW	[34]	[35]
A	**0.11±0.01**	0.21	0.17
F	**0.12±0.01**	0.30	0.15
K	**0.06±0.003**	0.19	0.08
M	**0.04±0.002**	0.11	0.07
W	**0.02±0.003**	0.08	0.03

	CASW	[34]	[35]
A	**0.15±0.02**	N/A	0.18
B	**0.18±0.01**	N/A	0.20
G	**0.16±0.01**	0.32	0.18
M	**0.23±0.04**	N/A	0.27
S	**0.09±0.002**	N/A	0.11

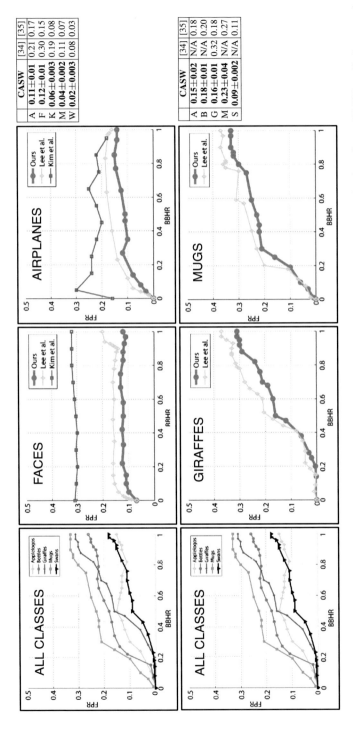

Fig. 27.5 Bounding Box Hit Rates (BBHR) vs False Positive Rates (FPR). *Top* is Caltech-101, *bottom* is ETHZ. *Left column* is our CASW on all classes, and *middle* and *right columns* show a comparison with [34, 35] on a specific class (*lower curves* are better). The tables show FPR at BBHR = 0.5. Caltech-101: A: Airplanes, F: Faces, K: Ketches, M: Motorbikes, W: Watches. ETHZ: A: Applelogs, B: Bottles, G: Giraffes, M: Mugs, S: Swans. (Best viewed in color)

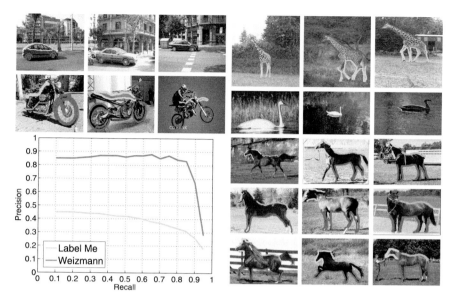

Fig. 27.6 Unsupervised detection and segmentation of objects in example images from LabelMe (*top left*), ETHZ (*top right*), and Weizmann Horses (*bottom right*). For LabelMe and ETHZ, each row shows images that are grouped within a unique image cluster by CASW in the first stage. Contours that are clustered by CASW in the second stage are highlighted with distinct colors indicating cluster membership. CASW accurately discovers foreground objects, and delineates their characteristic parts. E.g., for LabeMe *Cars sideview* CASW discovers two contour clusters (*yellow* and *magenta*), corresponding to the two car parts wheels and roof. (*Bottom left*) ROC curves for LabelMe and Weizmann Horses, obtained by varying the minimum allowed DTW similarity between pairs of matching contours which are input to CASW. (Best viewed in color)

move independently, hence, only one contour cluster is found. On the other hand, it finds $K = 2$ for *Giraffes, Swans* in ETHZ, *Cars side, Motorbikes* in Caltech and La-belMe, and $K = 3$ for Weizmann Horses. In Fig. 27.6, we highlight contours from different clusters with distinct colors. Figure 27.6 demonstrates that CASW is capable not only to discover foreground objects, but also to detect their characteristic parts, for example, wheels and roof for *Cars side*, wheels and seat for *Motorbikes*, head and legs for *Giraffes*, etc. The plot in Fig. 27.6 evaluates our object detection on LabelMe and Weizmann Horses. Detection accuracy is estimated as the standard ratio of intersection over union of ground-truth and detection bounding boxes, $(BB_{gt} \cap BB_d)/(BB_{gt} \cup BB_d)$, where BB_d is the smallest bounding box that encloses detected contours in the image. The average detection accuracy for each category is: [Face(F): 0.52, Airplane(A): 0.45, Motorbike(M): 0.42, Car Rear(C): 0.34], whereas [35] achieves only [(F): 0.48, (A): 0.43, (M): 0.38, (C): 0.31]. For Weizmann Horses, we obtain *Precision* and *Recall* of 84.9 ± 0.68 % and 82.4 ± 0.51 %, whereas [33] achieves only 81.5 % and 78.6 %.

The C-implementation of our CASW runs in less than 2 minutes on any dataset of less than 100 images, on a 2.40 GHz PC with 3.48 GB RAM.

27.7 Conclusion

We have argued in this paper that using contours as basic image features: (a) Facilitates capturing shape properties of objects; (b) Allows a unified computational framework that can jointly address object discovery, recognition, and segmentation; and (c) Enables efficient and robust learning and inference. Our claims are supported by the state-of-the-art performance of our shape-based approach to object discovery, recognition, and segmentation, which we have reviewed in this paper. Our approach clusters image contours based on their intrinsic geometric properties, and spatial layouts. The resulting clusters are interpreted as shapes of parts of discovered objects.

We have derived two key insights. First, shape alone is sufficiently discriminative and expressive to provide robust and efficient object discovery in unlabeled images, which even outperforms related point-based methods. As image contours are dimensionally matched with shape they are more suitable features for object discovery than point features. Second, due to background clutter, there could be many similar image features—both contours and point features—coinciding with true object occurrences and the background. To separate the background from foreground in object discovery, one usually makes the assumption that the background clutter cannot generate occurrences of similar spatial configurations of features in distinct images with a high probability. This probability is arguably lower for similar spatial configurations of contours than that of points, since contours have a lager spatial extent than points. Thus, identifying similar contour layouts in the images is expected to yield more accurate foreground-background separation than finding similar layouts of points. In summary, using contours facilitates discovering frequently occurring objects in images.

References

1. Payet N, Todorovic S (2009) Matching hierarchies of deformable shapes. In: Proc 7th IAPR-TC-15 workshop graph-based representations in pattern recognition (GbR), pp 1–10
2. Payet N, Todorovic S (2010) From a set of shapes to object discovery. In: ECCV
3. Payet N, Todorovic S (2011) From contours to 3D object detection and pose estimation. In: ICCV (oral presentation)
4. Fergus R, Perona P, Zisserman A (2003) Object class recognition by unsupervised scale-invariant learning. In: CVPR, vol 2, pp 264–271
5. Torralba A, Murphy K, Freeman W (2004) Sharing features: efficient boosting procedures for multiclass object detection. In: CVPR, vol 2, pp 762–769
6. Leibe B, Leonardis A, Schiele B (2004) Combined object categorization and segmentation with an implicit shape model. In: Workshop on statistical learning in computer vision, ECCV, pp 17–32
7. Agarwal S, Awan A, Roth D (2004) Learning to detect objects in images via a sparse, part-based representation. IEEE Trans Pattern Anal Mach Intell 26(11):1475–1490
8. Sudderth E, Torralba A, Freeman WT, Willsky AS (2005) Learning hierarchical models of scenes, objects, and parts. In: ICCV, vol 2, pp 1331–1338
9. Winn J, Criminisi A, Minka T (2005) Object categorization by learned universal visual dictionary. In: ICCV, vol 2, pp 1800–1807

10. Fei-Fei L, Fergus R, Perona P (2006) One-shot learning of object categories. IEEE Trans Pattern Anal Mach Intell 28(4):594–611
11. Opelt A, Pinz A, Zisserman A (2006) Incremental learning of object detectors using a visual shape alphabet. In: CVPR, vol 1, pp 3–10
12. Biederman I (1988) Surface versus edge-based determinants of visual recognition. Cogn Psychol 20(1):38–64
13. Williams LR, Jacobs DW (1995) Stochastic completion fields: a neural model of illusory contour shape and salience. In: ICCV, pp 408–415
14. Lindenbaum M (1995) Bounds on shape recognition performance. IEEE Trans Pattern Anal Mach Intell 17(7):666–680
15. Liu TL, Geiger D (1999) Approximate tree matching and shape similarity. In: Proc IEEE int conf computer vision, vol 1, pp 456–462
16. Shokoufandeh A, Macrini D, Dickinson S, Siddiqi K, Zucker SW (2005) Indexing hierarchical structures using graph spectra. IEEE Trans Pattern Anal Mach Intell 27(7):1125–1140
17. Keselman Y, Dickinson S (2005) Generic model abstraction from examples. IEEE Trans Pattern Anal Mach Intell 27(7):1141–1156
18. Siddiqi K, Kimia BB (1996) A shock grammar for recognition. In: CVPR, p 507
19. Sebastian TB, Klein PN, Kimia BB (2004) Recognition of shapes by editing their shock graphs. IEEE Trans Pattern Anal Mach Intell 26(5):550–571
20. Felzenszwalb PF (2005) Representation and detection of deformable shapes. IEEE Trans Pattern Anal Mach Intell 27(2):208–220
21. Zhu Q, Wang L, Wu Y, Shi J (2008) Contour context selection for object detection: a set-to-set contour matching approach. In: ECCV (2), pp 774–787
22. Kokkinos I, Yuille AL (2009) HOP: hierarchical object parsing. In: CVPR
23. Ling H, Jacobs DW (2007) Shape classification using the inner-distance. IEEE Trans Pattern Anal Mach Intell 29(2):286–299
24. Torsello A, Robles-Kelly A, Hancock ER (2007) Discovering shape classes using tree edit-distance and pairwise clustering. Int J Comput Vis 72(3):259–285
25. Trinh NH, Kimia BB (2011) Skeleton search: category-specific object recognition and segmentation using a skeletal shape model. Int J Comput Vis 94(2):215–240
26. Bai X, Wang X, Liu W, Latecki LJ, Tu Z (2009) Active skeleton for non-rigid object detection. In: ICCV
27. Shotton J, Blake A, Cipolla R (2008) Multiscale categorical object recognition using contour fragments. IEEE Trans Pattern Anal Mach Intell 30(7):1270–1281
28. Ferrari V, Tuytelaars T, Gool LV (2006) Object detection by contour segment networks. In: ECCV, pp 14–28
29. Perona P, Malik J (1991) Detecting and localizing edges composed of steps, peaks and roofs. In: ICCV, pp 52–57
30. Arbelaez P, Maire M, Fowlkes C, Malik J (2011) Contour detection and hierarchical image segmentation. IEEE Trans Pattern Anal Mach Intell 33:898–916
31. Felzenszwalb P, McAllester D (2006) A min-cover approach for finding salient curves. In: IEEE workshop on perceptual organization (POCV)
32. Russell BC, Freeman WT, Efros A, Sivic J, Zisserman A (2006) Using multiple segmentations to discover objects and their extent in image collections. In: CVPR
33. Todorovic S, Ahuja N (2008) Unsupervised category modeling, recognition, and segmentation in images. IEEE Trans Pattern Anal Mach Intell 30(12):1–17
34. Kim G, Faloutsos C, Hebert M (2008) Unsupervised modeling of object categories using link analysis techniques. In: CVPR
35. Lee YJ, Grauman K (2009) Shape discovery from unlabeled image collections. In: CVPR
36. Felzenszwalb P, McAllester D (2006) A min-cover approach for finding salient curves. In: CVPR POCV
37. Belongie S, Malik J, Puzicha J (2002) Shape matching and object recognition using shape contexts. IEEE Trans Pattern Anal Mach Intell 24(4):509–522

38. Lowe DG (2004) Distinctive image features from scale-invariant keypoints. Int J Comput Vis 60(2):91–110
39. Chib S, Greenberg E (1995) Understanding the metropolis-hastings algorithm. Am Stat 49(4):327–335
40. Lin L, Zeng K, Liu X, Zhu SC (2009) Layered graph matching by composite cluster sampling with collaborative and competitive interactions. In: CVPR, June 2009
41. Lee YJ, Grauman K (2008) Foreground focus: unsupervised learning from partially matching images. In: BMVC
42. Fei-Fei L, Fergus R, Perona P (2004) Learning generative visual models from few training examples: an incremental Bayesian approach tested on 101 object categories. In: CVPR
43. Russell BC, Torralba A, Murphy KP, Freeman WT (2005) Labelme: a database and web-based tool for image annotation. Technical Report AIM-2005-025, MIT
44. Borenstein E, Ullman S (2002) Class-specific, top-down segmentation. In: ECCV, vol 2, pp 109–124

Chapter 28
Schema-Driven Influences in Recovering 3-D Shape from Motion in Human and Computer Vision

Thomas V. Papathomas and Doug DeCarlo

28.1 Introduction

One of the fundamental questions in vision is how the visual system recovers a nearly veridical representation of the world, given that the retinal optic flow has an infinite number of possible interpretations, especially if one considers that there are moving objects in the environment. This one-to-many mapping from retinal optic flow onto the real-world surfaces and objects that provide the stimulation is known as the inverse problem in optics [35, 40, 45–47].

There is a long-standing debate in vision on whether visual perception, which is based on the solution to the inverse problem in optics, is influenced by schema-driven processes or it is entirely stimulus-driven and automatic. Helmholtz [26] was among the first researchers to hypothesize that perception is a process that involves "unconscious inference" at a time when it was commonly believed that perception was a purely data-driven process. This view has been adopted and extended by more recent formulations based on experimental evidence [11, 20, 22–24, 42, 52]. This view is also adopted by researchers who use a Bayesian formulation [8, 15, 19, 34, 71]; according to this view, the visual system uses "priors", such as the convexity bias [39, 60] or the "light-from-above" assumption [1, 6, 7, 36], to arrive at the most probable interpretation of the visual input, given the ambiguity of the solution to the inverse problem in optics. Proponents of this view posit that, in addition to the "bottom-up" processing that starts with data-driven sensory signals and activates progressively higher brain areas, there are also schema-driven "top-down" cognitive influences (such as experience, memory, suggestions, knowledge,

T.V. Papathomas (✉)
Department of Biomedical Engineering and Center for Cognitive Science, Rutgers University, Piscataway, NJ, USA
e-mail: papathom@rci.rutgers.edu

D. DeCarlo
Department of Computer Science and Center for Cognitive Science, Rutgers University, Piscataway, NJ, USA

S.J. Dickinson, Z. Pizlo (eds.), *Shape Perception in Human and Computer Vision*, Advances in Computer Vision and Pattern Recognition, DOI 10.1007/978-1-4471-5195-1_28, © Springer-Verlag London 2013

etc.) that start at higher brain areas that "interpret" their input and modulate the activation of lower brain areas ([3, 17, 30, 32, 41]; but see [18] for an argument against top-down influences).

One approach to studying the interaction of bottom-up (data-driven) and top-down (prior-knowledge-driven) processes is to select stimuli in which these two processes compete against each other, such that the percept elicited by the bottom-up signals is quite different from—and often opposite from—the percept that is favored by the top-down processes. Specifically, the value of visual illusions in this effort has long been recognized [5, 22–24, 52, 69]. Illusions have been used extensively to study normal brain mechanisms and stages of processing [2, 16, 20, 38, 49]. In particular, there is a fascinating class of three-dimensional (3-D) stimuli in which the data-driven cues elicit one depth percept while the schema-driven processes elicit a strong depth-inversion illusion. Two members of this class that produce very reliable illusions are the hollow mask [21, 27–29, 43, 70] and the reverse perspective [9, 42, 43, 55, 61, 67]. In this chapter, we will consider the role of top-down influences on the hollow-mask illusion both for human and machine vision. We observe that a face-tracking algorithm that recovers the 3-D shape from animation sequences of moving faces is susceptible to the hollow-mask illusion just as humans are, when it incorporates a top-down schema of convex faces, even though the data-driven motion parallax signals are adequate to recover the veridical concave 3-D shape. We discuss the implications of this observation.

28.2 The Hollow-Mask Illusion for Humans

The hollow-mask illusion, along with reverse perspectives, is one of the best-known depth inversion illusions, where one can distinguish cues and processes that give rise to competing percepts. In the case of the hollow mask, the prior knowledge of faces being convex, based on life-long exposure to faces, is the only schema-driven influence *in favor of* the illusion. It would be instructive to summarize briefly the basic data-driven influences that provide cues for the true depth structure, *against* the illusion, with the exception of the kinetic depth effect cue that provides ambiguous information (see item 2b.2 below). (1) There are two main extraretinal signals: (1a) *Vergence* is a binocular signal: it refers to the simultaneous but opposite-directed movement of the two eyes to achieve fixation of both on the point of interest. Since it can be expressed as an angle (vergence angle) that is formed by the two eyes' lines of sight, it is a single-valued function. (1b) *Lens accommodation* is self-explanatory monocular signal: the shape of the eye lenses has to vary in order to achieve the proper optical power, also single valued, to obtain a sharp "image" on the retina. Theoretically, at least, if viewers had access to the motor signals that control the muscles affecting vergence and accommodation, they could have used them as cues to depth, provided they were derived over time, as they fixate various points on the object/surface of interest. In practice, there is a long-standing debate on whether such motor signals are indeed used as cues to depth [4, 50, 68]. (2) We next move to some of the retinal-based cues: (2a) The most important binocular signal is the *stereoscopic disparity* between the two-eyes' "images", which comprises both horizontal and vertical components; disparity provides continuous 3-D shape cues that recover the true depth ordering of a scene or object; however, disparity needs to be processed further to yield true accurate depth information [51, 64]. (2b) Some of the monocular cues that are most relevant to the hollow-face illusion are: (2b.1) *Motion parallax*, due to the observer's self-motion as he/she views a scene, produces an optic flow field that also provides continuous 3-D shape cues with properties that are similar to those of stereopsis; they recover the correct depth ordering but they need to be scaled for recovering true depth [53, 54]. (2b.2) For a stationary observer, a moving object provides depth-from-motion cues, the so-called *kinetic depth effect* or KDE [31, 62]. KDE also provides continuous 3-D shape cues, but the depth ordering is ambiguous; as an example, a rotating wire-frame globe can be perceived either veridically, rotating in the physical direction, or in reverse depth, rotating in the opposite direction. (2b.3) *Occlusion* is a powerful cue to depth but it only provides depth-ordering information. (2b.4) *Shading* can also provide cues to the 3-D shape of an object [48, 65]. (2b.5) Finally, *image blur* can be used for assessing depth relationships in a scene [25, 66]. Blur is closely related to lens accommodation because only the point that the viewer fixates on and its close surroundings are in sharp focus, whereas more distant points are blurred. The degree of blur can be used to estimate the depth differential between a blurred image point and the fixation point, but it does not inform us of the depth polarity (is it in front or behind fixation). In addition, there are other depth cues in the general case (texture gradient, atmospheric perspective, size familiarity, etc.) that may not be strongly relevant in the hollow mask illusion. Nevertheless, the plethora of depth cues makes the problem of recovering depth too complex for a thorough scientific analysis. Here, we lump together all the depth cues that provide good estimates of depth (items 1a, 1b, 2a, 2b.1, 2b.3) and observe that they are more powerful at small viewing distances.

Thus, when observers view a hollow mask up close, the bottom-up signals of stereopsis, motion parallax, vergence eye movements and lens accommodation, among others, provide powerful signals that dominate and enable viewers to recover the veridical concave 3-D shape of the mask. These signals, however, become weaker as the viewing distance increases. At an adequately long viewing distance, the top-down influences—familiarity with convex faces in the case of a facial mask—dominate, causing depth relationships to be inverted; points that are physically further away appear to be closer than points that are physically closer. Consequently, concavities appear as convexities and vice versa, resulting in the percept of an overall convex face.

Figures 28.1a and 28.1b illustrate an essential feature of the hollow-mask illusion. Namely, even though the hollow mask of Fig. 28.1b faces to the left, the (mis-)perceived convex mask appears to face to the right (more details on this are provided later in reference to Fig. 28.2). This gives rise to two related motion illusions: (1) When a viewer moves laterally in front of a static hollow mask, the perceived convex mask appears to turn and "follow" the viewer. An explanation of

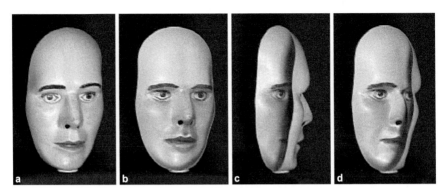

Fig. 28.1 (**a**) A convex mask that faces to the right of the viewer ($\theta = 22.5°$ in the notation of Fig. 28.2). (**b**) A concave mask that actually faces to the left ($\theta = 157.5°$) but it appears to be a convex mask facing to the right. (**c**) A mask with significant self-occlusion ($\theta = 117.3°$). (**d**) A mask that involves a marginal self-occlusion ($\theta = 135°$). See also Fig. 28.2

this illusory motion that is based on the depth inversion has been proposed by Papathomas [42]. (2) When the hollow mask is rotated in front of a stationary viewer, the perceived convex mask appears to rotate in a direction opposite to the physical direction of rotation. An extension of the explanation by Papathomas can be applied in this case. In this paper, we will concentrate on the second type of illusory motion that is elicited by a rotating mask for a stationary observer.

Figure 28.2a is a top view that illustrates the notation we use to describe the orientation of the mask. Angle θ specifies the spatial orientation of the mask, starting from zero when the convex side of the mask faces straight ahead toward the viewer, shown with solid lines, and increasing in the counter-clockwise (CCW) direction; a mask is shown in dashed lines as it rotates CCW by an angle θ_1. This mask orientation is very similar to the one used to obtain the image in Fig. 28.1a. In Fig. 28.2b the mask starts at $\theta = 180° - \theta_1$ (dashed lines) and it rotates CCW by an angle θ_1 to the straight ahead concave position at $\theta = 180°$ (solid lines). The viewer sees the concave side of the mask in this case. The image in Fig. 28.1b was obtained using a mask orientation similar to that at $\theta = 180° - \theta_1$. Notice that, if we think of the dashed-line hollow mask ($\theta = 180°$) as pointing toward the viewer, then the solid-line hollow mask of Fig. 28.2b points to the left of the viewer by an angle $\theta = -\theta_1$.

Importantly, as masks in Figs. 28.2a and 28.2b illustrate, for small rotation angles that avoid self-occlusions on the mask, and under orthographic projection, the image of the concave mask at $\theta = 180° - \theta_1$ is very similar to that of the convex mask at $\theta = \theta_1$. For example, the sizes of the left and right eyes of the masks will be roughly equal under orthographic projection. In contrast, for a perspective projection—which, after all, is what one obtains on the retina or with a camera— there are ample cues, for small viewing distances, to distinguish between the images obtained for the masks at $\theta = 180° - \theta_1$ and at $\theta = \theta_1$; this ability to distinguish between the two images decreases with increasing viewing distance.

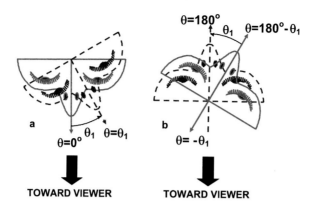

Fig. 28.2 Notation for the mask orientation. In these top views the viewer is at the bottom of the figure. For each mask orientation, the *straight-ahead solid arrow*—NOT the *thick arrow*—extending outward from the convex side is used to indicate its spatial orientation. The orientation angle θ is measured counter-clockwise from the reference position ($\theta = 0$), in which the convex mask faces the viewer. (**a**) The convex mask rotates CCW by an angle θ_1 from $\theta = 0$ (*solid lines*) to $\theta = \theta_1$ (*dashed lines*). (**b**) The mask rotates CCW by an angle θ_1 from $\theta = 180° - \theta_1$ (*solid lines*) to $\theta = 180°$ (*dashed lines*); both of these masks show their concave side to the viewer. The *dashed-line* mask in part a and the *solid-line* mask in part b were used to obtain the images of Fig. 28.1a and 28.1b, respectively

For example, for the dashed-line mask in Fig. 28.2a ($\theta = \theta_1$), the eye to the *left* of the viewer, being closer than the eye to the right of the viewer, will form a larger image. The opposite will be true for the solid-line mask in Fig. 28.2b ($\theta = 180° - \theta_1$); the eye to the *right* of the viewer will form a larger image than the eye to the left of the viewer. Of course, the size difference depends on the viewing distance of the imaging device (retina or camera) from the mask. This size difference between the left and the right eyes extends to the entire left and right sides of the face and the resulting size gradient can theoretically be used to recover the true 3-D shape. The images of Figs. 28.1a and 28.1b were obtained from a relatively large distance and, hence, these size differences are not evident.

The essence of the illusion is obtained when one compares what is perceived in the following two cases: (a) The convex masks starts from a straight-ahead position ($\theta = 0°$) and moves CCW by an angle θ_1 to position $\theta = \theta_1$, as in Fig. 28.2a. (b) The concave masks starts from a straight-ahead position ($\theta = 180°$) and moves CW by an angle θ_1, to position $\theta = 180 - \theta_1$, in the opposite direction to that shown in Fig. 28.2a. Under viewing conditions that favor the illusion, these two motions will produce the same percept, namely a convex masks that rotates CCW, because the concave mask will appear to rotate in the opposite direction to that of its physical direction of rotation. Notice that, because the kinetic-depth-effect cue (item 2b.2 in this section) is ambiguous, when we perceive the concave mask in inverted depth (convex), we perceive it rotating in the opposite direction.

The question is: will this size-differential cue, as well as other bottom-up cues (motion parallax, stereoscopic disparity, blur and possibly vergence angle and accommodation,[1] among others) overcome the schema of a convex face to recover the true concave mask shape? The answer is: it depends on several factors but primarily on the viewing distance. As explained above, the size gradient is negligible for large viewing distances and increases with decreasing viewing distance. The same is true for the differential signals provided by most of the bottom-up cues we mentioned earlier. Namely, the binocular disparity differential signals provided by mask features that are at different depths, such as the tip of the nose and lips, are very weak at long viewing distances and grow stronger as the distance decreases; ditto for motion parallax signals, and differences in vergence and accommodation. Because the strength of these bottom-up signals diminishes with increasing viewing distance, the prior experience with convex faces dominates and thus the prediction is that the illusion strength will increase with increasing distance. This is precisely what has been observed in experimental studies [21, 27–29, 43, 70].

28.3 The Hollow-Mask Illusion and Computer Vision

Most computer vision algorithms that have been developed to recover the 3-D structure of human faces include the schema for the convex form of faces as part of their knowledge base. Naturally, one would expect this schema to influence the recovery of 3-D shape when such algorithms are provided an animation sequence that involves a hollow mask. This is what we consider below for a representative face-tracking algorithm.

28.3.1 Model and Algorithm

The particular 3-D face model and tracking algorithm we used is that of DeCarlo and Metaxas [10]. The model itself is a handcrafted 3-D polygon model which has motion parameters that describe head movements (3-D translation and rotation) and facial motions (mouth movements, eyebrow raises, etc.), and shape parameters that enable the model to approximate the geometry of an individual's face. See Fig. 28.3. The 3-D face model uses about 80 spatial geometry variables (distance between eyes, length of nose, distance between upper lip and tip of nose, width of lips, etc.) that the algorithm adjusts to obtain a physical 3-D surface that conforms best to the face features that are present in the animation sequence being processed. The algorithm uses a combination of optical flow and feature alignment in order to maintain track of moving subjects. Essentially, the 3-D model, along with a simple model of image formation, is used to explain the changing appearance of a face in a series of images, in terms of its parameters.

---

[1] As Christopher Tyler commented, "vergence and accommodation would have to be derived over time by eye movements to provide shape information."

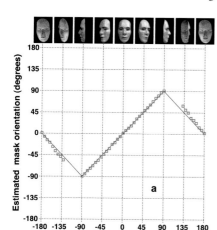
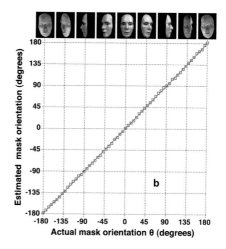

Fig. 28.5 The results of the algorithm under two different 3-D schemata, as applied to the animation sequence. The *horizontal axis* denotes the actual mask orientation of the stimuli during the rotation; *icons at the top* display the mask view for the corresponding orientation (the stimuli are identical in the two cases). The *vertical axis* denotes the mask orientation estimated by the algorithm. (**a**) Results with model 1 that assumes a convex mask schema. The algorithm tracks the mask well when the convex part is visible ($-90° \leq \theta \leq 90°$). However, the estimate is in the opposite direction from the actual motion (it approximately has slope -1), when the concave part is visible without any self-occlusions ($135° \leq |\theta| \leq 180°$). The algorithm experiences tracking problems and is unable to explain the image when parts of the mask occlude other parts (roughly in the range $90° < |\theta| < 135°$). (**b**) Results with model 2, a schema that accepts both convex and concave faces. The estimated mask orientation approximately matches the actual mask orientation for all 360 degrees (it has slope 1)

shape and spatial orientation of the mask over the entire range of 360°. Indeed, the slope of the line is 1 for $-180° \leq \theta \leq 180°$.

28.4 Discussion

In some sense, these findings can be thought of as evidence for the existence of schema-driven influences in visual perception for the particular case of human faces. Liberated from these top-down influences—in this case the knowledge that faces are convex—the algorithm uses the bottom-up signals to recover exactly the true shape and orientation of facial masks. However, when the algorithm is imbued with the knowledge of faces being convex, it behaves just as humans in being "fooled" by the hollow-mask illusion. As Theo Pavlidis [44] commented, "I have not seen any other demonstration where machine vision algorithms also suffer from optical illusions."

There are at least two pieces of evidence for top-down influences. The first is the inversion effect, that is, the reduced strength of the illusion when the hollow mask is displayed upside-down [27, 28, 43]. Apparently, the cause for the reduced strength

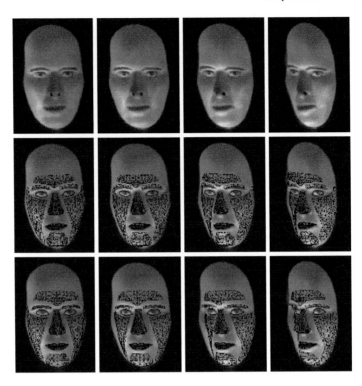

Fig. 28.6 Tracking results for the concave side of the mask. On *top* is the original sequence. In the *middle* are tracking results using model 2 (the convex-concave 3D model), which estimates the mask position correctly; it recovers a hollow mask rotating CW. On the *bottom* are tracking results using model 1 (the convex-face 3D model), which has the rotational direction reversed; it recovers a convex mask rotating CCW

is the lack of familiarity with inverted faces. The second piece of evidence is the reduced strength of the hollow-mask illusion in cases where the cognitive influences are impaired. Examples of such impairment are observed with subjects who are sleep-deprived [63] or under the influence of cannabis [13, 14, 56] or alcohol [58]. Schizophrenia (SZ) patients also experience a weaker illusion than controls, i.e., they tend to perceive the hollow mask as hollow [13, 33, 37, 57, 59]. One possible explanation is that SZ patients have a reduced ability to exert top-down influences in perception. Evidence for such weak feedback connections in SZ patients was presented by Dima et al. [11], based on fMRI data; Dima et al. [12] presented additional evidence on the basis of reduced P300 and P600 electro-encephalography (EEG) components, which signal late-stage processing, in SZ patients.

In addition to the explanation that the illusion is based on face familiarity, another possibility is that the illusion may not be stimulus-specific but instead may owe to a bias in favor of convexity [39, 60]. This hypothesis was tested by Hill and Bruce [28]. They reported that a hollow human mask produces a much stronger illusion than a "hollow potato" by comparing the switching distance, namely the average of the viewing distance at which the illusion breaks down on approach—starting with the illusory percept from a long distance—and the viewing distance at which the illusion sets in on retreat—starting with the veridical percept at a very close distance. Thus, the human mask enhances the bias to see concave surfaces as convex.

A third possibility, raised by Barlow [5], is that the sensory mechanisms analyze the redundancy that exists inherently in the sensory signals and the associations between input variables. According to Barlow, neural mechanisms respond to the "established associative structure in the input messages by recoding them ... [thus] making new structure more easily detectable" [5]. In the case of faces, he argues that our vast prior experiences resulting from moving past normal faces—as they themselves move or remain stationary—have resulted in an efficient neural coding scheme for the representation of our own motion and the visual motion signals generated by the 3D geometry and the parts of a normal face. Thus, when we move past a stationary hollow mask, this recoding scheme now works in the wrong direction to compensate for the visual motion that it expects. The result is that the scheme interprets the visual motion signals as elicited by a normal (convex) face that moves. The weaker illusion for an upside-down hollow mask is accounted by Barlow's [5] hypothesis as resulting from less exposure to upside-down faces and therefore less recoding mechanisms.

What happens for $90° < |\theta| < 132°$? Figure 28.1c shows a mask oriented at $\theta = 117.3°$. The algorithm, as well as the human visual system, is unable to recognize a normal face in this and other cases where there are extensive self-occlusions. Apparently, the algorithm that has a convex-face schema cannot resolve the discontinuities in the 3-D shape that are recovered by the optic flow and provides no output for a face. When the extent of the self-occlusions is limited, as in the marginal orientation of Fig. 28.1d ($\theta = 132°$), the algorithm can still—barely—recover a face. The same occlusion that acts as noise for tracking a convex face in the convex-face schema algorithm can be used as signal in the thin-mask schema algorithm.

At this point, we can conjecture about how a computer vision algorithm for scene perception would operate when presented with an animation sequence of a rotating reverspective. A reverspective is a 3-D piece that is constructed and painted realistically such that the painted perspective cues depict a depth structure that is exactly opposite to the physical structure, which is recovered correctly by binocular disparity and motion parallax signals [61, 67]. A computer vision scene analysis system that is driven mainly by data-driven signals (motion parallax, stereoscopic disparity, etc.) would recover the veridical 3-D structure. We conjecture that, if such a scene analysis system is endowed with schema-driven modules for perspective, it will likely experience the illusion that human experience, that is, perceiving the direction of rotation to be the opposite from the physical direction, in analogy with the behavior of the face tracking algorithm (see pertinent video animation in http://videos.springer.com).

This raises an interesting issue. Ideally, computer vision systems need to be endowed with some schemata that help them process the visual input more efficiently and accurately. For example, face-processing systems benefit greatly from a built-in deformable model of a generic face that is characterized by several deformation parameters. This allows the systems, when provided the input video sequence of a particular face, to optimize the parameters so as to fit the best possible model to that particular face. The price they pay is that such systems are fooled by the hollow-mask illusion, as humans are.

Humans, however, have the advantage of changing the viewing conditions (shorter viewing distance, binocular viewing, etc.), not to mention handling the stimulus by touch, to gain more knowledge about the true 3-D structure of the stimulus. We can see two extreme options for computer vision systems. The first—easy—approach involves endowing such systems with additional schemata, such as the schema of a thin facial mask in the case of face perception. The second—difficult—approach is to enable these systems to explore possibilities that are not covered by the initial repertory of schemata they were provided with at inception. In the case of face tracking algorithms, the system would have to analyze the optic flow in the video, recognize that it fails to arrive at a solution in some instances and search for alternative schemata that, if successful, it would add it to its own repertoire. The first approach is one of "spoon feeding" schemata to the system and it requires constant supervised learning; the second approach is one of "learning from experience" and it appears more promising but requires fundamental advances before it can be implemented. Of course, these two approaches are applicable to cases where we are limited to images derived from the visible spectrum only. Obviously, systems equipped with range finders can provide 3D signals to recover the true depth structure.

Acknowledgements We would like to thank Manpreet Kaur for conducting experiments on the hollow-mask illusion with human observers. We thank Christopher Tyler who reviewed the manuscript and offered valuable suggestions.

References

1. Adams WJ, Graf EW, Ernst MO (2004) Experience can change the 'light-from-above' prior. Nat Neurosci 7:1057–1058
2. Aglioti S, DeSouza JFX, Goodale MA (1995) Size contrast illusions deceive the eye but not the hand. Curr Biol 5:679–685
3. Ahissar M, Hochstein S (2004) The reverse hierarchy theory of perceptual learning. Trends Cogn Sci 8(10):457–464
4. Banks MS, Backus BT (1998) Extra-retinal and perspective cues cause the small range of the induced effect. Vis Res 38:187–194
5. Barlow HB (1997) The knowledge used in vision and where it comes from. Philos Trans R Soc Lond B, Biol Sci 352(1358):1141–1147
6. Berbaum K, Bever T, Chung CS (1983) Light source position in the perception of object shape. Perception 12:411–416
7. Berbaum K, Bever T, Chung CS (1984) Extending the perception of shape from known to unknown shading. Perception 13:479–488
8. Caudek C, Fantoni C, Domini F (2011) Bayesian modeling of perceived surface slant from actively-generated and passively-observed optic flow. PLoS ONE 6(4):e18731

9. Cook ND, Hayashi T, Amemiya T, Suzuki K, Leumann L (2002) Effects of visual field inversions on the reverse-perspective illusion. Perception 31:1147–1151

10. DeCarlo D, Metaxas D (2000) Optical flow constraints on deformable models with applications to face tracking. Int J Comput Vis 38(2):99–127

11. Dima D, Roiser JP, Dietrich DE, Bonnemann C, Lanfermann H, Emrich HM, Dillo W (2009) Understanding why patients with schizophrenia do not perceive the hollow-mask illusion using dynamic causal modeling. NeuroImage 46:1180–1186

12. Dima D, Dillo W, Bonnemann C, Emrich HM, Dietrich DE (2011) Reduced P300 and P600 amplitude in the hollow-mask illusion in patients with schizophrenia. Psychiatry Res Neuroimaging 191:145–151

13. Emrich HM, Leweke FM, Schneider U (1997) Towards a cannabinoid hypothesis of schizophrenia: cognitive impairments due to a dysregulation of the endogenous cannabinoid system. Pharmacol Biochem Behav 56:803–807

14. Emrich HM, Weber MM, Wendl A, Zihl J, Von Meyer L, Hanisch W (1991) Reduced binocular depth inversion as an indicator of cannabis-induced censorship impairment. Pharmacol Biochem Behav 40:689–690

15. Feldman J, Singh M (2006) Bayesian estimation of the shape skeleton. Proc Natl Acad Sci USA 103(47):18014–18019

16. Franz VH, Gegenfurtner KR, Bulthoff HH, Fahle M (2000) Grasping visual illusions: no evidence for a dissociation between perception and action. Psychol Sci 11:20–25

17. Gilbert CD, Sigman M (2007) Brain states: top-down influences in sensory processing. Neuron 54:677–696

18. Goldberg I, Harel M, Malach R (2006) When the brain loses its self: prefrontal inactivation during sensorimotor processing. Neuron 50:329–339

19. Goldreich D, Peterson MA (2012) A Bayesian observer replicates convexity context effects in figure-ground perception. Seeing Perceiving 25(3–4):365–395. doi:10.1163/187847612X634445

20. Gregory RL (1968) Perceptual illusions and brain models. Proc R Soc B 171:279–296

21. Gregory RL (1970) The intelligent eye. McGraw-Hill, New York, pp 126–131

22. Gregory RL (1980) Perceptions as hypotheses. Philos Trans R Soc Lond B, Biol Sci 290:181–197

23. Gregory RL (1997) Knowledge in perception and illusion. Philos Trans R Soc Lond B, Biol Sci 352:1121–1128

24. Gregory RL (2005) The Medawar lecture 2001 knowledge for vision: vision for knowledge. Philos Trans R Soc Lond B, Biol Sci 360(1458):1231–1251

25. Held RT, Cooper EA, Banks MS (2012) Blur and disparity are complementary cues to depth. Curr Biol 22:426–431

26. Helmholtz H (1910/1867). Handbuch der Physiologischen Optik, vol 3. Voss

27. Hill H, Bruce V (1993) Independent effects of lighting, orientation, and stereopsis on the hollow-face illusion. Perception 22(8):887–897

28. Hill H, Bruce V (1994) A comparison between the hollow-face and 'hollow-potato' illusions. Perception 23:1335–1337

29. Hill H, Johnston A (2007) The hollow-face illusion: object-specific knowledge, general assumptions or properties of the stimulus? Perception 36:199–223

30. Hochstein S, Ahissar M (2002) View from the top: hierarchies and reverse hierarchies in the visual system. Neuron 36:791–804

31. Jain A, Zaidi Q (2011) Discerning nonrigid 3D shapes from motion cues. Proc Natl Acad Sci USA 108(4):1663–1668

32. Jones MJ, Sinha P, Vetter T, Poggio T (1997) Top-down learning of low-level vision tasks. Curr Biol 7:991–994

33. Keane BP, Silverstein SM, Wang Y, Papathomas TV (2013) Reduced depth illusions in schizophrenia: Evidence for a weakened, state-dependent convexity prior. J Abnormal Psych 122(2):506–512

34. Kersten D, Yuille A (2003) Bayesian models of object perception. Curr Opin Neurobiol 13:1–9
35. Kersten D, Mamassian P, Yuille A (2004) Object perception as Bayesian inference. Annu Rev Psychol 55:271–304
36. Kleffner DA, Ramachandran VS (1992) On the perception of shape from shading. Percept Psychophys 52:18–36
37. Koethe D, Gerth CW, Neatby MA, Haensel A, Thies M, Schneider U, Emrich HM, Klosterkotter J, Schultze-Lutter F, Leweke FM (2006) Disturbances of visual information processing in early states of psychosis and experimental delta-9-tetrahydrocannabinol altered states of consciousness. Schizophr Res 88:142–150
38. Krekelberg B, Lappe M (2001) Neuronal latencies and the position of moving objects. Trends Neurosci 24:335–339
39. Langer MS, Bülthoff HH (2001) A prior for global convexity in local shape-from-shading. Perception 30:403–410
40. Palmer S (1999) Vision science: from photons to phenomenology. MIT Press, Cambridge
41. Papathomas TV (1999) The brain as a hypothesis-constructing-and-testing agent. In: LePore E, Pylyshyn Z (eds) What is cognitive science? Blackwell, Oxford, pp 230–247
42. Papathomas TV (2007) Art pieces that 'move' in our minds—an explanation of illusory motion based on depth reversal. Spat Vis 21:79–95
43. Papathomas TV, Bono L (2004) Experiments with a hollow mask and a reverspective: top-down influences in the inversion effect for 3-d stimuli. Perception 33:1129–1138
44. Pavlidis T (2012) Personal communication. December 15, 2012
45. Pizlo Z (2001) Perception viewed as an inverse problem. Vis Res 41(24):3145–3161
46. Poggio T, Torre V, Koch C (1985) Computational vision and regularization theory. Nature 317:314–319
47. Purves D, Lotto RB (2003) Why we see what we do. Sinauer, Sunderland
48. Ramachandran VS (1988) Perception of shape from shading. Nature 331:163–166
49. Ramachandran VS (1995) Anosognosia in parietal lobe syndrome. Conscious Cogn 4(1):22–51
50. Regan D, Erkelens CJ, Collewijn H (1986) Necessary conditions for the perception of motion in depth. Investig Ophthalmol Vis Sci 27:584–597
51. Richards W (2009) Configuration stereopsis: a new look at the depth-disparity relation. Spat Vis 22(1):91–103
52. Rock I (1983) The logic of perception. MIT Press, Cambridge
53. Rogers B (2009) Motion parallax as an independent cue for depth perception: a retrospective. Perception 38(6):907–911
54. Rogers B, Graham M (1979) Motion parallax as an independent cue for depth perception. Perception 8(2):125–134
55. Rogers BJ, Gyani A (2010) Binocular disparities, motion parallax, and geometric perspective in Patrick Hughes's 'reverspectives': theoretical analysis and empirical findings. Perception 39:330–348
56. Semple DM, Ramsden F, McIntosh AM (2003) Reduced binocular depth inversion in regular cannabis users. Pharmacol Biochem Behav 75(4):789–793
57. Schneider U, Borsutzky M, Seifert J, Leweke FM, Huber TJ, Rollnik JD, Emrich HM (2002) Reduced binocular depth inversion in schizophrenic patients. Schizophr Res 53:101–108
58. Schneider U, Dietrich DE, Sternemann U, Seeland I, Gielsdorf D, Huber TJ, Becker H, Emrich HM (1998) Reduced binocular depth inversion in patients with alcoholism. Alcohol Alcoholism 33:168–172
59. Schneider U, Leweke FM, Sternemann U, Weber MM, Emrich HM (1996) Visual 3D illusion: a systems-theoretical approach to psychosis. Eur Arch Psychiatry Clin Neurosci 246:256–260
60. Sherman A, Papathomas TV, Jain A, Keane BP (2011) The roles of perspective, angle polarity, stereo and motion parallax in perceiving 3D objects. Seeing Perceiving 25:263–285
61. Slyce J (2011) Patrick Hughes: perverspective, 3rd edn. Momentum, London

62. Sperling G, Landy MS (1989) Kinetic depth effect and identification of shape. J Exp Psychol Hum Percept Perform 15(4):826–840
63. Sternemann U, Schneider U, Leweke FM, Bevilacqua CM, Dietrich DE, Emrich HM (1997) Pro-psychotic change of binocular depth inversion by sleep deprivation. Nervenarzt 68(7):593–596. [Article in German]
64. Tyler CW, Kontsevich LL (1995) Mechanisms of stereoscopic processing: stereoattention and surface perception in depth reconstruction. Perception 24(2):127–153
65. Uttal WR, Liu N, Kalki J (1996) An integrated computational model of three-dimensional vision. Spat Vis 9(4):393–422
66. Vishwanath D, Blaser E (2010) Retinal blur and the perception of egocentric distance. J Vis 10(10):26
67. Wade NJ, Hughes P (1999) Fooling the eyes: trompe l'oeil and reverse perspective. Perception 28:1115–1119
68. Welchman AE, Harris JM, Brenner E (2009) Extra-retinal signals support the estimation of 3D motion. Vis Res 49:782–789
69. Westheimer G (2008) Illusions in the spatial sense of the eye: geometrical-optical illusions and the neural representation of space. Vis Res 48(20):2128–2142
70. Yellott JI Jr (1981) Binocular depth inversion. Sci Am 245:118–125
71. Yuille A, Kersten D (2006) Vision as Bayesian inference: analysis by synthesis? Trends Cogn Sci 10:301–308

Chapter 29
Detecting, Representing and Attending to Visual Shape

Antonio J. Rodríguez-Sánchez, Gregory L. Dudek, and John K. Tsotsos

29.1 Introduction

In 1962, Harry Blum wrote a report titled "An Associative Machine For Dealing
With the Visual Field And Some of its Biological Implications" [3]. The title re-
veals that he was not only inspired by, but also wished to impact biological vision.
Blum was later motivated by the Gestalt psychologists in developing algorithms for
extracting shape descriptors [4] and even tried to map his algorithm onto the results
of Hubel and Wiesel's [23] study of visual cortical neurons. Blum points out that the
Gestaltists used field theoretic concepts and proposed diffusion/propagation models.
These ideas motivated Blum, but he realized they were unsatisfactory as presented
due to their lack of precision and detail. Blum thus took those ideas and developed
the now well-known Medial Axis Transform (MAT or 'grass fire' algorithm). The
concept has reached its most sophisticated form in the shock graphs of Siddiqi et al.
[53]. Our research looks at the detection and description of single object 2D silhouettes, the same kind of silhouettes on which MAT or shock graphs might operate. In
our case, however, the quest is to develop a formalization of the stages of processing
the primate visual cortex uses for this task and to show the correspondence between
the computational result and the responses of single neurons to the same stimuli. In
addition to constraining our design by the biological plausibility goal, we are further
constrained by the quest to make the result amenable to attentional processes such
as those required for spatial and shape reasoning [33, 61].

A.J. Rodríguez-Sánchez (✉)
Intelligent and Interactive Systems, University of Innsbruck, Innsbruck, Austria
e-mail: Antonio.Rodriguez-Sanchez@uibk.ac.at

G.L. Dudek
Centre for Intelligent Machines, McGill University, Montreal, Canada

J.K. Tsotsos
Dept. of Electrical Engineering and Computer Science, and Center for Vision Research, York
University, Toronto, Canada

S.J. Dickinson, Z. Pizlo (eds.), *Shape Perception in Human and Computer Vision*,
Advances in Computer Vision and Pattern Recognition,
DOI 10.1007/978-1-4471-5195-1_29, © Springer-Verlag London 2013

Shape computation in the primate visual system may be considered as part of the object recognition pathway covering areas V1, V2, V4 and the inferotemporal cortex (or IT) in the visual cortex. The first studies in area V1 found neurons that respond to bars and edges [24]. Already in those studies, three cell-types were differentiated: simple cells, responding to bars at specific locations; complex cells, which respond to a bar irrespective of its position inside the cell's receptive field; and hypercomplex (today known as end-stopped) cells, sensitive to the termination of an edge or a bar. End-stopped cells were extensively studied in later studies [2, 31, 37, 38], which reported the existence of end-zone inhibitory areas.

V2 neurons respond to real and illusory contours [63] as well as angles, corners, and provide submaximal responses to bars [6, 26]. V4 is important for the perception of form and pattern/shape discrimination [36]. The series of studies by Pasupathy and Connor [40–42] showed that populations of V4 neurons would respond to shapes and their responses could be approximated with an angular position-curvature representation of the shape. Posterior inferotemporal (PIT) neurons integrate contour elements with both linear and nonlinear mechanisms [7]. That study showed that some contours had an excitatory effect on the neuron response, while for others, it had an inhibitory effect. Anterior inferotemporal (AIT) neurons are responsible for the representation of objects, including faces, hands and other body parts. This representation includes shape as one of its components, this area receives inputs from V4 and PIT neurons at different retinal positions [57], which may explain its scale, position and view invariant cell responses [5].

The developmental importance of shape is unquestionable [9, 19, 30, 49, 55, 56]. Spelke showed how in both adults and children, shape is an important component of object perception, and that Gestalt properties of shape are adhered to from a very young age. Smith et al. examined object name learning in young children (3 yrs) and found that learning object names tunes children's attention to the properties relevant for naming, namely, to the property of shape. Gershfokk-Stowe & Smith further showed this to be true for noun-learning in even younger children (17 months).

Finally, experimental work has clearly shown that humans and non-human primates can attend to shape [8, 10, 27, 50, 54, 59], and that this capacity interacts with other visual qualities or sensory modalities. Corbetta et al., using PET scanning, observed, that attention to shape activated the collateral sulcus, fusiform and parahippocampal gyri, and temporal cortex along the superior temporal sulcus. They concluded that selective attention to different features modulates activity in distinct regions of extrastriate cortex specialized for the selected feature. The disjoint pattern of activations suggests that perceptual judgments involve different neural systems, depending on attentional strategies. Todd, in a very nice survey paper, concludes that the perceptual representation of 3D shape may be primarily based on qualitative aspects of 3D structure that involve arrangements of salient image features, such as occlusion contours or edges of high curvature, whose topological structures remain relatively stable over viewing directions. He also points to empirical studies that have shown that the neural processing of 3D shape is broadly distributed throughout the ventral and dorsal visual pathways, suggesting that processes in both pathways are fundamental to human perception and cognition. Sereno & Amador found that during the presentation of a sample stimulus and test array to monkeys, some LIP neurons show stronger responses to the stimulus in the shape-matching task when the animal must attend to the shape of a stimulus, the first evidence that attention to shape can be seen in primate cortex. Cant & Goodale, using fMRI, showed that attending to shape activated the contour-sensitive lateral occipital (LO) area, whose organization seems complex, with neurons tuned not only to the outline shape of objects, but also to their surface curvature independent of contour. James et al. also found evidence that lateral occipitotemporal cortex (LO) is involved in representing object shape information. A specialization of LO, the tactive-visual area (LOtv) seems to integrate visual with haptic shape elements and even with auditory shape elements [27].

Although research on the detection and representation of shape has been strong over the years (see the chapters in this volume, for example), few shape models seem to support attentional processes beyond the usual region-of-interest kind of methods. A notable exception is the MetriCat model of Hummel & Stankiewicz [25]. It suggests two roles for visual attention in shape recognition: attention for binding and attention for signal-to-noise control. MetriCat implements both as special cases of a single mechanism for controlling the synchrony relations among units representing separate object parts.

Our goal is to develop a shape detection and representation methodology that supports the attentional processes as described by the Selective Tuning (ST) model of attention [60]. The choice of this model is that it includes a very broad set of attentional mechanisms and has already received very strong experimental support for the many predictions it has made regarding human and non-human primate visual processing [22, 60].

It is not difficult to use ST to constrain the quest for a shape detection framework. The requirements are all found in Tsotsos [60] and include both representation as well as processing constraints:

1. Visual representations (or areas to draw the direct comparison to cortical anatomy) are organized into a Lattice of Pyramids (or P-Lattice), defined in [60].
2. Receptive fields of individual neurons are spatiotemporally localized.
3. Objects, and their shapes, are presented using a parts-based composition of less abstract elements represented hierarchically in the P-Lattice.
4. The basic process of recurrent branch-and-bound operating over the P-Lattice is required for attentional tuning.

These are sufficient requirements for a shape representation scheme to be 'attentive' and thus play a critical role in the definitions of components that follow.

The next sections will briefly overview an early and then a very recent exploration into appropriate shape detection and representation ideas.

29.2 An Early Use of Curvature: Curvature-Tuned Smoothing

The original work on curvature-tuned smoothing (CTS) attempted to address this by representing shape in terms of curvature data and to allow a family of alternative interpretations via a nonlinear scale space [13, 14]. Since curvature is a differential property that must be inferred over noisy data, its extraction requires smoothing or regularization which, in turn, implies a biasing prior over the estimates to be extracted. The basis of the CTS approach is to employ a richer prior distribution than what is normally used. When one reflects on the importance of a prior, it is only a small step to realize that top-down influence can be used to moderate or accelerate the estimation process, a step that was not taken in the original work on curvature-tuned smoothing which was based on exhaustive consideration of all possible curvatures, but which relates to later work on attentive processing.

The perceptual relevance of curvature, particularly for 2D curves, has been apparent for decades while the use of a multi-scale representation sidesteps the issues of more simplistic representations. In prior work, the stable extraction and measurement of curvature information in the presence of noise was addressed in several ways, but was usually based on the assumption that there is a single unique curvature measurable at each point. While this is, of course, true in the analytic case, the assumption introduces significant difficulty for estimation problems involving noisy signals, such as those that occur in vision. Despite the respectable results that have been achieved by some researchers, the need for scale-specific operators to deal with noise problems (which also manifests itself as the need to choose a best smoothing scale, or the choice of an appropriate neighborhood for measurements) causes an inherent preference for certain ranges of curvature value and involves strong implicit assumptions about the underlying signal. The actual curvature of a signal depends on what we call noise and what we call signal, and hence may take on differing values depending on our goals.

The extent and shape of the neighborhood used for this processing asserts an implicit scale specificity as a result of the interpolant of support function used for estimation. For example, a polynomial model of a portion of a curve limits the number of inflection points over the region and hence bounds the amount of structure that can occur. In general, high curvatures with correspondingly small spatial extents relative to the neighborhood size will be lost or drastically attenuated. This attenuation is, in fact, the key objective of the non-local estimation methods. On the other hand, low curvatures may remain difficult to measure since the neighborhood being used will often be too small to reduce local noise. To a large degree, this too is the objective of non-local modeling: to discard structure at the wrong scale. The difficulty is compounded in practice by the fact that scale-specific constraints are usually stated only implicitly and the single correct scale is difficult to control or select. In most modeling problems, the objective is to map the data to its most likely causative models, that is, the most reasonable real curves that it could actually describe. In doing so we regularize the measurement process, discarding implausible structure in the data. The method described here exploits the relationship between curvature and scale to produce a set of alternative descriptions of the data based on structure at different scales.

Our approach begins with shape primitives that are extracted using a variational formulation called *curvature-tuned smoothing* [12–14]. This description has several desirable properties including its basis in perceptually-relevant curvature measurements [1, 32], and its properties in the face of sparse data or noise [43, 58]. The multi-scale nature of the representation allows multiple alternative possible descriptions for portions of a curve to be retained. It produces a description of a curve where a single region may be described in terms of one or more arcs of different curvatures (and hence sizes), and hence makes explicit information and different spatial scales (by the term scale we refer to the size or spatial extent of a processing operation or feature).

The curve representation is produced by repeatedly minimizing the following energy functional with respect to a piecewise C^2 solution $\bar{u}(t) = (x(t), y(t))$:

$$E\big(\bar{u}(t, c)\big) = \int_{l_e}^{k_e} \big\|\bar{u}(t) - \bar{d}(t)\big\|^2 + \phi p\big(\bar{u}(t)\big) + \lambda(c)\big(\kappa_a(t) - c\big)^2 dt$$

where t is arc length, $\bar{d}(t) = (x(t), y(t))$ is a list of initial data points estimating the input curve, $p(x, y)$ is a potential function derived from the input image (i.e., a measure of edginess), with ϕ being an associated weight, $\kappa_a(t)$ is the curvature of $\bar{u}(t)$, $\lambda(c)$ provides the relative weight of the stabilizing term, c is the "curvature tuning", and l is the stabilizing constant selected as a function of c. The term ϕ can be set to zero if pure 2D curves are the input data (as opposed to edges embedded in a larger image). This solution is determined for various values of c, denoted by c_i. The first two terms constrain the solution to be consistent with an initial input description and with image support for the curve position. The third term expresses an "internal" bias for a solution with a specific curvature given by c. The result is a multi-scale decomposition of a curve such that segments that can be interpreted as being characterized by different natural curvatures are simultaneously extracted. These are the regions having low energy in terms of the above functional. An example of the result is shown in Fig. 29.1. The figure shows a poison sumac leaf in silhouette and the portions of it that are detected at specific curvature tunings along the silhouette.

The matching methods most commonly used for curved data deal with recognition by organizing cues along the arc-length axis. That is, a correspondence between features is established as the curve is traversed in a given direction. The presence of structure along the curvature (non-linear scale) dimension is an additional and unique aspect of the description produced from curvature-tuned smoothing. For example, the leaves of the poison sumac plant are typified by large rounded leaf tops containing a particular arrangement of three "sub-bumps" at the same location.

By using the multi-scale representation to match curves in scale space, a potentially richer description was obtained that what would be extracted by comparable regularization-based smoothing techniques. These multi-scale descriptions could then be used for recognition, for example using dynamic programming [13]. Most notably, this representation using various prior expectations in curvature space can "tune" the regularization process. Whether this tuning should be applied selectively instead of exhaustively was never explored in the original work, but is a natural

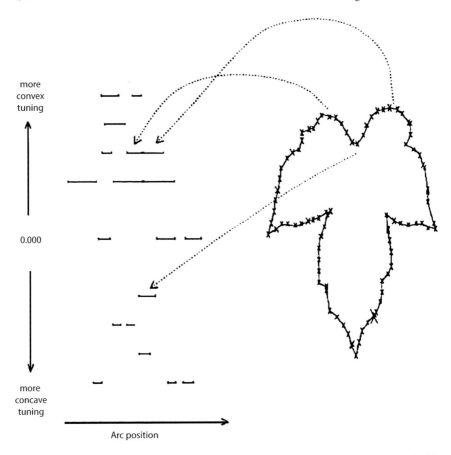

Fig. 29.1 Poison sumac leaf and scale-space. The CTS description of the poison sumac leaf is shown, with the segments corresponding to certain features on the leaf illustrated. Each line corresponds to a segment with discontinuities at its ends. The length of each line corresponds to the segment length

candidate of top-down bias in the interests of either computational efficiency of selective search and thus a natural hook into attentional processes.

29.3 2DSIL: End-Stopped and Curvature Computations for Silhouette Recognition

Our most recent efforts have focused on trying to create a shape model with biological relevance if not also plausibility. Recent experiments in area V4 [42] and TEO [7, 57] of the macaque monkey seem to agree with a recognition of objects by parts strategy, clearly suitably satisfying for constrains the ST attention model. In the case of V4 and TEO, those parts would be local curvatures [7, 40–42]. 2DSIL

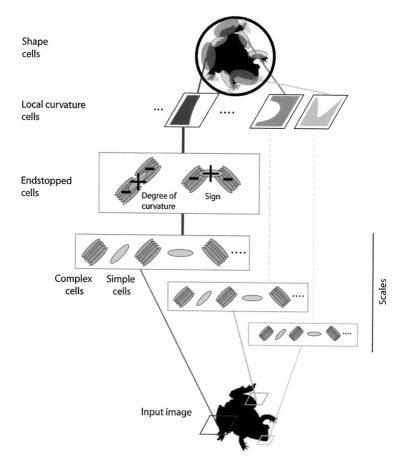

Shape cells

Local curvature cells

Endstopped cells

Degree of curvature

Sign

Complex cells

Simple cells

Scales

Input image

Fig. 29.2 Architecture of 2DSIL (see text and [47, 48], for more information)

[48] (see Fig. 29.1) is our resulting model. Different from other models, such as [44, 52], 2DSIL does not consist of the addition of new layers over the Neocognitron [18] with a repetition of S and C neurons. Rather, new types of neurons select for different curvatures and include inhibitory surround. Cell types comprising 2DSIL (Fig. 29.2) are the following:

- *Simple cells* of visual area V1 are sensitive to bar and edge orientations. Gabor filters [35] and Difference of Gaussians have been shown to provide a good fit when modeling simple cells from area V1, although a better fit to neuronal responses has been found with Difference of Gaussians [21]. The latter formulation is the one used in 2DSIL for modeling simple cells. 48 different groups of simple cells were designed, varying sizes, orientation and values of Gaussian width and length.
- *Complex cells* have a sensitivity for bars and orientations as well, but their receptive fields are larger than those of simple neurons. Hubel and Wiesel [23, 24]

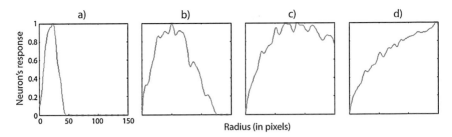

Fig. 29.3 Curvature selectivity from end-stopped neurons. Smaller cell sizes (**a, b**) are selective for sharper curvatures, larger neuron scales are selective for broader curvatures (**c, d**). Simple cell sizes that combined into end-stopped cells were: 40 (**a**), 80 (**b**), 100 (**c**) and 120 (**d**) pixels

found that simple cells have one or more subfields in which the response is either on or off while complex cells yield both on and off responses, which suggest that complex cells integrate the responses of simple cells. In our model, a complex cell is the sum of 5 laterally displaced model simple cells Gaussian weighted with position and later rectified (any value less than 0 is set to 0).

- *End-stopped cells* can be of two types. One provides band-pass selectivity for degree of curvature. The tuning for degree of curvature can range from very sharp to very broad as can be seen in Fig. 29.2 for four cell sizes. This type of cell is composed of a simple and two complex cells [11]. Complex cells are laterally displaced and provide an inhibitory input with respect to the centered excitatory simple cell. Depending on the orientation of the complex cell component with respect to the simple cell we obtain neurons that are selective to degrees of curvature (if that orientation is the same). The combination from smaller model end-stopped neurons is selective for sharper curvatures and the combination of larger cells responds strongly to broader curvatures (Fig. 29.3). The second type of end-stopped neuron is selective for the sign of curvature, by using displaced neurons at different orientations (Fig. 29.2).

- *Local curvature cells* are obtained due to the neural convergence of the two types of model end-stopped cells. By combining model end-stopped cells selective to the degree of curvature and model sign end-stopped cells responses, we obtain twice the number of curvature classes than the number of end-stopped cells. For example, if we have four types of degree of curvature end-stopped cells, through the use of the sign of curvature of those cells we obtain eight curvature classes. For the case where the response from end-stopped cells is small, a high response from a model orientation simple cell means the contour is a straight line, so its curvature is set to 0. Local curvature cells are computed at each location.

- *Shape cells* are at the top of the hierarchy (Fig. 29.2) and integrate the responses from local curvature cells. Shape-selective cells respond to curvature configurations with respect to their position in the cell's receptive field. A model shape cell will respond to a shape, and depending on how close the stimulus is to its selectivity, its response will be stronger or weaker. In the example provided in Fig. 29.2, the input to a shape cell that respond to the silhouette of a frog is composed of

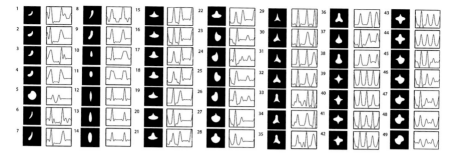

Fig. 29.4 Capability of shape neurons for encoding stimuli from Pasupathy and Connor [42]. Stimuli (in *black background*) were created using a Matlab program for that purpose provided by Dr. Pasupathy. Compare the plots at the right of the stimuli with the neural responses and plots in Fig. 3 from Pasupathy and Connor [42]

local curvature cells with high responses to sharp curvatures at the bottom (the right hand of the frog), local-curvature cells selective to broad curvatures at the left and top-left (two back legs), etc., providing a cell that has a high response to different local curvatures at specific locations. A similar shape would also provide a high response from the 2DSIL shape-selective cell.

2DSIL shape-cell responses were compared with the responses from neurons in area V4 [48]. Neurons in area V4 of the visual cortex encode shapes as curvature parts relative to their position in the object [42]. The stimuli used in that study were silhouettes created using convex and concave boundary elements to form closed shapes (see Fig. 29.4, silhouettes on black background).

Figure 29.4 shows the results of applying 2DSIL over the stimuli (left columns) from [42]. The encodings from model shape cells are in the right columns. The blue plots not only reproduce the curvatures for the stimuli that appear at their left but are also very close on how populations of V4 neurons encode shape, compare this figure with Fig. 3 of [42] or refer to [46]. When computing the difference from the plot values in Fig. 29.3 with those of [42], the reported error was of 0.074 ($stdev = 0.037$, $error\ range = [0, 1]$) which shows that the model shape cells in 2DSIL faithfully replicate the population results obtained in area V4 of the visual cortex.

We further tested 2DSIL on real images. We selected eight commonly used databases with clutter (Leaves from Fergus et al. [16], cars back, faces, motorcycles, leopards, bottles and airplanes from Caltech256, and cars from Leung [34]). The task was an object present/absent classification, where the model has to detect if the object in question is present in the image or not. We used the background database as negative (absent) samples.

The details of the test have been presented previously [47]. The key here is to simply show that the curvature cells in the model do indeed capture sufficient salient aspects of shape to enable classification. Values from local curvature cell responses were used to construct a feature vector (2640 elements) that was the input to an Adaboost classifier (300 iterations). Training consisted of presenting randomly half the images containing the object (positive samples: 93 for leaves, 263 for cars back, 258 for cars-MIT, 225 for faces, 95 for leopards, 50 for bottles, 413 for motorbikes and 537 for airplanes) and half the background images (negative samples: 225 randomly chosen images). The remaining images were used to test the model (same number as in training, but different randomly chosen images).

We obtained the percentage of correctly classified images (as containing objects or background). The model outperforms classical systems such as for most databases. Correct classifications were: 98.6 % for cars back (1.9 % false negatives and 0.9 % false positives), 96.9 % for cars-MIT (5 % false negatives and 0.9 % false positives), 89.2 % for faces (12 % false negatives and 10 % false positives), 94.0 % for leaves (10 % false negatives and 0.7 % false positives), 96.9 % for leopards (4 % false negatives and 2.6 % false positives), 83.3 % for bottles (35 % false negatives and 16.5 % false positives) and 92.8 % for airplanes (5 % false negatives and 1.2 % false positives). Results are similar as well to another biologically inspired model [51], and the very recent Bag-of-features approach by Han et al. [20].

Finally, since the ability to connect to an attentional system such as Selective Tuning provided key constraints for the overall design, it is important to show that these constraints are indeed satisfied. In Rodriguez-Sanchez et al. [45], we showed exactly this capacity demonstrating how the shape cells provide sufficient information for simple shape recognition in common visual search tasks. The performance of the overall shape attentive system was directly compared to psychophysical experimental data in common search tasks: a color similarity search where feature search can be inefficient if the differences in color are small and a set of feature and conjunction searches that show the continuum of search slopes from inefficient to efficient using stimuli such as circles, crosses, and letters. It was shown that the qualitative performance comparison was virtually identical.

29.4 Conclusions

Our foray into shape representation, detection and attentive recognition, has led to a sophisticated and successful model, 2DSIL, of processing in the early stages of visual cortex and also to a high performance computer vision shape framework. This work, however, suggests as many questions as it might answer. Questions that motivate the next stages of research include:

- How would higher order processes use 2DSIL as input, such as those examined by Brincat & Connor [7]?
- Can the model be extended to surfaces or 3D shapes, and precisely how? Although the CTS model was extended to operate over range data, how might it be applied to natural imagery with implicit 3D structure, and how could this extension be made for 2DSIL? Moreover, while curvature extrema regions of constant curvature and vertices are both computationally natural primitives with extensive evidence with respect to perceptual relevance, the choice of tractable yet perceptually-relevant descriptions for surfaces is much less clear. Despite extensive evidence for the importance of 3D structure, are the mathematically or com-

putationally elegant model extensions of 2D shape suitable for modeling human perception?

- Several researchers have reported selectivity for 3D shape in IT [28, 29, 62]). The lower bank of STS (superior temporal sulcus—a subarea of TE) was found selective to 3D shape, while lateral TE was selective to 2D shape [29]. How in the context of 2DSIL, can local curvature neurons be extended from curves in 2D-silhouettes to surfaces and shape cells to encode from shapes in a plane to shapes in 3D space [39, 64]?
- How can the model, which permits all potential shapes, be tailored via learning to represent the set of real objects in a given domain of interest? Should it be done through incorporating prior knowledge following the Gestalt principles (such as symmetry, proximity, and continuity)? Or should it be done through learning as infants seem to do [17]?
- Lastly, the models described here focus mainly on the representation of shape, and while each is validated using a recognition of classification mechanism, that important stage of processing remains to be more carefully examined, especially in a probabilistic context. With respect to recognizing 3D surfaces embedded in images, a natural extension would be to explore Markov Random Fields or Deep Learning as computational frameworks for recognition.

In answering these questions, the main inspiration, as was true with Blum's work, will remain the same: the belief that by understanding human visual processing better we may develop better computer vision methods.

Acknowledgements This research was funded by the Natural Sciences and Engineering Research Council of Canada and Canada Research Chairs Program.

References

1. Attneave F (1954) Some informational aspects of visual perception. Psychol Rev 61:183–193
2. Bishop P, Kato H, Orban G (1980) Direction selective cells in complex family in cat striate cortex. J Neurophysiol 43:1266–1283
3. Blum H (1962) An associative machine for dealing with the visual field and some of its biological implications. Air Force Cambridge Research Labs, L G Hanscom Field, Mass, Feb 1962
4. Blum H (1967) A transformation for extracting descriptors of shape. In: Wathen-Dunn W (ed) Models for the perception of speech and visual forms. MIT Press, Cambridge, pp 362–380
5. Booth M, Rolls E (1998) View-invariant representations of familiar objects by neurons in the inferior temporal visual cortex. Cereb Cortex 8(6):510–523
6. Boynton G, Hegde J (2004) Visual cortex: the continuing puzzle of area v2. Curr Biol 14(13):R523–R524
7. Brincat S, Connor C (2004) Underlying principles of visual shape selectivity in posterior inferotemporal cortex. Nat Neurosci 7(8):880–886
8. Cant JS, Goodale MA (2011) Scratching beneath the surface: new insights into the functional properties of the lateral occipital area and parahippocampal place area. J Neurosci 31(22):8248–8258
9. Clements DH, Sarama J (2000) What do Children Know about Shapes? In: Teaching children mathematics. April 2000, The National Council of Teachers of Mathematics, Inc, pp 482–488

10. Corbetta M, Miezin F, Dobmeyer S, Shulman GL, Petersen SE (1991) Selective and divided attention during visual discriminations of shape, color, and speed: functional anatomy by positron emission tomography. J Neurosci 11(9):2393–2402
11. Dobbins A (1992) Difference models of visual cortical Neurons. Doctoral dissertation, Department of Electrical Engineering, McGill University
12. Dudek G, Tsotsos JK (1997) Shape representation and recognition from multiscale curvature. Comput Vis Image Underst 68(2):170–189
13. Dudek G, Tsotsos JK (1991) Shape representation and recognition from curvature. In: Proc computer vision and pattern recognition, pp 35–41
14. Dudek G, Tsotsos JK (1990) Recognizing planar curves using curvature-tuned smoothing. In: Proceedings 10th international conference on pattern recognition, vol 1, pp 130–135
15. Durand JB, Nelissen K, Joly O, Wardak C, Todd J, Norman F, Janssen P, Vanduffel W, Orban G (2007) Anterior regions of monkey parietal cortex process visual 3D shape. Neuron 55:493–505
16. Fergus R, Perona P, Zisserman A (2003) Object class recognition by unsupervised scale-invariant learning. In: CVPR, vol 2, p 264
17. Fiser J, Aslin RN (2002) Statistical learning of new visual feature combinations by infants. Proc Natl Acad Sci USA 99:15822–15826
18. Fukushima K (1980) Neocognitron: a self organizing neural network model for a mechanism of pattern recognition unaffected by shift in position. Biol Cybern 36(4):193–202
19. Gershfokk-Stowe L, Smith LB (2004) Shape and the first hundred nouns. Child Dev 75(4):1098–1114
20. Han X, Chen Y, Ruan X (2010) Image recognition by learned linear subspace of combined bag-of-features and low-level features. In: ICIP
21. Hawken M, Parker A (1987) Spatial properties of neurons in the monkey striate cortex. Proc R Soc Lond B, Biol Sci 231:251–288
22. Hopf J-M, Boehler CN, Schoenfeld MA, Heinze H-J, Tsotsos JK (2010) The spatial profile of the focus of attention in visual search: insights from MEG recordings. Vis Res 50(14):1312–1320
23. Hubel D, Wiesel T (1962) Receptive fields, binocular interaction and functional architecture in the cat's visual cortex. J Physiol 160:106–154
24. Hubel D, Wiesel T (1968) Receptive fields and functional architecture of monkey striate cortex. J Physiol 195(1):215–243
25. Hummel JE, Stankiewicz BJ (1998) Two roles for attention in shape perception: a structural description model of visual scrutiny. Vis Cogn 5:49–79
26. Ito M, Komatsu H (2004) Representation of angles embedded within contour stimuli in area v2 of macaque monkeys. J Neurosci 24(13):3313–3324
27. James TW, Stevenson RA, Kim S, VanDerKlok RM, James KH (2011) Shape from sound: evidence for a shape operator in the lateral occipital cortex. Neuropsychologia 49:1807–1815
28. Janssen P, Vogels R, Orban G (2000) Selectivity for 3D shape that reveals distinct areas within macaque inferior temporal cortex. Science 288:2054–2056
29. Janssen P, Vogels R, Liu Y, Orban G (2001) Macaque inferior temporal neurons are selective for three-dimensional boundaries and surfaces. J Neurosci 21:9419–9429
30. Jones SS, Smith LB (1993) The place of perception in children's concepts. Cogn Dev 8:113–139
31. Kato H, Bishop P, Orban G (1978) Hypercomplex and simple/complex cells classifications in cat striate cortex. J Neurophysiol 41:1071–1095
32. Koenderink JJ, van Doorn AJ (1980) Photomettric invariants related to solid shape. Opt Acta 27(7):981–996
33. Kruijne W, Tsotsos JK (2011) Visuo-cognitive routines: reinterpreting the theory of visual routines as a framework for visual cognition. Technical Report CSE-2011-05, Dept of Computer Science & Engineering, York University
34. Leung B (2004) Component-based car detection in street scene IMages. PhD thesis, Massachusetts Institute of Technology, Dept of Electrical Engineering and Computer Science

35. Marcelja S (1980) Mathematical description of the responses of simple cortical cells. J Opt Soc Am 70(11):1297–1300
36. Merigan W, Pham H (1998) 4 lesions in macaques affect both single and multiple-viewpoint shape discriminations. Vis Neurosci 15:359–367
37. Orban G, Kato H, Bishop P (1979) Dimensions and properties of end-zone inhibitory areas of hypercomplex cells in cat striate cortex. J Neurophysiol 42:833–849
38. Orban G, Kato H, Bishop P (1979) End-zone region in receptive fields of hypercomplex and other striate neurons in the cat. J Neurophysiol 42:818–832
39. Orban G, Janssen P, Vogels R (2006) Extracting 3D structure from disparity. Trends Neurosci 29:466–473
40. Pasupathy A, Connor C (1999) Responses to contour features in macaque area V4. J Neurophysiol 82(5):2490–2502
41. Pasupathy A, Connor C (2001) Shape representation in area V4: position-specific tuning for boundary conformation. J Neurophysiol 86(5):2505–2519
42. Pasupathy A, Connor C (2002) Population coding of shape in area V4. Nat Neurosci 5(12):1332–1338
43. Rektorys K (1980) Variational methods in mathematics, science and engineering. Reidel, Dordrecht
44. Riesenhuber M, Poggio T (1999) Hierarchical models of object recognition in cortex. Nat Neurosci 2(11):1019–1025
45. Rodríguez-Sánchez AJ, Simine E, Tsotsos JK (2007) Attention and visual search. Int J Neural Syst 17(4):275–288
46. Rodríguez-Sánchez A (2010) Intermediate visual representations for attentive recognition systems. PhD, York University
47. Rodriguez-Sanchez A, Tsotsos JK (2011) The importance of intermediate representations for the modeling of 2D shape detection: endstopping and curvature tuned computations. In: Proc IEEE computer vision and pattern recognition, Colorado Springs, CO
48. Rodríguez-Sánchez A, Tsotsos J (2012) The roles of endstopped and curvature tuned computations in a hierarchical representation of 2D shape. PLoS ONE 7(8):1–13
49. Samuelson LK, Smith LB (2005) They call it like they see it: spontaneous naming and attention to shape. Dev Sci 8(2):182–198
50. Sereno AB, Amador SC (2006) Attention and memory-related responses of neurons in the lateral intraparietal area during spatial and shape-delayed match-to-sample tasks. J Neurophysiol 95:1078–1098
51. Serre T, Wolf L, Bileschi S, Riesenhuber M (2007) Robust object recognition with cortex-like mechanisms. IEEE Trans Pattern Anal Mach Intell 29(3):411–426
52. Serre T, Wolf L, Poggio T (2005) Object recognition with features inspired by visual cortex. In: IEEE conference on computer vision and pattern recognition
53. Siddiqi K, Shokoufandeh A, Dickinson SJ, Zucker SW (1999) Shock graphs and shape matching. Int J Comput Vis 35(1):13–32
54. Sigurdardottir HM, Michalak SM, Sheinberg DL (2012) Shape beyond recognition: how object form biases spatial attention and motion perception. J Vis 12(9):665
55. Smith LB, Jones SS, Landau B, Gershkoff-Stowe L, Samuelson L (2002) Object name learning provides on-the-job training for attention. Psychol Sci 13(1):13–19
56. Spelke E (2000) Principles of object perception. Cogn Sci 14:29–56
57. Tanaka K (1996) Representation of visual features of objects in the inferotemporal cortex. Neural Netw 9(8):1459–1475
58. Terzopoulos D (1986) Regularization of inverse visual problems involving discontinuities. IEEE Trans Pattern Anal Mach Intell 8(4):413–424
59. Todd JT (2004) The visual perception of 3D shape. Trends Cogn Sci 8(3):115–121
60. Tsotsos JK (2011) A computational perspective on visual attention. MIT Press, Cambridge
61. Ullman S (1984) Visual routines. Cognition 18(1–3):97–159
62. Verhoef BE, Vogels R, Janssen P (2010) Contribution of inferior temporal and posterior parietal activity to three-dimensional shape perception. Curr Biol 20(10):909–913

63. von der Heydt R, Peterhans E, Baumgartner G (1984) Illusory contours and cortical neuron responses. Science 224(4654):1260–1262
64. Yamane Y, Carlson E, Bowman K, Wang Z, Connor C (2008) A neural code for three-dimensional object shape in macaque inferotemporal cortex. Nat Neurosci 11:1352–1360

Chapter 30
Toward a Dynamical View of Object Perception

Mary A. Peterson and Laura Cacciamani

In this chapter, we review our research demonstrating that object perception is a dynamical, integrated process in which (a) high-level memory representations are accessed before objects are perceived; (b) potential objects compete for perception and only the winners are perceived; and (c) there is no clear dividing line between perception and memory. Our review begins with results that led us to reject the traditional serial hierarchical view of object perception as well as modern versions in the form of feedforward processing models. We then outline the accumulating evidence that led us to favor a more dynamical, interactive model that involves feedforward as well as feedback processing between high- and low-levels of the visual hierarchy. In our review, we highlight how our views changed over time.

30.1 Object Perception: What Happens When?

When objects are perceived, they appear clearly separated from regions of the visual field immediately outside their borders; those outside regions appear to simply continue behind the objects as local backgrounds, or as the space surrounding them. Since the time of the Gestalt psychologists, a commonly held assumption was that objects and their grounds are segregated very early in visual processing, and that memory representations are accessed later in time and only for objects, not for grounds (see Fig. 30.1). The Gestalt psychologists referred to objects as "figures;" subsequently, the term "figure-ground segregation" has been used by many investigators to refer to temporally early memory-free components of object perception. These scientists have assumed that figure-ground segregation occurs at low levels in the visual hierarchy, and that object memories are located in higher levels. The

M.A. Peterson (✉) · L. Cacciamani
Department of Psychology, University of Arizona, Tucson, USA
e-mail: mapeters@email.arizona.edu

S.J. Dickinson, Z. Pizlo (eds.), *Shape Perception in Human and Computer Vision*,   443
Advances in Computer Vision and Pattern Recognition,
DOI 10.1007/978-1-4471-5195-1_30, © Springer-Verlag London 2013

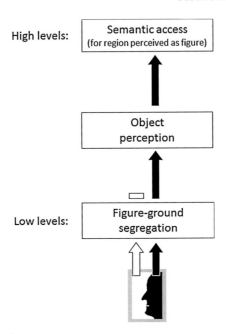

Fig. 30.1 Schematic illustrating the traditional serial hierarchical view of object perception in which figure-ground segregation occurs at low levels. For the bipartite black and white display, assume that at this low-level stage the black region is determined to be figure (i.e., the object) and the white region is determined to be the ground. On the traditional view, information pertaining to the region perceived as figure is sent via feedforward connections (*black arrows*) to higher levels where object memories and semantics are accessed (i.e., that the perceived object is a face, and associated semantics), whereas information pertaining to the region perceived as ground is not sent to higher levels (note the *white horizontal bar* illustrating truncation of high-level processing of the ground)

conflation of temporal order and hierarchical level is consistent with a serial hierarchical processing assumption in which visual processes are localized at a certain level in the visual hierarchy, processes located in lower levels are completed earlier in time than those located in higher levels, and there is no feedback from higher to lower levels. Indeed, many scientists refer to figure-ground segregation as an early, low-level *stage* of processing.[1]

There has never been any evidence that figure-ground segregation is a low-level *stage*, however. Certainly, ample evidence indicates that image factors such as convexity, symmetry, enclosure, and small area are sufficient for figure-ground perception, and that past experience is not necessary (e.g., [11, 15, 21, 23, 24, 30, 59, 73]). Such results were long taken as evidence that figure-ground perception is based on low-level assessments of image factors and precedes access to object memories. But this conclusion was not warranted: evidence that past experience is not necessary

---

[1] A figure-ground segregation stage could be placed at mid- rather than low-levels in the visual hierarchy, as in other models of visual perception that remain serial feedforward models (e.g., [35, 36]).

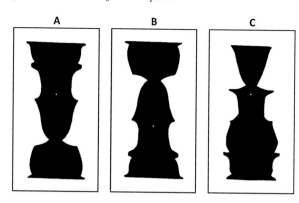

Fig. 30.2 Figure-ground displays used by Peterson et al. [50]. The white ground regions depict (**A**) (portions of) standing women, (**B**) portions of upside-down women, and (**C**) the parts of the standing women in (**A**) spatially-rearranged. Reprinted with permission from Peterson, M.A., Harvey, E.H., and Weidenbacher, H.L. (1991). Shape recognition inputs to figure-ground organization: Which route counts? *Journal of Experimental Psychology: Human Perception and Performance, 17*, 1075–1089, American Psychological Association

for figure-ground perception does not rule out the possibility that, when present, it influences figure-ground perception.[2] A systematic investigation of whether past experience (i.e., memory) can affect figure-ground perception (i.e., object perception) was lacking.[3]

30.2 Systematic Tests of Whether Past Experience Influences Figure-Ground Perception

My colleagues and I conducted a series of experiments to investigate whether object memory influences figure-ground segregation. Using a variety of stimuli and methods, we found strong evidence that it does (e.g., [9, 45–50, 52]). The set of displays used by Peterson et al. [50] are shown in Fig. 30.2. In each display, a central black region shares a border with a surrounding white region. The black region was closed, symmetric, smaller than, and enclosed by the white region; these image properties favored the percept that the center black region was the figure, and that the surrounding white region simply continued behind the figure as its ground. The critical manipulation concerned the white regions. In Fig. 30.2A, the left and right vertical borders shared by the black and white regions portray portions of well-known objects—women—in their typical upright orientation on the white side. Fig-

---

[2]Note that none of the image factors was shown to be necessary for figure-ground perception either.

[3]An experiment reported by Rubin [61] suggested that past experience can influence figure assignment, and a subsequent experiment by Schafer & Murphy [63] made the same claim for motivation, which was based on prior experience. These initial claims were rejected because they were open to alternative interpretations (e.g., [65]; see [40] for review).

ure 30.2B is an upside-down version of Fig. 30.2A; now the well-known objects (the women) on the white side of the border are portrayed in an unfamiliar upside-down orientation. In Fig. 30.2C, the parts portrayed on the white side of the border are the same familiar parts as in Fig. 30.2A, but they have been spatially rearranged so that the configurations they form are no longer familiar (in Fig. 30.2C, the parts arrayed from top to bottom are, using the part names from Fig. 30.2A: the woman's skirt; her shoulders and arms; her feet; and her head).

Peterson et al. [50] asked observers to report about reversals of perceived figure-ground status in the displays shown in Fig. 30.2. They found that the white regions were more likely to be perceived as figures at the borders they shared with the black regions when they portrayed portions of familiar objects that were upright (in their typically-experienced orientation) rather than inverted (Fig. 30.2A vs. Fig. 30.2B). Inverting the stimuli rendered the configurations on the white side of the border unfamiliar, but did not change other image features (e.g., convexity) known to affect figure assignment. Moreover, inverted familiar configurations are not permanently unfamiliar; it simply takes longer for inverted versions of familiar stimuli to be recognized (e.g., [16, 69]) because access to memory representations is delayed [37]. Thus, the finding that familiar configurations influenced border assignment when the stimuli were upright and not when they were inverted showed that object memories can contribute to figure-ground segregation, *but only when the object memories are accessed rapidly.* Finally, the presence of upright, familiar parts arranged in an unfamiliar configuration, as in Fig. 30.2C, did not result in more reports of the white regions as figure than in Fig. 30.2B, leading Peterson et al. to conclude that effects of past experience originated at high levels of processing where familiar configurations were represented and not at lower levels where familiar parts are represented. Notably, Peterson et al. [50] found that informing participants of the correspondence between the upright and inverted displays, or between the intact and part-rearranged displays, did not alter the pattern of results, indicating that *these effects of past experience required stimulus input; knowledge alone without fast access to memories of familiar objects was insufficient.*

The pattern of results described above was evident both in the duration that subjects *maintained* the white regions as figures once they were perceived as figures and also in the likelihood that the white regions were *obtained* as figures by reversal out of the black-region-as-figure percept. The latter result in particular led us to conclude that, contrary to the traditional assumption that figure ground perception precedes access to past experience, past experience exerts an influence on figure-ground perception, at least when it is accessed quickly via upright familiar configurations. Peterson and Gibson [9, 48] showed the same pattern of results when subjects reported their first figure-ground percept for briefly exposed displays.

The experiments reviewed above showed that representations of familiar configurations at high levels in the visual hierarchy are accessed sufficiently early in time to influence figure-ground perception. High levels were implicated because the receptive fields of cells mediating these effects of object memories had to be large enough to encompass the configuration of parts (up to ~5° of visual angle). For converging evidence using different stimuli and/or different methods see [45, 47, 49, 52].

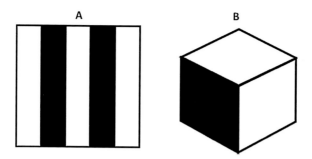

Fig. 30.3 Figure-ground perception is not the only possible outcome when two contiguous regions share a border. Shared borders can delimit regions of a flat pattern (**A**) or the corners of a three-dimensional object (**B**). Adapted from Goldreich, D., & Peterson, M.A. (2012). A Bayesian observer replicates convexity context effects in figure-ground perception. *Seeing and Perceiving, 25*, 365–395, with permission from Brill and Martinus Nijhoff

30.3 Where Is Object Perception Accomplished?

The results reviewed so far showed that figure-ground perception takes input from high-level representations, but they were agnostic as to where in the visual hierarchy figure-ground segregation takes place. At first there seemed to be no reason to reject the idea of a low-level figure-ground computation. Seemingly consistent with that view, Lamme and colleagues (e.g., [26, 75]) had shown that V1 neurons respond differentially when a figure versus a ground lies in their receptive fields (cf., more recently [74]). Therefore, we originally maintained the assumption that the computations leading to figure-ground perception took place in a low level in the visual hierarchy (V1 or V2) and that contributions from past experience were mediated by feedback from the higher-level regions implicated by the past experience effects we had observed (see also [26, 38, 39, 49, 71, 72]).

We later moved beyond the assumption that a figure-ground computation occurs at a low level in the visual hierarchy, and argued instead that figure-ground perception is simply one possible outcome of perceptual organizing processes [41], one that we now understand to span multiple hierarchical levels [1, 51]. We took this position because it is only sometimes the case that one of two abutting regions in the visual field is perceived as an object (figure) and the other region is perceived as a shapeless ground [10, 17]. Other outcomes are possible; for instance, two abutting regions can be perceived as sections of a two-dimensional pattern (Fig. 30.3A) or as two sides of a three-dimensional object, such as a cube (Fig. 30.3B). The perceived outcome depends on a host of factors, among them the context surrounding the abutting regions (e.g., [10, 53, 56]).

These observations call into question the notion of a figure-ground "computation" (or "process" or "stage"). As an alternative, we proposed that (1) candidate objects that might be perceived on opposite sides of borders are processed to high levels (e.g., object memories, semantics) in a first fast feedforward pass of processing in which properties relevant to object status (figural status) are detected; (2) these candidate objects compete to be perceived as the object (i.e., as the figure)

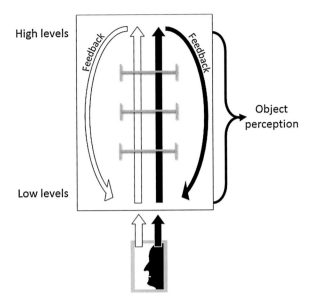

Fig. 30.4 In our current dynamical view of object perception, candidate objects that might be perceived on opposites sides of borders are processed to high levels (e.g., semantics, object memories) in a first feedforward pass of processing. (*Upward pointing black and white arrows* symbolize that this feedforward pass occurs for both the black region and the white region sharing a border in the bipartite stimulus below.) Feedback from high levels then influences processing at multiple lower levels (see curved, *downward pointing black and white arrows*). (For simplicity, the illustration shows feedback to one low-level region.) The opposing candidate objects compete for representation at many levels; the competition is inhibitory. (See the *horizontal gray bars with caps on the ends*.) The candidate object that wins the competition is perceived as the object shaped by the border (i.e., the figure). The losing candidate object is not perceived; its side of the border is simply perceived as a shapeless ground to the object. The outcome of the competition is represented across high and low levels of processing. Object perception emerges from this dynamical interactive system

at many levels in the visual hierarchy; and (3) the competition, and ultimately the perceived outcome, is influenced by context and by dynamical interactions between high and low levels of visual processing. Object perception—which may entail the assignment of a shared border as the edge of an object on one side but not the other (figure-ground assignment)—emerges from this dynamical interactive system. (See Fig. 30.4.) In the sections that follow, we review the evidence that led us to our current view.

30.4 Competition

We were not the first to propose that figure-ground perception entails competition. Sejnowski and his colleagues [19, 64] proposed the first competitive model of figure-ground perception. Their model included figure units separated by pairs of edge units facing in opposite directions (e.g., edge-left and edge-right units). These opposing edge units inhibited each other but engaged in mutual excitation with figure units lying on their preferred side. Kienker et al. [19] used focused attention as a seed to increase the activity in one set of figure units and their associated edge units; these edge units suppressed edge units facing in the opposite direction, which in turn suppressed the figure units on the opposite side of the edge. The authors concluded that this relatively enhanced activity in the figure units on one side of an edge was the mechanism behind figural assignment (see also [13, 14]; and more recently, [7, 22]). Vecera and O'Reilly [71, 72] extended Kienker et al.'s model to account for Peterson et al.'s [46–48, 50] effects of familiar configuration by using feedback from high-level cells to increase the activity of the feature units lying on one side of an edge. Although many of the competitive models reviewed above implement influences on figure-ground perception from levels somewhat higher in the hierarchy, none implements semantic influences and all assume that inhibitory competition occurs only between low-level edge units.

Peterson, de Gelder, Rapcsak, Gerhardstein, and Bachoud-Lévi ([44], see [55], for a review; [54]) proposed instead that object perception entails inhibitory competition between ensembles of object properties (i.e., familiar configuration and traditional image-based factors) on opposite sides of a border rather than, or in addition to, competition between edge units or figure units. In Peterson et al.'s framework, object properties on the same side of the edge cooperate, and those on opposite sides compete. We use the term "candidate objects" to refer to these ensembles of object properties on opposite sides of borders. Ceteris paribus, the more strongly cued side of the edge wins the competition and the border is perceived as a bounding edge of the candidate object on that side of the border. Critically, Peterson et al. proposed that the candidate object on the relatively weakly cued side of a border (the side that loses the competition for object (figure) status) is inhibited. They suggested that this inhibition accounts, in part, for the patently unshaped nature of grounds near the border they share with perceived objects. It is important to emphasize that none of the other models of figure-ground perception predicted the inhibition of a candidate object on the losing side of a border; they predicted inhibition of edge units facing in the ground direction, and enhanced neural responses to the features comprising the object (i.e., the figure).

In support of the competitive model proposed by Peterson et al. [44], Peterson and Skow [54] observed suppression of responses to object candidates on the perceived ground side of a border. Their participants classified line drawings as depicting real-world objects or novel objects. The line drawings were preceded by briefly-exposed silhouettes that were designed so that the inside, bounded region would be perceived as the figure/object: they were closed, symmetric, smaller in area than, and enclosed by a large surrounding white backdrop (see Fig. 30.5 for sample stimuli). A portion of a familiar configuration was suggested on the outside of half of these novel black silhouettes, but participants were unaware of these familiar configurations; they perceived the outside of these "experimental silhouettes" as a shapeless ground to the novel black silhouette (because the ensemble of object properties favoring the inside as the object was stronger than the familiar configuration cue on the outside). For the other half of the novel black silhouettes, no portion

Fig. 30.5 Sample stimuli used by Peterson & Skow [54]. Subjects categorized line drawings as portraying real-world or novel objects. (Only real-world objects are shown in this figure; line drawings of novel objects came from the Kroll and Potter [25] set.) Line drawings were preceded by small, symmetric, enclosed, black silhouettes with a novel shape. For half of these novel black silhouettes, a portion of a familiar object was suggested on the outside; these were experimental silhouettes (Exp Silh). Participants were unaware that these familiar objects were potentially present. A portion of a house is suggested on the outside of the experimental silhouettes in this figure. For the other half of the novel black silhouettes, no familiar objects were suggested on the outside; these were control silhouettes (Ctrl Silh). *Left panel*: the "Same Category" condition, where the familiar object suggested in white on the outside of the experimental silhouette (here, a house) was from the same basic-level category as the line drawing that followed (also a house). *Right panel*: the "Different Category" condition, where the familiar object suggested in white on the outside of the experimental silhouette (again, a house) was from a different category from the subsequent line drawing (here, a duck). The same line drawings also followed control silhouettes in both conditions. Reprinted with permission from Peterson, M.A., & Skow, E. (2008). Suppression of shape properties on the ground side of an edge: Evidence for a competitive model of figure assignment. *Journal of Experimental Psychology: Human Perception and Performance, 34(2)*, 251–267, American Psychological Association

of a familiar object was suggested on the outside. Participants also perceived the outside of these "control silhouettes" as a shapeless ground to the novel black silhouette.

Despite the fact that observers were unaware of the familiar object suggested on the outside of the experimental silhouettes, they took longer to classify line drawings of objects from the same basic level category as the unseen object rather than a different category. After ruling out alternative interpretations (including the interpretation that edge units facing toward the ground were suppressed), Peterson and Skow [54] attributed the longer response times to suppression of the candidate object that lost the competition for figural status. They suggested that the competition for figural status was an instance of the competition for representation investigated by Desimone and Duncan [6] and their colleagues, described next.

Moran and Desimone [31, 32, 60] found that the response of a neuron is reduced when two stimuli are present in its receptive field, even when one of the stimuli elicits a vigorous response when presented alone and the other elicits little or no response when presented alone. These effects are observed only when the stimuli lie close enough to each other to fall within the same receptive field [29, 32]. Desimone and his colleagues concluded that the response reduction they observed occurred because the two stimuli were competing for representation by the neuron. They found that the competition is resolved in favor of the stimulus that is higher in contrast or that is attended ([6, 8, 58]; see [57], for a review). For instance, if an animal attends to one of two stimuli within a neuron's receptive field, the neuron's response pattern changes to resemble the pattern obtained when only the attended stimulus is present (regardless of whether the attended stimulus elicits a strong or a weak response). Duncan and Desimone's model has come to be called the *Biased Competition Model of Attention* (although note that in addition to attention, contrast can bias the competition).

Peterson and Skow [54] considered it natural to extend the Desimone and Duncan model to figure-ground perception because the two objects potentially represented on opposite sides of a border necessarily lie in the same receptive field.[4] Moreover, like Desimone and colleagues, they found that responses to object properties that lose the competition are suppressed. Biased competition has been shown to occur at many levels of the visual system (i.e., V2, V4, TE, IT) via a variety of methods (i.e., single cell recording, event related potentials, and functional magnetic resonance imaging [fMRI]).

30.5 High-Level Object Memories and Dynamical Interactions Between High and Low Levels

Peterson and Skow's [54] results are consistent with the hypothesis that competition for object (i.e., figure) status can occur at high levels: In their experiment, the familiar configurations that lost the competition were approximately $3°$ in vertical extent; hence they are represented in high-level brain regions with large receptive fields. It is likely that competition for object (figure) status can occur in lower-level brain regions as well, given that simple image properties like convex parts, small area, and closure can influence figure assignment. We originally thought that familiar parts, represented in lower levels than familiar configurations, could not influence the competition for figural status, however. This was because in tests with neurologically normal individuals, no effects of past experience were evident when the (familiar) parts of familiar configurations were rearranged to form a novel configuration: Participants were no more likely to see regions portraying such part-rearranged novel configurations as figure than regions portraying inverted versions of familiar configurations (see Sect. 30.2 and Fig. 30.2C). Therefore, Peterson [42, 54] hypothesized that only familiar configurations and not familiar parts can affect figure

---

[4]We were not the first investigators to see a relationship between the biased competition model and figure-ground perception (cf. [18, 70]), but previous authors neither elaborated on nor explored their suggestion.

assignment. They further hypothesized that familiar configuration effects on object perception were mediated by brain regions such as V4 with receptive fields large enough to encompass their configurations.

A recent experiment by Barense et al. [1] caused us to change these views: Barense et al. showed (1) that a brain region higher than V4 is involved in effects of past experience on figure assignment and (2) that competition for figural status can be biased by part familiarity responses. They reached these conclusions after examining effects of past experience on figure assignment in patients with damage to the perirhinal cortex of the medial temporal lobe. The perirhinal cortex lies anterior to the brain regions traditionally thought to be involved in visual perception; it has long been thought to be involved in declarative memory only, and not in perception (e.g., [3, 20, 66–68]). An alternative view has emerged in the last decade—that the representations and computations in the perirhinal cortex subserve perception as well as memory when the task-relevant stimulus set contains many complex conjunctions constructed from similar features (e.g., [2, 4, 12, 28, 33, 34]).

To test whether the perirhinal cortex was involved in effects of familiar configuration on figure-ground perception, Barense et al. asked perirhinal cortex-damaged individuals to report the perceived figure-ground organization of displays like those in Fig. 30.6. Each display had a critical region and a matched complementary region. The critical regions depicted either intact familiar configurations (Fig. 30.6A); novel configurations created by rearranging the parts of the familiar configurations (part-rearranged novel configurations, Fig. 30.6B); or novel configurations composed of a novel ensemble of parts created by inverting the part-rearranged novel configurations (control novel configurations, Fig. 30.6C).[5] In contrast to non-brain-damaged participants, perirhinal cortex-damaged individuals perceived regions depicting part-rearranged novel configurations as figure approximately *equally as often* as intact familiar configurations and *more often* than control novel configurations (see Fig. 30.6D). In other words, participants with perirhinal cortex damage showed effects of familiar parts on figure assignment—an effect that has not been observed with non-brain-damaged participants.

To account for their results, Barense et al. [1] hypothesized that when part-rearranged novel configurations are present and the perirhinal cortex is intact (as in the control participants), the perirhinal cortex detects the mismatch between the familiarity of the parts and the novelty of the configuration and suppresses part-familiarity responses in lower levels of the visual hierarchy so that the familiarity responses at low and high levels correspond. As a consequence, part familiarity cannot exert an influence on the competition for object perception in part-rearranged novel configurations. However, when the perirhinal cortex is damaged (as it is in the patients), it does not distinguish between novel and familiar configurations; hence it does not inhibit low-level familiarity responses to the familiar parts in part-rearranged novel configurations. Because low-level part familiarity responses are

---

[5]Further exploration is necessary to determine whether the individual parts of the novel configurations are novel, but we do know that as an ensemble, the parts in the novel configurations are novel, whereas the ensemble of parts in the part-rearranged novel configuration is familiar.

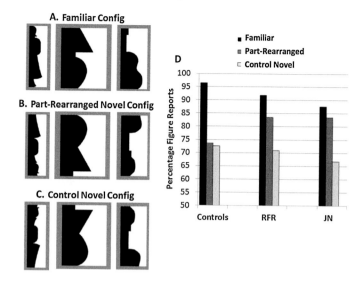

Fig. 30.6 (**A**)–(**C**) Stimuli Barense et al. [1] used to test effects of configuration familiarity on figure assignment. Each stimulus was divided into two regions by a central border. One of the two regions was a critical region. Here, the critical regions are shown in *black on the left*; black/white color and left/right location of critical regions were balanced in the experiment. (**A**) Familiar Configurations. The critical regions depict portions of familiar objects (from left to right: a woman, a lamp, and a guitar). (**B**) Part-Rearranged Novel Configurations. The critical regions in (**B**) were created by cutting the familiar configurations in (**A**) into parts at minima of curvature along the central border and spatially rearranging them into novel configurations. The parts in (**B**) are the same familiar parts as in (**A**), albeit in a different spatial relationship. (**C**) Control Novel Configurations. The critical regions are inverted versions of those shown in (**B**). Inversion is known to reduce familiarity of configurations; here we use it to reduce the familiarity of the parts of a novel configuration. The parts are unfamiliar when inverted, because the familiar configuration from which they were extracted has not often been seen in this orientation. (**A**, **B**, and **C** are reprinted with permission from Barense et al. [1] Fig. 1A.) (**D**) The percentage of trials on which subjects reported perceiving the critical regions as figures in the three types of stimuli. The data from two patients with perirhinal cortex damage (RFR and JN) are shown on the *right*. The data from age–matched control subjects are shown on the *left*. Config = Configuration. Adapted from Barense, M.D., Ngo, J.K.W., Hung, L.H.T., Peterson, M.A. (2012). Interactions of memory and perception in amnesia: the figure-ground perspective. *Cerebral Cortex, 22*, 2680–2691, with permission from Oxford University Press

not suppressed, their effects on the competition for object perception are revealed in figure reports regarding the part-rearranged novel configurations. Thus, familiarity responses at low levels can affect object perception, but tests of brain-damaged participants revealed these effects. For non-brain-damaged individuals, the effects of familiar parts and familiar configurations cannot be distinguished because feedback from the perirhinal cortex of the medial temporal lobe reduced low-level familiarity responses to familiar parts that are arranged to form a novel configuration.

Peterson, Cacciamani, Barense, and Scalf [43] tested Barense et al.'s [1] proposal using fMRI in non-brain-damaged participants. They found that, for stimuli presented in the right visual field, the perirhinal cortex does distinguish between intact familiar configurations and part-rearranged novel configurations, responding most strongly to the former and least strongly to the latter, with responses to control novel configurations in between. They also found a stronger response to the familiar parts in the low-level cortical region V2 (left hemisphere) when the familiar parts were arranged in a familiar configuration rather than a novel configuration. Peterson et al. took the differential responses to the same familiar parts in V2 as evidence of feedback from higher levels where the configurations were represented; the perirhinal cortex was a candidate given the similarity between its response pattern and the pattern observed in V2. Thus, the fMRI results confirmed the feedback model proposed by Barense et al. [1].

The results of the experiments by Barense et al. [1] and Peterson et al. [43] showed that memory representations at higher levels than previously supposed—the perirhinal cortex—are involved in effects of past experience on figure assignment. They also confirmed the hypothesis that object perception in general, and figure-ground perception in particular, is a dynamical, interactive process—one in which there is no clear dividing line between perception and memory.

30.6 Conclusion

Object perception seems immediate and unambiguous to human perceivers, yet it is neither. At first blush, it seems that serial processing assumptions and feedforward models can account for perception, yet they cannot. Our investigation of whether past experience can affect object perception revealed that object perception is the result of dynamical feedforward and feedback interactions between low- and high-level brain regions—both regions traditionally thought to be involved in perception and those traditionally thought to be involved in declarative memory only. A challenge for the future is to unpack the entire dynamical system, to identify (1) the levels where competition for object perception occurs (our recent results suggest it can occur both where part familiarity and where configuration familiarity are represented), (2) which levels only influence the competition (e.g., does the perirhinal cortex only influence the competition?), and (3) which levels reflect the outcome of the competition [a candidate for the latter is V1; see [27, 62], although critical computations may occur there as well (e.g., [5, 74])]. This is a fertile program of research, the results of which promise to elucidate object perception.

Acknowledgements   MAP acknowledges the support of NSF BCS 0960529 while writing this chapter.

References

1. Barense MD, Ngo JKW, Hung LHT, Peterson MA (2012) Interactions of memory and perception in amnesia: the figure-ground perspective. Cereb Cortex 22:2680–2691

2. Baxter MG (2009) Involvement of medial temporal lobe structures in memory and perception. Neuron 61:667–677

3. Clark RE, Reinagel P, Broadbent NJ, Flister ED, Squire LR (2011) Intact performance on feature-ambiguous discriminations in rats with lesions of the perirhinal cortex. Neuron 70:132–140

4. Cowell RA, Bussey TJ, Saksida LM (2010) Components of recognition memory: dissociable cognitive processes or just differences in representational complexity? Hippocampus 20:1245–1262

5. Craft E, Schütze H, Niebur E, von der Heydt R (2007) A neural model of figure-ground organization. J Neurophysiol 97:4310–4326. doi:10.1152/jn.00203.2007

6. Desimone R, Duncan J (1995) Neural mechanisms of selective visual attention. Annu Rev Neurosci 18:193–222

7. Domijan D, Setic M (2008) A feedback model of figure-ground assignment. J Vis 8(10):11–27

8. Duncan J, Humphreys G, Ward R (1997) Competitive brain activity in visual attention. Curr Opin Neurobiol 7:255–261

9. Gibson BS, Peterson MA (1994) Does orientation-independent object recognition precede orientation-dependent recognition? Evidence from a cueing paradigm. J Exp Psychol Hum Percept Perform 20:299–316

10. Goldreich D, Peterson MA (2012) A Bayesian observer replicates convexity context effects in figure-ground perception. Seeing Perceiving 25:365–395

11. Göttschaldt K (1938) Gestalt factors and repetition (continued). In: Ellis WD (ed) A sourcebook of Gestalt psychology. Kegan Paul, London

12. Graham KS, Barense MD, Lee AC (2010) Going beyond LTM in the MTL: a synthesis of neuropsychological and neuroimaging findings on the role of the medial temporal lobe in memory and perception. Neuropsychologia 48:831–853

13. Grossberg S (1994) 3-d vision in figure-ground separation by visual cortex. Percept Psychophys 55:48–120

14. Grossberg S, Mingolla E (1985) Neural dynamics of form perception—boundary completion, illusory figures, and neon color spreading. Psychol Rev 92(2):173–211

15. Hebb DO (1949) The organization of behavior. Wiley, New York

16. Jolicoeur P (1985) The time to name disoriented objects. Mem Cogn 13:289–303

17. Kennedy JM (1974) A psychology of picture perception. Jossey-Bass, San Francisco

18. Keysers C, Perrett DI (2002) Visual masking and RSVP reveal neural competition. Trends Cogn Sci 6:120–125

19. Kienker PK, Sejnowski TJ, Hinton GE, Schumacher LE (1986) Separating figure from ground with a parallel network. Perception 15:197–216

20. Kim S, Jeneson A, van der Horst AS, Frascino JC, Hopkins RO, Squire LR (2011) Memory, visual discrimination performance, and the human hippocampus. J Neurosci 31:2624–2629

21. Koffka K (1935) Principles of Gestalt psychology. Harcourt Brace, New York

22. Kogo N, Strecha C, Van Gool L, Wagemans J (2010) Surface construction by a 2-d differentiation-integration process: a neurocomputational model for perceived border ownership, depth, and lightness in Kanizsa figures. Psychol Rev 117:406–439

23. Köhler W (1947) Gestalt psychology. New American Library, New York. (Original work published 1929)

24. Kosslyn SM (1987) Seeing and imagining in the cerebral hemispheres: a computational approach. Psychol Rev 94:148–175

25. Kroll JF, Potter MC (1984) Recognizing words, pictures, and concepts: a comparison of lexical, object, and reality decisions. J Verbal Learn Verbal Behav 23:39–66

26. Lamme VAF, Rodriguez V, Spekreijse H (1999) Separate processing dynamics for texture elements, boundaries, and surfaces in primary visual cortex of the macaque monkey. Cereb Cortex 9:406–413

27. Likova LT, Tyler CW (2008) Occipital network for figure/ground organization. Exp Brain Res 189:257–267. doi:10.1007/s00221-008-1417-6

28. Lee AC, Yeung LK, Barense MD (2012) The hippocampus and visual perception. Front Human Neurosci 6:91
29. Luck SJ, Chelazzi L, Hillyard SA, Desimone R (1997) Neural mechanisms of spatial selective attention in areas V1, V2, and V4 of macaque visual cortex. J Neurophysiol 77:24–42
30. Marr D (1982) Vision. Freeman, San Francisco
31. Miller EK, Gochin PM, Gross CG (1993) Suppression of visual responses of neurons in inferior temporal cortex of the awake macaque by addition of a 2nd stimulus. Brain Res 616:25–29
32. Moran L, Desimone R (1985) Selective attention gates visual processing in the extrastriate cortex. Science 229:782–784
33. Murray EA, Bussey TJ, Saksida LM (2007) Visual perception and memory: a new view of medial temporal lobe function in primates and rodents. Annu Rev Neurosci 30:99–122
34. Murray EA, Wise SP (2012) Why is there a special issue on perirhinal cortex in a journal called Hippocampus?: The perirhinal cortex in historical perspective. Hippocampus 22(10):1941–1951
35. Nakayama K (1999) Mid-level vision. In: The MIT encyclopedia of the cognitive sciences, pp 545–546
36. Nakayama K, He ZJ, Shimojo S (1995) Visual surface representation: A critical link between lower-level and higher-level vision. Visual cognition: An invitation to cognitive science, vol 2, pp 1–70
37. Oram MW, Perrett DI (1992) Time course of neural responses discriminating different views of the face and head. J Neurophysiol 68:70–84
38. Peterson MA (1994) Object recognition processes can and do operate before figure-ground organization. Curr Dir Psychol Sci 3:105–111
39. Peterson MA (1999) What's in a stage name? J Exp Psychol Hum Percept Perform 25:276–286
40. Peterson MA (1999) Organization, segregation and object recognition. Intellectica 28:37–51
41. Peterson MA (2003) On figures, grounds, and varieties of amodal surface completion. In: Kimchi R, Behrmann M, Olson C (eds) Perceptual organization in vision: behavioral and neural perspectives. LEA, Mahwah, pp 87–116
42. Peterson MA (2003) Overlapping partial configurations in object memory: an alternative solution to classic problems in perception and recognition. In: Peterson MA, Rhodes G (eds) Perception of faces, objects, and scenes: analytic and holistic processes. Oxford University Press, New York, pp 269–294
43. Peterson MA, Cacciamani L, Barense MD, Scalf PE (2012) The perirhinal cortex modulates V2 activity in response to the agreement between part familiarity and configuration familiarity. Hippocampus 22(10):1965–1977
44. Peterson MA, de Gelder B, Rapcsak SZ, Gerhardstein PC, Bachoud-Lévi A (2000) Object memory effects on figure assignment: conscious object recognition is not necessary or sufficient. Vis Res 40:1549–1567
45. Peterson MA, Enns JT (2005) The edge complex: implicit perceptual memory for cross-edge competition leading to figure assignment. Percept Psychophys 14:727–740
46. Peterson MA, Gibson BS (1991) The initial identification of figure-ground relationships: contributions from shape recognition routines. Bull Psychon Soc 29:199–202
47. Peterson MA, Gibson BS (1993) Shape recognition contributions to figure-ground organization in three-dimensional displays. Cogn Psychol 25:383–429
48. Peterson MA, Gibson BS (1994) Must figure-ground organization precede object recognition? An assumption in peril. Psychol Sci 5:253–259
49. Peterson MA, Gibson BS (1994) Object recognition contributions to figure-ground organization: operations on outlines and subjective contours. Percept Psychophys 56:551–564
50. Peterson MA, Harvey EH, Weidenbacher HL (1991) Shape recognition inputs to figure-ground organization: which route counts? J Exp Psychol Hum Percept Perform 17:1075–1089
51. Peterson MA, Kimchi R (2013) Perceptual organization. In: Reisberg D (ed) Handbook of cognitive psychology. Oxford University Press, London, pp 9–31

52. Peterson MA, Lampignano DL (2003) Implicit memory for novel figure-ground displays includes a history of border competition. J Exp Psychol Hum Percept Perform 29:808–822
53. Peterson MA, Salvagio E (2008) Inhibitory competition in figure-ground perception: context and convexity. J Vis 8(16):4 (13pp)
54. Peterson MA, Skow E (2008) Suppression of shape properties on the ground side of an edge: evidence for a competitive model of figure assignment. J Exp Psychol Hum Percept Perform 34(2):251–267
55. Peterson MA, Skow-Grant E (2003) Memory and learning in figure-ground perception. In: Ross B, Irwin D (eds) Cognitive vision: psychology of learning and motivation, vol 42. Academic Press, New York, pp 1–34
56. Rauschenberger R, Peterson MA, Mosca F, Bruno N (2004) Amodal completion in visual search: preemption or context effects? Psychol Sci 15:351–355
57. Reynolds JH, Chelazzi L (2004) Attentional modulation of visual processing. Annu Rev Neurosci 27:611–647
58. Reynolds JH, Chelazzi L, Desimone R (1999) Competitive mechanisms subserve attention in macaque areas V2 and V4. J Neurosci 19:1736–1753
59. Rock I (1962) A neglected aspect of the problem of recall: the Hoffding function. In: Scher JM (ed) Theories of the mind. Free Press, New York
60. Rolls ET, Tovee MJ (1995) The responses of single neurons in the temporal visual cortical areas of the macaque when more than one stimulus is present in the receptive-field. Exp Brain Res 103:409–420
61. Rubin E (1958) Figure and ground. In: Beardslee D, Wertheimer M (eds & trans) Readings in perception. Van Nostrand, Princeton, pp 35–101. (Original work published 1915)
62. Salvagio E, Cacciamani L, Peterson MA (2012) Competition-strength-dependent ground suppression in figure-ground perception. Atten Percept Psychophys 74:964–978
63. Schafer R, Murphy G (1943) The role of autism in a visual figure-ground relationship. J Exp Psychol 32:335–343
64. Sejnowski TJ, Hinton GE (1987) Separating figure from ground with a Boltzmann machine. In: Arbib MA, Hanson AR (eds) Vision, brain and cooperative computation. MIT Press, Cambridge, pp 703–724
65. Smith DEP, Hochberg J (1954) The effect of "punishment" (electric shock) on figure-ground perception. J Psychol 38:83–87
66. Squire LR, Zola-Morgan S (1991) The medial temporal lobe memory system. Science 253:1380–1386
67. Squire LR, Wixted JT (2011) The cognitive neuroscience of human memory since H.M. Annu Rev Neurosci 34:259–288
68. Suzuki WA (2009) Perception and the medial temporal lobe: evaluating the current evidence. Neuron 61:657–666
69. Tarr MJ, Pinker S (1990) When does human object recognition use a viewer-centered reference frame? Psychol Sci 1:253–256
70. Vecera SP (2000) Toward a biased competition account of object-based segregation and attention. Brain Mind 1:353–384
71. Vecera SP, O'Reilly RC (1998) Figure-ground organization and object recognition processes: an interactive account. J Exp Psychol Hum Percept Perform 24:441–462
72. Vecera SP, O'Reilly RC (2000) Graded effects in hierarchical figure-ground organization: reply to Peterson 1999. J Exp Psychol Hum Percept Perform 26:1221–1231
73. Wallach H (1949) Some considerations concerning the relationship between perception and cognition. J Pers 18:6–13
74. Zhou H, Friedman HS, von der Heydt R (2000) Coding of border ownership in monkey visual cortex. J Neurosci 20:6594–6611
75. Zipser K, Lamme VAF, Schiller PH (1996) Contextual modulation in primary visual cortex. J Neurosci 16(22):7376–7389

Chapter 31
Modeling Shapes with Higher-Order Graphs: Methodology and Applications

Chaohui Wang, Yun Zeng, Dimitris Samaras, and Nikos Paragios

31.1 Introduction

Shape matching and inference aims at determining the correspondence between a source shape instance (or shape model) and a target shape instance (or the observed data where the target shape is embedded). It is a fundamental problem in computer vision, computer graphics, medical image analysis and has been widely investigated in numerous important applications such as 3D surface matching and reconstruction [5, 7, 12, 21, 30, 32], statistical shape modeling and knowledge-based segmentation [15, 16, 22, 34], feature correspondence and image registration [1, 20, 28, 38], shape similarity and object recognition [2, 3, 29]. Let $S \subset \mathbf{R}^3$ denote a shape.[1] The gen-

---

[1] The shape can also be associated with a texture model if photometric information is available.

C. Wang (✉)
Vision Lab, University of California, Los Angeles, USA
e-mail: ch.wang@cs.ucla.edu

Y. Zeng · D. Samaras
Dept. of Computer Science, Stony Brook University, Stony Brook, USA

Y. Zeng
e-mail: yzeng@cs.stonybrook.edu

D. Samaras
e-mail: samaras@cs.stonybrook.edu

N. Paragios
Center for Visual Computing, Ecole Centrale Paris, Châtenay-Malabry Cedex, France
e-mail: nikos.paragios@ecp.fr

N. Paragios
LIGM Laboratory, University Paris-East & Ecole des Ponts Paris-Tech, Marne-la-Vallée, France

N. Paragios
GALEN Group, INRIA Saclay - Île-de-France, Rocquencourt, France

S.J. Dickinson, Z. Pizlo (eds.), *Shape Perception in Human and Computer Vision*,
Advances in Computer Vision and Pattern Recognition,
DOI 10.1007/978-1-4471-5195-1_31, © Springer-Verlag London 2013
459

eral idea for solving this problem is usually based on an optimization problem as
follows:

$$\tau^{\text{opt}} = \underset{\tau \in \mathcal{T}}{\arg\min} \left\{ E_{S_1, S_2}(\tau) = \rho\big(\tau(S_1), S_2\big) + \chi(\tau) \right\} \qquad (31.1)$$

where $\rho(\tau(S_1), S_2)$ denotes a measure on the geometric and/or photometric difference (often referred to as *data likelihood*) between the transformed source
shape (model) $\tau(S_1)$ and the target shape S_2, $\chi(\tau)$ denotes a prior or regularization on the transformation τ, and $\mathcal{T}$ is the feasible solution set (e.g., diffeomorphisms).[2]

One main difficulty in solving shape matching and inference lies in the fact that
the shape is usually embedded in a high-dimensional space and exhibits large and
complex deformation/variance. This poses a challenge to the design of an efficient
algorithm for the search of the optimal transformation between two shapes or the
optimal shape model from the observed data. Another main difficulty originates
from the facts that the problem is inherently ill-posed and that the input data are
often noisy and can be partially occluded. That is why prior knowledge on the de-
formation/variance of the shape is often introduced to address the ill-posedness of
the problem and to make the algorithm more robust to noise. However, this raises
another challenge in the choice of the representation of prior knowledge, which
should be effective in the aspect of modeling and efficient in the aspect of learning
and inference.

31.1.1 Main Obstacle—Extrinsic Factors

A ubiquitous phenomenon in vision perception is that a single object can exhibit
infinite geometric variation in the observed data following the change of extrinsic
factors such as sensor parameters and global object pose.[3] In the case of 3D data
where the observation also lies in a 3D Euclidean space, different sensor parameters
and/or global object poses usually lead to observations that differ by a similarity
transformation (translation/rotation/scaling). In a broad sense, *extrinsic factors* refer
to all that would cause a shape to have different extrinsic manifestations which are
nevertheless intrinsically equivalent.[4] An extrinsic factor is often associated with a
certain transformation group G (e.g., the Euclidean group, the similarity group and
the isometry group) and globally affect the configuration of a shape. Accordingly,

---

[2]When a bijective mapping between $S_1 \subset \mathbf{R}^3$ and $S_2 \subset \mathbf{R}^3$ is required, the feasible solution can be
defined as all diffeomorphisms that map S_1 to S_2.

[3]Photometric variation can be caused by the change of illumination. We mostly focus on the geometric aspect here but the extension to the photometric aspect can be done analogously.

[4]The definition of the intrinsically equivalence depends on the problem to be addressed. For instance, when dealing with nonrigid 3D surface matching, we often assume that two surfaces differing by an isometric transformation (with geodesic metrics) are intrinsically equivalent.

for a shape instance, the set of all intrinsically equivalent shapes is the orbit of that instance under the corresponding transformation group G.

Actually, *extrinsic factors* pose a main obstacle to addressing the aforementioned challenges efficiently, in particular in the following two major aspects.

Regarding the problem complexity and the algorithm design, we can see from the above discussion that such extrinsic factors are a main source of shape variability [36], the removal of which will largely reduce the complexity of shape matching and inference. The problem can become much easier if we only need to deal with the *intrinsic shape variability*, which refers to the residual (e.g., intra-class variability, noise) after ruling out the effect of extrinsic factors.

The main issue in the design of the algorithm is how to define and minimize the cost function in Eq. (31.1) efficiently. To account for the effect of extrinsic factors, the most commonly used scheme in the literature is: decompose the transformation τ in Eq. (31.1) into a transformation $g \in G$ that corresponds to the extrinsic factors and a residual transformation r that accounts for the intrinsic shape variability, that is, $\tau = g \circ r$, then optimize g and r in a successive or alternating manner (e.g., EM-style approaches). A typical example is the *iterative closest points* (ICP) algorithms [5, 32] for rigid shape matching, which alternates between establishing correspondences given the Euclidean transformation and estimating the Euclidean transformation given the correspondences. Another important example is related to the incorporation of shape priors and will be discussed a bit later.

Such a scheme requires initializing g and is prone to be trapped at local minima during the alternating search. Therefore, it usually works well only when the two shapes are close enough under the given initialization of g. Another important limitation is that it cannot directly deal with the case where g is difficult to be explicitly represented (e.g., the isometric transformation that is often considered in nonrigid 3D surface matching). Last, the search for optimal r (i.e., the global minimum with respect to r) for a fixed g is actually difficult in general and its complexity increases sharply as g deviates from the true transformation.

Regarding the incorporation of the shape prior, extrinsic factors pose an obstacle for connecting the shape instance and the prior model in the matching and inference process. In fact, the prior information on a shape class lies in the residual transformation r after factoring out g corresponding to extrinsic factors from the transformation τ. Based on this, most existing shape prior models [22], for example, the well-known *active shape/appearance models* (ASMs/AAMs) [15, 16], are built by first aligning all the training samples into a reference space (to factor out the similarity group) and then learning the shape distribution on these registered samples.

However, such prior models often exhibit two main limitations. On the one hand, the estimation of the similarity transform g is required both in the training and the inference stages, since the learned model and an observed shape instance are in different coordinate frames in general. Besides the computational complexity, such an estimation also introduces certain bias on the learned prior model, since the optimal decomposition of τ into g and r actually is an ill-posed problem. One the other hand, the optimal search in the inference stage with such prior models requires initializing g and is prone to be trapped at local minima.

31.1.2 Key Strategy—Encoding Shape Invariance in Higher-Order Graphs

In fact, due to the intrinsic equivalence of the shape, the distance function in Eq. (31.1) should be invariant to extrinsic factors, that is, $\rho(\tau(S_1), S_2)$ and $\chi(\tau)$ should be g-invariant. Hence, if we can explore shape invariance with respect to extrinsic factors by choosing g-invariant data term $\rho(\tau(S_1), S_2)$ and prior model $\chi(\tau)$, then we will be able to efficiently search for the optimal transformation τ^{opt} without searching for g. In particular, when extrinsic factors correspond to a transformation group, such a scheme can be interpreted as representing a shape in an intrinsic shape space that is g-invariant and the correspondence is then determined in such an intrinsic shape space, where the shape variability is largely reduced.

To this end, we are particularly interested in discrete representations of shapes, which have been widely employed in the literature, where the transformation τ in Eq. (31.1) is represented by the correspondences between the points of two shapes. Then the shape matching and inference problem boils down to determining the correspondence from the target shape (or the observed image data) for each point on the source shape (model). Recent significant development in graph-based methods and inference techniques (e.g., Markov Random Field (MRF) inference algorithms [10, 25, 27] and graph matching [28, 37, 38]) have demonstrated their potential in solving such a correspondence problem. In particular, the newly developed techniques for higher-order models [17, 23, 24, 27] enhance significantly the applicable extent and the performance of graph-based methods. In such a context, we employ higher-order potentials to characterize measures/statistics that are g-invariant (e.g., similarity-invariant and isometry-invariant) and optimize the energy function using discrete optimization methods to address 3D shape matching and inference (e.g., [39–42]). One important advantage of such a scheme is that the problem can be solved in a one-shot optimization algorithm with optimality guarantee.

In the next two sections, we will show via our recent works [39, 42] how this methodology can be implemented for two typical problems: nonrigid 3D surface matching and knowledge-based 3D segmentation, and demonstrate the superior performance of our approaches. Finally, we will conclude the chapter with a discussion of future directions in Sect. 31.4.

31.2 Nonrigid 3D Surface Matching

We present our approach [42] to robustly establishing correspondences between two surfaces via a higher-order graph-based formulation, where the similarity between local structures and the distortion of global structures are isometry-invariant and incorporated together via singleton terms and third-order interactions, respectively.

Let us denote by $\mathscr{P}_1$ and $\mathscr{P}_2$ the two point sets from surfaces S_1 and S_2, respectively. Our goal is to find the correspondence from $\mathscr{P}_2$ for each point of $\mathscr{P}_1$, if it exists. This can be formulated as selecting a subset (referred to as *matching*) $\mathscr{M}$ from the set of all possible correspondences $\mathscr{A} \triangleq \mathscr{P}_1 \times \mathscr{P}_2$ that leads to the least dissimilarity while respecting matching constraints (e.g., one-to-one mapping). For each correspondence $a = (i, j) \in \mathscr{A}$, we assign a Boolean variable x_a to indicate if a is included in the matching $\mathscr{M}$ ($x_a = 1$) or not ($x_a = 0$). By doing so, the matching $\mathscr{M}$ can be represented by a tuple of Boolean variables $\mathbf{x} = (x_a)_{a \in \mathscr{A}}$. The feasible solution space $\mathscr{X}$ of $\mathbf{x}$ depends on the matching constraints. Here, we impose the constraint that each point in $\mathscr{P}_1$ is mapped to at most one point in $\mathscr{P}_2$ and *vice versa*, leading to the following feasible solution space $\mathscr{X}$:

$$\mathscr{X} = \left\{ \mathbf{x} \in \{0, 1\}^{|\mathscr{A}|} \,\middle|\, \sum_{i \in \mathscr{P}_1} x_{i,j} \le 1, \sum_{j \in \mathscr{P}_2} x_{i,j} \le 1, \forall i \in \mathscr{P}_1 \text{ and } \forall j \in \mathscr{P}_2 \right\} \quad (31.2)$$

The dissimilarity induced by a matching between two surfaces can be defined based on the distortion encoded within various numbers of correspondences. We then formulate the surface matching problem as finding the optimal matching that minimizes the dissimilarity function as follows:

$$\mathbf{x}^{\text{opt}} = \arg \min_{\mathbf{x} \in \mathscr{X}} \left\{ E(\mathbf{x}) = \sum_{a \in \mathscr{A}} \theta_a x_a + \sum_{(a,b) \in \mathscr{A}^2} \theta_{ab} x_a x_b + \sum_{(a,b,c) \in \mathscr{A}^3} \theta_{abc} x_a x_b x_c \right\}$$

$$(31.3)$$

In the following, we discuss the definitions of the potential functions in Eq. (31.3), which capture the information of both local structures and global deformation.

The singleton potential encodes geometric and/or photometric compatibility between the local structures of each correspondence. For simplicity, we use the Gaussian curvature curv(i) at point i as geometric descriptor, which is invariant to isometric transformation [14], as well as the texture value tex(i) at point i as photometric descriptor if texture information is available. Then, the singleton potential θ_a for a correspondence $a = (i, j)$ is defined as follows:

$$\theta_a = \big(\text{curv}(i) - \text{curv}(j)\big)^2 + \lambda_0 \big(\text{tex}(i) - \text{tex}(j)\big)^2 \quad (31.4)$$

where λ_0 is a positive weight that balances the contribution between curvature and texture information. Similarly, other features can also be considered within such potentials, such as multiscale heat kernel signatures [35] and eigenfunctions of the Laplace-Beltrami operator [33].

The higher-order potential encodes the intrinsic deformation priors of global structures which are invariant to isometric transformation. Theories in Riemann surface [19] reveal that when two surfaces are isometrically deformed from one to the other, the correspondences (mapping) between them can be sufficiently characterized by a *Möbius transformation*, which has only six degrees of freedom and can be uniquely determined by a triplet of point-wise correspondences. Hence, we can measure the deviation from isometry for the mapping (implied by the Möbius transformation) between two surfaces determined by a triplet of point-wise correspondences, which serves as an intrinsic deformation prior term that can be encoded in a third-order potential.

According to the uniformization theorem [19], any 3D surface can be flattened conformally to a canonical 2D domain. Then for any triplet of correspondences, $(p_i^1, p_j^1, p_k^1) \in \mathscr{P}_1$ and $(p_i^2, p_j^2, p_k^2) \in \mathscr{P}_2$, we first recover the associated Möbius transformation $m^1(z)$ and $m^2(z)$ that maps each triplet to a constant configuration $(e^{i\frac{2\pi}{3}}, e^{i\frac{4\pi}{3}}, e^{i2\pi})$. Under this transformation, each point p in the sets $\mathscr{P}_1$ and $\mathscr{P}_2$ is equipped with coordinates in $\hat{\mathbb{C}}$ (i.e., the complex plane $\mathbb{C} \cup \{\infty\}$) denoted by $z(p) \in \hat{\mathbb{C}}$. Similar to [30], we establish correspondences between $\mathscr{P}_1$ and $\mathscr{P}_2$ by searching the mutually closest point correspondences set $\mathscr{M}_{ijk}$ under the new coordinates, and define the deformation deviation from isometry as:

$$E_{ijk} = \sum_{(p_1,p_2)\in\mathscr{M}_{ijk}} |z(p_1) - z(p_2)|^2 \tag{31.5}$$

Then we define the intrinsic deformation prior term as follows:

$$\theta_{ijk}^{\text{Möbius}} = \begin{cases} E_{ijk}/|\mathscr{M}_{ijk}|^2 - 1 & \text{if } E_{ijk}/|\mathscr{M}_{ijk}|^2 < \delta \\ 1/|\mathscr{M}_{ijk}| & \text{otherwise} \end{cases} \tag{31.6}$$

Here δ is a lower bound value to rule out unlikely correspondences (in our experiment $\delta = 0.1$). Intuitively, if there are more matching pairs and the distances between those matching pairs are smaller, the potential will be lower. Such a prior term is invariant with respect to isometric transformation, due to the fact that E_{ijk} is computed in the canonical 2D domain and an isometric transformation applied to a surface will not change the representation of the surface in the canonical domain.

Since the mirror symmetry group is a subset of the isometry group, the intrinsic deformation prior term in Eq. (31.6) cannot resolve symmetry ambiguity. In practice, we often want to eliminate such an ambiguity, for which we can define another type of third-order terms based on the Gaussian map of the surface. The Gaussian map is defined as the mapping of the normal at each point on the surface to the unit sphere [14]. Due to the fact that two triplets have the same orientation of the Gaussian maps if and only if the determinant of their normals have the same sign, we can define the below higher-order term as a penalty for extrinsic orientation inconsistency:

$$\theta_{ijk}^{\text{Gaussian}} = \begin{cases} 0 & \text{if } \det(\mathbf{n}_i^1, \mathbf{n}_j^1, \mathbf{n}_k^1) \cdot \det(\mathbf{n}_i^2, \mathbf{n}_j^2, \mathbf{n}_k^2) \geq 0 \\ 1/|\mathscr{M}_{ijk}| & \text{otherwise} \end{cases} \tag{31.7}$$

where $\mathbf{n}_i \in \mathbb{R}^3$ denotes the normal at point i, and $\det(\mathbf{n}_i, \mathbf{n}_j, \mathbf{n}_k)$ denotes the determinant of the 3×3 matrix $[\mathbf{n}_i, \mathbf{n}_j, \mathbf{n}_k]$. With such an additional term, the third-order potential for each triplet of correspondences $(p_i^1, p_j^1, p_k^1) \rightarrow (p_i^2, p_j^2, p_k^2)$ is defined as a weighted sum of the two types of potentials, that is,

$$\theta_{ijk} = \lambda_1 \theta_{ijk}^{\text{Möbius}} + \lambda_2 \theta_{ijk}^{\text{Gaussian}} \tag{31.8}$$

Here, only singleton and third-order terms are considered for simplification. Pairwise potentials defined based on different metrics (e.g., geodesic [12], diffusion metrics [13] and commute time [31]) can also be considered in this general formulation to integrate more geometric information towards improving the performance.

Dual-decomposition-based optimization An advantage of the pseudo-boolean formulation is that higher-order terms can be reduced into a quadratic term and then be solved by existing efficient optimization algorithms such as QPBO techniques [9, 26]. Inspired by [38], the dual-decomposition optimization framework [4, 27] and the order-reduction technique proposed in [23] are adopted to deal with the problem in Eq. (31.3). More specifically, the original problem is decomposed into a *linear subproblem*, a *higher-order pseudo-boolean subproblem* and a set of *local subproblems*. The linear subproblem and the local subproblems used in the experiments are similar to those of [38]. Then, a higher-order pseudo-boolean subproblem is introduced to deal with the higher-order terms in Eq. (31.3). After solving the subproblems, the dual variables are updated using a projected subgradient method [27, 38] to maximize the lower bound.

Towards efficient dense surface matching, we propose a two-stage optimization pipeline which consists of *sparse feature matching* and *dense point matching*. In the sparse matching stage, we establish the correspondences between two small sets of sparse features using the high-order graph matching algorithm presented above. Since any three correspondences determine a mapping between the two surfaces and provide a correspondence candidate on S_2 for each point on S_1, a large number of correspondence candidates can be obtained for each point by considering all distinct triplets of correspondences in the sparse feature matching result. This can be followed by a clustering process to find the modes of the candidates so as to significantly reduce the number of candidates. Finally, a similar high-order graph matching scheme is employed to determine the optimal dense surface matching.

Experimental results The evaluation of our framework is done based on a number of challenging examples, which demonstrates its accuracy and efficiency, notably in challenging cases of very large deformations, or meshes that are partially occluded (see sample results in Fig. 31.1). Due to the lack of a ground truth regarding the dense correspondence, we quantitatively measure the quality of dense registration as follows: after performing the Delaunay triangulation of the points on the source surface, we compute the ratio of the area of each facet to the area of its matched facet (see Fig. 31.1). For natural deformations (e.g., expression change, stretched arms or bending fingers) such as those in our experiments, the local area is not expected to undergo abrupt change. Therefore the log area ratio is expected to be close to 0.

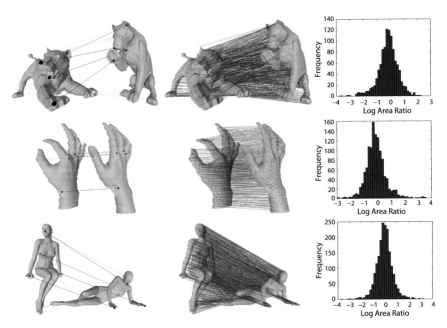

Fig. 31.1 Matching results (from left to right: sparse matching, dense matching and log area ratio) (figure partially courtesy of [42])

31.3 Pose-Invariant Prior and Knowledge-Based Segmentation

In this section, higher-order interactions are considered to build pose-invariant shape priors and are exploited for the development of a novel one-shot optimization approach for knowledge-based 3D segmentation in medical imaging [39].

Pose-invariant shape modeling The shape model consists of a set $\mathscr{V}$ of landmarks on the boundary of the object of interest. In the 3D case, we use x_i ($i \in \mathscr{V}$) to denote the 3D position of landmark i and $\mathbf{x} = (x_i)_{i \in \mathscr{V}}$ denote the positions of all the landmarks. Our goal is to learn priors on $\mathbf{x}$ from the training data that consists of a set of M shapes. Instead of registering all the surfaces into a reference space, we only assume that point-wise correspondences have been determined for the landmarks in the training set. We propose to learn statistics on similarity invariants, such as the relative distances between pairs of landmarks in a clique. Let $\mathscr{P}_c = \{(i, j) | i, j \in c \text{ and } i < j\}$ denote all the pairs for a clique c ($c \subseteq \mathscr{V}$ and $|c| \geq 3$) of landmarks, and $d_{ij} = \|x_i - x_j\|$ denote the Euclidean distance between points i and j ($(i, j) \in \mathscr{P}_c$). We compute the *relative distance* $\hat{d}_{ij}$ by normalizing d_{ij} over the sum of the distances between all the pairs of points involved in the clique c, i.e.,

$$\hat{d}_{ij} = \frac{d_{ij}}{\sum_{(i,j) \in \mathscr{P}_c} d_{ij}} \tag{31.9}$$

Since the distance $\hat{d}_{ij}$ is normalized (i.e., $\sum_{\{i,j\}\in\mathscr{P}_c} \hat{d}_{ij} = 1$), it is sufficient to consider a vector $\hat{\mathbf{d}}_c$ of relative distances corresponding to $|\mathscr{P}_c| - 1$ pairs of points. For instance, let us consider a third-order clique $c = \{i, j, k\}$ ($i, j, k \in \mathscr{V}$ and $i < j < k$), the corresponding three points compose a triangle $\triangle_{ijk}$ and $\hat{\mathbf{d}}_c$ denotes the relative lengths $(\hat{d}_{ij}, \hat{d}_{jk})$ of the sides (i, j) and (j, k), that is,

$$\hat{\mathbf{d}}_c = \left(\frac{d_{ij}}{d_{ij} + d_{jk} + d_{ki}}, \frac{d_{jk}}{d_{ij} + d_{jk} + d_{ki}} \right) \tag{31.10}$$

We can learn the statistics $\psi_c(\hat{\mathbf{d}}_c)$ of $\hat{\mathbf{d}}_c$ from the training data, with standard probabilistic models such as Gaussian Distributions, Gaussian Mixtures and Parzen-Windows. Finally, we build the higher-order shape model $\mathscr{S} = (\mathscr{V}, \mathscr{C}, \{\psi_c(\cdot)\}_{c\in\mathscr{C}})$, where $\mathscr{V}$ and $\mathscr{C}$ determine the topology of the model and $\{\psi_c(\cdot)\}_{c\in\mathscr{C}}$ characterizes the statistical geometric priors between the points contained in each clique $c \in \mathscr{C}$. In the case where third-order cliques are used, $\mathscr{C}$ is defined as $\mathscr{C} = \{\{i, j, k\}|i, j, k \in \mathscr{V}$ and $i < j < k\}$. Such statistical constraints can be easily encoded in a higher-order MRF with a set of cliques that includes $\mathscr{C}$, leading to a prior probability on the 3D configuration of the shape model as follows:

$$p(\mathbf{x}) \propto \prod_{c\in\mathscr{C}} \psi_c(\hat{\mathbf{d}}_c(x_c)) \tag{31.11}$$

where $\hat{\mathbf{d}}_c(x_c)$ denotes the mapping from the 3D positions x_c of the three points contained in the clique c to the relative distance vector $\hat{\mathbf{d}}_c$. It is easy to verify that $\hat{\mathbf{d}}_c$ is similarity-invariant. However, other similarity invariants (such as angles of a triangle) can also be adopted in the above shape prior model.

Landmark candidate detection In order to explore image support through feature vectors and to avoid a prohibitive computational complexity, we perform landmark detections to find a set of correspondence candidates in the observed image for each landmark i ($i \in \mathscr{V}$) in the 3D shape model. To this end, we first learn a classifier for each landmark, then compute a score for each possible location, and finally select the L positions that have the best scores to compose the candidate set for the landmark. We employed *Random Forests* [11] to perform the classification.

Higher-order MRF segmentation formulation The shape model, together with the evidence from the image support, is formulated within a higher-order MRF to perform image segmentation. To this end, we associate each node of the MRF with a landmark i ($i \in \mathscr{V}$), and the latent variable X_i corresponding to the node i denotes the 3D position of the associated landmark. The candidate set of each variable X_i is denoted by $\mathscr{X}_i$, which consists of the detected landmark candidates. Thus, the Cartesian product $\mathscr{X} = \prod_{i\in\mathscr{V}} \mathscr{X}_i$ denotes the candidate set of the configuration $\mathbf{x} = (x_i)_{i\in\mathscr{V}}$ of the MRF model. In order to introduce the pose-invariant shape prior (of third order) into the MRF formulation, we associate a triplet of landmarks to a third-order clique c and use the potential function of the clique c to encode the statistical geometric constraints between the three landmarks. Finally, the segmentation problem is transformed into estimating the optimal configuration $\mathbf{x}^{opt}$ of the higher-order MRF, which is formulated as a minimization of the MRF energy $E(\mathbf{x})$:

$$\mathbf{x}^{opt} = \arg \min_{\mathbf{x} \in \mathcal{X}} E(\mathbf{x}) \tag{31.12}$$

The energy of MRF is defined as a sum of singleton potentials $U_i(x_i)$ ($i \in \mathcal{V}$) and third-order potentials $U_c(x_c)$ ($c \in \mathcal{C}$), that is,

$$E(\mathbf{x}) = \sum_{i \in \mathcal{V}} U_i(x_i) + \sum_{c \in \mathcal{C}} H_c(x_c) \tag{31.13}$$

The singleton potential $U_i(x_i)$ ($i \in \mathcal{V}$) consists of the negative log-likelihood, imposing penalty for landmark i to be located at position x_i in image $\mathbf{I}$, that is,

$$U_i(x_i) = -\log p(\mathbf{I}|x_i) \tag{31.14}$$

$p(\mathbf{I}|x_i)$ is defined using the classifier's output probability value for landmark i to be located at x_i. The higher-order clique potential $U_c(x_c)$ ($c \in \mathcal{C}$) encodes the statistical geometrical constraints on the triplet c of points and is defined as:

$$U_c(x_c) = -\alpha \cdot \log \psi_c(\hat{\mathbf{d}}_c(x_c)) \tag{31.15}$$

where $\alpha > 0$ is a positive weight, $\hat{\mathbf{d}}_c(x_c)$ and $\psi_c(\cdot)$ have been presented previously. Regional terms can also be factorized and incorporated in such an MRF model [41].

Higher-order MRF inference We adopt the dual-decomposition optimization framework [4, 27] to solve the inference (Eq. (31.12)). More specifically, we decompose the original problem into a set of subproblems, each corresponding to a factor-tree [6] and perform the exact inference efficiently in each subproblem in polynomial time using the max-product belief propagation algorithm [6], with complexity $O(NL^K)$, where N, L and K denote the number of nodes, the number of candidates for each node, and the maximum order of the factors, respectively. The solutions of the subproblems are combined using projected subgradient method to solve the Lagrangian dual so as to obtain the solution of the original problem [27].

Experimental results The dataset for experimental validation consists of 3D MRI scans of the calf muscles of 25 subjects (Fig. 31.2(a)). Standard of reference was available, consisting of annotations provided by experts for the Medial Gastrocnemius (MG) muscle. To segment MG muscle from such images is challenging since there is no evident difference of tissue properties between neighbor muscles and boundaries between adjacent muscles are visible very sparsely and heterogeneously. We performed a leave-one-out cross-validation on the whole dataset. For comparison purposes, we considered those methods presented in [18]. Figure 31.2(b) shows two examples of the surface reconstruction results obtained using the estimated position of landmarks and *thin plate spline* (TPS) [8]. Figure 31.2(c) presents the average distance between the real and estimated landmark positions using different methods, which confirms the superior performance of the proposed similarity-invariant shape prior and the inference using higher-order MRFs.

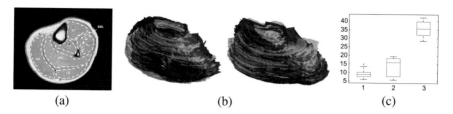

(a)   (b)   (c)

Fig. 31.2 Muscle segmentation. (**a**) A slice of a 3D MRI image of calf muscle with expert annotation. (**b**) MG muscle segmentation results (*green*: reference; *red*: result). (**c**) Boxplots of the average landmark error measure in voxel (*1*. our method. *2*. method in [18]. *3*. standard ASM method.). On each box, the central mark in *red* is the median, the edges are the 25th and 75th percentiles, the whiskers extend to the most extreme data points (figure partially courtesy of [18, 39])

31.4 Conclusion

We have shown, via two specific applications, the idea of encoding shape invariance in higher-order graphs for shape matching and inference, resulting in a one-shot optimization algorithm without initializing and estimating extrinsic factors. Similar ideas can be applied to address other extrinsic factors. For example, we introduced in [40] a unified paradigm for 3D landmark model inference from monocular 2D images to simultaneously determine both the optimal 3D model and the corresponding 2D projections without explicit estimation of the camera viewpoint. As the next step, it is interesting to study the optimal invariants and to recover the optimal subset of higher-order interactions that can best express the 3D geometric manifold. Besides, faster optimization algorithms of higher-order MRFs could be beneficial both in terms of the considered applications as well as in terms of modularity with respect to other shape matching and inference applications.

References

1. Ashburner J (2007) A fast diffeomorphic image registration algorithm. NeuroImage 38(1):95–113
2. Belongie S, Malik J, Puzicha J (2002) Shape matching and object recognition using shape contexts. IEEE Trans Pattern Anal Mach Intell 24(4):509–522
3. Berg AC, Berg TL, Malik J (2005) Shape matching and object recognition using low distortion correspondences. In: CVPR
4. Bertsekas DP (1999) Nonlinear programming, 2nd edn. Athena Scientific, Nashua
5. Besl PJ, McKay ND (1992) A method for registration of 3-d shapes. IEEE Trans Pattern Anal Mach Intell 14(2):239–256
6. Bishop CM (2006) Pattern recognition and machine learning. Information science and statistics. Springer, Berlin
7. Blanz V, Vetter T (1999) A morphable model for the synthesis of 3D faces. In: SIGGRAPH
8. Bookstein FL (1989) Principal Warps:Thin-plate splines and the decomposition of deformations. IEEE Trans Pattern Anal Mach Intell 11(6):567–585
9. Boros E, Hammer PL, Sun X (1991) Network flows and minimization of quadratic pseudo-Boolean functions. Technical report, RRR 17-1991, RUTCOR research report

10. Boykov Y, Veksler O, Zabih R (2001) Fast approximate energy minimization via graph cuts. IEEE Trans Pattern Anal Mach Intell 23(11):1222–1239
11. Breiman L (2001) Random forests. Mach Learn 54(2):5–32
12. Bronstein AM, Bronstein MM, Kimmel R (2006) Generalized multidimensional scaling: a framework for isometry-invariant partial surface matching. Proc Natl Acad Sci USA 103(5):1168–1172
13. Bronstein AM, Bronstein MM, Kimmel R, Mahmoudi M, Sapiro G (2010) A Gromov-Hausdorff framework with diffusion geometry for topologically-robust non-rigid shape. Int J Comput Vis 89(2–3):266–286
14. do Carmo MP (1976) Differential geometry of curves and surfaces. Prentice Hall, New York
15. Cootes TF, Edwards GJ, Taylor CJ (2001) Active appearance models. IEEE Trans Pattern Anal Mach Intell 23(6):681–685
16. Cootes TF, Taylor CJ, Cooper DH, Graham J (1995) Active shape models-their training and application. Comput Vis Image Underst 61(1):38–59
17. Duchenne O, Bach F, Kweon I, Ponce J (2009) A tensor-based algorithm for high-order graph matching. In: CVPR
18. Essafi S, Langs G, Deux JF, Rahmouni A, Bassez G, Paragios N (2009) Wavelet-driven knowledge-based MRI calf muscle segmentation. In: ISBI
19. Farkas HM, Kra I (2004) Riemann surfaces. Springer, Berlin
20. Glocker B, Komodakis N, Tziritas G, Navab N, Paragios N (2008) Dense image registration through MRFs and efficient linear programming. Med Image Anal 12(6):731–741
21. Gu L, Kanade T (2006) 3D alignment of face in a single image. In: CVPR
22. Heimann T, Meinzer HP (2009) Statistical shape models for 3D medical image segmentation: a review. Med Image Anal 13(4):543–563
23. Ishikawa H (2009) Higher-order clique reduction in binary graph cut. In: CVPR
24. Kohli P, Pawan Kumar M, Torr PHS (2009) P3 & beyond: move making algorithms for solving higher order functions. IEEE Trans Pattern Anal Mach Intell 31(9):1645–1656
25. Kolmogorov V (2006) Convergent tree-reweighted message passing for energy minimization. IEEE Trans Pattern Anal Mach Intell 28(10):1568–1583
26. Kolmogorov V, Rother C (2007) Minimizing nonsubmodular functions with graph cuts— a review. IEEE Trans Pattern Anal Mach Intell 29(7):1274–1279
27. Komodakis N, Paragios N, Tziritas G (2011) MRF energy minimization and beyond via dual decomposition. IEEE Trans Pattern Anal Mach Intell 33(3):531–552
28. Leordeanu M, Hebert M (2005) A spectral technique for correspondence problems using pairwise constraints. In: ICCV
29. Lin L, Liu X, Zhu SC (2010) Layered graph matching with composite cluster sampling. IEEE Trans Pattern Anal Mach Intell 32(8):1426–1442
30. Lipman Y, Funkhouser T (2009) Möbius voting for surface correspondence. ACM Trans Graph 28(3):72:1–72:12
31. Qiu H, Hancock ER (2007) Clustering and embedding using commute times. IEEE Trans Pattern Anal Mach Intell 29(11):1873–1890
32. Rusinkiewicz S, Levoy M (2001) Efficient variants of the ICP algorithm. In: International conference on 3-d digital imaging and modeling
33. Rustamov RM (2007) Laplace-Beltrami eigenfunctions for deformation invariant shape representation. In: SGP, pp 225–233
34. Seghers D, Loeckx D, Maes F, Vandermeulen D, Suetens P (2007) Minimal shape and intensity cost path segmentation. IEEE Trans Med Imag 26(8):1115–1129
35. Sun J, Ovsjanikov M, Guibas LJ (2009) A concise and provably informative multi-scale signature. based on heat diffusion. Comput Graph Forum 28:1383–1392
36. Sundaramoorthi G, Petersen P, Varadarajan VS, Soatto S (2009) On the set of images modulo viewpoint and contrast changes. In: CVPR
37. Torr PHS (2003) Solving Markov random fields using semi definite programming. In: International workshop on artificial intelligence and statistics

38. Torresani L, Kolmogorov V, Rother C (2008) Feature correspondence via graph matching: models and global optimization. In: ECCV
39. Wang C, Teboul O, Michel F, Essafi S, Paragios N (2010) 3D knowledge-based segmentation using pose-invariant higher-order graphs. In: MICCAI
40. Wang C, Zeng Y, Simon L, Kakadiaris I, Samaras D, Paragios N (2011) Viewpoint invariant 3D landmark model inference from monocular 2D images using higher-order priors. In: ICCV
41. Xiang B, Wang C, Deux JF, Rahmouni A, Paragios N (2012) 3D cardiac segmentation with pose-invariant higher-order MRFs. In: ISBI
42. Zeng Y, Wang C, Wang Y, Gu X, Samaras D, Paragios N (2010) Dense non-rigid surface registration using high-order graph matching. In: CVPR

Chapter 32
Multisensory Shape Processing

Christian Wallraven

32.1 Introduction

The vast majority of research into shape processing in the perceptual, cognitive, and neurosciences so far has dealt only with the visual modality. From a developmental standpoint, however, this strong focus on one modality only seems less well-motivated. Anyone who has watched an infant interacting with objects has observed multisensory processing in its purest form: usually objects are never only looked at, but picked up, turned around and looked at from all sides, squeezed, banged on the floor, taken in the mouth, thrown around, etc. In all of these interactions, the haptic modality is crucial. As soon as grasping, reaching, and touching objects become available to an infant, the sensory information about objects is vastly enhanced. The interaction that is made possible by this enables a host of material and object properties to be sensed and combined with the visual input (as well as input from other modalities). Examples of material and object properties that the haptic modality gives access to, include: weight, size, temperature, elasticity, and general information about the texture and shape (see [20] for an in-depth discussion of haptic perception; see also [21] for an interesting list of over 400 nouns and the way they relate to each sensory modalities, including vision and haptics). Indeed, haptic exploration thus can be seen as a bootstrapping for our visual expertise, given that analysis of these properties from visual information alone is either not possible at all (the weight of an object would be one example, small temperature differences another) or at best only in a comparative sense (for monocular vision, the two-dimensional projection of an object on the retina does not uniquely specify its size). Proprioceptive and kinaesthetic information, for example, provide an embodied reference frame in which one can immediately determine that an object fits into the hand, is at arm's length, etc. Similarly, texture information derived from

C. Wallraven (✉)
Cognitive Systems Lab, Dept. of Brain and Cognitive Engineering, Korea University, Seoul, Republic of Korea
e-mail: christian.wallraven@gmail.com

S.J. Dickinson, Z. Pizlo (eds.), *Shape Perception in Human and Computer Vision*, Advances in Computer Vision and Pattern Recognition, DOI 10.1007/978-1-4471-5195-1_32, © Springer-Verlag London 2013

the high-frequency sensors and temperature information from the nerve ends in the skin can be coupled to the observed visual texture to create material categories of "wood" and "stone" that can then be later recognized from visual input alone.

It is perhaps because of our finely tuned visual expertise which has been trained over many years in this fashion to allow easy, visual access to object properties, that research on how we learn and process shape and object representations has so far mainly focused on the visual modality. In recent years, however, this bias has become less pronounced and a large number of publications have appeared that focus on all aspects of visual and haptic processing in the perceptual, cognitive, and neurosciences. More specifically, with the advent of new technologies in computer graphics, virtual reality, and rapid prototyping, investigations are not limited anymore to low-level properties of visuo-haptic interaction, but are instead focusing increasingly on higher-level perceptual processing, including learning, as well as object recognition and categorization. The main topic of this chapter is therefore to provide an overview of results in the area of high-level multisensory processing using vision and touch. We have identified five key research areas that have led to a deeper understanding of how touch and vision interact for creating our highly tuned and efficient multisensory interpretation skills. These five areas are briefly sketched in the following.

32.2 Measuring Perceptual Spaces

When the brain is faced with the task of categorizing an object based on shape, a computational account of what needs to be done is as follows: first, shape features need to be extracted from the stimulus, which are then compared in a second step to stored representations of other objects or object categories. The closest match among the stored representations is then selected as the potential match candidate, unless the match strength is too low, in which case the object should be tagged as 'unknown'. Much of the success of this computational account hinges on defining a concept of similarity between shape representations in order to evaluate the match strength. Ever since the seminal work by Tversky [28], and especially Shepard [24, 25], similarity has been proposed as a core concept for object and shape representations in particular, and knowledge representations in general. Shepard proposed a "universal law of generalization" [24] derived from first principles in which objects are represented in a metric perceptual space, with distances between objects depending on their (dis-)similarity. Accordingly, similarity judgments have been used extensively to investigate visual shape and object representations and to relate them to physical properties (e.g., [4, 25]).

Edelman and Shahbazi (2012) discuss the importance of similarity for (visual) object representations from a computational modeling perspective. In their proposed computational framework, objects are represented based on a "chorus transform", which measures the similarities of any given object to a set of stored prototypes in memory. As the number of stored prototypes is usually much smaller than the

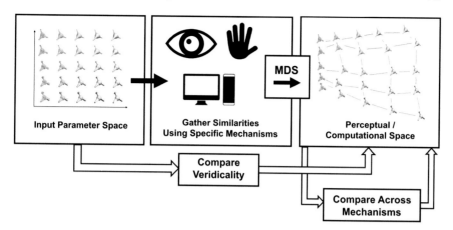

Fig. 32.1 Framework for investigating multisensory shape processing based on comparing parametrically-defined input spaces to perceptually reconstructed spaces via similarity ratings and multidimensional scaling. See text for more details

number of dimensions in which similarity is measured (say, pixels, or histograms of gradients in an image for visual comparisons), this chorus transform achieves dimensionality reduction and hence allows for efficient indexing. Critically, this way of representing objects is based on evaluating the similarity between objects in a (perceptual or cognitive) measurement space.

The general framework for investigating high-level mental representations (see Fig. 32.1) is based on obtaining similarity ratings of objects created from a parametrically-defined input space. These ratings are then analyzed with multidimensional scaling (MDS) which recovers a lower-dimensional embedding of the objects in a perceptual space. First, a well-defined parameter space of objects needs to be created—if the goal is to investigate shape representations, for example, some suitable parametric model for creating shapes is selected (the method of course works for any well-defined input parametrization of physical parameters). A critical decision at this stage concerns the number of parameter dimension and hence number of objects that will be of interest to the experimental question at hand. Since the main experimental task for participants will be to rate similarities between all exemplars, the number of trials will depend quadratically on the number of objects. The most common way to gather similarity ratings is to ask participants to rate similarity of two objects on a Likert-type Scale of 1–7 (where 1 means fully dissimilar and 7 fully similar). If one has N objects, this will result in $N \times N$ comparisons for a full design comparing object A to object B and vice versa. Alternatively, one could run a time saving version which only compares object A to object B thus resulting in $N + N \cdot (N - 1)/2$ comparisons—note, that this assumes perceptual symmetry in the comparison of object A to object B.

The similarity ratings are then used to create a matrix of perceptual dissimilarities. A good sanity check during this step is to confirm that participants, indeed, rated same object pairs (A–A and B–B) with the highest similarity rating. If this fails for a larger number of cases, something must have gotten mixed up in the data analysis or even in the experimental design. All MDS algorithms require as input a symmetric matrix for which the diagonal elements are all 1. This means that the experimental data may have to be re-normalized to fit this assumption.

As a next step, multidimensional scaling is used to embed each object in a lower-dimensional space, where object-object distances confirm as closely to the observed dissimilarity ratings as possible. The optimization of the embedding is performed according to one of several stress-functions as well as according to metric or non-metric distance relationships—the choice of stress-function and distance relationship is given by one of the flavors of MDS-algorithms available (see also [1], it is interesting to note that the "standard" MDS—the so-called classical, metric MDS—bears similarity to a principal component analysis (PCA)).

All MDS algorithms require the user to specify the dimensionality of the embedding space as an input parameter. Usually, however, this is an experimental unknown—that is, one would like to know how many perceptual dimensions are best suited for explaining the data. A post-hoc analysis consists of running the MDS algorithm with different number of dimensions and looking for a sharp dip in the stress output (cf. the method to determine the dimensionality in PCA according to the magnitude of Eigenvalues). For most flavors of MDS, the stress value is normalized between 0 and 1, and previous simulations have shown 0.2 to be an acceptable value [1].

The final step in MDS consists of comparing the perceptual representation to the input space—this, of course, can only be done if the dimensionality of both spaces is compatible. In doing so, one has to be careful that most MDS-algorithms determine only the inter-feature distances, leaving the reconstructed (perceptual) space ambivalent up to a rotation. Hence, both in interpreting the axes (dimensions) of the MDS solution, as well as in comparing the MDS solution to the input space, one needs to keep in mind that the solution may still need to be rotated. A typical algorithm for mapping the MDS solution to the input space is the Procrustes algorithm which finds the rigid rotation that best aligns the two spaces—the remaining (Euclidean) distance between the two spaces can be used together with the stress value to assess the veridicality of the perceptual representation.

As shown in Fig. 32.1, the same strategy can also be used to compare several perceptual representations among each other. One may, for example, compare results from an experiment obtained from visual similarity ratings with those obtained from haptic similarity ratings. If the resulting dimensionality and topology between the two perceptual representations is similar, then this may indicate similar processing strategies in the two modalities (e.g., [3, 12] and see below). In addition, the similarity ratings need not be obtained from human experiments—computational approaches can also be used to assess the similarity between two objects according to any number of features. Indeed, such an approach may help to identify potential processing strategies of the human mental representations by identifying algorithms that create similar MDS solutions to the human data.

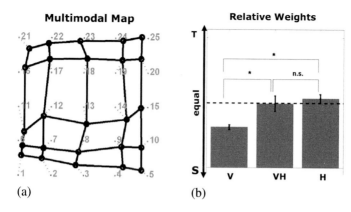

Fig. 32.2 (a) Combined modality-independent map reconstructed from visual, haptic, and visuo-haptic similarity ratings for 25 objects. The input parameter space is shown in *light grey*, the *black grid* represents the MDS solution. Note how close the perceptual reconstruction is to the input space. (b) Texture (T) and shape (S) weights for the visual (V), haptic (H), and visuo-haptic (VH) conditions for this experiment. Vision is slightly dominated by the shape dimension, whereas the other two conditions are equally weighted

32.3 Multisensory Perceptual Spaces

In several recent studies, similarity ratings have been used to investigate the link between physical and multisensory perceptual spaces with the help of parametrically-defined novel objects [3, 10–12]. The results of these studies have shown that visual and haptic perceptual spaces can represent highly complex physical shape spaces with surprising fidelity. In the following, we will briefly describe this work in the context of perceptual spaces in relation to a multisensory experience of shape processing.

In [3], the relative importance of shape and texture was investigated using a parametrically-defined set of novel, three-dimensional objects (shown in the left panel of Fig. 32.1). A base object was progressively smoothed to create variations in shape (or macro-geometry); similarly, texture was added gradually to introduce changes in texture (or micro-geometry). The resulting object-models were then printed to obtain tangible objects using a 3D printer. Similarity ratings were then obtained for visual, haptic, and visuo-haptic conditions of the same objects. In addition, objects had to be grouped into consistent categories in order to identify the relation between similarity ratings and category judgments. Interestingly, an MDS analysis of the data showed that two dimensions were sufficient to explain the data and that the reconstructed perceptual space was highly similar to the input space (Fig. 32.2a)). For the given stimuli, the shape dimension dominated over texture in the visual condition, while texture and shape were equally weighted in the haptic condition. In the bimodal condition, texture and shape were also weighted equally (Fig. 32.2b)). In addition, the resulting perceptual spaces of all conditions were highly similar, such that the data was very well explained by one single percep-

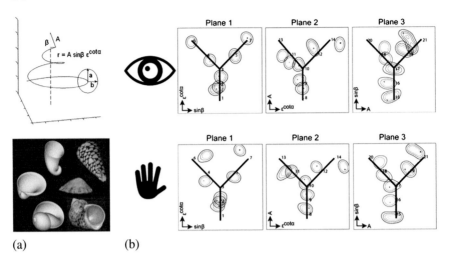

(a)   (b)

Fig. 32.3 (a) *Top panel*: Input space generation of shell-like objects according to a five-parameter equation. *Bottom panel*: Examples of computer-generated shells and real sea shells. (b) Visual and haptic reconstruction of the three y-shaped input parameter spaces. Note how well the perceptual reconstruction matches the input space

tual map (independent of modality), and modality-dependent weightings of shape and texture.

The framework was extended in [10–12] in order to investigate whether a more complex shape parameter space would still be able to be reconstructed using the visual and the haptic modality. For these experiments, a three-dimensional parameter space of shell-like objects was generated (Fig. 32.3a)). In the first series of experiments [12], the task was to rate the similarity between two sequentially presented objects. Using these similarity ratings and multidimensional scaling (MDS) analyses, the perceptual spaces of the different modalities were visualized. Interestingly, participants were again able to reconstruct the topology of this much more complex parameter space visually as well as haptically. Moreover, the visual and haptic perceptual spaces had virtually identical topology (Fig. 32.3b)).

As similarity is thought to underlie our ability to categorize, the next study included three different types of categorization tasks (free sorting, semi-supervised categorization, and fully supervised categorization) [10]. The results showed that the haptic modality was able to compete with the visual modality in all three tasks. Comparing the underlying perceptual spaces obtained from similarity ratings to the categorization behavior, the results demonstrated consistently that within-category similarity was higher than across-category similarity for all categorization tasks. In addition, the higher the degree of supervision in the task, the more the objects clustered together. This study showed that similarity rating tasks and categorization tasks can be viewed as lying on a continuum with similarity judgments producing the least and supervised categorization producing the most clustered perceptual representations.

The previous two studies used computer-generated, shell-like objects. In order to check how well the results would generalize to the real-world sea-shells, [11] repeated the experiments with a set of real sea shells (Fig. 32.3a)). Again, perceptual spaces were found to be extremely similar in the visual and the haptic domain. Although the natural shells vary in a variety of object features (including shape, color, texture, and material), haptic object exploration still resulted in a very consistent perceptual reconstruction. As these perceptual spaces showed a clear clustering, three categorization experiments were performed to test whether the similarity data would be able to predict categories. Again, the results clearly showed that the perceptual spaces are able to correctly predict human categorization behavior.

32.4 Visuo-haptic Face Recognition—The Role of Expertise

Faces are arguably one of the most common and socially most important stimulus classes for humans and hence have received special attention in the perceptual, cognitive and neurosciences. Faces are especially interesting as their variations in shape are relatively homogeneous compared to other natural object categories, such as different types of animals or plants, or artifactual categories, such as chairs or houses. The human brain therefore has had to develop special expertise for face recognition in order to fine-tune its machinery to deal with the relatively small intra-class variability. Indeed, research in neuroscience suggests that the brain possesses a dedicated processing area for faces.

From a developmental standpoint, it is interesting to note that perceptual expertise in face processing takes years to develop [6, 23]—one of the hallmark tests for this development is to compare recognition of upright and inverted (upside-down) faces. For adults, face inversion results in a remarkably large deterioration of recognition performance, which is commonly explained as the failure of the perceptual system to perform a so-called 'holistic processing' of the face in the inverted condition. Holistic processing in this context refers to the fact that each facial feature is processed in interaction with multiple other features (e.g., [5, 22]). In [6] it was found that 6–12 year old children still perform worse than adults on both upright and inverted faces, but that performance for upright faces improves during this period much more than performance for inverted faces. This tuning is interesting from a shape processing perspective as it relates to a specific strategy in which information about shape elements (such as facial features) is integrated at multiple levels. The face processing system, however, is faced with more challenges when it comes to dealing with environmental changes: faces have to be recognized under changes in illumination, pose, facial expression, accessories, etc. Several researchers have demonstrated that recognition performance under such changes is fairly robust for unfamiliar faces, but that performance is remarkably stable for familiar or famous faces (e.g., [26]). In other words, expertise not only plays a role during the development of shape processing skills for faces as opposed to other stimulus classes, but in addition, face processing becomes also optimized within the category of faces.

Studies with morphable models, which allow for efficient, high-level manipulations of shape and face attributes have shown that humans are highly sensitive to face shape [27]. Recently, several authors have used the unusual task of haptic or even cross-modal face recognition to shed light on uni- and multisensory processing of faces. In [15], it was shown for the first time that humans can haptically discriminate and identify faces at levels well above chance. These experiments were conducted with blind-folded participants using either live faces or face masks. Interestingly, the natural texture afforded by the live faces in contrast to the plastic face masks increased face recognition performance by only a small amount, showing the importance of shape information in recognition of these complex stimuli. A follow-up study showed that—similar to visual information—haptic face recognition was also orientation-sensitive [16], although this result is still under debate [8, 9]. Perhaps most interestingly, information can be shared across the haptic and visual modalities bi-directionally to a certain extent [2, 9, 15]. In [9], for example, it was shown that faces learned haptically can be recognized visually at equal performance levels—similarly, faces learned visually can be recognized haptically, albeit at a performance drop. In addition, overall, haptic face recognition was lower than visual face recognition. The study suggested that the haptic modality represents the bottleneck in this information transfer.

One of the reasons for the lower face recognition performance in haptics may be the nature of haptic exploration: in order to encode and recognize objects haptically, one needs to move the fingers and the hand over the object, integrating information in a serial fashion. Given the results mentioned previously about the quality of haptic shape encoding, the question arises whether the haptic modality is limited in terms of its shape processing capabilities, or whether it is limited due to serial encoding. This question was addressed in a recent study in which the *visual* modality was changed to serial encoding [8]. For this, face viewing was restricted to an aperture that could be moved via the mouse over the face. Surprisingly, visually restricted face recognition levels dropped to those of haptic recognition. Interestingly, for this exploration mode, the inversion effect disappeared, showing that serial encoding at this stage may solely rely on local processing of features. A series of follow-up experiments has investigated whether one may able to train face recognition in the serial encoding mode [29]. Participants were trained for a few hours on consecutive days in this (unusual) encoding mode. Interestingly, recognition performance improved very quickly, generalized well to other faces, was retained for at least two weeks, and even began to show signs of an inversion effect. Hence, at least for the visual modality, serial encoding can be trained very efficiently such that the efficient processing of complex face shapes becomes possible.

32.5 Summary and Open Questions

Shape is one of the most important features for the human perceptual system. Accordingly shape processing has evolved to expert levels allowing effortless learning and categorization of a large number of objects. Here, we have argued that shape processing should be regarded and studied as an innately multisensory problem. Most importantly, the development of shape processing is critically dependent on the haptic modality, which not only allows for interaction and manipulation with objects (coupling perception and action), but also affords the extraction of important object properties. These properties are either not accessible to the visual modality (temperature and weight), or they can be grounded in the haptic experience (texture and material properties, size). We have proposed a framework for studying the perceptual representation of shape through the use of similarity ratings and multidimensional scaling techniques. A number of experiments in this context has shown that haptic shape processing can be on par with that of visual processing in terms of the ability to capture and represent complex input shape spaces.

Of course, haptic processing, also has its limits—haptic recognition of face shapes, for example, is worse than expert visual face recognition. This may in part be due to the serial processing mode of haptic exploration (as opposed to the rapid, parallel processing of vision). Indeed, if vision is restricted to serial exploration, face recognition drops to haptic levels—interestingly, however, this drop can be quickly reversed through a few hours of training on face recognition. Whether this also holds true for haptic face recognition remains to be tested—nevertheless, even for shapes as complex as faces, some information can be shared across modalities.

Indeed, one of the central questions in multisensory processing is whether there are two separate object representations, or whether there is one amodal representation that combines information from two (or more) modalities [18]. Findings from several recent studies that have investigated the neural correlates of multisensory processing using fMRI together show that very similar brain areas are activated for both visual and haptic processing, but that the activation pattern differs depending on the modality [13, 17, 19]. More studies are needed to fully elucidate the nature of shape representations in the brain.

The following list summarizes some open questions for multisensory shape processing:

- What are the different mechanisms for multisensory shape and object perception in sighted, visually impaired and blind people?
- What are the complexity limits for shape and object representations in vision and haptics?
- To what extent are properties of visual object processing shared across modalities?
- What are the brain mechanisms responsible for shared representations across modalities?
- How can we use these results to create novel human machine interfaces?
- How can we extend the similarity rating framework to recent results from machine learning [7, 14]?

Acknowledgements This work was done in collaboration with Theresa Cooke, Nina Gaißert, Lisa Dopjans, and Heinrich Bülthoff. It was supported by PhD stipends from the Max Planck Society, and by the WCU (World Class University) program through the National Research Foundation of Korea funded by the Ministry of Education, Science and Technology (R31-1008-000-10008-0).

References

1. Borg I, Groenen P (2005) Modern multidimensional scaling, 2nd edn. Springer, Berlin
2. Casey SJ, Newell FN (2007) Are representations of unfamiliar faces independent of encoding modality? Neuropsychologia 45:506–513
3. Cooke T, Jäkel F, Wallraven C, Bülthoff HH (2007) Multimodal similarity and categorization of novel, three-dimensional objects. Neuropsychologia 45(3):484–495
4. Cutzu F, Edelman S (1998) Representation of object similarity in human vision: psychophysics and a computational model. Vis Res 38:2229–2257
5. Dahl CD, Wallraven C, Bülthoff HH, Logothetis NK (2009) Humans and macaques employ similar face-processing strategies. Curr Biol 19(6):509–513
6. de Heering A, Rossion B, Maurer D (2012) Developmental changes in face recognition during childhood: evidence from upright and inverted faces. Cogn Dev 27(1):17–27
7. DiCarlo JJ, Cox DD (2007) Untangling invariant object recognition. Trends Cogn Sci 11:333–341
8. Dopjans L, Bülthoff HH, Wallraven C (2012) Serial exploration of faces: comparing vision and touch. J Vis 12(1):6. (14 pp)
9. Dopjans L, Wallraven C, Bülthoff HH (2009) Cross-modal transfer in visual and haptic face recognition. IEEE Trans Haptics 200(4):236–240
10. Gaissert N, Bülthoff HH, Wallraven C (2011) Similarity and categorization: from vision to touch. Acta Psychol 138:219–230
11. Gaissert N, Wallraven C (2012) Categorizing natural objects: a comparison of the visual and the haptic modalities. Exp Brain Res 216:123–134
12. Gaissert N, Wallraven C, Bülthoff HH (2010) Visual and haptic perceptual spaces show high similarity in humans. J Vis 10(11):2. (20 pp)
13. Gallace A, Spence C (2009) The cognitive and neural correlates of tactile memory. Psychol Bull 135:380–406
14. Jäkel F, Schölkopf B, Wichmann FA (2009) Does cognitive science need kernels? Trends Cogn Sci 13:381–388
15. Kilgour AR, Lederman SJ (2002) Face recognition by hand. Percept Psychophys 64:339–352
16. Kilgour AR, Lederman SJ (2006) A haptic face-inversion effect. Perception 35:921–931
17. Kitada R, Johnsrude IS, Kochiyama T, Lederman SJ (2009) Functional specialization and convergence in the occipito-temporal cortex supporting haptic and visual identification of human faces and body parts: an fMRI study. J Cogn Neurosci 21:2027–2045
18. Lacey S, Campbell C, Sathian K (2007) Vision and touch: multiple or multisensory representations of objects? Perception 36:1513–1521
19. Lacey S, Tal N, Amedi A, Sathian K (2009) A putative model of multisensory object representation. Brain Topogr 21:269–274
20. Lederman S, Klatzky R (2009) Haptic perception: a tutorial. Atten Percept Psychophys 71(7):1439–1459
21. Lynott D, Connell L (2012) Modality exclusivity norms for 400 nouns: The relationship between perceptual experience and surface word form. Behav Res Methods, 1–11
22. Schwaninger A, Wallraven C, Cunningham DW, Chiller-Glaus S (2006) Processing of identity and emotion in faces: a psychophysical, physiological and computational perspective. Prog Brain Res 156:321–343
23. Schwarzer G (2000) Development of face processing: the effect of face inversion. Child Dev 71(2):391–401
24. Shepard R (1987) Toward a universal law of generalization for psychological science. Science 237(4820):1317–1323
25. Shepard R (2001) Perceptual-cognitive universals as reflections of the world. Behav Brain Sci 24(04):581–601
26. Sinha P, Balas B, Ostrovsky Y, Russell R (2006) Face recognition by humans: nineteen results all computer vision researchers should know about. Proc IEEE 94(11):1948–1962

27. Troje N, Bülthoff H (1996) Face recognition under varying poses: the role of texture and shape. Vis Res 36(12):1761–1771
28. Tversky A (1977) Features of similarity. Psychol Rev 84(4):327
29. Wallraven C, Dopjans L, Bülthoff HH (2012) Learning to recognize faces through serial exploration. Exp Brain Res 226(4):513–523

Chapter 33
Shape-Based Instance Detection Under Arbitrary Viewpoint

Edward Hsiao and Martial Hebert

33.1 Introduction

Object instance detection under arbitrary viewpoint is a fundamental problem in Computer Vision and has many applications ranging from robotics to image search and augmented reality. Given an image, the goal is to detect a specific object in a cluttered scene from an unknown viewpoint. Without prior information, an object can appear under an infinite number of viewpoints, giving rise to an infinite number of image projections. While the use of discriminative point-based features, such as SIFT [21, 28], has been shown to work well for recognizing texture-rich objects across many views, these methods fail when presented with objects that have little to no texture.

Objects range from being completely uniform in color, to having stochastic textures from materials, to repeatable point textures found on man-made items (i.e., soup cans). In the following, texture-rich objects refer to those where discriminative, point-based features (e.g., SIFT) can be extracted repeatably. Weakly-textured objects, on the other hand, refer to those that contain stochastic textures and/or small amounts of point textures, but which are insufficient for recognizing the object by themselves. Examples of objects of different texture types can be seen in Fig. 33.1.

Weakly-textured objects are primarily defined by their contour structure and approaches for recognizing them largely focus on matching their shape [12, 18, 24, 41]. Many object shapes, however, are very simple, comprised of only a small number of curves and junctions. Even when considering a single viewpoint, these curves and junctions are often locally ambiguous as they can be observed on many different

E. Hsiao (✉) · M. Hebert
Robotics Institute, Carnegie Mellon University, Pittsburgh, USA
e-mail: ehsiao@cs.cmu.edu

M. Hebert
e-mail: hebert@cs.cmu.edu

S.J. Dickinson, Z. Pizlo (eds.), *Shape Perception in Human and Computer Vision*,
Advances in Computer Vision and Pattern Recognition,
DOI 10.1007/978-1-4471-5195-1_33, © Springer-Verlag London 2013

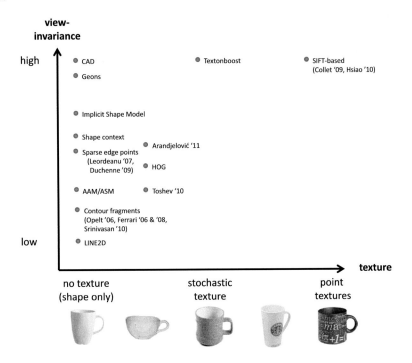

Fig. 33.1 View-invariance vs. texture for current state-of-the-art methods

objects. The collection of curves and junctions in a global configuration defines the shape and is what makes it more discriminative.

Introducing viewpoint further compounds shape ambiguity as the additional curve variations can match more background clutter. Much research has gone into representing shape variation across viewpoint. Figure 33.1 shows a rough layout of current state-of-the-art methods with respect to the type of texture they are designed to recognize versus how much view-invariance they can handle. Current models can roughly be divided into two main paradigms: *invariant* and *non-invariant*.

Invariant models create a unified object representation across viewpoint by explicitly modeling the structural relationships of high level shape primitives (e.g., curves and lines). *Non-invariant* models, on the other hand, use view-based templates and capture viewpoint variations by sampling the view space and matching each template independently. In this article, we discuss the advantages and disadvantages of invariant and non-invariant methods. We conclude that non-invariant approaches are well-suited for capturing viewpoint variation for specific object recognition since they preserve the fine-grained details. We follow with a discussion on additional techniques that are necessary for addressing shape ambiguities under arbitrary viewpoint.

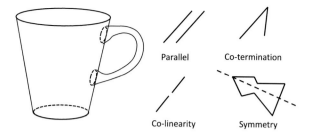

Fig. 33.2 Invariant methods consider properties of shape primitives that are invariant across viewpoint. Common invariant properties that are used are parallelism, co-termination, co-linearity and symmetry

33.2 Invariant Methods

Invariant methods are based on representing structural relationships between view-invariant shape primitives [4, 17]. Typically, these methods represent an object in 3D and reduce the problem of object detection to generating correspondences between a 2D image and a 3D model. To facilitate generating these correspondences, significant work has gone into designing shape primitives [3] that can be differentiated and detected solely from their perceptual properties in 2D while being relatively independent of viewing direction. Research in perceptual organization [29] and non-accidental properties (NAPs) [44] have demonstrated that certain properties of edges in 2D are invariant across viewpoint and unlikely to be produced by accidental alignments of viewpoint and image features. These properties provide a way to group edges into shape primitives and are used to distinguish them from each other and from the background. Example of such properties are collinearity, symmetry, parallelism and co-termination as illustrated in Fig. 33.2. After generating candidate correspondences between 2D image and 3D model using these properties, the position and pose of the object can then be simultaneously computed.

In earlier approaches, 3D CAD models [13, 24, 46] were extensively studied for view-invariant object recognition. For simple, polyhedral objects, CAD models consist of lines. However for complex, non-polyhedral objects, curves, surfaces and volumetric models [25] are used. In general, obtaining a compact representation of arbitrary 3D surfaces for recognition is very challenging. Biederman's Recognition-by-Components (RBC) [3] method decomposes objects into simple geometric primitives (e.g., blocks and cylinders) called *geons*. By using geons, structural relationships based on NAPs can be formulated for view-invariant detection.

Given geometric constraints from NAPs and an object model, the recognition problem reduces to determining if there exists a valid object transformation that aligns the model features with the image features. This correspondence problem is classically formulated as search, and approaches such as interpretation trees [16, 17], Generalized Hough Transforms [17] and alignment [6, 23] are used.

Interpretation trees [16, 17] consider correspondences as nodes in a tree and sequentially identify nodes such that the feature correspondences are consistent with the geometric constraints. If a node does not satisfy all the geometric constraints, the subtree below that node is abandoned. Generalized Hough Transforms (GHT) [17], on the other hand, cluster evidence using a discretized pose space. Each pair of model and image feature votes for all possible transformations that would align them together. Geometric constraints are combined with the voting scheme to restrict the search of feasible transformations. Finally, alignment-based techniques [6, 23] start with just enough correspondences to estimate a *hypothesis* transformation. *Verification* is then used to search for additional model features satisfying the geometric constraints. The hypothesis with the most consistent interpretation is chosen.

While CAD models and geons have been shown to work well in a number of scenarios, automatically learning 3D models is a considerable challenge [5, 16]. In addition, geons are unable to approximate many complex objects. To address these issues, recent approaches [26, 33] try to learn view-invariant features and non-accidental properties directly from 2D data. A common paradigm is to align and cluster primitives that have similar appearance across viewpoint. For example, the Implicit Shape Model (ISM) [26] considers images patches as primitives and uses Hough voting for recognition. To determine view-invariant features, images patches from all viewpoints of the object are clustered. Each cluster corresponds to a locally view-invariant patch and is associated with a probabilistic set of object centers. A match to a cluster casts a probabilistic vote for its corresponding object positions.

While patches are simple to extract, those on the object boundary contain background clutter and can result in incorrect matches. A more direct approach to modeling shape is to use contours. In the following, we use an approach we developed to illustrate the challenges of learning and using view-invariant curves for object detection. We follow the ISM approach and learn view-invariant curves by grouping curves with similar appearance together. Unlike patches which have a fixed number of pixels, the length of curves varies across viewpoint. We maintain the same number of points by using Coherent Point Drift [32] to generate point-to-point correspondences between curves of nearby views. Given a sequence of object images, we start with the curves of a single view and track the curve deformations by linking the pairwise correspondences. As each frame is processed, a new track is initialized if a curve fragment does not correspond to one that is already being tracked. Tracks are stopped if the number of unique points remaining is less than 50 % of the original curve. Each tracked curve is then represented by its mean and deformations, and is associated with a probabilistic set of object centers as shown in Fig. 33.3.

At recognition time, a modified Iterative Closest Point (ICP) [37] matches image curves with model curves, accounting for the local deformations. If an image curve matches a significant portion of the model curve, it casts a vote for all corresponding poses. The critical issue with allowing local deformations is that it is difficult to enforce global consistency of deformations without storing the constraints for each viewpoint individually. Figure 33.3d shows an example where the local deformations are valid but the global configuration is not consistent. If the constraints are defined individually for each viewpoint, however, the view-invariance is lost and the approach is equivalent to matching each view independently (i.e., non-invariant).

Another common issue with invariant approaches is that they rely on stable extraction of shape primitives. This is a significant limitation since reliable curve extraction and grouping [29] still proves to be a considerable challenge. While there has been significant development in object boundary detection [1, 8], no single boundary detector is able to extract all relevant curves. The Global Probability of

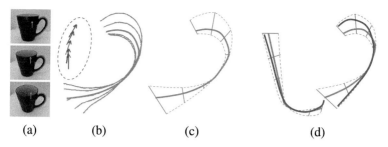

(a)   (b)   (c)   (d)

Fig. 33.3 Modeling the deformation of curves across viewpoint. (**a**) *Curves* tracked across viewpoint. The *arrows* specify the centers and upright poses of the object. (**b**) Aligned curves with their associated centers and pose. (**c**) Mean curve with deformations computed from aligned curves. (**d**) Global consistency is difficult to enforce without storing the viewpoint information

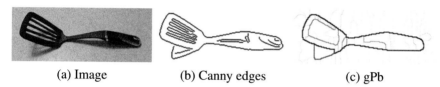

(a) Image   (b) Canny edges   (c) gPb

Fig. 33.4 Edge extraction. Current state-of-the-art methods in boundary detection (gPb) are unable to stably extract interior contours which are essential for recognizing specific objects. Canny, on the other hand, can detect these edges, but will also fire on spurious texture edges

Boundary (gPb) detector, which is designed to ignore stochastic textures, often confuses interior contours with stochastic texture as seen in Fig. 33.4. These interior edges provide distinctiveness that is necessary for recognizing specific objects.

Due to the challenges of creating 3D models, extracting shape primitives and learning geometric constraints from data, many recent approaches have moved away from using invariant shape primitives. In the next section, we discuss how non-invariant, view-based methods are able to address the above issues and why they are more effective for specific object recognition under arbitrary viewpoint.

33.3 Non-invariant (View-Based) Methods

Non-invariant methods represent an object under multiple viewpoints by creating a "view-based" template [35] for each object view (Fig. 33.5). Each template captures a specific viewpoint, only allowing slight deformation from noise and minor pose variation. Unlike invariant methods which define geometric constraints between pairs or sets of shape primitives, non-invariant methods directly fix both the local and global shape configurations. To combine the output of view-based templates, the scores from each view are normalized [30, 38] and non-maximal suppression is applied.

Non-invariant methods have a number of benefits over invariant ones. First, using view-based templates bypasses the 3D model generation and allows the algorithm

Fig. 33.5 Non-invariant
methods create a template for
each viewpoint of the object

to directly observe the exact projection of the object to be recognized. This has
the benefit of not approximating the shape with volumetric primitives (e.g., geons),
which can lose fine-grained details needed for recognizing specific objects. Secondly, template matching approaches can operate directly on low-level features and
do not require extraction of high-level shape primitives. Finally, many non-invariant
approaches achieve recognition performances on par or better than invariant ones,
while being relatively simple and efficient to implement. Recent results show that
they can be successfully applied to tasks such as robotic manipulation.

A number of methods exist for representing object shape from a single view.
These range from using curves and lines [11, 12, 39] to sparse edge features [18, 27]
and gradient histograms [7]. Methods which use curves and lines often employ 2D
view-invariant techniques, similar to the approaches described in Sect. 33.2, to reduce the number of view samples needed. Interpretation trees [17], Generalized
Hough Transforms [17] and alignment techniques [6] which are used for 3D view-
invariance are similarly applied to 2D geometric constraints. However, this representation suffers from the same limitations of using high-level shape primitives.

While some approaches use 2D view-invariance, others simply brute force match
all the possible viewpoints using low-level features. The Dominant Orientation Template (DOT) method [19] considers the dominant orientation in each cell of a grid.
Starting with a single template of an arbitrary viewpoint, new templates are added
if the detection score using the previous templates becomes too low. By carefully
designing the algorithm for efficient memory access and computation, the approach
is able to recognize thousands of templates in near real-time. More recently, the
LINE2D [18] approach has demonstrated superior performance to DOT while maintaining similar computation speeds. LINE2D represents an object by a set of sparse
edge points, each associated with a quantized gradient orientation. The similarity
measure between a template and image location is the sum of cosine orientation
differences for each point within a local neighborhood. While LINE2D works well
when objects are largely visible, Hsiao et al. [22] showed that considering only the
points which match the quantized orientations exactly is a much more robust metric when there are occlusions. Finally, the popular Histogram of Oriented Gradients
(HOG) [7, 10] approach represents objects by a grid of gradient histograms.

While using low-level features avoids edge extraction, a drawback is the loss of
edge connectivity and structure. For example, the HOG descriptor is unable to differentiate between a single line and many lines of the same orientation because their

Stable configuration   Unstable configuration

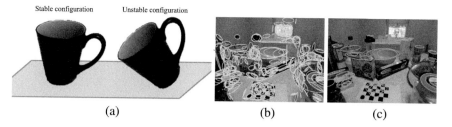

(a)   (b)   (c)

Fig. 33.6 Stability. (**a**) In static environments, most objects rest on surfaces. Objects detected in unstable poses can be down-weighted or filtered. We illustrate the usefulness of knowing the support surface orientation with an example of finding image ellipses that correspond to circles parallel to the ground in 3D. These circles are commonly found on household objects. (**b**) Raw ellipse detections. (**c**) Ellipse detections remaining after filtering with the ground normal

descriptors would be similar. The LINE2D method matches each point individually, resulting in high scoring false positives where neighboring edge points are not connected. These drawbacks, however, are often outweighed by the benefit of operating on low-level features and observing the exact projection of the object in the image.

An additional criticism of non-invariant methods is that they require a large number of templates to sample the view space. For example, LINE2D requires 2000 templates per object. While this many templates may have resulted in prohibitive computation times in the past, advances in algorithms [18, 19] and processing power have demonstrated that template matching can be done very efficiently (e.g., LINE2D and DOT are able to match objects at 10 frames per second). To increase the scalability, template clustering and branch-and-bound [19] methods are commonly used. In addition, templates are easily scanned in parallel and many can be implemented efficiently on Graphics Processing Units (GPUs) [36].

33.4 Ambiguities

Regardless of whether invariant or non-invariant methods are used, shape recognition under arbitrary viewpoint has many inherent ambiguities. Allowing corners and smooth contours to deform results in a wide range of contours that can match the background, especially for simple shapes. Without additional information, introducing view-invariance in shape recognition produces many improbable false positives that align very well to the image.

Objects in real world environments, however, do not appear in arbitrary configurations. Especially when recognizing multiple objects simultaneously, the relationships between object poses are constrained. An approach used in many scenarios is to determine the supporting plane [20] of the objects, such as road in outdoor scenes or table for indoor scenes. Given the supporting surface, the possible stable configurations (Fig. 33.6) of objects on the surface are drastically reduced. Object hypotheses that are in unstable configurations can be filtered or down-weighted.

More likely occlusion   Less likely occlusion

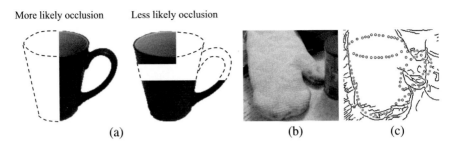

(a)   (b)   (c)

Fig. 33.7 Occlusion reasoning. Objects in natural scenes are often occluded by objects resting on the same surface. This information can be used to rank the occlusion configurations of an object. (a) The *left cup* has a more likely occlusion configuration than the *right cup*. (b) Example false detection window of a cup without occlusion reasoning. (c) Model points that match well to the edgemap are shown by *solid points* and those that match poorly are shown by *open points*. The occlusion configuration is unlikely

Other approaches, along these lines, reason about scene layout and object recognition together. Given a set of object hypotheses, the approach of [2] determines the best object poses and scene layout to explain the image.

Most shape-based recognition approaches focus solely on finding locations with good matches to the object boundary. However, not all object hypotheses with the same match percentage are equally plausible (Fig. 33.7). For example in natural scenes, the bottom of an object is more likely to be occluded than the top [9]. Methods for occlusion reasoning [17, 34, 40] range from enforcing local coherency [14] of regions that are inconsistent with object statistics [15, 31, 43] to using relative depth ordering [42, 45] of object hypotheses. Most of these approaches, however, require learning the occlusion structure for each view independently. Recently, our results have shown that explicitly reasoning about 3D interactions of objects [22] can be used to analytically represent occlusions under arbitrary viewpoint and significantly improve shape-based recognition performance.

Finally, while regions with uniform texture are often ignored for recognizing weakly-textured objects, our recent experiments show that they are actually very informative. In Fig. 33.8, the object shape aligns very well to the background, but the texture-less object interior matches poorly. By combining both region and boundary information, many high scoring false positives in cluttered scenes can be filtered.

33.5 Conclusion

Shape-based instance detection under arbitrary viewpoint is a challenging problem and has many applications from robotics to augmented reality. Current approaches for modeling viewpoint variation can roughly be divided into two main categories: *invariant* and *non-invariant* models. Invariant models explicitly represent the deformations of view-invariant shape primitives, while non-invariant models create a non-invariant, view-based template for each view. While invariant models provide

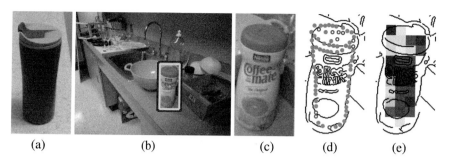

(a)   (b)   (c)   (d)   (e)

Fig. 33.8 Region information is necessary for robust shape recognition. The false positive shown aligns well to the edgemap but the interior matches poorly. (**a**) Model object. (**b**) False positive detection. (**c**) Zoomed in view of the false positive. (**d**) Edge points matched on top of the edgemap (*solid* is matched, *open* is not matched). (**e**) Activation scores of individual HOG cells [43]

a unified representation of objects across viewpoint, they require generation of 3D models and extraction of high level features which are challenges in themselves. Non-invariant methods are able to bypass these issues by directly operating on low-level features in 2D. They are also able to directly observe the 2D projection without needing to approximate the 3D shape. Recent advances in algorithms and processing power have demonstrated efficient template matching approaches which simultaneously detect thousands of templates in near real-time. Since shape recognition under arbitrary viewpoint introduces ambiguities that result in a large number of false positives, additional information such as surface layout estimation, occlusion reasoning and region information are needed for robust recognition.

Acknowledgements   This work was supported in part by the National Science Foundation under ERC Grant No. EEEC-0540865.

References

1. Arbeláez P, Maire M, Fowlkes C, Malik J (2009) From contours to regions: an empirical evaluation. In: Proceedings of IEEE conference on computer vision and pattern recognition
2. Bao SYZ, Sun M, Savarese S (2010) Toward coherent object detection and scene layout understanding. In: Proceedings of IEEE conference on computer vision and pattern recognition
3. Biederman I (1987) Recognition-by-components: a theory of human image understanding. Psychol Rev 94(2):115
4. Biederman I (2000) Recognizing depth-rotated objects: a review of recent research and theory. Spat Vis 13(2–3):241–253
5. Bilodeau GA, Bergevin R (2000) Generic modeling of 3d objects from single 2d images. In: Proceedings of international conference on pattern recognition
6. Cass TA (1998) Robust affine structure matching for 3d object recognition. IEEE Trans Pattern Anal Mach Intell 20(11):1265–1274
7. Dalal N (2006) Finding people in images and videos. PhD thesis, Institut National Polytechnique de Grenoble / INRIA Grenoble
8. Dollar P, Tu Z, Belongie S (2006) Supervised learning of edges and object boundaries. In: Proceedings of IEEE conference on computer vision and pattern recognition

9. Dollar P, Wojek C, Schiele B, Perona P (2009) Pedestrian detection: a benchmark. In: Proceedings of IEEE conference on computer vision and pattern recognition
10. Felzenszwalb P, McAllester D, Ramanan D (2008) A discriminatively trained, multiscale, deformable part model. In: Proceedings of IEEE conference on computer vision and pattern recognition
11. Ferrari V, Fevrier L, Jurie F, Schmid C (2008) Groups of adjacent contour segments for object detection. In: IEEE transactions on pattern analysis and machine intelligence
12. Ferrari V, Tuytelaars T, Van Gool L (2006) Object detection by contour segment networks. In: Proceedings of European conference on computer vision
13. Flynn PJ, Jain AK (1991) Cad-based computer vision: from cad models to relational graphs. IEEE Trans Pattern Anal Mach Intell 13(2):114–132
14. Fransens R, Strecha C, Van Gool L (2006) A mean field em-algorithm for coherent occlusion handling in map-estimation prob. In: Proceedings of IEEE conference on computer vision and pattern recognition
15. Girshick RB, Felzenszwalb PF, McAllester D (2011) Object detection with grammar models. In: Proceedings of neural information processing systems
16. Grimson WEL, Lozano-Perez T (1987) Localizing overlapping parts by searching the interpretation tree. IEEE Trans Pattern Anal Mach Intell 9:469–482
17. Grimson WEL, Lozano-Pérez T, Huttenlocher DP (1990) Object recognition by computer. MIT Press, Cambridge
18. Hinterstoisser S, Cagniart C, Ilic S, Sturm P, Navab N, Fua P, Lepetit V (2011) Gradient response maps for real-time detection of texture-less objects. IEEE Trans Pattern Anal Mach Intell
19. Hinterstoisser S, Lepetit V, Ilic S, Fua P, Navab N (2010) Dominant orientation templates for real-time detection of texture-less objects. In: Proceedings of IEEE conference on computer vision and pattern recognition
20. Hoiem D, Efros AA, Hebert M (2008) Putting objects in perspective. Int J Comput Vis
21. Hsiao E, Collet A, Hebert M (2010) Making specific features less discriminative to improve point-based 3d object recognition. In: Proceedings of IEEE conference on computer vision and pattern recognition
22. Hsiao E, Hebert M (2012) Occlusion reasoning for object detection under arbitrary viewpoint. In: Proceedings of IEEE conference on computer vision and pattern recognition
23. Huttenlocher DP, Ullman S (1990) Recognizing solid objects by alignment with an image. Int J Comput Vis 5(2):195–212
24. Ikeuchi K (1987) Generating an interpretation tree from a cad model for 3d-object recognition in bin-picking tasks. Int J Comput Vis 1(2):145–165
25. Koenderink JJ (1990) Solid shape. MIT Press, Cambridge
26. Leibe B, Leonardis A, Schiele B (2004) Combined object categorization and segmentation with an implicit shape model. In: Workshop on statistical learning in computer vision, proceedings of European conference on computer vision
27. Leordeanu M, Hebert M, Sukthankar R (2007) Beyond local appearance: category recognition from pairwise interactions of simple features. In: Proceedings of IEEE conference on computer vision and pattern recognition
28. Lowe DG (2004) Distinctive image features from scale-invariant keypoints. Int J Comput Vis
29. Lowe DG (1984) Perceptual organization and visual recognition. PhD thesis, Stanford University
30. Malisiewicz T, Efros AA (2011) Ensemble of exemplar-svms for object detection and beyond. In: Proceedings of IEEE international conference on computer vision
31. Meger D, Wojek C, Schiele B, Little JJ (2011) Explicit occlusion reasoning for 3d object detection. In: Proceedings of British machine vision conference
32. Myronenko A, Song X (2010) Point set registration: coherent point drift. IEEE Trans Pattern Anal Mach Intell 32(12):2262–2275
33. Payet N, Todorovic S (2011) From contours to 3d object detection and pose estimation. In: Proceedings of IEEE international conference on computer vision

34. Plantinga H, Dyer CR (1990) Visibility, occlusion, and the aspect graph. Int J Comput Vis
35. Poggio T, Edelman S (1990) A network that learns to recognize 3d objects. Nature
    343(6255):263–266
36. Prisacariu V, Reid I (2009) Fasthog—a real-time gpu implementation of hog. Department of
    Engineering Science, Oxford University, Technical Report
37. Rusinkiewicz S, Levoy M (2001) Efficient variants of the ICP algorithm. In: 3DIM
38. Scheirer WJ, Kumar N, Belhumeur PN, Boult TE (2012) Multi-attribute spaces: calibration
    for attribute fusion and similarity search. In: Proceedings of IEEE conference on computer
    vision and pattern recognition
39. Srinivasan P, Zhu Q, Shi J (2010) Many-to-one contour matching for describing and dis-
    criminating object shape. In: Proceedings of IEEE conference on computer vision and pattern
    recognition
40. Stevens MR, Beveridge JR (2000) Integrating graphics and vision for object recognition.
    Kluwer Academic, Amsterdam
41. Toshev A, Taskar B, Daniilidis K (2010) Object detection via boundary structure segmenta-
    tion. In: Proceedings of IEEE conference on computer vision and pattern recognition
42. Wang N, Ai H (2011) Who blocks who: simultaneous clothing segmentation for grouping
    images. In: Proceedings of IEEE international conference on computer vision
43. Wang X, Han TX, Yan S (2009) An hog-lbp human detector with partial occlusion handling.
    In: Proceedings of IEEE international conference on computer vision
44. Witkin AP, Tenenbaum JM (1983) On the role of structure in vision. Human Mach Vis 1:481–
    543
45. Wu B, Nevatia R (2005) Detection of multiple, partially occluded humans in a single im-
    age by Bayesian combination of edgelet part detectors. In: Proceedings of IEEE international
    conference on computer vision
46. Zerroug M, Nevatia R (1999) Part-based 3d descriptions of complex objects from a single
    image. IEEE Trans Pattern Anal Mach Intell 21(9):835–848

Index

S.J. Dickinson, Z. Pizlo (eds.), *Shape Perception in Human and Computer Vision*,
Advances in Computer Vision and Pattern Recognition,
DOI 10.1007/978-1-4471-5195-1, © Springer-Verlag London 2013

Printed in the United States
By Bookmasters